HARVARD SOCIOLOGICAL STUDIES

VOLUME I

THIS STUDY HAS BEEN AIDED BY A GRANT FROM THE HARVARD
UNIVERSITY COMMITTEE ON RESEARCH IN THE SOCIAL SCIENCES,
AND ITS PUBLICATION HAS BEEN FINANCED BY THAT COMMITTEE

THE STUDIES IN THIS SERIES ARE PUBLISHED BY THE DEPARTMENT
OF SOCIOLOGY OF HARVARD UNIVERSITY, WHICH, HOWEVER,
ASSUMES NO RESPONSIBILITY FOR THE VIEWS EXPRESSED

LONDON : HUMPHREY MILFORD

OXFORD UNIVERSITY PRESS

THE ESSENTIAL FACTORS
OF SOCIAL EVOLUTION

BY

THOMAS NIXON CARVER

PROFESSOR OF POLITICAL ECONOMY EMERITUS AT
HARVARD UNIVERSITY

CAMBRIDGE
HARVARD UNIVERSITY PRESS
1935

PRINTED IN THE UNITED STATES OF AMERICA

PREFACE

GOLFERS sometimes play against an invisible adversary named Par, formerly Bogie. Sociologists who take their work seriously find themselves engaged in a struggle against another invisible adversary, not yet named. It may be called The Sociological Press. The game consists in trying to keep up with the output of sociological literature as it pours from that Press. It is a pleasant game, if not too much prolonged. It is, however, somewhat tantalizing to realize that no matter how long one plays it, one can never really catch up, or read the last word written on the subject.

The writer has been engaged in this pastime for forty-two years. The present volume is a condensation of a mass of notes, quotations, citations, comments, and observations accumulated during that period. He had, at one time, hoped to publish a monumental work on the general subject of Social Evolution, but was finally convinced that the task was too great for any one not endowed with the genius of a Herbert Spencer. The present modest volume is a compromise between the writer's ambition and his ability.

No one can go very far in the study of the fundamental problems of sociology without discovering for himself that these are among the oldest problems of human speculation. Though the name, sociology, is relatively modern, the subject is ancient. Men have been puzzled about the essential problem of sociology, the problem of living and working together in large numbers, quite as long as they have been puzzled over problems of cosmogony or biology. They have made their guesses, and have supported their guesses as plausibly in this field as in the others. Most theological dogmas were scientific hypotheses in their day. They ceased to be scientific and became theological when they were adhered to in spite of lack of evidence or in the face of positive evidence to the contrary. Not only theologians, but philosophers, men of science, and economists have hazarded guesses on the basic problems of social origins, social conflict, the social nature of man, and the genesis of social institutions. No modest scholar will hold in contempt these early guesses or hypotheses. He will have contempt only for those who continue to cling to them as dogmas in the face of contradictory evidence.

To sift out of an accumulated mass of materials those which seem essential to an understanding of the processes of social evolution, has been no small task. The writer wishes to acknowledge his indebtedness, first, to his students who have, during thirty-eight years of college and university teaching, listened patiently to his expositions, raised difficult questions, supplied information and fruitful suggestions, and thereby contributed to whatever of consistency and constructive scholarship may be found in this volume. Mention should next be made of his colleagues in the Departments of Economics and of Sociology at Harvard for the great courtesy and consideration which they have shown while the writer was engaged in this work. The author feels justified in singling out for special mention the late Professor Allyn A. Young whose profound interest and understanding were a constant inspiration.

The author is under special obligation to the former Harvard University Committee on Economic Research and the present Harvard University Committee on Research in the Social Sciences. Grants made by these committees have made possible the research which was a necessary preliminary to the preparation of the manuscript.

For special and painstaking help in the preparation of manuscript, in looking up citations and verifying quotations, the author wishes especially to thank Mrs. Henry B. Stevens, Dr. Olive I. Reddick, and Mr. Bernard L. Gabiné; also his most patient and cheerful of helpers, Miss Helen Prescott. If he were to name all the others to whom he is indebted, the publishers might object to so long a list.

T. N. CARVER

Cambridge, Massachusetts
July, 1934

PART I

THE PROBLEM OF LIVING TOGETHER
IN LARGE NUMBERS

CHAPTER I

A PRELIMINARY SURVEY

SOCIOLOGY may be defined as the study of the efforts of human beings to live and work together in large groups called "societies." A society is something more than a conglomeration of individuals. It is an organized group, having a conscious purpose and, in the interest of that purpose, exercising some control over the behavior of its individual members. Even if its purpose be nothing more than its own perpetuation, that purpose can only be achieved by controlling its members, encouraging such behavior as tends to strengthen and perpetuate the group, and discouraging such behavior as tends to weaken the group, or to threaten its continued existence.

The continued existence as well as the growth of the group requires associated effort on the part of its members. This associated effort is essentially teamwork, though it may require some stretch of the imagination to conceive of a team as consisting of millions of men, women, and children, and to think of the multifarious associated activities of all these individuals as teamwork. Moreover, it is a team which plays a perpetual game called the "struggle for existence," and the stake is the survival or extinction of the team. This does not mean that the team is an end in itself, or that individuals exist for the benefit of the team. The team, even the great team called the "nation," exists for the benefit of individuals, but it has been found, through millions of years of experience on this planet, that individuals cannot live, or carry on successfully the struggle to live, except by teamwork in large groups. This has made it necessary for individuals to "play the game" as members of a team, to behave in the interest of the team, knowing that they as individuals — the vast majority at least — get on better as members of a successful than as members of an unsuccessful team. Any student who has been a member of an athletic team should understand this. If he does, he will understand the first and greatest of all the leading principles of sociology, namely, that social life is essentially teamwork, and that the essentials of teamwork are the same whether the team consists of eleven men or of millions of men, women, and children. Teamwork consists in doing with all one's might whatever is necessary for the success of the team. That is all that real, as distinguished from conventional, morality is,— or patriotism, or social obligation, or true religion,— for that matter. However, it must be remembered that the great team is the great society. More of this later.

Individuals may be led to behave in the interest of the team by several motives. First, their intelligence may enable them to see the superior advantage to themselves of belonging to a successful over that of belonging to an unsuccessful team. Second, they may develop a kind of emotional interest in or loyalty to the team to which they belong. Having been for untold centuries compelled by the necessities of existence to live and work in groups which we are here, temporarily, calling teams, it would have been strange if we human beings had not developed a certain capacity for teamwork, or even a certain love of it, which would seem to include an emotional loyalty to the team itself. That loyalty to the greatest of all teams is called patriotism. When it is felt toward smaller teams it goes by various names, such as sectionalism, sectarianism, Christianity, Romanism, Judaism, club spirit, gang spirit, class feeling, etc, etc.

The so-called humanitarian may dispute the statement that the nation[1] is the greatest of all teams, and insist that humanity is a greater one. "Above all nations is humanity" is a mouth-filling slogan, but humanity is not in a position to discipline any nation; in fact, humanity is not organized and therefore lacks one essential of a team. We may as well be frankly realistic and admit that humanitarianism is only a natural prejudice in favor of one's own kind,— a feeling which seems to be felt by all the higher mammals. Besides, if one insists on being so very broad-minded as to divest himself of all such prejudices

[1] Nation is here used in the American sense.

as nationalism, family feeling, or group loyality, why harbor such a prejudice as humanitarianism? Why not do as certain Orientals pretend to do and take all the kindly animals into the circle of our universal brotherhood? If one begins to show preferences, such as the preference for human beings as against other creatures, what logical reason can one give for stopping there and refusing to show other preferences, which Professor Giddings summarized under the term "consciousness of kind"?

A third method of inducing men to behave in the interest of the group is sometimes necessary. In those cases where the individual's intelligence and loyalty combined are not sufficient to induce the desired forms of teamwork or associative effort, the group itself must assume some active authority over the individual. It must inflict something unpleasant as a penalty for unsocial behavior, and award something pleasant for social behavior,— social behavior being the pedantic equivalent of teamwork.

The necessity for some degree of control by the group over the individual is universally recognized. In animal and insect societies, social behavior seems to be largely instinctive. Human beings, however, seem to be rather poorly equipped with instincts. At any rate, no human society seems able to dispense with intelligence, emotional loyalty, or even with positive law with penalties, as guides to social behavior. Every form of social life, whether in the human species or among lower species, is characterized by the behavior of individuals in the interest of the group. That socialized behavior may have become instinctive and automatic; it may be the result of intelligence which will lead individuals to sacrifice their lesser interests in favor of the larger and more durable interests which center in group life. It may be the desire for the good opinion of one's team-mates, and the fear of their displeasure. It may also be the result of the fear of punishment.

The notion that animals and primitive men enjoy unabridged and complete freedom of individual action is erroneous and unsupported by fact. Studies in insect, animal, and primitive human society clearly show that the individual's behavior is guided by certain outward as well as inward forms of inhibition which arise from the presence of other members of its own species. No individual can behave in a society exactly as he would if he were isolated. The rigidity of his behavior in a society of his own kind is exhibited by the complete coöperation of the members even of insect and animal societies in performing specialized functions that insure group survival. In primitive human society, especially, individual behavior is limited, and always within the bounds of social constraint. Individual motivation is so intertwined with social purpose that it seems to have no separate existence. Describing the social behavior of some of the most primitive of people, Malinowski says:

The natives (in the Archipelagoes of Melanesian New Guinea) obey the forces and commands of the tribal code, but they do not comprehend them: exactly as they obey their instincts and their impulses, but could not lay down a single law of psychology. The regularities in native institutions are an automatic result of the inheritance of the social forces of tradition and of the material condition of the environment.[1]

The same point of view is arrived at by Spencer and Gillen, W. H. R. Rivers, and others.[2]

Anthropologists and ethnographers clearly show the existence of a social organic structure in primitive society, at least in the most primitive societies which they are able to study, having a definite organization with its functions institutionalized just as in modern society. Social development, however, depends on the interactions between the individual and the social group to which he belongs. Both the individual and the group must be of an acquisitive as well as of a contributory character if society is to be of a dynamic nature. Each must make its demands upon the other and each must respond to the demands of the other.[3]

---

[1] Bronislaw Malinowski, *Argonauts of the Western Pacific* (George Routledge & Sons, Ltd., London, 1922), p. 11.

[2] Baldwin Spencer and F. J. Gillen, *The Native Tribes of Central Australia* (The Macmillan Co. Ltd., London, 1899). By the same authors, *Northern Tribes of Central Australia* (The Macmillan Co. Ltd., London, 1904).

W. H. R. Rivers, *Social Organization* (Alfred A. Knopf, New York, 1929).

For a good summary of the views of various authors on primitive social organization see *Revue de l'Institut de Sociologie Solvay*, March, 1922.

[3] "For the strength of the pack is the wolf
And the strength of the wolf is the pack."

In other words, a dynamic society may be conceived of as a continuum within which individuals work together, each making demands upon others and responding to their demands, and each making demands on the group as a whole and responding to its demands.[1] This, then, implies that social organization — the mechanism which crystallizes society in its functioning — is in a constant process of adjustment. Our study, therefore, since it has to do with organized groups called societies, may be defined, in more scholastic terms, as the study of social organization,— its nature and function,— and the process of adjusting the group organization to the needs of individuals, and of adapting individual behavior to the demands of the group.

Let it not be imagined that this is a new subject. Men were studying it for thousands of years before the word *sociology* was invented. As will be shown later, the attempt to systematize it and bring its various phases under one comprehensive survey is recent; but the essentials of the problem of living and working together in large groups called societies had not escaped the attention of philosophers, statesmen, and moralists of previous centuries.

Why it was necessary or advantageous to live and work together in groups seems to have been less puzzling at first than the question, why we have so much trouble when we try it. The advantages of group life have seemed so obvious as to need no explanation and to call forth no discussion. The advantage of numbers and organization in coping with the huge beasts which were the contemporaries of early man, and in the struggles for the possession of hunting grounds and pasture lands, must have left no room for verbal argument. Their advantages in modern industry are clearly set forth in treatises on economics; nowhere better than in Adam Smith's famous discourse on the Division of Labor. But the puzzling question for a long time was not why we live and work together in large groups, but why we have so much trouble with one another when we try it. It did not seem necessary for early students to explain the ad-

[1] (See p. 8).

vantages of that large-scale teamwork called social action. Students have very properly economized their energies by trying to answer questions which seemed to need answering rather than questions which seemed to need no answers.

Five great questions have perplexed students of the problem of living together in large groups, and directed their studies. They are arranged here in their logical order and not in the chronological order in which they have been studied.

1. How did men come to live and work together in those great groups called societies?

2. Why do they have so much trouble getting along with one another when it is so obviously to their advantage to live and work together?

3. Are we making any progress in the art of living together?

4. Have we a social nature, and if so, how was it acquired and in what does it consist?

5. How does group action help us to solve the great problem of trying to fit ourselves into the universe in which we find ourselves?

The modern student of sociology will do well not to assume a too supercilious attitude toward the various answers to these great and puzzling problems. Some of the old answers seem naïve to us now, but so, in all probability, will the most sophisticated answers of the ultra-modern students of today look to students of the future. It should be a sobering thought that, outside the fields of physical science and the mechanic arts, men are not able to do better work or to think any more clearly or comprehensively today than they did in the past — even in the remote past. No new social problems have arisen in recent times except those created by physical science and the mechanic arts, and, except for statistics based on printed records, themselves the product of a mechanical invention — the printing press — no new technique for studying social problems has been developed in modern times.

The first of the great questions stated above, How did men come to live and work together in those great groups called societies? has been approached from two different directions.

One group of students has tried to answer the question by study-ing historically and descriptively the forms of social organiza-tion, or the ways in which people have actually lived and worked together in different times and places. Another group has tried to understand the factors and forces which have compelled men to live and work together, and to change their ways of working to-gether to meet new conditions. The method followed by the first group is called historical or descriptive sociology. That of the second group is called dynamical sociology.

The central thought of the first group seems to be the accum-ulation of historical and archæological facts, and a comparison of the facts discovered. By putting these facts together they hope to gain some light on the question as to how group life started and the course of its development. It is obvious that, without this historical and archæological knowledge, no com-prehensive or complete answer to the problem can be found. However, this does not, alone, give us a complete answer. It can not tell us a great deal about the nature and function of social organization. To state the fact that a given social group at a given stage in its history lived under this or that form of organization, or that it had this or that form of religion, mar-riage, family organization, property, or government, does not tell us the reason for its existence, for its particular form of or-ganization, or for the institutions which it has developed.

In all purely descriptive statements we are likely, unless we exercise great care, to fall into the error of ascribing functional activities, or to imply that certain functional activities are in-herent in the forms we are describing. It is difficult, in other words, to be purely descriptive, no matter how strongly one may condemn attempts to interpret the phenomena described. Structure and function are so interdependent in every organism, especially in what has come to be called the social organism, as to make it difficult to separate them even for purposes of de-scription. One common implication is that social action is merely a manifestation of collective energy expressing itself in definite historical forms. Another is that social institutions are merely the instruments or the vehicles for the expression of social impulses of men. These are as truly "interpretations" as the assumption that types of social action as well as the institutions through which social action expresses itself came into existence sporadically, for no particular or assignable reason whatever, but survive, if they do survive, because they have survival value. They help to "keep the tribe alive" is a formula which the dynamical sociologist, as distinguished from the historical or descriptive sociologist, is fond of using. The dynamical sociologist frankly goes beyond mere structural description.

The forms and structures of institutions are, the dynamical sociologist believes, of less importance than the functions they perform. These must be carefully analyzed if we are ever to understand the nature of society. Whatever be the mechanism whereby one form of social organization has given rise to another, the processes involved in the transformation are essentially dynamic and causal. Institutions are not merely the expression of the whims or even the fundamental traits of the people who develop them. If that were true, we should have little trouble living together under our own institutions because our institutions would be the expressions of our own natures. Institutions are, however, sometimes imposed by circumstances entirely apart from human nature. Instead of being an expression of human nature, an institution imposed by the conditions under which human beings have to live, may be hostile to human nature, at least at the beginning. Human nature must then go through a long process of adaptation and re-adaptation until it is brought into harmony with the institutions which it has to adopt in order that men might survive.

Of course, any conception of social organization as a dynamic unity is incomplete without a knowledge of evolutionary history. Thus the two ways of looking at society — the historical description of the structure of society in different times and places, and the functional analysis — really supplement each other and are both essential to a proper understanding of society and its workings. Each approach, by itself, gives only one aspect of the process of social evolution.

All evolution proceeds, as suggested above, by a combination of two processes, namely, variation and selection. Without variation there can be no such thing as the selection of the more adapted and the extinction of the less adapted, for the simple reason that there would be no individuals who were either more adapted or less adapted than their fellows. This is as true of the evolution of societies as a whole and of social institutions as of biological forms. Human beings are known to be inventive and therefore capable of inventing all sorts of social institutions. A description of all such institutions as have existed in the past or as now exist is like a catalogue of biological variations. That, however, is only half of the evolutionary story. How these institutions work, and what is their survival value, are at least equally important questions to an evolutionary sociologist.

Not only social institutions, but moral codes, religions, educational systems, fashions, and everything else connected with social life must be considered as having a place, potentially at least, in the process of human adaptation. A social evolutionist must consider them very much as a biological evolutionist would consider teeth and claws, horns and hoofs, fur, feathers, blubber, and protective coloration, as having possible functions to perform in the survival or extinction of the species.

An analogy may be useful. A geologist, looking at a geographical spectacle like the Grand Canyon, is not content with a mere description of it as it now exists. Even if he were able to get descriptions of it at different stages of its existence, he would not be satisfied with them. He would desire to know how it came into existence. If he found that its form as described at different times was not always the same, he would want to know why it changed. When he tried to explain this question he would become a dynamical geologist. The significance of Darwin's work in biology lies in the fact that he was not content with a mere description and classification of species. He wanted to know how they originated and why their forms changed. In answering those questions he went beyond history and description and became what might be called a dynamical biologist. That is what it means to be a true evolutionist.

Similarly, the sociologist is not content with a description of forms of social organization at different times and places. He wants to know how and why they originated, and how and why they changed. He becomes a dynamical sociologist only when he tries to answer these questions. In order to answer such questions he must understand the factors and forces which produce social change. That is what it means to be a true social evolutionist.

This is clearly the method which must be used in order to find the answer to the first of our five great questions. No one can give a satisfactory answer to the question as to how men came to live together in societies by merely describing the forms or structures of primitive societies, important as such descriptions are. There must also be a study of the forces which bring them into existence and cause them to survive longer than disorganized masses of men. This question will be discussed more in detail in Chapter II.

To the second, also, of these great questions, namely, Why do we have so much trouble among ourselves when we try to live together in groups? two general answers have been given, though each has been elaborated and explained almost beyond recognition. 1. Men have trouble living together because of some taint or evil tendency which has entered human nature from the outside, or because human nature has been degenerated or debased by some outside influence. 2. The trouble is the result of the incomplete development, or the unfinished evolution of human beings; for if men are to live in societies they must become adapted to the conditions of social life just as they must become adapted to physical conditions which surround them; and this process of evolution or re-adaptation is not yet complete, consequently, we are only partially fitted for life in great groups.

The first answer is given, in somewhat different terms, by two widely separated groups of thinkers. Among certain Christian theologians, the outside influence which degenerated human nature was the Devil, and the degeneration took the form of original sin, human depravity, or the fall of man. Among more sophisticated social thinkers, the source of the degeneration is found in some of our social habits, institutions and tendencies, such as private property, commercialism, machine production, materialistic philosophy, or the doctrine of evolution. Among these modern thinkers, our social institutions, habits, and tendencies play the same rôle as the Devil in the older theology. Under both theories, human nature has been degenerated by outside influences which are not inherent in human nature itself.

The other answer, namely, that we have trouble living together because we have not yet evolved into a thoroughly socialized species, is more in harmony with the evolutionary philosophy of the day. It recognizes, or at least assumes, that we are an unfinished race of beings, still in process of becoming adapted to an unfinished universe; that, in this unfinished state, our race is only partially adapted to the conditions under which it has to live, and that there must be an adaptation of human nature to social as well as to physical conditions before we can live together in a state of social harmony. So long as the evolutionary philosophy prevails, this explanation of the source of conflict will seem more reasonable than the theory of human degeneration through the debasing influence of outside agencies.

Explaining conflict on the ground of human degeneration led to the formulation of policies and programs for economic and social improvement which left out of account some of the fundamental factors which now seem to limit and determine such improvement, with the result that the remedies suggested and sometimes applied now seem about as efficacious as patent medicines. Even those who account for the trouble on the ground of incomplete evolution do not always realize the full import of their theory. They are sometimes reluctant to surrender the idea that human beings live under a special dispensation and are not subject to the laws or observed tendencies of biological evolution. They point out, for example, that men can and do, within limits, adapt their environment to themselves and thus, to some slight degree, escape the necessity of being adapted. They fail to see that before men could assume this active rôle and begin remaking their environment to suit themselves, they had to go through a preliminary process of biological evolution which resulted in an erect posture, a hand adapted to other purposes than locomotion, and a large bulb on the upper end of the spinal cord, called a brain.   Nor do all who call themselves evolutionists realize that the sole and only process of evolution is trial and error, variation and selection, survival and extinction, success and failure, all of which mean the same thing, namely, that evolution comes because the less adapted fail and the more adapted succeed.   Up to the present moment, practically every social reform is a blind but determined fight against the only theory of evolution which has any scientific standing.

While, as suggested above, most social problems are old, and while no new technique, aside from statistics, has been developed for studying them, nevertheless modern science has given a new point of view from which to approach them.   This is called the evolutionary point of view.   They who take this point of view look upon all evolution as a process of adaptation of living forms to their surroundings.   The true social evolutionist looks upon organization and teamwork as a means of successful living, that is, of adaptation and survival.   The human species has carried this method of survival somewhat farther than other creatures, though some of the social insects could, if they were able to argue with us, support their claim to first place among social creatures with a respectable show of evidence.

The thesis that the reason we have so much trouble getting along with one another is because of some taint or special degeneration of human nature seems to be based upon the assumption that human beings are unique in the world of life and do not come under the same general biological laws as other animals. The evolutionary thesis looks upon the human race as an interesting biological species which has developed somewhat specialized but by no means unique methods of adaptation and survival. They who hold this point of view are willing, without being admonished like the sluggard, to "go to the ant" and to "consider her ways."   Much can be learned by the sociologist by reading such books as *Social Life Among the Insects*, by Professor William Morton Wheeler,[1] and other studies of animal and insect societies.

Rather obviously, a part of the process of adapting human life to a more or less hostile world was organized teamwork. This teamwork was necessary for the fight against powerful enemies and for the securing of adequate sustenance. Equally obvious, to a true evolutionist, was the necessity of adapting individuals to social life, that is, to teamwork on a large scale. If human beings were perfectly adapted to that kind of teamwork, we should have no difficulty getting along together. Since the process of evolving a social creature is not yet complete, we are only partially adapted to social life. Consequently, we have trouble which shows itself in all kinds of conflict among individuals in the same society.

Chronologically, the problem of conflict within the same society was studied earlier than the problem of the dynamic origin of social life. Conflict has been characterized as social friction. The overcoming of friction is a very pressing problem for social engineers,— variously called moralists, tribal leaders, lawmakers, and statesmen,— as well as for mechanical engineers. This problem will be more elaborately discussed in Chapter III.

The third of the great questions which have perplexed students of social problems, namely, Are we making any progress in the art of living together in large numbers? has been answered both yes and no. The answer has never been unanimous, even among intelligent students. At one time, one answer seems to be popular; at another time, the opposite. At one time the golden age seems ahead; at another, behind. At one time men look hopefully to the future; at another, regretfully to the past. The glory that was Greece and the grandeur that was Rome are at one time contrasted with the poverty and the sordidness of the present. At another, men "dip into the future, far as human eye can see," to glimpse the glory of the world.

From the discovery of America until the World War general optimism predominated in the Western World. The opening

---

[1] Harcourt, Brace & Co., New York, 1923.

up of new sources of food definitely removed the menace of famine. The gold and silver which poured into Europe from the Americas through Spain raised prices and stimulated enterprise. Power-driven machinery multiplied productive power. Colonies absorbed all the labor displaced by machinery. All these gave men a sense of mastery over their own fate and left little room for pessimism or despondency. Then came the doctrine of evolution, to give a philosophic justification for belief in progress. Evolution, to the average man, became a synonym for endless progress. Since the World War, however, a distinct note of pessimism is noticeable. Men have lost their belief in the certainty of progress and are even beginning to question its reality or even its possibility.

Whether it is called progress or not, there is no doubt that in the field of physical science the modern world knows many things which were unknown to the ancient world. In the field of mechanic arts, it is equally certain that men can now do many things that their ancestors could not do. Through physical science and the mechanic arts, men are solving one phase of the problem of living together in large numbers,— that of sustenance. We can supply the wants of large numbers of people more amply than was formerly possible; we can provision more and larger cities through superior means of transportation and more efficient instruments of production. Since one of the problems of living together in large numbers is that of economic subsistence, it may be said that, on this side at least, there has been some progress. Beyond that, there is not much that can be said without starting an argument.

The fourth of these great questions, Has man a social nature? has, likewise, been answered in two general ways. One answer is that man has no social nature, but that he is intelligent enough to see the advantage of teamwork,— of group action toward a common end. The other answer is that man has a social nature; that he, like other animals, has at least a preference for his own kind as compared with other creatures; that he at least prefers society to solitude, but that the scarcity of many desirable things creates a conflict of interests and causes him to quarrel with his fellowmen in spite of his inherently social nature.

Both answers seem to contain a measure of truth. It is difficult to see how even unsocial creatures could quarrel if their interests did not in some way conflict. It is easy to see how moderately social creatures might quarrel if the interest of one conflicted with that of another. When each is pursuing his own interest, and the success of one interferes with the success of the other, unless they are more thoroughly socialized than human beings are supposed to be, there will certainly be a conflict. On the other hand, it could be said that if human nature were thoroughly socialized, even scarcity could not produce conflict among individuals or between groups. That is, if every individual were so constituted as to be able to enjoy food on the palates of other people exactly as much as on his own, or on the palates of strangers exactly as much as on those of his own kin, even famine could not cause such individuals to quarrel. Probably, therefore, it would be safe to say that human nature is somewhat socialized, but not sufficiently to prevent a conflict of interests wherever a scarcity of desirable things shows itself.

The fifth question, namely, How does group action help us to solve the great problem of trying to fit ourselves into the universe in which we find ourselves? includes the first four and tries to bring them all together under a comprehensive system of social thought. The fact of adaptation in nature and man is so evident as to have been recognized from the earliest times of which we have any record. Theologians, philosophers, sages, thoughtful men everywhere have recognized and marvelled at it. The way things fit together, the harmony of the universe symbolized in such poetical expressions as "the music of the spheres," the interdependence of all forms of life, the nectar of the flower for the bee, the spreading of the pollen by the bee, the marvellous ways in which the various organs and glands of the body support one another and maintain the life of the whole, all these and thousands of other harmonious interdependencies have excited the wonder and admiration of thinking persons.

Unthinking brutes, lacking the capacity to marvel at anything, would never try to explain. Rational creatures simply could not help trying to explain any more than a fish could help using its swimming or a bird its flying organs.

Earlier students saw in these marvellous and minute fittings together evidences of design on the part of a supreme artificer designer. They could think of no other adequate explanation. The modern evolutionist recognizes the same set of facts, and has added to the list enough to increase our amazement and perplexity,[1] but he sees in them evidences of adaptation through the process of variation and selection, trial and error, a general shuffling and shifting about of materials with occasional and accidental fittings together. It almost looks as though matter were intelligently seeking adaptation, or opportunities for a fitting together of parts; but the more rigid evolutionists account for all adaptations on the ground of accidental combinations which, when favorable, survive. A particle of wind-blown dust, for example, can never rest in an exposed place. When it happens to find a low place or a sheltered spot, it remains quiet until the low spot becomes a high spot because of the wearing away of the high grounds which, for a time, protected it. An unadapted organism can not remain in a state of unadaptation. It must undergo changes, or become extinct. If it can manage to reproduce before it does, the species may live longer than the individual. Even the species must die, however, unless it can adapt itself. If an individual happens to be born which is adapted to its surroundings, and can reproduce itself, the species can live an unchanging existence until the conditions change. Then it must readapt or die.

The variations which take place among the new individuals that are born may be either accidental and sporadic, or they may center around a norm,[2] like bullet-holes around the bull's eye of a target. In the latter case, matter would seem to be

---

[1] One of the most striking additions to our knowledge of the intricate way in which things fit together is found in Walter B. Cannon's *The Wisdom of the Body* (W. W. Norton & Co., New York, 1932).

[2] Sometimes called orthogenesis.

intelligent, or, if not, some support would be given to the long-discarded doctrine of design. Evolutionists generally assume that natural variations are accidental and sporadic, and that natural selection is likewise unplanned and accidental, not like the purposeful selection of the plant or animal breeder. If a variation happens to fit into the general milieu, it survives, otherwise not. Even though the variation happens to be one of those extreme forms popularly called sports, but now called mutations by scientists, unless it fits into the general conditions of life it perishes. If it fits, it lives.

Deeply as the world has been impressed by the fact of adaptation, or the fitting together of parts, not only within the organism, but within a general milieu, including many organisms, nevertheless, it has not been able to close its eyes to another and seemingly contradictory fact, namely, maladaptation, or incomplete adaptation. So contradictory has the fact of incomplete adaptation in the midst of many adaptations seemed as to call for explanation. Until the concept of a continual process of adaptation and readaptation came with the doctrine of evolution, the only satisfactory explanation seemed to be a kind of mystic dualism, a belief that the universe was a battleground between rival and antagonistic forces. If the universe is complete, and not in process of creation by the method called evolution, how else could one account for the many obvious contradictions? Many things obviously fit together, indicating, it was believed, a beneficient design. But many misfits are equally obvious; what better explanation could be found than that of malevolent design? Ormuzd and Ahriman in the Persian dualism, God and Satan in the Hebrew dualism, personified these opposing forces.

The conception of evolution, or of creation by an endless process of trial and error, of variation and selection, destroys the necessity for any sort of dualism. An unfinished universe, still in process of evolution, must show many maladaptations or incomplete adaptations,— situations still in process of readjustment of parts. An unfinished race or species, still in process of adaptation to an unfinished world, must likewise show many incomplete adaptations.   Under this theory, Ahriman and Satan become superfluities.

Under this theory, if we still possess a vermiform appendix which gives us trouble, it is not because Satan put it where it doesn't belong, but because the process of evolution has not eliminated it from the human organism.   If we show inclinations to do unsocial acts, it is not because Satan tempted us, or introduced a taint into human nature to make us susceptible to wrong influences, but because the process of evolution has not yet bred a race of thoroughly socialized human beings.   Or it may be that we developed traits which adapted us, more or less closely, to the conditions under which we (our germ plasms) once lived, but which traits unfit us for the conditions under which we are now forced to live.   Under this theory evil becomes neither more nor less than incomplete adaptation.

Every species develops in the course of its evolution a group of characters which help it to survive in the environment in which it lives.   The long neck of the giraffe, enabling it to browse on the leaves of the mimosa tree, a kind of glorified alfalfa, is a classic example; but the long neck has to be accompanied by other anatomical and physiological readjustments. Intelligence is the human specialty, but intelligence also has to be accompanied by several anatomical and physiological readjustments, a large brain, organs of speech, an opposing thumb, an erect posture, and a skeletal and muscular development which permit the hurling of missiles.   But all these combined would not have given the human species its dominant position had it not also developed a capacity for teamwork.   This capacity for teamwork has never been analyzed into its elements, consequently it is impossible at the present moment, to say exactly in what this capacity consists.   Obviously intelligence has something to do with it.   Organs of speech have a great deal to do with it.   Apparently, also, there is what can only be named as a feeling of kinship, possessed by all the higher animals, especially the gregarious kinds.   Perhaps sympathy is a better name.

That living and working together in groups is a form of

adaptation which may help a species to survive is easily recognized when we study the social life of lower creatures, especially some of the social insects. It ought to be equally easy to see in social life a kind of human adaptation, a means by which human beings can live more comfortably and in larger numbers than would otherwise be possible. To one who understands this, with all that it signifies, it will also appear that those physical and mental characters which make it possible for men to live and work together are as definitely phases of adaptation as the long neck of the giraffe or the flippers of the seal.

Each of the five great questions which we have been discussing in this preliminary way, has, in its turn, attracted the attention of students of social life and given unity and consistency to their studies. Except for some unifying concept, students must have wandered over a wide range of subjects from linguistics to skyscrapers, all of which are the results of the efforts of human beings to live and work together in large numbers. The study of sociology should aim, not at encyclopedic information, but at understanding. The five great problems mentioned above have puzzled men for many generations. The answer to any of them will contribute to our understanding of that many-sided and complex thing called society. This understanding is what we want, rather than the collection of stores of information with which to make a show of erudition and which only befog or obscure the real facts about social phenomena.

The attempt to make sociology an encyclopedic collection of facts regarding everything done by men in society must necessarily lead to confusion. No one works or lives to himself alone. Everything done by human beings is done in society. If the sociologist were to take for his province every field and every product of social action, he would have to become an expert linguist, because speech is a social product; an expert architect, because architecture is a social product; an expert physician, because the study and treatment of disease is social work, etc. etc. This could only lead to confusion. So long, however, as the sociologist confines himself to the essentials of the problem of living together in large numbers, he will be prevented from wandering over the whole field of human knowledge. The essentials of that problem are found in the five specific questions outlined above. The writers who have made significant contributions to our knowledge of sociology have attempted to answer one or more of them. True, they have not all been called sociologists, but their contributions are none the less valuable on that account.

In this preliminary survey of the field of sociology we have glimpsed the general contour of the ground to be studied more in detail in the following chapters. The student who has read this chapter should have a pretty clear notion as to what sociology is, and what its leading problems are. The solution of each of these problems is a study in itself.

CHAPTER II

HOW MEN CAME TO LIVE TOGETHER IN SOCIETIES

THE fundamental and all-sufficient reason why human beings have always, so far as we know anything about them, lived together in those great groups called societies, is that it paid better than trying to live singly or in small groups. It paid better in the sense that they were safer against enemies of all sorts, and that they could provide more amply for their needs by associated than by isolated effort. This fact is basic and underlies every thing that may be said about social life, sociology, or social evolution. In spite of all the difficulties and conflicts that arise when men try to live and work together, they can not do otherwise and survive.

The basic fact is not that men have a social nature, or that human nature can express itself only in social life, but that the conditions under which men have had to live made group action or teamwork necessary. If men have even a partially developed social nature it must have come as a result of the fact that they have had to live and work and fight together for survival. They have had to evolve some capacity for teamwork in order to live in the only way they could live successfully, namely, in organized groups. This capacity for teamwork or associated effort is all that can properly be called a social nature. If human beings have made any progress in the art of living together in large groups it is partly because, through variation and selection, they have evolved a greater capacity for teamwork than their remote ancestors possessed, and partly because they have learned the art of government by means of which the more unsocial traits of human nature can be held in check.

If there is a creature which finds it, on the whole, unprofitable to live in groups, that creature is not only solitary in fact, but it has not developed a social nature for the reason that there was no survival value in a social nature. It has learned no way of influencing or controlling individual behavior in the interest of a group for the reason that there was no group to exercise such control. A possible case is the tiger; another is the eagle. Beyond mating and the process of reproduction, there is no advantage to either species in teamwork. Either can defend itself without help, and gather its food without coöperation. Besides, if there were too many of either species in the same neighborhood, they would frighten away the beasts or birds on which they prey. There would, therefore, not only be no advantage, but a positive disadvantage in trying to live together in large numbers.

Men, on the other hand, in common with many other species, have found a positive and overwhelming advantage in teamwork, or associated and organized effort. How they discovered it, may never be known. Lkie many other products of evolution, it may have been by the mere process of trial and error. They who managed, for any reason, to live and work together in groups, got on better than those who did not, and survived where others perished. Having somewhat higher intelligence than other animals, they could learn from experience, and eventually plan their teamwork.

The Familistic Theory. Just what form the first social groups took may never be known. Several reasonable conjectures may be made, however. A reasoning creature, who wants to know why things happen, is pretty likely to make guesses, otherwise called hypotheses, where final knowledge is impossible. One guess is that the first social groups were mere biological groups, called families, consisting of parents and children. With some species, the family, if such it can be called,— that is, the union of male and female for reproduction and the resulting union of parents and offspring,— is a very unstable and transient affair. The young grow quickly to maturity and begin to shift for themselves before others are born of the same parents. Sometimes mating is for a season only, though in other cases it is permanent. At any rate, the family does not approach in permanency that with which we are familiar under the name of the human family.

A physiological reason for the stability of the family among human beings is found in the prolongation of infancy. Among human beings the period of infancy accompanied by helplessness is so prolonged as to require parental care for a period of years. Parental feeling has evolved or been selected into the human race to provide a motive for the care of children during this prolonged period. Besides, younger children are born before the older ones are able to shift for themselves. This not only necessitates a prolonged period of parental care, but results in a group of several children to be cared for at the same time. Having learned to live together in a considerable group, it is not difficult to imagine them playing and working together, and engaging in teamwork of various kinds.

The writer who did most to impress upon students of sociology the vast importance of the prolongation of infancy was John Fiske.[1] He found the essential character of human evolution to be the growth of the psychic from the organic. In the complex life which human beings have to live there are more adjustments to be made than can be made by instinctive responses alone. Most of these responses and adjustments have to be learned, and there is a vast amount to be learned. The young bird or animal seems to be born with all the instincts it is likely to need to help it through a normal life. It does not need to learn a great deal, or, at any rate, it does not learn a great deal. Since it does not have to learn a great deal, it does not need a long learning period. Its capacity to make the few necessary responses is born with it and may therefore be called organic or instinctive. The human being, on the other hand, having so much to learn, needs a long period in which to learn it. Infancy is the learning period.

---

[1] See his *Outlines of Cosmic Philosophy* (Houghton Mifflin & Co., Boston, 1874. 2 vols.).

We need not here stop to appraise the philosophic value of this theory. It is conceivable that other creatures might find it to their advantage to learn many responses if they only had the capacity to learn. It is also conceivable that we human beings, in final analysis, really have no more which it would be advantageous to learn than other creatures, but having the capacity to learn, we learn. An individual living in a society of learners must needs learn or prove himself unfit for such a life. If unfit, he fails and, in the long run, perishes. Thus, it is quite conceivable that the capacity to learn came first, and the necessity to learn or be eliminated in the struggle for existence may have followed as a consequence. However, this is somewhat like the problem of the priority of the hen or the egg.

Waiving all questions of priority, there can be no doubt as to the vast importance of the prolongation of a learning period on the intellectual development of the human race, and of the prolongation of a period of helplessness on the social development of the race. The fact that the learning period and the period of helplessness are identical does not detract from its importance. As Bernard points out:

Very probably the prolonged period of infancy in the child has been selected into the race because of the greater adaptive intelligence of the human mother. Rather it would be more nearly correct to say that a prolonged infancy, involving the birth of the child prematurely from the standpoint of lower animal life, and immediate survival efficiency, has been selected into the race because of the ultimate survival value of a longer learning period or a more varied capacity to make adjustments (greater flexibility of characters) which permits the acquisition of a vastly greater store of adjustment technique.[1]

Moreover, as Fiske showed, the period of infancy is correlated with the growth of parental feeling. The growth of parental feeling he believed an important phase of progress; for, in this growth, he saw the germ of the family, and so of social life and all that is psychic. This significant fact is clearly recognized by all students of social psychology. Professor McDougal goes so

[1] L. L. Bernard, *Instinct, A Study in Social Psychology* (Henry Holt & Co., New York, 1924), p. 327.

far as to say that the parental attitude is the only truly altruistic element in nature.

It is no exaggeration to say that this one instinct (parental) is the mother of both Intellect and Morality. For without it, Intellect could not have been evolved; and its impulse is the only truly altruistic element in nature; and, though many philosophers have ignored the fact, the moral tradition, by which all moral character is shaped, could never have been built without this altruistic factor.[1]

Fiske's contribution to family history, his account of social origins, has finally become so largely associated with his name, that it overshadows somewhat a very vital background. It is well to remember that he laid great stress on the family partly because he saw in it the essential training ground for the developing of human sympathy. This was too narrow an assumption. He was a personal cambatant of selfishness; and he tried to strike at it, sometimes quixotically, in his writing. The important part of his work — the part, at least, that might lead the sociologist for a very great distance — is his theory that progress consists in the growth of the psychic, in the increasing complexity and effective organization of intelligence. The prolongation of infancy and the development of the family are important as they relate to the growth of the life of the mind.

Lest it be too hastily assumed that Fiske was a psychologist rather than a sociologist, it is necessary to call attention to the vast scope of his work. A striking personality, a contributor to the sum of human knowledge in several fields, including history, government, biology, philosophy, and even cosmology,— it is difficult to classify him. While his theory of the growth of the psychic from the organic may seem to be primarily a contribution to psychology, yet he connected it so closely with biology, physiology, and sociology as to give it a wide significance. The prolongation of the learning period called infancy carried with it the necessity of a long period of parental care. This in turn necessitated a more or less permanent association of individuals

---

[1] William McDougal, *Outline of Psychology* (Charles Scribners Sons, New York, 1923), p. 130. See also his *Social Psychology* (John W. Luce & Co., Boston, 1921), pp. 170–171, 274–275.

in a family group and became one of the dynamic factors in the development of domestic institutions. The central position of domestic institutions in organized society is attested by the large number of studies that have been made and of books written about them.[1] The prolongation of infancy becomes, therefore, one of the original data for the study of sociology.

The prolongation of infancy, supplemented, as Professor Wheeler has pointed out,[2] by the prolongation of the lives of parents, constitute two biological facts which, in combination, give us a considerable overlapping and intermingling of generations.[3] The long period of dependence of the young compels them to remain under the control of their elders. The long period of maturity on the part of the parents enables them to exercise that control. There is a long period of contact between the old and the young, the mature and the immature, the teachers and the learners; between those who have already learned through contact with their predecessors and those who are in process of being taught by contact with their elders. The elders thus become the transmitters of the accumulated wisdom and superstition, knowledge and prejudice, sence and nonsense, skill and awkwardness of the past, while the young become the transmittees.

Says Goldenweiser:

The significance of the family as a transfer point of civilization cannot be overestimated. In the socio-psychological domain it serves as a bridge between the generations, between fathers and sons. Truly organic, biological in its foundation but with important psychological and sociological correlates, the family is thus seen to be an universal possession of mankind.[4]

Anthropological studies clearly indicate that the family lies at the root of the cultural inheritance of primitive social life. "Biologically speaking," says Raymond Firth, "human society is

[1] Some of the most scholarly works ever published in the field of sociology have been on the subject of the family. Their titles would fill a small catalogue.
[2] *Social Life Among the Insects* (New York, 1923), p. 10.
[3] See also Galton, *Hereditary Genius* (D. Appleton & Co., New York, 1870).
[4] Alexander A. Goldenweiser, *Early Civilization* (Alfred A. Knopf, New York, 1922), ch. XII, p. 239.

founded on the family of parents and children, a group which has its ultimate beginning in the union of two individuals."[1] The family, thus, is not merely an extension of the sex-function. In actuality it has a far deeper significance in influencing the character of social formation and enabling society to maintain its continuity unimpaired. In transmitting to its children, through education, the characteristic ways of behavior called family tradition, a definite mental attitude or social culture pattern is established and social heredity is made possible. In short, prolonged infancy is one of the basic factors in the mechanism of social heredity. It is natural then that society, far more than the individual, becomes a creature that looks before and after.

Nothing in the whole field of sociology can exceed in importance this long period of overlapping and intermingling of generations. It gives a continuity to social life and social practices comparable to that given by the instincts to the life and practices of lower creatures. And yet it is less rigid than instinct in its operation. If there is a learning period, there must also be the possibility of learning new ways of behaving,— a possibility that seems to be lacking in those creatures whose behavior is controlled by instinct. We are often reminded of the rigidity of social tradition. We need to be further reminded that it is also plastic as compared with instinct. As a member of the family [says Bogardus], the child learns fundamental rules of conduct, gains respect for the law, and acquires principles of coöperation. Since the family has the characteristics of a social microcosm, the child in a social visioned family acquires many of the habits basic to constructive participation in public life.[2]

Yet the plasticity of the youthful mind is not left to be molded wholly by the haphazard experiences of time and place. The learning period makes it possible to test even the old traditions, to "prove all things." This tends to develop an attitude of crit-

---

[1] Raymond Firth, *Primitive Economics of the New Zealand Maori* (George Routledge & Sons, Ltd., London, 1929), p. 106.
[2] Emory S. Bogardus, *Fundamentals of Social Psychology* (The Century Co., New York, 1924), ch. v., p. 49.

ical reflection, and thus paves the way for diversity and originality so essential to progress. For just as in the organic life, so in the life of society, variability whether minute in character, or so extreme as to be called mutation, is the fundamental principle of development. On the other hand, the overlapping of age on youth makes it possible to "hold fast that which is good." The learning process, therefore, has two aspects which, in a proper state of balance, make progress possible. First, the young can learn of their elders. Second, they can discover.

Learning is largely by imitation. The overlapping and intermingling of generations have given to imitation the vast importance which led Tarde[1] to regard it as the essential social fact. It may be objected that as a general rule society tends to hold on too fast, that it tends too much toward an unerring conformity to the social heritage. But as Professor Karl Pearson points out:

> One of the strongest factors of social stability is the inertness, nay, rather active hostility, with which human societies receive new ideas. It is the crucible in which the dross is separated from the genuine metal, and which saves the body-social from a succession of unprofitable and possibly injurious experimental variations.[2]

The accumulation of social habits, traditions, customs, and *mores*, to which William G. Sumner devoted his prodigious learning, and which seemed to him the very essence of sociology, was made possible by the prolongation of the contact of the plastic minds of youth with the molding attitudes of age. Before the age of printed books there was a vast body of lore handed down from parent to child on the thin air of oral instruction. Some of it, of course, was false, as is much of that which is preserved in printed pages, but this body of lore and the responses of individuals to it, constitute what is sometimes called the social mind. Assuming that there is, as every physical scientist believes, an objective test for distinguishing truth from falsehood, progress might be said to consist in a gradual clearing of the social mind of accumulated falsehoods and the substitu-

---

[1] Cf. Gabriel Tarde, *The Laws of Imitation*, tr. E. C. Parsons (Henry Holt & Co., New York, 1903).

[2] *The Grammar of Science* (Adam and Charles Black, London, 1911), p. 1.

tion of accumulated knowledge.   Another aspect of the significance of imitation is the fact that diffusion as well as the building of culture,— material and ideological,— is due primarily to
it.   As McDougal says:[1]

> If imitation, maintaining customs and traditions of every kind, is the
> great conservative agency in the life of societies, it plays also a great and
> essential part in bringing about the progress of civilization.   Its operation
> as a factor in progress is of two principal kinds:
> 1. the spread by imitation throughout a people of ideas and practices
> generated within it from time to time by its exceptionally gifted members;
> 2. the spread by imitation of ideas and practices from one people to
> another.

As to the mechanism of imitation itself, its nature and origin,
I shall merely quote the statement made by one of the out-
standing psychologists in the field of educational psychology.
Says Professor Thorndike:

> On the whole the imitative tendencies which pervade human life . . .
> are, for the most part, not original tendencies to respond to behavior seen
> by duplicating it in the same mechanical way that one responds to light
> by contracting the pupil, but must be explained as the result of the arousal,
> by the behavior of other men, of either special instinctive responses or
> ideas and impulses which have formed in the course of experience connec-
> tions with that sort of behavior.   Man has a few specialized original
> tendencies whose responses are for him to do what the man forming the
> situation does.   His other tendencies to imitate are habits learned nowise
> differently from other habits.[2]

Human society in its functioning seems to show that there
is nearly always some semblance of intelligent awareness of
certain ends that are being pursued.   Yet it is a sad fact that,
in most of our social behavior, something of the element of
purposelessness tends to persist.   Activities are carried on in
all of our groups and societies which are more in the nature of
imitation pure and simple with no intelligent motive behind
them.   Pareto's emphasis on the fact that most human social

---

[1] *Social Psychology* (Methuen & Co., London, 1926), p. 341.
[2] Edward L. Thorndike, *The Original Nature of Man* (Teachers College, Co-
lumbia University, New York, 1913), p. 122.   See also M. Sherman and Irene
Sherman, *The Process of Human Behavior* (Williams & Norgate, Ltd., London,
1930), pp. 103–113.

actions are illogical, or rather allogical,— *i.e.* no coördination of actions and ends,— is too true to reality, and must be recognized in explaining social behavior. It must be borne in mind, however, that in some cases and in some forms imitation is essential to the maintenance of social unity and social cohesiveness. Likewise is it true that in trying to explain social behavior Sidgwick's cautious remark that "imitation will not explain everything, but explains a good deal" is perhaps the sounder approach to reality. But, discarding the various theories of causation of social behavior such as "Imitation" of Tarde, "Consciousness of Kind" of Giddings, or the "Collective Representations" of Dürkheim, the fact remains that one of the main factors in social behavior is the desire for uniformity and the fear of non-conformity which motivates human actions.

The prolongation of infancy and of parenthood, with the resulting overlapping and intermingling of generations, provides a physiological basis for the transmission from generation to generation of the vast body of lore which goes by the name of custom and tradition,— forms of imitation which constitute the greater part of civilization. Before the invention of writing and the keeping of records, that body of lore could only be transmitted by word of mouth. Without a long learning period and a wide overlapping of generations, the transmission of such a body of lore could scarcely have been possible. The broad contacts between generations supply a conductivity for the transmission of ideas over long periods of time, somewhat analogous to the high conductivity of certain metals for the transmission of physical energy. The family, based on the prolongation of infancy, becomes, under this theory, not only the original form of social grouping, but continues, down at least to the age of printing, the chief agency for the prolongation of civilization.

A learning period, however, would not be of much use without the capacity to learn. Lester F. Ward has suggested another physiological modification of the human species quite as important as the prolongation of infancy, namely, a superior brain development. Endowed with a plastic mind, "wax to receive and marble to retain," the prolongation of the learning period made the human race a conserver of tradition and a storehouse of accumulated knowledge.

2. *The Intelligence Theory.* According to Lester F. Ward, the genesis of human society lay in the fact that man early "perceived the advantages" which association yields. It derives its existence "only in proportion" as its advantages become actual and are perceived by the individual.[1] It is obvious that he means by the genesis of human society not the precise historical form in which it first appeared, but the underlying reason for its appearance and its continuance. These two concepts, that of the first form in which social life showed itself and the reason why it showed itself, while closely linked, are not identical and are logically separable. Ward's theory that the genesis of human society is found in the intelligence which perceived the advantages of group life does not contradict the theory that the first actual form of group life was the family, beginning with parents and children and enlarging to include a considerable group of kindred. The success of groups thus formed may have convinced human intelligence of its advantage.

Groups may have been brought together under other circumstances than those of mating, birth, or descent from a common ancestor. However they were formed, if they proved advantageous there would be empirical evidence to appeal convincingly to human intelligence. Furthermore, some modern anthropologists would be inclined to doubt whether primitive men were as intelligent as Ward seems to assume. However the first groups may have been formed, the fact that the individuals who belonged to them flourished and survived, increased in numbers and spread over more land, driving out smaller groups as well as isolated individuals, would be a sufficient explanation

---

[1] "This, then, is the essential prerequisite to all true social union, that there shall be sufficient brain development to enable the individuals interested to perceive, however dimly, the advantages of association." *Dynamical Sociology* (D. Appleton & Co., 1898), vol. i, p. 452.

"We are compelled to reject the doctrine of Aristotle, so prevalent everywhere, that man is naturally a gregarious animal, or, as it is less objectionably stated, that man is naturally a social being. Civilized man is undoubtedly a social being, but this quality has been the result of a long and severe experience by which a great change has been produced in his constitution." *Ibid.*, vol. ii, p. 221.

of the fact that all men now live in groups. Those who did not were long ago exterminated.

On the other hand, the hypothesis that the first actual groups grew out of the family may have been based on an overemphasis on the solidarity of the family. It is at least conceivable that the prolongation of infancy may have been a product as well as a cause of group life. Since infants could not survive a prolonged period of dependence unless there were something on which to depend, it looks as though there must have been some form of or approach to group life before infancy could have been greatly prolonged. Besides, in mild or semi-tropical countries, the period of infantile dependence is less prolonged than we northerners are in the habit of thinking. Where shelters are cheap and transient, where food requires a minimum of cooking, and where hearthfires are not indispensable to physical comfort, the family as we northerners know it, is a rather unstable and transient affair. Few of us realize how important to family life, and to group life as well, is a permanent shelter and a hearth or fireplace. The sacred fire, tended by the Vestal virgins, was apparently a Roman recognition of the fundamental importance of the hearth. Here was a gathering-place for those seeking comfort and cheer in cold weather. Here was the one place where every one felt physically comfortable and mentally cheerful, where every one liked to be. This feeling of comfort and cheer came to be associated with the persons one met in that place. Hence family affection and group loyalty.

Cooking also, in a cold climate, becomes an important ceremony. In connection with the fireplace as a place of congregation, came the eating place and the common meal as a place of satisfaction. The socializing influence of a common meal is fully appreciated by practical persons, if not by academic sociologists. A good dinner is known to be an excellent means of securing a "meeting of the minds" when agreement on important matters is desired. The sacrament of the Lord's Supper is probably a religious idealization of this fundamental fact, just as the Vestal fires were of the socializing power of the hearth.

The hearth, the common meal, and the permanent shelter called the home, are factors in the solidarity of the family, and possibly in the beginnings of group life, at least in northern latitudes. These factors, in combination, may be more important even than kinship. That is to say, those who are brought into close association by a combination of these three factors may be more closely bound together than those who are united by blood relationship. To be sure, there is likely to be a combination of blood relationship and all these other factors, but where, for any reason, there is not, there is likely to be a stronger emotional basis of unity among those who are closely associated under a common shelter, before a common hearth and around a common table, than among those not so associated but united by ties of kinship.

In southern latitudes, however, these factors are of less importance than in northern. Consequently, family solidarity is not so conspicuous and does not figure so convincingly as an explanation of the historical origin of group life. Shelters are not only less permanent but less necessary than in northern latitudes, fires are less necessary for comfort, and besides, the custom of eating together around a common table is less prevalent than among northern peoples. The expressions "home" and "home fires" do not call forth the same emotional responses as among northern peoples. The word "family" does not suggest the same idea. The suggestion that the origin of group life is found in the family does not thrust itself on the student of life among the southern races.

After all, there is no reason for assuming that group life everywhere began in the same way. Under some conditions, it may have begun with the family which later grew into a clan and a tribe based on kinship. Such historical illustrations as the "seed of Abraham" which developed into a cluster of tribes and later into a nation, do not touch the real point. Abraham himself came out of an ancient eastern city to start a cattle ranch in the Far West of Palestine. The city from which he came had developed a civilization in many respects as highly evolved as our own. As well argue from the Mayflower Compact that social life began with formal contracts as to argue from the case of Abraham that it began with the family. However, there are other evidences which are more convincing. Studies of clan organization seem to indicate that some societies may have been based on descent from a common ancestor, which, in turn, would suggest a familistic origin for some societies, but not necessarily for all.

One difficulty is to determine at what stage in their development our ancestors could really be called human. The most primitive tribes yet studied have at least developed a language. This development was probably an elaborate process extending over long periods of time. They also possess all the peculiar anatomical characters which we are accustomed to associate with the word *human*. If we assume a brain development which makes a language possible, it is reasonable also to assume a degree of intelligence which would enable men to see the advantage of group life when it was once demonstrated in real life. Intelligence may very well be included among the original factors in the development of social life.

3. *The Militaristic Theory.* Another plausible theory is that group life may have grown out of the necessity for protection against enemies. That ten men fighting together are more powerful than one, and that a hundred, if well organized, are more powerful than ten, must have been sufficiently obvious to appeal to the intelligence of any creature that could properly be called human. Even if that were not true, the fact that those who happened for any other reason,— such as kinship or subjection to a bully,— to fight in organized bands, commonly prevailed against those who did not, would have been sufficient. The only survivors, in the long run, would be those who fought in bands.

Strength in fighting both against other human beings and against huge beasts,[1] has two aspects, both promotive of group

---

[1] Native African hunters, armed only with javelins, do not hesitate to attack the lion if they can hunt in bands. When the lion charges, a number of javelins are hurled at him. At least one is likely to strike him, whereupon he invariably turns to attack the javelin, giving the hunters ample opportunity to dispatch him.

life and action. One is the possession of a situation, such as a cave, a cliff, or a lake village suitable for defense. The other is an organized group with a technical equipment suitable both for attack and defense. The balance of power between attack and defense has shifted back and forth, even down to the latest wars. The classical example is, of course, the mediaeval castle which, before the invention of gun powder, gave the defenders the advantage, but, when cannon came into use, were easily battered down around the defenders' ears, thus changing the whole political and social organization of Europe. The promptness with which Belgian forts were demolished by German cannon at the beginning of the World War seemed, for a time, to show that the balance of power was still on the side of attack. However, defense came out ahead when the art of trench warfare was developed. One evidence of this is the fact that, in spite of all the improvements in the technique of killing, a smaller percentage of those engaged were killed than in any other great war. The contest between the makers of cannon and the makers of armor plate is another illustration of the same age-long shifting of the balance between attack and defense. The above allusions are merely by way of illustration.

From the most primitive times, this balance has been shifting. Those people who tried to live in settled habitations were successful only so long or in so far as they were able to beat off the wandering bands of fighters. They were successful, apparently, only when they occupied positions which were easily defended, such as caves, cliffs, and lake villages supported on piles driven into lake mud.

Another phase of the military theory is found in the suggestion that organized society may have begun, in some cases at least, as a band of fighters under a war chief. The war chief may have won a following by pommelling weaker men, women, and children into subjection and organizing them under his arbitrary rule. If he possessed not only brute strength but some degree of organizing ability and intelligent foresight, the group thus formed might grow in power and numbers. The modern gangster may be a throwback to the founder of that form of early social life.

Instead of a mere bully, the primitive strong man may have been a leader in battle. Partly because of his power to compel obedience, and partly because of a popular recognition of his ability as a leader, or admiration of his prowess, he was able to organize a group of followers. If his ability was real, and his group was successful, his following would grow and become, eventually, a large and well integrated social group. The war chief and his following in certain modern fighting tribes may be a modern reproduction of the early beginnings of group life.

This strong-man theory does not necessarily contradict the familistic theory. The strong man may easily have been the head of a family which, because of his success as a leader, grew into a considerable group. His many wives and children, together with accretions from outside the family, of those seeking his protection and of others conquered by him and subjected to his government, could conceivably grow into a great society, especially if the head of the group were something of a statesman who could organize it into a superior fighting and producing organization.

One thing is certain, namely, that however the first groups came to be organized, no group could grow, or even survive in competition with other groups, unless it were efficiently organized either for fighting or producing, or both. This is rather more important than the question of the way in which the very first groups happened to start. In all probability, groups started in various ways and took on various forms. This variation among groups would play the same part in the evolution of groups that variation in biological organisms played in the evolution of organisms. But variation, in either case, must have been accompanied by selection if there was to be evolution in the Darwinian sense. Selection, in the evolution of social groups as well as in that of individual organisms, is determined by the ability to meet the conditions of life. Two conditions especially must be met: first, it must avoid being killed by enemies; second, it must avoid being destroyed by starvation.

No social group can survive, or be selected for survival, if it fails in either of these particulars. Therefore, it must be effectively organized for defense and for subsistence. Primitive statesmanship must have met this test, however the group happened to be organized in the first place.

In fact, this seems to have been the fundamental reason why men came to live together in groups. From the standpoint of fighting, no individual could defend himself against an organized group. They who lived and fought together could kill or dispossess any one who tried to live and fight alone. That being the case, it was certain that, in the course of time, no land could be held by isolated individuals if any group happened to want it. The process must have gone on, the stronger or more efficiently organized groups destroying or dispossessing the weaker or less efficiently organized, until surviving groups began to approach the optimum size. With poor means of transportation and communication, a group might outgrow the capacity of its statesmen. When that point is reached, it could not extend, or even defend its frontiers against the more compact groups which surrounded it. A kind of balance, resembling what the biologist calls the "balance of nature" would result.

4. *The Economic Theory.* As just suggested, one limiting factor in the growth of efficient organization is and always was the means of transportation and communication. Another is the capacity of the people for organization. This latter factor will be discussed in Chapter V on The Social Nature of Man. Transportation as a factor in determining the size of social groups has two aspects: first, the transportation of people to their food supplies; and second, the transportation of food to the people. The scarcity of food in any spot must have necessitated foraging over wide areas. Obviously, the people must have wandered in search of food, or they must have sent out foragers to bring food to their settled habitations, if there were settled habitations. Some fairly primitive people are known to have lived in caves. In those cases at least there were settled habitations necessitating the bringing in of food.

It used to be assumed, rather widely, that primitive men

lived by hunting and fishing, and, at a later stage, by herding. The only thing of which we can be reasonably certain is that primitive men must have lived, as the higher animals do, on what they could find. If the findings in the form of fruits and vegetables were good, they hunted for fruits and vegetables. If the findings were better in the form of shell fish, they hunted for shell fish. The vast extent of the kitchen middens found in various parts of the world would indicate that considerable numbers of men, over long periods of time, must have lived largely on shell fish. If, however, there were supplies of food in the form of animals that had to be stalked or chased, or fish that had to be lured and caught, men turned to hunting or fishing in the active sense.

The meagerness of the food supplies that could be found, before men learned to till the soil, made it impossible to support large groups in fixed settlements, unless there were means of carrying food from wide areas to the settlements. Before men learned to build boats there were no such means. Consequently, fixed settlements must have supported small groups. Wandering groups could, by following the food supply, forage over wider areas and thus support somewhat larger groups. Because of their numbers, these larger groups must have had the advantage in fighting, unless the smaller groups were well fortified in caves, cliffs, and other fastnesses. The villages built on piles over lakes were also well situated for defense. But wandering groups left few marks of their existence for archaeologists to study. Those groups who lived in well fortified places, such as caves and cliffs, or lake dwellings, were, apparently, the only ones who left durable evidences of their work. This may have given us of today an exaggerated notion of the importance of the cave, cliff, and lake dwellers.

Wandering groups which could follow the game as it followed the grass, or move to rivers when fish were running, and back to the hunting grounds when game was migrating, could support larger numbers of people than stationary groups until the latter found means of increasing their food supply. The cultivation of food crops, or the building of boats were, evidently, the first means of supporting large numbers of settled people.

The superior fighting power of wandering over settled people may have been, for a long time, the effective reason for the frequent failure of settled people to survive. This superior fighting power was, in turn, the result of the larger numbers which could live together in one group by wandering in search of food and foraging over wider areas. The discovery of maize, or Indian corn, is now believed to have been the basis of the first civilizations of inland America. This discovery solved the food problem, temporarily at least, and enabled large numbers of people to live together in one place. It must have been a precarious existence, however, as evidenced by the fact that, except where protected by water or mountain fastnesses, as around the lakes of Mexico and the mountains of Peru, those civilizations decayed, or the settlements disappeared. A failure of the maize crop, or its destruction by enemies, would have meant wholesale starvation.

In other parts of the world, water transportation seems to have given fixed settlements a somewhat safer source of food. Perhaps it was a combination of cheap transportation and the protection afforded by a water front. Wandering nomads, not having boats, were stopped by water. The settled village, having boats, could bring food from greater distances. It is, apparently, no accident that, in most parts of the world outside of America, the first permanent or durable settlements were located on rivers or other waters where transportation by boat was easy.

This suggests another theory as to how men first came to live together in groups or societies. It may be called an economic theory, to distinguish it from the familistic and the militaristic theories already considered. The economic theory is that the necessities of economic existence may have brought men together in certain places. A source of food, such as an oyster bed or a clam flat, may have drawn men to a certain spot, as sources of food will draw animals, birds, and insects. The mere fact of geometrical propinquity and a common interest in the food supply, without regard to family or kinship, may have been a sufficient basis for group consciousness and associated effort. Assuming a sufficient degree of intelligence to see the advantage of peace and coöperation, when once demonstrated, we have an adequate explanation of group activity and teamwork.

However, as suggested above, there is no compelling reason to think that group life everywhere began in precisely the same way. It may have begun in different ways in different times and places. The biological family may, and very likely did, in many cases, develop into a larger social group called the family, the clan, or the tribe. In other cases, a war chief may have gathered around himself a considerable body of fighters and servants, with their women and children. In still other cases, men may have reasoned it out and got together and agreed to live and work together, both for defense and subsistence. In still other cases they may have been drawn to the same spot by the presence of food, and, from the fact of actually being together with a common interest, may have learned to work together. Doubtless other ways can be suggested. It can not be too frequently repeated, however, that no matter how they first came to live and work together, the habit could not have spread and become universal if there had not been survival value in it.

If group life is so superior to isolated living as to make the latter impossible in any spot of land coveted by a group, why do men have so much trouble living together in groups? Why, in other words, is there so much conflict among people in the same group? One might easily understand how there might be conflict between groups. When one group becomes so great as to need more land as a source of subsistence, it has a motive for trying to get more land. If, in order to get it, it has to dispossess another group, the other group, also needing more land, will have a motive for resisting. This is clear enough, and it may throw some light on the source of conflict among members of the same group. That, however, will be discussed in the next chapter.

CHAPTER III

CONFLICT

1. *The Reality of Conflict.* It is difficult to imagine any human relationship — whether between individuals within a group, or between groups, societies or nations — that does not contain, in some form or other, elements of conflict as well as elements of harmonious coöperation.[1] This applies to the most intimate and tender of all human relationships, as well as to the most perfunctory, business-like or diplomatic. Even the relationship between husband and wife,— if they permit themselves to think of such things,— has elements of conflict, arising from an antagonism of desires or interests. Such questions as the division of the income, who shall have the auto on a given afternoon, the selection of names for the children, whether to go to the theatre or stay at home, contain elements of potential conflict. Likewise does their relationship have many elements of harmony. Each needs the other; they complement each other. There are large fields of activity in which their interests do not compete but rather coöperate, and in a great multitude of ways each gains in proportion as the other gains. Whether they live in peace and harmony or in a state of antagonism will usually depend upon which aspect of their relationship they let themselves think about most frequently. If they permit themselves to forget their need of one another and the many ques-

[1] See T. N. Carver and H. B. Hall, *Human Relations* (D. C. Heath & Co., Boston, 1923), p. 239.

43

tions on which their interests harmonize, and to think only of the questions on which there is a conflict of desire or interest, they are not likely to live a harmonious life.   If, on the other hand, those questions on which there is a unity of interests occupy their minds to the exclusion of those questions on which their interests conflict, they may expect nothing but peace and harmony.

Likewise, the most perfunctory and businesslike relationship has its elements of harmony as well as of conflict.   The producer, for example, needs the consumer, and the consumer needs the producer.   The producer gains in proportion as the consumers increase in number and in purchasing power.   To that extent at least, it is to the producers' interest to see the consumers prosper.   If they prosper, they are likely to make better customers for the producer.   It is likewise to the interest of consumers to see producers increase in number and efficiency. In their own interests the consumers must contribute to the prosperity of the producers by paying prices that will stimulate productive activities.   In many other ways it is easy to demonstrate that the interests of producers and consumers are in harmony.   But, on the other hand, when they meet face to face as bargainers, the price which suits the one is very likely to displease the other.   In the price-making process they discover a very definite conflict of interests.   The producer would like to sell at a high price; the consumer would like to buy at a low price, and there may be a great deal of higgling of the market. At such times, in the heat of argument, they may forget the larger field in which their interests harmonize.   If they forget their need of one another, and fail to see that there is somewhere a price which will partially harmonize the interests of both and probably create the least sum total of dissatisfaction on both sides, the conflict may become destructive to the interests of both, in which case, the psychology of conflict may displace the psychology of coöperation.

It is a part of the psychology of conflict to be willing to suffer injury if only we can inflict greater injury on our opponents.   In conflict we seek what may be called a negative profit, that is, a smaller loss or injury than we cause to the enemy. It is a part of the psychology of peace to seek a positive profit, that is, to be willing that the other fellow should gain if only we can gain by the same transaction. It makes a vast difference in all social relations whether we are under the general motivation of war or peace, of conflict or coöperation.

As stated in Chapter I, this fact of conflict in human relations was, chronologically, the first great social problem to attract the attention of students. A more complete statement would probably be to the effect that it was the baffling fact of a combination of harmony and conflict,— obvious harmony in some cases and obvious conflict in other cases,— which attracted the attention and puzzled the minds of students. So baffling was this apparent contradiction as to tempt men to try to eliminate it by shutting their eyes to it. In this world of harmony, they said, there is and can be no real conflict of human interests. To assert that there can be any real conflict is to impugn the beneficient Creator of the universe, is a more extreme statement of the same thesis. On the other hand, others said that human relationships are only another manifestation of "Nature, red in tooth and claw," "Man eating man, man eaten by man," etc. "Big fish eat little fish" is said by such pessimists to be the formula of human as of marine life.

To those extremists who assert one or the other of these views, it does not seem to occur that human relationships are sometimes harmonious and sometimes inharmonious. Common observation should convince any one of this. One problem of the sociologist is to explain the situation. However, this situation had been discussed voluminously before the term *sociology* was coined.

2. *The Psychology of Conflict.* It has been stated on good authority [1] that war is the natural condition of mankind. Something depends, of course, upon the way we define the word *natural.* That men as well as other creatures have always had

---

[1] The gist of this paragraph is elaborated in ch. VI of the author's book entitled *The Present Economic Revolution in the United States* (Little, Brown & Co., Boston, 1928).

to struggle for existence is now an axiom of biology. Among the ancestors of the peoples of Europe this struggle was carried on against enemies, both human and non-human, as well as against the impersonal factors of their physical environment. In the earlier stages of the human struggle for existence some of the non-human enemies were huge and ferocious beasts. As Sumner so forcibly expresses it: "When man came to take his seat at the banquet of life, he found the places all occupied, and to get a seat he was forced to expropriate a crowd of table-companions who were no less ravenous than he."[1] In the later stages the enemies which we fight against are mainly of the invisible sort, such as disease germs.

In fighting against our ancient enemies, the huge and ferocious beasts, the same fighting temper was required that was necessary in fighting against human enemies,— those rival tribes which were invading our hunting grounds or seeking to exterminate us in order that they might have more room for themselves. An enemy in that primitive kind of warfare was something to be killed. The more they were thinned out the better it was for us. The killing of such enemies required a violent exercise of the fighting muscles and these had to be driven by a fighting temper. Those who lacked either fighting muscles or a fighting temper had a very poor chance of survival and in the long run were exterminated. In Europe and the greater part of America the survivors were those who were psychologically as well as physically fitted for fighting.[2] The processes of natural selection, therefore, tended in those primitive times to breed a race with a fighting temper as well as with fighting muscles. A fighting temper, no less than fighting muscles, had survival value.

It sometimes happens, however, that a quality which has great survival value under one set of conditions proves to be a serious handicap under changed conditions. This may be true

---

[1] Sumner and Keller, *The Science of Society* (Yale University Press, New Haven, 1927), vol. I, p. 96.

[2] The Eskimos of the Far North, and other tribes that were content with a habitat too poor to tempt invaders, escaped this form of struggle and therefore escaped the necessity of evolving a fighting temper.

of emotional as well as of purely physical qualities. The fighting temper, for example, however necessary it may have been for survival, may prove a handicap in the stage which we hope[1] we are now entering, in which fighting — at least of the old type — is unnecessary. It is difficult to see how a berserker rage can help us very much in our war against disease germs, or in our efforts to overcome the law of diminishing returns from land. And yet it doubtless had its value in the kind of warfare that required a violent exercise of the fighting muscles. It is like a narcotic drug which paralyzes the higher centers of control, destroys caution, and enables men to show what looks like reckless courage, which has its place on the battlefield where soldiers are asked to make a desperate charge or lead a forlorn hope. The same drug, however, would be entirely out of place in a machine age when caution rather than recklessness should be promoted. If a drug could be found that would cause automobile drivers and others in responsible positions to show unusual caution, there would be something to be said for promoting its use.

This fighting temper sometimes drives us to fight when there is no wisdom in fighting. When we become extremely irritated toward anything we want to fight it. The child beats or breaks its mechanical toy when he cannot make it work. The grown man kicks the chair over which he has stumbled, an act which may not do the chair any harm, and which certainly does not do his shins any good. Grown men have been known to break their golf sticks not because their wisdom told them that it would improve their game, but merely because it was a natural expression of the fighting temper. Muleteers have been known to swear at their mules even though wisdom would counsel gentler measures. In short, the fighting temper is a useful quality so long as we are dealing with things that need to be exterminated. It is entirely useless when we are dealing with things that need to be cultivated, improved, or increased in

---

[1] The hope exists, even though it may prove to be an irridescent dream. If it proves to be such a dream, the inheritance of a fighting temper may be one of the reasons.

quantity. It is particularly troublesome when we are dealing with those irritating friends who are on the whole useful though sometimes stubborn and intractable.

In our larger social relations the fighting temper gives a great deal of trouble. When producers give way to their fighting temper in dealing with consumers they are doing themselves harm rather than good. The only satisfaction they could possibly derive would be that they might do consumers more harm than they did themselves. If producers are seeking a positive gain for themselves, they will want to see consumers increased in numbers and purchasing power. When laborers give way to their fighting temper in dealing with employers they make the same mistake. The last thing that laborers want is to see employers exterminated or even thinned out. What they want,— if they are wise,— is to see employers increased in number and in purchasing power.

Most of the "enemies" so-called that are developed in class wars are the kind that we need to increase rather than to diminish. If we are laborers, our so-called "enemies," the employers, need to be increased. When employers increase in number it is worse for each of them because there is more competition among them. It is better for the rest of us because there are more employers competing for our labor. It is obvious that here we are dealing with a kind of "enemy" with which our inherited fighting temper unfits us to deal. The fighting temper fits us to deal with enemies whom we want to exterminate or thin out. It leaves us bewildered and helpless in our dealings with the so-called "enemy" whose power is weakened as he increases in numbers and strengthened as he decreases in numbers.

If we are employers and are engaged in a modern class war, we weaken our so-called "enemy," the laborers, by increasing their number, by stimulating immigration or encouraging a high birth-rate among them. We strengthen our so-called "enemy" by thinning them out, either by restricting immigration or by encouraging birth-control among them.

Of course one may contend that these so-called "enemies" in

a modern class war are not really enemies. However, it takes intelligence and a process of reasoning to arrive at any such conclusion. Economic behaviorism,— the ordinary automatic response to a general situation,— regards them as enemies. In other words, our economic behaviorism is partly a product of the fighting temper which was bred into us through millions of years of social selection. Anything that irritates us' even though it be a niggardly customer who refuses to pay a satisfactory price for what we have to sell, is likely to arouse our fighting temper. We hate it and desire to do it an injury. "Hates any man the thing he would not kill?"

In international and other inter-group relations the same mixture of conflict and harmony exists. It is easy to show that both groups are interested in an exchange of specialties or in the territorial division of labor. But that does not obscure the fact that there are also questions on which their interests conflict. Boundary questions, trade balances, international debts and their terms of settlement, all require forbearance and courtesy and extremely careful diplomacy to prevent actual hostilities. No amount of subtlety or sophistry can argue these conflicts of interest out of existence. The question of intergroup peace or war depends upon which element in these intergroup relations the people of both groups permit themselves to think most about.

Whether the groups under consideration are territorial or class groups, we find questions on which their interests harmonize and others on which they conflict. Laborers need employers and employers need laborers. They complement one another as truly as do husband and wife, teacher and pupil, producer and consumer, manufacturer and farmer. Nevertheless, there are other questions on which their interests conflict. If laborers would work willingly and cheerfully for low wages, employers would gain. If employers would willingly and cheerfully pay high wages, laborers would gain. To bring about a harmonious compromise sometimes requires the utmost tact and diplomacy. Employers frequently find it to their interest to import cheap foreign labor; laborers find it to their interest to exclude it.

In brief, throughout the entire range of human relations, we find elements of conflict as well as elements of harmony. This fact, namely, that both conflict and harmony exist side by side in all our social relations, has forced itself upon the attention of students of social affairs. Prophets, theologians, philosophers and sociologists have clearly realized its significance and have sought to find some explanation of it. As Professor Hobhouse says:

> In living together, consciously and unconsciously we exert pressure and constraint upon one another, and consciously and unconsciously we coöperate and draw out from each other capacities which would otherwise be dormant. . . In every actual society harmony is shot through with disharmony and in the social relations there is more or less constraint, distortion, or mere indifference.[1]

The fact of harmony may be more fundamental than the fact of conflict, but it does not force itself so dramatically upon the attention of the student. As a storm is more impressive than calm, so conflict is more impressive than peace. It is not strange, therefore, that human conflict was one of the first topics to puzzle serious minds and to receive the attention of students. Why do storms occur? was more likely to be discussed by moderately rational creatures than, Why don't they occur? Why is there human conflict? was also a more ready theme for debate than, Why is there peace? The earliest sociological theories were theories of conflict. These were embodied in legends, allegories and myths before they were set forth in thesis form. This observed phenomenon of conflict between races, between cultures, between groups and between individuals within groups so strongly impressed itself upon their minds that they considered it in itself to be an ultimate reality. A deeper insight, however, discloses the fact that conflict in itself is not primary but is the result of a more fundamental factor which is strictly of an objective nature rather than subjective or purely psychological. This, then, leads to a study of the objective source of

---

[1] L. T. Hobhouse, *Social Development* (Henry Holt & Co., New York, 1924), p. 70.

conflict and the various explanations given as to its nature and function.

While the fighting temper unquestionably intensifies conflict, and, once developed, may even be a secondary cause of conflict, it can not in any evolutionary sense be called a primary cause of conflict. It seems to have been itself a result of conflict, that is, a product of a situation in which fighting was necessary, and in which the possession of a fighting temper had survival value. This, however, does not explain what there was to fight about, or why it was necessary to fight. Without some such necessity there could have been no survival value in a fighting temper. We must look deeper for the ultimate source of conflict.

So glaring has been the fact of conflict as to lead many writers to identify it with the problem of evil. As such it was the first problem in sociology to receive the serious attention of students, seers, philosophers, and theologians.[1] They were puzzled to know the source of the difficulty and they sought for an answer in a way that gave some unity to their thinking. Some found the answer in the doctrine of "original sin" and the remedy in religion. Others, like Plato,[2] found the answer in the institution of property, leading men to think in terms of *meum* and *tuum*, and the remedy in justice. Others found the answer in scarcity and the conflict of interests which result from it.[3] While this problem of conflict is a distinctly sociological problem, the early writers who discussed it did not call themselves sociologists.

3. *Scarcity.* Much has been written in a moral vein on the subject of man's ever expanding economic and social wants.

---

[1] The author is here referring to that body of literature and tradition which has come down to us of the western world and which constitutes our own literary heritage. Men of every type and state of civilization have thought seriously about all the things which occupy the minds of modern sociologists. Wherever men wrote at all, they have written about these things. Research in other literatures— Egyptian, Babylonian, Indic, Chinese, Arabic — will yield excellent fruits. The present discussion relates only to modern European and American writings.

[2] See the dialogue as set forth in Plato's *Republic*, Book V.

[3] See the author's *Essay in Social Justice* (Harvard University Press, 1914), ch. II, on "The Ultimate Basis of Social Conflict," where it is shown that the central problem of justice grows out of the necessity of distributing things that are scarce, that is, insufficient to satisfy men's desires.

The usual statement is that people want too much, but the meaning of this statement has never been sufficiently analyzed. It obviously means that there is some lack of coördination between man's desires and nature's means of satisfying them. When this lack of coördination is looked at from one point of view, it is called scarcity. When viewed from another point of view, it is called self-interest or selfishness. Considered as a whole, however, it reveals itself as what Dean Pound calls "the central tragedy of human existence."

That scarcity in one form or another is the ultimate basis of human conflict is the thesis which will be discussed in this section. The other side of the shield, called selfishness, will be discussed in a later section. Around these two facts of scarcity and self-interest are grouped practically all our moral ideas and all our laws and institutions for the control or mitigation of human conflict. They underlie all theories of economic value and to some extent also social value.

This idea is remarkably well expressed by Roscoe Pound [1] in the following language: "From an earthly standpoint, the central tragedy of existence is that there are not enough of the material goods of existence, as it were, to go around; that while individual claims and wants and desires are infinite, the material means of satisfying them are finite; that while, in common phrase, we all want the earth, there are many of us but there is only one earth. Thus we may think of the task of the legal order as one of precluding friction and eliminating waste; as one of conserving the goods of existence in order to make them go as far as possible, and of precluding friction and eliminating waste in the human use and enjoyment of them, so that where each may not have all that he claims, he may at least have all that is possible. Put in this way, we are seeking to secure as much of human claims and desires — that is, as much of the whole scheme of interests as possible,— with the least sacrifice of such interests."

The word *scarcity* has a relative rather than an absolute mean-

---

[1] *The Spirit of the Common Law* (Marshall Jones Co., Boston, 1921).

ing. A thing may be very abundant, speaking absolutely, and yet if there is not as much of it as people want, it is scarce relatively to human wants. Again, there may be very little of it, but if that little is more than people want, it is not ordinarily said to be scarce; certainly not in the economic sense. Finally, scarcity is always a question of time and place. No matter how much there may be of a thing, if it is not found when and where it is wanted, it is then and there scarce. The fact of scarcity, however, can never be completely intelligible and its meaning apparent until its relation to the size of population is made clear. Between the two factors there is the closest interaction. Scarcity is both limited and modified by the factor of population, and in turn limits and modifies the size of every population.

Sex and hunger [1] are brought into conflict by two other great facts: first, the fact that a "natural" birth-rate is higher than a "natural" death-rate; second, the fact that increasing applications of labor to the cultivation of a given area of land do not give proportionally increasing returns. By a "natural" birth-rate is meant such a birth-rate as results wherever the powerful sex impulse is not repressed or, at least, kept under rational control. By a "natural" death-rate is meant such a rate as would result if every individual lived out a normal lifetime, say his alloted three-score years and ten, or four-score years, and died a "natural" as distinguished from a tragic or an untimely death.

The average pair, for example, can have a total of only two deaths, but if they live out a normal span of life and do not control the sex impulse, they will have more than two children. Their children, likewise, will continue reproducing more than their own numbers. Wherever population is stationary, the birth-rate and the death-rate must balance. This balance means either that the death-rate is abnormally and tragically high, to balance a "natural" birth-rate, or that the birth-rate has been reduced to balance the death-rate. Among all the lower crea-

[1] As Schiller pointed out, the animate world is carried on "durch Hunger und durch Liebe," but there is a conflict between them.

tures and the lower orders of men, there is neither the intelligence nor the morale which would make it possible for them to reduce their birth-rate. It goes on at a "natural" rate, that is, reproduction is a physiological or an animal process, and in no sense a rational or a moral process. But, sooner or later, the death-rate must rise to balance this enormous birth-rate, otherwise the species would soon lack standing room.[1]

Of course there never was a highly developed human society that did not, in one way or another, limit its birth-rate. Marriage is the most nearly universal method of keeping the birth-rate under some degree of control. By suppressing promiscuous breeding and exercising some degree of ceremonial control over marriage, a measure of control over the birth-rate is automatically established. Where, along with ceremonial control of marriage, there is also an enforced responsibility on the part of parents for the support of their own children, a somewhat more effective control of the birth-rate is established.

Among all creatures which are incapable of exercising intelligent foresight,— and this includes human beings of the lower grades of intelligence,— reproduction is a purely physiological process. It begins at puberty and continues until the sterility of advancing age intervenes. But in every human society where ceremonial marriage prevails, and where the *mores* enforce parental responsibility, reproduction does not begin at puberty and does not proceed at the rate which is physiologically possible.

As already pointed out, sex and hunger are thrown into conflict by the fact that the quantity of food that can be grown on an acre of land is limited. So long as this fact exists, the number of wants which can be satisfied by the produce of that acre will also be limited. When, therefore, the gratification of sex leads to an increase of numbers in a given area, the people must either manage to draw their food from wider areas or they must work harder and harder to grow enough produce in the original area.

---

[1] Cf. E. A. Ross, *Standing Room Only* (The Century Co., New York, 1927). Also T. N. Carver and Hugh Lester, *This Economic World* (McGraw-Hill Book Co., New York, 1928), chap. I.

Not only is the quantity of food that can be grown on a given area limited, but long before that limit is reached, the soil begins to yield diminishing returns to intensive cultivation. That is, you cannot go on doubling your crop on a given area by simply doubling the labor used in cultivating it, or quadrupling the crop by quadrupling the labor, and so on indefinitely until the limit is reached.

Putting these two great facts together, namely, the fact that a "natural" birth-rate is higher than a "natural" death-rate, and that land yields diminishing returns to labor, we have an explanation, adequate for the moment, of the universal fact of scarcity. Of course, one might carry the inquiry further by asking why we are so constituted as to make a natural birth-rate higher than a natural death-rate. An approximate answer would be that during the long period of our development on this planet, the conditions of living were so hard, our enemies so numerous and so deadly, as to produce a high death-rate among us. A high birth-rate was necessary if we were to avoid extinction. A powerful sex impulse was necessary to insure a high birth-rate. By some process of adaptation which the evolutionist does not understand any better than any one else, this powerful sex impulse was developed or inherited from pre-human ancestors, who also needed a high birth-rate to prevent extinction. Beyond this, it seems futile to push the inquiry.

We might also, and with equal futility, inquire why land is so scarce, or why it is so constituted as to yield diminishing returns. We must, apparently, accept these facts as among the primary data of sociology. At least we may, in this discussion, regard them as starting points for the study of human conflict.

This ever present and persistent fact of scarcity has a great deal to do in directing our conscious and planned behavior. Much of our behavior is, of course, purely automatic. Much that is not automatic is spontaneous and not consciously planned, being of the nature of play or self-expression. Much of it, however, is planned and consciously directed toward desired ends. The greater part of this is directed toward the getting or utilizing of something that is scarce,— of which we do not have as

much as we want. For the great mass of mankind, this constitutes the serious business of life. Getting and using; getting in
order to have a more ample supply; using economically, in
order that our supply may go as far and satisfy our desires as
fully as possible; these occupy the greater part of the waking
time and direct the working energies of the masses of mankind.
Very few ever escape from this imperious necessity, and they
who do seldom amount to much.

That there are possibilities of evil in this situation has been
felt by moralists of many times and places. The desire to get
more than one has of a substance which is scarce is pretty likely
to conflict with the desire of some one else. Acquisitive efforts
bring people into conflict, thus producing moral, social, legal,
and political as well as economic problems. An interesting illustration of the effect of scarcity on "morals" is furnished by
Worth E. Shoults in his account of the Adelie penguins of
Antartica.[1]

An Adelie's nest consists of a loose pile of small stones, quite unadorned
or softened with lining; but unfortunately for the peace of the avian community, there is not in the near vicinity a sufficient supply of such building
material to go around. Thus does temptation enter into the life of a
penguin. . . . He longs to supply his wife with more and better stones
for the construction of their little love nest, but there are none to be had,
with honor.

Soon he covets those within his neighbor's stone pile, and, having thus
broken one commandment, he skids further along the downward path and
before long is engaged in taking what he can while his neighbor isn't looking.

Constant vigilance is the price that must be paid for keeping a stone
bungalow under one's feathers in a city of penguins.

Various ways out of the difficulty have been suggested either
as preachments or as practical measures. One is the repression
of desires; another is the increase of goods that are scarce. In
so far as desires can be repressed, or prevented from expanding,
in so far will scarcity be alleviated and the conflict of desires
softened. In so far as goods can be multiplied, the same results

[1] *National Geographic Magazine*, February, 1932, p. 260.

occur. Both seem to fall short of the complete elimination of conflict.

We cannot afford to pass over without protest the idea, too frequently held by certain popular moralists, that the development of character is the aim and purpose of life. If that were accepted, we might be led rather easily to the conclusion that the rigors of a harsh climate, and of meager subsistence, with the necessity for industry, frugality, and forethought which those rigors impose upon us, were designed to produce these virtues, or a type of man possessing them. It seems more in harmony with the theory of evolution to regard character merely as a means to an end, a means of survival in an environment where self-discipline is necessary.

Instead of regarding the virtue of industry as an end, and a niggardly environment as a means of developing that virtue, it seems more reasonable to regard survival as an end, a niggardly environment as an actual condition, and the virtue of industry as a means of attaining the end under the condition. Instead of regarding the virtues of thrift as an end and long winters as a means of developing that virtue, it seems more reasonable to regard survival as an end, long winters as an actual condition, and the virtue of thrift as a means of attaining the end under the condition, or merely as a necessary means of surviving long winters. All the virtues that go to make up what we commonly call character, and even character itself in its totality, must apparently be regarded as means of survival under harsh conditions, as means of adapting ourselves to a physical environment to which we are not naturally adapted. The painfully acquired ability to work and to control our appetites is a kind of adaptation analogous, in the animal world, to the blubber of the whale, the fur of the seal, or, in the human world, the ability to eat and digest large quantities of fat food as a means of keeping warm.

3. *Man and Nature at War.* Any leaning which we may have toward a deep-lying harmony between man and nature is easy enough so long as we contemplate only the civilized races that dwell in temperate climates. We, in this climate, with our

well constructed shelters, heating appliances, and clothes, have evidently through work achieved a higher degree of physical comfort than have most dwellers in the tropics where shelter, clothes, and fires are unnecessary. But our belief is likely to receive a shock when we consider the hyperboreans. These dwellers in the Far North are certainly under the chastening hand of a rigorous Nature. If the discipline of natural forces is what men need to develop character, they certainly are under that discipline. If necessity is the mother of invention, they should be very inventive. If plain living always stimulates high thinking, the intellectual lives of these people should be on an exceedingly high plane. Yet, according to our standards at least, their intellectual life is at a low level, their inventiveness, while thoroughly respectable, can hardly be said to be greater than ours or even comparable with it. Their civilization, according to any standard which may be taken as a rational criterion, has never reached an advanced stage.

Though we are accustomed to thinking of our own climate as somewhat harsh and the physical conditions under which we live as somewhat rigorous, they can hardly be shown to be more harsh and rigorous than the conditions of the tropics. The harshness and the rigors of our climate are of a different sort than those of warmer climates. It is by no means certain that the climate of the tropics is any milder than ours. The cold is less intense but the heat is fiercer. Certain tropical countries are, of course, prolific in their supplies of food. But this same terrific fecundity produces innumerable enemies as well as friends of the human race. These enemies include not only ferocious animals and reptiles but many invisible ones as well. The hookworm, the mosquito, and unnumbered kinds of harmful bacteria imperil the lives of the dwellers in the tropics quite as much as the east winds do the lives of New Englanders. Besides, it is probably easier to guard against the east wind than against the invisible and intangible enemies that flourish in the tropics. The amount of intelligence that is necessary to enable us to fight against cold is probably much less than that required to fight against the anopheles, the hookworm, the germs of the sleeping sickness and other tropical enemies.[1] In any tropical country, man is certainly as much out of harmony with his environment as in any part of the United States or Europe.

On the whole, it would be quite as easy to maintain the thesis that the civilized races of the temperate zones are less out of harmony with their natural environment than are the less civilized races of the Far North or of the tropics,— in other words, that the most civilized races occupy those parts of the globe where the necessity of work is least,— as it would be to maintain the opposite thesis, namely, that civilization is stimulated by harsh conditions, and the necessity for actively controlling and modifying these conditions. This would go a long way toward destroying the thesis that it is good for the human race to be compelled to work hard to modify its environment. It would probably be nearer the truth to say that it is good for the human race to live in an environment where the amount of work necessary to bring the environment into harmony with human requirements is at the minimum, where nature encourages men to work, first by providing him with abundant raw materials, second, by responding vigorously to his efforts to grow food. A favorable environment, in other words, is one that responds promptly and beneficiently to a relatively small amount of work; where a minimum of clearing of the ground and of tillage is necessary to produce an abundant crop, where a minimum of labor in forests and mills, quarries or brickyards, is necessary to provide building materials that are adequate for shelter; where fuel is abundant and easily secured; where, in

[1] The following description of life in a tropical jungle is likely to increase our satisfaction with our own climate, harsh as it may seem at times. The tropical jungle abounds with life, it is true, but much of it is predatory to man rather than useful to man.

". . . Then there was every kind of noxious insect — mosquitoes without end, gigantic leeches dangling from every leaf which made a specialty of attacking the eyeballs, ticks, stinking caterpillars, immense blue-bottles which swarmed in clouds over any food left uncovered, crickets which ate a man's clothes up in a night, and a plague of minute bees which settled in myriads on the heated face of the traveller. Above all, there was the rain. The whole country was water-logged by the flooding rivers and incessant deluge. In the dry season the average rainfall was about two and a half inches a day." John Buchan, *The Last Secrets* (T. Nelson & Sons, Ltd., London), 1923, p. 252.

short, it takes the smallest possible amount of intelligence to
see the advantages of active adaptation,— that is, of controlling the environment and making it over to fit the requirements
of the human organism.

That ancient civilizations arose in regions where labor applied
to land was highly productive is a commonplace in history.
The fertile river valleys of Egypt, Mesopotamia, India, and
China supported civilizations when our European ancestors were
still savages.   Here food was so abundant that men had time
to do other things besides satisfying their immediate daily needs;
or, rather, a part of the population could produce food enough
to support the rest while the latter gave their time to other
things.   Art, architecture, philosophy, religion, and government
could therefore flourish.   The civilizations which have since
grown up in latitudes farther north may not have exceeded
those earlier civilizations in physical magnificence, but they
have exceeded them in all that makes for the comfort and well-
being of the average man.

On the other hand, the overpowering influence of the terrific
productiveness of nature in certain tropical regions is sufficient
to discourage man's enterprise.   Kipling's story "Letting in the
Jungle"[1] gives a vivid picture of the way in which the jungle
struggles to re-assert itself,— to flow back, as it were, upon a
cleared area and overwhelm it as with a flood of rank vegetation.
Concerning India, Buckle writes:

Besides the dangers incidental to tropical climates, there are those noble
mountains which seem to touch the sky, and from whose sides are dis-
charged mighty rivers which no art can divert from their course and which
no bridge has ever been able to span. There, too, are impassable forests,
whole countries lined with interminable jungle, and beyond them, again,
dreary and boundless deserts,— all teaching man his own feebleness and
his inability to cope with natural forces. Without, and on either side,
there are great seas, ravaged by tempests far more destructive than any
known in Europe, and of such violence that it is impossible to guard against
their effects. And as if in those regions everything combined to cramp the
activity of man, the whole line of coast from the mouth of the Ganges to
the extreme south of the peninsular does not contain a single safe and

[1] In *The Second Jungle Book.*

capacious harbor, not one port that affords a refuge which is perhaps more necessary there than in any other part of the world.[1]

In contrast to India, Buckle points to Greece as a country where everything invites man to dominate. There is nothing to terrify or overwhelm him. Everything tends to exalt the dignity of man, while in India everything tends to depress it.

Whatever opinions we may hold on the deeper question of an underlying harmony between man and the environment in which he lives, there is no doubt whatever that individual human beings frequently have a feeling of discomfort; that is to say, they are sometimes cold, hungry or sick, and these discomforts would be much greater than they are now if men did not work and go to great pains to prevent them. But work, if carried beyond a certain limit, is also disagreeable, causing fatigue and interfering with various forms of enjoyment. In this dilemma, where the choice is between other forms of discomfort and the disagreeableness of hard work, the finite mind will have difficulty in appreciating the doctrine of a complete harmony between man and his environment. With its limited vision, the apparent maladaptation seems quite real.

When we approach the problem from this point of view, the whole economic struggle becomes a vast, united effort to attain to a harmony which does not naturally exist. If men are hungry because their environment does not spontaneously yield food enough, they try to improve on the natural food supply by causing it to grow in greater abundance. If they are cold, they try to make a warm climate next to their bodies. They accomplish this by holding heat in the body by means of clothes and shelters, and by producing artificial heat in their dwellings by burning fuel. However, the way of complete escape from discomfort by means of work is limited by the intervention of fatigue. The choice has to be made between two forms of discomfort,— that which arises from a lack of goods, and that which arises from an excess of labor. So long as the lack of goods causes more discomfort than the excess of labor, we keep

[1] *History of Civilization in England* (D. Appleton & Co., New York, 1908).

on working.   When the excess of labor begins to cause more discomfort than the lack of goods, we stop working.[1]

However, the superabundance of some things may be as great a cause of discomfort, or as distinct a phase of mal-adaptation between man and nature, as the scarcity of other things.   Things that are positively harmful to man are always superabundant, from his point of view, no matter how small the quantity. However, there are relatively few of such things.   Poisons, noxious insects, disease germs, and a few others might be named. But highly useful things may become nuisances where they exist in too great abundance.   Water in a rain-drenched, swampy country may be as great a source of discomfort as its lack in an arid country.   Men will work as hard to reduce its supply in the one case as to increase its supply in the other case. Superabundance is in one case as clear a form of maladaptation as scarcity is in another.   Moreover, conflicts of interest among human beings are as certain to arise in the effort to get rid of that which is superabundant as in the effort to get more of that which is scarce.   However, the number of cases in which superabundance is a cause of strife are small as compared with the number in which scarcity is the cause.

The term "environment" is somewhat indefinite, as any comprehensive term is likely to be.   So far as the individual is conscious of his environment, it is only at certain points where he is in contact with it.   These points of contact he is likely to visualize as physical objects.   His attitude toward his environment is concentrated on certain of these physical objects. Toward them his attitude is one of repugnance, of indifference, or of desire.   The following outline includes them all.

Objects of repugnance (nuisance or "illth")	{ 1. Harmful { 2. Useful but too abundant
Objects of indifference	{ 1. Useless but not harmful { 2. Useful but sufficient (free goods)
Objects of desire (wealth)	Useful and scarce

---

[1] The economist, of course, works out the equilibrium of marginal disutilities with great nicety.

Economists have generally concentrated their attention upon that class of objects which, in the above outline, are called objects of desire,— which are both useful and scarce,— or wealth, and upon man's efforts to acquire them. The second group listed under "Objects of indifference," namely, objects which are useful but amply sufficient, and not too abundant, he calls free goods, and then dismisses them from further consideration. Objects of repugnance are scarcely discussed at all, though efforts to get rid of them are clearly economic efforts. Killing of weeds or of beasts of prey may well be regarded as parts of the industry of growing crops and herds, or of alleviating the scarcity of useful things. Killing disease germs which attack the human body is somewhat more difficult to bring under the production of wealth, though it clearly improves the relation between man and his environment. Destructive nuisances, predatory plants and animals constitute, from one point of view, a problem of superabundance. From another point of view, they interfere with the production of useful things and may be regarded as factors in the problem of scarcity. The problem of value, in any positive sense, is a problem of scarcity, since nothing has a positive value unless it is scarce. There is, however, such a thing as negative value, sometimes called nuisance value. This phase of value, however, has attracted comparatively little attention either from economists or sociologists.

5. *The Law of Personal Preference.* As already pointed out, even the scarcity of desirable things could not produce conflict among human beings who had no personal preferences. If we could imagine a race of men who cared equally for all persons, for others as much as for self, for distant as much as for near relatives and neighbors, for members of other social groups as much as for their own fellow citizens or members of their own social groups, we could scarcely imagine them in a state of conflict with one another. The personal preferences which ordinary men show are generally summarized under the term self-interest. This is not an accurate term because it does not leave sufficient room for genuine interest in others, ranging all the way from passionate affection to casual friendship; but more of this later.

For the present it is sufficient to note that at least two factors are necessary to produce a conflict of interests: first, scarcity; and second, a preference for some persons as compared with other persons. Self is generally in the preferred list.

It is not uncommon to attribute conflict to self-interest alone, but this is incorrect. As pointed out already, scarcity, as truly as self-interest, is a factor. When either factor is missing, the result — conflict — does not ensue. In this sense, both are equally important. Again, an intense interest in a person other than self may lead one to fight as hard for that other person as for self. It is the fact of personal preference, rather than of self-interest, that counts. It is undoubtedly true that most of our personal preferences center around ourselves. This fact gives whatever justification there is for such terms as selfishness or self-interest.

The term self-interest does not seem to be very well understood, probably for the reason that it has never been sufficiently analyzed. It is not necessary to spend much time on a hair-splitting discussion of the old philosophical riddle as to whether altruism is or is not a form of selfishness. It is argued, according to this highly sophisticated method, that the altruistic individual is presumably altruistic because he prefers to be so, and that since he gratifies his preference he is to be accounted, to that degree, selfish. Such an unnatural conclusion could result only from an overemphasis upon motive rather than upon conduct, or perhaps more accurately, from a failure to see that a motive derives whatever value it has from the conduct which results from it. It may be true from a purely subjective standpoint and without any regard whatever to the problem of living together in large numbers, that the man who gets more delight from the taste of food upon the palates of his children than upon his own is as truly selfish as the man who gets no pleasure at all from the taste of food on any palate but his own. But when we look at it from the standpoint of his relation to other individuals and consider the way in which he fits into a social environment, there is no doubt as to which kind of a father would be better for children. That, after all, is the only thing that matters. There is no doubt that the man who takes some pleasure in the happiness or well-being of his neighbors fits somewhat better into a neighborhood than the man who takes no pleasure in anything except his own sensual gratification. The qualities which enable one to function properly as a neighbor and a member of society are the ones which a society should value highly and try to cultivate in its members. One way to cultivate such qualities is for society to show its approval of them and its disapproval of their opposites. Juggling the names of these qualities does not get us anywhere toward the solution of the problem of living together in large numbers.

Discarding all subjective quibblings, we may state, at least tentatively, that benevolence is a quality in the individual which enables him to take pleasure in the pleasures of others and to suffer pain or at least mental discomfort when others suffer pain. He who possesses this quality will normally, without compulsion, behave in ways which will give pleasure to others and avoid giving them pain. Selfishness, on the other hand, is a quality which prevents one from taking pleasure in the pleasures of others or suffering pain from the pains of others. He who is of such a quality is not likely to do much to increase the pleasure or decrease the pains of other people.[1]

It must be borne in mind, however, that both benevolence and selfishness are relative terms, depending upon the degree of self-preference,— the degree to which one prefers self to others. If, by complete benevolence is meant the quality which gives absolutely no preference to self as compared with other creatures, however far removed, then it is safe to say that such a thing as complete benevolence does not and never did exist except, perhaps, in myth and fable. The oriental saint who gave his body to feed the tiger merely because the tiger was hungry would perhaps be an example of absolute benevolence in this sense. On the other hand, such a thing as complete

---

[1] Benevolence is, of course, closely related to sympathy, which Adam Smith made the basis of social behavior.

A brief and good exposition of the Scottish school of ethicists including Adam Smith's Concept of Sympathy is given by Ethel Muir in *The Ethical System of Adam Smith* (J. Bowes, Halifax, N. S., 1898).

selfishness does not exist if that term means a quality which shows absolutely no regard for the interest of any other person than self.

What are called benevolence and selfishness as actual facts in the world are really found somewhere between the two extremes, one of which allows no preference whatever for self, and the other of which allows no interest whatever in any other being. Any one, however benevolent, will show some preference for self when his interests conflict with those of disease germs, noxious insects, the lower animals, and even of the higher animals, all of which are God's creatures but against which even benevolent persons have been known to wage war.

We can probably go further and say that every one, however benevolent, will show some preference for self or those near him where his or their interests conflict with those of other human beings rather distantly removed in space or kinship or like-mindedness. The same individual who would not sacrifice his own interests in favor of a dweller at the antipodes or a stranger who lives a long way off, might be willing to do so for those who are peculiarly near and dear to himself. In other words, every one, however selfish, will show some regard for some other person, perhaps very closely related to himself. He would not be a benevolent man,— he would scarcely be human, but rather an angel of love,— who would be willing to go hungry in order that he might relieve the mild hunger of another man of a different race or color whom he never saw. He would not be a selfish man or anything human, but a devil of hate, who would not be willing to deny himself some trifling satisfaction in order to save from starvation or extreme suffering some near relative or neighbor. Neither angels of love nor devils of hate actually exist in human form, though there may be pretty close approximations to both.

From this it will appear that the real difference between the benevolent and the selfish man is a difference of degree [1] rather than of kind. The benevolent man may be said to have a mild

---

[1] See the author's *Essays in Social Justice* (Harvard University Press, 1914), p. 62 *et seq.*

or moderate preference for self or for those peculiarly close to self, and the selfish man to have a strong or immoderate preference for self. To put it in another way, the benevolent man may be said to have a wide circle of beings in whom he is interested, or to be so much interested in them that he will deny himself things of considerable importance in order to meet their slightly greater needs. The selfish man, on the other hand, may be said to have a narrow circle of beings in whom he is interested, or to be so little interested in them that he will deny himself only trifles or things of little importance in order to meet their much greater needs. The individual's benevolence, then, may be said to increase directly with the radius of the circle which includes those in whom he is interested, and with the intensity of his interest in all those who are found within that circle. Likewise, one's selfishness may be said to increase with the narrowness of the circle and with the feebleness of his interest in those who are found within the circle.

The following diagram illustrates this principle:

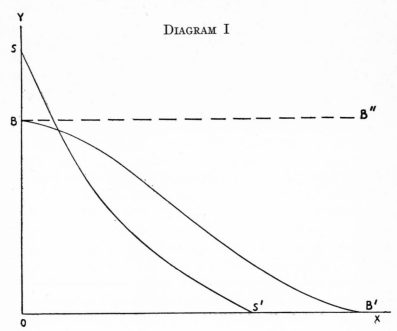

DIAGRAM I

Along the line OX of the above diagram, measure the radius of the circle of one's interests, with one's self at the centre O, with other persons ranged along the line in the order in which one is interested in them. Along the line OY measure the intensity of one's interest in each person within that circle. Assume, further, that the line OS measures the intensity of S, the selfish man's interest in himself, while the line OB measures B, the benevolent man's interest in himself. They in whom S and B are interested are ranged along the line OX, those nearest these two persons being the ones in whom each is most intensely interested, and those farthest away being the ones in whom each is least interested. The radius of the circle of S's interests would then, we shall assume, be measured by the line OS' and that of B's by the line OB', and the curve SS' would represent the intensity of S's interest in other beings, while the Curve BB' would represent that of B in others. S becomes satanic in proportion as the curve SS' approaches the line SO, while B becomes divine in proportion as the line BB' approaches the dotted line BB'. Being human, their curves are found somewhere between these two extremes.

Let us now see exactly what is meant by the radius of the circle of one's interests, or by the terms "nearness to" and "distance from" self. In some way it will occur at once that the radius of the circle has something to do with the number of people who are included in it. If the circle of the benevolent man's interests is greater than that of the selfish man, it means that the one is interested in a larger number of people than the other. In either case, those within the circle of one's interests will be found to be in some sense nearer to self than are those who are outside that circle; and those within the circle in whom we are most interested will be found to be, in some sense, nearer to self than those in whom we are least interested. But in what sense can we use such a geometrical term as "nearer to" to express a moral or social fact? In the first place, it can be used in a strictly geometrical sense, meaning physical or geometrical propinquity. They who are nearer to one in space usually, though not always, command more of one's attention and interest than they who are farther away. We normally care more for members of our own household than for members of other households, more for our near neighbors than for our distant neighbors, using the words *near* and *distant* with respect to space.

Again, we may use the words *near* and *far* with respect to time, and say that those who are near to us in point of time command more of our attention and interest than those who are far from us. We are more interested, for example, in our contemporaries, other things equal, than in those who have lived or are to live in remote times, in our immediate parents than in our remote ancestors, in our immediate children than in our remote descendants.

But there is another, and very important sense in which these terms are used which is not so easily expressed as are the concepts of space and time. They may be used with respect to similarity and dissimilarity. Other things equal, we care more for those who are like ourselves than for those who are unlike ourselves. That is to say, we normally care more for our own flesh and blood than for others, for our near relatives than for our distant relatives, for our own fellow citizens than for foreigners, for those who profess our own religion than for pagans, for human beings than for animals, for the higher than for the lower animals, etc. etc.

This may all be summed up by saying that we are more interested in those who are near to ourselves in point of space, in point of time, and in point of similarity and dissimilarity than in those who are distant from us in these three senses. It will, of course, inevitably happen that these three concepts of nearness will often be in conflict. Those who live near us in point of space may happen to be distant from us in point of dissimilarity. In this case the ties of kinship may prove stronger than the ties of neighborhood, or vice versa; that is, in case of conflict, we may side with those who are near of kin, though distant in space, rather than with those who are near in space but remotely of kin, or vice versa. We are frequently, for example, more moved by the sufferings of an animal which is near in point of space than by the equal sufferings of a human being who is distant, though if both were equally near in point of space we should be more deeply moved by the sufferings of the human being, since he is nearer in point of similarity. Because of these distinct factors in the determination of our interests, all of which may be working in harmony or in conflict, the problem of determining the actual circle of one's interests becomes a perplexing problem in permutations and combinations.

In order to test himself on this question of preference, let the reader answer the following questions:

1. Do you care equally for every individual in the world, or do you care more for some than for others?

2. Will you do as much for those for whom you care little as for those for whom you care much?

3. If there is a conflict of interests between some of those for whom you care little and some of those for whom you care much, will you be indifferent or will you take one side or the other? Which side?

A little self-examination will show that one's interest in others may lead one into conflict quite as freely as one's interest in self. But, one's interest in others is likely to be greater in those who are "near" to self than in those who are distant from self. In that sense, our interests are self-centered.

Let us now see exactly what is meant by a preference for self, or by self-centered interest in others. In order to be as concrete as possible, let us begin by considering the interest which one has in the utilization of his income, remembering, however, that there are other interests in life besides income. It will be generally agreed that as a man's income increases, other things equal, his appreciation of each dollar will diminish. That is to say, if he has only three hundred dollars a year, he will guard each dollar pretty carefully because the loss of a single dollar would deprive him of something necessary for his subsistence. Moreover, he will not spend a dollar for things for which he does not have a strong desire. But if, with the same disposition, his income were three thousand dollars, each dollar would mean somewhat less to him than when he had only three hundred dollars. Again, if his income should be still further increased to thirty thousand a year, each dollar would be still less highly appreciated. This principle may be illustrated by Diagram II.

DIAGRAM II

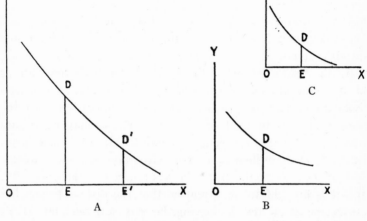

Let his income be measured along the line OX beginning at O, in Figure A, while his appreciation of a dollar is measured along the line OY. As his income increases his appreciation will fall, and this fall will be represented by some sort of a descending curve, say the curve YDD'X. That is to say, where his income is measured by the line OE, his appreciation of a dollar is represented by the line DE; but when his income is enlarged to OE', then his appreciation of a dollar is represented by the line D'E'.

In a similar way, Figure B may represent *his* appreciation of his *neighbor's* need of an income, or the need of some one peculiarly near to himself in some of the senses noted above. If the other man's income were as large as his own, that is, if each had an income of OE, he would not be inclined to divide with the other man. His appreciation of the *other man's* need of a dollar would be represented by the line DE in Figure B, while his appreciation of his own need of a dollar would be represented by DE in Figure A. However, if his income were much larger than the other man's; say that his is OE' in Figure A, while the other man's is OE in Figure B, in which case his appreciation of his own need of a dollar is represented by the line D'E' in Figure A, and of his neighbor's need of his marginal dollar by the line DE in Figure B, he then appreciates the other man's need of his marginal dollar somewhat more highly than his own and, acting accordingly, gives him a portion of his own income. In this case, he would ordinarily pass as a benevolent man, but he would still be somewhat self-interested or self-centered.

Again, if some one whom he does not ordinarily recognize as his neighbor, or as near to himself in any sense, say some person living a long way off, and belonging to a different branch of the human race, is brought to his attention, he may appreciate that person's need according to Figure C. If their incomes are equal, he will ordinarily pay no attention whatever to the distant person's need. But if he has a larger income, say OE', and it is brought to his attention that the distant person has no income at all and is starving, he may surrender one of his many thousand dollars in order that the distant person may have one dollar's worth of goods to keep him alive. In the diagrams, his appreciation of his own need of a dollar is represented by the line D'E' in Figure A, while his appreciation of the distant person's need of a dollar is represented by the line OY in Figure C. Even in this case he would ordinarily pass as a benevolent man, doubtless more benevolent than the average man in any community past or present, yet he would be decidedly self-centered.

The following series of figures may serve to illustrate and summarize the whole theory of self-centered appreciation. To understand their meaning it is necessary to read the formulae across as well as up and down. Reading across formulaes I, II, III, and IV, and referring each part of each formula to the figure above it, we get the law of self-centered appreciation in all its essential variations. I, for example, relates to the individual's appreciation of his own present and future needs. II relates to his appreciation of his own needs as compared with those of his contemporaries and others removed in point of time. III relates to his appreciation of his own needs as compared with those of his neighbors and others removed in point of space, while IV relates to his appreciation of his own needs as compared with those of others near to him in point of similarity as well as those removed from him in point of dissimilarity.

DIAGRAM III

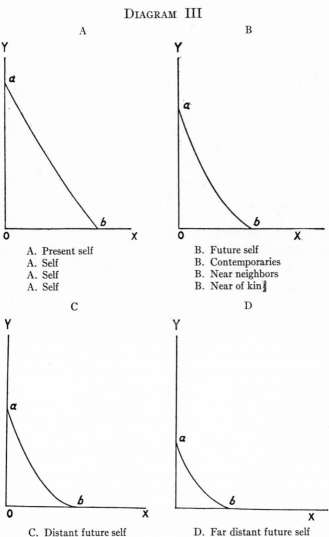

A
A. Present self
A. Self
A. Self
A. Self

B
B. Future self
B. Contemporaries
B. Near neighbors
B. Near of kin

C
C. Distant future self
C. Other generations
C. Distant neighbors
C. Distant of Kin

D
D. Far distant future self
D. Remote generations
D. Far distant neighbors
D. Far distant of kin

In each of the figures, I, II, III, and IV, let the line OX measure the quantity of means of satisfying a desire of any kind, and the line OY the intensity of one's appreciation of the importance of each unit of that quantity. Then the curve *ab* in each figure will represent the diminishing appreciation of each unit of the supply, as the supply itself increases. But in figure I the curve *ab* represents the diminishing appreciation of each unit of the supply when applied to the satisfaction of the desires of the self or of the person doing the appreciating, while in each of the other figures the curve *ab* represents the diminishing appreciation of each unit of the quantity of the means of satisfying the desire when applied to the satisfaction of other persons than the one whose appreciation is measured. I, for example, may be doing the appreciating, in which case the curve *ab* in figure I will represent my appreciation of the importance of different units of my income when applied to my own gratification. But in each of the other figures, the curve represents *my* appreciation of the importance of satisfying other people's desires, or, as in the first case, of the desires of my future as compared with my present self.

With this understanding, then, it can be made perfectly clear just what my benevolence would consist in if my supply of the means of satisfying a given desire were measured as in figure I by the line Ob. The last unit of that quantity would have a negligible utility for me, that is, I could surrender it with no sacrifice whatever. At the same time, if my near neighbor possessed absolutely none of it, I should have interest enough in him to appreciate his need, at least to such an extent as would be measured by the line Oa in figure II. Since by depriving myself of one unit at the point *b* in figure I without any loss whatever, I can satisfy myself to the extent of the line Oa, figure II, by contributing to B's supply, I would very easily choose to allow B to have at least one unit of my supply, rather than keep it myself. I do this, of course, because I personally get more gratification from the consumption of that unit by B than I would by its consumption by myself. From one point of view I could be said to be acting selfishly, and from another point of view I could be said to be acting generously. As will be seen clearly by the foregoing argument and the above diagram, there is an element both of benevolence and selfishness in every such act. The difference between the benevolent and the selfish man would be shown by the difference between the curves *ab* in the different figures I, II, III, and IV. The greater the difference between the height of the curve in figure I and in the other figures, the greater the selfishness.[1]

In sections 2 and 3 of this chapter the sources of conflict have been shown to be: first, scarcity of desirable things; second, self-preference, self-centered appreciation, or differential generosity. There being fewer of certain things than people desire — people uniformly preferring their own satisfaction, or that of those near to them to the satisfaction of other people — the conflict of interests is unavoidable. This self-preference or differential generosity is only a manifestation of the limitations of the finite mind. Being finite, it is impossible for it to visualize things distant as vividly as things present, things unfamiliar as things familiar. For the same reason, namely, its finiteness, it can not feel as keenly the joys and sufferings of distant people as of near people. People may be near or distant in space, in time, in kinship, in similarity, and in likemindedness.

6. *Manifestations of Conflict.* It is impossible to avoid seeing that this conflict of interests among human beings is a phase of that universal struggle for existence on which the Darwinian theory of evolution is based. So universal and relentless is that struggle as to have convinced the thinking world of the futility of all attempts to eliminate it. In some minds this seems to have produced a kind of despair, in others a disposition to close the eyes to its existence. The world itself is wiser than either of these groups of thinkers. The fact that there is a conflict of interests is not blinked. That this conflict of interests must necessarily result in some form of rivalry, competition, or struggle is not questioned. Practical statesmanship has turned its attention to the problem of mitigating the struggle, eliminating its

---

[1] Differential generosity is a better and more accurate term than selfishness.

more destructive features, and turning it into productive fields.

That there are productive fields within which the struggle for existence, for advantage, or for gain, can be carried on can be shown by the following outline, which merits careful study.[1]

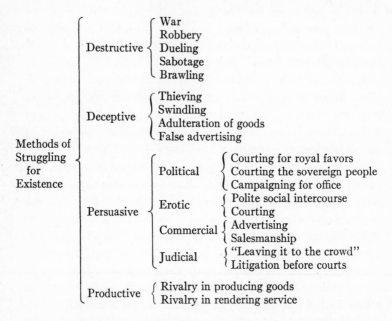

The methods of conflict named in the above outline may be explained and illustrated as follows: By destructive methods are meant all those whereby one succeeds by virtue of one's power to kill, to hurt, or to inspire fear of physical injury or pain. "War," "robbery," "dueling," "sabotage," and "brawling" are names for methods of destruction as carried on by human beings; but it must be remembered that animals also kill, rob, inflict injury, and inspire terror. By the deceptive methods are meant all those by which one succeeds by virtue of one's power to deceive, to swindle, or to cheat. Animals practise deceit, though we do not call their forms of deceit by such names as "swindling," "counterfeiting," "adulteration of goods," etc.

---

[1] This diagram is taken from the author's previous work, *Principles of National Economy* (Ginn and Co., Boston, 1921), p. 49.

By the persuasive methods are meant all those methods whereby one succeeds by virtue of one's power to persuade or to convince. One may beat one's rival by being a more persuasive talker, whether one is striving for favors from the sovereign person or from the sovereign people, whether one is striving for the hand of a lady, the decision of a jury, or the trade of a possible customer. This form of conflict would remain even if we could eliminate all other forms. Even under the most complete form of communism there would remain abundant room for the persuasive forms of conflict. By the productive methods are meant all those methods whereby one may beat one's rivals, or gain advantages, by virtue of one's power to produce, to serve, or to confer benefit.

The same persons may resort to more than one of these methods in order to gain an advantage. When two farmers compete in growing crops they are struggling for existence or for economic advantage, by a productive method. When they quarrel over a line fence and take their quarrel before court for adjudication, they are struggling by a persuasive method. When they secretly alter or remove landmarks in order to gain an advantage in their litigation, or when they bribe jurors, they are struggling by a deceptive method. When they fall to fighting either with fists or with weapons, they are struggling by a destructive method. When they change their methods in the order just described, they are sinking lower and lower in the scale; that is, they are resorting to worse and worse methods of struggling for existence or advantage. When they rival one another in growing corn, there is more corn grown as the result of that rivalry; the country is better fed and every one is better off except possibly the one who is beaten, and even he may very likely be better off than he would have been if he had not competed at all. When two farmers quarrel over a line fence and take the case into court, no one gains any benefit except the lawyers, and what the lawyers gain the litigants lose. No new land is created by that conflict. No new wealth is produced. The community is no better fed, and the litigants have wasted their time. To change from persuasion to deception or from deception to physical force is so clearly to sink to a lower level that it is unnecessary to pursue the topic further.

Among the lower creatures there are no rules of the game, no organized efforts to mitigate, regulate, or soften the struggle for existence. It will be apparent to any one who will study the diagram that among animals the destructive and deceptive methods are the characteristic forms of struggle. They kill, maim, injure, rob, and deceive one another with no moral or legal restraints. They may sometimes rise to the level of persuasion, as in the courting process, but never to the level of production; that is, no animal ever tries to beat its rival by producing a larger and better product or rendering a greater or better service. Among human beings who have no moral sense and who are unrestrained by law and justice, the destructive and deceptive methods of struggle are precisely the things that morals and laws are designed to prevent.[1] In any civilization worthy of the name and under any government worthy to stand over night, men are actually restrained by their own moral feelings, by the respect for the good opinions of their fellows, and by the fear of legal penalties, from attempting to promote their own interests by destruction or deception.

In the interest of its own success, the group must suppress

---

[1] The non-moral struggle in all its grimness and lack of standards was probably never more vividly expressed than by Robert Louis Stevenson in *The Woodman:*

> Thick 'round me in the teeming mud
> Briar and fern strove to the blood.
> The hooked liana in his gin
> Noosed his reluctant neighbors in:
> There the green murderer throve and spread,
> Upon his smothering victims fed,
> And wantoned on his climbing coil.
> Contending roots fought for the soil
> Like frightened demons: with despair
> Competing branches pushed for air.
> Green conquerors from overhead
> Bestrode the bodies of their dead:
> . . . .
> So hushed the woodland warfare goes
> Unceasing; and the silent foes
> Grapple and smother, strain and clasp
> Without a cry, without a gasp.

all dectructive and deceptive methods by which any of its own members might gain advantage for himself to the detriment of of the group, and encourage, so far as possible, the productive methods. Its success as a group, its growth, and even its survival in the struggle with other groups, will depend, in no small degree, upon its success in suppressing destructive and deceptive methods and in turning the energies of its people into, productive channels. In terms of the above diagram, the principal function of organized society is to cancel the brackets labelled destructive and deceptive. This will limit its individual members to those brackets labelled persuasive and productive.

Much ink has been wasted in moral treatises on the evil of selfishness. There is no more merit in such a treatise than there would be in a treatise on the evil of gravitation, of electricity, of the expansive power of steam or incandescent gases. No engineer would be gutily of such a treatise, though he realizes that these forces may do harm. He sees also that, under control, they may serve men's purposes. His problem is to control them and make them work, not to condemn or to pass moral judgment upon them. The law of personal preference, which some call selfishnessi is a motivating force, and it operates according to certain observed tendencies which can be roughly calculated. The problem of the statesman, who, at his best, is merely a social engineer, is to recognize this motivating force and harness it to useful work. If the social engineer can show every individual that he can help those for whom he has a preference more effectively by earning an income than by robbing, swindling or any non-productive method, then every individual will try to earn, that is, to create as much wealth as he gets. The more intense his interest in himself and those for whom he cares, the more he will try to produce in order that he may get. The social engineer who achieves such a result as this will make a larger contribution to the success of his social group than any mechanical inventor ever made.

7. *Inter-group Conflict and Group Survival.* It may sound paradoxical to say that one compelling reason for the suppression of destructive and deceptive methods of conflict among the

individuals of a group is the desire to enable the group itself to wage successful conflict against other groups. Really there is nothing paradoxical about it. An army, for example, whose soldiers fought among themselves in time of battle, or tried to deceive one another, would not be very successful. If, on the other hand, they vie with one another in deeds of prowess or bravery against the common enemy, that kind of individual rivalry would contribute to the success of the army. Such rivalry is as truly a form of conflict as fighting among themselves, but it is a kind which strengthens the group. It is, in that sense, analogous to the productive forms of rivalry in an industrial society.

There is inter-group rivalry in time of peace as well as in time of war. There is international competition for markets. The number of people who can live in one country or under one flag, will depend to some extent on the success of that kind of competition. There have been in times past (and they are not unknown at present) international conflicts over land for colonization purposes. The number of people of a given race, language, or civilization, who can live in the world depends pretty definitely on the land areas they can control or colonize. Even when a nation lives a pent-up life, seeking expansion neither in the direction of wider markets nor wider territorial sovereignty, its growth will be affected by its success in suppressing wasteful conflicts among its own citizens. The more its citizens rival one another in productive competition and the less in destructive or deceptive competition, the more people it can support and the more abundantly it can provide for them.

The motive of self-interest may be made to promote the general interest of the whole under a government which takes a rational point of view and pursues rational policies. In so far as the individual can be made to see that his best or his only chance of promoting his own interest is to do something useful for the group and seek a fair reward for it, in so far will he be moved by his own self-interest to do useful things. The more the men within a country are motivated to do useful things, the more people the country can support or the more amply they can be supported. It is only under a rational and well enforced system of criminal law that men are led "as by an invisible hand," (to use Adam Smith's celebrated phrase) to promote the general interest while trying to promote their own. It cannot be too much emphasized that there is no natural harmony of interests. There is a very real conflict, but a semblance of harmony can be created by law. When the individual whose interest would otherwise lead him to use destructive or deceptive methods can be made to see that this would lead to severe punishment, it will then be to his interest to refrain. He may then, in the pursuit of self-interest, turn to useful conduct.

The sociologist can not escape the need of understanding human nature. In studying social life, he is certain to find guidance in the work of psychologists. Yet he must not be allowed to forget that psychology does not pretend to solve purely sociological problems. His ultimate concern with man's social nature is in its survival value. Men would never have evolved a social nature if sociability and group life had not proved to have survival value in the struggle for earthly existence. How could human beings ever have acquired the capacity to work together, if coördinated effort had not proved more efficient than isolated effort in their fight for food and their struggle against enemies? Antipathy *might* have played a more important rôle than sympathy in survival. The consciousness of kind *might* have produced a feeling of repulsion rather than attraction. Tigers have survived with not too social a nature.

The German biologist, W. Bölsche,[1] assumes that human origins must have been in a kind of "paradise" environment where the struggle for existence was not severe. Otherwise, he holds, so "extravagant" a thing as a large brain could never have got a decent start in evolution. For "brawn" would never have been sacrificed for brain in a too brutal world. Assume that sociability might have developed under "paradise"

---

[1] *Das Liebesleben in Natur* (E. Diederichs, Jena, 1922).

conditions of life; it would still be true that sociability would have to prove its survival value in the struggle for existence, once men wandered out of paradise. And men are known to have wandered far on the earth.

Bölsche's theory, however, is not universally accepted. The late Henry Adams,[1] among others, attributes the growth of mind to a degradation of energy. In other words, intelligence is a kind of degeneration which he attributes to the "Progressive degradation of energy by dissipation and the leveling of intensities." This is an application to the study of human biology of Thompson's thesis published under the title of *A Universal Tendency in Nature to the Dissipation of Energy.*[2]

According to Mr. Adams and the authorities whom he quotes, the earth is already rather far gone on its way toward death. As a place favorable to life it reached its zenith in the Miocene period. Vegetation reached its climax in the carboniferous age. During the Miocene period there was sufficient lush vegetation to support those huge beasts whose vital energy and will to live vastly exceeded anything that is left on this decrepit planet. Then degradation began, and most of the splendid creatures that had once flourished either became extinct or degenerated to mere runts. One took to extracting a precarious living from an impoverished world by the exercise of cunning, flatteringly called intelligence. That degenerate creature took to calling himself *Homo Sapiens.* This is a form of degeneracy because intellect is a lower form of energy than will, lower even than instinct.

We need not waste time discussing such words as *lower* and *higher.* If the world is cooling off so that life becomes harder, the new conditions must be met in some way by any creature that hopes to survive. If one survives by growing smaller, through the process of selection, there is no good reason for saying that he has degenerated. If another survives by developing sharper wits or a shrewder cunning, or by building shelters

---

[1] *The Degradation of Democratic Dogma* (The Macmillan Co., New York, 1919), p. 152 *et seq.*
[2] London, 1852.

and kindling fires, there would seem to be no good reason for calling this a form of degeneration. It has simply met the conditions of a changing environment, and met them successfully, as shown by the fact of survival.

The thing to remember, however, is that the ever intensifying struggle to survive in a dying world, where the conditions of life grow ever harder, may have required ever increasing intelligence of a creature which once started in that direction. The rate at which *Homo Sapiens* is using up the mineral, forest, and soil resources of the earth suggests, at least, that the intelligence which enabled him for a time to meet the conditions of a decaying world is merely accelerating the rate of decay. If that be true, he must either perish or develop ever increasing intelligence to meet the ever increasing difficulties of living on an exhausted planet. This calls for greater and greater economies of human energy, or the progressive elimination of waste. One of the great wasters of human energy is conflict, working at cross purposes. How to eliminate conflict and save what energies we have for the work of extracting a living from our meager environment becomes one of the greatest of human problems. The elimination of conflict is a problem of team work, of group control, and of group survival.

The problem of social evolution, of social progress, is as much concerned with survival values as is the problem of biological evolution. The two problems, in fact, are synthesized by their common concern in the question of group survival. Social evolution has taken place, in the course of history, through the survival of groups best adapted to their environment. Groups have secured adaptation through the organizing of their group life, through effective team work. They have survived according to the success of their group organization, their customs, mores, and institutions. But organization, in turn, has proved effective as a means of group survival only in the measure that men have been organizable. In order to survive in groups, men had to evolve a kind of social nature. They had to evolve, if you will, social instincts; or, if not instincts, they had to exhibit a conditioned social behaviour, or simply an intelligent acceptance of group life. Organization and organizability were both necessary for group survival. The study of social survival is capable of giving to sociology the all-inclusive aim that was the dream of its founders.

The problem of the survival of social groups seems to be largely a problem of economizing human energy. Group life itself is merely a means of economizing energy, storing it, insuring its effective use.[1] Moreover, every phase of group life has been subjected, in the course of social evolution, to the "economy" test of survival. It has had to justify itself by economizing human energy. Institutions, customs, laws, moral ideals, which did not economize the energies of a group, became a handicap and threatened the group's extinction in the political struggle of groups. The survival value of economizing group energies is a theme that will assume great importance in any treatise on sociology which aims at thoroughness and comprehensiveness. The importance of the theme, it is hoped, will convince the reader that sociology rests on economic foundations. Even morals, in so far as they are rational and not merely conventional, must be looked upon as ways of economizing human energy.

It is not possible to go very deeply into the study of the problem of economizing human energy without discovering that human beings waste an amazing amount of energy in quarreling over conflicts in their individual desires and interests.

8. *Conflict and the Problem of Evil.* That there is some connection between the problem of conflict and the problem of evil

---

[1] R. W. MacIver speaks of the changes in the *social forms* under which human interests are pursued as revealing a "principle of communal economy."

"If we use the term 'economy' in the widest sense," he says, "to signify the conservation of values not only material but spiritual, the conservation of life itself, the conservation of the means of life, and the conservation of personality or the intrinsic values of life, we may call the principle which these changes reveal the principle of communal economy. There is throughout the development of community a constant transformation of social relationships which can be understood only as fulfilling this principle. . . . Economy is relation to purpose and intelligence. . . ." *Community* (The Macmillan Co., London, 1928), pp. 334–335. See further ch. VI, "Second Law of Communal Development: The Correlation of Socialisation and Communal Economy."

is perhaps apparent by this time. From the evolutionary point of view, evil will seem to be almost another name for maladaptation. In essence, maladaptation means the failure of successful completion of the activities essential to the preservation and promotion of the life of an individual or group. A sentient creature out of harmony with its surroundings is certain to suffer some form of unpleasantness commonly called pain. In a state of complete harmony there will certainly be no sense of positive unpleasantness; and this state would be regarded by optimists as positive pleasure, by pessimists of the Schopenhauer type, as negative pain. In either case the state of harmony would seem more desirable or less undesirable to a sentient creature than a state of disharmony or maladaptation. A creature with intelligence as well as feeling and will would certainly be striving for adaptation rather than maladaptation, for harmony rather than disharmony. This is rather obviously the motivating force of all industry.

A little less obvious, perhaps, but none the less true, as pointed out several times in this chapter, is the fact that scarcity is a reason for the emergence of conflict of interests among individuals as well as among groups of individuals. To the biologist this great fact appears as the struggle for existence; to the economist, as the basis at least for competition and the all-sufficient reason for regulating the struggle for existence in such ways as to eliminate the destructive and preserve the productive forms of competition. To the sociologist, who approaches his subject from the biological and economic points of view, we have here the factors which compel organization and teamwork on pain of extinction, and which to a considerable extent determine the forms of organization and teamwork.

From this point of view the two great factors in the problem of evil,— at least in its social and moral implications,— are self-preference and scarcity. Given these two factors, conflict becomes inevitable between individuals and groups; and with this kind of conflict comes every moral or social problem with which any one is acquainted.

After running the whole gamut of explanations,— theological, metaphysical, and naturalistic,— the student may as well settle down to the conclusion, specifically stated by several authors, that evil is essentially maladaptation, which, in turn is only incomplete evolution. Man is an unfinished being, trying to adjust himself to an unfinished universe. There is an evolutionary lag: the process of evolution does not keep up with the changing environment, especially the rapidly changing social environment.

As a result of this evolutionary lag, there are still many maladaptions or disharmonies:

A. Between man and his environment. These have in themselves no moral or social quality, but may give rise to other disharmonies, *e.g.*

B. Between man and man. These are moral and social in their nature. They grow out of scarcity and show themselves in the form of conflicting interests, and result in all sorts of trouble, wars, litigations, rivalries, defeats, heart-burnings, jealousies.

C. Between the conflicting desires, emotions, and interests of the same individual. These give rise to the necessity for economy, self-control and self-discipline, that is, for choosing which interests shall be satisfied,— the essence of economy,— for suppressing or sacrificing the smaller interests in favor of the larger,— which is the essence of self-control and self-discipline.

CHAPTER IV

PROGRESS IN THE ART OF LIVING TOGETHER

A. THE CONCEPT OF PROGRESS

WE have seen that early commentators on social phenomena were not only convinced of the necessity of living together in societies, but also perplexed by its difficulties. Many of them could not reconcile two apparently contradictory facts, namely, the necessity of social life, and the inevitableness of conflict. The dream was cherished that there was a possible state, either in a long forgotten past or some golden future, where men did or could live together without conflict, and in a state of peace and harmony. They who located that state in the past frequently despaired of ever restoring it, though some conceived with Milton of regaining a paradise once lost. They who located the state of social harmony in the future were probably the first progressives.

The world has generally been divided on the question as to whether the human race is progressing or degenerating. It was not until the middle of the nineteenth century that the Western

World turned definitely and almost unanimously to the idea of progress. When this idea dominated the thinking of students it was natural that they should attempt to explain away conflict, either as non-existent, as due to the shortsightedness of men, or as doomed to disappear in the process of time. This does not imply that there were not individuais who had, long before, proclaimed their belief in human progress, but it had not impressed the popular mind so deeply as had the fact of conflict.

In the eighteenth century the Age of Reason was proclaimed, and men began,— a few at least,— to build great hopes on its possibilities. As Dean Inge points out, "In the seventeenth century a doctrine of progress was already in the air. . . . But it was only in the eighteenth century that Western Europe began to dream of an approaching millennium without miracle to be gradually ushered in under the auspices of a faculty which was called reason."[1]   But, by the middle of the nineteenth century the "popular divinity" of Western Civilization was beginning to be called Progress.[2]   This new divinity dominated every field with the possible exception of theology.   Not only science, but philosophy, literature, and even industry bowed before her throne.   Progress had dethroned Reason — the goddess of the revolutionists of the eighteenth century — or, as others put it, the Age of Reason had been but the harbinger of the Age of Progress.

The reasons for the rise of the idea of progress to its place of dominance in the nineteenth century are not difficult to understand.   To begin with, there was undoubted and verifiable advancement of knowledge in the fields of physical science and the mechanic arts.   There was no disputing the fact that men were find,ng out things in physical science which had not been known before, and were doing things in the field of mechanic arts which had never been done before.   In the second place, there was a growing sense of mastery which the new knowledge gave.

---

[1] W. R. Inge, *The Idea of Progress* (The Clarendon Press, Oxford, 1920), p. 7.
[2] See Carl Kelsey, *The Physical Basis of Society* (D. Appleton & Co., New York, 1928), p. 449.

The sources of both these new elements in human life may, of course, be traced far back in history, but their results were becoming apparent to every one by the middle of the nineteenth century. The discovery and colonization of the New World had, three centuries before, opened up new sources of food and made living conditions easier.[1] New supplies of the precious metals had stimulated commerce.[2] Later, the steam-engine and power-driven machinery had still further increased the feeling that men were gaining a mastery over their own destiny and were no longer the victims of circumstances over which they could exercise no control. The Western World at least felt emancipated from fatalism and became buoyantly optimistic. Feeling able to control their own destiny, to direct their own future, people naturally became interested in problems of future development.

Then came the Darwinian theory of evolution. The idea of evolution, in the sense of historical continuity and unbroken development, was, of course, very old. Darwin accomplished two things. First, he described a natural and understandable method by which evolution *could* take place,— the method of variation and selection. Second, he convinced the world that evolution actually did take place. The thinking of the world was fundamentally changed by the publication of the *Origin of Species*. Since that time the idea of evolution has been taken as a matter of course.

1. *The Elevationists.* For a long time it was assumed that evolution was necessarily "upward." Evolutionists became almost automatically elevationlsts. The evolutionary process was assumed to carry life to higher and higher levels. The evolution of life itself from a previously existing physical and

---

[1] The relief of overpopulation in Europe has never been sufficiently appreciated.
[2] The great price revolution which followed the importation of gold and silver into Europe through Spain, is only beginning to be appreciated, largely through the exhaustive studies of Dr. E. J. Hamilton. Cf. "American Treasure and Andalusian Prices, 1503–1660," *Journal of Economic and Business History*, November, 1928; "La Monnaie en Castille, 1501–1650," *Annales d'Histoire Economique et Sociale*, March and May, 1932; "Imports of American Gold and Silver into Spain, 1503–1660," *Quarterly Journal of Economics*, May, 1929.

chemical but non-biological *milieu* was assumed to have been a step "upward," and the evolution of man from some "lower" form of life was a later step in the same "upward" direction. As F. S. Marvin remarks: "To Darwin, to anyone who had studied the facts of life from the new perspective (evolution), progress was no less real, it was a palpable and concrete thing, but its reality could and should be measured by the adaptation of the living being to its environment, including in its environment those fellow creatures with whom it lives."[1] To substantiate his contention Marvin quotes Darwin's statement: "the ultimate result is that each creature tends to become more and more improved in relation to its conditions.[2] This improvement inevitably leads to the gradual advancement of the organization of the greater number of living beings throughout the world."

Herbert Spencer, however, substituted another formula,— that of increasing complexity,— which avoided all question-begging implications. Nevertheless, in the popular mind at least, evolution was generally identified with progress. Too often it assumed that progress was not only a fact but an inevitable fact,— that there was something in the evolutionary process which could neither be helped nor hindered by anything we could do. As Herbert Spencer puts it: "Progress is not an accident, not a thing within human control, but a beneficent necessity."[3] Only a few grasped the possibility of self-directed evolution by one creature, namely, man, that had evolved upward to an intellectual plane.

Others have questioned, and are questioning in increasing numbers, not only the identity of evolution and progress, but the fact of progress itself, at least during the last few millennia. In his recent book *Culture and Progress*[4] Professor W. D. Wallis remarks:

[1] F. S. Marvin, *The Century of Hope* (The Clarendon Press, Oxford, 1927) pp. 159–160.

[2] Perhaps he should have qualified by saying that it is either improved in relation to its conditions or becomes extinct.

[3] *Progress, its Law and Cause, Essays, Scientific, Political, and Speculative* (D. Appleton & Co., New York, 1892).

[4] McGraw-Hill Book Co., New York, 1930, pp. 210–214.

We usually assume that western civilization makes progress, for progress is fundamental to our culture; but is this assumption correct, or are we on a treadmill of futile repetition? Our scientific achievements, already unparalleled, increase with an acceleration born of genius and application. In all fields knowledge grows. Industry, as represented by both capital and labor, attains organization and power not realized before. Facts of this order touch the imagination and appeal to us as a demonstration of progress. But do these really constitute progress, or have we failed to grasp the significance of these culture changes?

In comparing the achievements of the present with those of the past, the question is, In what fields do men of today excel or even equal those of the past? The only clear and definite answer is the one already given, namely, in the fields of physical science and the mechanic arts. In these two fields there can be no intelligent dispute. Men of today know things that were not known before, not because men of today are superior mentally or have higher intelligence quotients, but because there is more accumulated scientific knowledge. This knowledge has been discovered by reason of the fact that modern men have had superior mechanical instruments, such as the telescope, the microscope, the spectroscope, and a multitude of others. This knowledge has been preserved, accumulated, and made widely available by means of another mechanical instrument, namely, the printing press.

Through a fortunate combination of circumstances, physical science and the mechanic arts have supplemented each other. An astronomer of today may know vastly more about the heavenly bodies than Sir Isaac Newton ever knew or could have found out, to say nothing of Copernicus, or any of the ancients. But this superior knowledge is the result of superior mechanical instruments and not of superior intelligence. These superior mechanical instruments are supplied by the mechanic arts. A chemist of today may, for the same reasons, know vastly more about chemistry than Michael Farraday ever knew. A historian of today may write more comprehensive and more accurate histories than Herodotus could have written. The reason is that he has better libraries — products of the mechanic art of printing from movable type — than Herodotus had at his disposal.

Select any field of intellectual achievement in which mechanisms do not help, and we cannot find modern examples of work which are better than the ancients did.   If a modern philosopher taught more comprehensive and penetrating philosophy than Plato or Aristotle, it would be because he was a greater philosopher than they, not because he had better mechanical instruments.   If a poet of today composed greater poetry than Homer and Vergil, it would be because he was a greater poet than they; but there are no greater poets than those of antiquity.   If a painter of today could excel the old masters, it would be because of his own greatness, not because of superior instruments.   If his pictures last longer it will be because modern chemistry has provided him with better pigments.   Aside from this, modern paintings do not show any superiority.   In short, there is no achievement of modern men which excels that of men who labored hundreds of years ago, except, as already indicated, in the fields of physical science and the mechanic arts, or fields served by them.   If music is the only fine art that has made progress, it is probably because modern musicians have better instruments than the ancients had.

As Joseph McCabe says: "Our age is in this respect (scientific achievement) incalculably beyond any age that preceded it. In philosophy we cannot equal Greece. . . ."[1]   "In art one may doubt if the world will ever again reach the highest Greek and mediaeval standards, much less surpass them.   That is not a sign of loss of power, and it is foolish to flatter ourselves that we are rising higher by opening new and eccentric (Futurism, Cubism, etc.) . . ."[2]   "Socially and morally the comparison is more difficult.   We are bound, if we have even a sound elementary knowledge of the matter, to abandon the old idea that we Europeans of today are superior to the men and women of Egypt, Babylonia, Greece, and Rome."[3]   Not only do we not

---

[1] *The Evolution of Civilization* (G. P. Putnam's Sons, New York, 1922), p. 121.
[2] *Ibid.*, p. 129.
[3] *Ibid.*, p. 130.

excel or compare with the Greek thinkers or the mediaeval artists, but are, according to authorities in these fields, actually declining. "Indeed," says A. Clutton Brook, "one might say that there has been a continual slow decline in all the arts of Europe, except music, since the year 1500." Even modern music owes more than is commonly admitted to clever mechanical devices such as the piano and the organ. In spite of these, music itself has been slowly declining since the death of Beethoven.[1]

It is easy to overlook the contributions of physical science and the mechanic arts to other fields. Take the field of morals, for example. The modern world is inclined to pride itself on its superior generosity or willingness to share its prosperity with people who are the victims of some disaster, such as an earthquake, a flood, or a famine. But it is because of the advance in physical science and the mechanic arts that we have such abundance as to make it easy for us to share it with our fellow men and such means of communication and transportation as to make it easy to send them our aid. If we were ourselves as near the hunger line as men were before the age of invention, it is uncertain how much we would be willing to share. "We have other proofs," says Joseph McCabe, "that from four to five thousand years ago the standard of character was much as it is today." He quotes from the *Book of the Dead* the following: "I have not oppressed the members of my family; I have not wrought evil in the place of right and truth. . . . I have not made it the first consideration of each day that excessive labor should be performed for me. I have not ill-treated servants. I have not caused pain. I have made no man suffer hunger. I have made no one weep. I have not inflicted pain upon mankind."[2]

Again, the peace movement has been cited as evidence of moral progress. But, to begin with, it has not been very successful either in diminishing the frequency or the bitterness of

[1] F. S. Marvin, arranged and edited, *Progress and History Essays* (Oxford University Press, Humphrey Milford, 1916), p. 22.
[2] Joseph McCabe, *op. cit.*, p. 45.

war. In the next place, we do not have anything worth fighting about, owing to the abundance resulting from modern inventions. Every animal, including the human animal, is reasonably good-natured when it is well fed. It is a mistake to identify a comfortable feeling of distention with morality. Suppose that we were hungry a good deal of the time, and the rest of the time didn't know how many meals we had ahead, we might not be so generous or good-natured. Self-preservation is still the first law of nature.

On this point we misjudge the so-called savage. Suppose we were living under an economic system in which the food supplies were somewhat meager. Suppose also, that owing to freedom from pestilence, our numbers were increasing rapidly and that game was becoming scarce. Moved by the cries of our children for food, we might be tempted to invade the hunting grounds of another tribe. But the other tribe would realize that this would mean hunger for its own people. It would probably fight to protect its hunting grounds. It would have some reason for fighting. What comparable reason for fighting has any nation with a high mechanical development? In other words, much of our so-called morality is merely the by-product of applied science and mechanical efficiency.

It is difficult to think in terms of progress without introducing one's own prejudices, sometimes called value judgments. It is equally difficult to insulate one's own value judgments from those of the social group of which one is a part unless one is highly individualized. This year's fashions will seem to us, as individuals, preferable to those of past years, not because they are superior but because we cannot help thinking as the group thinks about such things. There are fashions in art, literature, philosophy, and morals quite as definitely as there are in millinery and haberdashery. The way fashions are changing always seems progressive to the average mind simply because the average mind lacks the power to think otherwise. As Robert H. Lowie points out:

> Human beings generally act and think as they do for no other reason than that they have picked up such behavior and thoughts from some

social group of theirs. The superstitious notion that evolution constitutes spontaneous progress has bewitched not only the average mind, but also enslaved certain scientists and philosophers prefering a world of phantasy and wish to actual analysis. Only when some special and, on the whole, improbable cause enters the scene, does anything new happen — and then as likely the organism is destroyed as made fitter. The principle holds for culture. A change for the better — in any conceivable sense of that vague term — never occurs without due cause, and a change for the worse is quite as probable.[1]

Similarly, the general direction of any social change must seem progressive to the average mind.

As a tentative plan for avoiding this crowd hypnotism and for arriving at an objective test, progress has been defined as human adaptation — a gradual change as a result of which men are better fitted to live in the environment in which they find themselves, or the environment is better fitted to them. This is, of course, the process of social evolution.

However, as has been pointed out, "The essential process, according to the evolutionary hypothesis, is adaptation to conditions, and the conditions may be such as will lead to change for the worse just as easily as to change for the better."[2] It is, however, possible within limits to change the conditions, if not for the better, at least to suit our whims. Again, even though the changed conditions may necessitate a change for the worse in human life, that does not tell the whole story. Adaptation to the new conditions may leave human beings in a less desirable state than they were before the outward conditions changed, but, after the outward conditions have changed, those human beings who adapt themselves to the new conditions will be more comfortable than those who fail thus to adapt themselves. Thus adaptation, even to worse conditions,— provided they are unavoidable,— may be considered desirable, and, in that sense, or to that extent, progressive. Survival itself may require adaptation to changed conditions, even though the con-

---

[1] *Are We Civilized?* (Harcourt, Brace & Co., New York, 1929), pp. 291–292.

[2] C. M. Case, *Social Process and Human Progress* (Harcourt, Brace & Co., New York, 1931), p. 3.

ditions have grown worse, as it is assumed that they will when the earth shall have grown colder in future geologic ages.[1]

Let us suppose, for example, that a return of the ice age should force living forms in the north temperate zone to undergo a process of readaptation. This readaptation might take the form of a reduction of size, or some other form which we should now, with our present standards, evaluate as degenerate. Even after the readaptation had taken place, the conditions of life might be worse than they were before the ice sheet moved southward. Nevertheless, the living forms which went through the process of readaptatoin would certainly find themselves more comfortable than would have been the case if they had not been readapted. Even social adaptation might force us to live as the Eskimos. A change to that way of living would, from one point of view, be called retrogressive, yet, from another point of view, it would be called progressive. That is, we might live more comfortably in a frigid climate by imitating the Eskimos than we could if we failed to imitate them. Progressiveness, in that sense, would mean changing our ways to suit new conditions, even though the new conditions were growing worse. Even morals might have to change or to be reformed. "New occasions teach new duties." A new ice age would certainly be a new occasion. It might require a new code of morals, with new duties, new rights, and a new set of moral values.

While no two writers seemed to agree in their definitions of progress, yet each of a considerable group was able to formulate a theory of progress and to write consistently about it. The first writers to use the term *sociology*, or to call themselves *sociologists*, were those who wrote on social progress or social evolution. In its first beginnings as a subject for formal study, and in the minds of its creators, sociology was mainly a theory of progress.

2. *The Degradationists.* Even at the beginning of the twentieth century, when the belief in progress seemed almost universal, there were voices crying in the wilderness, proclaiming

---

[1] *Supra*, Chapter III, p. 43.

that civilization was a disease, that our so-called morality was self-destructive because it was filling the world with fools and weaklings, "too poor to tax, too numerous to feed," and that the world itself was in the last stages of decrepitude. There were religious leaders who held that the human race was sinking deeper and deeper in the mire of wickedness, as a race it was beyond redemption, and that the sole purpose of religion was to salvage as many individuals as possible from the wreck. There were scientists also who held that civilization was dysgenic, sterilizing its own architects, who alone could be classed as builders of civilization, and bidding its weaklings to be fruitful and multiply and replenish the earth — with weaklings. There were philosophers who preached a doctrine of uncompromising pessimism and excoriated the silly optimism which closed its eyes to the stupendous evil of the world.

Schopenhauer[1] stands out as the most unflinching of the pessimists. "I know of no greater absurdity," wrote he, "than that propounded by most systems of philosophy in declaring evil to be negative in its character. Evil is just what is positive; it makes its own existence felt."

Even more specific is the following:

There is nothing more certain than the general truth that it is the grievous *sin of the world* which has produced the grievous *suffering of the world* . . . Accordingly, the sole thing that reconciles me to the Old Testament is the story of the Fall. In my eyes, it is the only metaphysical truth in that book, even though it appears in the form of an allegory.

He says further that the fundamental difference among religions is not monotheism, pantheism, etc., but optimism and pessimism, that is, whether they praise and value the existence of the world, or recognize that it is the consequence of our guilt and properly ought not to be. The power by which Christianity overcame Judaism and the heathenism of Greece and Rome was Christian pessimism. Paganism was optimistic.

Other degradationists substitute an unfavorable physical or

---

[1] *Studies in Pessimism*, T. B. Saunders translation (Swan Sonnenschein & Co., London, 1891), pp. 1, 24.

social environment both for an internal taint in human nature and for a malignant spiritual power as an explanation of human degeneration.   One of the most profound of these is the late Henry Adams who, in his stimulating book on *The Degradation of the Democratic Dogma*,[1] attributes it to the "progressive degradation of energy by dissipation and leveling of intensities." Adams quotes profusely from physicists, astronomers, and geologists in support of the "Law of Degradation."   Perhaps the most striking of these quotations is from Flammarion's *Astronomie Populaire*.[2]

Life and human activity will insensibly be shut up within the tropical zones.   Saint Petersburg, Berlin, London, Paris, Vienna, Constantinople, Rome, will successively sink to sleep under their eternal cerements.   During many centuries, equatorial humanity will undertake vain arctic expeditions to rediscover under the ice the sites of Paris, of Bordeaux, of Lyons, of Marseilles.   The sea-shores will have changed and the map of the earth will be transformed.   No longer will man live, no longer will he breathe, except in the equatorial zone, down to the day when the last tribe, already expiring in cold and hunger, shall camp on the shores of the last sea in the rays of a pale sun which will henceforward illumine an earth that is only a wandering tomb, turning around a useless light and a barren heat.   Surprised by the cold, the last human family has been touched by the finger of death, and soon their bones will be buried under the shroud of eternal ice.   The historian of nature would then be able to write, "Here lies the entire humanity of a world which has lived!   Here lie all dreams of ambition, all the conquests of military glory, all the resounding affairs of finance, all the systems of an imperfect science, and also all the oaths of mortals' love!   Here lie all the beauties of earth!"— But no mortuary stone will mark the spot where the poor planet shall have rendered its last sigh!

Concerning our boasted intelligence Adams proceeds:
. . . By the majority of physiologists, Thought seems to be regarded — at present — as a more or less degraded Act,— an enfeebled function of Will:[3]

"Thought comes as the result of helplessness," says Lalande in his volume on "Dissolution" (Paris, 1899, p. 166); "Thought, as Bain says, is the refraining from speech or action.   The truth is, therefore, that action comes first; the idea is an act which tends to accomplish itself, and which, when

---

[1] The Macmillan Co., New York, 1919, p. 152 *et seq.*
[2] Paris, 1905. (See Adams, *op. cit.*, p. 182.)
[3] *Ibid.*, p. 203. Even the intellect, according to Adams, is a degenerate form of energy.

stopped by some obstacle before its realization, finds a new form of reality in that stoppage. Jean Jacques Rousseau said: "The man who thinks is a depraved animal"; and in this he expressed an exact view of psychology. As far as he is animal, the thinker is a bad animal; eating badly; digesting badly; often dying without posterity. In him the degradation of vital energy is flagrant. (La Depravation de la nature physique est visible chez lui.)[1]

. . . The historian is required either expressly to assert, or surreptitiously to assume, before his students, that the whole function of nature has been the ultimate production of this one-sided Consciousness,— this amputated Intelligence,— this degraded Act,— this truncated Will.[2]

Sociological writers, at least since Comte, have as a rule spent little time in trying to solve the riddle of existence, or even in speculating on the ultimate results to human society of the second law of thermodynamics. They have rather inclined with the men of ordinary common sense to say, "We don't know why we are here; but here we are. We don't know how this universe began or how it will end; but we are in it and can't get out except by suicide. We don't know whether the universe is kind or not, but we have discovered that we can be more comfortable or less comfortable according to the way we behave." Whether the universe is kind or unkind, it seems to be more kind or less unkind to those who adapt themselves to it than to those who fail to adapt themselves. At least, those who adapt themselves suffer less discomfort than those who do not.

Among those degradationists who attribute man's low estate to the degenerating influences of civilization, Max Nordau[3] deserves first rank because of his outspoken and unflinching pessimism, tempered, it is true, by a wholesome belief in the purgative powers of natural selection. The influences of city life, with its constant nerve strain, its multifarious poisons in

---

[1] An equally poor opinion of intellect seems to be implied in the account of the trouble that resulted from eating of the fruit of the tree of knowledge. Pandora's curiosity also caused a lot of trouble, according to another story.

[2] *Ibid.*, p. 205.

[3] See especially his *Degeneration* (D. Appleton and Co., New York, 1895). In his later works a more optimistic view was expressed. See his *Morals in the Evolution of Man*, tr. M. A. Lewenz (Cassell & Co., London and New York, 1922), in which he takes his place among the elevationists.

the form of alcohol, nicotine, opium, poisonous foods, and bad air, produce a degeneration of morals and manners simply because the majority become degenerate. They give tone and set standards, they lead the fashions not only in millinery, but in politics, dramatics, literature, art, and philosophy. The sober, steady-going, sound, healthy, and sensible minority are laughed out of countenance by the degenerate mob. For a time it looks as though civilization is about to decay. The social world looks as sickly as the physical world in its last stages looks to Flammarion. But there are curative powers at work. The degenerates are weeded out by the inexorable laws of natural selection. "God is not mocked." "The soul that sinneth it shall die." The sound and sensible, the domestically inclined, eventually take control of the situation, give tone and set standards, lead the fashions in politics, dramatics, art, literature and philosophy, and the processes of recovery and elevation begin. If, however, there should not be a sufficiently large remnant of sound and healthy people to be the progenitors of a new and better population, civilization is doomed.

. . . In the civilized world there obviously prevails a twilight mood which finds expression, amongst other ways, in all sorts of odd aesthetic fashions. All these new tendencies, realism or naturalism, "decadentism," neo-mysticism and their subvarieties, are manifestations of degeneration and hysteria, and identical with the mental stigmata which the observations of clinicists have unquestionably established as belonging to these. But both degeneration and hysteria are the consequences of the excessive organic wear and tear suffered by the nations through the immense demands on their activity, and through the rank growth of large towns. . . .[1]

Thus even vice itself becomes an agent of moral adaptation by acting as a fool killer to weed out those who can not withstand the degenerative forces of our complex civilization. They who can be in the world but not of it, who can keep themselves unspotted from the world, who, in the midst of the demoralizing influences of modern civilization with its great cities can re-

---

[1] Max Nordau, *Degeneration, op. cit.*, (D. Appleton & Co., New York, 1895), bk. I, chap. IV.

main immune to their contagion, are to survive, reproduce their kind, and build the civilizations of the future.

> It is [says Philip Gibbs] some unconscious or semi-conscious knowledge — some intuition or foreboding — of this exhaustion of the very sources of energy leading to a desperate struggle for existence in which Empires, States, and people may perish, which is accountable for the waves of melancholy spreading over the western world since the last great war. . . . It has found expression in pictorial art which denies beauty; in drama which goes to brutality, cruelty, and vice for its pictures of life; in music which revolts against the charm and melody and rhythm of former ages, and expresses modern life in strange and violent cacophonies; and it is stated starkly by novelists, essayists and philosophers.[1]

Bowden[2] lists some of the pessimistic pictures of America, of which the following are brief summaries:

1. "The American soul is pitifully small and undeveloped in comparison with American shrewdness and energy . . . smothered by our extreme mechanization and standardization of all our functions, individual and collective. A creeping paralysis is spreading over every Spiritual impulse."

2. Ralph Adams Cram voices the belief that "Great leaders are no more; democracy has reduced all to a dead level."

3. Lothrop Stoddard concludes that high civilization produces racial impoverishment, and one vast night of barbarism is impending: "Our civilization has grown so complex that it is a burden too great to be borne, we shall be crushed beneath it."

4. Spengler expounds: "A cycle theory of history — which dooms us to the sad fate of Nineveh and Tyre, attributing our decline to the machine instead of dysgenic breeding."

5. According to Count Keyserling: "The individual is ceasing to exist as a result of standardization of manners and morals. The old cultures are disappearing."

6. Religion has become vague and sterile — an uplift movement.

---

[1] *The Day After Tomorrow* (Doubleday, Doran Co., New York, 1928), p. 119.
[2] Robert Douglas Bowden, *In Defense of Tomorrow* (The Macmillan Co., New York, 1931), pp. 9–11.

Sociologists, however, at least in the early stages of the development of their subject, allied themselves on the side of the elevationists. The belief in the possiblity of progress, coupled with a desire to discover its laws, stimulated the first students who called their subject sociology. Even later writers, though they have grown chary in the use on the word *progress*, find difficulty in ridding themselves of the concept. All are conscious of a process of social change, development, growth, or evolution, even though they refuse to call it a progressive change in any sense which would imply a change for the better. A study of the factors which produce change,— physical, biological, and social,— especially when this study is carried on by one who has a clear understanding of adaption and all that it implies, may yet give us a positive theory of progress free from all value judgements.

B. Sociology as a Theory of Progress

1. *Auguste Comte and Social Harmony.* There are two philosophers who stand out in the early history of social science because they were among the first to give it a name and a place in the world of thought,— to give it some substantial unity and aim. Auguste Comte and Herbert Spencer deserve first place in this chapter; for it was their idea of social progress which gave consistency to the first really scientific attempts to study society.

Comte left no plan for an encyclopedic assembling of all possible data relating to social life; he branded social science as the study of facts that might throw light on the one essential problem of social progress.[1] He defined progress as the gradual approach to harmony in human relations, and studied how it might be promoted. He turned the attention of social philosophers and moralists from the problem of conflict (evil), the topic of Chapter III of this book, to the problem of producing harmony out of conflict.

---

[1] "All that can be rationally proposed in our day," he said, "is to recognize the character of positivity in social as in all other science and to ascertain the chief bases on which it is founded. . . ." *Positive Philosophy,* tr. Martineau (C. Blanchard, New York, 1855).

As a contribution to the methodology of his subject, rather than to its content, Comte outlined his famous three stages of intellectual development. In the approach to sociological as well as to physical problems, men began by attributing changes to supernatural agencies. This Comte called the theological stage. Next they attributed these changes to some principle of action which they posited or assumed to exist. This he called the metaphysical stage. Finally, they began observing and testing to find out what actually happened and how it could be made to happen again or prevented from happening. This he called the scientific or positive stage. In this stage, men are not much concerned with final causes, or ultimate ends. They are bent rather on finding out how to bring to pass what they want to bring to pass.

In the study of sociology, the theological stage is represented by the doctrine of an over-ruling providence leading men on by ways which they know not to goals which they can not foresee.[1] The metaphysical stage is represented by the various philosophies of history. The scientific or positive stage, which Comte believed he was ushering in, was to be a stage wherein students observed the order of sequence in human events, to the end that they might know what was necessary to bring about such conditions as they desired. He was, of course, normative as well as positive in his approach, as every writer who ever wrote a worthwhile treatise has had to be. He was interested in the relation of means to ends, but he could not avoid studying the relation of cause to effect in the most scientifically positive manner.

Social progress, as he boiled it down to its most concentrated form, meant a development of order in the structure of society, of harmony in the social relations of human beings. In a very important sense he began where the theory of conflict left off. Instead of trying to explain conflict he tried to trace the processes by which harmony developed out of conflict. In his more

---

[1] Providence and Nemesis seem to have root meanings somewhat alike: namely, management.

scientific moments, he argued that he looked forward to no ultimate perfection of this order and harmony. Progress, he admitted, must always be a purely relative idea. He saw, as well
as later writers, that historical development depends upon the
working of the environment on individuals, and the reactions and
responses of individuals to the impact of their surroundings. The
environment, however, is a changing thing. So long as it is
changing, how can there be perfect harmony between men and
their environment? Human beings would have to continue their
efforts to bring themselves into harmony with an ever changing
universe.

2. *Herbert Spencer and Social Differentiation.* Herbert Spen
cer, like Comte, developed his system of sociology around a
theory of progress. Like Comte, also, he played the part of
architect far more than stone mason in the building of sociology.
He was more a systematizer of knowledge than a scientist, pure
and unalloyed. He organized the data of social life about one
gigantic hypothesis, a universal law of evolution, a formula of
progress.

Although Spencer made frequent use of the word "progress,"
he preferred the word "evolution" for describing the development of the whole universe, inorganic, organic, and superorganic. Here was needed, he thought, a word free from the
anthropocentric meaning which was attached to "progress."[1]
It actually seems, however, that he made the two words practically synonymous. At least, if he considered evolution as
something more than progress, he considered progress as a
result of evolution.

That progress, to Spencer, was synonymous with change into
more and more complexity, is indicated by the following passage:

Heterogeneity is still increasing. It will be seen that as in each event
of today, so from the beginning, the decomposition of every expended force
into several forces has been perpetually producing a higher complication;
that the increase of heterogeneity so brought about is still going on; and

---

[1] See footnote in Duncan, *Life and Letters of Herbert Spencer* (D. Appleton
& Co., New York, 1908), vol. II, p. 329.

that progress is not an accident, not a thing within human control, but a beneficent necessity.[1]

His concept of social progress is that of change in social structure and function itself regardless of any teleological consequences. He says:

> The current conception (of social progress) is a teleological one. The phenomena are contemplated solely as bearing on human happiness. Only those changes are held to constitute progress which directly or indirectly tend to heighten human happiness. . . . But rightly to understand progress, we must learn the nature of these, considered apart from our interests.[2]

This is probably a wise — possibly an inescapable — point of view. Even modern philosophers who deny "progress," and speak of "adaptation" instead, think of adaptation as the result of an evolutionary process. Spencer was, above all, combating, in his evolutionary formula, a theological view of morality as unchanging. His more formal definition of evolution was ". . . an integration of matter and concomitant dissipation of motion during which the matter passes from an indefinite, incoherent homogeneity to a definite, coherent heterogeneity; and during which the retained motion undergoes a parallel transformation."[3]

The brilliancy of this concept and the comprehensive knowledge which Spencer brought to its defense, made a profound impression upon the intellectual world. It modified not only the thinking of scientists, but of theologians and literary men as well. The frequently quoted verse [4] by W. H. Carruth

---

[1] Herbert Spencer, *Essays, Scientific, Political, and Speculative* (D. Appleton & Co., New York, 1892), p. 60.
[2] *Ibid.*, p. 9.
[3] *First Principles* (D. Appleton & Co., New York, 1885), p. 396.
[4] A fire-mist and a planet
 A crystal and a cell,
 A jelly-fish and a saurian,
 And caves where the cavemen dwell;
 Then a sense of law and beauty,
 And a face turned from the clod—
 Some call it Evolution,
 And others call it God.

could scarcely have been written except in a world already tinctured with Spencer's philosophy.

This progress formula is full of holes of a philosophical nature. It is couched in terms of very general application. Early in his life, Spencer became convinced that everything in the universe is related to everything else. He tells in his "Filiation of Ideas," how, standing by the side of a pool one day where a gentle breeze was blowing, he began to watch the undulations of the water. This led him to think of other undulations, other rhythms; and he thought, Is not the rhythm of motion universal? Yes, he answered to himself, and went on thinking about motion.[1]

In the next few days he found himself gathering together a number of ideas that had been lying about in his mind. The conservation of force, the instability of the homogeneous, the multiplication of effect,— these truths he discovered were all aspects of one universal truth, the tendency of the simple to become complex, of the homogeneous to become heterogeneous. The idea of evolution as one universal transformation process came to him almost in a flash. From that time on, his life was devoted to the stupendous task of treating astronomy, geology, biology, psychology, and sociology in successive order from one point of view.[2] The same fundamental law, he believed, could be used to explain the development of astronomical systems from a primitive fire-mist or star-dust; of the earth and the planets from primitive nebulae; of biological forms from a primitive protoplasm; of intelligence from primitive reactions of matter sensitized to stimuli; and of a complex social life from the primitive, simple, undifferentiated life of the horde. It is not at all or exclusively a sociological truism. It would, in fact, be difficult to expound it much or discuss it critically without running into the danger of obscuring the one point it was put in here to emphasize. This formula of progress, this

---

[1] The philosophy of Spencer has been voluminously discussed, but rarely adequately. Perhaps the best estimate of its defects — as well as its merits — is to be found in Josiah Royce's *Herbert Spencer, an Estimate and Review* (Fox, Duffield & Co., New York, 1904).

[2] See Duncan, *Life and Letters, op. cit.*, pp. 327 ff.

evolution idea, was the correlating thread on which were strung all the facts that Spencer brought together in his three stout volumes on the *Principles of Sociology.*

Like many another student of human affairs, Spencer looked forward to an ultimate state of social harmony, but he expected it to come, not through supernatural but strictly natural processes, and through the process of evolution and not through legislation. As a result of the evolutionary process, men would become so thoroughly socialized as to be perfectly fitted for social life. The lag in the evolution of human nature would be overcome, human evolution would catch up with the conditions under which human nature was evolving, adaptation would be complete.

. . . there must be produced [he said] a kind of man so constituted that while fulfilling his own desires he fulfils also the social needs. . . . The ultimate man will be one whose private requirements coincide with public ones. He will be that manner of man who, in spontaneously fulfilling his own nature incidentally performs the functions of a social unit; and yet is only enabled so to fulfil his own nature by all others doing the like.[1]

This, apparently, was Spencer's conception of perfected human nature living in a perfected society, of progress as ultimate — that men might some day be so richly gifted with knowledge of social welfare, and a will for it, that they could be allowed perfect freedom to act for themselves. Social harmony would automatically result. Since Spencer believed in the inheritance of acquired characters he could hold that the practice of "social goodness" would have an effect in physically transmitting it. And, since the effect would be cumulative, he could argue that men might become socially perfect.[2] Spencer's critics are unable to see a necessary connection between his formula of progress and his hope for an ant-like social perfectibility of men. The first seems capable of giving direction to the scientific study of society; the second is suspected of being only a dream of something that the universe has never given an observable sign of

[1] From the closing paragraph of the *Principles of Sociology.*
[2] See Chapter VI on Adaptation, *infra.*

producing except perhaps in the case of certain social insects. Comte and Spencer set an intellectual fashion. It had been startling at first to think of studying scientifically a thing like morality; yet the latter nineteenth century finally caught up the idea and magnified it. Literally scores of writers began to make plans for a science of society. Most of them, in one way or another, elaborated on Comte and Spencer. They could not get much beyond fabricating some theory of evolution as a test of progress without finding themselves hopelessly lost. Four American writers in particular ought to be mentioned: John Fiske, Lester F. Ward, Simon N. Patten, and Walter F. Willcox.[1]

3. *John Fiske and the Growth of the Psychic from the Organic.* Fiske, like Comte and Spencer, had a theory of progress. Like them, also, he constructed a system of philosophy which included the development of human societies as a part of one universal process of cosmic evolution. Like them, he saw social institutions growing according to cosmic law.[2] Like them, too, he was accused of tucking in ideas of his own about human perfection as the goal of evolution. Yet, beyond his general theories and fond hopes, he left an idea which was full of pointers for the social scientist. Whether true or not, it was worth proving or disproving.

He labelled progress a growth of the psychic from the organic. He saw, as Spencer insisted, that, as animal organisms grew more and more complex in their physical makeup, their reactions to their environment became, of necessity, more and more complex. Far back in universal history, these reactions had been simple, inborn, instinctive, biological; but by the time man appeared they had become so many, so complicated, that they

---

[1] This is not to disparage or even to overlook the scholarly and fruitful work of another group of pioneers in sociology, such as William G. Sumner, Franklin H. Giddings, Edward A. Ross, Albion W. Small, Frank W. Blackmar, and many others in the United States, or of Vilfredo Pareto and L. T. Hobhouse in other countries. The author is here grouping those writers who developed their sociological systems around a theory of progress. It is the belief that sociology owes its first beginnings as a separate discipline to writers on social progress or evolution.

[2] See especially his *Outlines of Cosmic Philosophy* (Houghton Mifflin & Co., Boston, 1874. 2 vols.).

had to be learned after birth, by experience. A complex intelligence became all important. With man, evolution became essentially psychic, and less and less organic.

Allusion has already been made in Chapter III to the important place which Fiske gave to the prolongation of infancy in the enlargement and stabilization of the family, and to Professor William Morton Wheeler's additional suggestion that the prolongation of parenthood was also a factor. Fiske's first use of the prolongation of infancy was, however, in connection with his theory of progress as a growth of the psychic from the organic. The complexity of the reactions of men to the stimuli which came to them from the outside made it necessary for men to learn these reactions after birth. They could not be inborn. The learning of these reactions required a long learning period. Hence the prolongation of infancy. He says:

. . . while the nervous connections accompanying a simple intelligence are already organized at birth, the nerve connections accompanying a complex intelligence are chiefly organized after birth.

Thus there arise the phenomena of infancy which are non-existent among those arrivals whose psychical actions are purely reflex and instinctive. Infancy, psychologically considered, is the period during which the nerve connections and correlative ideal associations necessary for self-maintenance are becoming permanently established. Now this period, which only beigns to exist when the intelligence is considerably complex, becomes longer and longer as the intelligence increases in complexity. In the human race it is much longer than in any other race of mammals, and it is much longer in civilized man than in the savage.[1]

4. *Lester F. Ward and the Increase of Happiness.*   After Herbert Spencer, the greatest name among those who made progress the central theme of sociology is Lester F. Ward.[2]

---

[1] *Ibid.*, vol. II, p. 342. There is an extensive quotation from Fiske's *Cosmic Philosophy*, concerning the prolongation of infancy, in Carver's *Sociology and Social Progress* (Ginn & Co., Boston, 1905).

[2] 1841–1913. The important sociological writings of Ward are: *Dynamic Sociology* (New York, 1883. 2 vols.). *Psychic Factors of Civilization* (Boston, 1893). *Outlines of Sociology* (New York and London, 1898). *Pure Sociology* (New York and London, 1903). *Applied Sociology* (Boston and New York, 1906). *Glimpses of the Cosmos* (New York and London, 1913–18).
The *Outlines* is the best book for beginning a study of Ward.

A trained geologist and botanist, understanding physics and chemistry well, he used, too often perhaps, highly technical terms that simply served the purpose of analogy. Yet approaching sociology as a practising scientist in several branches of knowledge, he showed a philosophic grasp of its place in the world of the sciences; and left ideas for attacking the study of social life that are still important — indeed dominant and compelling.

He framed sociology in a theory of progress at once so simple and so definite and yet so difficult to expound that he caused much thinking to be done in his day. "Human progress," he said, "may . . . be properly defined as that which secures the *increase of human happiness.*"[1]

This sounds, at first, like some wild hope — the kind of thing that put no small confusion into the work of Spencer and Comte. How could any one study the factors in social life which increase human happiness, and reduce them to law? A person would have to have at least an idea of what happiness is. Ward did the only thing he could do, and hold the sociologist to his proper business. He made happiness a measurable thing.

All happiness consists [he said] in the gratification of desire. . . . There are two ways, therefore, by which the happiness of a being can be increased: first, by affording the opportunity for exercising existing faculties; and second, by the creation of new and additional faculties, and extending these opportunities to the exercise of these also.[2]

In making the increase of human happiness the criterion of progress, Ward was adapting to sociological purposes what Bentham had laid down as the foundation of law and morals. Ward was not, however, a psychological hedonist. That is, he did not, as Bentham is accused of doing,[3] insist that men are

---

[1] *Dynamic Sociology, op. cit.,* vol. II, p. 174. See also Bentham, *Principles of Morals and Legislation* (The Clarendon Press, Oxford, 1907), ch. I.

[2] *Ibid.,* vol. II, p. 176.

[3] The accusation is unjust, and is based on an unfair interpretation of Bentham's words: "Nature has placed mankind under the governance of two sovereign masters, *pain* and *pleasure*. It is for them alone to point out what we ought to do, as well as to *determine what we shall do. Op. cit.,* p. I.

actually governed in their choices by a calculus of pleasures and pains. He was, however, as are most modern moralists, an ethical hedonist. That is, he believed definitely that the final test of right and wrong as well as of progress, was utility, or the excess of pleasures over pains, of happiness over unhappiness.

Ward did not clarify, as fully as is desirable, his concept of happiness as consisting in the gratification of desire. He recognized the difference between the desire for action and the desire for objects whose consumption or possession gives pleasure. Being essentially of the West, he did not take any too seriously the oriental concept of happiness as consisting in the eradication of desire, or in emancipation from craving. To the western mind, the possibility of killing desires by satiation seems much more pleasant than that of killing them by eradication. Ward placed the desire for action, or the exercise of our faculties, on a higher plane than the desire for consumers' goods. The possibilities of the increase of happiness seemed to him to lie mainly in the direction of a fuller exercise of our faculties and the development of new faculties.[1]

But not all exercise is pleasurable. It is still necessary, in order that certain desires may be satisfied, that many kinds of action shall be carried beyond the point where the pleasure of action gives way to the unpleasantness of fatigue, confinement, or monotony. Action is then called work. These forms of unpleasantness help to cancel some of the pleasures derived from the things produced. After this cancellation is made, the balance of pleasantness and unpleasantness may be illustrated by the following diagram.

Let us measure the quantity of desirable things which may be won by labor along the line OX, and let the quantity of such things which a given individual is able to earn be represented by the distance OB. Then let the pleasure to be got from them be measured along the line OY. Under the principle of diminish-

---

[1] Later in this chapter we shall consider the relation of this concept to that of culture,— culture being defined as the exuberant exercise of the *higher* faculties.

ing utility, the total pleasure to be derived from the quantity OB may be represented by the surface YDBO.

To this quantity of pleasure must be added the pleasure of the work of earning the goods, in so far as the work is pleasurable. From it must be subtracted the unpleasantness of the work, in so far as the work is unpleasant.

DIAGRAM IV

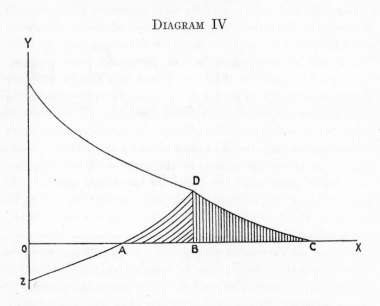

Let the curve ZAD represent the diminishing pleasantness and the increasing unpleasantness of the work. The work of producing goods up to the point A (distance OA) is pleasant, but decreasingly so, and beyond the point A (Distance AB) it is unpleasant, increasingly so. Accordingly, the surface OAZ is to be added to the pleasure of the individual but the surface DBA must be subtracted.

Still another subtraction must be made. The individual still has many desires which he can not satisfy. The quantity of things necessary to satisfy these desires, but beyond his reach, is represented by the distance BC. The intensity of his desire for each unit of this quantity is represented by the series of perpendicular lines extending from the line BC to the curve DC.

In other words, the shaded surface DCB represents the sum of unpleasantness which results from unsatisfied desires.

This individual's surplus of happiness, in so far as it is dependent on what he can get by his own effort, is represented by the excess of the surface YDAZO over the surface DCB. (The small surface DBA represents neither surplus nor deficit).

This may introduce an important qualification to the too easy assumption that there is a correlation between the increase of wants or desires, on the one hand, and the increase of happiness on the other. An increase of desires, without some increase in the means of satisfying them, merely adds to the area DCB, and subtracts from the excess of pleasantness over unpleasantness. Emerson's famous essay on *Compensation* introduces other forebodings, including the regret at the thought of leaving so pleasant a world, to reduce the excess of pleasantness over unpleasantness. Schopenhauer, of course, goes even further in his doctrine that the satisfaction of a desire is only negative pleasure, consisting in the cessation of the pain of an unsatisfied desire.

The attempt to use the increase of happiness as a measure of the rate of progress does not commit one to any theory as to the final good. Happiness may or may not be an end in itself. It may conceivably have a purely instrumental value. It can be regarded as a lure to induce us to do whatever is necessary in order to keep the germ plasm alive, as unhappiness is a warning to induce us to avoid whatever threatens the life of the germ plasm. Thus, happiness is *for* something, just as pain is. Neither is an end in itself. But even though happiness may have an instrumental, or a derived value, it may still be the most convenient quantum for measuring progress. We use weight, or physical dimensions, as convenient bases for measuring quantity without committing ourselves to the proposition that the property or dimension chosen is the only essential property or dimension of the thing we are trying to measure. If we are convinced that there is a fairly close correlation between the rate at which happiness increases and the rate of progress, and if we think that we can measure the rate of the increase of happiness, we may logically use happiness as a basis of measurement. But both "ifs" in that proposition are important.

What, now, finally stands out as really clear and simple in Ward's sociology? To study the conditions of increasing human happiness; to measure the opportunities of satisfying more desires; to note how much the increase of happiness is dependent on the growth of the intellect in the control of social life; to do all this, before dealing in human futures, is a task big enough, he said, for social science. He made the scientific study of society something definite; he gave it an aim, a theory of progress for others to find true or false. He was extremely cautious about putting rash hopes into his work that were not scientifically verifiable. He was more of a scientist than either Comte or Spencer or Fiske.

To Comte, perhaps, or Spencer — it is uncertain which — sociology owes its birth in the fructifying idea of progress. But it owes its somewhat naïvely scientific youth to the truths it was given by Fiske, Ward, and other men who were moved by the spirit of the time to think of human progress.

5. *Simon N. Patten and the Transition from a Pain to a Pleasure Economy.* One of the most stimulating of modern writers, both in economics and sociology, is the late Simon N. Patten. A man of remarkable originality, he challenged the thinking world in several fields. His best known contribution to sociology is his theory of social progress, which he defines as the transition from a pain economy to a pleasure economy. This generalization, while resembling somewhat Herbert Spencer's famous contrast between the militant and the industrial types of society, is somewhat more dynamic in its treatment. "Beings in a pain economy," says Patten, "have vigorous motor powers but a low development of the sensory powers."[1] When survival depends primarily on escape from enemies and the avoidance of pain, the forms of thought and the ideals created are such as will aid the people to combat these evils. There grows up

[1] *A Theory of Social Forces*, ch. v (American Academy of Political and Social Science, Philadelphia, 1896).

a pain morality which inhibits such behavior as may weaken men in their defense. There grows up a pain religion also, either to invoke the aid of higher powers, or to enforce discipline necessary for defense. Patten does not imply that men in the pain of economy are constantly thinking of fear and pain, but even their pleasures are such as not to interfere with the discipline necessary for defense or escape.

The purpose of the state, in the pain economy, is to protect the people from enemies. Everything within the state must be subordinated to the supreme need of defense. Religion and morals must combat all forms of pleasure which may expose people to attack from enemies, or weaken them in their fight against harsh circumstances. Morality in that stage is essentially ascetic.

Since the human race developed under a pain economy, and has lived for millions of years under the rigid necessity of self-protection, most of the institutions, religions, and mores are such as have survival value in the presence of enemies, both human and subhuman. The pious Christian has not only prayed for a time when none should "molest us or make us afraid," he has deliberately tried to inure himself to such conditions so long as they are unavoidable. Only recently has a small part of the human race emerged into conditions where it is safe or even possible to forget the presence of enemies or other sources of imminent danger. The Western World is now in a transition state. It is emerging into a condition in which men are motivated more by pleasurable than by painful anticipations,— by hope rather than by fear. Conscious fear is in a process of being banished, and the only effective motive to action is the hope of some form of satisfaction. The titillation of the appetite has displaced the satisfaction of hunger as the food motive. Self-adornment rather than protection from cold or insects is becoming the purpose of clothing. Self-expression rather than self-discipline is the goal of life.

When harsh winters or long dry spells brought starvation to the unthrifty, thrift had survival value. Since only the thrifty who had intelligence enough to store food for times of scarcity could survive, their virtues survived with them. Thriftlessness perished with the thriftless type of individual. In these days of superabundance, the old type of thrift seems to the average person unnecessary. While another type of thrift, namely, investment in new instruments of production, is increasingly necessary, there is a tendency to turn that function over to a few far-sighted individuals while the common run of men live a carefree, grasshopper sort of existence, and complain because of the unequal ownership of means of production.

During this period of transition we are already puzzled and confused. No one seems able to predict the end. We already lead carefree lives to a considerable extent. Neither invading armies, bears, wolves nor Indians, are left to molest us and make us afraid. Others save and invest for us, so that we do not need to think of the morrow. When harmful bacteria are all traced to their lairs and exterminated, as the larger beasts of prey have been, we may learn to forget about hygiene as we have already forgotten about morals and decency, and each one may feel free to do that which pleases him in defiance even of the laws of health. Already we are clamoring for old-age and unemployment insurance in order that we may be saved the trouble of thinking about rainy days to come.

However, every state or condition requires some sort of morality, that is, some sort of modification of individual behavior. Even the pleasure economy will require the difficult choice between the less and the greater pleasure, the ephemeral and the durable, the lower and the higher. The choice between two goods is quite as difficult as the choice between two evils.

That the pleasure economy has its difficulties is apparent when we consider that no nation has ever survived it for a long time. As Patten remarks, "Nation after nation has gone down when utilities instead of pains have become the supreme object of interest. Individuals as well as nations show the deteriorating influence of pleasure as soon as they are freed from the restraints of pain economy."[1]

---

[1] *Op. cit.*

One is here reminded of Carlyle's suggestion that for every one who can stand prosperity there are twenty who can stand adversity. When interpreted in terms of human ecology, this does not mean that prosperity is inherently more difficult to endure than adversity. It only means that the human race has had more experience with adversity than with prosperity. For millions of years, adversity has been exterminating those who could not stand it and preserving those who could. We are now a race which has become, through this long process of selection, at least partially immune to the demoralizing influences of adversity. It may take a million years of prosperity to build up a race, by the process of variation and selection, which is equally immune to the demoralizing influences of the pleasure economy. One of two things is certain. Either prosperity will destroy our race as it has destroyed others, or we shall develop the power to resist its destructive influences.

While admitting that the transition from a pain to a pleasure economy is a form of progress, Patten does not cater to our optimism by holding out the hope that progress may be permanent. In some respects his resembles a cyclical theory of civilization. Like a plant, civilization produces its flower and fruit, but in the process destroys itself. It differs from a cyclical theory, however, in that it does not hold that progress is inevitable. Tribes and peoples have apparently lived in a low state of civilization for millions of years. Their progress, if they ever made any, has either stopped long ago or has been by slow and imperceptible stages. But once let a group start definitely upward in its progress from a pain to a pleasure economy, it seems to run its course and destroy itself in the process.

Among other degenerative tendencies may be mentioned the exercise of the inventive faculties on the problem of separating sex from childbirth, to the end that the pleasures of sex may be enjoyed without the penalties of childbirth, or the cares, responsibilities, and expenses of parenthood. This rationalizing tendency naturally shows itself first among those most capable of reasoning, namely, the most intelligent classes. This results in a differential birth-rate. The function of reproduction is largely turned over to the least fit until intelligence is bred out and stupidity bred into the race, and one episode in the rise and fall of civilizations has come to an end.

C. THE MEASURE OF PROGRESS

1. *The Neo-Darwinians,— La Pouge, Kidd, Gumplowicz, Ratzenhofer, Durkheim.* Sociology would have advanced slowly to the position of a systematised discipline among other sciences, in spite of the good introduction it had been given by such eminent philosophers as Comte, Spencer, Fiske, Ward and Patten, had it not been for a formula that now goes by the name of Darwinism.[1] The idea of evolution in general is usually associated with Darwinism and is commonly taken to be synonymous with it; but this is scarcely accurate. The reason for this is well explained by Professor Hogben. He says:

Forced into the forum as a propagandist the biologist gave less attention to the logical structure of the new theory than to its apparent implications for social philosophy. The ethical concept of progress became entangled in the evolutionary idea. In the writings of Herbert Spencer and the evolutionist philosophers Darwinism has left a lasting impress upon contemporary thought.[2]

The essential idea of social evolution, as expounded by writers like Comte and Spencer in making clear their ideas of progress, is as old as philosophy. Darwin, who was primarily a biologist, did not invent the idea of social evolution. What he did was to make evolution more than a philosophic hypothesis. He developed it into a scientific formula that accounted for the origin and growth of the human body and mind as well as of plant and animal species.[3]

---

[1] The philosophers themselves, many of them, were influenced by ideas that are now labelled "Darwinian." They arrived at these many times independently of Darwin. This was not strange, since the general idea of evolution was so much in the air. It was Spencer, for instance, who coined the phrase "survival of the fittest."

[2] Lancelot Hogben, *The Nature of Living Matter* (Kegan Paul, Trench, Trubner and Co., Ltd., London, 1930), p. 127.

[3] Although he wrote nothing under the title of sociology, he made a notable contribution to sociological thought in his *Descent of Man*. This was a treatise

He had, back of him, not only the work of scientists, especially in the field of geology, who had taught that the present form of the earth's crust was the result of a long process of orderly development, but the work of practical animal breeders like Bakewell, the Collings, Tompkins, and Coke. The significance of the work of these men is sometimes overlooked. Before Darwin these men had proceeded on what are now called "Darwinian" lines. Aware of the universal fact of variation among animals of the same species, they had simply used the method of selection, or selective breeding. By this method they had, in half a century, produced strikingly new breeds of farm animals. It occurred to Darwin, after reading Malthus, that there was selection in nature as well as in the farmer's breeding pen. He called the one natural selection to distinguish it from the artificial selection of the animal breeder.

This formula of Darwin's has become so much of a truism in biology that it is difficult to realize what an important part it played, during an age still ruled by theological dogma, in turning the idea of evolution into a scientific tool. Biologists have already gone far beyond Darwin. They are asking now, What causes variation? What makes individuals different? They believe if they can only learn how to control variation, they can, knowing the requirements of a given environment, make adaptation, and so survival, more or less automatic — for whom you will. They simply ask to be given a free hand with the germ plasm.[1] They took their hint, none the less, from Darwin.

It would have been strange if a convincing demonstration of the method of biological evolution had not been full of leading strings for the sociologist. Remember — the idea of social evolution, in Darwin's time, while existing, was hardly more than a philosophic hope. Social progress was an idea hardly more substantial than a dream. The writers who took up the Darwin

on the evolution of human traits and institutions that was simply overshadowed in importance, by the *Origin of Species*. He saw no unbridgeable chasm separating human institutions from animal habits, nor civilized institutions from savage. He attempted to explain them all in terms of an evolutionary process.

[1] See *infra*, Chapter V, on Adaptation.

formula and applied it to the study of society were able at least to demonstrate an exact method by which social evolution could proceed as Darwin had shown how biological evolution could take place. As Karl Pearson remarks: "The insight which the investigations of Darwin, seconded by the suggestive but far less permanent work of Spencer, have given us into the development of both individual and social life, has compelled us to remodel our historical ideas and is slowly widening and consolidating our moral standards."[1]

We thus find, for instance, that Vacher de Lapouge organized the facts of social life rather neatly around Darwin's theory.[2] He simply transferred and applied the Darwinian concept of evolution to human societies considered as living entities. In racial evolution, he argued, there is variation and selection just as there is in all the world of life. Races are varieties of men that struggle for survival. They cannot all live and expand for lack of space and food. If there is such a thing as human progress, it is because the race that is better adapted than others to its environment lives longer as a race and prospers, while the others fade away into historical oblivion. Men, he reasoned, have no more of an innate tendency to progress than have plants and animals. If progress comes, it comes because the unfit fail to propagate their kind.

This sounds like pure biology. But Lapouge explains that human evolution is social and not biological, because the human environment is social and not merely physical. Life in general has to adapt itself to a purely physical world; nature is the only judge of what varieties of life shall survive. Human beings, as individuals, have to adapt themselves to social institutions — to war, politics, economic competition, the church, morals, legal control, jails and gibbets. It is conformity to social standards which determines what individuals shall prosper. Only indirectly

---

[1] *The Grammar of Science* (Adam & Charles Black, London, 1911), p. 1.

[2] The three important books of Lapouge are: *Les Selections Sociales* (Paris, 1896); *L'Aryen, son rôle sociale* (Paris, 1899); *Race et milieu sociale* (Paris, 1909). The first is enough to give even the more than average student of sociology a sufficient idea of Lapouge's general theories.

and ultimately is physical nature the arbiter of individual survival.

But what determines which groups shall survive? This is a question which is not likely to occur to any but a trained sociologist. He realizes that the process of selection is the weeding out of social groups as well as of individuals. While the individual's survival depends, to a considerable degree, upon the conformity *to* the mores of the group, the survival of the group depends, to an equal degree upon the conformity *of* its mores to the conditions which surround it. When surrounded, for example, by hostile groups who have easy access to its hunting grounds, the group's survival will depend to a considerable extent upon its fighting power, and this, in turn, upon a multitude of factors — mores, institutions, organizations — which contribute to that fighting power. When surrounded by barriers which shut out invaders, or when occupying a territory so poor as not to tempt invaders, its survival will not depend so much on fighting power as on productive power. Productive power, in turn, depends upon factors different from those which contribute to fighting power.

There are variations among groups as among individuals. There is also selection of the favorable variations and extinction of the unfavorable variations among groups as well as among individuals. The actual process, that of variation and selection, by which the evolution of social groups proceeds is identical with that by which individual evolution proceeds. The difference is in the factors which determine group survival on the one hand and individual survival on the other hand.

Lapouge seems to have outlined a rather clear-cut course for the sociologist to follow. It seems quite logical to argue that the race best adapted to its social surroundings is the one that is victorious in war and politics and economic competition. The race that is made less prosperous or less fertile by the morality or religion to which it conforms is handicapped in the struggle for existence. Analyze, therefore, the factors that make the military success of a race,— its material prosperity, its fertility, its morale,— and you have the key to social adaptation and social progress. The job is something definite.

Yet there is much in Lapouge's work that is of very questionable value. There is not much doubt that he made a fundamental error in picking out the survival of race rather than the survival of the social group as the key to social evolution. There may be such a thing as race.[1] If social institutions affect the survival of one race or another, racial evolution may be called social. But social evolution is much more than the survival of races best adapted to social institutions; it is also the survival of social institutions themselves, of political systems, religions, moralities, and other organized means of social control. Social institutions are themselves socially evolved through the struggle of political rather than racial groups for political ascendancy. Political groups are socially more fundamental than racial groups.[2]

Benjamin Kidd caught at this idea. He wrote, it is true, about all kinds of struggles for existence — among individuals, classes, races, nations.[3] This much, at any rate, he emphasized to the profit of sociology: the struggle of social groups for survival results in the success of the socially efficient groups. Social progress is possible, but only through the sacrifice of individuals and of groups that are least adapted to social life.

Leaning always on Darwinism, Kidd developed his theory that religion has played a leading rôle in social progress. While men were still animals, he argued, and struggling with other animals for survival, the human brain evolved; and reason, evolving, was victorious in the struggle. But men, with their greater intelligence, while they were slowly becoming social creatures, were not at all exempt from a struggle for survival; there was struggle among individuals within a group and between groups. In the struggle for group survival, individuals

---

[1] In biological evolution race has clearly been important.

[2] Almost never has a political group been a race in itself.

[3] See the excellent account of Kidd by Bristol in *Social Adaptation, op. cit.*, pp. 85 ff. Bristol discusses, among other things, Kidd's law of "projected efficiency" which it does not seem necessary to consider here.

have to be sacrificed. Now how, asks Kidd, could intelligent individuals accept the sacrifice that the struggle involved? Is it not true that intelligence is egotistical? Would there be any rational motive for hermit-minded, egotistical individuals to sacrifice themselves for the group in order that sociable groups might survive? Kidd saw that social progress necessarily involved the sacrifice. Religion explained for him what seemed quite incomprehensible. Religion he saw as the irritational faith that could lead men to accept social life, at any cost; religion made men socially efficient.

> No form of belief [he said] is capable of functioning as a religion in the evolution of society which does not provide an ultra-rational sanction for social conduct in the individual. . . . A religion is a form of belief, providing an ultra-rational sanction for that large class of conduct in the individual where his interests and the interests of the social organism are antagonistic, and by which the former are rendered subordinate to the latter in the general interests of the evolution which the race is undergoing.[1]

Kidd did not altogether substantiate his theory that religion is the leading factor in social progress. He showed, perhaps, that a group held together by strong religious institutions might survive a group weak in sociability, because it lacked churches. He did not show convincingly that other institutions might not take the place of churches, that a group might be held together, not by an ultrarational faith, but by a perfectly rational conviction of the usefulness of coöperative labor. He did not see, for example, that men might be led to give active assent to an abstract principle of distributive justice,— such a principle as this: that each should share in the joint product of industry in proportion to his contribution to that joint product. Knowing that one man can contribute more than another, the majority may accept smaller individual shares than go to the minority, and not insist on killing the goose that lays the golden eggs by trying to grasp larger shares for themselves and destroying the motive for efficiency on the part of more gifted individuals. Perhaps Kidd might have insisted that assent to such a principle of distributive justice is a kind of religion.

[1] *Social Evolution* (Macmillan & Co., New York & London, 1894), pp. 101, 203.

A more questionable assumption of Kidd was that the great mass of individuals must necessarily be sacrificed under economic competition. The possibility that competition might be so controlled and directed as to enable the great mass to succeed and only the defective minority to fail, seems to have escaped him. He never grasped the fundamental difference between economic competition and the struggle for existence as it is carried on in the sub-human world. His insufficiencies, however, ought not to be allowed to overshadow the importance of the problem which he was, in all his work, trying to solve,— the problem of social efficiency and its survival value in the struggle of social groups.

Another example of an attempt to explain social processes in terms of the Darwinian principle of conflict is Ludwig Gumplowicz. In his book *Pure Sociology* Ward makes the following comment:

Gumplowicz and Ratzenhofer have abundantly and admirably proved that the genesis of society as we see it and know it has been through the struggle of races. I do not hope to add anything to their masterly presentation of this truth, which is without question the most important contribution thus far made to the science of sociology. We have at last a true key to the solution of the question of the origin of society. . . . It is the only scientific explanation that has been offered of the facts and phenomena of human history. It proceeds from a true natural principle which is applicable to man everywhere, and which is in harmony with all the facts of Ethnology and Anthropology. Finally, this principle proves to be a universal one, and is the one on which are also explained all other natural phenomena.[1]

No less stern a critic of Gumplowicz than H. E. Barnes makes the following comment: "His thorough analysis of the social process, viewed as the interaction of conflicting groups, is one of the most fundamental notions which has yet been brought forward by sociology and constitutes a contribution of the greatest permanent value."[2]

[1] Lester F. Ward, *Pure Sociology* (The Macmillan Co., New York, 1903), pp. 203–204.
[2] H. E. Barnes, "The Struggle of Races and Social Groups"; article in *Journal of Race Development* (Clark University, Worcester, Mass., 1918–19), vol. IX, pp. 400–401.

The chief criticism that may be raised against Gumplowicz's theory is that it overestimates the working of "blind natural laws" in the formation of the social process as well as in the making of social institutions, to the exclusion of planned progress, or of what Ward calls "Collective Telesis." In human society the effort to escape from environing conditions is rather in the nature of a positive attempt to control and better the condition than that of mere blind acceptance and passivity. Gumplowicz is also accused of underestimating the fundamental fact of mutual aid as a factor in social development. He could reply, however, that mutual aid is mainly confined to members of a group and is therefore a factor in its success in its struggle with other groups. There is mutual aid, *par excellence*, in a well organized and disciplined army, but it is a means of fighting successfully against other armies. Mutual aid is a form of teamwork. It is highly developed in a colony of ants or bees, but it does not extend to members of rival colonies. His utter denial of social progress as a whole reminds one of the most gloomy dictum of Ralph Waldo Emerson in his essay on *Self-Reliance*. Says Emerson:

Society never advances. It recedes as fast on one side as it gains on the other. Its progress is only apparent like the workers of a treadmill. It undergoes continual change; it is barbarous, it is civilized, it is Christianized, it is rich, it is scientific; but the change is not amelioration. For everything that is given, something is taken.

Some over zealous environmentalists object to Darwinism because it stresses heredity. Granting all that may be said as to the passivity of the individual's reaction to the stimuli which come to him from his social environment, we can not get away from the basic, biological fact of variation among individuals. Without this variation there is no evolution. With this variation, there is a difference in the reactions of different individuals to the same environment. A social environment which stimulated a Newton or a Faraday to a certain type of mental activity, failed absolutely to stimulate millions of others to any such mental activity. In short, no two individuals react in precisely the same way to a given environment. A great deal, therefore, depends upon the kinds of individuals we are breeding. That will be an important factor in determining how the next generation will react to the social environment we are building for them.

The problem of group survival leads to the vitals of sociology. It would be difficult to overstress the importance of the neo-Darwinians who first gave half-valid hints concerning factors that might have survival value for a human group in its struggle with other groups for political ascendancy.[1] The neo-Darwinians threw out a profitable leading string for the sociologist. They illustrated a method by means of which social progress could take place. They gave some consistency to the study of social life.

Sociologists — most of them — have come to accept the idea of social evolution as a truism. They see how social progress, if there has been such a thing at all, has taken place. Now they want to hasten progress. Leaning on Darwinism, they are ready to go far with it. They are centering their attention on the slow changing of social institutions — the mechanism of social variation, just as biologists are studying the changing of the germ plasm — the mechanism of physical variation. Social institutions are the means by which political groups adapt themselves to their environment. Sociologists want to control institutional change.[2] If they learn to do this, as far as they can predict the demands of a given environment, they feel that they ought to be able to make social adaptation certain and social progress as swift as their wisdom. They know that legislatures have it in their power to change social institutions. They believe that political legislation should be backed by social science. Their job is to analyze the factors that have caused groups to survive in most of the tight pinches of human history, to make a scientific study of social variation. The job

---

[1] They are too numerous to discuss further in this chapter. The work of L. Gumplowicz and J. Novicow is as important as Kidd's and Lapouge's. A book such as P. Sorokin's *Contemporary Sociological Theories* (Harper & Brothers, New York, 1928), contains a great deal of reference material on the subject. See especially chs. v and vi.

[2] Remember Lester F. Ward's "Social Telesis."

done, they are in a position to advise politicians about making changes in social institutions with a view to hastening social progress.

2. *Walter F. Willcox and the Statistical Measure.* The Darwinian formula convinced the world, rightly or wrongly, of the possibility of progress. It showed how evolution could take place and presented convincing evidence that it did take place. Evolution came to be identified with progress. It is one thing, however, to accept the possibility of progress and quite a different thing to recognize it when one sees it. The discussion has tended, recently, therefore, to center around the question of the criteria of progress. What are its earmarks and how may we determine, at any given period, whether we are progressing, retrograding, or merely moving in circles?

The earlier writers had not ignored this question. Comte identified progress with the growth of harmony in human relations. He did not, however, leave us a very satisfactory method of measuring the degree of harmony or disharmony. Spencer identified progress with the growth of complexity. This lends itself to mechanical measurement somewhat better than Comte's idea of harmony. However, it seems too mechanical to suit most utilitarians who are more interested in human happiness than in mechanical complexity. Ward's concept of happiness as the test of progress satisfies those who realize their own automatic responses to painful and pleasurable sensations, but happiness is singularly difficult to measure.

A more fundamental objection to happiness as a measure of progress is based upon the ecological fact that happiness or pleasure, like pain, has an instrumental value. Pain is a warning which leads us to avoid whatever may be destructive and endanger our survival. Pleasure is a lure which leads us to do whatever is necessary to insure our survival or that of our germ plasm. Thus neither pleasure nor pain are ends in themselves, but are means to an end, which end is survival. Survival may or may not be the final end, but it is at least the end of which pleasure and pain are the means. In that important sense, survival is one step nearer than happiness to the *summum bonum*. Ecologically speaking, it *is* the *summum bonum*.

Survival also has the advantage of being a physical fact, and much less elusive than happiness. It is, of course, pertinent to ask, what is survival for? It is equally pertinent to ask, what is happiness for? To the latter question the ecologist has a ready answer. It is for survival. It lures men on to do those things on which survival depends, just as pain warns and deters men from doing those things which treaten extinction. No equally prompt and definite answer can be given to the question, what is survival for? One can not say that survival is for the sake of happiness without begging an important question, namely, is life worth living, or does survival bring more happiness than unhappiness? Optimists assume that to be true, pessimists deny it categorically. So long as the argument is a strictly logical one, it results in a stalemate.

There is, however, a universal urge in all living creatures to keep on living and reproducing their kind. All living creatures seem to behave as they would behave if they were thoroughly convinced that life was worth while and survival a thing supremely to be desired. The ecologist sees pleasure and pain as agencies to aid and guide sentient creatures, luring them or prodding them, to do those things which make for survival and to avoid those things which hinder survival. To a living creature, life seems the chief thing in terms of which everything else is evaluated. Moreover, as pointed out in an earlier chapter, the feeling that life is worth while has, itself, survival value because those who have this feeling are more likely to survive than those who lack it. The jury is being packed by natural selection.

A view which is in complete harmony with this theory was expounded by Professor Walter F. Willcox in a brilliant article entitled "A Statistician's Idea of Progress."[1] This article, it is safe to say, contains one of the most definite, clear-cut, and constructive contributions ever made in the field of sociology.

[1] *International Journal of Ethics*, vol. XXIII.

While not committing himself on any such abstract question as the *summum bonum*, Professor Willcox definitely insists that progress must be tested by something that can be measured and counted. The number of people can be counted by census enumerators, and the kinds and quantities of desirable things which they enjoy can also be inventoried. A civilization which is increasing the means of subsistence, permitting more and more people to live and to have more and more of the things which they desire is, according to this test, a progressive civilization. Even though their desires are not approved, they at least have a wider choice than people who, because of poverty, must needs be satisfied with very little.

This fits in with the theory of survival values in that the first requisite of survival is subsistence. A group of people who are so motivated and organized as to increase the means of subsistence has at least that advantage over a group so motivated and organized as not to be able to increase the means of subsistence. This test of progressiveness applies to their social system and not to their individual capacities. In comparing the American Indian with the European colonist, for example, it is not necessary to assume anything as to the physical or mental superiority of an Indian over a European, or of a European over an Indian. The question is, which had the better social, economic, and political organization,— the "higher" civilization? Different philosophers might give different answers. To a practical philosopher who is also an economist and a statistician, the answer is clear. The European colonists were equipped by their civilization to produce more subsistence, to support more people and to give each person more desirable things than the Indian's civilization equipped him to do.

Since this argument does not even hint that a man and an amoeba are of equal value, it is hardly a valid answer to say that there are more amoebae than men in the world. As to the relative values of men and other creatures, men may be pardoned for showing a certain prejudice in favor of their own kind, as other creatures do. Since men write treatises on this subject for other men to read, this prejudice may be assumed.

Let us forget this prejudice, however, when we are discussing purely human affairs, and assume that, man for man, an Indian is exactly as valuable as a white man. The fact that the white man's civilization enables a hundred white men to live and make a living where the Indian's civilization permitted only one Indian to live or make a living, would seem to argue for the superiority of the white man's civilization. To deny this would imply that one Indian is worth as much as a hundred white men, an opinion not free from prejudice. Here is a measurable quality of the two civilizations. They who, on the other hand, assert the superiority of the Indian's civilization, have no similar basis of measurement. They must fall back on their own prejudices or preferences.

Let us apply this comparison to the present and the future of the same civilization. Granting that the average individual living at one time is worth exactly as much as the average individual living at another time, if the civilization is so changing as to equip men for the production of more subsistence, so that more can live at a later than at an earlier time, and live as well or better, it would be a progressive civilization; otherwise not.

Walter Bagehot goes even further and applies the biological test of survival as a measure of progress.[1] Sophists might discuss the causes and cures of the disease called civilization, but there is no doubt that civilized men can take land away from uncivilized men whenever they want it. When Europeans came in contact with Tasmanians, the latter disappeared. When Europeans came in contact with American Indians or native Australians, the latter lost their lands, and would have starved to death except for the doles allowed them by those who took their lands. In Darwinian terms, the Europeans are more "fit," that is, more able to survive than the Tasmanians, Australians or Indians. These races live, if at all, because of the forbearance of the civilized races. Yet it is not so much a matter of individual as of social fitness. The Europeans have a superior

[1] *Physics and Politics* (D. Appleton & Co., New York, 1912), pp. 205–224.

social, economic, and political system. It is a matter of group survival, and group survival depends upon the organization of the groups rather than upon the individual prowess of its members.

Very naturally, there is an extreme reluctance to accept either the statistician's or the biologist's idea of progress. Every one has his own notions as to what is good and desirable. Even though all his notions are inherited, they are none the less dear to him. He can not conceive of progress except in terms of his own standards. Consequently the average person will conceive of progress as a change in the direction of some standard of his own. If he is the devotee of a certain religion or a certain type of culture, progress to him will consist in the spread of that religion or that type of culture. If he is a pacifist, progress will consist in the cessation of war. If he is a militarist, it will consist in the building up of a fighting machine and the building of a great empire through the spread of military power. If he is a scientist, it will consist in the improvement of the mechanic arts, etc. etc.

Any one, however, who insists that progress consists in the development of higher standards is under obligation to explain what a "high" standard is, and why it deserves to be called "high." It is conceivable that a high standard is one which makes it possible for a great many people to live and to satisfy a great many interests of each individual. A high standard of goodness in individual character, for example, may be one which conforms to a statistician's definition of progress. In other words, a "good" person is one who does things which make it possible for many people to live and to satisfy many interests. A bad person is one who does things which have the opposite effect. A "good" habit is one which, in proportion as it spreads, makes it possible for many to live and satisfy many interests. A bad habit is the opposite. Under this concept of goodness, its spread could be tested by the statistician.

A religious revival, for example, if worth while, should leave its results in forms which a statistician could measure. It should result in a diminished death-rate, and an increased birth-rate among those who possess the kind of talent that is needed as evidenced by the demand for and the price of it. It should result in better farming and better workmanship, both of which could be measured by the statistics of production. It should result in harder study of useful subjects, which could be measured by the statistics of attendance upon schools, of election of courses designed to make students more useful, and of grades in courses.

On the other hand, a religious revival would be vicious and not beneficent if it resulted in nothing more than an ebullition of religious feeling, in a renewed interest in the discussion of questions having no possible connection with problems of human adaptation to the earthly environment, if it encouraged schools and courses of study which taught young people to fiddle while the world was on fire, to seek an esoteric culture when there are multitudes of unemployed who need highly intelligent and highly trained employers who alone can solve their problems of unemployment for them. In short, a change of standards, either through a religious revival or the slow process of education, can not be said to be progressive unless it produces desirable results which can be measured by the statistician.

The general reluctance of experts in education to subject their educational frills to a statistical test is evidence of their lack of scientific interest. Do undergraduates who have been subjected to a tutorial system or a house plan do better work in graduate or professional schools, or in after life, than those who have never had those "advantages?" That question has not yet been put to a valid statistical test. Needless to say, a consensus of opinions of tutors and house-masters is not a valid test. The general reluctance of religious organizations to apply the statistical test to themselves evidences a similar lack of scientific attitude. Do Christians, for example, make better farmers, workmen, or business men than non-Christians? Do Catholics contribute less proportionately to the criminal and prostitute class than Protestants? Even to suggest such reasonable statistical tests is to provoke a storm of protest and to be accused of religious bigotry. The Mormons, the Jews, and the

Christian Scientists at least seem to be willing to meet such a test.[1] Other religious bodies might well follow their example. The devotees of this or that esoteric form of culture might well be checked up by a statistician. Whatever may be said for or against their cult, unless it, to some measurable degree, assists in the great problem of human adaptation, it can present no convincing reason to the intellect for its acceptance as a factor in progress. Its appeal must be wholly emotional. Needless to say, the success of its demogical appeals to the emotions is no valid test. It is what happens after conversion to a religion that counts, and a statistician is the one to make the count.

Professor Willcox has at least pointed the way to a final test of progress. He may not have said the last word, but certainly no one hereafter is entitled to be heard on the subject of progress until he has considered the possibility of measuring it by some objective test. Between some sort of objective or statistical test, and the mere assertion of personal approval of a given change, there is no middle ground.

A qualitative change in social organization may be suggested which, when checked by a statistician, would produce measurable results. A transition from the destructive and deceptive forms of competition to the productive forms, might reasonably be said to be a progressive change. A nation which succeeds in bringing about such a transition could be said to be a progressive nation.

Destructive forms of competition[2] are those under which the individual succeeds in getting what he wants by the exercise of his superior powers of destruction, by his ability to kill, to hurt or to inspire fear. Deceptive forms are those under which the individual succeeds in getting what he wants by reason of his superior powers of deception, by his ability to deceive, defraud, or outwit. Productive forms of competition are those under which the individual succeeds in getting what he wants

---

[1] See *The Fruits of Mormonism*, by Franklin Stewart Harris and Newbern Isaac Buth (The Macmillan Co., New York), 1925.

[2] Supra, Ch. III, Sec. 6.

by reason of his superior powers of production or service, by his ability to supply what others want.

The nation which succeeds in reducing to the lowest minimum the percentage of individuals who use their energies in destructive and deceptive forms of competition, and in increasing to the maximum the percentage of those who use their energies in productive or useful forms of competition, will, in the long run, outstrip all others in the numbers that can be supported and in the abundance of things enjoyed by each individual. It is all involved in the simple formula: he that would be successful or great, let him earn his success or his greatness by being useful, not by deception or by terrorism. Here is a standard which produces measurable results and does not depend for its validity upon a mere personal prejudice.

Even Ward's social telesis, or planned evolution, must wait until we have valid measurements. Some feeble and rather vapid suggestions of social telesis are found in recent proposals for a planned economy. A rationally planned economy must obviously begin with a planned population, but this is the last thing which the economic planner wants to see planned.

CHAPTER V

THE SOCIAL NATURE OF MAN

1. *The Concept of Sociability.* Do men hang together because of social feeling or because they see that if they do not they will, as Franklin suggested, hang separately? Do men live in groups because they are by nature social, and yet quarrel among themselves because they are intelligent enough to see that, wherever there is a scarcity of any desirable thing, their interests conflict; or do they live in groups because they are intelligent enough to see the advantage of it, and yet quarrel among themselves because of an inborn anti-social feeling?

In Chapter III we have tried to show that there is an inherent antagonism of economic interests which is sufficient to give rise to conflict among members of the same society unless these members are superhumanly altruistic, that is, altruistic beyond the capacity of any finite mind. The opinion was expressed that men were social in the sense that they preferred society to solitude, that they preferred their own kind to other creatures, and that they were anatomically and psychologically constructed for communication, which is a form of association; but that they were not sufficiently social to overcome or control, in all cases, the explosive tendencies growing out of the antagonism of economic interests wherever scarcity existed. In this chapter we shall consider, in somewhat greater detail, this social nature of man.

In the study of social progress, it is impossible to go very far without running into various problems concerning "human nature."[1] If there was survival value in social life, it would have been strange if the process of evolution had not bred sociable human beings, that is, beings with some capacity for social life. Sociability has had survival value, for it has given to large social groups cohesion and organic unity. There must be some cement to hold the parts of a group together, some common interest to furnish a motive for common action. In the struggle among rival groups for survival, success must have come to those groups which were best cemented, best organized for efficient group action, either in war or in industry. One problem of the sociologist is to find what are the elements in efficient organization which have survival value. Talkativeness may be one such element; a sound system of jurisprudence may be another; a sound code of morals, an efficient industrial system, a social disposition on the part of a group of individuals, may be other elements. The last-named seems the most fundamental of all and will here be discussed first.

"Man — the political animal — according to the definition of Aristotle, lives and must live in society. A human being outside the pale of society is an inconceivable thing."[2] This does not mean at all that a man would cease to be human if he were isolated after his mental habits were formed, or that Robinson Crusoe was any more human after he met Friday than before. It means simply that men are the product of social living; that they have become, through social living, very different creatures from what they would have been had they developed, biologically, in isolation. An individual of a race thus developed in and adapted to social life, but removed from social life from

---

[1] Cf. especially C. H. Cooley, *Human Nature and the Social Order* (Charles Scribners Sons, New York, 1902).

[2] From the *Political Doctrine of Fascism*, by A. Rocco (translated and published by the Carnegie Endowment for International Peace, New York, 1926), p. 16.

birth, would be as helpless as a bird without air to fly in or a fish without water to swim in.

It is obvious that certain anatomical features of the human body have evolved in connection with a social mode of life. Vocal organs, for instance, evolved because they were of service in group action. The gift of speech would hardly have been acquired by men had there been no occasion for using it and had it not proved to have survival value. Similarly, it seems that human beings would never have evolved the forward set of the eyes in the head, which prevents their seeing behind them and on all sides, had it not been for the fact that they were able to lead a social existence. They did not need to see on all sides. Each could use his fellows for sentinel duty. Most animals, unless, like the lion, they are so strong that they scarcely need to keep a roving eye out for enemies, or the owl which is protected by a mantle of darkness, are equipped with a set of eyes which enables them to see in all directions. Man has not evolved such acute hearing as many other creatures because he has not had to rely altogether on himself to hear. The brain of man seems to have developed as an organ for perceiving the advantages of teamwork and making the most of them. Most animals, lacking thumbs, an upright posture, and other anatomical characters for a brain to use, have little need of a large brain.

Sociability is not by any means purely anatomical. It is psychic, however much the psychic may be correlated with the anatomical. "But beyond the superiority of his physical nervous system, and the mode in which that renders his psychic functions possible or makes an element of their behavior, it is in his mentality and his mental life that he especially distances the others."[1]

In what, then, does sociability essentially consist? What is it that seems to make man enjoy always [2] the mere presence of

[1] Henry Osborn Taylor, *Human Values and Verities* (The Macmillan Co., New York, 1928), p. 121.

[2] This statement is limited only by the principle of satiability. Too much society, like too much food, music, or religion, may create a temporary desire for respite.

others of his kind, to prefer society to solitude most of the time? Naturally, if sociability has untold survival value, social scientists are eager to know about the human capacity for teamwork, how to cultivate it. This has become a major problem in sociology. The attempt to analyze the social nature of man has played a large part in giving consistency to the study of social life — perhaps equal in importance to the part that the analsysis of conflict and of progress have played.

From the days of Aristotle, students have attributed the human capacity for large-scale teamwork to something organic in man, to an inclination to live in cities, to gregariousness, to an instinct of sociability, to some inborn proclivity. Lester F. Ward sharply challenges this conclusion, as do his two most brilliant disciples, J. Q. A. Dealey and E. A. Ross. To them the capacity for teamwork is primarily the intellectual ability to see the advantage of it. In the opening sentences of their *Text Book of Sociology*,[1] Dealey and Ward say:

Man is not *naturally* a social being; human society is purely a product of his reason and arose by insensible degrees, *pari passu* with the development of his brain. In other words, human association is the result of the perceived advantage which it yields, and came into existence only in proportion as that advantage was perceived by the only faculty capable of perceiving it, the intellect.

Ross, in *Social Control*,[2] which is dedicated "To my Master, Lester F. Ward," says

Intellect has come to fix the range and closeness of association instead of feeling. . . . The great social expansions have occurred, not in the most gregarious varieties of mankind, but in those races that have sense enough to perceive the advantages of association, and wit enough to construct a good social framework.

Here, as elsewhere, Ross recognizes that large groups demand of their members a larger measure of intelligence than small groups do.

The "four pillars of natural order" Ross calls sympathy, so-

---

[1] The Macmillan Co., New York, 1905.
[2] The Macmillan Co., New York, 1901, pp. 17, 66. See especially chs. I–VI.

ciability, sense of justice, and resentment. Sympathy and sociability which have been built into the nervous system by selection and heredity are themselves inadequate for complex group life. Here a distinction must be drawn between biologico-social relationship, as in the case of animal group life which is merely organic, and the psychologico-social relationship which though deep-rooted in the former yet is the real foundation of our complex society. The Teutonic race, for example, which has built the strongest social structures has weaker social instincts than the Veddahs who have achieved only simple group life.

Just how it could be shown that the Teutons have weaker social instincts, as Ross suggests, than the Veddahs, would be difficult to say. We are here faced with the fundamental problem of the relation between the cohesive and the explosive forces which exist in every human group. Is the apparent lack of social behavior among the Teutons the result of greater intelligence which enables them to perceive the essential conflict of economic interests, or because of weaker social feelings? Is the apparently social behavior of the Veddahs the result of greater social feeling or of the lack of intelligence to see wherein their individual interests conflict? It might be urged, with some show of reason, that the gregarious behavior of certain animals is not so much the result of strong social feeling as of low intelligence. If they knew enough to realize that numbers made for scarcity and hunger, they might not be so peaceably inclined toward one another. How the cohesive and explosive forces in society are held in a state of balance will be shown in a later chapter.[1]

2. *The Sense of Justice.* Ross goes further and says that western group organization is utilitarian, purposive, economic. Sociability, the preference for one's own kind, the attraction of like for like,— these are important but are not the basis of the social order. What is fundamental is a sense of justice based on self-control and reflection. It is here that the Teutons excel.

[1] *Infra*, Chapter VIII.

"While the long-skulled blond of central and northwestern Europe is mediocre in power of sympathy and weak in sociability, he is strong in that most important of political aptitudes — the will to justice." Ross says that a man from Mars attempting to forecast our codes would better work out from interests than sentiments, and know the conditions which work smoothly in the social machinery rather than the human heart. "For the key to the interpretation of social pressure is, after all, not righteous impulse but utility."

The term "sense of justice," appears to be somewhat inadequate. Whatever it is, it is probably acquired, like a sense of decency, and is not inborn. Besides, it is doubtful if it is any stronger in the Teutons, who seem to be able to live in large groups, than in the Veddahs, who are not successful as empire builders or even as nation builders. The truth seems to be that the Teutonic peoples have succeeded in developing somewhat more rational ideas as to what justice is than most other races. It appears that the "sense of justice" is about as varied as the sense of decency, of modesty, of etiquette, or any acquired social habit. But there is great survival value in a "sound" idea as to what justice is. In fact it is "sound" only when and in the sense that it has survival value.

The race which, either through superior intelligence or by lucky accident, happens to develop an idea of justice which has survival value has a great advantage over one which does not. There are always conflicting interests to be adjudicated. If they are not adjudicated at all by some tribunal or umpire, they will be settled by resort to wasteful physical or mental conflict; "might will make right," as it is popularly expressed. This will cause much waste of human energy not only in wasteful or destructive combat, but it will fall far short of giving the maximum encouragement to useful conduct. The strong or the cunning will be encouraged to prey upon the weak or the dull, and the latter will be discouraged from exerting their useful or productive powers to the maximum.

Again, even where there is a developed "sense of justice," with tribunals and sanctions, the rules for the adjudication of conflicting interests may be irrational in the sense that they do not lend the maximum encouragement to the kinds of conduct which promote group life. It is always difficult to determine just what rules will promote group life. Opinions will always differ on such questions, and even when they are left to majority opinion there is no certainty that they will be settled rationally. When, as is more likely to be the case in the early stages of social development, the rules for the adjudication of conflicts are formulated by the strong man who is able to enforce his judgments, they are pretty certain to be wrong, that is, to favor some class or type of persons rather than to favor the growth and prosperity of the group as a whole. When once formulated and adopted, they become a part of the *mores*. Then they *seem* right to every one except a few sporadic reformers, and even these are more likely to be irrational than rational. At any rate, they are likely to be suppressed. Thus every one has a "sense of justice" no matter how irrational his ideas of justice are. However, as suggested above, those groups whose ideas of justice are such as to promote the group growth and group prosperity are more likely to grow and prosper than are those groups whose ideas of justice hinder growth and prosperity.

One inadequate conception of justice which, even in the most advanced society of today, is still struggling for recognition is the notion that an individual is entitled to anything which he is smart enough to get. Another equally inadequate conception is that each one is entitled to anything which he is helpless enough to need. The idea that mere ability, without due reference to social usefulness, is entitled to reward has survived altogether too long. It becomes an absurdity as soon as we realize that it takes ability to be a great and successful criminal. Even when a smart man keeps well within the law he does not always earn all he gets. It doubtless takes an able man to put over a big business deal, but neither his ability nor the size of the deal is any measure of his usefulness to society. It all depends on what kind of a deal it is. If it results in giving greater bargaining power to some huge concern,— power to beat down prices to producers or to beat up prices to consumers,— the able man has merely built up a predatory organization, and his ability has done harm rather than good. He has earned considerably less than nothing.

It doubtless takes great ability,— at least able salesmanship,— to fool people into buying useless nostrums, into voting for foolish legislation, into reading salacious books; but that is a kind of ability without which the world could get along rather well. The question to be determined is not how smart a man is, but how useful he is. How much does he enrich his group by his activities? The idea of ability based on the principle of private right has no place in our modern interdependent society. It must give way to the concept of ability interpreted in terms of social utility. This is so obvious, when once stated, as to need no discussion, and yet it is constantly forgotten. Every day we hear of the remarkable ability of this or that dealer on the exchange, of the uncanny skill of this or that card sharper, of what a good judge of horses this or that race track gambler is,— always in a tone which implies that his ability justifies his gains. Why does this idea persist in spite of its logical absurdity?

The answer is probably in the fact that we all admire smartness, whether it is exercised usefully or harmfully. This admiration for smartness is pretty deep-seated, and probably requires an anthropological explanation. During the greater part of the life of men on this planet, our ancestors were dealing with huge creatures with which they were no match physically. Their only chance of success against the cave bear, the sabre-toothed tiger, and the mastodon was to outwit them. Smartness had survival value and needed to be cultivated. This is said to explain our admiration for such notorious rascals as Reineke Fuchs and Br'er Rabbit. It was morally scandalous the way these clever rogues took advantage of the stupid beasts with whom they dealt. Why do we all, old and censorious as well as young and wayward, unite in our admiration of such roguery?

Well, they were, to begin with, such adept rogues. Again,— and this is more important,— the creatures on whom they imposed were such big brutes. Neither Reineke nor Br'er Rabbit was a match for them physically. Our admiration merely expresses our delight in the triumph of mind over matter, of brain over brawn, of intellect over brute strength. It was a step upward when men began to glory in the dominance of mentality over brutality, even when mentality was not handicapped by a conscience.

There is another contest, however, in which civilized men are compelled to take an interest. That is the contest between production and predation. Artistically, it is still in the stage of melodrama, where it is presented as the conflict between virtue and vice, between honesty and villainy. One trouble is that the virtue which triumphs and the vice which is put to shame are of a somewhat conventional and stereotyped sort. It is not always easy to see the connection between the conflict on the stage and the conflict between the productive and the destructive forces in industry.

Another difficulty is that intellectual people are not supposed to take an emotional interest in melodrama, much less in the triumph of honesty over villainy. That is for people who have had good mothers and such commonplace things, who have been taught to revere George Washington and other stereotyped heroes,— who have, in short, been inoculated with the virus of morality. But all people, intellectuals as well as lowbrows, villains as well as heroes, from Beacon Hill to Central Africa, can appreciate and glory in the triumph of cleverness over brute strength. Its appeal is universal and not limited to those who have become emotionally moral.

However we may explain the origin of the idiotic notion that a man is entitled to all he is smart enough to get, so long as he does not fall foul of the courts, it has outlived its usefulness. The survival of our civilization requires that we protect production against predation, usefulness against harmfulness, and that we fully accept the notion that ability is entitled to a reward only when it is exercised usefully or productively.

In *Principles of Sociology* [1] written some twenty years later, Ross states that in its early years psychologists failed to give

---

[1] The Century Co., New York, 1920, esp. ch. 32.

sufficient emphasis to "the instincts and emotions — man's social side." Nevertheless, in discussing "resemblance" as a socializing factor, and particularly Giddings' phrase, "consciousness of kind," he maintains that it is not the perception of general likeness, but of likeness in specific matters that calls forth fellow-feeling.[1] He puts much greater emphasis on gregariousness than he did in *Social Control*, and says: "What is necessary in order that men should feel themselves to be one . . . is that they should be aware of essential common traits distinguishing them from others, or of a momentous common interest which can be protected and advanced only by collective effort." In this he seems to place consciousness of kind as of equal importance with the perception of utility in association. Ross maintains, however, that man, unlike the ant, coöperates not from instinct but from reason, and therefore there has been a "chronic shortage" of coöperation. He also holds that while small groupings may be the outgrowth of sociability, no large or permanent group persists unless it is of utility to its members, however great may be their consciousness of kind. That is at least parallel to the biologists' admissions that however mutations arise they can not persist and spread unless they have survival value.

3. *Rallying in the Presence of Danger.* Ross's position [2] that coöperation for defense, or for utilitarian reasons rather than from consciousness of kind, is the basis of large organization may be admitted, but is this primarily a result of intelligence or of something deeper or, at any rate, more nearly automatic? It may be true that, genetically, the habitual resistance attitude towards danger plays an important rôle in bringing about social relationship and thus making possible the growth of consciousness of kind. Even animals, birds, and insects rally in face of a common danger. But it is questionable whether it is fundamental to the cohesiveness of a social structure and the maintenance of its stability. In the case of animals we find that as

---

[1] The present writer has suggested "self-appraisal" as underlying and conditioning the consciousness of kind.

[2] *Principles of Sociology, op. cit.*, p. 405.

soon as the danger is over the social relationship, resulting as it does from the fundamental urge — fear — which compels them to unite, soon ceases to exist. This is also true of some of the most primitive peoples. "The Bushmen," says Elliot Smith, "have no tribal organization and no permanent chiefs.[1] In face of danger the nearest clans or families combined to resist the foe, under the most courageous and capable leader, but as soon as the need of combination ceased, the alliance came to an end." Cohesion, stability of human society, however high or low in the scale of development and complexity, depends primarily upon the strength and intensity of the consciousness of the collective life ingrained in each individual member of the group.

Apparently the ancient habit, common to animals and primitive men, of rallying for group defense in the face of danger, exists also among the most civilized and sophisticated nations. We have only to remember the outburst of patriotism whenever war is declared, and the lapse into extreme individualism as soon as the war is over. Those who remember what took place during the World War will recall the high moral fervor of that time. The extreme reaction toward cynicism and selfishness is indicated by the post-war habit of calling the patriotism and moral fervor of the war period by such names as war hysteria. From the social point of view, our people were living at their best during the war. They were, with some glaring exceptions, willing to sacrifice personal appetites and privileges for the common good. From the same point of view, they sank to their lowest level soon after the danger was past. Patriotism and moral fervor became bywords. During the war, opposition to such beneficent legislation as the restriction of immigration was swept away, and the quota law was passed. Since the war, every selfish interest that fattens on cheap labor and docile parishioners has been unceasing in its attack upon that law. Other legislation designed for the common good was soon repealed.

[1] G. Elliot Smith, *Human History* (Jonathan Cape, Ltd., London, 1930), p. 204.

This universal trait, common not only to all sorts and conditions of men, but to gregarious animals and birds as well, of rallying for common defense against an enemy, and then quarrelling among themselves afterward, helps to support the thesis that sociality grew out of the necessities of defense. Another fact is that military groups are more perfectly organized than any other kind. For military purposes, men will submit to more rigorous discipline than for any other purpose; they will also make greater personal sacrifices, and act more in accordance with the principles of teamwork.

There must have been survival value in this practice of rallying for group defense or it could not have become so nearly universal. Having survival value, those human beings who possessed in the highest degree the ability to rally promptly and to act vigorously, were themselves selected for survival. Thus there seems to have been bred a type of man who could spontaneously respond to the call to arms.[1] This trait may not yet have acquired the characteristics of an instinct, but it is at least conceivable that it is an undeveloped, or a partially developed instinct — a trait in process of becoming an instinct.

Obviously it is something more than an intellectual perception of economic advantage. Napoleon was disappointed to find that the Bavarians clung to the Prussians although their economic interests seemed more allied to the French, demonstrating that "blood"[2] counted. Other factors than community of interests seem to have determined the policy of the French-Americans toward the English Colonists in the eighteenth century. Ross's view[3] that no degree of likemindedness would hold individuals together in an organization which was not doing anything for them seems to disregard the observable fact that the average man tends to be loyal to those whom he has helped more than to those who have helped him.

---

[1] There also develops a form of parasitism. If there are enough who respond promptly to make the life of the group safe, others may survive by not rallying but playing safe.

[2] A common language, in this case.

[3] *Ibid.*, p. 238.

It is dangerous to dogmatize regarding social origins or the ways of primitive men. Since the first enthusiasm with which the theory of evolution was accepted, no one who weighs his words will say positively that the lower races of the present are more primitive than degenerate. Again it is not easy to show from an objective study of their actions that their social behavior is more the product of their intellect than of their feelings. No one really knows whether men first became social because their intellects understood the advantages of associated effort, or whether they learned the advantages of associated effort from practices which were first instigated by sympathy, consciousness of kind, imitativeness or some other social propensity. If large-scale teamwork had survival value, as all seem to agree, it would follow that those men who practised it would survive, whether they practised it for mental or emotional reasons.

4. *Talkativeness.* In discussing the problem of the social nature of man, it is easy to overlook the obvious and seek the occult. It is an obvious fact that man is endowed with the gift of speech. This is partly anatomical and partly psychical. And, as Lester F. Ward points out, "in one sense the faculty of oral speech must be regarded as a physical development, since along with it there had to be developed a physical organ, the larynx . . . but the power of articulate speech has chiefly been acquired by the exercise of the rational faculty."[1]   George Barton Cutten brings out this point very strikingly in his statement:

It is not unlikely that the power of articulate speech was one of the chief factors in the rise of man to his human status. In connection with this there are two things to be noted: first, that the power of speech depends not upon the vocal organs, which were well developed in the apes, but upon the brain and mind adjustments and progress; and second, that the development of the centers of motor speech in the brain was not sufficient in itself, but certain co rdinate and related centers had to be developed before the motor speech centers could function.[2]

[1] Lester F. Ward, *Dynamic Sociology*, vol. II, p. 180, *lib. cit.*   For a discussion of the psychological aspect of speech see article by John Dewey, "Knowledge and Speech Reaction," *Journal of Philosophy*, 1922, vol. 19, no. 21, p. 561.
[2] *Mind: Its Origin and Goal* (Yale University Press, New Haven, 1925), p. 52.

The weight of authoritative opinion seems to strengthen the view that speech and the accompanying morphological modification is the result of "brain-organization." As E. B. Tylor expresses it: "It is not merely that the highest anthropoid apes have no speech; they have not the brain-organization enabling them to acquire even its rudiments."[1]

> The evolution of speech [says G. Elliot Smith] enormously emphasized the significance of man's dependence on his social environment. . . . A mould of the brain-case of the earliest and most primitive members of the Human family at present known to us (Pithec-anthropus) reveals a very conspicuous and precocious expansion of an area precisely corresponding in position to the part of modern man's brain which is concerned with the appreciation of spoken language. The only inference is that speech is as old as man himself. . . . The powerful instrument of speech completely transformed man's mode of behavior.[2]

Even on the anatomical side, the gift of speech creates a craving for association. Having talking muscles, they call, as do other muscles, for exercise. This need for exercise of the talking muscles creates a need for some one to talk to. Both on the anatomical and the psychological side, speech must be regarded as a social faculty. It is a gift which could not develop except in association, and without which association would be limited to very simple or primitive forms. It is a gift which marks man as the preëminently social animal. Lonesomeness, when cut off from opportunities to communicate, is one of the most poignant of human emotions. Solitary confinement is sometimes looked upon as "cruel and inhuman" punishment.

In debating the question of the social nature of man, the fact that he possesses organs of speech is of no small significance. There is a satisfying finality to such physical evidence which is not possible in regard to more subjective phenomena. If one argues from the presence of "social" instincts, emphasizing gregariousness, parental affection, love of approbation and the like, the question of other instincts, some of them anti-social,

---

[1] Edward B. Tylor, *Anthropology* (Watts & Co., London, 1930), vol. 1, p. 42.
[2] *Human History* (Jonathan Cape, Ltd., London, 1930), pp. 49, 50.

e.g., the fighting instinct, may arise to be reconciled. The inconclusiveness of introspection, from a scientific point of view, has been urged to a greater or less extent with varying success by divers scientists. But the existence of man's vocal organs is a fact, and perhaps the most conclusive evidence that he is by nature social. An apparatus specialized for communicating with one's fellows and the existence of those fellows are inseparable phenomena in a world governed by the evolutionary principle.

Perhaps talkativeness, having great survival value because of its relation to association and coöperation, was the trait which pulled selection into the channel it took. Not merely the superior intellect of man is concerned in this. Perhaps men coöperate at a task not alone because they perceive the advantages of teamwork, but because they like to talk. At any rate there are innumerable instances where men do actually work in company although the task of each is physically quite independent of that of the others. Talkativeness, and its developed forms of reading and writing, spread the ideas and the judgments of the group among all its members and unify their thinking and activity. A common language is fundamental to a developed common life.

On the other hand it may be argued that language is one of the products of associated effort, that it is virtually a code of signals gradually evolved as an aid to teamwork, and later, greatly elaborated in order to satisfy the craving for communication. "Obviously the human speech," says Sir Richard Paget, "has grown up by a process of natural evolution; obviously also it was a common accomplishment of mankind at the beginning since all known races of men (however primitive) are found to use speech for the expression of their ideas. . . . But if human speech has been evolved, it must have come from some pre-existing accomplishment of the animals from which man himself was evolved."[1] Now, this accomplishment was probably due to the constant living in association.

[1] Sir Richard Paget, *Babel, or Past, Present and Future of Human Speech* (Kegan Paul, Trench, Trubner & Co., London, 1930), p. 12.

Granted the existence of any thing which could be called intelligence, it is demonstrable that it is increased and magnified both by association and speech. On the theory of probabilities, ten thinking creatures will think of more things than one, a thousand more than ten, a million more than a thousand, and so on. But, no matter how many ideas were conceived, unless they were communicated to and shared by others, no individual would have any ideas but his own. When, however, the ten, the thousand, or the million were living in close association with one another, and, through speech, in constant communication with one another, the thought of one becomes the thought of many. Each individual has the benefit not only of his own ideas and inventions, but also of those of all his associates. The intellectual activities and accomplishments of each is multiplied by association. It is doubtful if human intelligence could have developed except through the association that goes with numbers living in juxtaposition or without the communication that goes with speech.

In a whimsical but brilliantly incisive book,[1] Clarence Day suggests a prehuman or simian origin for the propensity to talk. He also attributes to this inherited simian trait many of the characteristics of modern civilized men, and many of their most cherished institutions. No right, for example, is quite so dear to us, relatives of chattering apes, as the right to chatter. No interference is quite so bitterly resented or stoutly resisted as interference with freedom of speech. The right of private combat might have been our most cherished right if we had been descended from cats.

So precious [says Day] [2] to a simian is the privilege of making sounds with his tongue, that when he wishes to punish severely one of those men he calls criminals, he forbids them to chatter and forces them by threats to be silent. [Day continues:] . . . Whatever a simian does, there must always be some talking about it. He can't even make peace without a kind of chatter called a peace conference. Super cats would not have had to "make" peace: they would just have walked off and stopped fighting.[3]

[1] *This Simian World* (Alfred A. Knopf, New York, 1927).
[2] *Ibid.*, p. 20.
[3] *Ibid.*, p. 21.

The pride we take in our gift of speech is embodied in most of our schemes for higher education. As if learning one language were not enough for one lifetime and as if there were not other things of vastly greater importance to be learned, we compel our young banderlog to spend decades learning duplicate systems of "chatter." "Those who thus learn several different ways to say the same things, will command much respect, and those who learn many will be looked on with awe — by true simians."[1]

However much we may affect to despise mere chatter, the fact remains that the development of a language is probably the greatest achievement of the human race up to the present moment. Only a trained linguist can appreciate the marvelous intricacy, precision, and expressiveness of a developed language. A mere sociologist, however, may appreciate how much of a social product it is and how fundamentally necessary it is to a highly developed social life. The more we look into it the more we are likely to be convinced that the whole of civilization, in its dynamic or "going" aspects, is pretty largely a stream of talk, if under talk we may include writing and printing.

5. *Sympathy.* The gift of speech is not the only inborn character that marks human beings as social creatures. Adam Smith, for instance, writing as a moralist, suggested that men are predisposed by nature to work together because they are organically endowed with fellow-feeling or sympathy. In his *Theory of Moral Sentiments*, Smith accounts for a large part of human conduct neatly in two sentences: "Upon these two different efforts, upon that of the spectator to enter into the sentiments of the person principally concerned and upon that of the person principally concerned to bring down his emotions to what the spectator can go along with are founded two different sets of virtues. The soft, the gentle, the amiable virtues, the virtues of candid condescension and indulgent humanity, are founded upon the one: the great, the awful, and respectable, the virtues of self-denial, of self-government, of that command of the passions which subjects all the movements of our nature to what

[1] *Ibid.*, p. 42.

our own dignity and honour, and the propriety of our own conduct require, take their origin from the other."[1] Not only does sympathy make men willing to help one another, but it makes each sensitive to the opinions of his fellows, and so makes each individual amenable to social control. "How selfish soever man may be supposed," wrote he,[2] "there are evidently some principles in his nature which interest him in the fortunes of others, and render their happiness necessary to him, though he derives nothing from it except the pleasure of seeing it." These "principles" in human nature he includes under the word *sympathy*, though pity, compassion, and fellow-feeling are also used to describe some of them. Sympathy is a broader term and describes our tendency to experience pleasure in the pleasure of others as well as sorrow in their sorrow. The existence of this feeling he takes as a matter of course, being, as he says, "too obvious to require any instances to prove it." It is not confined to the virtuous and humane, though they doubtless feel it more keenly, but it is shared by the greatest ruffians and the most hardened violators of the laws of society.

He points out that it requires an imagination to be able to share in the feelings of others. Having no immediate or physiological experience of what others feel, we can form no idea of their states of happiness or sorrow except by imagining how we should feel if placed in like circumstances. It is not our physical senses alone, but our imaginations playing upon our physical senses, which tell us what others feel. This is one of the deepest lessons we learn from our experiences of life. Early in life the child will ask, when trying to excite sympathy, "How would you like it if you were in my place?" or the unscrupulous lawyer, defending a criminal, will use all his skill to prevent the jurors from imagining themselves in the place of the injured persons, and to cause them to imagine themselves in the place of the accused. Old athletes find their muscles sore after watching a close game or contest. In imagination they were in the places

[1] Edition of 1808, Edinburgh, vol. I, p. 41.
[2] *Theory of the Moral Sentiments*, ch. I.

of the players and were actually, without knowing it, straining their own muscles. In thinking of sickness men have been known to become sick themselves or at least to develop some of the symptoms of sickness. Presumably they may, within limits, become well or remain well by avoiding such thoughts or imaginings. Our interest in fiction and the drama probably has its roots in the same feeling. We are made to share the joys and sorrows, the thrills and the passions of the characters. The fact that it is only play-acting is not sufficient to prevent a feeling of deep depression after the catastrophe of the tragedy, or of elation after the satisfactory ending of the melodrama.

This feeling of sympathy, this ability to enter into and share the thoughts and feelings of others, is not only a cement which helps to bind together the parts of a great society; it is also adapted to preserve it, or help to secure its continuity. Of all the tragedies that occur, none move us more powerfully than those which happen to the young. The death or injury of a child who has not yet had its chance at life, the frustrating of the hopes and aspirations of youth which has not yet functioned in the life of the great society,[1] sadden us more than when similar physical accidents occur to the mature or the aged. The play and the laughter of the young likewise produce in us a more intense pleasure than similar expressions from their elders. Even this feeling of special sympathy and solicitude for the young has its social function and must be regarded as an important element in the social nature of man. It helps to "keep the tribe alive."

Our ability to enter into the thoughts and feelings of others is affected by distance. It is easier to imagine oneself in the place of another who is near in point of space, time, kinship, or likemindedness. This is probably one of our mental rather than one of our emotional limitations — if there be a difference. It is more of a strain upon our imagination to put ourselves in the position of an angleworm than in the position of a fellow human, or even in the position of one of the higher mammals.

---

[1] In *Kim*, by Rudyard Kipling, the bearded Afghan chief criticizes Kim for his immaturity. "At his age," said he, "I had killed my man and begotten my man."

It is not so difficult to imagine ourselves in the position of one of our own kin as in that of a member of another race, in the position of a contemporary as in that of one of the ancients, in the position of a near neighbor as in that of one who lives a long way off.

6. *Imitation.* Adam Smith was only a precursor of a number of writers who have tried to find some social tendency or feeling in human nature and to make it the key to an understanding of social life. Important among these pioneer psychological sociologists is Gabriel Tarde.[1] Society, to him, meant the psychic interpretation of the relation between mind and mind; and the key to this interpretation lay in the tendency of human beings to imitate. An idea, a belief, or a desire, appearing in the mind of one tends to be repeated in the mind of another — and then another and another; the idea spreads in a wave of imitation.

Imitation, according to Tarde, actually constitutes social life.

No one will deny [he said] that whatever we say, do, or think, once we are launched in the social life, we are forever imitating some one else, unless, indeed, we are ourselves, making an innovation — an event that rarely happens; it is easy, moreover, to show that our innovations are, for the most part, combinations of previous examples, and that they remain outside of the social life so long as they are not imitated. There is not a word that you say which is not the reproduction,— now unconscious, but formerly conscious and voluntary,— of verbal articulations reaching back to the most distant past, with some special accent due to your immediate surroundings. There is not a religious rite that you fulfill, such as praying, kissing the icon, or making the sign of the cross, which does not reproduce certain traditional gestures and expressions established through imitation of your ancestors. There is not a military or civil requirement that you obey nor an act that you perform in your business, which has not been taught you, and which you have not copied from some living model. There is not a stroke of the brush that you make,— if you are a painter,— nor a verse that you write,— if you are a poet,— which does not conform to the customs or the prosody of your school, and even your very originality itself is made up of accumulated commonplaces, and aspires to become common-

---

[1] 1843–1904. His most important books are: *Les lois de l'imitation* (Paris, 1890) (Eng. tr. E. C. Parsons, New York, 1903); *La logique sociale* (Paris, 1894); *L'opposition universelle* (Paris, 1897); *Les lois sociales* (Paris, 1898) (Eng. tr. H. C. Warren, New York, 1899); *L'opinion et la foule* (Paris, 1901).

place in its turn. Thus, the unvarying characteristic of every social fact whatsoever is that it is imitative.[1]

Tarde, it is worth noting, was very much concerned in basing his social laws upon the essential elements of all science. Science consists, he said, "in viewing any fact whatsoever under three aspects corresponding, respectively, to the repetitions, oppositions, and adaptations which it contains, and which are obscured by a mass of variations, dissymetries, and disharmonies."[2] Imitation, he showed, is merely the manifestation, in the social world, of the repetition that goes on everywhere in the universe. In the organic world, repetition shows itself through reproduction and heredity, in the way organisms reproduce their like. Among physical phenomena, waves of sound or light spread by periodic vibrations that are a kind of repetition. Undulation in the inorganic world, reproduction in the organic world, and imitation in the social world are the observed uniformities with which science must concern itself. There are also the resistances, deflections, and emergences of new and unexpected combinations to be studied.

This is only a mere sketch of what Tarde held to be essential to the understanding of social life. He used vague terms, it is true, that are not now considered precise enough for scientific use. Like most of the pioneers in sociology, he was more of a philosopher than an experimenting scientist. He led other writers, however, to analyze more carefully the tendency of human

---

[1] *Social Laws, op. cit.*, pp. 40–41. Tarde, in the emphasis he puts on imitation, allies himself with Fiske, who stressed the importance of a long period of infancy in the development of mind. For infancy may be best understood as a "learning period." And imitation has a great deal to do with learning.

"The imitative relation," Tarde is careful to say, "was not, in the beginning, as it often is later, a connection binding one individual to a confused mass of men, but merely a relation between two individuals, one of whom, the child, is in process of being introduced into the social life, while the other, an adult, long since socialized, serves as the child's personal model." (*Ibid.*, p. 44.)

[2] *Ibid.*, p. 5. The *Social Laws* of Tarde is freely quoted, rather than his other works, because the book is brief and especially concise. ". . . I am to give," Tarde said in the preface to the *Laws*, "not a mere outline or *résumé* of my three principal works on general sociology, but rather the internal bond that unites them." The *Laws* is strongly recommended to the reader unfamiliar with Tarde.

beings to imitate.[1] His work is of very great value, from the point of view of this chapter, because it gave some consistency to the study of society, in showing how men are able to live and work together. Imitation explains much of the growth of language and customs, the spread of fashions, the acceptance of law and social control.[2] The opposition to imitation explains much of human discord; it is the "moving principle of the bloodiest wars." The harmonizing of imitations in the mind of the individual explains the source of social change; it is the social germ plasm that gives birth to all that is new in social institutions.

While imitation is, in some of its forms at least, clearly rational and purposive, in other forms,— especially in subconscious imitation,— it seems to border closely on instinct. In fact William James regarded the imitative impulse as an instinct.[3] It is at least significant that even the child does not imitate everything indiscriminately, but seems to show a congenital tendency to imitate certain things rather than others. Giddings has called attention to the tendency of most animals as well as man to imitate its own kind more readily than other creatures, which led him to posit the "consciousness of kind" as a more fundamental fact than either sympathy or imitation. From the point of view of psychology, therefore, it is doubtful whether it may be considered an instinct. As Dashiel says, "imitation is not to be conceived as instinctive or innate, but as an acquired reaction."[4] Professor McDougal makes the following remark:

M. Tarde and Professor Baldwin have singled out imitation as the all important social process, and Baldwin, like most contemporary writers,

---

[1] See for instance, among many others, J. M. Baldwin, *Social and Ethical Interpretations in Mental Development* (The Macmillan Co., New York, 1908); E. L. Thorndike, *Educational Psychology* (The Science Press, New York, 1903), vol. I; E. A. Ross, *Social Psychology* (The Macmillan Co., New York, 1908).

[2] The reader should consult, in this connection, Tarde's *Laws of Imitation*, translation of E. C. Parsons, *op. cit.*

[3] *Principles of Psychology* (Henry Holt & Co., New York, 1890), vol. II, p. 408.

[4] J. F. Dashiel, *Psychological Bulletin*, vol. XVIII, p. 395. It is easy to overlook the fact that there must be an ability to acquire before there can be an acquired reaction.

attributes it to an instinct of imitation. But careful consideration of the nature of imitative actions shows that they are of many kinds, that they issue from mental processes of a number of different types, and that none are attributable to a specific instinct of imitation, while many are due to sympathy and suggestion.[1]

Whatever the student may think as to the completeness of Tarde's explanation of social life, there can be no doubt as to its importance.

Imitation [says McDougal] is the prime condition of all collective mental life. . . . In the simpler forms of social grouping imitation is the principal condition of this profound alteration of the individual's mental processes. And, even in the most developed forms of social aggregation, it plays a fundamental part . . . in rendering possible the existence and operation of the collective mind, its collective deliberation, emotion, character, and volition. . . . All that constitutes culture and civilisation, all, or nearly all, that distinguishes the highly cultured European intellectually and morally from the men of the stone age of Europe is then summed up in the word "tradition," and all tradition exists only in virtue of imitation . . . it is only by imitation that any improvement, conceived by any mind endowed with that rarest of all things, a spark of originality, can become embodied within the tradition of his society. Imitation is, then, not only the great conservative force of society, it is also essential to all social progress.[2]

A better understanding of mob behavior is probably arrived at from a study of the relation of power to responsibility. It seems that man in a mob behaves very much as he would behave alone if he could experience the same weakening of the feeling of responsibility and the same augmentation in the feeling of power. Place an individual in a position of irresponsible power whether he reaches that position through his membership in a mob, through the political tradition that the king can do no wrong, or merely through the fact that he has become a popular idol and is therefore not to be held accountable for what he does, and you have an individual who is liable to do violent and unscrupulous things. In a mob, the individual feels only a fraction of the responsibility for what the mob does. At the same time, so long as the mob can act together with a single

[1] *Op. cit.*, p. 94.
[2] *Op. cit.*, pp. 333–336.

purpose, he feels a vast augmentation of power. He will therefore behave as unscrupulously as Beelzebub himself. The same feeling of diminished responsibility and augmented power came, with the same results to the monarch under the old tradition that he could do no wrong. A popular idol, like Lord Nelson, could flaunt his mistress before the public and force even respectable society to recognize her. "The Devil is never very far," said Gustavus Adolphus, "from the man who is responsible to God alone."

This simple and easily understood fact that a man in a mob feels little responsibility for what the mob does and, at the same time, feels that the mob has power to do anything it sets out to do, seems a sufficient explanation of mob behavior. It does not seem necessary to fall back on any occult reason, or even on hypnosis. However, any one who has had the experience of attending a religious revival, a partisan rally, a meeting of undergraduates called and conducted for the purpose of working up enthusiasm for a football game, or any other meeting where feeling was intense, must have felt his individuality melting in the fervent heat of the crowd. There seem to be certain common elements in these meetings, ranging all the way from Pentecost down to football rallies, though there are also, of course, vast differences.

And yet there are other phases of mob psychology which seem to be so clearly imitative, and subconsciously so, as to resemble hpynotism. It is well known that persons in a hypnotic state can be made to imitate in an apparently mechanical way the motions of the hypnotist. The influence of the crowd upon an individual seems, sometimes, to resemble that of a hypnotist upon his subject. This is supposed to explain the behavior even of intelligent and generally self-contained individuals in a crowd in a time of strong emotion or sudden panic. The fact, alluded to above, of multiplied power and divided responsibility, may be a better explanation in some cases, but can hardly explain the Crusades, the dancing manias of the Middle Ages, or a Democratic National Convention.

It is not, however, in these spasmodic forms of group behavior that imitation plays its greatest rôle. Language itself is almost wholly imitative, so also are the great bodies of tradition, the customs, the mores, the legal codes, the ancient precedents so carefully followed by courts, the religious rites and ceremonials, the music, dances, and games, the industrial processes, and above all, that mysterious thing called fashion,— all of those actions in fact which we are in the habit of calling social. Man, especially civilized man, is the most imitative of all creatures.

7. *Instinct.* The drift of opinion seems to be away from the theory that sociability is, in any true sense, instinctive. We have seen that certain anatomical features which seem to favor group life are inborn, but these can scarcely be called instincts. Sympathy seems to be acquired, but the power to acquire it seems to be inborn as truly as the power to learn to speak. The same seems to be true of the power or capacity to learn or to imitate. Tarde left a large part of the social nature of man un-analyzed. It remained for a more objective psychology than his to account for social behavior on a broader basis than the imitations and inventions of the human mind.[1] The functional psychology that first studied human actions, without isolating thought, went beyond Tarde. Writers like William McDougall, who analyzed the working of the mind and studied the origins and purposes of a whole hierarchy of instincts, had an influence in advancing a better understanding of the social nature of man.[2] McDougall's classification of the instincts is sometimes

---

[1] Pitirim A. Sorokin remarks: "The purpose of sociology (according to Tarde) is not to explain the trans-subjective events of history or of the behavior of men in their concrete psycho-physical form, but in the dynamics of ideas, beliefs, desires, and other inner experiences. Men's behavior, relationship, historical and social events, as trans-subjective phenomena, are interesting to Tarde's sociology only so far as they are a manifestation of mental phenomena, and as far as they may influence the psychic processes of invention, opposition and imitation." *Contemporary Sociological Theories, op. cit.*, p. 639.

[2] ". . . psychologists must cease," says McDougall, "to be content with the sterile and narrow conception of their science as the science of consciousness, and must boldly assert its claim to be the positive science of the mind in all its aspects and modes of functioning . . . the positive science of conduct or behavior." *Introduction to Social Psychology*, rev. ed. (J. W. Luce & Co., Boston, 1926), p. 15. James ought to be mentioned as a pioneer in this field. In his two volumes on the

regarded as arbitrary, and his work of pioneer incompleteness. It is, nevertheless, representative of a type of study that has given leading ideas to the sociologist.[1]

In the course of studying the native capacities of the human mind, certain psychologists came to recognize that the instincts, important as they are, ought to be looked upon as merely the stuff from which social behavior is made. Man has a social nature, it seems, not so much because he has social instincts as because his natural impulses have been conditioned to social life by a learning process. This learning process, the so-called "conditioning of response," has become the special interest of a number of psychologists known generally as behaviorists.[2] There is not much in behaviorism that had not been talked about by psychologists long before it was born. Its special importance to the social sciences is the remarkably objective method it promises to develop for the study of human nature. Beyond that, in the emphasis it puts on the influence of the social environment, it is simply a good antidote for the ills of the instinct school.

Thorough-going behaviorists do not pay much attention to what goes on within the mind. What they do is to observe the

Principles of Psychology, New York, 1890, he made a study of instinct and will and habit that cleared the ground for a better understanding of the social nature of man. The social self, he showed, developed, through the personal contacts of social life, from basic "social self-seeking impulses," from instincts like imitation, emulation, sympathy, love, jealousy, shame, curiosity, and so on.

[1] The sociologist who is eager to study human instinct should read, in addition to the authorities cited, and as representative of a very large amount of psychological literature, E. L. Thorndike, *The Original Nature of Man* (New York, 1913); R. S. Woodworth, *Psychology*, rev. ed. (Henry Holt and Co., New York, 1929); S. Freud, *Group Psychology and the Analysis of the Ego*, tr. J. Strachey (London, 1922); W. Trotter, *Instincts of the Herd in Peace and War* (T. F. Unwin, London, 1916). Also such critics of the instinct school in psychology as C. C. Josey, *The Social Philosophy of Instinct* (Charles Scribners Sons, New York, 1922); L. L. Bernard, *Instinct* (Henry Holt and Co., New York, 1924); and J. B. Watson, *Behaviorism*, rev. ed. (W. W. Norton & Co., New York, 1930).

[2] The inspiration for behaviorism came from the Russian, I. Pavlov. In this country, it was especially the books of J. B. Watson that started the behaviorist crusade. Important as Watson's work is, it goes to absurd extremes. The *Social Psychology* of F. H. Allport, (Houghton Mifflin Co., Boston, 1924) and the *Human Nature and Conduct* (Henry Holt & Co., New York, 1922) of John Dewey ought not to be neglected by any one interested in behaviorism.

connection between a stimulus that causes a person to act, and the kind of action that follows the given stimulus. Their task, according to J. B. Watson, is "given the stimulus, to predict the response — given the response, tu predict the stimulus."[1] The task is by no means simple. There are thousands of stimuli in the environment of a human being and innumerable ways of reacting to them. Moreover there are many things that will not act at first as stimuli for producing a certain kind of reaction. A person may learn through experience to react differently to the same thing; he may be conditioned to show fear of darkness and dogs, even though, before he learned to do so, he showed no fear. A child of a few months may be conditioned to catch its breath and cry at the sight of the toy it has played with.

The behavior of grown-up men, the behaviorist says, is built up about a few fundamental, unlearned, unconditioned reactions to a few definite stimuli. Watson's experiments show that an infant, unconditioned to any stimuli, will show fear of a loud voice and the loss of physical support; anger, at the hampering of bodily movement; love, at the stroking contact of skin. Using such raw material — say the fear response to a loud noise — the behaviorist demonstrates how any stimulus can be made to arouse a fear reaction.[2]

We select some animal . . . [says Watson] which has never aroused any emotional reaction in the child. Next we allow an assistant to carry this object to the child . . . in a covered tray. The instant the object is uncovered and the child begins to reach for it a second assistant strikes on a steel rod or dishpan behind the child's head. Instantly the child . . . stiffens, catches its breath, begins to cry. . . . We quiet the child . . . repeat the test. The same thing happens. After only a few tests we show the object but do not make the noise. Instantly the child reacts to the

[1] *The Ways of Behaviorism* (Harper and Bros., New York and London, 1928), p. 2. It is, of course, the musician's first task to find out the relation between the stroke on the instrument and the instrument's response. When he has learned that, he can get the response he wants, if the instrument is capable of giving it. Nevertheless, it is of some importance that he know something about the character of the instrument.

[2] The behaviorists lean here on a real "instinct theory," in spite of themselves. For the conditioned response is built on the unconditioned response, call this latter thing instinct, or a prepotent reflex, as you will.

neutral object as it would react to the noise.   A conditioned emotional response has been established.[1]

The behaviorist offers tempting solutions to a good many sociological problems.   The sociologist, in studying human nature, may want to discover, for instance, how men can be made to feel a wholesome fear of the law.   The behaviorist says: Study stimuli and response.   Learn how to control the conditioning of behavior by studying how the proper stimuli can be presented in proper sequence to potential good citizens in the process of their growing up.   Make the idea of law arouse a fear response.   Expose a boy to the joint stimuli of a loud noise and a frown, then a frown and policemen, then policemen and an idea of duty. He will become — roughly speaking — a law-abiding citizen.

To say that the method of behaviorism cannot completely solve sociological problems is not to belittle much that is valuable in the method.   What a person thinks is as important as what he does;   at least thinking certainly affects acting.   The organism that responds is certainly as important as the stimulus. Moreover, although man is versatile in his teachability, although most of his behavior is learned and the instincts he possesses at birth are few and simple, it is still true that there is a physical, an organic base to all his behavior that is not much modified by any process of conditioning response.   Individuals — and peoples — vary in their physical make-up; and they vary, therefore, in their teachability.   The student of human nature must bear this always in mind.

8. *The Consciousness of Kind.*   The analysis of the social nature of man was still further advanced by those psychological sociologists who found through a study of instincts some one mental factor in terms of which they explained society.   One of these was Franklin H. Giddings, a thinker of rare ability, who coined the phrase "consciousness of kind"[2] to express his conception of the basis of group life.

---

[1] *Ibid.*, p. 57.   "The mistake the psychologists made . . .," insists Watson, "was to look upon emotions as 'mental states' and not as ways of behavior which had to be learned like other sets of habits" (*ibid.*, p. 47.)   Possibly Watson attributes less importance to the power to learn than it deserves.

[2] *Principles of Sociology* (The Macmillan Company, New York, 1896).

The original and elementary subjective fact in society [said he] is the *consciousness of kind.*[1] By this term I mean a state of consciousness in which any being, whether low or high in the scale of life, recognizes another conscious being as of like kind with itself. . . . In its widest extension the consciousness of kind marks off the animate from the inanimate. Within the wide class of the animate it next marks off species and races. Within racial lines the consciousness of kind underlies the more definite ethnical and political groupings, it is the basis of class distinctions, of innumerable forms of alliance, of rules of intercourse, and of peculiarities of policy. Our conduct towards those whom we feel to be most like ourselves is instinctively and rationally different from our conduct towards others, whom we believe to be less like ourselves.[2]

Giddings devoted himself to working out a complete interpretation of social life on the basis of this subjective fact of "consciousness of kind."[3] The secret of gregariousness he found to be quite fundamentally in perceptions of likeness and unlikeness. Any creatures, including men, he argued, who are alike, or enough alike, whether from kinship or similar organic make-up, to react in like ways to like stimuli, enough alike to be sensitive to mutual stimulation, or to react in the same ways to the same stimuli, are ready to enter into social life. The consciousness of likeness is the starting point for the growth of sympathy. It makes imitation easy.[4]

Like Ward, he recognized the great importance of pure reasoning power. He set great store by the "reflective sympathy" that social life had evolved in human beings.

[1] "Sociology," Giddings wisely said, "must work out a subjective interpretation (of society) in terms of some fact of consciousness or motive and an objective interpretation in terms of a physical process (i.e. of *evolution* through the equilibration of energy). These two interpretations must be consistent, each with the other, and must be correlated." *The Principles of Sociology, op. cit.,* p. 16.

[2] *Ibid.,* pp. 17–18.

[3] He did not avoid talking objectively, of course. He was interested in showing how social life transforms, *evolves* human nature; and so he was forced to give attention to objective facts like *association* and *communication,* to relate changes in the consciousness of kind to changes in the form of association, etc., etc. He did not neglect social "process."

[4] Giddings points to the socializing effect of imitation in a special sense, in the sense of converting impressions of unlikeness as into impressions of likeness. See the *Principles, op. cit.,* p. 103.

Human beings [he explained] have acquired the power to think, to form conceptual ideas, to reflect, to put ideas together in trial and error combinations,— which is to reason. With the power of thinking they have acquired the power to talk, and have developed conversation. They are able, therefore, to become acquainted. They can not only compare the behavior of one with the behavior of another, but also they can get at and compare one another's ideas, tastes, sentiments and purposes. . . . In a general way they are of one kind, and know it. In lesser ways, they are of different kinds and each knows his own kind. . . . Therefore, they not only consort but also associate, each choosing with some range of freedom his associates, his *socii*. Accordingly, acquaintance, talk, and the consciousness of kind are, as was said, the specific determiners of association, an essential factor in which is a certain measure of mental freedom, of power to detach oneself in thought (and to a less degree in habits) from a *solidaire*, undifferentiated herdmindedness.[1]

Giddings, in his analysis of human nature, gave profitable hints to sociologists looking for guidance in the study of social life. Sociology, in his hands, became the study of factors which cause the expansion of a rational consciousness of kind.[2] "It is conscious association with his fellows," said he, "that develops man's moral nature."

That the consciousness of kind, as expounded by Giddings, is a more fundamental factor than sympathy will appear when we realize that sympathy can scarcely exist except when one is able to put oneself, in imagination at least, in the position of another. It is much easier to imagine oneself in the position of another creature whom we recognize as having something in common with ourselves, than in that of a creature with whom we do not seem to have anything in common. This is a phase of what Sorokin[3] has called social distance, and what the present writer has called nearness[4] in point of similarity. It will appear also to be more fundamental than imitation when we consider that it is easier to imitate those whom we resemble in other ways than to imitate those from whom we differ widely. In fact the consciousness of kind seems to determine the degree

---

[1] *The Scientific Study of Human Society, op. cit.*, pp. 33–34.
[2] "Subjectively," said Giddings, "progress is the expansion of the consciousness of kind." *Principles, op. cit.*, p. 359.
[3] *Social Mobility* (Harper & Bros., New York, 1927), ch. I.
[4] *Essays in Social Justice, op. cit.*, ch. III.

of sympathy felt and the extent to which imitation is carried on.

All our class distinctions, race feelings, religious prejudices, clannishness, and most of our loyalties are determined or at least limited by the consciousness of kind. Even the humanitarian is governed by it in that he shows a preference for, literally, a prejudice in favor of human beings as compared with other creatures. A brutarian, if there is such a thing, would be "broader" minded than the humanitarian, in that he would show a less narrow prejudice in favor of his own kind, but would take the entire animal creation into the circle of his "kind."

It is probable, of course, that later psychologists would refuse to admit that the consciousness of kind was instinctive. It seems more closely related to intelligence than to instinct. At least there must be a perception of some points of resemblance before there can be consciousness of kind. These points of resemblance may be physical or mental, natural or cultural. They may include merely the color of the skin, hair and eyes, or they may include only cultural standards or religious beliefs. To perceive a resemblance of cultural standards, for example, would surely require intelligence. The feeling resulting from that perception of resemblance may be difficult to classify.

The consciousness of kind is one of the most clarifying concepts ever introduced into sociological discussions. It is the key to the understanding of a great many problems both of a theoretical and a practical nature. It gives us a clue for the unravelling of the problems of race, of labor and capital, of democracy, of crime waves, and a multitude of others. Much use will be made of it in the remainder of this volume.

9. *Reasonableness.* Thus far in this chapter we have been considering those qualities in human nature which are supposed to draw people together into groups. Little attention has been given to factors of their own devising which serve to bind them together. It is at least plausible that groups are held together by two sets of forces; first, those inner impulses or emotions which create the desire for association; second, those outward coercions which compel them to associate. Even these outward coercions, however, are dependent upon a certain willingness to

be coerced, or an amenability to discipline. The interactions of objective and subjective factors in group life present a puzzling problem which will be discussed more fully in a later chapter on the Balance of Social Forces.

One important part of the amenability to discipline is undoubtedly the intelligence to see the necessity of discipline. It is not all a matter of intelligence, however. It is in part a matter of emotion. Even a very young child is angered by a restraint of its muscular freedom. Adults find any kind of restraint or frustration more or less irritating. To be stopped by a traffic policeman is more or less disagreeable, but fortunately most people are reasonable enough to suppress their feeling of irritation and conform to regulation. It is conceivable, however, that some very intelligent people who call themselves high-spirited,— which is a euphemism for irritable,— may let their feelings override their intelligence and refuse to follow any regulation which they find irritating. Reasonableness includes something more than intelligence, though intelligence is an essential part of it.

There are a great many writers who have made much of the human intellect in their study of man's social nature,[1] and especially of the exercise of that intellect in organizing systems of control over individual behavior. Naturally, the intellect cannot be separated from the instincts it controls and the habits it supervises, except by an analytical abstraction. When behavior, however, is cut up for analysis, the intellect appears to play an important part in making men sociable. When human

---

[1] J. P. Lichtenberger points to a good comparison between Plato and Aristotle that shows what place the intellect may be thought to have in social life:

"Plato was surrounded by a society which responded in some measure to ideals and he produced the philosophy of an ideal state. He conceived of the social order as a fabric of the human mind. It was conscious, utilitarian, purposive. He assumed that men knew what they wanted and that society was a coöperative device to obtain it. . . . Aristotle perceived that society was not quite so simple; that the cause of society was not primarily a perception of *utility*, or an *instinct of utility*, but *an instinct of sociability*. It was therefore not in the brain of man but in his organic nature that an explanation of his social relations must be sought. Society is, then, a growth rather than an edifice." *Development of Social Theory*, (The Century Co., New York, 1923), p. 206. The reader may be reminded of the importance that Comte gave to the intellect.

beings acquire a large measure of intelligence, they rationalize on the advantages of teamwork; they work together, and compel recalcitrant individuals to join them, however small is the pure emotional loyalty they feel for one another and their group.

When, after the death of Cyrus, Xenophon had thrust upon him the task of rallying the ten thousand and of extricating them from their dangerous position, he had to create a feeling of solidarity. In his appeals he did not stress emotional loyalty so much as the necessity of sticking together and obeying orders. The appeal was primarily to their intelligence, though he did not refrain from reminding them that they were all Greeks in a land of barbarians.

If there are racial differences in intelligence, it would not be improbable that intelligence would play a larger part in securing social behavior in some races than in others. If Xenophon had been appealing to a less intelligent group, he might have had to appeal, as did Peter the Hermit, to religious emotion, or to personal loyalty, as did Gustavus Adolphus and Napoleon, instead of to the intelligence of his followers. Sociologists have been too prone, perhaps, to assume that all races are alike in that they all respond to the same stimuli in the same way. There is no positive proof as yet either of the affirmative or negative of that assumption. Meanwhile, it is as dangerous to assume one as the other as the basis of any sweeping generalization. What is true of Europeans is not necessarily true of Asiatics or Africans, though it may be.

It was the opinion of Henry Thomas Buckle [1] that the progress of civilization in Europe was one with the "increasing influence of mental laws." Buckle recognized two separate but interacting realms of development, each with its own laws: namely, nature and mind. In parts of the world, specifically outside of Europe, the latter has been subordinated to the former; man has been secondary to the external world in in-

---

[1] 1821–62. Probably the most learned man of his time. Known chiefly for his *History of Civilization in England.* The quotations are from vol. I of the second London edition published in two volumes by D. Appleton & Co., New York, 1858. See pp. 112–131.

fluencing history. But in Europe the order is reversed and mind — or man — is of first importance because it has progressively dominated nature. Increasing knowledge has led to a diminishing pressure from nature because mind has learned to foretell nature's acts and control its agents.

Buckle, who was primarily a historian, treated history dynamically, and thereby became what might be called a historical sociologist. And, as we have seen, in his view the dominant force molding society, at least in Europe, was man's intellect. This emphasis on intelligence in the development of group life, that is to say, on the recognition by human beings of the advantages of sociability, or of coöperation in individual survival, is found in the work of that pioneer sociologist, Lester F. Ward, who called the birth of the intellect "a third cosmic epoch in the history of life." The intellect he saw as the directive element of society, the "only means by which the social forces (the feelings) can be controlled." The essential prerequisite to all true social union, he argued, is "sufficient brain-development to enable the individuals interested to perceive, however dimly, the advantages of association."[1]

All through his several books, Ward again and again emphasized the advantages and economies of what he called "the indirect method of conation"— the intellectual method of gaining a desired object.[2] Animals without intellect, he argued, get what they want by a direct expenditure of pure muscular energy. And they find that a direct application of muscle serves their ends very well, until obstructions appear in the way of a desired object that they cannot clear away by any amount of their own muscular force. Unthinking creatures, time and again, are forced to exhaust their energies without gaining their ends. Men differ from animals in that they are able to get what they want in a round-about way. If the direct expenditure of muscular energy proves ineffective in satisfying their desires, they are still able, with their intellect, to

---

[1] *Dynamical Sociology, op. cit.*, vol. I, p. 452.
[2] *Ibid.*, vol. II, pp. 99 ff.

figure out a chain of means for achieving an end. Above all, they are able to invent ways by which they can make natural forces work for them.

The intellect in social life is, according to Ward, as yet not used as it might be. Individual behavior is in a large measure intellectual; but the individual only rarely uses his intellect for pursuing the ends of society. Not until men use their intellectual powers for gaining society's ends, Ward insisted, will the intellect begin to have its greatest share in social life. The social desires, the social forces, must act under the guidance of a social mind.[1] The social mind is the governing body of society which aims, by means of the art of government, to induce the members of a social group to act always for the good of the group.

> The desires, passions, and propensities of men are bad [wrote Ward] only in the sense that fire lightning are bad . . . if society only knew how, it could utilize these forces, and their very strength would be the measure of their power for good. Society is now spending vast energies and incalculable treasure in trying to check and curb these forces without receiving any benefit from them in return. (This checking and curbing is the unintelligent, brutish method of directly applying force to gain a desired end). The greater part of this could be saved. . . .
> The principle that underlies all this is what I have called "attractive legislation." But it is nothing new or peculiar to society. It is nothing else than the universal method of science, invention, and art that has always been used and must be used to attain telic results. (This is the intelligent, indirect method.)[2]

There has been more of this intelligent social engineering than even Ward appreciated. By social engineering is meant such control and direction of social forces as will make them produce results that are desired. This is quite parallel to the physical engineer's control and direction of physical forces. The real engineer does not waste time expressing moral approval or disapproval of the forces with which he is working. He accepts them as forces and tries to harness them to his own purposes. The real social engineer, likewise, wastes no time in moral appraisal of the social forces with which he works. Such a moti-

---

[1] Ward used the language of innumerable writers who speak of society as an organism.

[2] *Outlines of Sociology, op. cit.*, pp. 272-273.

vating force as self-interest is a force to be used for the social good, not to be approved or disapproved. Like any other force, it may, if uncontrolled, do harm to the group, but, like any other force, it can be used. It can be made to motivate men to do useful work. Convince every one that he will be rewarded for any useful work which he does, and punished for any harmful work, and the trick is done. His self-interest will then lead him to do useful work. Having earned a reward, he must be permitted to use his legitimate reward for the benefit of those for whom he cares, even though he includes himself in his preferred list. In this way he is led, "as by an invisible hand," to use Adam Smith's expression, to promote the public good while trying to promote his own. This must be the first and most fundamental step in all social engineering.[1]

That this is sound engineering will appear to any one who will ask himself the following questions and answer them categorically.

1. Does the average individual care more for some persons than for others?

2. Will he work harder for those for whom he cares much than for those for whom he cares little?

3. Can he be induced to work for the benefit of the general public which includes many for whom he cares very little?

The answers to questions 1 and 2 are too obvious to need discussion. The answer to question 3 is: He can be induced to work for the general public on two conditions: first, if he is paid for his work; and second, if he can use his pay in the interest of those for whom he cares most.

10. *Modesty.* Nothing is more distinctively human nor more distinctively social than modesty.[2] Therefore no discussion of

---

[1] It is identical in meaning with a rule laid down by a higher authority than Adam Smith: "He that would be great among you, let him be your servant." The desire for greatness or success was not condemned. Success was merely to be earned by useful work.

[2] In common use modesty has two widely different meanings. In one sense it is almost synonymous with meekness, humility, or self-effacement. This use of the term has very little in common with the other use which is more closely associated with shame. As discussed in this chapter modesty means the feeling of propriety, especially with respect to such matters as nakedness and sex.

the social nature of man, or of the evolution of morals, would be complete without a consideration of modesty and all that it connotes.

Modesty is distinctively human because it is practically non-existent among the lower animals. Letourneau[1] says: "Modesty is *par excellence* a human sentiment, and is totally unknown to the animals." Lester F. Ward in *Dynamic Sociology*[2] says: "Sexual modesty is based on a quite different principle from such a quality as neatness, amounting to a kind of modesty, in animals. Sexual modesty exists only in the human race — but in the *whole* human race." These writers leave no doubt that they believe that modesty is a peculiarly human trait. Something resembling it is occasionally noticeable among animals, especially domestic animals; but it is difficult to know whether it has been acquired through association with humans or handed down from wild ancestors. A collie, for example, when shorn of his coat, shows at first unmistakable signs of shame,— at least it is so interpreted by human beings. He usually remains in hiding for several days until what we interpret as the feeling of nakedness has worn off. However, care must be taken not to read into the behavior of animals our own feelings.

Certain writers, however, find the source of modesty in animal life. William I. Thomas in *Sex and Society*[3] says: "A minimum expression of modesty, and one having an organic rather than a social basis, is seen in the coyness of the female among animals." Behavior which we can easily interpret as coyness is observable, but how closely it is associated with modesty is difficult to say. The entire lack of sex feeling at certain periods would seem to explain her avoidance of anything resembling sex expression. Winwood Read in *The Martyrdom of Man*[4] traces propriety to cleanliness, and "Cleanliness," he says "is a virtue of the lower animals, and is equivalent to decoration. . . .

[1] In *The Evolution of Marriage* (Charles Scribners Sons, New York, 1904), p. 56.
[2] (D. Appleton & Co., New York, 1924), p. 635 *et seq.*
[3] University of Chicago Press, 1907, p. 208.
[4] E. P. Dutton & Co., New York, 1929, p. 452.

It is a part of animal cleanliness to deposit apart, and even to hide, whatever is uncleanly. . . ." With all due respect to such high authorities, it seems that the feeling of disgust for uncleanness is widely different from modesty. Human beings share that feeling of disgust for bad table manners, for dirty ears and noses, and yet these forms of uncleanness are seldom regarded as immodest.

Modesty is distinctively social in that it is a product of association, is acquired and not inborn, and is a peculiarly sensitive form of subservience on the part of the individual to the behavior patterns imposed by the group. Having once been acquired through association, however, it may easily affect the behavior of individuals even when they are in isolation. It is pretty clear that each particular rule of modesty is conventional. That in itself, however, would not prove that the essence of modesty is wholly conventional. It is well known that young children exhibit no signs of modesty until they are taught. On the other hand, the fact that they can be taught may imply something — possibly more than those are willing to admit who hold that modesty is purely conventional. However, there can be no doubt that modesty is social in the sense that it is an expression of sensitiveness on the part of the individual to the attitudes of others toward himself.

Of all specific rules of individual behavior, those coming under the general name of modesty are probably the least rational and at the same time the most rigidly enforced and the most difficult to change. Even when the rules prescribed by modesty do happen to change, the changes are difficult to predict in advance or to account for after they have occurred. Even the original form of modesty is not known, though there are many opinions on the subject. These opinions, however, are in the form of conjectures, unsupported by adequate evidence.

Popular opinion in the Western World generally associates modesty with clothing, or the shame which nakedness produces. The weight of anthropological authority is to the effect that modesty is not universally associated with clothing. There is no uniformity among races as to whether clothing should be worn or not. Even among those whose rules prescribe the wearing of clothing there is no uniformity as to what should be worn, and there is the widest diversity as to what parts of the body should be covered. There is not even a minimum of agreement on this point. That is, there is no one article of clothing, however small, which is universally prescribed, and there is no part of the body which is universally covered. Yet modesty, in some form, seems to be universal. That is, so far as known, there is no race that does not have a feeling of modesty and certain rather rigid rules with respect to it. Franz Boas says, in his foreword to Margaret Mead's *Coming of Age in Samoa:* "Courtesy, modesty, good manners, and ethical standards are universal, but what constitutes courtesy, modesty, good manners and ethical standards is not universal."

If modesty is universal, the conclusion seems irresistible that there must be some common human trait or organic need which calls for modesty. The probabilities would seem to be overwhelmingly against the conclusion that modesty itself is wholly accidental, irrational, or conventional, with no organic or universal reason to support it. We may not be able to point to any common practice which modesty universally requires, but that does not conclude the argument. There is the possibility that we have not observed closely enough or analyzed minutely enough. Certainly the mere observation that there is no universal agreement as to what constitutes nakedness does not exhaust the subject. Secrecy concerning certain bodily functions seems to be more nearly universal than the mere covering of the body. Universality even here, however, has not been observed or recorded but this line of inquiry may be pursued with advantage.

Most writers on this subject are content to describe customs as they find them. Their observations and descriptions are so varied as to show that modesty is deeper than mere clothing. O. Finsch in his *Ethnologische Erfahrungen,* (I 92), as quoted by Sumner and Keller in *Science of Society,*[1] says, "Despite full

---

[1] Yale University Press, New Haven, 1927, p. 1243.

nudity the natives are extremely decent and modest people whose morality may serve as an illustration to show that nakedness and modesty may very well exist side by side." Westermarck in his *History of Human Marriage* [1] gives numerous examples of nudity and no sense of shame. While it is fairly clear that there is no uniformity with respect to clothing or nakedness, it is impossible to find in the descriptions of travellers and others who have studied the manners and customs of people any single basis of uniformity in the expression of modesty. However, it may be necessary to consider certain things which we know must take place and which no traveller or social observer ever sees. The things which are not described may prove to be the significant ones.

Next to the belief that modesty is associated with clothing, the most popular notion with respect to it is that it is peculiarly a feminine trait. This has the support of such an eminent authority as Havelock Ellis, who says [2] "that modesty — which may be provisionally defined as an almost instinctive fear, prompting to concealment, and usually centering around the sexual nature — while common to both sexes is more especially feminine, so that it may almost be regarded as the chief secondary sexual character of women on the psychic side." Elsewhere in his *Evolution of Modesty*,[3] Ellis cites Venturi as holding that modesty is possessed by women alone, men exhibiting a sense of decency. On the other hand, he cites Viazzi and Sergi as believing men are more modest than women, and Madame Celine Renooz as believing that modesty is not really feminine but "masculine shame attributed to women." Sumner and Keller [4] point out that, "as a broad generality, among the most uncivilized peoples it is the men who are more decorated than the women." The absence of decoration produces a feeling of nakedness which is supposed to be associated with modesty.

---

[1] 2d edition, The Macmillan Co., New York, 1894, p. 187 *et seq.*
[2] *Op. cit.*, p. 134.
[3] F. A. Davis Co., Philadelphia, 1910, p. 3.
[4] *Op. cit.*, p. 2139.

T. Waitz in *Anthropology* [1] says, "If dress were the result of a feeling of shame we should expect it to be more indispensable to woman than to man, which is not the case." Barth in his *Reisen* [2] says, "I have observed that many heathen tribes consider a covering, however poor and scanty it may be, more necessary for man than for woman."

It appears, therefore, that those writers who connect modesty with clothing and attribute it particularly to women are mistaken. There seems to be no uniformity on either subject. In some tribes men are naked and women clothed; in some women are naked and men clothed; in some all are naked; and there is every possible variation. In some, women are naked prior to marriage and naked after. If, in the society to which we belong, modesty seems more pronounced among women than men, the conclusion must be that it is the result of convention. It is probably worth noting that all those opinions as to the modesty of the female were written before modern fashions as to feminine attire came into vogue.

One of the most persistent phases of the theory that modesty is connected with clothing is found in the statement rather frequently made by amateur anthropologists that clothing is the cause of modesty as well as of shame. If it were found that people who wear no clothes have no sense of modesty or feeling of shame, there would be some ground for such a statement. There seems, however, to be rather less evidence in support of this theory than of the opposite, namely, that modesty is the cause of clothing. It is practically certain, however, that after the habit of wearing clothes once developed, their absence would produce a feeling of shame. In that case, modesty as well as comfort would prescribe their continued use.

As to the origin of clothing, a great many theories have been advanced. Each one is supported with some evidence, but none is supported with sufficient evidence to convince us that it is the one and only origin. The probabilities are that there have

[1] Ed. J. F. Collingwood (Longman, Green, Longman, and Roberts, London, 1863), p. 300.
[2] Vol. II, p. 473.

been many reasons for the wearing of clothing in different times and places, and that we need not waste time looking for one universal origin. Herbert Spencer, enlarging upon his well known statement that ornament precedes use, gives a purely ceremonial reason for the origin of clothing. First come trophies;[1] trophies lead to badges, and finally to dress, worn at first to excite admiration. He adds, however, that a "rudimentary aesthetic sense which leads the savage to paint his body, has doubtless a share in prompting the use of attractive objects for ornaments."[2]

It is worth observing that many of the writers who have discussed or described the clothing of primitive tribes have found their primitive tribes in tropical climates where the use of clothing for warmth would be absent. There are fairly primitive peoples living in the Far North, such as the Eskimos. It does not require a great deal of inventiveness or erudition to discover why the Eskimos wear clothes or how they got the suggestion. To say that people in cold climates wear clothes for aesthetic reasons would be about as rational as to say that they build fires for the same reasons. Yet there is undoubtedly a certain amount of aesthetic pleasure in looking at a fire and enjoying the light, the brightness and the cheer which surround it.

The suggestion that clothing was invented as a means of increasing sex appeal by creating an air of mystery is more prurient than erudite. To attribute such subtle and insidious reasoning to primitive people, engaged in the grim struggle of keeping alive, of finding food and eluding enemies, is an evidence of naïveté rather than of sophistication. Any such use of clothing came rather late in social development, after males began winning their wives by their power to provide economic support, and when women began using the arts of fascination to win husbands.

So long as we are dealing with tropical races it is possible to

---

[1] *Principles of Sociology* (D. Appleton & Co., New York and London, 1929), vol. II, pp. 179–192.

[2] *Ibid.*, p. 192.

say that clothing was at first almost wholly ornamental. Spencer and others have pointed out that painting and tatooing for ornament seems to have preceded clothing, then movable ornament was substituted so that man could gratify his taste for change. This certainly furnishes an interesting background for the phenomenon of changing fashions in millinery and haberdashery at the present time. Sumner and Keller state:[1]

It seems clear enough, then, that clothing has taken its origin largely in ornament and so goes back to the motive of ostentation. . . . Minimal coverings of the most backward people . . . are assumed when the individual has passed childhood, not because he or she then arrives at sexmaturity . . . but because at that time individuality is first attained and must be proclaimed.

T. Waitz says:[2] "The original motives, however, of painting and tatooing the body could hardly have been to cover nakedness from a feeling of shame; the former was resorted to for ornamentation, the latter to mark the tribe or the family." Westermarck in the *History of Human Marriage* [3] expresses the view that tatooing is for the purpose of making men attractive to the women. Men usually adorn themselves more than women do among primitives, and this is because men run a greater risk than women do of not attaining a mate. He thinks that Spencer's explanation, based on trophies and badges, is only occasionally true. Havelock Ellis in the *Psychological Review* [4] says:

Herbert Spencer, followed by Sergi and others, regarded modesty simply as the result of clothing. This view is overturned by the well-ascertained fact that many races which go absolutely naked possess a highly developed sense of modesty. These writers have not realized that psychological modesty is earlier in appearance, and more fundamental, than anatomical modesty.

William G. Sumner, however, in *Folkways* [5] in spite of the above quotations, seems to hold that amulets really preceded

---

[1] *Op. cit.*, pp. 2140, 2142.
[2] *Op. cit.*, p. 301.
[3] 2d edition. The Macmillan Co., New York, 1894.
[4] Vol. VI, p. 134, note.
[5] Ginn & Co., Boston, 1911, p. 429.

ornaments, or at least that superstition was as early as vanity in causing dress. "At the earliest stage of the treatment of the body we find motives of utility and ornament mixed with superstition and vanity and quickly developing connections with magic, kin notions, and goblinism. Modesty and decency are very much later derivatives." J. G. Frazer in the *Golden Bough* [1] remarks that "amulets often degenerate into ornaments."

The need for clothing for protection in cold climates is so clear as to have called forth no discussion. It has not occurred to most of those writers who account for clothing on aesthetic or ceremonial grounds that there is extreme need for clothing even in the tropics. Any one who realizes what a menace to health, comfort, and even to life itself the insect pests of the tropics are, will have no difficulty in understanding this. Even painting and tatooing the body may have developed from the habit of rolling in ashes or of spreading clay upon the body as a protection from flies and other insect pests. Karl von den Steinen in *Unter den Zentral-Brasiliens* is quoted in Thomas, *Sex and Society*,[2] as reporting the use of coverings as protection from insects.

The advantage of a covering which can be changed, burned, or boiled as compared with fur in an insect-infested environment, must be apparent to any one who has ever stood before a monkey cage in a menagerie. The survival value of substituting an artificial for a natural covering may account for the natural nakedness of the human body. In short, protection against insects is as plausible a reason for the origin of clothing in warm countries as protection from cold is in cold countries. It is even possible that a frequent change of clothing may have had an intensely utilitarian use long before it became fashionable.

In view of all the evidence, the present writer is of the opinion that clothing was worn first as protection before it came to be worn either for adornment or to satisfy the claims of modesty. It was needed for protection against flies and other insects even

[1] The Macmillan Co., London, 1913, vol. II, p. 156, note.
[2] The University of Chicago Press, 1907.

where it was not needed for warmth. Having become customary, it came to have an added use as adornment, and its absence came to produce a disagreeable feeling of nakedness or shame.

Since there is ample evidence that modesty exists even among tribes that go naked, we cannot agree that modesty resulted from the wearing of clothes. Neither do we believe that clothing resulted from any innate sense of modesty, but rather from definite needs presented by the physical environment. The fact that nowadays, for most peoples, modesty has become closely associated with questions of clothing is entirely a matter of the specific mores which have grown up,— different in different groups. Presenting oneself in a garb — or in a situation — other than the one prescribed by one's society is embarrassing. But for the origin of modesty we turn to a wholly different source — namely, fear.

Several writers agree that modesty is akin to fear, or is, in fact, a form of fear. We shall do well to look into this a little further. ". . . Fear may safely be regarded as the sentiment which lies at the bottom of human modesty."[1] Ward's theory is that in the beginning the males fought for the females; the victor carried off his prize to a place of safety from attack by his rivals. Eventually the secrecy of the sex act became customary; and any breaking of custom is accompanied by shame. Modesty is an early form of shame.

Among all the higher animals, masculine rage, or jealousy, is excited by the act of engendering. In every species, some special provision, habit, or custom exists for the protection of procreants. Among human beings, the only protection is secrecy.[2] Here we find an adequate source of modesty. It is one of a great variety of animal customs which reduce the danger from the jealous rage of rival males.

It has become evident enough, perhaps, in the course of reviewing these widely differing interpretations of the social nature of man, that there is a measure of truth in them all. The

---

[1] L. F. Ward, *Dynamic Sociology*, 2d edition (D. Appleton & Co., New York, 1924), vol. I, pp. 632 ff.

[2] Cf. The slaying of Zimri and Cosbi in Numbers xxv: 6–15.

puzzling problems of social life cannot be solved without reference to some analysis of all the elements that enter into it, including instinct, intelligence and all that come between. Charles Darwin said this long ago in words that are well enough chosen to epitomize all the knowledge that has since been gained of human nature. He maintained that man's peculiar position in the world, his dominance over all other animals, is due to "his intellectual faculties, his social habits, which lead him to aid and defend his fellows, and to his corporeal structure."[1]

---

[1] *Descent of Man* (D. Appleton & Co., New York, 1871), vol. i, p. 131. ". . . as the reasoning powers and foresight of the members (of a tribe) became improved," said Darwin, "each man would soon learn from experience that, if he aided his fellowmen, he would commonly receive aid in return. From this low motive he might acquire the habit of aiding his fellows; and the habit of performing benevolent actions certainly strengthens the feeling of sympathy, which gives the first impulse to benevolent actions." *Ibid.*, p. 157.

CHAPTER VI

HUMAN ADAPTATION

A. THE CONCEPT OF ADAPTATION

1. *Fitness.* The word *adaptation* and the ideas that cluster around it are destined, in this century, to play an important part in social science,— as important a part as they played in biological science during the last century. If social adaptation can be defined in terms which are scientifically objective, it may give us a basis for a positive theory of social development, that is, a theory which is not based on a value judgment.[1] We need not even say that survival is desirable when we affirm that survival depends upon adaptation. We may positively, and without any taint of cosmic teleology, state the truism that the world will be peopled, if at all, by those human beings who, if any, manage to survive. We may go further and say that,

---

[1] This does not imply that value judgments have no place in science. Problems of finding means to certain ends occupy a good part of the time, even of a laboratory scientist, though these may not be his major problems. The whole science of medicine assumes certain ends as desirable, but it does not lose either its respectability or its scientific character because of that fact.

in the long run, those who adapt themselves to the conditions, or adapt the conditions to themselves, are more likely to survive than those who fail in either form of adaptation. It is a positive theory that those who think that survival is desirable are more likely to strive desperately to meet the conditions of survival, that is, to adapt themselves to conditions or conditions to themselves, than are those who think that survival is undesirable.

Even when it comes to expressing a value judgment as to the desirability or undesirability of survival, it looks as though an increasing majority would agree that it is desirable. The jury is, as it were, being packed by the processes of selection. They who think survival desirable, and try to survive, are more likely to survive and transmit their optimistic temperament to others than are those who think survival undesirable. That certain value judgments have greater power of survival than others is a positive and not a normative theory. This aspect of the problem of survival values probably comes as near to giving us a positive theory of morals as it is possible to go. It is easy enough to show that certain moral codes contribute to survival, but the question then arises, why does one desire to survive? The answer is, the *desire* to survive will survive with the people who feel it; the desire not to survive will not survive because the people who feel it will not survive. The desire to survive will, therefore, in the living world, dominate over the desire not to survive; and, in the long run, the desire to survive will tend to become universal among the living. At this point we must turn the problem over to the metaphysician.

As to the concept of adaptation, it may, in general terms, be defined as the fitting together of parts. How do we know, or how can we know whether the parts fit together or not? It is difficult to say without bringing in the ideas of purpose and function. To say, for example, that two cogwheels fit together because they harmonize in color is manifestly absurd. To say that they fit together because their friction produces a musical note is likewise absurd unless their purpose is to produce musical notes. When it is known that their purpose is to transmit power, they may be said to fit together when they transmit the desired quantity of power with the minimum of friction or loss.

Again, how do we know whether an animal is adapted to its environment or not? To say that it fits into its environment merely because it is sufficiently decorative to please the eye of an artist is hardly sufficient. Certainly such a reason would not satisfy an evolutionist. In the biological sense, adaptation has some relation to the survival of organisms. An organism is adapted to its environment if the environment provides for all its needs in such ways and such forms as it can use for its own maintenance, survival, and multiplication.

The process is a passive one in the sense that it is "unwilled" by the evolving organism. Human beings do not escape entirely from the necessity of passive adaptation. In order to thrive, they must be physically adapted to their natural and to their social environments. Like all animals, they must be organically adapted to their physical environment and to an atmosphere of social customs, laws, and institutions as well. Social life, from the very beginning, required such passive modification of human anatomy and physiology as would fit men for a social existence. The ability to use language, for instance, which is so important for the highest success in gregarious living, involved the evolution of special vocal organs. A person organically unadapted to group life is as much a misfit in his world as a fish out of water. A person who, for example, lacked organs of speech or the mental capacity to make use of them, or who lacked the power to sympathize or imitate, would be unfitted for social life.

Organic fitness for a social-physical life, however, is not all that human adaptation means. There are factors in the fitting of human life to its environment which the biologist, as such, is not equipped to study. Human beings, for one thing, are adapted to their world through group life. They would fare ill if the life of the group itself were not well adapted to its own environment. The group exists in its customs, mores, and institutions; through these the group survives.

An institution, a custom or a religion may, however, for a

time at least be a hindrance rather than a help in the process of adaptation. If so, it is likely to be temporary because it lacks survival value, or possesses negative value. Suppose that a nation is surrounded by hostile nations eager to prey upon its natural resources. Suppose that an institution such as the church has enough influence to place a real social censure upon men who show a militaristic temper, who are eager to fight to keep the nation's resources. Such a religion would endanger group survival. Imagine, for the sake of simplicity, that there is no league of nations for settling inter-group quarrels, that war is the only method of settling disputed rights. Is it not obvious that a militaristic church, a church eager to crusade for political advantage, willing even to promise a glorious Valhalla to those who fall in battle, might help to fit the group to its social surroundings?

The fitness of social customs, mores and institutions for promoting the existence of a group in a particular environment is a matter of great concern for the sociologist studying human adaptation. The process by which such fitness is attained is to a certain extent analagous to the passive process of biological evolution. Social customs and mores and institutions vary. Some are more successful than others in meeting the demands of a given environment. The more successful are selected by the environment for a social survival.

Human adaptation does not take place entirely through a passive process, through organic evolution, or through the mere survival of institutions which best adapt this group or that to some particular environment. Human beings are able, because of their intelligence, to assume an active rôle. Instead of waiting always for institutions to reveal their fitness for a particular environment by their survival or their ability to outlast other institutions, men are able somewhat to anticipate how a given institution will work in a given environment, to frame institutions which they "think" will survive.[1] The ways by which they are able to adapt their world to fit themselves and the

---

[1] Cf. Sumner's distinction between crescive and enacted institutions. *Folkways* (Ginn & Company, Boston, 1906), p. 54.

methods by which they are able to create workable social institutions, to organize their own group life in the interests of group survival, lie beyond the horizon of the biologist, but are very much the concern of the sociologist.

The power of men to assume the active rôle, it must always be remembered, is itself the result of a passive physical evolution. The power to think, to devise, to invent is connected, in a way as yet not very well understood, with the organic development of a complex brain. Mental and physical adaptation are not at all exclusive in their action. They are at least interdependent, if not merely different aspects of the same thing. The mind is an aid to the body; but the body also aids the mind. Social life, to the extent that it becomes intelligent, relieves the burden of individuals who might otherwise need to develop stronger arms, or fleeter legs and feet, or a less delicate digestion. But individuals, in turn, are not exempt from physical adaptation to a social environment when a good brain and a body fitted to the strains of social life are more and more at a premium. They cannot afford to be born into a civilized society with the brains of monkeys, or even of savages.

The active method by which human beings change their environment to fit themselves is a much faster and less painful method of securing adaptation than the passive method of organic evolution, by which animals must wait to be fitted to their surroundings. If a species of animal is forced to migrate from a cold to a warm climate in search of food, it may acquire immunity to the ravages of heat and to the diseases of the tropics, but the process is the long and painful one of variation and selection, the survival of the fittest for the new environment and the extinction of the least fit. An unpredictable number of generations may have to be born with new physical variations before a creature really well adapted to heat appears in the transplanted species. The extermination of the less adapted involves a painful ordeal, a fight against disease and starvation.

Human beings, on the other hand, if they are dwellers of the North, and are forced in search of food to the tropics, are able to carry refrigeration with them. They can eat and digest new kinds of food, because they have discovered, with their intelligence, the art of cooking, which is really a form of pre-digestion. They do not have to wait for generations to be born with immunity to tropical diseases. They wage war upon the insects that act as carriers in the transmission of the fatal fevers. And, if finally they find that the heat is too much for them, they have intelligence enough to create, on a small scale, a climate in which they know they can live. Climate, to a large extent, they make for themselves. In a wintry world, they surround themselves with walls and floor and roof, and warm the space within by means of fire; or, out of doors, they surround their bodies with eight layers of cloth. In a summery world, they make a wind blow with electric fans, and keep their houses at an even, spring-like temperature with piping that cools the air.

To mold the environment requires work, it is true; and the species that assumes the active rôle in adaptation is doomed to a perpetual life of work. Work, however, is less painful to energetic people than extermination; and more desirable to crea-tures that hold life itself in high esteem. For life, in a very real sense, means the avoidance of pain, and a high death-rate is associated with an increase of pain or other forms of un-pleasantness.

Adaptation, in the active sense, means the devising of new ways for satisfying a need and reaching an end. It is an im-portant process just because the world happens to be a changing world. Old ways of doing things have to be scrapped, not be-cause they are merely out of date, but because they actually cease to function. Animals are able to satisfy their needs only if the world changes slowly enough for organic evolution to keep up with the changes,— sometimes only if organic variation and selection produce adaptations in their bodies very quickly. When an ice sheet is creeping down from the north, animals in temperate climes may be doomed to extinction if too many generations are born unfitted for life in an icy world. If the creatures emigrate south, they are still in need of a compara-tively swift change in their organic make-up. Intelligent crea-tures are well fitted for meeting change in their environment.

It does not seem to matter very much to them what happens in the course of the years. If there are droughts or the stock market crashes, if circumstance takes any surprising turn, they are clever enough to adjust themselves to the new situation, to devise new ways and means of living.

A study of active adaptation,— it has doubtless become evident,— is most easily divided into two parts. First, is the active material adaptation, the adapting of the material environment to human needs. Industrial achievement, the harnessing of the world of matter to human uses, the production of "goods" — this is all an important part of human adaptation. Active material adaptation merges closely into the second form, which may be called, for lack of a perfectly apt phrase, active social or group adaptation. Human beings adapt themselves to their world not merely by harnessing nature to the production of the material goods they desire, but also by means of an active, social organization, by the intelligent creating of social institutions that make group adaptation effective.[1] They have to adapt themselves to a world that is both social and material by means of social tools. They cannot go far in any kind of industrial achievement until they have begun to produce goods by actively organizing group industry. Economists have long insisted on the high production value of a division of labor among the members of a group.

Active social adaptation means more than an intelligent group organization of industry. It means, for instance, the organization of the church for social usefulness — the substitution of an intelligent faith in the possibilities of earthly life for a blindly mystic and dogmatic religion which pictures the Kingdom of Heaven beyond this world. It means that groups, through agencies of social control, through government and law, make social institutions such as will aid the survival of groups.[2] In-

---

[1] "Social Telesis," as Lester F. Ward called it.

[2] All social institutions are, to the extent that they contain within themselves an intelligent directing principle, agencies of social control. Institutions, in a sense that should not be confusing, create themselves. Government, as an agent of social control, creates itself as an institution, a definite social structure — say democracy, or autocracy, or socialism. Parthenogenesis is no more extraordinary as a phenomenon in sociology than in biology.

telligent groups do not wait to be fitted to their environment, any more than intelligent individuals do, by the passive process of evolution.

Enough has been said to indicate that the problem of human adaptation is a wide-ranging one. In any study of social life it appears in a number of guises, all of which are important. In any thorough-going consideration of it, the details are bound to be somewhat confusing. A diagram may therefore be useful to outline the subject as the sociologist must study it:

KINDS OF ENVIRONMENT

		Physical	Social
		1	2
Kinds of Adaptation	Passive	Biological Evolution or Genetics	Moral Development or the Evolution of a social nature
	Active	Industrial Achievement or Economics	Social Control or Government
		3	4

J. Novicow, in his *Les Luttes entre Sociétés Humaines*,[1] introduced into a study of social life a diagram somewhat similar to this. The author knows of no sociologist, other than Novicow, who has made independent use of a diagrammatic representation of the problem of human adaptation so like his own. Novicow's diagram is this:

ADAPTATION

Phenom.	*Passive*		*Active*
Biolog. Millieu Physique	{ Organisation Science	Production	{ Outillage biologique Outil. social du 1er degré Adaptation de la Planète
Psychol. et sociaux Milieu Social	{ Imitation....	Amour.....	{ Charité Propagande

[1] *F. Alcan* (Paris, 1896), p. 41. In order to grasp fully the somewhat complicated interpretation of this diagram which Novicow gives, the student must necessarily turn to *Les Luttes*, especially ch. VI of bk. I.

The present writer's Diagram divides the field of sociology into four Sectors, and each sector is a special field for the study of human adaptation. Sector 1 is the field of the biological evolutionist or the geneticist. His technique must be used in the study of the adaptation of human bodies to their material environment. Sector 2 is the field of the moral evolutionist who tries to explain in dynamic terms the factors and forces which determine the variation, selection, and survival of moral systems. Sector 3 is the field of the economist and, to a certain extent, of the technologist, who tries to understand how men make over their environment to suit themselves. Sector 4 is the field of government, or of efforts to remodel the social environment, to make it conform to the needs of men.

The first three sectors all together do not offer a complete solution to the problem of living together in large numbers. So long as some human beings even occasionally bolt the bounds of morality and behave in unsocial ways, the sociologist is concerned with the study of some method by means of which their behavior can be controlled. The group cannot, in the interests of its own survival, afford to wait for individuals to become passively and organically modified to fit social life — to the extent of their becoming automatically "good." The group must assume the active rôle and undertake by government, legal organization, laws, rewards and penalties, to compel men to behave in ways which they would not if they followed their own natures or even the dictates of the mores.

A similar concept is developed by Lippert in his "Lebens-fürsorge." The urge to live and function in such a way as to assure life is, according to him, the organic element or source of all human achievement (successful adaptation) and the very basis of social and cultural phenomena. He says:

> The unity and continuity of cultural development is in accord with the single basic impulse of all culture. This single dominant fundamental impulse in culture history "is the care for life." It unites and distinguishes man and the brute. It is manifested in different degrees in animal instinct and human reason.[1]

[1] J. Lippert, *The Evolution of Culture*, translated by George Peter Murdock (The Macmillan Co., New York, 1931), p. 3.

By these means, so far as they are relevant, each member of a social organization is being made better fitted for functioning, or playing his part towards maintaining or advancing the group. All living beings are the creatures of fundamental drives. These drives are what John Dewey calls life-activity. This life-activity in the process of its fulfillment is constantly met with obstructions and this gives rise to desire. In other words, desire is the necessary tendency of an organism to overcome obstacles and seek that which it needs for its survival.[1] Living organisms are "active agencies, prompted by hunger and love and the will to live, seeking more life in their developing, growing, and multiplying, and rarely ceasing to be insurgent against environing difficulties and limitations."[2] Unless plants and animals have means for obtaining the most important things they seek in the world which surrounds them, they are not well fitted to the environment in which they live. Scientific studies, replete with facts regarding the interrelations of plants, animals, and their environment, clearly show that every living species must be in equilibrium with the natural conditions under which it lives. The demands a species makes on its environment, and the means it employs to utilize the environment, and the adjustment of its structure and function to that purpose are in the nature of a balanced relationship; and when the environment undergoes a change to which it cannot adapt itself, it will be expelled by other species or exterminated. Modification of structure and specialization of function are the most conspicuous characteristics of the interrelationship between a living species and its environment.

The way in which living organisms fit the air and the water and the earth, the heat and the cold, is nothing short of spectacular. Surprising means are fashioned in nature for satisfying

---

[1] According to psychological definition the word "desire" is used somewhat promiscuously here. The reader will, however, catch the meaning quickly enough. It is perfectly possible, of course, to make a distinction between desire and conation in general. Cf. H. B. English's *Students' Dictionary of Psychological Terms* (Antioch, 1928); *Psychology, Simplified* (London, 1928), p. 116. For purposes of this chapter, Dewey's less technical definition seems adequate.

[2] Thomson and Geddes, *Life* (Harper & Bros., New York, 1931), vol. I, p. 1.

the desires of every kind of life in every kind of clime. It is amazing to think, for instance, of the vast variety of devices that serve for weapons of defense, that protect even the smallest creatures against their own peculiar array of enemies.

Here, a weak, stupid animal is sheltered under a shell or carapace, leading its narrow life in the very shadow of fierce and powerful animals, yet effectively protected from them. Here, another flits from limb to limb lightly, pecking its food daintily, hiding its eggs carefully, and skillfully, deceiving or diverting its wily and more powerful enemies. Here, a sleek and lazy creature, without shell or armor, wings for flying or claws for fighting, keeps its enemies at a distance by the production of an acrid or repellent odor. Here a slipping, sliding thing effects by fangs and venom what its neighbor accomplishes by a barbed skin or a repulsive emanation. Here, a huge forest prowler, muscled as with whipcord, survives by sheer strength, while another, lacking this strength, depends upon the fleetness of its limbs, the keenness of its eye, the acuteness of its hearing, living on its wits as verily as any human adventurer. Here, a delicate little creature, like the field mouse, preyed upon by everything in its neighborhood — snake, hawk, and owl, lacking any of the more powerful defenses, survives by the sheer fact of its great fertility. Here the elephant, slowest of breeders, being superior to attack (by right of sheer bulk) stalks unmolested through the forest.[1]

It was the adaptation that appears in nature which first caught the attention of scientists. Animals and plants live by means of different kinds of cell structures that fit together, hands and feet, nerves, cartilage, blood corpuscles, lungs and intestines, leaves and bark. There is a definite functional relation of one cell structure to another. More than that, there is a functional relation between the whole living organism and the world which it inhabits, that makes breathing possible, and eating and digesting and breeding. There is a functional relation between the organism and its topographical surroundings,— the climate, the soil,— and between the organism and its organic environment, between plant and animal, host and parasite, hunter and prey. Most of all, this adaptation in nature is common knowledge.

It is the infinite amount of detail in the whole business, how-

---

[1] G. W. Crile, *Man — an Adaptive Mechanism* (The Macmillan Co., New York, 1916), p. 27.

ever, that is really remarkable, and this escapes the notice of people who are not looking for it. Darwin, for instance, was amazed by the form of eggs of certain sea-birds, like the guillemots and razor-bills. The eggs are laid on the narrow ledges of precipitous cliffs. If they were of ordinary shape, they would roll away to a smash at a puff of the wind or a jostle of a careless parent. But they are shaped like a top, so they rotate on a short axis whenever they are hit, instead of tumbling to perdition. The razor-bills are bringing up a family, and even their eggs are adapted to the ways of the world where they live, to their topographical surroundings.[1]

No one can help wondering why so many things under the sun fit together. It seems, at least it used to seem, as though something is planned about all the adaptation in nature. It has always been difficult for men to believe that it just happened, though modern scientists account for it easily enough by the doctrine of spontaneous variation and natural selection proceeding through millions of years. Yet even wise men cannot be sure whether Nature is a super-human creator-designer; nor, if so, to what end she performs her feats of artistry. That she has some purpose, they find it difficult to doubt. She behaves, anyway, remarkably like man, who is all purpose, adapting means to ends. Perhaps that is why man reads purpose into the process of evolution. Science, however, excludes from its purview the question of an "Ultimate Design," finding it of little or no assistance in grasping the significant fact of the existence of adaptation and maladaptation in nature. As to the value of the speculative theories about "purpose" he may remark with Hume that:

if we take in our hand any volume of divinity or school metaphysics, for instance, let us ask, Does it contain any abstract reasoning concerning quantity or number? No. Does it contain any experimental reasoning

---

[1] See J. Arthur Thomson, *Darwinism and Human Life* (Henry Holt & Co., 1910), p. 197. If the reader is further interested in amazing illustrations of the adaptation in nature, he will find a great many such scattered through *Evolution and Adaptation* by T. H. Morgan (The Macmillan Co., New York, 1903). But there is illustration enough in any biology textbook.

concerning matter of fact and existence? No. Commit it then to the flames; for it can contain nothing but sophistry and illusion.[1]

It was once, more than it is now, an anxious concern of Christian theology to show that nature's purpose is clearly homocentric. According to Biblical authority, God — the spirit of nature — had prepared the earth for man and had given him dominion over it. If ever his destiny seemed perverse to him, it was the business of religion, the Comforter, to dispel his doubts and fears and inferiority complexes and "Justify the ways of God to man." What better way could be found than to illustrate, somehow, strikingly and insistently, the fitness of the earth for his habitation? If he could only be made to see the tremendous scale and the infinite detail with which the world had been made for his benefit, he might forget his hard knocks and illumine his difficult path with faith in the beneficence of Heaven. So the church built cathedrals, and filled them with oratory and drama, poetry, painting, music, sculpture — all to picture the goodness of God to man.

In spite of this, the ways of God were sometimes difficult to understand. From a human point of view, nature seemed fickle. She was gracious, time and again, backing human schemes, creating the mind. Yet, as often, her purpose was obstinately opposed to human wishes. She seemed like a kind of omnipotent Procrustes, to delight in making life fit her own iron bed — stretching limbs until it hurt, and arbitrarily cutting off extruding members. Today the church is somewhat less dramatic and less emphatic about proclaiming the special making of the earth for human happiness. Its confidence that man is the chief concern of the universe has been a bit shaken by science.

Today, evolutionists are not disposed to accept the idea of a former perfect state from which men have fallen. The obvious maladaptations which exist are explained, as stated in Chapter I, rather on the ground of incomplete evolution. The material universe and man himself are still evolving, still seeking equilib-

---

[1] *Essays, Moral, Political and Literary* (Longmans, Green & Co., New York, 1898), p. 135.

rium, still undergoing adaptation and readaptation. If the world was "prepared for" man, it was, in a number of particulars, rather inadequately prepared. If, on the other hand, man is being adapted to the world, he is, in a number of particulars, rather poorly adapted, or at least, not yet completely adapted. Sceintists, therefore, are not inclined to give serious consideration to the doctrine of design. Some, however, venturing frankly beyond science into the field of philosophic speculation, are expressing some concern. J. Arthur Thomson, for example, while admitting that the idea of "preparedness for" is not, in the strictest sense, a scientific idea, yet when we pass from things to living creatures, the question "why" becomes insistent. The study of function is, in a sense, the study of the "why" of something. In particular, when we come to study ourselves as living things, it is difficult to exclude the question "why," "not the philosophical 'why' as to ultimate meaning, but the scientific 'why,' objectively teleological."

But, again, the scientific critic may say, Are you not repeating the mistake of the naïve old lady who saw providential design in the way so many fine rivers flowed through so many large towns? — we are not sure that this does justice to the big fact that the chemical and physical conditions of nature have been conspicuous'y favorable to the order and progress of organisms. It is easy to assert that with other elements with other properties, there "might" have been other living creatures, very different from those we know, yet just as well adapted to their environment, just as marvellous and beautiful. But no one has produced examples to demonstrate this possibility.

The scientist, as such, may not be primarily interested in the question whether the environment was made to fit man or man was molded by the environment. The observable fact of a mutual fitting together is enough to begin with. When two things are observed to fit together, it is at least pertinent to inquire whether both are equally plastic or whether one is rigid and unyielding, like the mold, and the other plastic, like wax, and capable of being molded. When this line of inquiry is carried too far it leads us into dangerous fields of metaphysical speculation.

2. *Plasticity.* Some one may object here that scientists might quite as reasonably try to discover how the environment is made to fit life as to find out how living things are made to fit the environment. How is it possible to say, from a glance at a fish swimming about in water, that a fish is any more fitted to water than water is fitted to a fish?[1] By this we do not mean to underestimate the significance of ecological studies attempting to find out the influence of environmental factors on the nature of adaptability. It is a universal property of environmental factors to limit and modify adaptability in a manner which makes it seem as though there is only the direct action of the environment. But as Professor L. J. Henderson remarks:

> Darwinian fitness is compounded of mutual relationship between the organism and the environment. Of this, fitness of environment is quite as essential a component as the fitness which arises in the process of organic evolution; and in fundamental characteristics the actual environment is the fittest possible abode of life.[2]

> Whatever may be the final judgment of natural science upon either organic or inorganic harmonies, biological fitness is manifestly a mutual relationship. For, however present order may have developed out of past confusion, the organism and the environment each fits and is fitted by the other.[3]

This, then, implies that the functional rôle of environment in influencing the process of adaptation is not altogether direct, acting in a free and unrestricted manner. And as Thomson and Geddes point out, "Evolution is no mere yielding of life to its environment, in simple self-adjustment so far as may be. . . .

---

[1] In a book entitled *What Is Adaptation?* (Longmans, Green Co., New York and London, 1914), R. E. Lloyd asks, substantially, such a question. The introductory remarks and the first chapter of the book are especially interesting, even though the argument is not convincing.

[2] L. J. Henderson, *The Fitness of the Environment* (The Macmillan Co., New York, 1924), Preface, p. v.

[3] L. J. Henderson, *The Order of Nature* (Harvard University Press, Cambridge, 1925), Introduction, p. 3.

Fundamental though environment is, the progress of evolution is ever marked by active adaptation, with increasing domination of environment accordingly."[1]

Yet biologists, it is true, have been more impressed with the adaptation of life to its environment than with the fitness of the environment for life. They take more than a glance at the fish, they give little attention to the nature of water. They see life not as an accomplished fact of the moment but as a changing process of the years. A mere glance at the world — or a static view of life — reveals simply a certain degree of fitness of all things; it makes a study of adaptation seem as futile to science as the quest for a knowledge of God and immortality. It is only the long-run analysis — or the dynamic view — which reveals the comparative fitness of things and brings out into bold relief the real nature and essence of fitness. Life is change; and, in the changing process, mated things do not always change together. Mated things become mismated, if one changes more quickly than the other. And it is the quickly changing one that is charged, always, with solving the mating problem. It must readapt itself to its slowly changing mate. If the earth and the life that fits it always changed together, as time brought change, they might forever be adapted to each other. It would then be easy to think of either one as especially fitted to the other. But the air and the sea and the land change very slowly, while life runs on ahead, changing at every birth, never begetting its exact duplicate.[2]

Birth is the great radical of nature. New life is always being born with new organs and new ways of behavior; new satisfactions are demanded of a world that cannot yield them fast enough. Only the new desires that can be fulfilled in the world as it is are satisfied; the others perish in being born. But death is merely the device of nature to make more life; it does not

[1] Thomson and Geddes, *Life, Outlines of General Biology* (Harper & Bros., New York, 1931), vol. I, p. 48.
[2] The change is difficult to detect in unicellular, uniparental life; but it does occur. See the article by H. S. Jennings, "Can We See Evolution Occuring?" in *Creation by Evolution*, compilation by F. Mason (The Macmillan Co., New York, 1928).

seem to matter if one combination of germ plasm fails to fit the environment; tomorrow a new combination will be born, and it may fit better than any other that has gone before. The organism is like wax that can be shaped until it fits its mold. The mold does not change to fit the wax. When the supposedly dog-like progenitors of the seal developed a hankering for the sea, they had to undergo a physical modification to fit them for life in the sea; the water did not change to fit them. Compared to the plastic germ substance of their bodies, the water was rigid and unchanging. Indeed, the environment is simply the conservative of the universe; it does not change to fit each radical new aspirant to life. It seems that the radical does not always know exactly what it wants. The environment furnishes a standard, and the progressiveness or unprogressiveness of all change may be measured by it. In the case of all lower creatures it is the organism that is plastic, adaptable, and easily molded. It must be fitted to its environment, not its environment to itself.

The fitting of human life to its environment is the great concern of the sociologist. He is eager to study the ways by which men may acquire means for satisfying their desires in the social world which they inhabit. They are physical organisms; and their world-social milieu is a complicated one, and quickly changing, but it changes without regard to the needs of individual men. They must conform even to a changing environment.

To describe society in its functioning with anything approaching completeness the sociologist must make constant reference to attributes and characteristics the very essence of which is inseparable from the concept of a dynamic adaptation. Human beings must consider themselves in terms of their environment and must endeavor to make their relation to that environment one of harmony. Deep down at the very spring of human fitness there is the more fundamental relation of a two-fold character — the biologic and the sociologic — in which it expresses itself. In human adaptation, natural inheritance, fundamental as it is in determining successful or unsuccessful adjustment, is supplemented by another important factor conditioning its success or failure: social inheritance. The former might be called the subjective factor, the latter the objective. The social fabric, however, is never a reality in the same sense as the biologic make-up, although adjustment to it is essential to effective existence. A nice balance between the specialization and the plasticity of the social fabric is vital to its existence.

B. The Method of Adaptation

1. *Variation.* Passive physical adaptation, it is now agreed, is the result of organic evolution. Were it not for the fear of reviving the doctrine of design, or of attributing a rational purpose to a natural process, one might almost say that adaptation was the end of every phase of evolution. Certainly an organism that becomes perfectly adapted to its environment is not expected to evolve any further, until the environment changes. Even under perfect adaptation of the species as a whole there will surely be variations among individual organisms, but every variation from the normal type would be less fit for the environment than the normal, the standard, or the typical individual. Hence none of the variants would be selected for survival at the expense of the typical individuals. There would be no remolding or further modification of the organism to fit it better for its environment.

a. Darwin. Darwinism has thus far, perhaps, been made to appear a sufficient description of the evolutionary process. But Darwinism has had, since its first promulgation, a great many critics who have added much to scientific knowledge of passive physical adaptation.[1] There were four important facts about the world that Darwin tied together in his theory of evolution; it may be well to list them briefly, even at the expense of repeating them, so that Darwinism as it stands today, somewhat amended, may be easily compared with the original.

[1] It seems hardly necessary to make note of the books and articles that appear from time to time, presenting evidence against the doctrine of evolution. These books are not generally written by practising scientists. In a compilation by E. M. Phelps, *Evolution* (H. W. Wilson Co., New York, 1926), there is a bibliography of anti-evolutionary literature.

First, Darwin learned from Malthus to correlate two great facts, 1. that life tends to reproduce itself in large numbers. 2. That only a limited number of any form of life can live in a limited area.

Second, he realized that when food grows scarce there is a struggle to possess it.

Third, the issue of the struggle depends somewhat on the powers and capacities of the contestants.

Fourth, those contestants whose powers and capacities give them an advantage in the struggle survive. The environment sifts out and eliminates those with inferior powers for carrying on the struggle. The social evolutionist sees that the same set of facts determine the survival and development of social groups. Groups as well as individuals evolve by variation and survival.

Most biologists admit [remarks J. A. Thomson] [1] what Darwin himself clearly recognized, that in strictness the real process is natural elimination. As an American biologist says: "The fit are not selected — it is the unfit who fail to survive, and the fit are merely the survivors. . . . A railway train selects its passengers in the same sense — those who come in time get aboard, those who do not get left." (Thus) . . . although the process is negative, the results are in part positive.

If there is any one in doubt as to the reality and effectiveness of natural selection, he should consult the evidence which Thomson presents quite briefly in this same book.

The critics of Darwin to be considered at this point are biologists who have centered their attention on the part of the evolutionary process which accounts for the way individuals vary physically, from one generation to another.

Natural selection [says R. A. Fisher in his recent book] is not evolution. Yet ever since the two words have been in common use, the theory of natural selection has been employed as a convenient abbreviation for the theory of evolution by means of natural selection, put forward by Darwin and Wallace. . . . The overwhelming importance of evolution to the biological sciences partly explains why the theory of natural selection should have been so fully identified with its role as an evolutionary agency, as to have suffered neglect as a principle worthy of scientific study . . .

[1] *Darwinism and Human Life, op. cit.*, p. 193, footnote.

when the theory was first put forward, by far the vaguest element in its composition was the principle of inheritance. No man of learning or experience could deny this principle, yet, at the time, no approach could be given to an exact account of its working.[1]

They agree that, fundamentally, Darwin was correct as far as he went, that he simply did not go far enough. It seems incredible to these critics that the amazing ways in which the myriad parts of life are made to fit together, both in structure and function, can be accounted for by a theory of evolution which assumes that the natural selection of chance variations is the really important part of the process by which adaptation is secured.

Such a theory seems to them almost as incredible as the older theological dogma of design by some supreme intelligence. "When the onlooker asks the biologist for a straightforward exposition of the present status of the evolutionary hypothesis, he is frequently met with the guarded statement that biologists are no longer so sure that they know how evolution occurred, but are more certain than ever that it has occurred."[2] There must be some principle, they say, that will explain the origin of variations. Such a principle, if found, will explain how adaptation takes place. They seem, some of them at least, reluctant to accept chance or sporadic variation as a means of explaining how the fit came to be born. For how, they ask, can natural selection choose the fittest — or even the fitter — organisms for survival, until at least the fit are born? Control birth, they argue; control variation; learn how the "fittest" come into the world. Then it will be possible to predict how natural selection must inevitably act, how adaptation can be secured to life. All this does not mean that Darwin's critics believe natural selection ever ceases to be a factor in evolution. They believe simply that a process going on in the birth of life, determining variations, is antecedent to and quite as important

[1] R. A. Fisher, *The Genetical Theory of Natural Selection* (The Clarendon Press, Oxford, 1930).

[2] L. Hogben, *The Nature of Living Matter* (Kegan Paul, French, Trubner & Co. Ltd., London, 1930), p. 129.

as natural selection; that selection is not the prime evolutionary process. To quote again from Fisher: "To treat natural selection as an agency based independently on its own foundations is not to minimize its importance in the theory of evolution. On the contrary, as soon as we require to form opinions by other means than by comparison and analogy, such an independent deductive basis becomes a necessity."[1] In other words, they take up the problem which Darwin tried to solve in his theory of pangenesis. They call that problem fundamental, and attempt to correct and expand Darwin's solution of it. "The central problem of evolution," says Professor Gates, "is still the nature and causes of variation while the practical problems of Eugenics centre about heredity. Variation in past ages has already endowed the human race with an infinite variety of types and characters, many of the latter alternative in their inheritance."[2]

b. Lamarck. The problem cannot be adequately discussed until some mention is made of the theory of inheritance that was formulated by Darwin's eminent predecessor in the study of evolution — Jean Baptiste de Lamarck. Lamarck's work has had great influence on biological thinking.[3] Modern geneticists, a small number of them, who reject Darwin's pangenesis theory, go back still to the premises of Lamarck as being essentially correct. Lamarck accounted for the origin of variations in the action of the environment. Almost any one knows that potatoes grown in good soil are larger than those developed in poor soil. The largeness or smallness of the plant is an effect of the environment. Lamarck believed that such an effect can be inherited. Thus the progeny of well nourished wheat or potatoes start life more robust than was the parent stock at birth; they are born with a variation in their physical make-up toward robustness,

---

[1] L. Hogben, *op. cit.*, p. x.

[2] R. Ruggles Gates, *Heredity in Man* (The Macmillan Co., New York, 1931), p. 1.

[3] His matured views are set forth in his *Philosophie Zoologique* (Dentu, Paris, 1909). For a study of the gradual development of his views, see A. S. Packard, *Lamarck the Founder of Evolution* (Longmans, Green and Co., New York, 1901), chs. XVI and XVII.

which had its origin in the action of the environment, in the richness of the soil where the parent stock grew.

Furthermore, Lamarck argued, the effect of the environment may be cumulative through inheritance. Plants, made more robust by life in a rich environment, produce seedlings more robust at the start of life than their ancestors were. The seedlings, growing more robust, produce seedlings even more robust. Then the process repeats itself, at least until the environment changes enough to start a train of variations in a new direction. Lamarck did not recognize the effect of the environment as being quite the same in the case of animals as of plants. The effect on plants is direct, acting on the constitution of the organism principally through nutrition.

In the case of animals, changes in the environment affect the body indirectly by causing changes of habit. Changes of habit affect the use or disuse of certain organs. The effects of the use and disuse, Lamarck believed, are inherited. In this way he accounted for the origin of variations in animal life. If the food supply on low bushes in a given habitat, for instance, grows scarce, and certain animals are forced to seek their food on trees, there follows a change in grazing habits. The change involves a stretching of the neck; constant use of the neck for stretching results in an elongation of the neck. This elongation is inherited. A slight variation thus makes its appearance in the animal world. The process repeats itself many times, until the origin of a very long neck like the giraffe's can be accounted for, according to Lamarck's theory. There was another way in which Lamarck explained the origin of variations which has not been very much accepted by biologists. He believed that new physical wants are constantly being felt by living creatures which cause changes in their habits. The need of new organs then causes the organs to be born. The need for some kind of gregarious living among men would, by the logic of Lamarck's argument, have necessitated the exercise of vocal organs and this in turn would have caused them to grow or to take on special forms.

All in all, Lamarck's explanation of the cause of variations, which is well summed up in the phrase "the inheritance of acquired characters," presents a theory rather appealing for its apparent logic. And that is true in spite of the fact that common experience is full of instances which indicate that acquired characters are not inherited. The children of parents who have spent their lives using their brains are not necessarily born with better brains than the children of parents who have used their hands all their lives. Cases where this seems to be true are easily accounted for. Persons of superior mentality are more likely to choose intellectual pursuits than are persons of inferior mentality. It is the inborn superior mentality, not the acquired mentality, which is transmitted to children. The tails of sheep have been docked for generations; and yet sheep are not born dock-tailed. A striking instance of the non-inheritance of acquired characters occurs in the case of the bee. How can the worker bee transmit the habits she acquires during her life, or any physical attribute? For the worker bee never reproduces, but is produced in each generation by a queen and a drone quite differently constituted from the worker.

Yet what a perfect solution for the problems of the sociologist Lamarck's theories offer, if they were only true! The sociologist wants to discover how men can become well adapted to their environment. Among other things he is eager to know how to cultivate their social nature, how to make them even approximate the "ultimate man" of Herbert Spencer, a man so well socialized that his private desires coincide with the public good. The Lamarckian can offer this theoretic solution: Let men only practise social goodness, and their children will start life more social of disposition than their parents did. Let the children continue the practice. Their children, in turn, will be born more socialized than they were. The practice of social goodness will have a cumulative effect through inheritance, until human beings are born so physically constituted as to be automatically "good" in the social sense.

c. Weismann. The opponent of Lamarck who did most to show the inadequacy of his explanation of the origin of variations was August Weismann. Weismann reached the conclusion that the germinal substance was the sole conservative force and determiner of development. Hence, modifications due to environmental factors affecting only the external body calls cannot, by their very nature, be inherited. This Weismann substantiated by a number of experimental evidences which indicate that transmission of acquired parental modification to offspring does not take place.

He went further and investigated the origin of sex cells — Hydromedusae, and attempted to prove convincingly that the hereditary units, "germ plasms," in all sexually propagating species are continuous and remain unchanged. These hereditary units are, according to him, the sole factors in the formation of the make-up of the individual. They are capable of assimilation, growth, and multiplication through the process of reproduction by cell division. He says:

> It is their influence which determines the nature of the cell, which, so to speak, impresses it with the specific stamp, and makes the young cell a muscle-cell or a nerve-cell, which even gives the germ-cell the power of producing, by continued multiplication through division, a whole multicellular organism of a particular structure and definite differentiation, in short, a new individual of the particular species to which the parents belong.[1]

Weismann studied the mechanism of heredity until he concluded that there is no way by means of which the environment can affect the germ which gives birth to life. All the bodily characteristics of an organism develop from a fertilized egg, from "determiners" in the germ. As the fertilized egg divides into cells which become bone or muscle, or heart or brain, there are a few cells that remain like the original germ cells. These cells that remain undifferentiated from the original germ substance give rise to the egg or sperm that gives birth to a new generation. They never become a part of the body of the parent; they are simply encased by the parent body, live in it, generally, though not always, unaffected by outside influence. Variations, if they arise, originate in the germ plasm, and then appear in the grown organism.

---

[1] A. Weismann, *Vortrage*, translated by J. Arthur Thomson (Edward Arnold & Co., London, 1904), p. 287.

HUMAN ADAPTATION 205

Heredity is the transmission of the physical nature of the parent to the offspring. We have seen that this transmission affects the whole organism and extends to the most trifling details, and we also know that it is never complete, and that the offspring and parent are never identical, but that the former always differs more or less from the latter. These differences give rise to the phenomenon of variation, which forms an integral part of heredity, for the latter always includes the former.[1]

The mechanism of variation he explains as follows:

The elements of germ plasm — i.e., the biphors and determinants — are subject to continual changes of composition during their almost interrupted growth, and these very minute fluctuations which are imperceptible to us, are the primary cause of the greater deviations in the determinants, which we finally observe in the form of individual variation.[2]

The Lamarckian still has something to say for his side. He has at least offered an explanation of the origin of variation. To explain that a variation exists because it possesses survival value in a given environment does not explain its emergence. Weismann with all his attempts offered only a refutation of Lamarckism rather than a very positive theory of the origin of variation. There is strong evidence in favor of the truth of his refutation, more evidence than there is space to give here. For instance, Castle and Phillips have transplanted the ovaries of a young black female guinea-pig into the body of a mature albino deprived of her ovaries. The grafted animal was mated with an albino male. Had she not been deprived of her ovaries, it is certain that she would have given birth to albino young. Instead, between six months and a year following her operation, she produced three litters, six individuals altogether, all black. It seems that if outside influence in the body of the mother could have affected the transplanted ova some indication of the influence would have evidenced itself.[3]

Lamarck's theories, however successfully they were refuted by Weismann and his followers, filled none the less a gap in

[1] A. Weismann, *The Germ Plasm, A Theory of Heredity*, translated by W. N. Parker (Walter Scott, Ltd., London, 1893), p. 410.
[2] *Ibid.*, p. 417.
[3] See Castle, *Heredity in Relation to Evolution and Animal Breeding* (D. Appleton and Co., New York, 1911), ch. II.

the story of evolution which Darwin tried to fill by "pangenesis," and which Weismann himself recognized and attempted to fill. Weismann remarked, ". . . I should like once again to call attention to the deficiency which is necessarily involved in the assumption of any selection, sexual selection included, namely, that the first beginning of the character which has been intensified by selection remains obscure."[1] Weismann, in other words, felt the need of explaining how variations arise that are well enough adapted to their environment to survive at all, to say nothing of what causes the fitter or the fittest variations to be born. He finally adopted two theories, one of which, especially, modern biologists have come to recognize as important.

It has always seemed remarkable, even to strict Darwinians, that there should arise spontaneously in the germ plasm variations that cause exactly the same line of change to take place in the organism as the environment has demanded for survival. Selectionists, for instance, who argue that the long neck of the giraffe is the result of the selection of long-neck variations appearing spontaneously in the germ plasm, find it difficult to maintain that these variations toward long-neckedness are mere chance, that there is no connection at all between the environment and the formation of the germ. Weismann, in order to account for the origin of variations similar to what the environment demands of the body for its survival, concluded that the environment might affect the body and the germ plasm at the same time; he invented an hypothesis of the parallel modification of body and germ. In this way, he did not need to discover any mechanism by means of which environmental effects on the body could be transferred to the germ.

Are variations purely sporadic, or is there a tendency to vary in the direction of adaptiveness? Pure and unmodified Darwinism assumes that variations are sporadic. Those which happen to fit, survive; those which do not happen to fit, perish; in the course of time, the only ones left are those which fit. In the absence of evidence to the contrary, it was assumed to

[1] *The Evolution Theory*, tr. J. A. and M. R. Thomson (Edward Arnold, London, 1904), vol. I, p. 38.

be safer to accept chance or sporadic variations as the explanation. To assume that there is a tendency to vary in the direction of adaptation, rather than to vary sporadically, is to assume
something which looks very much like intelligence in material
things. Cannon has given a title to his recent book *The Wisdom
of the Body* which, from a different angle, points towards the
same idea.

However, there have been a number of experiments in recent
years which seem to prove that the environment may affect the
germ directly, even without affecting the body.[1] Tower, for
instance, has experimented with potato beetles and similar insects. He varied the temperature and humidity of their environment, and found that hereditable variations in pigmentation
arose in the offspring, even though the bodies of the parents were
not affected. Experiments of Stockard seem to show that
alcohol may affect the germ cells as well as the body of animals;
that the germs of guinea-pigs intoxicated regularly with alcohol
are so weakened that offspring are born weak and sickly.[2] However, this may be the result of pre-natal poisoning. Experiments
of Müller with Drosophila (fruit-fly) show that X-rays may
cause alterations in the germ — even to the extent of causing
changes in particular "genes" (units of the germ).[3]

Weismann went further in accounting for the origin of variations than the setting forth of his theory of the parallel modification of the body and the germ substance. He surmised that

[1] Most of the illustrations following are taken from Castle, *Genetics and Eugenics*
(Harvard University Press, Cambridge), 1921, especially from ch. III, "Are Acquired Characters Inherited?"

[2] See the *Journal of Heredity* for June 1929, which is entirely devoted to the
discussion of the effects of X-rays and Radium in producing changes in genes
and chromosomes. Castle remarks in connection with the work of Muller, "None
of these occurrences (changes in the germ) is different in kind from such as are
observed in untreated pedigreed cultures of Drosophila, but their rate of occur-
ence is increased, Müller estimates, up to as much as 150 times, the amount of
increase varying with the X-ray dosage."

[3] H. S. Jennings, in his *Biological Basis of Human Nature* (W. W. Norton &
Co. Inc., New York, 1930), remarks, ". . . germ cells carry cytoplasm as well as
genes (the units of the germ, determining inheritance), and . . . poisons in the
body of the parent might injure this cytoplasm in such a way as to make the
individuals developed from these germ cells defective without actual injury to
the genes" (p. 333).

there may be, among the unit determiners of heredity in the germ, a struggle for nourishment as the germ develops. He does not try to say how the determiners are determined, or how they vary; and it seems to be a matter of chance which determiner gets nourishment, grows and gives rise to a "plus" variation in the body of the organism. If a determiner is not nourished, no variation arises in the body to correspond to the determiner. Such germinal selection, through the nourishment of the developing germ, provides variations from which natural selection chooses individuals for survival.

Perhaps it may have become evident, in the course of this rather complicated account of heredity, that neither the school of Weismann nor of Lamarck really escapes the ultimate fact that there is something inherently variable in the very nature of germ plasm which is the root and origin of variation. It is here that we find the plasticity which enables life to be molded by its environment. Meanwhile, there can be no harm in suggesting that variation is only another name for imperfect heredity, or the inexact reproduction of parents in offspring. If children resembled their parents exactly, all the children of the same parents would be exactly alike, but they are not. If we could find a species of organism that had lived in an unchanging environment for a few million years, it would be interesting to study the variations which exist in the same generation. Comparison could then be made with the variations which exist in a relatively new species which has not yet begun to "breed true."

d. DeVries. A Dutch botanist at the very beginning of the twentieth century did a great deal to set the world thinking about the spontaneity of variations. Hugo deVries distinguished between what he considered temporary fluctuating variations and mutations. The first, he believed, appear in a plant as a result of changes in nutrition. A "garden environment," he thought, is a cause of variation, and may even affect the germ, but only temporarily. The selection of variations of this fluctuating type, minor differences of size, for instance, may modify a whole plant species, change the average appearance; but the plant returns to its original condition if selection ceases to be effective.[1] Mutations, deVries held, are variations that arise spontaneously in the germ. They do not have their origin in the environment; they are never necessarily fitted to the environment where they arise. The environment simply determines which mutations are to survive. Mutations are not minute variations; they are large, well marked changes. They are the real raw material of evolution and selection; they are permanent variations, capable of giving rise to new species. In the case of the evening primrose, which deVries studied more carefully, these extreme variations which he called mutations, may give rise, rather abruptly, to giant or dwarf species, to smooth-leaved or red-veined types, etc. etc.

The mutation theory, the doctrine that large, well defined variations, arising spontaneously in the germ, are the "stuff" of evolution, has undergone modification. Before anything is said, however, of the modern interpretation of mutation, it is perhaps worth noting, by way of parenthesis, how the idea of spontaneous variation has been helped along by C. Lloyd Morgan in his work on *Emergent Evolution.*[2] Morgan is primarily a philosopher and psychologist. For that reason, he has contributed to an understanding of biological evolution from a philosophical and psychological point of view. In the course of evolution, he holds, life itself and all its forms have "emerged"; they have arisen as new entities that cannot be explained in terms of anything that has ever preceded them into the world. They are a synthesis of what has gone before, just as water is a synthesis of hydrogen and oxygen. Water, however, cannot be explained in terms of the properties of hydrogen and oxygen; it has properties of its own that "emerge," that result from the combination of the two gases. So life cannot be explained in terms of the physics and chemistry of matter, from which it has emerged; nor can conscious life be explained in terms of the biology of unthinking life, from which mind has emerged.

[1] See also Galton, *Hereditary Genius* (D. Appleton & Co., New York, 1870), pp. 363–376.
[2] Williams and Norgate, London, 1923.

It follows, from the logic of Morgan, that every new organism born on earth may be regarded as an "emergence" in evolution, as a new life synthesis. If that be true, since life emerges through a germ substance, the synthesis must arise somehow through the germ.[1] Geneticists know enough about the birth of life to believe that there are units — genes and chromosomes — in the germ that are variously combined in the fertilization of the egg by the sperm. The secret of emergence may lie in the spontaneous and unpredictable way the genes combine in the germ to form new life. New characters are known to appear as the result of germinal changes in the alignment of genes and chromosomes. Once having appeared these changes may in turn give rise to realignments and new synthesis, to variations without end.

Morgan goes beyond logical proof in his phillsophy of evolution. He confesses it; for he acknowledges emergent evolution as the expression of Divine Activity, omnipresent and evident in all the "emergences" within his scheme. There is what he calls a "nisus" joining matter to life and mind and leading to the emergence of "deity" in spritual man. " . . . it may be urged," he says "that what at the outset I spoke of as the comprehensive plan of sequence in all natural events, is surely of itself sufficient evidence of Purpose, and this implies, it is said, some mind through whose Activity . . . the course of events are directed."[2] Accepting as he does the directive activity of God in evolution, Morgan introduces something into his account of the development of life which makes it difficult to think of biological variations as spontaneous emergences.[3] It is perfectly legitimate to say that since the quality

[1] In certain forms of life, such as unicellular organisms, the germ is one with the body. It is possible, in the case of unicellular life, that Lamarckism may explain the origin of variations. Lamarck and Morgan do not necessarily offer contradictory theories.

[2] *Ibid.*, p. 32.

[3] William McDougal in his *Modern Materialism and Emergent Evolution* (D. Van Nostrand Co., New York, 1929), asks "What makes emergents emerge? Morgan's answer is the directive activity of God. "But," says McDougal, "It is very difficult to reconcile this with his explicit repudiation of every form of vitalism . . ." (p. 152) McDougal's book contains a general discussion and

of deity has emerged in spiritual man, the genes were combining, from their first emergence, to produce finally that emergent quality of deity. It is legitmate, however, only on philosophical assumptions. It is questionable how far these assumptions will lead the geneticist.[1]

Biologists have not given up the idea of spontaneous variation; but they have considerably modified the ideas of deVries concerning mutation. DeVries labelled only large changes, appearing all at once in the organism, as mutations. These, he thought, must involve such general changes in a living thing as would cause the origin of a new species each time they occurred. Modern students of genetics have studied such mutations, until they feel reasonably certain how they arise. Conspicuous variations, involving sometimes many characters of an organism at once, appear to involve conspicuous changes in the germ that gives them birth. The characters of an organism are determined by units in the germ that have many times been mentioned already as genes. These genes — if the matter may be explained very simply without technicalities — line up in the germ into bars or strings called chromosomes. In the realignment of the chromosomes that takes place when the egg is fertilized by the sperm, there are known to occur changes in the number of sets of chromosomes (they usually appear in two sets); or else there may occur a change in the structure of a particular chromosome, a breaking in two of a chromosome and a fusing of a section of one with another, involving a realignment of the genes within the chromosome.[2] These chromosome

criticism of emergent evolution and should be read. See especially chs. v–vi, and the notes in the Appendix which refer to various versions in the theory of emergence.

[1] McDougal comments: "The principle of creative synthesis seems to be true of Mind or of mental events, and the term 'emergent' may conveniently be applied to the products of such synthesis. But there has been no emergent evolution in the physical realm. . . . There has been no evolution of mind from the physical realm, but evolution of mental capacities; and this evolution has been characterized by a progressive differentiation of the powers of mind rather than by emergence of new kinds of relation, causal or other. Mind everywhere at all levels is teleological, cognitive, conative and affective." *Ibid.*, p. 155.

[2] *Op. cit.* See especially ch. xiv, "How the Inherited Constitution Becomes Changed. The Origin of Diverse Organic Types." See also Castle, *op. cit.*, ch. vi.

changes cause simultaneous changes in a large number of characters in an organism, — as many characters as are represented
by the genes which are contained in the lost or duplicated or
split chromosome. Chromosome changes, apparently spontaneous are undoubtedly the cause of such mutations as impressed
deVries. Yet Castle says, "This kind of mutation cannot be
regarded as a satisfactory general explanation of the origin of
species, the thing which deVries had in mind when he proposed
the theory, because except among the higher plants comparatively few species differ from each other by whole chromosomes
and become incapable of interbreeding, when they do."[1]

Geneticists believe now that there are mutations more important, in the study of general evolution, than chromosome
variations. There are mutations, apparently spontaneous variations, in single genes that have a vast cumulative effect on
evolution. These changes are "discontinuous," in the way
deVries defined mutation: — *i.e.*, they are stable in inheritance.

Intensive experimental study of heredity [says Castle] shows that small
genetic differences are inherited no less strongly than large ones, and that
actual species, when they can be crossed, are found to differ in a large
number of small particulars rather than in a few large ones. . . . Mutation on this present-day view, is *any heritable change*, whether it affects
only a single inheritance unit (gene) . . . or whether it affects whole
chromosomes . . . fluctuating variability is not to be regarded, as it was
in the view of deVries, as something impermanent and fleeting. In it may
be found minor genetic changes which are permanently mingled with
environmental effects which are transitory. Only selection can serve to
distinguish and separate the former from the latter.[2]

The point has now been reached in this discussion of the
origin of variations, where the question obtrudes itself: What
has genetic study actually discovered that is really of much
help to the sociologist concerned with the problem of passive

---

[1] Castle, *Genetics and Eugenics* (Harvard University Press, Cambridge), 1930,
p. 330. The higher plants that have been studied with great profit for the knowledge that has been gained of chromosome mutation are the evening primrose by
Gates and others; roses by Harrison and others; and the jimson-weed by Blakeslee.
See both Castle and Jennings.

[2] *Op. cit.*, p. 126.

physical adaptation? Have geneticists really added much of positive value to Darwinism? Have they showed at all convincingly that physical variations in their origin are pre-adapted to the environment in such a way that natural selection has not the primary importance which Darwin gave to it? The answer, it must be admitted, is for the most part inconclusive. The most that can apparently be said for Lamarckism — which, if it were true, would offer a very clear-cut answer to the question and relegate Darwinism to quite a secondary place as a description of the evolutionary process — is that the environment is known directly to cause variation, but not necessarily of an adaptive sort. The effects of use and disuse have not yet been convincingly shown to be inherited.

e. Morgan. There seems, in fact, a degree of spontaneity in the variability of the germ, whether it be in the way the genes combine in the fertilization process or in the substance of the genes or in both together. The spontaneity is not absolutely unpredictable; it is relative, the variations waver always about a mean line of change. From a philosophic point of view, Lloyd Morgan suggests that evolution has taken place along a "nisus" leading to God. From a scientific point of view, it is possible to say, as Müller suggests, that the cause of variation is not God, but the radiations which the earth sends forth. Variations none the less occur along an average line of variation. However changeful is the universe, the nature of change is never such that the occurrence of variation cannot be reduced, in the long run, to general law. Darwin is somewhat confirmed — although in a righteous spirit of agnosticism on the part of still incredulous biologists — in his belief that natural selection, acting like a seive on all kinds of physical variations, separates the adapted from the undapted; that natural selection is a truly vital process in the adaptation of life to its environment. The direction which the average line of variation is to take in evolution is determined by natural selection.

f. Mendel. The modern theory of mutations cannot be understood apart from Mendelism. Variations, large or minute, although they appear constantly and spontaneously in the germ, occur within a system of inheritance that is regular and to a very large extent predictable, lawful, and not wholly "spontaneous." This system is called Mendelism. Gregor Mendel was an obscure monk-gardener and teacher of physical science at Brünn who was clever enough to pick out plants for breeding which were almost identical in their traits. They differed in one or two characters so markedly that the behavior of these traits in inheritance could be easily watched. Most scientists before Mendel had not watched the genetic behavior of a simple, well marked trait; so they were puzzled to account for the inheritance of a hundred characters all at once that never seemed to behave in a definite way. It is fair to say, in passing, that other plant breeders discovered what Mendel did, independently of him — deVries, Correns, Tschermak. Mendel's work, in fact, was not known until the re-discovery of it by deVries some forty years after it had been first published (in 1866), when the Austrian Abbot was given credit for his pioneering.

Mendel experimented with the breeding of ordinary garden peas. He found that if two varieties of pea, differing in some marked trait, are bred together, the offspring bear the trait as it appears in only one of the parent plants. A pea with a yellow seed, for instance, may be crossed with a green-seeded pea. Yellow-seeded peas, Mendel found, resulted from the cross. But he found further, if plants are bred from these yellow-seeded offsprings, by the self-fertilization of the plant or by crossing with plants of the same ancestry, there are produced peas that do not all have yellow seeds; they are born yellow-seeded and green-seeded in a three to one proportion. The green-seeded ones breed true to green, if crossed among themselves. And one-third of the yellow breed yellow. But the other yellow, if breed among themselves, produce yellow and green seeds in a three to one proportion. Mendel called the yellow character "dominant" and the green "recessive."

He believed that for each trait in a plant there is a determiner in the germ which gives it birth. In the crossing of yellow and green-seeded peas, the socalled F_1 (first filial) generation, he thought, receives a determiner for yellow seeds (y) and a determiner for green seeds (g) — one for each parent. But the y determiner is dominant; and so y, and not g (recessive) expresses itself in the grown-up pea. The F_1 generation, however, produces germ cells that carry, half the y determiner and half the g. The determiners are thus segregated, so when these germs breed, if there be granted an equal chance for a germ cell carrying a y determiner to join a germ carrying a y or a g, and for a g to join a y or a g, it follows that plants carrying yy, yg, gy, and gg determiners will be born. Since y is dominant, the peas of the F_2 (second filial) generation will bear yellow and green seeds in the proportion of three to one.

Mendelism, it is obvious, becomes increasingly complicated as the number of unit characters in which the parent stocks differ becomes larger. It remains, none the less, a statistical method of foretelling, so far as the unit characters of the parent stock are known, the traits which will appear in the offspring of a plant or animal. It enables the biologist to predict rather accurately the variations of heredity. But Mendelism, as it has been so far described, is a rather crude biological tool. The doctrine has been modified and enlarged by biological research since the days of Mendel, until now the original laws of heredity look like mere skeletons.

In the first place, Mendel did not know, in the 1860's, the mechanism by which the determiners, for yellow- and green-seeded peas — for instance, could segregate in the germ cells of the F_1 generation in such a way that the F_1 peas were born yellow- and green-seeded in a 3:1 proportion. It has since been found that the determiners, or factors of heredity, are carried in the chromosomes of the germ. A plant or animal is born with pairs of chromosomes, one of each pair contributed by each parent; the F_1 peas carry thus in a pair of chromosomes determiners for both yellow and green seeds. Now it is known that, in the maturing of the F_1 germ cells, the pair of chromosomes separates by a mechanism which gives to each mature germ only one of the pair of chromosomes. The process by which this happens can be described only in technical language which is best used by the biologist; the essential point to remember here is that the separating of the chromosome pairs explains how a mature germ of an F_1 pea carries the determiner for green or for yellow seeds only. It can be understood then how such germs when self-fertilized can give rise to an F_2 generation carrying either pure yellow or pure green or yellow-green determiners in the germ plasm.

Complications in the heredity mechanism bring about variations in offspring beyond what a simple description of Mendelism would imply. Determiners originally found in the same chromosome ("linked") may later become separated through the splitting or breaking apart of a chromosome, producing in consequence a combination of characters in the offspring theretofore impossible. A single trait may be dependent not upon one, but upon many determiners, with the result that a great many combinations become possible; although this acts in a normal Mendelian way, the inevitable variety in the offspring is confusingly great. Conversely, a single determiner may affect more than one trait, and these in varying degrees. Or a trait may have two independent determiners which when combined in the same individual produce a sort of intensification of the trait. The Mendelian ratios — the 3:1 and the 9 : 3 : 3 : 1 ratios — are invariable only as to the final units in heredity; since almost any human trait is the result of a combination of heredity units, and since rarely would two individuals differ in only one of these units, the whole heredity process becomes exceedingly complex. Nevertheless, within the mechanism of inheritance lies the origin of much physical variation, in the re-shufflings and re-arrangements of the genes and chromosomes and all the intricate changes that take place in the germ plasm through its maturation and fertilization. Mendelism offers a method of plotting these variations; and of foretelling the physical makeup of the offspring, when the germinal makeup of the two parent organisms is completely and accurately known.

As to the adequacy of the Mendelian laws of heredity for explaining the origin of all variation there is grave doubt among geneticists today. The genes themselves apparently possess an inherent and spontaneous tendency to mutate which science has not satisfactorily explained. Changes of temperature, treatment with X-ray, and other environmental influences have been found to cause mutations in germ plasm, but whether these are real variations or a hastening of the expression of a difference already inherent is not clear.

We know [says Hogben] that x-rays will produce mutant changes in the chromosomes of the germ cells. . . . If applied sufficiently early in the course of development, radiation with x-rays would then produce bodily changes of a transmissible nature. This possibility resides in the fact that the agent is capable of acting on all the cells of the body in the same way.[1]

But although combinations, reshufflings and duplications of existing genes may give rise to many mutations, they can hardly account for the vast changes which have taken place in organic evolution. In a complete theory the first origin and diversity of these factors must be accounted for. . . . Mutuation . . . must be based on the addition to, subtraction from, or alteration in the factors of inheritance. . . . Since ordinary external stimuli seem to alter the factors but rarely, if at all, it may yet be some day shown that alterations in the genes are due to the inherent instability of the atoms composing them and to the action of certain radiations pervading the environment.[2]

We have called attention to the growing interest in the problem of variation, especially in those extreme variations called mutations. The best opinion among geneticists seems to be to the effect that mutations are the positive, or creative, factors in evolution. Selection, while of great importance, is a negative factor, or at most, permissive. Only those mutations survive which happen to fit the environment. But the occurrence of mutations is the great fact to be accounted for. The study of mutations is, in a sense, the study of nature in her radical or experimental moods. It is in this field of study that the student is likely to stumble on new and previously undreamed-of possibilities. Mutations are the news items in biological history. In the study of selection, we are, in a sense, observing nature in her conservative, skeptical and critical moods. However, this

[1] *Op. cit.*, p. 186.
[2] "Evolution," *Encyclopedia Britannica*, 14th ed., 1929. See the *Proceedings* of the National Academy of Arts and Sciences, vol. xv, 1929, pp. 623 ff., for an account of the work of E. B. Babcock and J. L. Collins on natural radiations and spontaneous mutation.

is a field of study which cannot be neglected by the sociologist.

2. *Sifting.* There is one fact which it is time now, after the origin of variations has been discussed in some detail, to repeat for the sake of emphasis. Variations do not appear in their origin to be preadapted to their environment. They seem to occur spontaneously in the substance of the germ plasm. And they manifest themselves in an almost endless variety of forms through the constant reshuffling and recombining of factors in the germ. The question then intrudes itself: Have biologists offered any real solution to the problem they believe Darwin left unsolved? Darwin held that the course of evolution is determined primarily by the selection for survival of the varieties of life that are best adapted to their environment. His critics say: "Selection is real enough. But equally important as the survival of the fittest is the "arrival of the fittest" (as deVries puts it). Concerning the arrival of the fittest, the origin of variation, geneticists have revealed that, while variations appear to arise quite at random and cannot be shown to be necessarily of an adaptive nature, they are almost always very minor changes. They occur for the most part in small doses within a system of inheritance that is regular, lawful, predictable. So much Mendelism has made clear. Mendelism has explained in a measure how the fit, as well as the unfit, arrive and has thus supplemented Darwinism.

One of the objections that has often been raised against Darwinism is that it does not account for the survival of useless variations. Darwin himself, in the *Descent of Man*, remarked: "I had not formerly sufficiently considered the existence of many structures which appear to be, as far as we can judge, neither beneficial nor injurious, and this I believe to be one of the greatest oversights as yet detected in my work."[1]

Geneticists since Darwin's day, have corrected the oversight satisfactorily enough. If variations appear spontaneously, without relation to the demands of the environment, it is clear that many useless traits may arise. And Mendelism has now

---

[1] Ed. of 1871 (D. Appleton & Co., New York), vol. I, p. 146.

suggested how they may survive, even though they be slightly harmful: they may be correlated, "linked," with useful traits in inheritance. But the useless traits need not even be so linked, provided they are not actually so harmful as to make a difference in the survival or non-survival of their possessors. Useless traits are simply experiments for selection to work upon. They may not always, of course, be as useless as they appear. They may be related in a way not understood with some vital body function. Useless traits appear to be what might be called incomplete adaptation.

Concerning such useless traits, Lester F. Ward remarks: "A character which required to be complete before it could be advantageous could never be acquired by natural selection. All such characters as are acquired must be advantageous in proportion as they are complete."[1] This explains well enough why the initial stages in the development of a trait may seem useless. They need to be advantageous only in a proportionate sense. Moreover, as Ward suggests, general traits, possessed in common by all organisms, can develop more completely than special traits possessed by a given species in relation to a definite environment. Complete development in the one case would not mean, as in the other, specialization at the expense of organic plasticity. This explanation of the survival of apparently useless traits in biological evolution may have an important bearing on the survival of purely cultural traits in social evolution. Yet Mendelism, while it has gone beyond Darwin, points back to the important Darwinian doctrine that it is the selection of organisms, varying in the direction of fitness for their environment, their survival and propagation, which determines the course of evolution.

It may be asked, What about the variations that arise spontaneously in the substance of the germ? Can it be said that these vary in a direction that is favored and determined by selection? According to Castle, it can not. But surviving varia-

[1] From an essay, "Incomplete Adaptation as Illustrated by the History of Sex in Plants," included in *Glimpses of the Cosmos* (G. P. Putnam's Sons, New York and London, 1913–18), vol. II, p. 317.

tions, he says, may occur chiefly or exclusively in the direction of utility. He insists that the modern theory of mutation is a theory of evolution by mutation in single genes. Whole chromosomes may split and rearrange themselves in heredity; but there are only a few species where such splitting occurs with any frequency, and such splitting almost never represents wholesale mutation of germ substance. Changes in single genes may occur spontaneously, the frequency of mutation being determined perhaps, as Müller suggests, by natural radiation. It follows, in any case, says Castle,

> that a blending character, which by hypothesis depends on the joint action of many independent genes, will vary only gradually, since mutation in a gene at a time will produce only minor changes. Mutation in such cases will not be mutation at all except in name, but will consist of a gradual change in the direction favored by selection.[1]

The attention of scientists has frequently been taken away from selection and placed more exclusively upon mutation, simply because it has not been recognized how tremendous the effect of selection may be, acting through thousands of generations on very small variations. The two processes are in no sense contradictory or in conflict. Mutation (i.e. change, great or small, in the gene content of the germ cells) produces heritable variation; natural selection determines *what* heritable variations shall survive. If variation is infinitesimal from one generation to another, it seems hardly credible that the selection of this rather than that variation can make much difference in evolution. Variations, it seems, must appear from time to time sufficiently marked to be recognized as qualitative differences, one arising possibly out of another but of so different a nature that the one can by no known mathematical or scientific method be described in terms of the other. A variation, it is true, may represent a synthesis of what has gone before (this may be true of gene mutation), rather than a purely additive result (as in Mendelism); but the variation may be slight. And selection acting on such variations may in time produce stupendous re-

[1] Castle, *op. cit.*, pp. 330–331.

sults. Matter need not "jump" to life; nor life to mind; nor species to species. The point cannot be dwelt upon. DeVries in biology, Lloyd Morgan in psychology and philosophy, represent a "cataclysmic" school of evolutionists who have led students to exaggerate the "jumps" in evolution and so to underestimate selection.

It was said, a good many pages back, that the sociologist is concerned in the physical fitness of human beings for life in the world which surrounds them. Because men are physical organisms, like all living creatures, the social scientist cannot escape an interest in the way plants and animals are made to fit their environment in nature. Passive physical adaptation, biologists agree, is secured to living things through organic evolution. They disagree, however, concerning the method by which evolution takes place. Darwin has so far led the field in his description of the method. His work, however, has been supplemented by a great amount of important experimenting and theorizing, especially in the direction in which Mendel led the way. By way now of summarizing the theories that have been discussed concerning the method of evolution, a quotation from Julian S. Huxley is brief and to the point: "Although we know a good deal more about the method of evolution than did Darwin or any of his immediate successors, we are still in doubt as to a great many points. But we are not in the least doubt as to the fact of evolution."[1]

C. Fitness for Social Life

It is perhaps clear now that the sociologist, with the problem on his hands of molding physical human nature to a complex world, is not faced with an altogether simple solution. The genetic knowledge for which he counts on the biologist for help is still largely hypothesis and uncertainty. The time will no doubt come — and possibly soon, for geneticists are hard at work — when enough will be known concerning determinate variation, or perhaps the inheritance of acquired characters.

[1] "Evolution." *Encyclopaedia Britannica*, 14th ed., 1929, vol. VIII, p. 916.

What is at present known concerning the origin of new variations points to the importance of selection in determining their survival only, not in causing their production. The social scientist is bound to accept the conclusion of biology that selection is an indispensable agency in evolution and hence in adaptation. Using selection as a guiding principle, he has Mendelism to help him anticipate the result of selection. He is faced with difficult questions from the very start.

What are the human traits, the sociologist is bound to ask, that have the highest survival value in the human environment? And how can these most economically, by selection, be made to inherit the earth? J. Arthur Thomson, in his book *Concerning Evolution,*[1] suggests that the selective process is a rather complicated one in nature; that nature, in determining what shall live or die, puts living things through more than one sifting process.

The sifting [of Natural Selection] will vary according to the nature of the "struggle," whether it is between fellows of the same kith and kin, or between foes quite different in nature; or it may be non-competitive — the organism pitting itself against the callous physical fates. Or the sifting will vary according to the need which brings about the clash. It may be for food, for foothold, for a place in the sun, for a mate or for a harem, or for room for a cradle. The struggle may be for luxuries; it may be for self-satisfaction and self-preservation, or it may be concerned with the welfare of the offspring. Even among animals it may rise into an endeavor after well-being.

More than this, there is change in the criteria of survival, the physical qualities demanded for success in living. It may be, now, brains or speed or cunning; at another time, muscle or the ability to lie low, or sheer fertility. But there is still another way of looking at the facts. The evolutionary sieve itself evolves. Food requirements persistently shift. Then there are peculiarities of the physical environment, like temperature, that occasionally come into great prominence as sieves. There is the animate environment,— the competitors, neighbors, partners, parasites of an organism,— that sift its life possibilities.

[1] Yale University Press, New Haven, 1925, p. 137.

Flora and fauna are sieves to one another. There is the sieve of sexual selection. A social environment is another sieve that concerns man very much.[1]

> The fact is, we are returning to an appreciation of the subtlety of Darwin's concept of selection [says Thomson]. It is not one process, but many — lethal and reproductive, for instance; it operates in relation to an intricate web of life . . .; there has been an evolution of sieves as well as of the material to be sifted . . . the struggle for existence, in the course of which selection occurs, includes not only competitive but symbiotic — not only egoistic but altruistic reactions, and both pay![2]

This whole selective process going on in nature affects man because he is a part of nature. Yet, as Thomson says, there is a sieve that affects man especially. Human beings have to pass through the meshes of a social environment or else perish. Nature sifts men in groups; survival in a group, from the point of view of the individual, means survival in nature. The individual is put through the process of a social sifting, of proving himself fit for social life. And groups also are being sifted. Ultimately the individual is concerned with the survival of the group in which he exists, with the fitness of the group for existence in the physical world of nature. The selective process, as it applies to man, is unique; and yet man is ultimately enmeshed in the universal sifting of nature.

The social environment, the peculiarly human sieve in the selective process, is pliable in the hands of man. Within limits, men can construct their own sieves. Human beings, it was pointed out at the beginning of this chapter, have acquired, with the development of intellect, a power of active adaptation. They are not entirely dependent on the passive process of biological evolution for securing to themselves a fitness for living. Instead of waiting to be organically fitted to their environment, they change the environment to fit themselves. They can design a sieve for the sifting of men in order that the kind of men the ruling power does not like can be extinguished, and those

---

[1] See Thomson, *op. cit.*, pp. 139–143.
[2] *Ibid.*, p. 145.

whom the ruling power happens to approve may be selected for survival. Such is the effect of every criminal code.

The sociologist cannot forget this, even in his study of passive physical adaptation. Since man has it in his power to change the environment to fit himself, he has his own survival, to that extent, in his own hands. It was said some pages back that it is life which is charged always with the problem of adaptation because, relatively to the environment, life is a plastic thing. The intellect of man renders the environment relatively plastic, and so the growth of intellect is the beginning of a revolution in evolution. Before the intellect grew to a measure of strength, it was always the environment that picked this or that variety of plant or animal for survival, according to its fitness for life in its particular surroundings. The environment set a standard of fitness for individual survival. With the appearance of man and mind on the evolutionary scene, one species of animal is able to create its own environment.

Man could say, "The kind of human beings who are fitted to this standard of ours will survive." He set his own standard of fitness for survival. That standard meant, above all, that those human beings who were best fitted for the existing type of social life or social environment would survive. It happened so because the man's power of active adaptation came to be rather directly proportionate to the strength of his group life. The power of man to set his own standard of fitness for survival has increased with the age-long growth of his mind; yet it must never be forgotten for a moment that the power is limited, now as it always has been. For the human standard ultimately conforms to nature's standards; and if there is serious conflict, it is the human standards that must adapt themselves to those of nature. Man can say, "This, and not that, kind of human being has the traits that will be allowed to survive in this social group or that." He can set what standard he will for individual survival in a group. But he is helpless as a determiner of what type of group life shall survive. The group itself has to face the rigid physical demands of nature; the group must struggle with other groups for survival, and nature is the ultimate and impartial arbiter in the struggle. Thus it is that, if man is wise, the standard of fitness that he sets for individual survival will never be such as will weaken the survival chances of the group. It will be such, rather, as will promote the group's survival.

Passive physical adaptation does not become a superfluous field of study in sociology, just because man has it in his power to control his environment, in a measure, and so to set his own standard of fitness for survival. Human beings simply have to be adapted organically to a man-made rather than to a purely "natural" environment. It becomes the job of the sociologist to make a study of the physical and psychical traits which must be demanded by the group for individual survival in the group — that is, if the group itself is to survive. He must decide two things: first, what individual traits, in surviving, will promote the survival of the group; and, second, how can these be cultivated in the human organism? The first problem is sociological; the second genetic and must be solved by the geneticist.

Again, the analogy of the athletic team is useful. The members of the team must be selected, and they must be trained. Those candidates most likely to contribute to the success of the team must be accepted and those less likely must be rejected. No great and enduring society can be built on any other foundation. The captain or the coach of an athletic team has definite ideas as to what kind of men he wants, and how he wants them trained. In general, he wants men who can be trained to do, with vigor and precision, what he wants them to do. The members of the great society are not chosen in the same way. They are chosen first, by being born into it and second, by being permitted to reproduce. If they are intelligently chosen it is by the eugenic laws and practices. What kinds of men are needed in the building of a great society or a great nation? On this point the geneticist is not so well qualified to speak as the sociologist, and even he finds it a very perplexing problem.

Next to general health, strength and intelligence, the most desirable quality in members of a great society is that which may be called sociability, or liking for his own kind. How much of this quality is inborn and how much is learned is impossible to say. Even if it is learned, it can not be too often repeated, there has to be an inborn capacity to learn. Besides, it is more easily learned in some circumstances than in others.

It occasions no surprise to see animals of the same species living together in peace and harmony; they do not seem to have to learn to tolerate, or even to like one another. It does occasion surprise to see, in actuality, a lion and a lamb, a cat and a mouse, or any collection of unlike creatures — the "happy family" of our circus days — living in a similar state of harmony. They seem to have to learn even to tolerate one another. If it is true that certain gregarious animals do not have to learn to tolerate or to prefer one another, it must imply some inborn character which makes members of their own species seem more attractive or less repulsive than members of other species. Even if gregariousness is in part learned, still, it seems easier to teach an animal to like its own kind than other kinds. That difference in the ease of learning seems, at least, to be inborn. If so, the gregarious animal, and likewise man, has been to that extent modified, passively, to fit it for group life.

The history of animal domestication seems to show that tractability, which is the essence of sociability, may become an hereditary, organic trait. It is true that if animals domesticated for many generations are turned loose and allowed to run wild on the plains or in the forest for a generation, they seem to become as wild as others which have never been domesticated. Wild cattle of the South American pampas or the western plains of North America seem as wild as bison; the mustang seems as wild as deer or elk. Yet when the "wild" cattle are captured and kept under control for a short time, they soon become tractable and can be yoked, and the females can be used as milch cows. The wild horse, descended from the tame horses brought to this continent by the Spanish conquerors, but escaping to the plains, became, apparently, one of the wildest of animals. No wild creature was more difficult to capture, more swift, wary and cunning in eluding pursuit. Yet, once captured, controlled and ridden, the wild horse very quickly accepted man's dominion and a condition of domestication.[1] Nothing of this kind could ever be so quickly done with a truly wild animal like the bison. It seems logical to believe that through a very long selective process the ancestor of the modern wild horse became domesticated, and that tractability,— variations in that direction having been chosen for breeding purposes,— had long been an hereditary equine trait which a generation or more of wild life could not eradicate.[2] It seems logical to believe that the ease with which an animal may be tamed depends on the previous sociability of its habits,— in other words, artificial selection or animal breeding,— in order to make a start in the breeding of the character called tractability.[3]

If so much is true of domesticated animals, why is it not possible that human beings may be selected for survival because of their innate domesticity, their tractability, their sociability? Experience seems to show that such selection has occurred. The development of a type of man so constituted as to find in himself social impulses is a phase of passive physical adaptation. There is no doubt that sociability may be in a measure trained in human beings; it need not be, for the survival interest of the group, entirely innate. There is, none the less, something organic about it, an innate receptivity to social training, which can be biologically cultivated.

The problem as to how these traits may be most effectively

---

[1] Washington Irving, in his *Tour on the Prairies* describes the quickness with which wild horses are tamed. "Nothing surprised me more," he says, ". . . than to witness how soon these poor animals, thus taken from the unbounded freedom of the prairie, yielded to the dominion of man. In the course of two or three days the mare and the two colts went with the led horses and became quite docile" (J. Murray, London, 1835, p. 228).

[2] Darwin, in the concluding remarks of his work on *The Variation of Animals and Plants under Domestication*, says: "Complete subjugation generally depends on an animal being social in its habits, and on receiving man as the chief of the herd or family. In order that an animal should be domesticated it must be fertile under changed conditions of life, and this is far from being always the case" (O. Judd & Co., New York, 1868, vol. II, p. 400).

[3] "The ease with which most birds, except those of prey, may be reduced to domestication is due to the remarkable intensity of their sympathetic motives," says N. S. Shaler (*Domesticated Animals*, C. Scribner's Sons, New York, 1895).

cultivated is one that must be solved on lines which genetic study suggests. Genetics points to the importance of selecting for breeding purposes parental stock that is the bearer of the traits it is desired to cultivate. The selection of parental stock is a step of the first importance; for succeeding generations will be born with the traits of the parents combined in a definite and predictable way. Genetic study has found this to be true of all kinds and varieties of life. In the case of man, the laws of heredity and the principle of selection work as inevitably as they do in the case of all bi-sexual plants and animals. Genetics, unhappily, knows less about man than about the fruit-fly, and for good reason. The human organism is, for one thing, so complex a bundle of heredity as to elude easy or accurate analysis. Man, moreover, reproduces so slowly as to require centuries, instead of weeks or years, to follow through the behavior of his germ plasm. And he is rather inclined to guard the sacredness of his person; he is reluctant to submit himself to biological dissection. In spite of such difficulties geneticists have been able to learn a great deal about the way human traits combine in heredity. Given two parents, they know roughly what their children will be like. The selection of human parents with such traits as good health and good brains biologists regard as the first step, and the fundamental step, in the cultivation of such traits. If human beings desire to be physically fit for life, children must be produced by parents that are fit. For, as Dr. Bauer points out:

If a nation or a particular stratum of a nation has an inferior hereditary equipment, . . . education and cultural influences may improve individual members of the nation or the stratum, but they cannot alter the stock. The recognition that the extant hereditary equipment of an individual must be regarded as almost inalterable . . . which cannot be modified or eliminated by rearing and education — conflicts sharply with preconceived opinions which are widely current. But neither the biologist nor the physician must allow his scientific insight to be beclouded by such political prejudices.[1]

[1] Bauer-Fischer-Leng, *Human Heredity* (George Allen & Unwin, Ltd., London, 1931), pp. 41–42.

The problem of selecting human parents that are most fit for reproduction involves the human power of active adaptation. It involves the creating of a social environment which will provide the incentive for men and women to marry those who possess traits that are socially desirable. It involves not only marriage laws that will prevent the unfit from breeding, but social customs that will shower social approval on the marriage of the fit. Most biologists are seriously disturbed because, as the life of human beings becomes more and more surrounded with physical comfort, individuals who are physically weak and defective are allowed to live and propagate, when in the struggles of nature they would quickly die and never breed their weaknesses. "Improved conditions," says Jennings, "do not cause genes to become defective; they merely preserve and perpetuate genes that have become defective from other causes. What is required then is to stop perpetuating the defective genes."[1] This clearly implies the importance of selecting good human stock for parenthood. Men and women bearing defective germ plasm must not be allowed to become the parents of future generations.[2] For, as Professor Schiller rightly points out: "If a race becomes progressively feebler in body and mind, it must sooner or later arrive at a condition in which the best doctors cannot save it from the microbes, and the best teachers cannot implant into the young duffers of the next generation the knowledge needed to save society."[3]

[1] *The Biological Basis of Human Nature, op. cit.*, p. 356.

[2] "The fact that most gene mutations are harmful," warns Jennings, "appears disconcerting when applied to man. Civilized men live under conditions resembling the domesticated conditions in which even harmfully mutated breeds of animals survive and propagate . . . it seems to imply the necessity of selective elimination on a vaster scale than is agreeable to contemplate in connection with man" (*ibid.*, pp. 324–325).

[3] F. C. S. Schiller, *Eugenics-Politics* (Houghton Mifflin Co., Boston, 1926).

CHAPTER VII

MORAL ADAPTATION

1. *Morals and Group Survival.* On what ground can you say that one "ought" to be honest, industrious, temperate, brave, or anything else that one "ought" to be? There is only one rational ground on which you can say that one ought to be any of these things. This is on the ground that it contributes to group strength when individuals behave in these ways, and to group weakness when they behave otherwise. In the interest of its own success, or even of its own survival, the group must manage to make its individual members feel that they "ought" to be all these things. It must find some way to give individuals the feeling of "oughtness."[1]

How can the individual be made to feel the sense of "oughtness"; to feel, for example, that he "ought" to be honest, industrious, brave, or temperate? It is the business of the group to make him feel that way. Its survival as a group depends upon its ability to make individuals behave in ways that are good for group life. There are several means by which the group tries to make one feel the sense of "oughtness." They are generally summarized under the name of *mores,*— the social customs, traditions, and conventions, handed down from genera-

---

[1] Of course there are all sorts of groups, and their functions overlap in so many ways as to be very confusing. We may avoid some confusion by summarizing them all under the one word state, as it is used by European writers, or nation, as it is used by American writers to distinguish it from the states of the Union. Under either name we mean the group which determines its own functions and is under the legal control of no other group.

tion to generation. These customs, traditions and conventions are supplemented by such agencies as taboos, religions, and schools.

Those who cannot, by these means, be made to feel the necessary sense of "oughtness," must be controlled. They have to be made to feel a sense of "mustness." Laws, courts, prisons, gibbets, as well as the wrath of neighbors, are means to this end.

While this is the only rational ground for saying that one ought to be this or that, a more compelling reason has been needed. Not every one is rational enough to be convinced by this kind of reasoning. The average person has had to be appealed to in other ways. He can be made to feel that a thing is right or wrong by the *mores*. The average individual is incapable of feeling otherwise than as his group, through its laws, customs, habits, moral standards and religious traditions, have taught him to feel. Nevertheless, there is nothing infallible about the mores. While the mores can make anything seem right, there is no certainty that they are right. All we can say is that if the mores favor conduct which weakens the group, the group will ultimately fail in its struggle with other groups. If the mores favor conduct which strengthens the group it has a much better chance of succeeding. In the long run, those groups will succeed whose mores are such as to promote group strength and those will fail whose mores are such as to promote group weakness. It is in this matter of group strength or group weakness that we must look for a rational basis for ethics.

It is this basis for ethics which Sir Leslie Stephen emphasized in his *Science of Ethics*.[1] He says: "The criterion which I have accepted is, briefly that a man is virtuous or the reverse so far as he does or does not conform to the type defined by the healthy condition of the social organism." Stephen expresses in graphic language the inexorable law of nature according to which strength is rewarded by survival, from which one must conclude that to be strong is the first necessity and the highest virtue of the group: "The law of nature has but one precept, 'Be strong.'

[1] G. P. Putnam Sons, New York, 1882, p. 397.

Nature has but one punishment, decay, culminating in death or extirpation, and takes cognisance of but one evil, the weakness which leads to decay . . . the great law, 'Be strong,' has two main branches, 'Be prudent' and 'Be virtuous' ''.[1]

We see, then, that a law of nature in this sense — that is, in the sense of deriving its authority from its being indispensable to survival — is not necessarily eternal and immutable, but is relative to the conditions of the society in question. As Stephen says, a habit may be a law of nature in the making. Whether it is or is not depends upon whether it does or does not promote the welfare of the group. Just as the biological adjustment of an organism is not to some imaginary environment but to that in which it actually finds itself, so moral adaptation is not to some ideal society living in some ideal environment, but to the needs of the group as it is. For it is the actual group which must somehow manage to survive by using means available to it. Thus morality is "the best relative adjustment, and not the nearest conformity to an ideal standard suited to a perfect state of society. . . . To set up a perfect morality . . . is to set up not only an impracticable, but a false standard, since the only true standard is the relative sociological one founded upon the historical principle of adjustment."[2] However, it must be the best adjustment judged by the objective standard of survival, and not merely what the group may happen to think is right. If that which the group thinks is right is really good for it, the group is fortunate and has a good chance of surviving. If that which it thinks is right is really bad for it, the group is unfortunate and must pay the penalty for its unwisdom.

For long ages human beings, naïve and believing, have imagined that morality was the voice of some god speaking to them in occult ways, telling them, through oracles, medicine-men, prophets, and priests what was good and what was evil, thus ordering their lives. "He hath showed thee, O man, what is good," said the Hebrew Micah, "and what doth the Lord

---

[1] *Ibid.*, p. 172.

[2] Malcolm Guthrie, *On Mr. Spencer's Data of Ethics* (Modern Press, London, 1884), pp. 71–72.

require of thee, but to do justly, and to love mercy, and to walk humbly with thy God?" In the development of morals, this represents what Comte called the theological stage. The time came in Western nations when men grew too self-conscious or too sophisticated to listen to the word of God on the lips of self-appointed intermediaries between man and God. Religious awakenings like the Reformation convinced individuals that God could speak to each one intimately in the inner temple of his own conscience. Only comparatively recently in human history have philosophers dug down deep into the sources of morality and discovered that the source of morality is not external to men, nor a voice speaking to them like a father to his children. God is more likely to be thought of by the modern world as imminent in man. And morality is the voice of groups of men, speaking to individuals in the mores.

When a sufficient degree of sophistication is reached, men are inclined to throw off the belief that the moral law is the voice of God. They, the sophisticates, come to regard that idea as a clever invention of priests and rulers to keep the people in subjection. They no longer fear the wrath of God because they do not believe that there is a God. When they reach this conclusion there is danger that they may also conclude that since there is no God to hand down a moral law there is, therefore, no moral law. Such a conclusion is, however, the product of sophistication rather than of scientific comprehension.

The study of morals soon passed into the metaphysical stage, in which attention was concentrated on some assumed faculty which was named "will." Much time was wasted discussing such futile questions as freedom or determinism. Such discussions are futile, first, because there is no tangible or measurable basis for an answer, and, second, because the answer, even if there were one, would be of no possible use to anybody. No practical policy depends upon the answer. If men are free to choose, the law and the mores may provide reasons for choosing as the group wants them to choose. If men are automata, responding passively to such stimuli as are brought to bear upon them, the law and the mores can provide such stimuli as will result in the kinds of responses that are desired.

The positive stage is reached when students realize that, in the interest of group life, certain kinds of conduct are desirable and others not, and when this realization is followed by a study of ways and means of increasing the desirable and decreasing the undesirable kinds of conduct.

That men must behave differently when they try to live and work together in groups than would be necessary if they lived and worked in isolation should be apparent to any one with any experience of group life or teamwork. In a rather definite sense, rational morality is conformity to the necessary conditions of teamwork. The principles of teamwork, as stated in Chapter I, are fundamentally the same, whether the team consists of eleven men or a hundred and twenty-five million men, women, and children. They differ in details, but all agree in requiring the individual to do whatever promotes the success of the team and to refrain from doing anything which interferes with that success. When this is once understood to be the real basis of morality there will be no more confusion as a result of mere sophistication.

"There may be no Gods;" wrote Lafcadio Hearn,[1] "but the forces that shape and dissolve all forms of being would seem to be more exacting than Gods. To prove a "dramatic tendency" in the ways of the stars is not possible; but the cosmic process seems nevertheless to affirm the worth of every human system of ethics fundamentally opposed to human egoism."

James Anthony Froude, in his famous essay on *The Science of History* says:

What, then, is the use of history, and what are its lessons? . . . First, it is a voice forever sounding across the centuries the laws of right and wrong. Opinions alter, manners change, creeds rise and fall, but the moral law is written on the tablets of eternity. For every false word or unrighteous deed, for cruelty or oppression, for lust or vanity, the price has to be paid at last, not always by the chief offenders, but paid by some one. Justice and truth alone endure and live. Injustice and falsehood may be

[1] *Kwaiden* (Houghton Mifflin Co., Boston, 1904), p. 240.

long-lived, but doomsday comes at last to them, in French revolutions and other terrible ways.[1]

The Victorian flavor of Froude's language may sound strange to post-war ears. Even a moral evolutionist may not quite like the implication that the moral law is something apart from the process of adaptation, imposed upon us by command and disobeyed at our peril. If Froude had said that whatever is "written on the tablets of eternity" is, *per se*, the moral law, the language would still be somewhat turgid, but would be more nearly in accord with evolutionary thought.

The sum and substance of the whole matter would seem to be that the laws of natural selection are determining the survival and extinction of social groups as definitely as they are determining the survival and extinction of biological organisms. Those social groups survive which manage to get their individual members to behave in ways which make for group strength and survival. Those become extinct which fail to get their members to behave in such ways or which succeed in getting them to behave in other ways. In this sense, at least, the moral law is to be found in the very nature of group life. That is as definite as that the laws of bodily health are embodied in the very nature of the human organism.

The moral law is to be discovered by the same logical methods as the laws of health, or any other series of natural sequences. The study must be objective and not subjective, in both cases. The discovery of the moral law will come from a series of studies of survival values, but the emphasis must be placed on group survival rather than on individual survival.

There is no inherent reason why morals should not be the special study of the biological evolutionist who is a specialist in plant and animal ecology, except that the study of social organization and teamwork requires a technique somewhat different from that required for the study of the adaptation and survival of physical organisms. In fact, some of the most significant contributions to the understanding of the foundations

[1] Chas. Scribner's Sons, New York, 1886.

of morals have been made by biologists.[1] "The Natural History of Goodness"[2] is an important chapter in the Natural History of Man. But whether the subject is developed by biologists or men with a different training, nothing worth while will ever be found out about morals except by men who approach the subject with the attitude and some of the equipment of a physical scientist. The right is a matter of objective fact, of the adaptation of a living organism to its physical environment, but of a living organism which has learned the trick of organized teamwork as a means of adaptation and survival. As a kind of behavior (and the means of promoting it) which makes teamwork possible and efficient, "right" conduct is something to be discovered by observation and inference. In this respect the study of morality is like every other scientific study.

Several decades ago, Clifford applied the principle of natural selection to group morals in an essay, "On a Scientific Basis of Morals."[3] In this connection he used the idea of the tribal self —"a conception in the mind of the individual which serves as a peg on which those remote desires are hung which were implanted in him by the need of the tribe as a tribe." This tribal self he conceived as capable of approving or disapproving the individual's acts, according as they were or were not good for the tribe. By this approval of certain acts, a man is made to acquire a motive according to which he refers acts to the family or tribal self as supreme. His tribal self may say, "I like that thing that you have done." Then if a man habitually does things for the good of the tribe, his tribal self will go further and say, "In the name of the tribe, I like you." This is what Clifford calls approbation.

[1] Reference has already been made to William Morton Wheeler's *Social Life Among the Insects*.

[2] Cf. the remarkable address of William Morris Davis before the Phi Beta Kappa Society of Harvard in June, 1922, published under the title "The Reasonableness of Science" in the *Harvard Graduates Magazine* for September, 1922. It was preceded by an equally remarkable address before the same society in 1895 by John Fiske on "Ethics and the Cosmic Process" and published in *Through Nature to God* (Houghton Mifflin Co., Boston, 1899).

[3] W. K. Clifford, *Lectures and Essays* (The Macmillan Co., London, 1879), vol. II, pp. 112-20. Clifford was led, he says, by certain remarks of Darwin's.

But the matter of ethics does not end with approval — and here is where natural selection shows itself — for "right actions are not those which are publicly approved, but those whose public approbation a well-instructed tribal self would like." And this matter is not left to sentiment. ". . . natural selection will in the long run preserve those tribes which have approved the right things; namely, those things which at that time gave the tribe an advantage in the struggle for existence." Further, "The matters of fact on which rational ethics must be founded are the laws of modification of character, and the evidence of history as to those kinds of character which have most aided the improvement of the race."

Ethical maxims, then, do result from experience, but from the experience of the tribe, not of the individual. To the individual they seem intuitive; his "conscience gives no reasons;" but they are also, in reality, conditional. Although our moral system may say that we must do certain things if we want to live together in complicated social ways, it is conceivable to reply that we do not care to so live, and will not obey the rules. But then, because we are members of a group, it is equally conceivable, and rather more rational for the group to answer, "Then in the name of my people I do not like you," and to show its disapproval in appropriate ways.[1] Although the morals are conditional, Clifford says, "the absence of the condition in one born of a social race is rightly visited by moral reprobation."

Clifford's statement of the essential fact that moral systems are not only factors in the survival of individuals within the tribe, but must, in turn, stand the test of natural selection, is clear and concise. Some objection may be raised to the use of such terms as "tribal self." Everything which Clifford explains by means of the term "tribal self" can be expressed by deleting the word *tribal*. The individual has a desire for the approbation of his tribe. If he secures that approbation he is pleased with

---

[1] "And the offender, being descended from a social race, is unable to escape his conscience, the voice of his tribal self which says, 'In the name of the tribe, I hate myself for this treason that I have done.' " *Ibid.*, p. 120.

himself. By giving or withholding its approbation, the tribe can furnish him with a reason for conformity.

It makes a difference to individuals whether the morals of the group in which they live actually promote social welfare or not. Individuals in the aggregate depend for individual success on the success of the groups to which they belong. The group acts as a shield or carapace for men — and a cupboard. Through teamwork, through adaptation to social life, they adapt themselves to the physical world, and brave the dangers and difficulties of their existence. The group stands between them and nature whenever nature goes about selecting the kind of human life that is fit to populate the earth. The group, not single human beings, must stand the test of natural selection. The laws of the universe demand this in the sense that the contour of the land demands that water shall flow in a certain direction. Group welfare is actually promoted, a group lives long as a group, according as its morals are well or ill adapted to the demands of the physical world in which it lives. But how, the question arises, do morals become adapted? This is the question that it is the real concern of this chapter to answer. There is something more, however, to be said concerning the social significance of morality[1] — something that will bring to light a connection between moral adaptation and physical adaptation.

2. *The Shifting Basis of Morals.* That the conditions of social life change from time to time is well known. That moral standards and practices must change to meet new conditions is a generalization rather widely accepted. There is less willingness to apply this generalization to specific cases than could be desired. Let us begin with an illustration sufficiently remote to be disarming. When the children of Israel in the wilderness were fed upon manna, which came fresh every morning and spoiled if stored, there was no survival value in thrift. If they had lived long enough under these conditions to have developed a system of morals which fitted the environment, thrift would

---

[1] It seems that such a view of morals dissolves the surface dualism of contending moral theories, such as Naturalism vs. Humanism and Theism, Utilitarianism vs. Intuitionism, and Stoicism vs. Epicureanism.

not have been listed as one of the virtues. When the people were transplanted to a region of cold winters or long dry spells, the morals of the manna era would prove inadequate. There would be survival value in thrift. Only those who practised it could survive. Not only would thrift become a virtue in the sense of being approved socially, but means would have to be provided for the protection of the thrifty against the thriftless, otherwise the thriftless would survive on the stores of the thrifty.

Another illustration, less remote and more likely to stir our feelings, is found in the case of modern classes who receive wages, salaries, interest, rent, and other contractual incomes. They come to expect these incomes to fall as from heaven with the regularity of manna. They are as resentful if it fails as the Israelites probably would have been if manna had failed. Instead of laying the blame on Heaven, these modern classes are likely to lay the blame on our social system. But the fact that large numbers of people in these days can, in good times, live on the daily manna of wages, salaries, etc. and therefore do not need to be thrifty, does not prove that thrift is unnecessary. It is more necessary than ever, but, under our extreme specialization, it may be performed for the whole of society by a special group. The accumulation of capital, by whomsoever it is done, is essentially an act of thrift.[1] Those who depend upon the thrift of others have no more reason to complain than those who depend on the professional or mechanical skill of others.

One of the most baffling of those environmental changes which necessitate a change of morals, is the change from a condition of poverty to a condition of wealth. In seeming contradiction to Carlyle's famous dictum prosperity is not only easier to stand but less demoralizing than adversity. The reason why there are more people who can stand adversity than prosperity is because they have had more experience with and training for adversity. During the greater part of the history of our race we, that is, our ancestors, were struggling with adversity. We as a race have learned something from that long experience.

[1] Thrift does not now and never did mean deprivation. It means devoting resources to future rather than to present purposes.

They who did not learn how to stand adversity were eliminated generation after generation. By this combination of the learning and the selective processes we became adapted to adversity. We have not yet had time to learn much about prosperity.

One lesson which men were forced to learn was that it paid better to work in organized groups than as separate individuals. Another thing was that if they were to work as organized groups, individual behavior had to be modified. Unfortunately, (or fortunately) they did not find themselves equipped with a set of instincts which would lead them automatically to behave in the ways which group work required. Neither were they intelligent enough to reason out, in every one of the multitudinous cases that arose, just how a member of a group ought to behave in the interest of successful teamwork. Something was needed to bridge the gap between instinct and intelligence, something which would cause a man to behave in certain social exigencies as he would behave if nature had endowed him with a set of social instincts adequate for the emergency, or with an intelligence which would tell him just what to do in those particular exigencies.

This gap has been bridged by systems of morals,[1] as it were, in group memory. Every group that ever amounted to anything has found ways of influencing its members to behave as social beings, that is, to do, even to their personal disadvantage, what was to the advantage of the group. There is, to choose a single example, no instinctive love for truth nor horror of lying. Neither are we intelligent enough to decide instantly in a critical case that the long-run social advantage of truthfulness is great enough to overbalance the immediate and personal advantage of lying. There must be created within us an emotional horror of lying if we are to be expected to tell the truth at all times. This emotional horror of lying, and all other emotional horrors, are social products. They are part of the mores, or the customary morals and religions of social groups.

[1] "Reason is but a weak antagonist," wrote Oliver Goldsmith (on The English Clergy and Popular Preachers) "when headlong passion dictates: in all such cases we should arm one passion against another."

One of the important phases of human adaptation is that of becoming emotionally adjusted to the conditions of life under which one has to live. It is as necessary to develop a set of emotions as it is to develop purely physical or mental qualities that possess survival value. One who does not feel a more or less unreasoning loyalty to the group to which he belongs is not likely to be a very valuable member of that group, especially in sudden or great emergencies. On such occasions it is necessary to act promptly and to reason about it afterward if one has not done his reasoning long before. When the emergency arises it is time for action and not for investigation. Unless there is an inherited instinct to compel action, an acquired emotion is the only thing that will serve in such a case. One must sometimes act very much as a horse shies. For thousands of generations wild horses had to dodge enemies. The horse that stopped to investigate before it jumped did not have as good a chance of survival as the horse that jumped first and investigated afterward.

The mores or customary morals of our group were built up during countless centuries of struggle with adversity. The fact that we have finally conquered the adverse forces and risen into a state of relative prosperity is pretty conclusive evidence that our mores were sound. They enabled us (our ancestors) to meet the conditions of life successfully. They gave us the moral brace we needed to withstand the demoralizing tendencies of poverty and adversity. The question now is, and upon this question the future of civilization depends, will the same moral discipline which once fortified us against the demoralizing tendencies of adversity now fortify us against the demoralizing tendencies of prosperity? There is no compelling reason to think that it will. The great need of the time is a new moral discipline which will save us from the evils of prosperity as our old moral discipline saved us from the evils of adversity. This is the greatest question now before the civilized world. It is more acute here in America than anywhere else. The answer must be found here.

The whole theory of human adaptation may be summed up

in the proposition that the group has a hand in selecting the type individual which is to survive, but conditions outside the group, its environment, select the type of group which is to survive. The individual must conform to the standards set by the group, but the group must conform to standards set by the outside conditions, called the environment. The group, with its standards, customs, religions, laws, is an important part of the environment to which the individual must conform or be exterminated. The conditions outside the group are the environment to which the group must become adapted. In short, the group, that is, the sovereign group, is subject to natural selection with all its rigors. The individual is subject only in part to natural selection. In a much more imminent sense he is subject to social selection.

The group may, it is true, in ignorance give its approval to individual conduct which is harmful to group life, or its disapproval to conduct which would be beneficial. It may persecute its saints and reward its sinners for the simple reason that it may have perverted notions as to what constitutes sainthood and sin, but it cannot avoid the consequences of its own mistakes. From the sociological point of view, goodness, or even sainthood, consists in doing the things which contribute to the life of the group, and badness consists in doing things which subtract from the life of the group, or weaken it, or endanger its survival. In the language of an Indian chief, "Goodness is that which keeps the tribe alive."

An athletic team, for example, may select its members, but something else "selects" the teams that survive an elimination contest. The team that does not select wisely when it chooses its recruits will not survive such a contest. A tribe that persecutes or otherwise handicaps those who are most capable of adding to its strength will not last long in inter-tribal conflict. Again, an athletic team may presumably adopt whatever training rules it chooses, and the individual must conform or be put off the team; but whether those rules are good or bad does not depend upon the opinion of the group but on the way in which they affect the success or failure of the team. If the team's training rules are irrational, and if it eliminates from its personnel those who do not conform to its rules, it is doubly certain to fail as a team. So with all groups, even the great society or the national group.

In a militant age, when groups had to fight for the possession of land and the means of subsistence, the group whose mores did not approve of courage and all the other military virtues would stand a poor chance of survival. In an industrial age, a group whose mores did not approve of industry, foresight and common honesty would stand a poor chance of prospering, or even of being able to feed its people. In periods of high death-rate due to constant wars or recurring plagues, groups which insist too strongly on monogamy, or even on chastity, do not get on as well as groups which relax somewhat their austerity.

3. *Standards of Fitness.* The most important function of every great social group, and of its government, is to set up and maintain a rational standard of individual fitness for survival. It can call fit whomsoever it pleases, and help him to survive. It can call unfit and extinguish whomsoever it chooses. Conventionally, the fit individuals are those whom the society approves and helps, and the unfit are those whom it disapproves and hinders. Society has ways of favoring those whom it calls fit and extinguishing those whom it calls unfit. The operation of its criminal law works toward the extermination of those whom it calls unfit, through executions which kill the body and with it the germ plasm, through imprisonments, which tend to kill the germ plasm by preventing procreation, and by other handicaps and hardships which reduce the power to earn a living. *But,* in order to save its own life, the great group must decide rationally whom to call fit and whom to call unfit.

In the last analysis, or in biological terms,— which are more fundamental than political formulae,— the function of the concept and the administration of justice by the great society is to set up and maintain a social or rational standard of individual fitness for survival. In the absence of such a standard, the expression "survival of the fittest" is a biological expression and carries no moral significance whatsoever. Fangs, venom, claws and other destructive characters make an animal "fit" to survive if they enable him to survive. A concept of justice, adequately administered, may destroy all survival value of destructive powers so far as the struggle for individual survival within the group is concerned, and give survival value to powers which, in the natural world, would have no survival value at all. By hanging or otherwise repressing all those individuals who struggle for survival by using their powers of destruction against their fellow members, and safeguarding all those who struggle for survival by using their powers of production, a new standard of fitness for individual survival is set up,— a standard not found in the biological world, or known to the biologist.

The tribe which succeeds in giving survival value to those individual powers which are useful to the tribe as a whole, and in destroying the survival value of those individual powers which, when exercised, are injurious to the tribe as a whole, has a better chance of surviving as a tribe than any tribe which fails in this respect. In the long-time struggle for survival among tribes, only those survive which have, in some measure, succeeded in setting up and maintaining such a rational standard of individual survival. Other standards tend to disappear with the tribes that adopted them. Those which have not yet disappeared are weak, backward, primitive, and will live only so long as stronger tribes,— that is, the civilized nations with more rational standards,— refrain from taking their land.

This explains why there seems to be less variation in the concept of justice among civilized nations than in most moral concepts. The concept of justice is so vital to tribal survival as to preclude the possibility of national growth and power to any tribe which varies widely from the standard suggested in the preceding paragraph. There may be wide variations in dress, table manners, marriage ceremonies, religious observances, and a multitude of other social habits without affecting tribal or national survival. There can not be such wide variations in the concept or the administration of justice. Those tribes which have made such a success of their tribal life as to grow to positions of great power have had to develop a concept of justice

and a system of administering it that would give survival value
to those individual powers which, when exercised, made for
tribal strength and survival. When stated in this way, the
formula seems almost self-evident,— even banal,— yet it is even
yet seldom publicly recognized. The idea prevails, though
abundantly disproved, that the true concept of justice is to be
discovered by looking inward upon our own sentiments rather
than outward upon the efforts of men to live and work together
in large numbers. We need to study these efforts in order to
see how and why they succeed or fail. The good, in this rational
sense, is as truly a matter of discovery as is the true in the
scientific sense. Moreover, the discovery of the good is achieved
by the same methods as the discovery of the true.

But what is a fit society? What kind of individual is to
survive is a question on which society has a great deal to say.
It can set its standard of individual fitness, and preserve those
who conform and exterminate those who do not. What kind
of society is fit to survive is another question. On this question
societies themselves have little to say. They must meet requirements not of their own designing, and conform to conditions not
of their own creation.

Of course the word *group* is a loose term with a great variety
of meanings. It includes everything from vast and loosely bound
international or inter-racial groups, such as Islam, Catholocity,
Christendom, or the "civilized world," down to small neighbor-
hoods. It includes definitely organized, self-determined national
groups, with definite geographical boundaries, constitutions, and
governments, exercising sovereignty over definite populations
and territories, subject to no higher group and obeying no human law except those of their own making. It also includes
loosely organized groups exercising no power of compulsion over
their own members, subject to the control of some larger group
with its military forces and police powers, and enjoying the
protection likewise of that larger group.

The rigid and unmodified operation of natural selection is
limited to such groups as possess what is called sovereignty.
They alone are self-determined, self-protected, and free from

control by higher human authorities. Other groups enjoy some measure of protection from sovereign groups and are therefore not subjected to the rigid operation of natural selection. They are not free to adopt their own rules, even for the disciplining of their own members. In short, all other groups except those which enjoy sovereignty are, in part at least, subject to social selection, in which respect they are in a position somewhat similar to that of individuals. Some larger group,— say the sovereign group,— can call these other groups into existence, and can put them out of existence. The larger group can also protect these smaller groups from extermination by external or internal enemies.

While it is not possible to dispense with such words as "society" or "the community" or "the group" in sociological discussions, there are certain principles which apply rigidly only to sovereign groups. In such cases it is perhaps better to use such terms as the tribe, the state, or the nation. The sovereign group, since it must look out for itself and stand the test of natural selection, must insist, in the interests of its own survival, that its members possess some capacity for teamwork. The group must allow only such men as measure up to a standard of social fitness to survive within itself.[1] If it is wise, it insists, first of all, that its members be organically fit for a social existence. The preceding chapter urged all this.

It is obvious to any observer that men are not by instinct perfectly social; they are quite capable of acting in their own self-interest without any concern for social welfare. It is also obvious that the native, untutored intelligence of individuals is not acute enough always to tell them how to behave in a way that promotes group welfare. What is it, then, that fills the gap which instinct and the native intelligence of the individual

---

[1] Darwinian sociologists, remember, do not insist that those men who happen to be born social misfits ought to find starvation and early death their lot. Only in a eugenic sense need they die, that is, their germ plasm must die. From a human point of view, social selection seems less cruel than the selection of nature. The first is not less drastic, however, than the second. Under natural selection the weak are simply prevented from populating the earth by tragic death. In social selection, the unfit may be prevented from multiplying by less tragic devices.

do not fill? What else is capable of making men sociable? The answer is: Morality or group wisdom. The group may insist that its members possess a capacity for teamwork. But, if sociability is at least in part a function of the intelligence, the individual must be tutored by the group's experience of social welfare; or his capacity for teamwork will be blundering, experimenting, amateurish, only potentially able to promote the well-being of the group. Morals may be taught each rising generation by the generation that is grown to social wisdom. The mores are a factor in the success of group life because they obviate the necessity of men's being organically perfectly social.

4. *How "Good" Does One Need To Be?* The question arises, of course, Why is it not desirable that men should be organically perfectly social? How instinctively social does a human being need to be? And how much does his sociability need to be trained in him? Is it desirable that he should be as instinctively social as Lafcadio Hearn pictures ants? In his essay on Ants, Hearn says:

What I want to talk about is the awful propriety, the terrible morality, of the ant. Our most appalling ideals of conduct fall short of the ethics of the ant,— as progress is reckoned in time,— by nothing less than millions of years! . . . Most of us have been brought up in the belief that without some kind of religious creed — some hope of future reward or fear of future punishment — no civilization could exist. We have been taught to think that in the absence of laws based upon moral ideas, and in the absence of an effective police to enforce such laws, nearly everybody would seek only his or her personal advantage, to the disadvantage of everybody else. . . . These teachings confess the existing imperfection of human nature; and they contain obvious truth. But those who first proclaimed that truth, thousands and thousands of years ago, never imagined a form of social existence in which selfishness would be *naturally* (organically) impossible. It remained for irreligious Nature to furnish us with proof positive that there can exist a society in which the pleasure of active beneficence makes needless the idea of duty,— a society in which instinctive morality can dispense with ethical codes of every sort,— a society of which every member is born so absolutely unselfish and so energetically good, that moral training could signify, even for its youngest, neither more nor less than waste of precious time.[1]

[1] See Lafcadio Hearn, *Kwaidan* (Houghton, Mifflin Co., Boston, 1904), pp. 222, 232. Spencer, it will be remembered, believed that human beings would

It may be said, of course, that the social instincts of ants are so developed that their social behavior is perfectly automatic. Can there be such a thing as moral goodness in an automaton? The rational sociologist says, Yes. But that is because he thinks of moral goodness in terms of behavior, behavior that is good for the health of a group, behavior that promotes group survival. Ants have natures that lead them automatically to do what ant societies need to have done in order to survive. The ants are morally perfect. If men had happened to be made with instincts which led them to do, automatically, exactly the same things which they actually are taught to do, their conduct would be as good in one case as in the other. The test of moral goodness is simply the effect of conduct on the vitality of social life. Beneficience simply means behavior that advances a group's chances of long life; maleficence means just the opposite. Ants are not without interest in their own creature comforts; yet, in satisfying their own needs, they also satisfy the needs of their ant society.

From the point of view of an ant society, the conduct of individual ants is all that could be required of creatures with their limited capacity. They do with all their might, or up to the limit of their capacity, what their society needs to have them do. They are so extremely good that they could not be tempted to do anything else than that which is good for the ant society to which they belong. They are so good that they do not need government, rewards, and punishments, fear of the loss of social esteem, moral codes, religions — or even consciences — to keep them from doing wrong, that is, from doing what is harmful to the general interest of the ant society. They need no inducement or any kind of objective reward to persuade them to do what is beneficial. They have not been taught goodness or been converted to a virtuous way of life; they have come to lead a life of sanctification through the slow process of evolution. Their conduct does the ant society as much good

ultimately evolve into creatures innately as morally perfect as ants. Cf. *supra,* Chapter IV. See also William Morton Wheeler, *Social Life Among the Insects, op. cit.*

as it would if they were strongly tempted to do otherwise, but through religious or moral teaching or the fear of punishment, they were led to do precisely the same thing which they now do automatically. Why may not the sociologist parry the suggestion that an automaton cannot be morally good by suggesting that there may be such a thing as a good automaton, that is, one that does what we want it to do?

The objection may be raised that the automatic goodness of a social insect is as narrow as it is intense. The members of an ant society, for example, show no fellow feeling toward members of another society, even of the same species. There is, apparently, nothing in ant morality which is even synonymous with our feeling of common humanity. Their morality is distinctly a group morality. But (why mince matters?) so is ours. In an ant society there is, so far as we can discover, only one group that counts, which is the ant colony. There is consequently only one group loyalty. With us, there are many overlapping groups, beginning at the top with that vague group called humanity, toward which we feel an exceedingly vague and ineffective loyalty, and, ending at the bottom, with unions of two individuals for various purposes. We have so many conflicting group loyalties as to cause us many perplexities and internal emotional conflicts. These internal emotional conflicts growing out of conflicting group loyalties we call conscience — for want of a better name.

The question still remains, Do human beings *need* to be so automatically good as the social insects? Do we need to be instinctively moral? The answer is: first, man will never evolve into an innately perfect creature morally unless there is some survival value in being so terribly good; but, second, man will be good enough to survive if he is good enough to respond favorably to such stimuli to good behavior as society can easily provide; and, third, the society that succeeds in getting such response from its citizens will be as good and as likely to survive as a society in which citizens need no moral stimuli, no ethical codes, to induce them to be socially good.

It is possible to illustrate this position effectively by a physical analogy. From a certain point of view, we might say that a man has a superbly good physique if he can live a healthful life in our climate without any artificial aids in the way of clothing, shelter, or heating appliances. But does he need to be so terribly healthy as that? To put it differently, we might be said to be physical weaklings because we require, for a healthy existence, these artificial aids. Because we are dependent upon clothes, shelter, and heating appliances, we are to that extent less strong than we would be if we did not need them. If human beings had never had any such things, the people alive today, if any, would be the descendants of those who were strong enough to live without them. But, in evolutionary terms, is there any survival value in being so strong as that? Probably not. We have good physiques, that is, good enough physiques, if we can live healthy lives with such artificial aids as our industrial civilization can provide for us. We shall probably survive fully as long if we go on making clothes, building shelters, and using fire for artificial heat, as we would if we were to dispense with such things and permit only such people to live and multiply as could live without them. In short, there would be no survival value in being so terribly strong as to need for the body no artificial protection from winter blasts. By analogy, at least, we may be said to be good enough morally, if we always react favorably to such aids to good behavior as society can furnish us in the way of governments, ethical laws, social rewards and punishments, religious precepts — even prisons and gibbets.

This point may, perhaps, be clarified by considering two extreme and somewhat antagonistic views, those of the individual perfectionists and the social perfectionists. The individual perfectionists expect or hope for the perfection of the individual, the social perfectionists hope for or demand the perfection of society. The perfected individual is one who requires no social stimuli to induce favorable responses. He is as automatically "good" as a social insect. The perfected society is one which brings to bear upon each and every individual just the stimuli which will invariably secure favorable responses. If we had perfect individuals, as thus defined, they would need no aids

to "goodness" in the form of special stimuli. If we had a perfected society, as defined, it would not be necessary to improve
human nature. Such a society could get favorable responses
(good behavior) even from the most degenerate or unsocial
individuals.

It is conceivable, or theoretically possible, that the most
hardened criminal of today might have become a good and
useful citizen or team-mate if just the right stimuli had been
applied at just the right times. Omniscience might have applied
the right stimuli; but omniscience is not found among human
beings. This has led some extremists to say that every criminal
is a living proof of the ignorance and stupidity of our laws and
institutions. If by ignorance and stupidity is meant merely
the lack of omniscience, our laws and institutions may as well
plead guilty. With equal rationality the individual perfectionist
can say that if men were reasonably advanced on their way to
perfection they would behave socially even with such laws and
institutions as we have, and that if they were perfectly socialized
they would not need any laws or sanctions. A practical person
could go further and point out that nearly everybody now responds favorably to social stimuli and that if we were to so re-
vise all our laws and institutions as to get favorable responses
from those who are now criminals we would very likely get unfavorable responses from a good many of those who now behave
themselves reasonably well.

The wise policy seems to be to aim at the perfection neither
of the individual nor of society, but at a compromise between
the two. Such a compromise would be effected if we could
breed up a race of men who would respond favorably to such
stimuli as could be designed and applied by our limited wisdom,
and, at the same time, to design and apply the most effective
stimuli we can invent to secure favorable responses from the
great mass of such individuals as we have succeeded in breeding.
This is a fitting together of the individual and his social environment by a process of gradual modification of each. Each would
be so modified as to bring it into closer harmony with the other.

5. *Moral Experimentation.* Very little has been said so far

about creative moral conduct. Too much stress, perhaps, has been put upon the social significance of mere conformity to moral codes and too little upon the significance of the moral reformer. It must not be assumed that only the man who conforms his behavior to social wisdom is moral. He behaves, presumably, in a way that is good for society because he orders his life according to a composite human experience of social welfare. At least there is a presumption in favor of the view that the accumulated wisdom of the group is superior to that of its average individual. But there are ways in which an exceptional man can be moral in a higher sense without being a perfect conformist. He may be a moral innovator.

We must be on our guard against the temptation to regard every moral innovator as a moral leader or prophet. That is even more dangerous than to regard every innovator as an enemy of the human race. The fact is that most moral innovations, like most variations in the biological world, are unadapted and therefore fail. If one biological variation in ten thousand should happen to be adapted and survive, there is evolution. If one moral innovation in ten thousand should be a real improvement upon the mores, morals would improve pretty rapidly.

While it is unsafe either blindly to reject all innovations or blindly to accept them, the latter is vastly the more dangerous of the two. He who blindly rejects every innovation will be right — blindly so — in the vast majority of cases, while he who blindly accepts them all will be blindly wrong in the vast majority of cases.

The innovator is supposed to possess the virtue of originality, but originality alone is of doubtful value. It is one of the easiest things in the world to be original. It is not so very difficult to be sensible. To be both is to be a genius, and there are not many geniuses. To be original one needs only to do or say strange or startling things. Much originality is heard in a madhouse, or among drunken men and fools. To be sensible one only needs to say obvious things, to deal in truisms and platitudes, or to follow the beaten track. He who does this will be, in the great majority of cases, not only sensible and right, but uninteresting. Once in a while he will be both wrong and uninteresting. The power to discover new truths, or even new facts, and to state them in an interesting way is given to few, and they are the world's geniuses. The power to map out new kinds of behavior which will really make a better society is given to still fewer, and they are the world's few great founders of enduring religious and moral systems.

The point to be emphasized is that neither the innovator nor the stand-patter has any monopoly of either virtue or wisdom. They who are alarmed for the safety of civilization, whose hearts are heavy for the Ark of God, whenever an old habit or attitude is changed, are at least as rational as those who are always willing to try anything once. Some things have been tried often enough to convince any well informed person of their futility. "Experience teaches a dear school but fools will learn in no other." Yet Franklin, who wrote thus, was something of an innovator. He merely recognized the fact that a well informed person learns from the experience of the past and does not have to try everything for himself.

When a new experiment in any field is proposed, there are always people who say it won't work. Afterward, if it happens to work, some of them are pretty certain to claim that they started it. This formula is generally considered a sufficient answer to the objectors whenever any new experiment in government, in education, or in morals is proposed. It is not a sufficient answer for the reason that the objectors, even the blind objectors who without reason proclaim that any new scheme won't work, are more frequently right than wrong. The simple statistical fact is that most experiments don't work. If one in a thousand succeeds, the experimenters are doing pretty well.

Of course, this is no argument against continued experimentation. If we only try experiments enough, even though only one in a thousand succeeds, we shall make fairly rapid progress. In fact, that is the way most progress is made. The world tries thousands of wrong ways of doing nearly everything before it happens to hit upon the right way. Progress is slow where few experiments are made; it is rapid where many are made, even though they are made somewhat blindly, provided we know enough to give up an experiment when it has shown itself a failure. By discarding the numerous failures and preserving the few successes, the world advances.

The greatest inventors are not the greatest scientists in the academic sense; they are the indefatigable experimenters. Edison and Burbank achieved prodigious results by continuous and tireless experimentation. Most of their experiments accomplished nothing more than to show them what not to do again. By everlastingly trying this and that and the other way, they actually found the right way or at least a better way of doing a number of important things. But they had to know enough not to try the same experiment over and over again after it had proved unworkable. Some of our social experimenters are not so wise.

This method of trial and error is really the way of evolution, even of so-called emergent evolution. In the biological world, most mutations perish because they are not adapted to the environment in which they happen to be born. Once in a while one is born which happens to fit into its environment, it survives, reproduces its kind, and a new species emerges. In human affairs, the method of experimentation, or of trial and error, is the equivalent of variation and selection in the plant and animal world. Even those extreme variations called mutations are, after all variations, and these mutations perish unless they happen to fit their environment.

The world has been a great experimental laboratory in the moral and social field.[1] A great many "new discoveries" are made in the field of morals; most of them have no survival value

---

[1] There are a good many classics on the history of morals that are packed with illustrations of moral variation: W. E. H. Lecky, *History of European Morals* (Longmans, Green & Co., New York, 1869); Herbert Spencer, *Descriptive Sociology* (Williams & Norgate, London, 1930); E. Westermarck, *Origin and Development of the Moral Ideas* (The Macmillan Co., New York, 1908); L. T. Hobhouse, *Morals in Evolution*, 3d edition (H. Holt & Co., New York, 1916); W. G. Sumner, *Folkways, op. cit.;* W. G. Sumner and A. G. Keller, *Science of Society* (Yale University Press, New Haven, 1927). The whole literature of anthropology is crammed with samples of moral variation.

and they perish, or the people who try them perish, which amounts to the same thing. Once in a great while a "new discovery" is made which happens to work. A new system of morals or a new religion is born which fits its devotees for survival, and a new moral force is introduced into the world. This is, however, a poor argument in favor of adopting every new moral idea which is proclaimed. Most of them really are wrong in principle because they won't work. Only a few have shown any survival value. Most of the "new" ones have been tried and have been proved unworkable. If we knew as much as our great experimentors in physical science know, we should learn not to repeat the same failures over and over again. That is one reason why persons with a historical perspective are generally conservative. At least they do not proclaim that they are willing to try anything once. A monkey is willing to do that. A real sociologist knows that many of these so-called new schemes have already been tried many times and have always failed.

It is chastening for any group of mortals to know the whole story, because they know then that the way they behave in their land and in their generation is not the only possible way to squeeze satisfaction out of living — or necessarily the best way. They acquire a healthy, eager, inquisitive, exploring attitude toward morality. They know that morals must change to keep pace with a changing world. And so they learn the value of moral inventiveness. But they learn, too, that they cannot look very far into the future to see the far-flung consequences of change. And so they learn, also, the value of standing pat by ancient wisdom in the matter of morals, of experimenting with care and circumspection. They know that "whatever is" in the moral world is not necessarily right; but only possesses an actuarial probability of being right because of the fact that it has survived the test of time,— of moral selection.

Yet moral innovations we must have if there is to be progress. They are the variations which are the raw materials of selection. The mores must be modified from time to time for two reasons. In the first place, they may be wrong and may always have been wrong in many particulars. In the second place, they may need to be changed in order to keep up with a changing environment. The moral code must be a changing thing because the environment with which it needs to keep in tune is a changing thing. Group ways of behaving have to be altered in order to keep in touch with group welfare, in order to be continuously adapted to the changing life conditions a group must face.[1]

One reason why so few moral innovations have any social value is, first, that they are generally based on an irrational conception of morals and their purpose, and second, they assume a subjective rather than an objective test of what is good. It has become the fashion, for example, to decry self-interest as immoral. The man who acts from motives of self-interest, even though he does very good and useful things, unless he also does spectacular things, finds himself less lionized by society than the Rotarian who does exactly the same things, but says he is doing them for a bigger and better Main Street.[2] Yet, if the thing done is just as regularly and calculably good for society if done from one motive as from another, one motive is as good as another. What are motives good for except to move men? One motive, of course, may move them to do useful things more efficiently and regularly and calculably than a second. The first, then, is a better, a more "moral" motive; it does its work better. A physical analogy may help to make the point

[1] Cf. *supra*, Chapter VI, p. 367. To a certain extent, through active adaptation, the group is able to change the environment to fit its morals. But, because morals are plastic, relative to the environment, even more plastic than the biological organism, it is the morals which must ultimately be adapted to the environment, and not the environment to them.

[2] John Dewey, writing a chapter on America as a "house divided against itself," and speaking of the contradiction between our practice of a pecuniary culture and our professed Christian horror of economic determinism, says:

"We praise even our most successful men, not for their ruthless and self-centered energy in getting ahead, but because of their love of flowers, children, and dogs, or their kindness to aged relatives. Anyone who frankly urges a selfish creed of life is everywhere frowned upon. Along with the disappearance of the home, and the multiplication of divorce in one generation by six hundred per cent, there is the most abundant and most sentimental glorification of the sacredness of home and the beauties of constant love that history can record. We are surcharged with altruism and bursting with desire to 'serve' others." *Individualsim Old and New* (Minton, Balch & Co., New York, 1930), pp. 13-14.

clear. Any soil is good soil which grows good produce. We do not say that a product is good because it comes from good soil. We say that the soil is good because it produces good products. If we were to reason about motives and conduct as clearly as we do about soil and products, we should rather say that a motive is good because it regularly and calculably produces good conduct. It is wise to emphasize the words "regularly" and "calculably" to eliminate the exception when accidental good comes from a bad motive. A bad motive, bad because it regularly and calculably results in harmful conduct, may, under accidental circumstances, result in something good. A piece of very sterile soil may yield meteoric iron if a meteor should happen to plunge into it.

The realistic sociologist does not waste time calling self-interest positively moral or immoral. He reasons that it may regularly move men to creative work that is socially useful. Like the engineer, he sees in it a force which may be used. To be sure, he does not think of self-interest as a complete lack of interest in any other creature. It is merely, as shown in Chapter III, a certain degree of preference for one's self and those near to one's self, as compared with those farther removed from self. The argument in favor of a moderate degree of self-interest can be stated categorically somewhat as follows:

1. Human interests will be best safeguarded and provided for when each particular interest is promoted by the particular person who is able and willing to safeguard and provide for it most effectively.

2. Generally speaking, but with a few exceptions, every interest can be safeguarded and provided for most effectively by the person who knows that interest most intimately.

3. Generally speaking, but with a few exceptions, the individual of mature years and sound mind knows his interests more intimately than he knows the interests of other people.

4. Generally speaking, but with a few exceptions, the individual of mature years and sound mind knows the interests of his contemporaries better than those of later generations, and of near generations better than those of remote generations.

5. Generally speaking, and with few exceptions, he knows the interests of his near of kin better than those of his distant or his very distant kin.

6. He knows the interests of those who are like-minded with himself better than he knows the interests of those who are unlike-minded with himself; that is, he knows the interests of those whose moral and mental qualities, purposes, and ideals are similar to his own, better than he does those whose moral and mental qualities, purposes, and ideals are different from his own.[1]

In some respects, social distance is being overcome. "In a world reduced to a neighborhood by machine communication and travel," says R. W. Sockman,[2] "the Christian moral sense must be held to account for human beings starving or freezing on the other side of the world just as certainly as the two explorers of the Nobile expedition were expected to explain the death of the Swedish scientist whom they left lying in the snow at their feet. The codes of Sinai are given immeasurably new margins of experiment by the codes of Marconi."

There is some obvious truth in these remarks. The codes of Marconi rather than codes of morals have, roughly speaking, made men far distant from each other in point of space, neighbors in like-mindedness. The amount of neighborliness between human beings on opposite sides of the world, however, can be tremendously exaggerated — witness neighborly quarrels in Geneva. There is such a thing as having near neighbors a little too near for our peace and comfort.[3] In any case, the principle that no one can effectively promote interests of which he is on the whole ignorant is not changed in the age of the machine. And the question, "Who exactly is our neighbor?" is a question of fact, not opinion. It is unhappily true that the age of machine communication has so quickly widened the field of our

---

[1] Quoted from the author's *Essays in Social Justice, op. cit.*, pp. 79–80.

[2] *Morals of Tomorrow* (Harper & Bros., New York and London, 1931).

[3] Good fences make good neighbors is a wise rural saying.

contacts with people that our loyalties are very much confused. Sockman, recognizing this, goes on to say:

> But while it is true that the narrower loyalty presses upon us more powerfully, it is equally true that the narrower field usually offers us the sphere and instrument of our most effective service. The honest seeker after a moral solution will therefore first search his own motives to make sure that he is not being self-deceived by self-indulgence, will scan the horizon for the largest possible interests to be served, and then will study his own aptitudes and near-by associations for the best means to be used.[1]

In view of our limited mental capacity, we cannot possibly know the interests of other people, especially if they be far distant from ourselves, as accurately or as intimately as we know our own interests. We can imagine no greater chaos than for every man to ignore his own interests, which he knows best, the interests of his immediate neighbors which he knows next best, and devote all his time to the promotion of the interests of other people of whom he is on the whole rather ignorant.[2] There would be so much misdirected energy and wasted benevolence as to result in an economic and a moral disaster.

But how selfish, or how unselfish, ought a person to be in order to be moral? He should be selfish enough to accord with his limited ability to know and appreciate the interests of others, selfish enough to look first after those interests which he knows best and next after those interests which he knows next best. To be more selfish than this, he must neglect the interests of others when he knows them well and can promote them efficiently. To be less selfish than this, he must try to promote interests which he does not understand very well and cannot promote; in other words, he must be a bungler. If complete and unqualified unselfishness combined, as it would have to be, with limited intelligence and information, should result in a great deal of misdirected and wasted effort, the individual who is unmitigatedly unselfish is a bad man. If a moderate degree of self-preference leads to more useful and beneficient action than complete unselfishness, then the moderately self-interested man

[1] *Op. cit.*, p. 256.
[2] *Ibid.*, p. 257.

is a better man than the completely unselfish one. He promotes group welfare.

The test to apply is not whether he is more interested in himself than in others, but whether he has a sufficient interest in others to be willing to stake his own self-interest on his ability to minister to their interests. In the language of the street, it is whether he is willing to give value for value. If he is a worker, is he willing to give a good day's work for a good day's pay or will he skimp his work and try to get more without earning more? If he is a professional man, is he willing to give his best ability in order to win the fees that will satisfy his own self-interest or will he try to win the fees without giving the best service within his power? If he is a producer of goods, is he willing to make the best goods he can in return for good prices or is he willing to adulterate, to use shoddy, or otherwise cheat the purchaser?

It is possible to look at self-interest in a light which makes it appear more moral than perfect beneficience; for beneficience can scarcely be thought of as moving men automatically to act for the public good. Those individuals who care very little for themselves or those "near" to them, and feel disposed to spend their time doing for others what they, the doers, think ought to be done, waste a great deal of energy in doing futile things, giving people presents which are not wanted, meddling with the affairs of people who would rather be let alone, always trying to do what their limited mental capacity makes it impossible for them to do efficiently, that is, to promote interests which they do not understand very clearly. On the other hand, individuals who are moderately self-interested can be counted upon to do useful things because they understand the interests they try to promote. Individuals, of course, who are so extremely self-interested that they are not willing to stake their own prosperity on their ability to promote the interests of any one other than themselves made bad citizens. They try to gain at the expense of others, cheating, giving less than they receive, robbing, getting without giving anything, harming society.

Plato said long ago that one cannot will to be bad, knowing

the good.[1] If this be true, motive is largely a matter of intelligence. A man wills, it seems, to act out of harmony with
society's good, only when he has no idea of what that may be,
or when he has not the wit to see that his own good is bound
up in the fortunes of society. If human beings are intelligent,
they are morally sensitive; they care for the good of the group
that has given them social nourishment. Most men will to be
good. But their knowledge of social welfare — even in this age
of education — is limited. So they are forced, in order to be
good, to uphold more or less unreasoningly the moral code.
For the most part, they as individuals are not wise enough to
be creative of great moral reforms. They go about their own
business, moderately self-interested, unconsciously changing
morals with slight personal touches here and there, slowly in
the end, creating moral evolution by their collective wisdom.
When they bolt the moral code, they have to be judged, not by
their motives, but by their conduct. Only if that be too bad
or thought to be too bad for the health of society to stand, do
they go to jail, to be socially exterminated as ants would have
to be if they were tried and found wanting in social instinct.

The typical citizen in a reasonably progressive society must
necessarily be a reasonably good citizen, else his society would
not be progressive. His conduct must be such as to promote
the public good more than to hinder it, otherwise his society
would be retrograding. He is behaving reasonably well because
he is responding reasonably well to such stimuli as society can
bring to bear upon him. He is reasonably self-centered, looking
first after those interests which he knows best, and second, after
other interests which he does not understand quite so well. He
does not pretend to care equally for all human beings. If he
thinks about it at all, he knows perfectly well that he can't
care equally for all. He has his preferences and prefers to work
for those for whom he cares. He is willing, however, to give
good measure in return for what he gets, to earn the means of
doing good to those for whom he cares.

[1] Cf. Protagoras, in Jowett's *Plato* (The Clarendon Press, Oxford, 1871), p. 358.

What more can any society ask of its members? To preach against this degree of preference and demand absolute unselfishness is to preach moral anarchy. In this, as in many other cases, the practices of men in reasonably progressive societies are much better than their preachments. Their practices are based on thousands of years of human experience. They have had survival value for their group. Their preachments are too frequently the results of an idealism which does not fit the world of reality.

6. *The Moral Prophet.* We are interested in the processes by which morals evolve rather than in a description of the types of moral practice at different stages of social development. A biological evolutionist who merely catalogued all the variations and mutations which had occurred, or of which he could learn, would not be much of an evolutionist. Even an accurate description of the changes which had taken place in the structure of a given plant or animal over long periods of time covers only a part of the evolutionary process. Some account must be given of the factors and forces which brought about the change. Darwin's illuminating term, natural selection, is more significant than volumes devoted to cataloguing variations or describing changes. Natural selection suggests a dynamic factor in the process of change and is not a mere description of change. Neither description of social and moral variants, nor a history of social and moral changes, constitutes a study of moral evolution. We need some clue to the factors which produced or forced the changes — something which will illuminate the discussions of moral evolution as the idea of natural selection illuminated the discussions of biological evolution.

"An authoritative code of morals has force and effect," says Walter Lippmann in his *Preface to Morals*,[1] "when it expresses the settled customs of a stable society: the pharisee can impose upon the minority only such conventions as the majority find appropriate and necessary. But when customs are unsettled, as they are in the modern world, by continual change in the

[1] The Macmillan Co., New York, 1929, pp. 317-318.

circumstances of life, the pharisee is helpless. He cannot command with authority because his commands no longer imply the usages of the community. They express the prejudices of the moralist rather than the practices of men. . . . It is useless to command when nobody has the disposition to obey. It is futile when nobody knows exactly what to command. In such societies (when customs are unsettled) wherever they have appeared among civilized men, the moralist has to be an administrator of usages and has had to become an interpreter of human needs. For ages when custom is unsettled are necessarily ages of prophecy. The moralist cannot teach what is revealed; he must reveal what can be taught. He has to seek insight rather than to preach."

There is, however, no reason for believing that there is any more prophesying in ages when custom is unsettled than in ages when it is settled. The real fact seems to be that the prophet gets more of a hearing. When the "cake of custom"[1] has formed and every one is smugly satisfied with the mores, the prophet gets no hearing, he is merely "a voice, crying in the wilderness." When the cake of custom is broken by some catastrophic process, men feel like sheep without a shepherd or, more literally, without a corral. They are in a mood to listen to prophesyings in strange tongues. They are fortunate, or wise, if they succeed in distinguishing between the mad prophets who would lead them further astray, and the one who, in such an exigency, could lead them in the one safe way. It cannot be too often repeated that there are thousands of ways of going wrong and only one way of going right; that there are many more prophets trying to lead in the wrong ways than there are trying to lead in right ways, simply because there are more wrong than right ways. It is easy to make mistakes in any enterprise because there are so many possible mistakes; it is difficult to avoid mistakes and find the right way, because there are so few right ways. "Strait is the gate and narrow is the way" that leads to sucess in social as well as in individual affairs.

---

[1] See Bagehot, *Physics and Politics* (D. Appleton & Co., London, 1879), p. 27.

There has never been a society, or an age, in which there has not been something of a battle going on between the pharisee and the prophet. The pharisee says that men are good enough if they simply obey the letter of their established customs, if they conform to the mores. He is primarily a ritualist. The prophet sees that ancient customs can become decrepit, unfitted to changing circumstances, and he says the spirit of the moral code must change. He tries to keep morality fitted to the actual needs of men, though, for actuarial reasons, he is usually wrong. If one prophet in a thousand happens to be right, and if the people know enough to follow the right one, progress is assured. The prophet — or the pharisee — usually sits in a seat of moral influence according as the environment in which a society lives is more or less rapidly changing. The pharisee, to be sure, always has a few listeners because the world never changes so quickly that fundamental group ways of behaving, authoritative with age, become completely unfit for use all at once.

The prophet, too, always has his few disciples because, however slowly the world changes, it never comes to a standstill. There is always room for improving morality and, what is more to the point, there are always some who think so. There is no doubt that the pharisees of the modern world are not being listened to as men who speak with authority. They preach about customs that were made almost two thousand years ago in Jerusalem or in the East, in a far-away past,[1] and they preach about these in spite of the fact that the circumstances of life have been changing with unbelievable speed, even in the last half century. Human beings with their own minds and hands have changed the face of their physical surroundings. Their morals, they begin to realize, are not in tune with the new world they have created. They have put themselves in a predicament from which they are struggling to escape. They are listening

---

[1] It must not be overlooked that many a so-called prophet is rebelling against the newer tendencies and harking back to an older and long-discarded morality. Rather frequently, "Israel went a whoring after false gods" and had to be called back by a prophet.

now to moral prophets — and Lippmann among them — more eagerly than to the pharisees.

Since the word *prophet* seems to imply the Hebraic variety, it may be well to see what the Old Testament prophets stood for. The following summary may start the student on the road to a useful enquiry.

I. In general, the message seems to be against idolatry and things Egyptain, Babylonian, etc. It is a call to "return to Jehovah," and a picture of the coming woe and destruction.

II. There is some idea of "backsliding," of disobeying specific laws, such as keeping the Sabbath and giving tithes, as well as "the law" in general.

III. There are messages against the "false prophets," but they are false because they claim to speak for Jehovah when he has not sent them, not because of their message; or rather the former point is stressed, and not the latter, except in the case where they say "Peace" when there is no peace.

IV. The call of the prophets to the people is "back to" righteousness much more than to observance of the law; and this righteousness is largely social. There are many references along this line, where specific social sins are mentioned.

V. In general the prophets' message seems to be a "calling back" to fundamentals, rather than to the old way. There is not much stress on particular rules or laws.

Thus, the "prophet" seems to be as frequently a reactionary as a progressive; his message is as frequently a calling back as a trumpet call to new things.

Ralph W. Sockmann, writing an excellent account of the mistakes of modern moralists says:

Moralists have not sensed the full implications of the industrial revolution, which not only transferred our citizenry from the soil to the city, but changed the patterns of thought from dependence upon nature to the control of production. . . . City minds which live amid the fluctuations of markets and the fickleness of fortune do not give the same heed to the moralists who talk about "whatsoever a man soweth that shall he also reap.". . . The half-mythical mood of those who "wait upon the Lord" of the harvests is not known to those who wait for street cars and watch the ticker tapes. However much we may generalize about the idea that human nature never changes, the fact is that the man on the street is not the same material for the moralist as "the man with the hoe." [1]

The use of the terms pharisee and prophet tends, unfortunately, to create an emotional attitude on the part of the reader which prevents him from reaching a scientific conclusion. The term pharisee tends to create the sensation of disapproval. The pharisee has never been held up as a model, or described in a way to create admiration, but always in a way to create contempt. The term prophet, on the other hand, tends to create a sensation of approval. By insinuating that the pharisee represents all those who try to conserve the ancient moralities, by which test Cato and other stern old Roman moralists would be classed as pharisees, and that the prophet represents all those who stand for change, one can very neatly beg the question at issue in any controversy over a proposed change or modification in the moral code.

Every moral innovator likes to think of himself as the prophet of a new order, the harbinger of a new and better day. They could not all be properly described in such terms because their innovations are of different sorts, and they attempt to lead in different, sometimes in opposite directions. They are simply the moral variants. Progress depends upon the selection of those few whose proposed variations represent real improvements and the rejection of the multitude whose proposals are merely "original" but otherwise devoid of merit.

It is easy for immature minds to jump to the conclusion that because some moral innovators have turned out to be true prophets, and some who have defended the old morality have turned out to be wrong, therefore every innovator must be a prophet and every defender of the old morality must necessarily be a pharisee. Any old system of morality which has stood

---

[1] *Morals of Tomorrow, op. cit.*, p. 7. There is some doubt about the exact meaning of the last sentence. It is very questionable just how much human nature actually changes in the course of years. There is no doubt, however, that human nature is molded by its environment. And so the man plus the street (or in relation to the street) is different material for the moralist from the man plus the hoe.

the tests of time and experience, which has enabled the society that adopted it to grow and gain some control over its physical environment, which has enabled large numbers to live and work together with some degree of harmony and not over much internal conflict, is likely to have a great many good elements, in fact, more good than bad elements in it. On the theory of probabilities, therefore, the moral innovation is rather more likely to be attacking some of these good than some of the bad elements. The enemy of the old is, for this reason, rather more likely to be attacking some of these good than some of the bad elements. The defender of the old is, on the same ground, rather more likely to be defending the good than the bad.

Instead, therefore, of using such question-begging terms as pharisee and prophet, it would seem better to use neutral terms if any can be found. The author suggests the retention of such terms as conformist and non-conformist, or conservative and radical. One is trying to conserve; the other to uproot. Such terms do not imply that the thing which some are trying to conserve and others to uproot is either good or bad.

Another quotation, from a writer who realizes that he cannot preach about ancient customs to the twentieth century, will show how deep-seated are the mistakes of modern pharisees. The quotation particularly concerns Americans because it pictures discontent with the very foundation of their morality, its pioneer individualism.

The scene in which individuality is created [says John Dewey] [1] has been transformed. The pioneer . . . had no great need for any ideas beyond those that sprang up in the immediate tasks in which he was engaged. His intellectual problems grew out of struggle with the forces of physical nature. The wilderness was a reality and it had to be subdued. The type of character that evolved was strong and hardy, often picturesque, and sometimes heroic. Individuality was a reality because it corresponded to conditions. . . .

But it is no longer a physical wilderness that has to be wrestled with. Our problems grow out of social conditions: they concern human relations rather than man's direct relationship to physical nature. The adventure

[1] *Individualism — Old and New, op. cit.*, pp. 92, 932.

of the individual, if there is to be any venturing of individuality and not a relapse into the deadness of complacency or of despairing discontent, is an unsubdued social frontier.

Other writers also glibly dispose of individualism by the easy method of pointing to the differences between a physical and a social frontier. They explain *why* sturdy individualism gives way to something else without taking the trouble to find out whether it actually does or not.

But the transition from a sturdy pioneer or rural individualism to an urban, sophisticated social-mindedness is by no means so simple as it is sometimes described. In fact, it cannot be shown that there is any less individualism, sturdy or otherwise, among the most urbanized populations than there was on our early western frontier. Certain manifestations of individualism have had to be given up or repressed, but they have broken out in new if not worse forms as populations have grown in density and sophistication, and as living conditions have grown easier. It is true that as men grow less dependent on their physical surroundings and more dependent on markets, employers, and other parts of their social environment, they learn how to adapt themselves to their fellows,— that is, to a social environment,— and lose some of their ability to adjust themselves to a natural, physical environment. But that does not tell the whole story.

Individualism, as a personal reaction, can be best defined as impatience of restraint, a desire to be let alone, a willingness to shift for oneself. As a political doctrine it may or may not reflect that personal attitude. It sometimes happens that persons of the most individualistic temperament are most vociferous in demanding governmental interference with other peoples' business, and, at the same time, most vehement in their protests against interference with their own business — that of talking or writing. The manufacturer who asks the government to keep its hands off and let him run his business to suit himself is no more of an individualist than the editor who asks the same thing, or the writer or teacher who insists on freedom of speech — that is, on a *laissez-faire* attitude on the part of the government toward the business of talking.

Herbert Spencer had frequent occasion to comment on the individualism in dress, hair, beards, and manners to be observed in socialistic meetings. Communistic societies, where not held together by a powerful religious bond or loyalty to a religious leader, have generally broken up because of the individualistic attitudes of their members, showing that political or economic opinion is one thing, and personal reaction to restraint quite a different thing.[1]

Impatience of restraint seems to grow rather than to decrease with the passing of the frontier and its pioneer attitudes. The restraints of domesticity seem to be resented more strongly in urban than in rural centers and in old rather than in new urban centers. Growing impatience of this form of restraint is shown in celibacy, prostitution, and divorce. Here is a form of individualism which increases not only with urbanization but with sophistication. It is more noticeable among the intelligentsia than among other groups. The desire to do as one pleases does not seem to decline as urbanization increases, though the desire to interfere with some one else probably increases.

Efforts to curb the business of selling habit-forming drugs by high pressure salesmanship are more deeply resented and more effectively resisted by urban than by rural peoples, in old than in new communities, and by persons of European birth and parentage than by the descendants of the pioneers. In this one particular, individualism grows and does not decline with the passing of the frontier, the growth of cities, or the arrival of populations who never knew a frontier. These new manifestations of individualism may be less sturdy and more pettish than those which showed themselves among pioneers, but they are none the less individualistic.

Nevertheless, it is true, and it must always be true, that

---

[1] See the three leading accounts of American communities: *Communistic Societies in the United States*, by Charles Nordhoff (New York, 1875); *History of American Socialisms*, by John Humphrey Noyes (Philadelphia, 1870); *American Communities*, by W. A. Hinds (Chicago, 1908).

changing conditions, either cosmic and geographical, or social and economic, must be accompanied by readaptations of morals — readaptations and re-readaptations. So long as the discussion is limited to the use of generalities it is not likely to result in controversy. That social conditions change is sufficiently evident to all. That changing social conditions require corresponding changes in standards of conduct seems altogether likely, at least to minds which have accepted the general idea of evolution. "New occasions teach new duties." This seems to the modern mind like an almost self-evident proposition; at any rate it has never provoked much controversy. It is only when we descend from generalities to particulars that differences of opinion are likely to arise. However, the generalities have no value until they are particularized. What the world wants to know is what are the new occasions and, specifically, what new duties do they teach? What new duties in particular does the present occasion teach? What specific changes in the mores are required to fit the new industrial conditions? Every answer to such questions as these is certain to be violently combatted. Yet such answers must be given if there is to be any progress. The very violence of the discussions is an evidence that the cake of custom is breaking up.

The oldest code now generally accepted throughout Christendom is the Decalogue. It was apparently intended to state the ten most important rules of individual conduct. We need not discuss the question of its adaptability to the conditions of the time and place of its promulgation. The question is, Does it give us the ten rules whose observance are of first importance in the country in which we are living in the second quarter of the twentieth century? If any moralist, either pharisee or prophet, were asked to draw up what he regarded as the ten most important rules of individual conduct, or the ten best fitted to the conditions of his own country in his own time, would he merely repeat the Decalogue, would he introduce some changes, or would he lay down an entirely new set of rules?

Very few, even of those who express reverence for that ancient code, would, if put to a real test, affirm that each and every

one of those ten rules is more important in his day and generation than any other which might be substituted. Those who
do insist verbally upon the supreme importance of those ten
rules over all others, could easily be shown by their actions to
think otherwise. Let us suppose, for example, that some moral
innovator should suggest that a new commandment, "Thou
shalt not get drunk," in this day of high speed, and in our
interlocking civilization, with its minute interdependence of one
upon another, might well displace the third commandment,
relegating the latter to a place among the less important rules
in the moral code. Such general statements as that moral
codes must change to fit new conditions would not save the
innovator from violent and widespread attack.[1] Yet there
would be much that could reasonably be said in favor of such
an innovation. The only valid objection is on the ground that
the Decalogue has long ceased to be an active code supported
by the effective sanction of public opinion. Those who obey
all its rules receive no more public esteem than those who
regularly and habitually break some of them, especially the
third, fourth, fifth, and tenth. Instead of an active code it
has become a literary monument which it would be sacrilege
to attempt to edit, alter, or bring up to date. That would be
like proposing to edit, or bring up to date, The Mayflower
Compact, The Declaration of Independence, or the Gettysburg
Address. The very fact that the Decalogue has ceased to be
an active code illustrates the general statement that moral
codes change in conformity to other social and industrial changes.

Without even intimating that the Decalogue needs editing,
we may discuss the relative importance under present conditions, of a rule, whatever its source, like the third commandment which is interpreted, perhaps incorrectly, as forbidding
swearing, and the rule suggested above against drunkenness.
Whatever any one may say on that subject when he is considering only generalities, when put to a practical test, he would
show less fear or disapprobation of the man who swears than

---

[1] The author knows because he has had experience.

of the man who gets drunk. If asked to choose between riding behind a locomotive engineer who was likely to swear and one who was likely to get drunk, there are not many who would choose the latter. If asked to make a similar choice in the matter of automobile drivers, drug clerks, bank cashiers, or any one else in a responsible position, the person's drink habits are likely to seem more important than his habits with respect to swearing. In short, in a social condition when we are so dependent upon one another as we are today, dependability must rank as a major virtue. Anything which destroys dependability must rank, therefore, as a major vice. Nothing except killing, lying, and stealing so effectively destroys dependability as drunkenness.

Even among those who agree perfectly on the general statement that new conditions require new moral codes, violent quarrels are likely to arise over each and every specific change wherever and whenever it is proposed. One might go beyond the vague and general statement and lay down some fairly definite principles, and still not start a riot. The reader is advised to try an experiment. Let him say to any group of friends that our civilization is characterized by great interdependence. That is so apparent as to be bromidic. Let him go further and say that dependability is necessary if there is to be interdependence. That will be accepted by those who have not lost interest in such commonplace remarks. Anything which destroys dependability, such as lying and stealing is, therefore, not only on conventional but on purely rational grounds, to be condemned by any group which hopes to be civilized. Even that may be accepted without dispute. The further remark that a drunk man, or even one who is half drunk, is undependable, may provoke some attention, but it could scarcely be denied. Yet to state the obvious conclusion that to be drunk, or even partially drunk, is to be condemned on the same ground as lying or stealing, and that a man who gets drunk is as bad as a liar or a thief, would be likely to start a riot, especially among the intellectual aristocrats.

Not only are there long-time trends in the changing moral

order, but occasional breaks with moral tradition which go under the name of *moral vacations*. The strain of living under strict rules of whatever sort is sometimes relieved by a recess. Early rising and the punching of time-clocks may be relieved by lying in bed on Sunday; imprisonment in shops and offices by going fishing; attendance upon classes, listening to dull lectures and poring over uninteresting books by an occasional escapade for the vexation of the dean. The value of all these forms of relaxation depends, of course, on our ability to return to our routine work with improved morale, until time for another outbreak. It is a somewhat dangerous experiment, but no one yet knows whether an occasional moral vacation might not conduce to a more socially useful life between vacations. On the other hand, a moral vacation that requires the aid of a narcotic drug to bring relaxation is artificial and cheap. It is clearly possible to carry the idea of moral adventuring too far.

No human personality has ever been more creative of moral change than was Jesus of Nazareth. Yet moral history pictures him once obscure and humble, the son of a carpenter, a prophet unheard in his own country. He was a moral malcontent in his generation. He brought down upon himself the disapproval of the pharisees,— the ritualists and popular leaders of his day,— and the punishment that the Roman government was content to give to thieves. It would be possible to multiply instances of obscure and humble people who have been the cause of moral changes,— people like the forty Rochdale workmen who began the great English coöperative movement; like the feminists who, within the last half century, have ventured away from the home into the business world and politics, and on to tennis courts, and who, even earlier, entered the field of moral reform. Yet it must not be too hastily assumed that because a moral variation has been accepted and embodied in the mores it has passed the final test. No group is infallible. The real test comes later. If, as a result of the acceptance and adaptation of the moral variation, the group suffers, grows weaker, or does not keep pace in its growth and power with rival groups, the moral variation was vicious and not good.

Your "prophet" was a false prophet who led the people astray. The old fogies, such, for example, as Cato, who resisted the moral innovation, were right. On the other hand, if the innovation was of the kind that released human energy and directed it to the upbuilding of a stronger group, the innovator was a true prophet and those who resisted it were "stand-patters" in the bad sense of that term. However, the fact that a moral innovation is rejected and never embodied in the mores does not finally and irrevocably condemn it. The group may be merely committing group suicide by rejecting the innovation that might have kept it alive. Yet it can not be too often repeated that most innovations are of the wrong sort, for the simple and sufficient reason that there are more wrong than right ways of doing anything. This consideration is recommended to those innovators who remind themselves of Jesus.

Sometimes great moral leaders arise who consciously set about inventing new ways for human beings to behave, seers like Savonarola who made a funeral pile of the vanities in Florence, like Martin Luther, like Jesus — as the New Testament pictures him — coming to give a more abundant life to men on earth. The great moral leader has more than personal needs in his mind; he is conscious of the needs of a whole group of people, if not humanity at large. And he is consciously inventive of moral variations which he thinks will satisfy these needs as they change. The ways of behaving which he invents are not necessarily foreordained to prove socially useful, or to satisfy human needs, any more than the moral inventions of the individual who is quite unconscious of his moral creativeness, are destined to satisfy human needs. However, a moral variation, no matter where it arises, must prove socially useful or else it will eventually die. Either it will not be imitated by human beings and will die of social disapproval, or, if adopted by a tribe, it will, if given time enough, kill the tribe. The moralities of sovereign states, changing and evolving, reflecting the sum total of moral change going on within them, find themselves involved in a struggle for social prestige and physical survival within a circle that finally includes the known world.

There is one thing a moral variation must do to survive in its passage through this labyrinth of selection. It must help the individuals and groups to survive,— individuals to survive within groups and groups to survive in inter-group struggle. If it fails in this, it fails in everything. Just as, in the physical world, physical variations that survive the natural sifting process must help organisms to satisfy their needs in a physical environment; so, in the social world, the moral variations that win social prestige must, if they have real survival value, help groups of human beings to satisfy their needs in an environment of rival groups. The question immediately arises: Is there any kind of measuring rod which indicates exactly how well a new way of behaving will satisfy human needs? There are slowly coming into life rules of behavior which all men on earth may some day accept without question as fundamental to social life at its fullest. Then all humanity may become an effective group, as it is not now. When fundamental rules of international law and order, of justice and coöperation are accepted by all the nations of the earth, then an international parliament may evolve to take the place of war as the instrument of selection. It may judge the behavior of those groups now called nations.[1] The judging will be by the measurable test of social usefulness, the effectiveness of behavior in providing human life with sustenance and security. And the means by which the judging will be made effective will be by loss of prestige, by the subjugation of nations who do not behave in ways that are good for the health of a greater society. The loss of prestige will make itself felt most painfully in loss of national income. A nation can be controlled through its pocketbook.

To naïve and trusting mortals, who are still confident that right and wrong can be proclaimed by their own infallible intuitions or by the authoritative word of priests — or even by their own reasoned self-interest — to such the idea of moral evolution must be disturbing. To such the evolving moral

---

[1] Needless to say, some means must be found for controlling population and the movements of population before international rivalries can be settled on a peaceful basis.

world must seem a tottering, uncertain, or unreasonable place in which to live. Yet even such might gain confidence, from an understanding of moral evolution, that there is a kind of solidity in moral law that can anchor their perplexed minds and keep their souls from being tossed into Hades or an Anarchy on Earth. There are morals that have stood the test of time and of moral selection longer, that have survived more universally, than others. These morals are *relatively* unchanging; they can be clung to with a conservative, rigid faith in their present rightness, because they answer human needs that are relatively unchanging. It is possible to say that *any* sound system of morals must approve certain fundamental ways of behaving, not because they are thought to have been graven on stone on Mount Sinai, but because in the course of evolution they have stood the test of moral selection. Groups of people who have behaved in such ways have survived, have been able to conquer or exert a psychic command over other groups that have behaved differently. Survival is the earmark of moral solidity, of rightness.[1]

It would be possible to catalogue morals according to their survival value and the amount of change they have undergone in the course of evolution. But it will be enough here to suggest a few that have survived Methuselah and changed very little. There are three groups of them in particular which must be mentioned because they have been more important than others in adapting men to life. There are, for instance, those morals that forbid men who live together to use violence in their dealings with one another. The use of violence among the members of a team or a social group must be strictly limited, put under the ban of rule and regulation, allowed only under rare circum-

---

[1] M. J. Savage, *The Morals of Evolution* (Geo. H. Ellis, Boston, 1880), "Rights and Duties in Matters of Opinion," pp. 146–160. "It does not make any difference what you believe concerning matters that are purely speculative. . . . The minute you come into practical affairs, to those that . . . touch character and conduct, then opinion means life and death, and it is not a slight affair at all. . . . "You have no right to an opinion because it is your opinion. If there were only a vagrant law in the intellectual realm, the great majority of opinions that are walking up and down the earth would be arrested for lack of 'visible means of support.'"
"You have no right to tolerate a false opinion in me" (pp. 151–152).

stances which gentlemen of honor would agree demand sword, pistol, or gloves; or else violence within the group must be altogether banned. For if men were forced to go constantly armed against their neighbors in fear of their lives, their energies would be taken from productive labors and consumed in the task of protecting their skins. The elimination of violence within the group is a first and always important prerequisite for the maintenance of any kind of social order, or successful group life. So important to the success of group life are those morals which outlaw violence among members of the group, so high is their survival value, that no group that does not enforce them can compete for long in a struggle with another group that obeys them — other circumstances being equal. These morals can be accepted now on faith as being full of righteousness; for they have always and universally stood up under the test of moral selection, relatively unchanging.[1]

Morals that forbid the use of fraud among neighbors in their dealings with one another must always rank as high in their survival value as those forbidding violence. Lying and thieving gain entrance to society under many apparently respectable aliases; but no society can afford to tolerate them in any guise. For men who can not trust one another can not live together as successfully as men who can. Morals that ban lying and thieving put a brake on the elemental anarchy in human nature. They are rather negative, however, in their appeal. There are morals of a more positive kind that give fraud a bad name, morals that make trustworthiness and dependability esteemed in society. Dependability is a large name for a good many kinds of behavior that are of unrivalled importance to the success of group life. It includes common honesty. It includes sobriety; for the drunken man can not be trusted. It includes the giving of value for value in trade.

---

[1] The use of violence in the dealings of nations with one another can be said to be proving itself more and more morally wrong, as the whole world of man becomes more and more a social group, as nations live and struggle together as neighbors against world enemies, and not against one another. Nevertheless, it is still true that violence within the group is more fundamentally destructive of the possibilities of human life than violence between groups.

If social life had not made it possible for a person to specialize in his job of earning bread, to do one useful thing well, to sell his talent and then depend on other men for producing most of his heart's desires, trustworthiness would not be so indispensable an item in any moral code. When social life is simple, to be sure, and each man shifts more or less for himself, dependability is not quite so vital as when men become more and more interdependent, as their relations with one another become less face-to-face and more complex and intangible. When the economic world is small and simply organized, it is well enough to say, "Let the buyer beware." Presumably he knows when to be on guard and for what. He can depend a great deal on his own judgment. But when industry gets to running on a large scale, when it becomes so intricately organized that no one knows very much about the case history of anything he buys, when a person can not be wise enough to save himself from being cheated on all sides, he would starve if he could not trust his neighbors. Self-sufficient human beings, particularly those close to the soil, do not need to count on their neighbors for very much, except in hard times. But always when food is scarce, or war is in the air, they have to depend on one another. Morals that forbid the use of fraud among neighbors and make dependability a valued kind of behavior have for so long and so universally passed the test of moral selection, have survived so unchanged that they can be believed in now as right.

Morals that forbid the use of violence and fraud among neighbors appear as old standbys in the history of moral evolution. There are others that must be ranked along with these as being both venerable and irreproachably righteous. Human beings do not begin to live together very successfully until they become reasonable and accommodating in their dealings with one another. Morals that demand reasonableness in human behavior are of stupendous importance to the success of group life. Such morals demand the thoughtful consideration of disagreements, the viewing of a dispute from every angle, the settling of quarrels without fists or tears, with reason and not pure emotion, by discussion, by arbitration. In our day these morals take the form of parliamentary government, of pleadings at the bar of justice, of meetings between laborers and capitalists, of polite debate among friends. The use of reason enables people to see just how they can help themselves and others at the same time most efficiently. It releases human potentialities, and within social bonds, for men who can use their heads to compromise their disagreements can exert the force of their personalities without crippling one another either in body or mind. No one is a total loser by a reasonable compromise. It takes two to mend a quarrel; both win. Morals that make reasonableness in human behavior fashionable have always passed the test of moral selection. For so long they have helped men to survive, to adapt themselves to the difficulties of living, that they can now be called right, on faith.

If, as has been argued in this chapter, a sound system of morals has survival value for the tribe, it must follow that a true moral reformer or prophet is, in a rather literal sense, a savior of his people — a savior, that is, from earthly destruction. He is a true reformer or prophet only when he sees vital weaknesses in the morals of his tribe which endanger its survival, and tries to persuade the people to so change their ways as to make the group stronger,— to keep the tribe alive. Otherwise he is a false prophet and no true Messiah.

If he is a true Messiah it is because he tries to give them a system of morals which will economize their energies, or turn every ounce of tribal energy into constructive channels, where it will contribute to the life of the tribe and make it possible for larger and larger numbers to live together in harmony, and to supply their needs more and more amply. Such a leader, if followed, will be the builder of a great nation, which will eventually free itself from the dominion of other tribes with weaker moral systems. No other kind of Messiah has any place in a world of scientific reality.

CHAPTER VIII

CULTURE AND SURVIVAL

1. *Two Aspects of Culture.* In the earlier stages of the development of social groups, survival was the final test of social efficiency. No matter how strongly we, with our prejudices, our acquired likes and dislikes, and our subjective standards of merit, might approve a given type of society, if that type uniformly failed to survive, there would not be much to be said. Our only alternative would be either to change our minds or to fall back on the assertion that the universe was evil and selected the evil rather than the good for survival. But in our modern, highly advanced societies, it is not always easy to realize how vital the question of group survival is. Our attitude toward that question is somewhat like that of a man with abounding health and energy toward the question of hygiene. We have grown careless, feeling that there is no danger of our society being extinguished, and if it decays, the tragedy will not take place in our day. In such a state of mind, we cease to evaluate social institutions, customs, mores, and religions on the basis of their relation to group survival. There is therefore a tendency to evaluate them on the basis of our own subjective standards without regard to social efficiency.

One group of sociologists is, accordingly, concentrating its attention on that phase of social life which goes under the name of culture. In its larger aspects, culture is a synonym for civilization. In this sense, culture has been written about by historians and philosophers long before the word sociology was coined. A study of civilization in all its aspects is too much for any single student to undertake. Those writers who have succeeded in adding to our knowledge of this vast field have generally concentrated on some restricted part of it. Others, like Henry Thomas Buckle,[1] have developed special theses regarding the general laws which determine the progress and character of civilization. Still others, like Herbert Spencer,[2] have attempted to catalogue and describe all the artifacts, institutions, and customs of all the peoples of the world, but have found the task too great.

The two synonyms, culture and civilization, may be defined as everything which the individual has to learn from his social surroundings. We have seen, in our discussion of the prolongation of infancy or the learning period, that the human individual is not endowed with instincts enough to enable him to do all that is necessary in his complicated life. He must learn by contact and experience. But his contacts are of two sorts. He has contacts with the physical objects which surround him and must learn how to adjust himself to them. He also has contacts with other human beings and must learn their ways. Sooner or later he must learn that these other human beings, like himself, had to learn from their fellows and predecessors. He learns also that there are certain standardized ways of doing things which are handed down from generation to generation, with new additions and subtractions from time to time. Some things are done with tools, and he must learn their uses, or some of them. Some ways are handed down by oral tradition and he must listen and learn. Other ways are told in printed books and he must learn how to use books.

One of the best attempts to describe and contribute to our understanding of culture in this wide sense was made by the late William G. Sumner[3] in his *Folkways*. This may seem like

---

[1] See his great work on *The History of Civilization in England* (D. Appleton & Co., New York), vol. I, 1857, and vol. II, 1861.

[2] See his monumental but unfinished *Descriptive Sociology* (D. Appleton & Co., New York, 1873 and 1910).

[3] *Op. cit.*, also Sumner and Keller, *The Science of Society, op. cit.*

a narrowing down of the subject, but it need not be. Anthropologists are likely to confine themselves to a study of the ways of primitive folk, and, in so far as they succeed, they avoid rambling over the entire field.

If the student will take the trouble to write a list of all that he has found out for himself, or learned to do without being taught by some one else, and subtract this list from the sum of all that he has learned to know or to do, the remainder will be what he has learned from his social surroundings. It has been handed down to him on the thin air of oral tradition, in the printed book, or in the form of various objects which other men have made. All this that he has learned, and much more that is there to be learned, if he ever gets around to it, may be called culture in its wide sense. It is the equipment, in the way of knowledge, technique, and artifacts with which he is provided by the society of which he is a member.

Part of this equipment is directly and immediately useful for survival. Fighting instruments and the technique of making and using them, tools of production to aid in the gaining of subsistence, and the technique of making and using them, clearly have survival value for the social group. So also has the morale, both military and industrial, of the group. So have many of the moral standards,— the social approval of courage, honesty, and industry, and disapproval of cowardice, dishonesty, and laziness. These and many other phases of culture in the widest sense, help to keep the tribe alive, to enable nations to grow in power, wealth, and numbers.

Not all students of the cultural aspects of sociology have identified culture with civilization. There is a tendency to define culture in a narrower sense as consisting of the adornments, embellishments and amenities of social life, having its sources in certain personal and spiritual qualities. From a sociological point of view, this narrower concept derives its value from its emphasis on "culture" as one of the "non-utilitarian ways," so to speak, in which surplus energy, individual and social, expands itself. As Cowan points out: "It is probably in this source (surplus energy) that we must look for the rise of 'art' in the widest sense of the term. . . . In the young of men and animals the instinct expends itself in the universal instinct of 'play,' but later on, may express itself not only in the gaudy coloring of the butterfly, the mid-day song of the lark, and the midnight passion of the nightingale, but equally in the corroboree of the native Australian, in the dance of the dervish, in the rough drawings of mammoth and reindeer by the most primitive man as well as the picture by Raphael, in the earliest savage recital and the last play by Shakespeare."[1]

The thesis of this chapter may as well be stated in advance. *Culture is the dissipation of surplus human energy in the exuberant exercise of the higher human faculties.*

The wider aspect of culture has the dignity of authority on its side. It is only fair, therefore, that the eminent authorities which identify culture with civilization, or all that an individual acquires from his social group, should have a hearing. Tylor gives a most inclusive definition. He says: "Culture is that complete whole which includes knowledge, belief, art, morals, custom, and other capabilities acquired by a man as a member of society."[2] In other words, the complete whole of group activities in their manifold expression. Social life produces group-ways of living; it is these that constitute culture in the broadest or the anthropological sense.[3] They are not the same the world over. There are cultural differences that interest the curious-minded. "Why do Siberian nomads milk cows while their Chinese neighbors do not? Why do early tools from India resemble so amazingly those from far-off Spain? What made Californian life so different in Indian days from what it is now?"[4] Anthropology exists just to answer questions like these about culture.

[1] Andrew Reid Cowan, *Master-Clues in World History* (Longmans, Green and Co., New York, 1914).

[2] Edward B. Tylor, *Primitive Culture* (Estes and Lauriat, Boston, 1874), vol. I, p. 1.

[3] This sounds like what William G. Sumner called "Folkways."

[4] R. H. Lowie, "Are We Civilized?" *Human Culture in Perspective* (Harcourt, Brace & Co., New York, 1929), p. 6.

Clark Wissler, in presenting the typical anthropological view of culture, says:

We speak of the mode of life of this or that people as their culture. . . . We say that the Eskimo has a culture of his own because . . . (in his daily activities) . . . we see new and surprising practices not to be found among other groups of people. Thus, he lives in a snowhouse, uses a peculiar boat called a *kayak*, rides upon sleds drawn by dogs, heats his house with seal oil lamps . . . etc. etc. Likewise, his methods of greeting strangers . . . ethical ideals, standards of beauty . . . are peculiarly different. . . .[1]

The term culture [says Dixon] has come to be used by anthropologists, sociologists . . . as a designation for that totality of peoples' products and activities, social and religious order, customs and beliefs which, in the case of the more advanced, we have been accustomed to call their civilization . . . the culture of any people comprises the sum of all their activities, customs, and beliefs.[2]

Cultural anthropologists include under the term culture "all the phenomena of human thought and feeling as embodied in human action," and taking form in institutions. To use Lippert's phrase, "Everything that man does to raise himself even in the slightest degree above his natural limitations, is a bit of culture."[3] In brief, the anthropologist does not isolate culture as one aspect only of the achievements of the human mind, but rather as synonymous with it. J. K. Folsom says, in different words: "Culture is the sum total of all that is artificial. It is the complete outfit of tools, and habits of living, which are invented by man and then passed on from one generation to another. It does not include any of the inborn biological characteristics of man."[4] This suggests that culture is, quite simply, something superorganic. But there are still difficulties of interpretation. Superorganic phenomena appear, in the work of Herbert Spencer, as social institutions; E. de Roberty, on the other hand, classifies the superorganic as social thought or abstract knowledge.[5]

---

[1] *Man and Culture* (Thomas Y. Crowell Company, New York, 1923), pp. 1 and 2.

[2] Roland Dixon, *The Building of Cultures* (Charles Scribner's Sons, New York, 1928), p. 3.

[3] J. Lippert, *The Evolution of Culture*, trans. by George Peter Murdock (The Macmillan Co., New York, 1931), p. 3.

[4] *Culture and Social Progress* (Longmans, Green and Co., New York, 1928), p. 15.

[5] *Connaissance.* See P. Sorokin, *Contemporary Sociological Theories* (Harper & Brothers, New York & London, 1928), pp. 439, 448-449.

Culture historians also make a kind of verbal carry-all of culture. "A culture," says Dawson, "is a common way of life — a particular adjustment of man to his natural surroundings and his economic needs. In its use and modification it resembles the development of a biological species. . . . It is primarily due, not to change in structure, but to the formation of a community, either with new habits, or in a new and restricted environment."[1] According to Dawson, the rise and formation of a culture is brought about by four fundamental interacting factors:— (1) "race, *i.e.* the genetic factor; (2) environment, *i.e.* the geographical factor; (3) function or occupation, *i.e.* the economic factor; (4) thought, or the psychological factor." They take it to mean everything that civilization means. Just to illustrate — Egon Friedell, in a recent *Cultural History of the Modern Age* outlines it as follows:[2]

"And thus we arrive at the following as a broad presentation of human culture:

	Man	
Acting	Thinking	Creating
in economy and	in discovery and	in art, philosophy
society, state and	invention, science	religion"
law, church and	and technology	
custom		

2. *Culture as Adornment.* Most of us, however, do not con-

---

[1] Christopher Dawson, *The Age of the Gods* (Houghton Mifflin Co., Boston, 1928), pp. xiii–xiv.

[2] *A Cultural History of the Modern Age*, translated from the German by C. F. Atkinson (A. A. Knopf, New York, 1930), vol. 1, p. 21. German *Kultur* historians, especially, use "culture" in the sense of "civilization." One of them, Kurt Breysig, remarks: "Die Kultur, die ich meine, umfasst, im buchstäblichen Sinne des Wortes, alle sozialen Institutionen, wie alles geistige Schaffen (Vorwort *Aufgaben und Masstäbe einer allgemeinen Geschichtsschreibung*). Again, W. Foy says, "Die Kulturgeschichte ist die Wissenschaft von der kausalen Entwicklung alles dessen, was das geistige Leben und die äussere Lebens Fuhrung sämtliches jetzt oder einst lebender Völkes der Erde ausmacht." (*Kulturgeschichtliche Bibliothek.* Vorwort des Herausgebers, p. viii.) Wilhelm von Humboldt makes an exceptional distinction between *Civilization* and *Kulture;* "Die Civilisation ist die Vermenschlichung der Voelker in ihren ausseren Einrichtungen und Gebräuchen und der darauf Bezug haben den inneren Gesinnung. Die Kulture fügt dieser Veredelung des gesellschaftlichen zustandes Wissenschaft und Kunst hinzu." (Quoted from Gobineau, Vol. I, pp. 81–82).

nect culture with everything that might be called civilized or a product of civilization. We do not think of the New Yorker as more cultured than the Hottentot; at least the word culture does not suggest that contrast. We are more likely to contrast the rude manners of the backwoodsman with the polished manners of the educated urbanite, or the dweller in the East Side of New York with the resident of Park Avenue. We think of culture as a personal adornment acquired, however, from contact with a social environment which places a high valuation on certain thoroughly standardized forms of behavior, dress, or speech. It may be associated with certain formal mannerisms, swallow-tail coats, peculiarities of accent, or knowledge of certain esoteric subjects. "People who talk about culture," John Bright remarked in one of his speeches, "by which they mean a smattering of the two dead languages of Greek and Latin, . . ."[1]

Educational frills, of course, are never intended to be very useful. "Thank God here is something which is of no use to anybody," is supposed to express a purely cultural ideal of education. A knowledge of such subjects, like the secrets of free masonry, is supposed to admit one to the mystic circle of the cultured. Such knowledge is supposed to be more or less ornamental. Technologically, the practices of cultured people are of a ceremonial nature.[2] As Lester F. Ward[3] remarks: "The education of culture aims to supply the mind with something, with some knowledge even, but it is a kind of knowledge which has no practical value."

Men dress their children's minds [said Herbert Spencer] as they do their bodies, in the prevailing fashion. As the Orinoco Indian puts on his paint before leaving his hut, not with a view to any direct benefit, but because he would be ashamed to be seen without it; so, a boy's drilling in Latin and Greek is insisted on, not because of their intrinsic value, but that he

---

[1] Quoted by Matthew Arnold in *Culture and Anarchy* (Smith, Elder & Co., London, 1869), p. 1.

[2] The connection between the words *cult* and *culture* is more than a purely etymological one.

[3] *Dynamical Sociology, op. cit.*, vol. II, p. 565.

may not be disgraced by being found ignorant of them — that he may have "the education of a gentleman."[1]

Spencer did not approve of an ornamental education. Neither did Mr. Bright. They were both men who were more interested in the obvious necessities of life than its superfluous adornments. It is because practical men — the mass of men — associate culture with the ornamental and ceremonial that they do not hold it in high esteem. They like common sense which answers well enough for them the most insistent questions of their existence — what to eat and when to sleep and what to wear for comfort, health, and decency. On the other hand, culture in the sense of a cult of exacting ceremonial observance, of standardized forms of behavior, is not without its devotees. To gain admission to the mystic circle of such a cult becomes an obsession. Once admitted, to insist on exacting standards for the admission of others, in order to keep the numbers few and select, becomes a business. It is a part of the universal desire for distinction, for separation from the common herd. Culture in this sense, far from being a form of progress, is a sign of decrepitude. It belongs to old and wornout civilizations — at least it is found in its highest perfection where social degeneration is far advanced.

It is still difficult for the devotees of this kind of culture to imagine how anyone can lead a life of elegant leisure without cheap servants to relieve him of all routine or disagreeable work. But the more cheap servants there are the more poverty there is. Consequently, that ideal of culture is built on the poverty of servile masses. How, it is asked, can one entertain graciously without a train of servants to wait on the guests, but in our crude Western democracies, servants demand such high wages as to put them beyond the reach of any but the very rich. The further East one goes, the more cheap servants there are. The

---

[1] *Education, Intellectual, Moral and Physical* (D. Appleton & Co., New York, 1866), p. 23. Spencer did not like, in the education of women, the immense importance of "accomplishments" which were so much more ornamental than useful. See also Huxley, *Science and Education* (D. Appleton & Co., New York, 1904), especially the Essay on Science and Culture.

crude democracies of the West have to depend on machines to do the work which cheap servants perform in the old and cultured East. True, machines do it better, but they do not give tone to social life as well-trained and liveried servants do. A machine is not obsequious and therefore does not contribute to one's sense of personal superiority over others.

It is, of course, true that men can give free play to their higher faculties only when they are relieved of the disagreeable necessity of expending their limited energy in heavy muscular work or in soul-killing routine and drudgery. Slaves and cheap laborers were once a means of relieving the cultured few of all drudgery, they were the only means available before the age of mechanical inventions. If culture is defined in the esoteric sense of personal refinement, slavery or cheap labor may be said to have been essential to the development of culture; but, of arithmetical necessity, culture under such conditions was essentially aristocratic,— a concentration of the surplus energy of the whole group in a few select individuals. For the masses who had to do not only their own rough work but that of the cultured few, there was no surplus energy,— no energy to spare for the adornments, embellishments, and amenities of social life.

From whatever point of view the study of culture is approached or whatever definition of culture is adopted, if the study is carried far enough, it becomes evident to the student, first, that it is a phase of social activity, and second, that it is a kind of activity which indicates that there is a surplus of energy not required for the grim business of keeping alive. In a rather ultimate sense, its study might be said to be a branch of human energetics.[1]   But, rather obviously, the larger the proportion of the population that can show this surplus of energy, the greater the total surplus will be.

Among creatures who are incapable of thinking and planning for the future, no such surplus of energy is ever possible. Among them there is equality, so far as classes are concerned, but it is an equality without a standard of living. They all live on or

---

[1] See the author's *The Economy of Human Energy* (The Macmillan Co., New York, 1924).

near the minimum of subsistence, and, in times of drouth or cold, are all in imminent danger of starvation, the weaker actually starving. One reason why they never can rise above such conditions is that they have no prudence in the matter of reproduction of numbers. Multiplication is with them a purely biological function, unrestrained by prudence or standards of living. Another reason is that, even if a few were prudent enough to reduce their progeny or increase their productivity in order to have plenty for themselves, the communism which exists among them would give the prudent no advantage over the imprudent. Food supplies would still be at the mercy of the most reckless breeders or the most wasteful consumers. Any surplus, however great, would soon be dissipated by overmultiplication, or overconsumption on the part of the imprudent masses.

Among creatures, however, with enough prudence to think of and plan for the future, it is possible to keep numbers well within the means of subsistence and therefore to enjoy a surplus. This surplus is reducible to a surplus of energy. Not all the energy of the race is required to get food enough to maintain itself. There is energy left for other things. But we are here faced with the great fact of differential prudence. Prudence, like other qualities which have been bred into the race by evolution, is the product of natural selection. But natural selection cannot proceed except where there is variation. In short, one of the twin pillars on which the theory of evolution rests is differentiation or variation. In order that a high degree of prudence might evolve, the more prudent individuals had to be selected for survival and the less prudent exterminated.

Under the primitive communism which exists among the lower animals, as pointed out above, even prudence in the multiplication of numbers, if practised by a few, would do them no good. Their limited progeny would have to take pot luck with the unlimited progeny of the reckless spawners. It is only where the more prudent can have some advantage over the less prudent that natural selection can favor the more prudent and help to breed up a prudent race. In the matter of storing food, for example, if every store accumulated by the prudent were the common property of all, it would be eaten up by the numerous progeny of the imprudent breeders. It was not until property came into existence that prudence began to have any survival value; and, of course, until it began to have some survival value, natural selection could not favor the prudent.

The contemporaneous development of prudence, and of institutions which give prudence some survival value, halted the universal tendency to dissipate surplus energy in the process of multiplication and bring the whole species down to a common level of misery on the margin of subsistence. As this process of dissipation was retarded, a surplus of energy, available for other things than subsistence, was possible. This surplus is the dynamic factor in civilization — of culture in its broadest sense — as well as of culture in its narrowest and most supercilious possible sense. There is neither civilization nor culture except where there is a surplus of energy which a race, or a fraction of the race, is free to use as it pleases.

The type of culture, of course, depends on the purposes for which the surplus energy of the race or class is used. It may be used in the building of tombs for its kings, as in Egypt; in supporting a priestly class with leisure to develop a vast system of religious ceremonialism, as among the great religious cults of the world; in supporting artists who develop the fine arts, as has been done wherever they have flourished; in building vast political and legal systems, as has been done in all great empires. It may even be used in building machines for carrying people from place to place at high rates of speed, in adorning men's bodies with strange and expensive gewgaws, or in games and amusements of various kinds. In whatever way the surplus energy is used, or whatever kinds of civilization may be developed, the basic fact remains that some men have had a surplus of energy which enabled them to do some of the things which they wanted to do for the pleasure of doing. This is true of the noblest and of the most degenerate of civilizations, and of the broadest and the narrowest types of personal culture. It is true of those engaged in "the frivolous work of polished idleness" and of those who are driven by an Odyssean urge "To follow knowledge, like a sinking star, Beyond the utmost bounds of human thought."

It is clear, therefore, that culture, in a higher or in a lower sense, or in some sense not at all tinged with value judgments, is a product of surplus energy.[1] There is also an element of exuberance in the expenditure of this surplus energy whenever it exists. Culture, therefore, in the widest and most comprehensive sense, may be defined as the exuberant exercise of our faculties. In the highest sense, it is the exuberant exercise of our highest faculties; in a lower sense it is the exuberant exercise of some of the lower faculties. This definition, properly understood, is broad enough to include civilization and all its artifacts, institutions, and religions; it is also specific enough to apply to those frills, material and immaterial, with which the individual who aims at personal culture tries to bedeck his body or his mind. In every case, the civilized man uses surplus energy, not needed for keeping alive, in the exuberant exercise of some of his faculties.

Our definition has something in common with Matthew Arnold's suggestion that culture consists in "an inward condition of the mind and spirit, not in an outward set of circumstances;"[2] but it goes further and tries to bring the idea of culture into harmony with biological, even with Darwinian facts. Culture in the broader sense of civilizatoin and all its products is, of course, a large and important subject, but it belongs to the historian and the anthropologist. Culture, even in the narrower sense of adornment, social polish, ceremonial gentility, or educational frills, is yet something of profound interest to the sociologist. It suggests something in excess of the biological needs of existence. It implies a surplus of social energy not needed for the sheer purpose of keeping the individual and the class alive. It flourishes only where there is such a surplus of

[1] A discussion of the agencies which make a surplus of energy possible, would require a volume. A beginning was made by the author in his *Economy of Human Energy* and in his *Essays in Social Justice*.

[2] *Culture and Anarchy, op. cit.*, p. 14.

energy. It is an advertisement of the solvency of a group, class, or coterie.

3. *Culture as Play.* The exuberant exercise of any faculty,— exercise for the mere joy of exercise,— is play. There is no prudential purpose that directs exuberant action. What is work, as distinguished from play, but simply the exercise of any faculty for other purposes than the joy of action, for ends that concern life and death, and bread and butter? As Henry Berr points out, "the modalities of play are virtually as many as the powers of the individual; and, as a fact, there is the play of the physical organs, the play of the different senses, and the play of the various higher faculties; everything which has seemed to protect and maintain life has afterwards served in its expansion. . . . Play is the spontaneous employment of the living being of superabundant energy. . . . From the moment there is energy (surplus) available this energy tends to employ itself for the pleasure of being so employed, for the relief of this expansion itself. The surplus energy permits of active play."[1]

Matthew Arnold was very much disturbed by John Bright's conception of culture. In his essay, he set out to offer a better one. Without much doubt, he succeeded; but he made culture seem a confusingly vague and abstract thing. On the first page, he quoted Mr. Bright with disapproval; after fifty pages, he remarks:

"I have been trying to show that culture is, or ought to be, the study and pursuit of perfection; and that of perfection as pursued by culture, beauty and intelligence, or, in other words, sweetness and light, are the main characters."[2]

Culture is too frequently defined in just such philosophic words: S. N. Patten in *Culture and War*[3] says for instance, "Life is a pulse, not an equilibrium. Culture is the unification and acceleration of this pulse."

A recent book on *The Meaning of Culture* by John Cowper

---

[1] Foreword to *Art in Greece*, by A. De Ridder and W. Deona (Alfred A. Knopf, New York, 1927).

[2] *Culture and Anarchy*, p. 51.

[3] P. 55.

Powys, probably as sanely and beautifully philosophic as any that has been written, leaves the impression again, that culture is something tenuous and vague. It is, to be quite brief, the expression of the personality — whatever that may be.

Culture and self-control are synonymous terms. . . . What culture ought to do for us is to enable us to find somehow or other a mental substitute for the traditional restraints of morality and religion. . . . It is the application of intelligence to the difficult imbroglio of not being able to live alone upon the earth.[1]

What has been suggested in this book is a view of culture, by no means the only possible one, wherein education plays a much smaller part than does a certain secret, mental and imaginative effort of one's own, continued . . . until it becomes a permanent habit belonging to that psyche or inner nucleus of personality which used to be called the soul.[2]

. . . the fluctuating and malleable creed of culture will imply a constant refining upon our powers of imaginative analysis, in regard to the Protean truth of things, and a constant refining upon our powers of perception, in regard to the mysterious beauty of things.[3]

A dog plays by using his fighting muscles, not in self-defense but in a spirit of pure rivalry with his dog-opponent.[4] A horse plays by using his running and kicking muscles to race with and fight just imaginary rivals. But, fighting muscles have survival value for the dog, and so have running and kicking muscles for the horse. Every creature, including man, plays by exercising such powers and faculties as he has acquired in the process of evolution. Culture is a variety of play — not the exuberant exercise of *any* faculty, only of the *higher* faculties. Higher simply means more scarce in nature.[5] Among living

---

[1] P. 235.

[2] P. 275.

[3] P. 251.

[4] Professor William McDougall speaks of an "impulse of rivalry" as essentially an "impulse to playful fighting, the impulse of an instinct differentiated from the combative instinct in the first instance in the animal world to secure practice in the movements of combat." *An Introduction to Social Psychology* (J. W. Luce & Co., Boston, 1926), p. 117.

[5] The adjective *scarce* is used here in an economic sense; it means rare in relation to a demand for use. The ability to cross the eyes may be a rare faculty in nature, but not scarce, because not needed for any special purpose. The distinc-

things, the capacity to eat and sleep and run is common enough; but only one creature has the power to use his brain to create or his tongue to speak a language.

It happens that the scarcest faculties are the peculiarly human ones that distinguish men from all other creatures. It is perfectly true that a few animals possess scarce abilities peculiar to themselves. A few insects have rather scarce gregarious instincts which they probably exercise for the fun of it. For all we know, they have their Rotary Clubs and Sewing Circles, and so possess the rudiments of culture. Yet it will be convenient simply to remember these potentialities, and to speak of scarce faculties and culture as distinctly human.

A parenthesis here may not be amiss. There are a few people who are called cultured, not so much because they have put on educational frills, as because they are professionally engaged in making frills for other people. The painter and the writer and composer, Beau Brummel, even, might object that the practice of culture is not play but a serious matter. The play-view of culture will not agree that it can be practised at all professionally. The artist is not cultured because of his profession, but only because he takes pleasure in the mere exercise of his creative faculties. The actual painting of a picture, the actual writing of a book, the chiselling of a statue — all this is work; but it has no more to do with culture than the digging of a ditch. The artist is usually a more cultured man than the ditch-digger simply because the work of the artist is often inspired by the exuberant exercise of a faculty more scarce than the ditch-digger possesses — a power of seeing things to which most men are blind. The practice of culture is by no means restricted to those who call themselves artists. Everyone is cultured who exercises his distinctly human faculties for the pure joy of using them.[1] The

tion may seem subtle, but its importance will become evident in the discussion that follows concerning the survival value of culture. In sociology the demand for use concerns, especially, survival and adaptation. Expensive automobiles are more rare than loaves of bread; but not more scarce in famine time.

[1] Mr. Rudyard Kipling, in "L'Envoi," by virtue of his authority as poet and seer, suggests that there will come a time when

". . . no one shall work for money, and

more scarce are the faculties he exuberantly exercises the more cultured, the more human, he is. Most men can throw a ball or a missile with some accuracy, and take an amazing amount of pleasure in it; but only a very few read Shakespeare for fun.

It may not be clear, at this point, why a study of sociology is concerned with play and culture. Is it not an intellectual indulgence for the sociologist to be speculating about anything that seems to bear no obvious relation to problems of adaptation? Does the use of a faculty for the mere joy of using it help any creature to survive? How does play help to fit any form of life to its environment?

The modern world, which tries so hard to be rational, is beginning to look upon play with a scientific eye. Play, in fact, threatens to become a serious matter. Something important is recognized about the value of exercise for its own sake. Play appears to have survival value. The tendency to play, which so many animals show, keeps their faculties fit for meeting the requirements of their existence. Faculties which are needed for survival purposes have to be kept in good running order; they have to be used or they will atrophy. They may need to be used only occasionally for serious business, for matters of life and death; but they must be in condition to meet grave situations. If they are exercised every day for the fun of it, they will be ready for use at any time and, most vitally, when survival hangs in the balance.

There are powers of self-defense, for instance, which are needed only in the face of an enemy, like the ability of the wild horse to run. He may wander for days without meeting a hostile eye; yet, when he does meet danger, it is important for him to run swiftly. He has to keep in good running order. If

no one shall work for fame,
But each for the joy of working . . ."
This time, unhappily, is not to come quite soon — only "When the youngest critic has died"; and, after that, even, we must wait for an aeon or two. But then —
". . . those that were good shall be happy; they shall sit in a golden chair;
They shall splash at a ten-league canvas with brushes of comets' hair;
They shall find real saints to draw from — Magdalene, Peter, and Paul;
They shall work for an age at a sitting and never be tired at all!"

he runs for the fun of it every day, he will be ready to run for his life. If his ability to run has survival value, then in so far as the exuberant exercise of his running muscles increases his ability to run, the exuberant exercise has survival value, too.

Not only does play keep a faculty in condition for work, but it develops a faculty before it can be used for work.[1] In puppy-hood, when the dog cannot fight in order to hold his own in the world, he is preparing, by mimic fighting, for a time when he will need to give battle in self-defense. It is a part of his psychological make-up that he can find pleasure in the mere exercise of his fighting muscles. These must be developed by play before they are ready for work.

If play has survival value, because it puts important faculties in condition for work, culture must have the same kind of value since culture, as we are considering it, is a form of play. Culture is simply the exuberant exercise of the faculties that have given man dominion over other creatures. If these scarce faculties are sometimes needed for survival purposes, and are kept in good condition only by being used for the fun of it, then culture has survival value, because it provides the fun. For instance, the ability to use an elaborate code of signals, called a language, is a scarce faculty which doubtless developed, in the human species, because it had tremendous survival value. It enabled men to work together in large numbers. Only by speech can they work together now, and provide themselves against the pangs of hunger and the onslaught of diseases. The man who can use words eloquently, who can convince his fellows that his needs are their needs also, is the man who stands an excellent chance of surviving in his struggle for a place in the world. And the group of people that can talk best about common needs is the group that can work best together, and survive.

[1] Karl Bücher suggests this idea when he notes: "Industrial activity seems everywhere to start with the painting of the body, tattooing . . . and gradually in advance to the production of ornaments, masks . . . and similar play products. . . . The taming of domestic animals . . . begins not with useful animals, but with such species as man keeps merely for amusement or the worship of gods . . . in play . . . technical skill is developed . . . play is older than work, art older than production for use." *Industrial Evolution* (Henry Holt and Co., New York, 1912), pp. 27–28.

It would be easy enough to illustrate again and again the survival value of culture. There are a number of faculties, vital to human existence, which, like the ability to speak, need to be kept in condition by the exercise which culture provides. Especially is this true of the power of abstract thinking, the scarcest and most distinctly human faculty found on the face of the earth.[1] The ability to think in abstract terms seldom shows itself in a highly developed form; yet it has tremendous survival value because it has made science possible. The animal that made the intellectual leap from an accidental use of a lever to an understanding of the abstract principle underlying its use, and was thus able to use it for a variety of purposes, was able to win consistently and decisively in his life-and-death struggle with the rest of the world. Science is a powerful weapon of defense in his hands. The ability to reason, however, which is so important to man's success in living, is a faculty he must develop and keep in good order by very frequent use. The more he reasons, the more adept he becomes in reasoning. He may find it unhealthy and nervously exhausting to keep up serious thinking for long stretches at a time. Yet, if he can turn from serious thinking and go on using his intellect for the fun of it, with no damage to his nerves, he will have sharper wits than if he did not get so much practice in thinking. That is why people ought to be encouraged to play with their powers of reason — in bridge, or dreams of Utopia,— in charades, riddles, or cross-word puzzles,— in dominoes, magic squares, or the calculus. The sharper their wits become, the better are their chances of success in struggling against the grave obstacles of existence. In fact, all those forms of culture that sharpen the wits, like chess, unprofessional experiments in science, attempts at literary expression, and philosophy, have proved to have such great survival value that modern men are indulging more and more in intellectual play. Other forms of culture, which once had tremendous survival value, are losing in popularity.

[1] It is interesting to note its dependence upon the power of speech.

For instance, communal dancing appears to be almost disappearing, except from the faraway corners of the earth. The ability of a number of creatures to dance rhythmically together is a scarce faculty in nature. Probably because it is dependent upon a primitive kind of intelligence, it developed only in man. It developed because it helped him to survive. It strengthened his tendency to be sociable, heightened his emotions, helped him to live in a crowd.[1] Any one familiar with mob psychology will recognize how potent the influence of communal dancing can be.[2] Morris Ginsberg summarizes very concisely the whole theory of mob psychology:[3]

The fact that individuals in a crowd behave and think differently than when in isolation is simply a particular case of the responsiveness of individuals to environment. In the presence of others, there is a heightening of the social instincts, producing a vague exaltation which urges leaders to take the lead and to "let themselves go" in doing so and in others to follow the lead. This exaltation makes both more suggestible, the leader to the mood of the mob, and *vice versa*. The suggestibility varies according to the objects of attraction. In all, the knowledge that our ideas and feelings are shared by many is encouraging. Thus a process of cumulative suggestion goes on, which tends to inhibit conflicting ideas and emotions and to give to those in the focus dynamic force and energy. Accompanying this exaltation is a feeling of omnipotence and a consequent loss of the sense of personal responsibility. There is also to be noted a concentration of attention and a narrowing of consciousness which results in the absence of the usual controlling ideas and ideals. When to this is added the fact

[1] For an excellent short bibliography on Mutual Aid as a factor of evolution, see W. M. Wheeler's *Social Life Among the Insects, op. cit.,* p. 285.

[2] Any one unfamiliar with mob psychology ought to read that classic on the subject, *The Crowd,* by Gustave Le Bon (translated from the French as far back as 1896). In the first chapter, appears the much-disputed theory that, in a crowd, a new mind comes into being, which is different from the minds of all the individuals who compose it.

Psychological literature is full of explanations which are put forward to account for the apparently unaccountable way a crowd behaves. E. A. Ross, in his *Social Psychology* (The Macmillan Co., New York, 1921), especially Chapters III, IV, V; William McDougall, in the *Group Mind* (G. H. Putnam's Sons, New York and London, 1920), especially Chapter II; E. D. Martin, in *the Behavior of Crowds* (Harper and Brothers, New York and London, 1920); Gabriel Tarde, in *L'Opinion et La Foule* (F. Alcan, Paris, 1910); Scipio Sighele, in *La Foule Criminelle* (F. Alcan, Paris, 1901), are only a few of the authors who have paid a great deal of attention to the mob.

[3] *Psychology of Society* (E. P. Dutton & Co., New York, 1921), pp. 135–136.

that the intellectual level of a crowd is generally low owing to the fact that only the qualities common to all are appealed to, it will be seen that all the phenomena usually noted in mobs and simple crowds can be accounted for.

Fancy a tribe in danger of attack from a hostile band. The warriors of the tribe feel, beforehand, only a lazy peace in their hearts. The day is fine for pursuing their individual ways, for fishing, or sitting in the sun, or hollowing out a tree for a canoe. Why should they be at war? But the drums begin to beat. That is a signal for them to form in a circle, and to begin a slow shuffling of their feet, a slow swaying of their bodies, all in time to the beat of the drums. The movements grow faster, more violent. The rhythm is intoxicating.[1] The individual begins to forget himself. He is conscious, above all else, of being one of a crowd. His personality is lost in the crowd. He is ready to follow where the crowd goes; his will counts for almost nothing. His power to reason grows weak; but his emotions grow stronger and stronger. The leader of the mob, the only one who keeps his head a bit, can exhibit any emotion; and the emotion will be felt by the mob. The war chief suggests danger, betrays pugnacity; the tribe will follow him to battle with the will of one man and the strength of many.

4. *The Power of Idealization.* There is another variety of culture that ought not to go unconsidered. It is the saving grace of civilization, the favorite creation of a faculty which human beings exercise for the fun of it more than any other they have — the capacity of the mind to idealize, to make believe, to make things seem other than they are.

This idealizing capacity has a good many serious uses. It

---

[1] Any one who has never felt the intoxication of rhythm should hear an orchestra play the "Bolero" of Ravel. The drums beat time to a simple dance theme that is repeated again and again, at first slowly, then faster and faster, until the most sophisticated audience has been known to rise to its feet, literally drunk with the rhythm.

Wilhelm Wundt remarks: "The earliest aesthetic stimuli are symmetry and rhythm. (Primitive man) derives pleasure even from the regularly repeated movements involved in making the straight lines of his drawings, and this pleasure is enhanced when he sees . . . the figures . . . the result of his movements." *Elements of Folk Psychology* (The MacMillan Co., New York, 1916), p. 103.

gives people the ability to visualize a new world of their own, if they happen not to like the world as they find it. And so, in giving them a picture of better days, it provides incentive enough for their minds to get to work devising ways and means for making a new world come true. Their making an ideal of the future, actually shapes the future, because the ideal is just reality in embryo.[1] When day-dreaming — roughly speaking — concerns itself with better ways of earning bread and butter, the survival value of the idealizing faculty becomes apparent. In fact, a great deal of serious make-believe has been the boon companion of the intelligence in inspiring all those experiments of science which have given men, from a survival point of view, a prominent position on the earth.

But the idealizing faculty does even more than provide suggestions for improving human destinies. In the face of evils for which the mind seems powerless to conceive a remedy, it gives a real sustenance of faith in the possible rightness of the world, and inevitably lends courage to human striving. If a man feels completely baffled by incongruous circumstance, his imagination has a way of making whatever happens to him seem the best that could happen, after all. If he begins to feel that the necessary labors of existence are disagreeable, his imagination can make them seem noble. The capacity for make-believe has survival value because it helps humanity to help itself. Humanity has needed that kind of help so badly that its idealizing powers have very often been called into serious use.

Particularly in the tragic exigencies of life, when fate seems to have one cornered, when there is no physical way of escape, the power of idealization provides the next best thing,— a way of mental escape. "The vision of the Christ," an intense form of idealization, has enabled men to face unflinchingly ordeals before which mere flesh and blood would quail. A sense of personal honor has served others in similar crises, yet, to a realistic eye, personal honor is of little use to a man after he is dead. The slogan "England expects every man to do his duty"

---

[1] There is no philosophic implication intended, concerning the *reality of the idea*.

derived its soul-compelling power from the idealization and magnification of Duty.

For most tribes and nations war has always seemed a necessity from which there was no apparent escape. For the greater part of mankind, who had to live under conditions which incessant war imposed, it was a great advantage to be able to forget the gruesome and horrible aspects, and to glorify it,— to believe it a noble business, almost a good in itself. This ability to make a virtue of necessity tended to relieve the mental distress of those whose destinies were made hideous, to a realistic mind, by war. The strength of a tribe which had to fight to exist was increased by the fact that the warrior was glorified and that war was made to seem less horrible than it really was. This attitude made better warriors of the men who loved honor and distinction. It made war the goal and ambition of youth. In so far as it made every youth look forward with joy to the day when he could become a soldier, it helped the tribe to survive.

Work is still a necessity as imperious as war ever was. On a fine morning, it seems unreasonable that we should not be lying in the sun or playing. Yet, if we use our idealizing faculty, as we have been taught, and persuade ourselves that work is a blessing, dignified and honorable, if every youth can be made to look forward with joy rather than dread to the day when he can go to work, our willingness to work will tremendously increase and our chances of survival are obviously multiplied.[1]

So important, indeed, is the idealizing faculty to human success in surviving the difficulties of life that it is vital for people to cultivate this faculty,— to get into the habit of using it. If they can get fun out of using it, they will increase their ability to use it. They may find the world quite satisfying most of the time. Their imaginations may not be stimulated, from the sheer necessity of unhappiness or impending danger, to fancy it otherwise. Yet the day is certain to come, when life is far from satisfying, when some one will begin to realize that it is

---

[1] These last two paragraphs are adapted from the introduction to the author's *Sociology and Social Progress* (Ginn & Co., Boston, 1905), pp. 11-12.

a pretty dull routine, when it will take all his power of idealization to gild the treadmill of existence. If he has got into the habit of making believe, for the fun of it, he will not be reduced to despair because he will know how to give himself a dose of courage.

There are a great many varieties of culture that are really no more than the playful exercise of the faculty of make-believe. All those gracious adornments to living that go by the name of ceremony are at heart such. Eating, by way of illustration, is really a rather tedious and very ordinary animal affair. It does not add to our sense of dignity or make us feel "a little lower than the angels." But because most people allow their imaginations to play with the process, it becomes an important and somewhat dignified ceremony. It becomes indecorous merely to masticate and swallow. Conversation and other social graces are made to overshadow the mere process of taking nourishment. Politeness, showing preference for others, make the ceremony of eating a school of sociability. Conversation is never allowed to touch upon the tragic depths of life. It does not matter how hungry a person is; he must appear, out of consideration for others, neither ravenous or apathetic about the food that is placed before him. The table is training ground for developing one's powers of make-believe and of idealizing and dignifying the animal processes.[1]

The playful exercise of the imagination in ceremony happens again and again, even in the ordinary doings of people. There are forms of address which they constantly use and physical gestures which patently gloss their lives with make-believe coloring.[2] They laugh when they feel least like laughing. They

---

[1] These remarks obviously refer to truly ceremonial dining. Unhappily, from many points of view, a great deal of eating is accomplished in the circle of the family without ceremony.

[2] "Originally simple," Herbert Spencer remarks, "these observances become progressively complex. . . . Primitive descriptive names develop into numerous graduated titles. From aboriginal salutes come, in course of time, complimentary forms of address adjusted to persons and occasions. Weapons taken in war give origin to symbols of authority, assuming little by little great diversities in their shapes. Simultaneously there is progress in definiteness; ending, as in the East, in fixed forms prescribed in all their details. . . . The advance in integration, in

rise when some one quite unknown to them enters a room, an act that would seem, if it were not playfully done, a somewhat paradoxical mark of respect. When they are introduced to a stranger, their words are far more suggestive of pleasure than their realistic minds would confess. They make pretty compliments, though they know they are joyfully lying. They meet an acquaintance, and are as solicitous for his health as if they really cared very much. If their personal likes and dislikes are questioned, they answer as convention demands.

Most of the significant acts and events in man's life are surrounded by ceremony. It is one of the most powerful instruments of social control. Its awe and mystery subject the individual to the influence of the leadership of an individual or group, so that his whole personality may be completely dominated. As Bogardus points out: "Ceremony as a tool of the autocratic leader puts the average individual into a more or less helpless situation. If he challenges the leader's ability to control, he is at once accused of taking the group's symbol in vain, and punished. Ceremony is the group visualized and magnified."[1] According to Sumner and Keller ceremonies "are not the product of conscious reflection and rational selection any more than is the body of mores of which they form a part. However, there is expediency in them or they could not have persisted so universally over the earth."[2]

Then, there are a great many festive occasions which are veiled in ceremony, when the imagination gets a good bit of playful exercising, at dances and weddings and wakes. These events are crowded with a symbolism that is designed to make life appear other than it is, to idealize it, to make it seem more gay or more majestic, or more everlasting. The dance is always a kind of masquerade, where the revellers cover up their everyday faces with powder and paint, or a riotous expression of the

---

heterogeneity, in definiteness, and in coherence (characteristic of all evolution), is thus (in ceremony) fully exemplified." *Principles of Sociology* (D. Appleton & Co., London, 1882), vol. II, pp. 211–212.
[1] Emory S. Bogardus, *Fundamentals of Social Psychology* (The Century Co., New York, 1924), p. 353.
[2] Sumner and Keller, *The Science of Society, op. cit.*, vol. III, p. 1695.

features.[1] Costuming is as various as the regions of the earth, but everywhere the dancers dress to idealize their own beauty.[2] They make-believe, for a time, that they really are the people they would like to be.

A wedding is a kind of masquerade full of the same pageantry of costume. The bride is dressed to symbolize purity, and her attendants personify youth and charm and beauty. The ring is a symbol of bondage or fidelity. The confetti and rice and old shoes that are showered on the bride and groom are signs of good luck. It is all make-believe. Wedding ceremonies in all their manifold forms, according to Sumner and Keller, "converge upon a single final termination, consequence or utility, namely, publicity. The expediency of publicity lies in the recognition and safeguarding of the group-interest as distinguished from the individual interest or even that of the family."[3] "Ceremony is, then, a solemn determination explicitly expressed, less in words for the ear than in equally well or better understood action and symbolism for the eye. It makes sure of a deliberate and publicly avowed will."[4] Ceremonies, according to the author, are devices of the imagination for blurring the disagreeable recognition of a fact, or of elevating it above the commonplace, instead of means of facing the fact itself.

In the face of sorrow, too, and even death, there is still ceremony and make-believe. The living, to assuage their grief, like to fancy that the dead are living somewhere beyond their ken. And so the funeral service, because it is full of symbols of the resurrection of the body, or the spirit, allows the imagination to play with thoughts of immortal life. Death being the most inescapable of all events, and being, on the whole, disagreeable to a creature with the capacity for living, the prospect ahead

[1] Ceremony, because it is very often connected with the coming together of people in a crowd, has had some share in making social life attractive, and in stimulating a liking for acting in a crowd. And so it has a survival value of the sort that communal dancing has. The dance, at this point, however, is brought in to illustrate the part it plays in giving exuberant exercise to the idealizing faculty.

[2] The relation that costuming often bears to magic is another point, of course.

[3] *Ibid.*, p. 1695.

[4] *Ibid.*, p. 1698.

of us would seem rather dreary were it not for our power either to forget it or to idealize it. Creatures that look before and after cannot altogether forget its inevitable approach. But with the aid of poetry, hymnology and religious ceremony, we can make it seem not so dreadful after all. Thus, in spite of our gift of foresight, we can approach the inevitable hour with a nonchalance comparable to that of the lower creatures who lack all power of anticipation.[1]

Quite as important as these various forms of ceremony for giving playful exercise to the idealizing faculty, is art. It is the purpose of art to picture the world as it is not, to make it seem more colorful than it is — or more gay, or more tragic, or more mysterious,— to idealize it.[2] The artist is forever exercising his imagination to give emphasis to the things in life that seem so choice to him, to soften or obliterate details that do not please him. The painter exaggerates a color here and softens an angle there; the sculptor shapes the body in proportions more perfect than are ordinarily born in flesh, or else makes a caricature of it; the poet and the novelist pick out a situation, an emotion, a theme, and with all the wizardry of words, hyperbole and metaphor and alliteration, with rhyme and rhythm, make them seem other than they are,— more important, more intense, more exalted.[3]

In giving embodiment to the fancies of his mind, however, the artist creates something that helps to cultivate the make-

[1] Like Pope's lamb:
"Pleased to the last, he crops the flowery food,
    And licks the hand just raised to shed his blood."

[2] "The greatest turning point in the spiritual history of man consists in the stupendous achievement which inaugurates the heroic age. I refer to the creation of the *ideal man*, the hero, and of the god in whom heroic characteristics are magnified into the super-human and demoniacal. Here lies the beginning of a real history of art. . . ." From *Folk Psychology*, by W. Wundt, *op. cit.*, p. 451.

[3] Egon Friedell, in the Introduction to his *Cultural History of the Modern Age* (translated from the German by C. F. Atkinson, New York, 1930), cleverly argues that all history, even, is legend, that it should be, in fact, an artistic exaggeration, a "spiritual costume — history." And he quotes from Oscar Wilde, "To give an accurate description of what has never occurred is not merely the proper occupation of the historian, but the inalienable privilege of any man of parts and culture."

believe habit in others.[1] Day after day and year after year, countless people swarm to the Louvre and gaze at the *Mona Lisa*, and try to imagine the sort of woman she was. What experience could she have had of life, they wonder, that should have implanted so questionable a smile upon her lips? There is the same playful make-believe, as the same unnumbered people stand by the rail which holds them at a respectful distance from the Venus. They exhaust their imaginations in puzzling over the secret of her beauty. If she could come to life, one asks himself, would she "launch a thousand ships," like Helen? And another thinks, If I could only look like her, I'd be "Miss Universe." There is the same stimulus to make-believe in Rodin's *Burghers of Calais*. No one can look at the haggard faces without fancying the story of their starving. No one can know the Madonna of the Italian painters and not feel something of the religious mysticism which inspired her creation. Drama is, in the same way, a stimulus to the imagination. At the play, has any one ever been able to resist a temptation to fancy himself in the rôle of hero? The novel, too, cultivates the make-believe habit. A person does not read a well told story without living it in his own mind, and adding details and changing the plot, even, according to his own fancy.[2]

Both aspects of art,— the art which aims at the reflection of reality, reproducing it as well as possible, and the art which recreates reality embellishing it in idealized form,— have their origin in the exuberance of play. This "make-believe" in its inception is an organically useful activity and is the basis for

---

[1] The artist himself, it is safe to remark, however seriously he may use his idealizing faculty in the professional process of picturing the world other than it really is, finds that his work is often most successfully inspired at times when he catches himself using his imagination in idealizing just for the fun of it.

Karl Groos remarks: "Indeed, it (play) is present in all creative activity, gilding earnest work with a sportive glitter. . . . Although highly developed art does so transcend the sphere of play, it too is rooted in playful experimentation and imitation. . . ." *The Play of Man* (D. Appleton & Co., N. Y., 1901), p. 394.

[2] Literature, in addition to this part which it plays in giving exuberant exercise to the idealizing faculty, has a share in providing playful exercise for the faculty of speech. Reading increases any one's capacity for understanding the meaning of words. And so its survival value must be very high.

all the higher forms of aesthetic activities. At bottom, the manifold forms of culture are expressions of self-realization widening and deepening life through play; it is play sublimated, diversified, and refined. Culture derives its existence from the fact that human life cannot in great measure be lived except under the stimulus of escape from (its) reality. And as Overstreet remarks, "better a dish of illusion . . . and a hearty appetite for life, than a feast of reality and indigestion therewith."[1] The way of escape from life's "reality" into its "unreality" as a necessary human contrivance is co-eval with man and played an important rôle in social organization and social development. The myriads of impermanent "needful falsehoods," idols of one kind or another, which man has shaped through all his existence (and which he probably will continue to shape) must spring from a tendency deep-wrought in the human fibre,— the tendency to dissipate surplus energy in the exuberant exercise of his higher faculties.

In short, through our power of idealization we are able to live, or to believe that we live, in a world of our own creation. Much in life that would seem gruesome and horrible to a realist can be made to take on a glamor of beauty and pleasantness. Pollyanna represents, in not greatly exaggerated form, a valuable and as yet unappreciated capacity of every mind. Without this capacity not many of us would care to live and to "bear the slings and arrows of outrageous fortune."

As to the survival value of culture, the following observations seem pertinent. Next to death, the most unavoidable thing for most of us is work. Except in limited quantities, most necessary work is, on the whole, disagreeable. We need not here go into an elaborate analysis of the mixture of agreeable and disagreeable elements in work. Suffice it to say that agreeable activities are really play, and that to be compelled by necessity to engage in one kind of activity when we would rather be doing something else is disagreeable. The prospect ahead would seem rather dreary for most of us were it not for our power

---

[1] H. A. Overstreet, *The Enduring Quest* (W. W. Norton & Co., New York, 1931), ch. xv, p. 197.

to idealize our work. Literally this is an exercise of the power to make-believe.[1] Through its exercise, life not only becomes more endurable to ourselves, but in addition to that, we work with more zest and enthusiasm than would otherwise be possible.

The power to idealize was present when war was necessary for tribal as well as individual survival value. Work is still necessary for national as well as individual survival. The power to idealize it still has, and will probably continue to have, survival value. Even the power to idealize death probably contributes to our efficiency by enabling us "ever with a frolic welcome" to take "the thunder and the sunshine." Certainly the power to idealize such necessary animal functions as eating and begetting gives us a better opinion of ourselves by enabling us to forget, in part at least, our likeness to and kinship with the lower animals. These are practical exercises of the power of idealization which undoubtedly have survival value.

But this power, like other necessary powers, needs to be developed by play, that is, by exuberant exercise, when it seems to serve no other purpose than to give joy to the actor. The most beautiful and refined products of culture are the products of this kind of exuberant exercise of the idealizing faculty. They include not only play-acting, but the best there is in all the fine arts.

5. *Non-Survival Values.* One of Darwin's significant contributions to sociology was his study of sexual selection in relation to man.[2] In this study he pointed out not only that sexual selection had played an important part in biological evolution but that it had been a major factor in the development of human institutions. As a phase of natural selection it had helped to determine animal forms through the struggle for mates. It was shown to be a factor in determining what individual characters should be transmitted to future generations.

---

[1] The older theological doctrine that work was a curse imposed upon men for Eve's sin of fecundity and Adam's sin of being accessory, had at least one element of realism in it. The modern preachment that work is a blessing is a product of the power to make-believe.

[2] *The Descent of Man*, second edition (A. L. Burt, New York, 1874), pp. 634–708.

In post-Darwinian terms it may be stated that the survival of the individual's germ plasm depends quite as definitely upon the ability of the individual to mate as upon his ability to escape death. Failure to mate destroys the germ plasm as effectually as failure to live. Sexual selection, therefore, is a factor of as great importance in determining the character of a species as the selection of individuals in the struggle to live. The struggle for mates is as vital to the survival of the germ plasm as the struggle for existence. Post-Darwinian discoveries have, in other words, added to the importance which Darwin attached to sexual selection.

In some mysterious way the economy of nature has managed to motivate animals to struggle for mates as powerfully as they are motivated to struggle to live. And yet the refinements and graces of social life, even in the most polite, refined, and gracious human circles, are all associated with sexual selection, or the courting process of mating. It was this aspect of social life which led Professor Giddings to remark: "Therefore all social intercourse, however gracious and refined it may be, is shadowed by potential tragedy, and will be shadowed by it to the end of time."[1] In short, even in the most refined circles of polite society, the man or woman who is beaten in the struggle for a mate has his or her germ plasm as effectually destroyed as though he or she had been shot, stabbed, poisoned, or starved.

Darwin and his followers have amassed a wealth of information regarding sexual selection. In this mass of facts it is possible to find the biological beginnings of what certain students of human society have called culture. In this struggle and the resulting sexual selection certain characters have survival value for individuals which have no value for the species or the organized group as a whole. These characters which help the individual to mate are as likely to be transmitted as are the characters which enable the individual to live. Thus characters are stamped on the species which seem to have no value to the species or the group as a whole, because they are of no apparent

---

[1] *Principles of Sociology* (The Macmillan Co., New York, 1896), p. 102.

use in escaping from or defending itself against its enemies, or in extracting nourishment from its environment. Within the species, the possession or non-possession of a certain character may determine whether a given individual can mate or not, but it may have no bearing whatever on the question of the ability of the species or the group as a whole to survive.

There are, of course, many cases in which success in the struggle for mates depends upon the possession of characters which are obviously useful to the group. In general, where males contend for females by the ordeal of battle, the superior fighters win mates and the inferior fighters remain mateless. The same fighting organs which make for success in mating may very likely prove useful in defense against the enemies of the tribe. In that case the same characters which have survival value in sexual selection also have survival value for the group. The fighting powers of the wild stallion, which enable him to drive all inferior stallions away from his group of mares, is also useful in defending them and their colts against wolves and other enemies.

On the other hand the plumage of the peacock by means of which he fascinates the female, would seem to be a handicap rather than a help in every other phase of the struggle for existence. So far as the species as a whole is concerned, the brilliance of the plumage is something to be enjoyed,— at least by the feminine half,— an andornment to be cherished for purely aesthetic reasons, having no value in the grim struggle for group survival. Yet from the standpoint of the individual male, plumage is a matter of life and death — for his germ plasm — and the characters which it carries. From the standpoint of the species it is an indication of the exuberance of life, of conditions under which the struggle for individual survival is not so intense as to require the maximum economy of vital energy merely to keep alive, under which there is a surplus of energy available for pure display and for no other use.

It is impossible for the thoughtful not to see a great social significance in this distinction between characters whose value is limited to sexual selection and those which have survival value in the more primitive phases of natural selection. Wherever there is, in any human society, an exuberance of vital energy, more than is needed for the mere business of keeping alive, there invariably develops a tendency to display this exuberance in pleasurable activities which have no apparent relation to the struggle for existence. This appears to be as automatic and unplanned as the development of a livelier iris on the burnished dove in the spring when food is superabundant, and the serious business of feeding new mouths has not begun. It even affects our mental attitudes and our philosophies of life. Wherever the conditions of life are hard and most of the energies of men are required for the strenuous business of keeping alive, survival depends upon stern discipline, either imposed from above or self-imposed from within. Those who survive do so either by submitting to the Draconian rule of a powerful leader, or by developing an austere and somber morality which suppresses dissipation and other wastes of human energy.[1]

Those groups who manage to survive by either method soon face a new dilemma. The same discipline which so economized their energies as to save them from extinction now makes them so prosperous as to leave them with a surplus of energy not needed for mere survival. By slow degrees the old discipline is relaxed, the old somber morality becomes "liberalized," the pursuit of positive pleasure displaces the old avoidance of pain and disaster, men forsake the steep and stony path of progress and pursue "the primrose path of dalliance to the everlasting bonfire." Eventually the forces of dissipation overbalance the forces of conservation. Duty, "stern daughter of the voice of God," gives way to self-expression, production no longer exceeds consumption but consumption exceeds production, and

---

[1] "The Eskimo sees no need for effort not connected with the pursuit of daily food, so he smokes and eats and tells tales. He has no printed literature; his only classics are those of legend and fable. Yet why is not the spoken fable of the Bunting and the Snowy Owl enough for the soul whose great ambition is to kill a walrus or caribou, to keep comparatively comfortable in *tupek* or igloo, or to drive the dog team properly? And why should the Eskimo have a greater ambition, so long as he is happy?" George Miksch Sutton in *The Atlantic Monthly*, July, 1932.

each year sees a depletion of the national patrimony. The end of this course is national death unless a moral or religious revival causes the people to turn aside from the pursuit of passive pleasure and rouses them to the joys of strenuosity in productive action. In the latter case, the cycle is repeated. The more thorough-going the revival, the more swift the growth in wealth and power, and the sooner the processes of dissipation and decay set in again.

These alternations of storing and dissipation of social energy come as near to constituting an inevitable cycle as anything connected with human behavior, outside the purely physical and unavoidable cycles of night and day, of the tides, the seasons of the year and possibly of the sun spots, and of birth, growth, decay, and death. In human as in animal and plant life, a surplus of energy not needed for getting food or keeping alive is easily dissipated either in reproduction or in luxury. In either case there is an exuberant exercise of certain powers. The energies which are exercised in gaining subsistence and those which are exercised in dissipating it are seldom in a state of exact equilibrium. Something equivalent to the two physiological processes of anabolism and katabolism goes on continually in the social body. But they are neither mechanical nor purely physiological. They are psychological at least to the extent that they depend upon mental reactions to the stimuli of outside circumstances. Under the pressure of need, men store up subsistence. The habit may persist until it is necessary to build larger barns. But when the barns are bursting with abundance, the almost inevitable reaction is to say, "Soul, take thine ease, . . . eat, drink and be merry"— until the surplus is dissipated. In a purely physiological form, the process shows itself in the sub-human world in some phases of sexual selection. It takes the form of the development of characters which have no use except for the winning of mates. In such cases, the species is able to support characters which have no survival value for it. Such species are the "nouveau riche" of the animal creation.

Reluctant as we may be to admit it, the fact is that none

of the fine arts, as distinguished from the useful arts, or the arts which have survival value for the group, has ever flourished except where wealth was abundant and subsistence easy, at least for the cultured classes. The artist may affect to despise the *bourgeois*, but without the *bourgeois* or his equivalent art never did and never can flourish. The ancient and the mediaeval cities where art flourished were rich cities. They were either made rich by the *bourgeois* virtues of industry, frugality, and sagacity, or by the less commendable activities of military men whose exploits "did the general coffers fill." The fine arts in such cities were the livelier iris on the burnished surface of the body politic.

6. *Culture and Sexual Selection.* The connection between sexual selection and culture goes even further than we have yet indicated. In the sub-human world, wherever bi-sexual reproduction occurs, two main classes of powers have proved to be effective in sexual selection, powers of capture and powers of fascination. By powers of capture are meant mainly organs of prehension by means of which the male, (it is usually the males who struggle for mates) captures and holds the female for the purpose of impregnation. By powers of fascination are meant various forms of prowess which impress the female, various adornments which catch and please her eye, various vocal powers which attract her attention and please her ear.

In the human world these two classes of powers persist. In the lower stages of social development they are the principal powers exercised by males in securing mates. Wife-capture has been widely practised, though it is later superseded by wife-fascination, as in the courting process. In the higher stages of human development both are superseded by another power, namely, the power to provide economic support.

So completely has the method of capture been superseded in advanced societies, and yet so persistent are certain ancestral traits, that it has been found necessary to brand rape as the most repulsive of crimes and to punish it with the most severe penalties. While the method of fascination has by no means been superseded, yet it is kept subordinate to the method of economic support. To win by fascination without assuming economic responsibility is called seduction and is frowned upon, at least by the great majority, and pretty generally punished.

In those species where the power of capture is the dominant factor in sexual selection, the result of selection is to develop in the males powerful organs of prehension, which may be of no use to the species as a whole. The possession or the lack of such organs determines the ability of the individual male to mate. They help his germ plasm to survive, but they do not help him to survive as an individual, nor to preserve the species from extinction. Where powers of fascination are the determining factors in sexual selection, as powers of prehension are in the case of capture, the result is the development of organs of fascination in the males. In general, these are of no use to the species as a whole; they are merely means of determining which males are to mate and transmit their qualities to succeeding generations. The possession of these powers does not help to keep the individual or the tribe alive, though it keeps the individual's germ plasm alive.

Where the power of fascination takes the form of prowess, it may or may not be of use to the species as a whole. Where the prowess which fascinates the female requires strength, agility or intelligence which may also be used in eluding enemies, fighting them off, or in securing food, it may serve a double purpose. It may enable its possessor to mate and transmit his power; it may also enable him and his progeny to succeed in the non-sexual struggle, that is, in the struggle for individual survival and in the struggle of the tribe as a whole to avoid extinction. In so far, however, as the powers of fascination consist merely in the power to strut, to pout, to caper about, or even to sit on a branch and warble, there is no reason to believe that they are of any value, other than aesthetic, to the species as a whole.

Men have passed through three stages in which successful mating depended upon the power of males: (1) to capture wives, (2) to fascinate them, and (3) to provide economic support. In this latest stage, successful mating depends upon qualities which are of value to the tribe or the nation as a whole. We may ignore that small parasitic group that lives on unearned wealth and consider the great mass who live on wealth which they have earned by the exercise of their own productive power. Obviously the efficient producer contributes to the success of the nation as a whole. The man who can make two blades of grass to grow where one grew before is certainly worth more than the man who can't, unless the latter can excel at some other equally useful work. It is also true that the nation should be more interested in breeding good producers than poor producers. Consequently, in that stage of sexual selection where the struggle for mates among males is a competition in productivity or earning power, those who succeed in winning wives are likely to transmit to future generations those wealth-producing qualities which the nation needs. At least this is true in somewhat primitive agricultural communities where productivity and earning power are closely related, and where both are highly esteemed.

This is true even in the hunting stage. The successful hunter whose prowess wins him mates transmits to his offspring the qualities which make a successful hunter, which are precisely the qualities needed to keep the tribe alive. The same is true of the successful herdsman, farmer, or mechanic. It is only in the more complex societies, where there are so many specialties, where some useful functions become so immaterial as scarcely to appear useful at all, and where, through inherited wealth and other special advantages, some may provide economic support without doing anything useful, that men begin to doubt whether the power to provide economic support is a useful power for the preservation of society.

It would be interesting to catalogue the various powers and organs of fascination, but such a catalogue belongs in a treatise on zoology or ornithology rather than in a treatise on sociology. They range all the way from manes, antlers and beards to plumage and musical voices in the subhuman world. In the human world they include personal beauty, a musical voice, poetic fervor, and everything which goes to make up personal charm.

The important point, from the sociological angle, is that they are the early beginnings of the cult of beauty. Figuratively, they are nature's first attempts to achieve beauty apart from utility. In non-teleological language, they represent the development of other than survival values.

Even in the human world, there is a closer connection than is commonly understood between the arts of fascination as developed by sexual selection and the striving for beauty in even the highest cultural sense. As has already been observed, play consists in the exuberant exercise of our powers. This is as true of those powers of fascination which are developed through sexual selection as of any other powers. When not needed for purposes of survival they are exercised for the sheer pleasure of the exercise. In the abounding wealth of our times, with its accompanying freedom from danger, there are relatively few occasions when we need to exercise our fighting powers.[1] Play in the form of competitive sports furnishes pleasure and is scarcely necessary as a means of keeping us fit. Similarly, in these days when economic support is so generally substituted for the power of fascination as a means of winning mates, the powers of fascination come to be exuberantly exercised with no thought of their biological purpose. Fascination is forgotten in the sheer joy of exercising those powers which were long ago developed for the biological purpose of winning mates.

The substitution by males of economic support for fascination as a means of winning mates has produced a striking revolution, almost a biological revolution. The male everywhere has assumed the active rôle in the mating process. Consequently, it was the male who first developed such special organs of fascination as were needed for the winning of a mate. Even in the lower economic stages of human development, it is still the male who develops a beard or a mane, who adorns himself with paint, feathers and brilliant raiment. The female is commonly of duller plumage, is less adorned with what Darwin calls secondary sexual characters, than the male.

---

[1] See William James, *The Moral Equivalent of War* (American Association for Internal Conciliation, New York, 1910).

In the higher economic stages of human development, when the function of providing economic support is commonly assumed by the male, the process is reversed. The males cease to adorn themselves so gaudily; they dress in more sober colors; they shave their beards and crop their hair; in general they give less attention to singing, dancing, and poetry. On the other hand, the women take up the arts of fascination. They develop remarkable skill in self-adornment, and tend on the average to excel the men in their appreciation of music, dancing, and poetry.

However, not all the men have forsworn the arts of fascination for those of economic production. There are still those who resent the so-called commercialism of the economic phase of courtship and marriage, and who cultivate in themselves the arts of fascination. They give themselves to artistic self-expression in music, dancing, and poetry, they retain such secondary sexual characters as long hair and beards, and they show a liking for more color in their raiment than the fashions of the day prescribe. In military as well as in artistic circles,— in non-business circles generally as well as in those populations where the industrial type of society has been slow in developing,— the male is the sex which adorns itself and retains the adornments with which nature provided it. Even some religious circles seem to show a leaning toward masculine rather than toward feminine adornment. At least one seldom sees members of a religious sisterhood clothed in bright colors. These are reserved for the brotherhoods.

As to feminine adornments, it is a striking fact that the fashions in such matters are set in those centers where the competition among females to fascinate the males is most intense. The demi-monde of great commercial cities lives on the profits of the art of fascination, and the competition for such profits is intense. Under the stimulus of this competition the art of fascination has reached a high state of development. Women everywhere find it necessary to follow the leadership of the demi-monde in this art, though applying it to legitimate purposes. In general, however, as in other phases of our subject, this art is cultivated with no idea as to its origin or of its biological

318 THE ESSENTIAL FACTORS OF SOCIAL EVOLUTION

or social purpose. Most of its devotees naively imagine that they are cultivating this art for its own sake, or that they are devotees of the cult of beauty, and that "beauty is its own excuse for being," whereas its real excuse is the necessity of winning a mate.

The study of that which men have done exuberantly, with no immediate realization of its survival value, is a very important part of sociology; some writers seem to regard it as the most important part. In one sense it is a sign and symbol of man's success in freeing himself from the coercion of nature. In so far as he has gained a mastery over his environment, and is able to make it do his bidding and is not himself the slave of circumstances, he becomes free to do as he pleases. He is no longer compelled to do what is necessary to keep alive but is able to do what he enjoys doing and because he enjoys it.

While all this is true, it does not completely divorce culture from survival, or culture values from survival values. Most of the powers which we possess, and which we so much enjoy exercising, were developed and handed down to us because they had survival value. Moreover, the pleasure we find in exercising them is a means of luring us on to the exercise and development of these inherited powers in order that they may be trained and ready for use. When our ancestors needed to use them for survival purposes, there was survival value in having them trained and developed. Play was the method of training. Survival may be a necessary condition to pleasure, but, in a rather fundamental biological sense, pleasure is necessary to survival. That is, the pleasure of exercising our powers gives us a motive for keeping fit for emergencies. Like all other forms of pleasure, it has an instrumental value and is not an end in itself.

PART II

ACTIVE ADAPTATION OR CONTROLLED EVOLUTION

CHAPTER IX

THE BALANCE OF SOCIAL FORCES

A MAN can not, by taking thought, add a cubit to his stature,—that is, not directly. Men have, however, learned the secret of indirection. By indirection they can achieve the seemingly impossible. By playing with the laws of heredity, huge animals and plants can be produced from small ones. No geneticist would deny the possibility of producing a race of giants from middle-sized men. If he were given a free hand to use the same methods which the animal and plant breeders have used in the production of new animal and plant varieties, the geneticist could produce new varieties of men. The laws of reproduction and of inheritance can not be changed, but they can be so manipulated and directed as to produce surprising results. In engineering, likewise, the forces with which we deal are too much for us to change or nullify. We can, however, by manipulating a few pieces of matter, turn these forces into new channels. When thus turned, the immutable forces of nature can be made to do work which we could not do directly with our own muscular power.

When analyzed, the method of indirection is found to be nothing more than disturbing the balance among forces and tendencies. Holding the balance of power, as it were, we can, by shrewd diplomacy, turn some of the stupendous forces of nature to fighting our battles for us or doing our work for us. To the unscientific mind, the rubbing of Aladdin's lamp did not produce more mysterious results than rubbing a match and touching off a mass of gunpowder. In both cases, a very little muscular work lets loose stupendous energy. Then the problem is, in either case, to make the energy that is released do the work which we want it to do. The difference is that the scientist knows how to repeat the match and gunpowder experiment so as to get the same results, but does not know how to repeat the lamp experiment.

1. *The Concept of Balance.* Balance or equilibrium is one of the most familiar concepts in every field of science. In sociology it is implied at least in every discussion of conflicting tendencies. The concept of an unopposed force acting on a physical body is unthinkable. The only concept of force possible to the finite mind is that which overcomes resistance. A force tending to produce movement is opposed at least by inertia and friction. An unopposed social force is likewise impossible to imagine. The inertia of custom, if unopposed by forces tending to produce change, would result in unchanging social stability. Any of the forces of change, if unopposed by social inertia, custom or tradition, would produce instantaneous and violent transformations of social conditions. On the other hand, it is impossible to conceive of an equilibrium except where there are opposing forces. This has led sociologists to use such terms as *social statics* and *social dynamics;* social statics being a study of the balancing of opposing forces resulting in a social equilibrium; social dynamics being a study of disturbances of equilibrium because one force or group of forces changes and thus disturbs the equilibrium, overbalancing those which oppose it.

Too much emphasis can not be laid on the proposition that every system, in order to be a system, must have the power of maintaining itself in a balance, or of restoring its balance when it is once disturbed. Except for this power of self-restoration, or of restoring a balance, any disturbance would destroy the system. In the solar system, for example, the approach of a comet, or the impact of a large meteorite upon a planet, would result in chaos were it not for the physical fact that, though the existing balance may be disturbed or temporarily destroyed, yet the forces continue to operate and a new balance is reached. The orbit of the earth, for example, is determined by the balance between the centripetal force of gravitation, pulling it toward the sun, and the centrifugal force of momentum which tends to throw it further from the sun. So long as there are no disturbing factors, the orbit remains unchanged. The arrival of a comet in close proximity, however, might change the balance, so that the path of the earth around the sun would be in a smaller or a larger orbit. But, unless the disturbance were so catastrophic as to practically destroy the earth, it would continue to move in a new orbit, or return to the old one. In a new orbit, however, there would again be a balance of the centripetal and the centrifugal forces. The solar system would still be a system, with slight changes.

In the physiological field also, there is a healing process, and numerous others which tend to restore the physiological system to a balance after every disturbance. Professor Cannon[1] has demonstrated this fact so clearly as to leave little to be said on the subject. The way the temperature of the body is maintained is only one of numerous illustrations of the balance of physiological forces.

Even outside the individual body there is what J. Arthur Thomson has called a "System of Animate Nature." In this *system* there is what may be described as the balance of nature. This term, balance of nature, is somewhat more useful to the sociologist than the "static state" which is borrowed from physics. They who write about the balance of nature conceive of equilibrium in terms of a state in which a system maintains itself. It is not a state in which there is no motion but one in which motion proceeds at an unchanging rate. Such, for instance, is the case when we speak of population equilibrium or a balance between births and deaths. We shall employ the term equilibrium in this sense,— the biological concept of balance.

The balance which nature maintains in many of its phases has amazed all who have contemplated it. As we have already

[1] *Infra.*

observed, the human body itself furnishes a striking example of this. Here we have a uniform temperature preserved under the most varied conditions of external heat and cold. An almost uniform weight of the body persists, often for years. The chemical make-up of the body remains unchanged, regardless of what chemicals it must produce or expel in order to achieve this. The body itself is a remarkable balance among all its organs, where parts differing in the extreme are unified through their functions, and form an interdependent whole. Professor Cannon[1] has coined the word *homeostasis* to designate this physiological constancy. Regarding the forces producing the homeostatic state he writes:

> If a state remains steady it does so because any tendency towards change is automatically met by increased effectiveness of the factor or factors which resist the change. Thirst, the reaction to a low blood sugar, the respiratory and circulatory responses to a blood shift towards acidity, the augmented processes of heat conservation and production, all become more intense as the disturbance of homeostasis is more pronounced, and they all subside quickly when the disturbance is relieved.[2]

In the last chapter Professor Cannon makes some important applications to social homeostasis.

In whatever direction we turn throughout the world,— animal, human, individual and social,— we observe the same phenomenon: the phenomenon of equilibrium. If we look deeper into the structure and function of any system we find first that the interaction of its parts, the processes of their function, the responses which they make to certain conditions of the system as a whole, are such as to preserve a balance or to restore it when disturbed. Second, we also find that the system as a whole — as an integrated unity of particular elements — maintains a balance relation with its environing systems. The system of rainfall and evaporation keeping the sea at a constant level, rivers feeding lakes, other rivers draining them, the plant's capturing of substances from air and earth, which start on an

---

[1] *The Wisdom of the Body* (W. W. Norton & Co., New York, 1932).
[2] *Ibid.*, p. 281.

endless round of reincarnations; the remarkable balance nature holds between male and female births; the nice balance in
the struggle for existence among plants and animals, so that the
slightest variation may be sufficient to start one species toward
survival at the cost of another; — innumerable instances would
be given of this remarkable characteristic of nature.

J. Arthur Thomson,[1] among many scientists, has been struck
by the remarkable interdependence and balance of factors
which he summarizes as follows:

The hosts of living organisms are not random creatures, they can be
classified in battalions and regiments. Neither are they isolated creatures,
for every thread of life is intertwined with others in a complex web. This
is one of the fundamental biological concepts — the correlation of organisms in the web of life — and it is as characteristically Darwinian as the
struggle for existence. No creature lives or dies to itself; there is no in-
sulation. Long nutritive chains often bind a series of organisms together
in the very fundamental relation that one kind eats the other. All things
are in flux, there is a ceaseless circulation of matter; all flesh is grass and all
fish is diatom; and so the stuff of the world goes round from one incarnation
to another. . . . In short, we get a glimpse of Nature as a vast system
of interlinked lives — a Systema Naturae in a new sense — a web with a
pattern . . . just as there is a correlation of organs in the body, so there
is a correlation of organisms in the world of life.

Emerson, not being a biologist, pictured a perfected world from
which spiders should be excluded. Thomson points out, however,
that the absence of spiders which snare so many insects that are
harmful to man, would involve the absence of many other
things besides spiders, *perhaps man himself.* He recounts numerous cases in which men have destroyed one enemy only to
invite another and more destructive one. Most of us in America
know of towns that have protected and propagated squirrels,
only to find that squirrels destroy the nests of woodpeckers,
and that, in the absence of woodpeckers, borers destroyed the
shade trees.

It is true that men can influence the balance of nature to
their own advantage. In the seventies of the last century the

[1] *The System of Animate Nature* (Williams & Norgate, London, 1920), vol. 1,
pp. 58–60.

cereal crops of the Mississippi Valley were threatened by the chinch bug. The situation seemed hopeless until a scientist discovered a parasite which caused the chinch bug to sicken and die. For several decades it seemed that the chinch bug was about to become extinct. On the other hand, men make mistakes. In the nineties of the last century the coyotes were a pest to sheep and poultry owners of California. A bounty was offered for coyote scalps. Hunters thinned them out. Rabbits at once began to multiply inordinately, to the great injury of the orchards and vineyards.

Thomson uses even more striking illustrations of the danger of disturbing the balance of nature by men who do not understand the web of life. One of the most striking is that of the mongoose in Jamaica. In some unknown way the European rat was introduced into the island, where he found an environment peculiarly suited to his needs. He became a major pest. The mongoose was imported to prey upon the rats, which he proceeded to do until he had practically exterminated them. Then he turned upon the birds, with the result that the insects and ticks which the birds used to eat became a menace greater even greater than the rat had been. The ticks attacked even the mongoose himself, making life a burden and tending to re-establish the balance of nature.

To the sociologist, human society is a web of social life. The interrelation of social factors impresses him as deeply as the web of life does the biologist. The chain of causation, so vividly pictured in the House that Jack Built, is a chain of social rather than of biological causation. The student will do well, therefore, to familiarize himself with the concept of a social equilibrium.

It is not impossible to make use of the principle of balance in the social world as the grain growers of the West did in the case of the chinch bug. If we ever bring ourselves to a realistic view of government and its functions, we shall find many such opportunities. It is possible, for example, to play the vote-getter against the money-getter and the hijacker against the rumrunner. We need not stop to argue the question as to which is the disease and which the antidote. We only need to know that one invites the other. If money-getters get too rapacious, they are certain to become unpopular. The professional vote-getter can always be relied upon to be keenly aware of the situation. An attack on money-getters is a good vote-getting policy, and the vote-getter is certain to make use of it. On the other hand, if he pushes his campaign too far, and begins to make smaller money-getters uneasy, he will lose votes and be compelled to halt his campaign. Thus a balance is maintained, at least in a democracy where votes count.

2. *The Man-Land Ratio.* In their great work entitled *The Science of Society*, Sumner and Keller[1] make the man-land ratio one of the starting points for the study of the subject of social science. This man-land ratio involves a concept of equilibrium quite analogous to, if not identical with, the balance of nature as conceived and developed by the biologist. Malthus may not have been the first writer to call attention to this balance. He was at least the first to force it upon the attention of the world and compel its consideration.

The two essential factors in determining the man-land ratio are, as stated in a previous chapter, first, the tendency of births to exceed deaths and second, the law of diminishing returns from land. The reason why there is a tendency of births to exceed deaths lies in the fact of fecundity. The fact of fecundity, combined with the fact that only a limited quantity of food can grow on a given acre, led Malthus to the famous generalization which he stated as the universal tendency of all animated life to increase beyond its means of subsistence. After more than a century of continuous discussion, our final conclusions on the population question may be summarized as follows: There is, to begin with, a powerful motive force leading to the rapid multiplication of numbers. Opposing this is the law of diminishing returns from land, furnishing an elastic limit to the numbers that can live from the produce of a given area. When numbers have increased until subsistence begins to run

[1] Yale University Press, New Haven, 1927.

short, the death-rate balances the birth-rate, and there is a stationary population. When an improvement is discovered which makes it possible to get more subsistence from the same area of land, the death-rate falls or the birth-rate increases, resulting in an increase in numbers until a balance is restored. When, through the depletion of the soil or the increasing aridity of the climate, subsistence decreases, the death-rate increases or emigration takes place until there is a decrease in population. Other forces than famine also affect the death-rate. Incursions of enemies, the slaughter of populations by invading armies, the spread of disease and pestilence in overdense populations,— all serve to thin out the people and produce a stable population in spite of the powerful forces which make for multiplication.[1]

Before we can proceed very far with our discussion of balance we must arrive at a fairly clear notion as to what a social force is. The term "force" in the physical world is simply the capacity to move matter. Non sentient matter can be moved only by a force which can be measured in footpounds or similar units. A balance of such forces is easily understood. Creatures with nerves and organs of locomotion can be "moved" by means of irritation or stimulation. It is not so very difficult to visualize a balance of counteracting irritations, even though we have no unit of measurement for irritation to correspond to footpounds of pressure in the strictly physical field. Whipping a weary horse may easily effect a balance between the irritation of the lash and that of the fatigue in his tired muscles. On a still higher level is the motivating force of anticipation. A weary slave may anticipate the irritation of the lash and that of fatigue. He may have to decide between them and act accordingly. Pleasant anticipations are also motivating forces, and a free

[1] Guy Murchie, in his stimulating book, *Men on the Horizon* (Houghton, Mifflin Co., Boston, 1932), mentions the fact that in China before the introduction of vaccination, a mother with eight or ten children playing around would say, if asked how many children she had, "Two or three." When asked about all the others, she would reply, "Oh, they have not had smallpox yet." Don't count your children before they have had smallpox, is a somewhat gruesome variation of the old adage, "Don't count your chickens before they are hatched."

It looks as though vaccination was saving Chinese children from smallpox in order that they may later die of starvation.

man may have to choose between pleasures to be derived from a larger income and those to be enjoyed with greater leisure.

In the main, social forces are systems of human motivation, and human motivation consists largely of anticipations of future pleasant and unpleasant sensations. Social systems differ from one another mainly in the kinds of anticipations which they try to arouse in individuals. Under a militant system [1] men are made to anticipate painful sensations as the penalty for disobedience to orders. Under the industrial system they are, in the main, led to anticipate pleasurable sensations as a reward for accepting an offer. In the industrial system especially is there a general balancing of advantages and disadvantages.

3. *The Balance of Cost and Utility.* The idea of balance runs through most of the economists' explanations of the phenomena of value and price. These phenomena generally reduce themselves to a balancing of opposing motives. There is, on the one hand, the desire for utility in one form or another, impelling to productive action. Opposing this there is, on the other hand, the desire to avoid cost or disutility in one form or another, acting as a brake or a drag on productive action. In the last analysis cost is psychological and may be called by such general terms as disinclination or repugnance. In one of the simplest possible illustrations of this principle it may be said that the individual worker, who can choose his own time for working and the number of hours per day that he will work, is impelled to work by the desire for the product of his labor and repelled by the desire to avoid fatigue. Except for the repulsion of fatigue he would work long hours in order to secure more and more of a desirable product or more and more wages. On the other hand, except for the impelling desire for products or wages, he would not work after he began to feel fatigue or any other form of unpleasantness. Being impelled to work by the desire for goods and repelled from work by the desire to avoid fatigue, he works, in theory at least, up to the point where the increasing

---

[1] Cf. Spencer's famous chapters on the Militant and the Industrial Types of Society in his *Principles of Sociology* (D. Appleton & Co., New York, 1892), Part V, chs. xvii, xviii.

fatigue or the desire to avoid it overcomes his decreasing desire for additional products. Except for the repulsion he would work on indefinitely. Except for the impulsion he would not work at all beyond the point where fatigue begins to be felt. A similar balancing of forces is found in mass behavior. The desire to avoid fatigue and other disagreeable things connected with work retards mass production.

In the earlier and more naïve stages of economic discussion little use was made of the concept of the equilibrium. The tendency of economic writers was to "base" value upon cost, wages upon subsistence, interest upon abstinence, profits upon risk, etc. etc. There are still some naïve discussions as to whether price is based on cost or on utility, but the more sophisticated have arrived at the conclusion that price is not based on either but is determined by an equilibrium between the two, *i.e.*, upon an equilibrium of forces, one group of forces tending to increase production, the other group tending to retard production; one group tending to increase consumption, the other group tending to retard consumption. One group of forces is summarized under the general term "desirability of goods"; the other under the general term "cost of producing goods" or undesirability of working, waiting and risking, all of which are involved in the production of goods. The balance of trade, the balance of international payments, and similar terms indicate that economists have for a long time, on certain subjects at least, been thinking in terms of a balance or an equilibrium.

As suggested above, a static condition is an equilibrium of forces. In the social world, as in the physical, the forces are never all driving in the same direction. There is opposition and interplay. Neither are the forces all of the same intensity. They reinforce, divert, or check one another. If all the forces thus interacting remained the same in strength and direction for a sufficiently long time to work out their combined effects, we would have not merely a static but a stationary condition. In such a case the study of the forces and their effects would be simplified. As a matter of fact, this does not happen. At any moment, the multitude of social forces are equilibrated;

at any moment, the social situation is the balance produced by these forces; it is an equilibrium though generally a moving equilibrium. But a moment later new forces may have entered, or there may be an augmenting or subsiding in the strength of those already exerted, or some of these may be diverted. There is soon a new balance or would be if it were not disturbed before it was established. The disturbance of the equilibrium and the settling of the forces into a new balance reveals the social state as dynamic.

We thus see society as the result of a balancing and constant rebalancing of social forces. A slight shift in any factor compels a readjustment of all the others. Society is dynamic; it is constantly changing. But the dynamic is best described as a disturbance of the static, and can be understood only through a study of successive equilibria and of the particular forces which have balanced one another. The fact that the social situation is always changing, that equilibrium follows equilibrium in a never-ending and rapid succession, gives importance to the question of the possibility and advisability of manipulating those forces in such a way as to influence the new equilibrium in socially desirable directions. When it is realized that a comparatively small shift in a single factor may have rather widespread results, the question becomes even more important.

At the same time, an understanding of the interplay and the balancing of social forces will convince the student of the extreme difficulty of reform. New and unexpected developments follow any disturbances of the social balance as of a biological balance. The increase of bootlegging under prohibition, and its reaction on other forms of crime, are now familiar topics. Poor relief has been found to have far-reaching and profound results on the degeneration of the population. Spencer pointed out that one result of any policy of protecting fools from the results of their folly is to fill the world with fools. When the world is dominated by fools there can be only a fool's civilization — if any. It has been reasonably suggested that the extreme cruelty of the old English criminal law, under which men were hanged for more than sixty different offenses, had something to do with the present law-abiding character of the English people. It extinguished those least amenable to social control and left the law-abiding element to reproduce its kind.

A realistic view of the function of the criminal law will reveal that it is not the absolute prevention of crime but rather a disturbance of the balance of social forces in a direction which is deemed desirable. By adding appreciably to the reasons against performing a certain act, the law may cause larger numbers to refrain from performing it than would otherwise refrain. If some individuals who would otherwise find it to their advantage to engage in predatory activities, find, under the law, that the reasons against are greater than the reasons for such activities, the law has performed its function, in part at least. It has changed the balance somewhat in favor of productive and against predatory activities. As Professor Hocking remarks: "It is said that the effect of the criminal law should be estimated not by crimes punished so much as by the far greater number of crimes prevented; but this estimate is still too small. For a crime is not prevented unless it is first contemplated; and the greatest effect of criminal law is in displacing the contemplation by training the planning energy of the community into noncriminal alternatives."[1]

4. *Reform by Shifting the Balance of Forces.* The first problem requiring the attention of the student of society, especially in his rôle of reformer, is to segregate and examine all the forces whose combined action and reaction produce the particular situation in question. This, of course, is not entirely possible. The forces are too numerous and their interplay too complex. Often forces which were too obscure to be noted have, upon release, greatly altered the anticipated direction of change. One reform, however meritorious, is very likely to disturb the balance of social forces and to necessitate several other reforms to correct the disturbances caused by the first one. But increasing scientific knowledge, combined with care in interpretation, reduces the difficulty. The attentive student will be able

[1] William E. Hocking, *Man and the State* (Yale University Press, New Haven, 1926), p. 39.

to disentangle the complicated net-work of cause and effect sufficiently to analyze the more obvious elements at least. And his success in altering society will be limited by his success in understanding the intricate web of causation. By using the method of manipulating causal forces, two advantages are gained. First, there is an important saving of energy, because the forces themselves, once slightly changed, work out the far-reaching results without further human effort.[1] And, secondly, by this more natural process, many evils which would follow a direct attack may be avoided.

Probably no farmer ever understood all the factors and forces that are involved in the growing and maturing of a crop. Experience has taught him, however, that by preparing a seedbed and planting seed at the proper time, a crop may be expected in a large enough percentage of cases to make planting worth while. Yet he only disturbs a few of the factors involved in plant growth. Similarly, even though a student of sociology may never understand all the social forces which are in a state of balance in any actual situation, it is not too much to hope that he may learn enough to know that when certain specific changes are made in some of them, certain desirable results are likely to follow. It is upon this belief that every intelligent piece of social legislation is tried.

This question of understanding the social forces which are in a state of equilibrium, in any case where a social change is desirable, may be well illustrated by the question of raising wages. We shall assume that it is socially desirable to raise the level of wages; how can this be done most effectively? Professor Marshall [2] has elaborated the concept of an equilibrium price as the price at which the forces of supply and demand balance each other. Price, demand, supply,— all three,— are interrelated as both causes and results. No one of these can be altered without necessitating a readjustment of

---

[1] Böhm-Bawerk, in his *Positive Theory of Capital* (Macmillan Co., New York, 1891), has emphasized and elaborated this point under the title "The Round-about Process of Production."

[2] *Principles of Economics*, The Macmillan Company, London, 1907, bk. v.

334 THE ESSENTIAL FACTORS OF SOCIAL EVOLUTION

the others. Wages are the price of labor. The equilibrium wage will be that at which the employers will hire as many laborers as are willing to work at that wage. A higher than the equilibrium wage will result in unemployment because it will induce more laborers to offer themselves than employers are willing to hire. What are the forces whose manipulation will automatically affect the equilibrium favorably to labor?

One is the standard of living. What standard do men insist upon maintaining, to which they subordinate marriage and family? Any group of laborers who are satisfied with a very low standard of life will marry early, even upon a small wage, and rear many children. From their ranks they pour more and more laborers onto the labor market; the potential supply of labor, even at a low wage, then seems inexhaustible. But any group of laborers who will not rear a family until they have achieved a degree of economic independence — evidenced, perhaps, in a savings account, a home, an automobile, or a life insurance policy,— will necessarily postpone marriage, and probably otherwise limit the size of the average family. Thus, in this case, the supply of labor which is available at a very low wage is *nil;* and the potential supply enlarges only in response to a comparatively high price, or wage. If, then, the standard of living can be gradually elevated, the supply of labor that would offer itself at the old wage will gradually decrease, and the wage scale will rise.

Suppose, on the contrary, there had been an artificial increase in wages, by decree. This wage, for a time at least, would not be the equilibrium price of labor, since it would destroy the balance between the supply and demand,[1] strengthening the former and weakening the latter. These two would eventually have to find their balance again, either at the new rate, by an

---

[1] It is customary to speak of a balance of demand and supply, or of equalizing demand and supply. These are convenient formulae, but they should be used with care, otherwise they may prove inaccurate and therefore misleading. Strictly, an equilibrium price is a price which will induce buyers to continue buying exactly as much as it will induce sellers to continue selling. So long as this is what is understood by a balance of demand and supply, no harm can result from using the latter formula.

alteration of other factors, or at the old rate again, or at some other, depending upon the interplay of all the forces. The important point is that the artificial rate could be maintained only if it became the equilibrium rate. If there were no change in the social outlook or economic standards of the recipients of the larger wage, they would find themselves in a position to support more people than before at the same level, and the new wage would result in earlier marriages and the multiplication of numbers. Besides, assuming there were no barriers, laborers from other groups or other countries would be lured by the wage increase. Thus the supply would be augmented. But as the change was produced artificially, and the economic situation did not justify the higher wage, the demand for labor would be no larger. It would probably become smaller, since employers could not afford to hire so many at the higher price, or, to put it otherwise, they would have a stronger motive for economizing labor. Thus, instead of a permanent increase in the wages and the amelioration of the workers, the old low standards are re-established. If, however, a gradual increase in wage takes place *pari passu* with, or more especially, as a result of a gradual rise in the standard of living, the supply of labor is kept down and the equilibrium wage remains high.

Another factor affecting the supply of labor is immigration. If there is a source of cheap labor outside of the country, and if its entrance into the country is unrestricted, so that many foreign laborers will offer themselves for employment at a low wage, the potential supply of labor is enormous. A higher standard of living on the part of the native laborers will merely eliminate them as competitors in these fields of employment for which immigrant labor is suitable. By thus forcing native laborers to concentrate in other fields, the scale of wages in all occupations will be depressed.[1] An artificial increase of wage would only tend to increase the number of immigrants. But if

[1] It has been maintained that "white" laborers will not work in the vegetable fields of Southern California, or on railway track construction. The fact doubtless is that they will not work at the wage offered to and accepted by Mexican peons whose standard of living is relatively low.

immigration itself is checked in a progressive country, wages of native labor will rise automatically because of a decrease in the total supply. Exclusion of immigrant labor disturbs the balance and results in a new equilibrium wage at a higher level.

A third factor affecting the supply of labor in a particular locality or a particular trade is mobility. If there are no barriers of ignorance or inefficiency, a supply of labor which is too large and which is therefore compelled to accept a low wage may be quickly reduced by offering it better opportunities in other fields. At present the degree of mobility is strictly limited. Even with the means of communication so highly developed as they are in the United States, workmen, especially of the lower ranks, are largely uninformed of favorable conditions of labor elsewhere.[1] The result is that there is often considerable disparity of wage between two sections of the same country.

The disparity of wages between two levels of employment, resulting from the vertical immobility of labor, is still greater. So long as educational opportunities are lacking to large numbers of the population, there must be a congestion in those occupations in which little or no education is required. When large numbers have no choice but to enter the unskilled occupations, the result is that there will be as large a supply of labor as employers are willing to employ even at low rates of wages. If an increase in income — from whatever source — were used by these families to educate their children for more useful work, vertical mobility would be increased.[2] Each would have a slightly wider choice of employment. But if an increase in income were dissipated in increasing the numbers of the group, on the old economic level, they would be worse off than ever. On the other hand, if an adequate system of education offered free opportunities to all children to fit themselves for the skilled occupations, so that their own mental capacities were the only limits to their achievements, the supply of labor in the unskilled

---

[1] There are other factors making for immobility, such as family ties, risk involved in change, cost of moving, and the like.

[2] See Professor Sorokin's remarkable treatise on *Social Mobility*, (Harper & Bros., New York, 1927), especially chs. XVII, XVIII and XIX.

trades would fall relatively to that in the better paid occupations. The increasing mobility of labor would so distribute the supply as to increase the wage in the poorly paid occupations. Even if men in every grade of labor were enabled to lift themselves only slightly in the scale, the effect upon the wages in the various grades would be considerable.[1]

There are other factors influencing the supply of labor, such as personal efficiency, and the many traits of which it is made; death-rates, especially in relation to birth-rates; and general health and vigor. When the sociologist desires to explain equilibrium or disequilibrium as the result of higher wages he must consider all of these factors. But this is still only one-half the picture. There are factors which influence the other side of the balance, namely the demand for labor. The wage may be raised by increasing the demand for as well as by decreasing the supply of labor.

The economist pictures the various factors of production as complementing or replacing each other. They are combined, in any one use, in such a way as to produce an equilibrium among themselves, the supply of some factors constituting the demand for others. Thus if we desire to increase the demand for labor, we may do so by increasing the supply of the other elements which combine with it, chiefly the supply of managerial skill. In other words, one reason why labor does not command a higher price than it does is that the men who can employ labor in such a way as to make it productive are extremely few. If only relatively inefficient business men are available they can manage only second-rate industries and pay only second-rate wages. If both the numbers and the average ability of business men are increased, the number of workmen they will be able and willing to hire at a high wage (*i.e.* the demand for labor) will be increased, and a higher equilibrium wage established.

It thus becomes apparent that all those social traditions and prejudices which influence the choice of career made by the superior members of a group have a pronounced effect upon

---

[1] For a somewhat more detailed discussion see the author's *Principles of National Economy* (Ginn & Co., Boston, 1925), ch. xxxv.

the workers' wages. In some countries a business career is thought to be demeaning, and thus many able men are dissuaded from entering it. Sometimes it is made socially attractive to retire from business at as early an age as possible. Often able men from the lower social ranks find opportunities for an independent industrial career closed to them. Any social or economic policy which will fill the ranks of business men with capable individuals, and keep those successful enterprisers in active service as long as they have the necessary vigor, will automatically increase the demand for the labor of the masses. If, at the same time, the standard of living of the masses can be raised and their birth-rate lowered, the supply of labor will be reduced. There really is no other way to raise, permanently, the wages of the masses.

The concept of the equilibrium wage,— a wage at which all the various forces which combine to create the demand for and supply of labor are in a state of balance,— has been discussed at considerable length both because of its own importance and because it serves as an illustration of the great fact of balance or equilibrium of social forces, which occupies our attention in this chapter. The illustration has served to bring out the point that the forces at work are many and various — strong or weak, immediate or remote. Nevertheless, they find their equilibrium. If this equilibrium is artificially disturbed, the new condition is temporary and balance must be restored or a new balance established. Therefore if a different point of equilibrium is desired — as, for example, a higher equilibrium wage — the surest and most efficient way of securing it is by altering the economic forces in a manner that will start a chain of consequences which will automatically produce a higher equilibrium wage.

5. *The Level of Civilization.* The notion of a balance of forces, which is so common in the field of physics and biology, and which we have just illustrated in the field of economics, is familiar as well as useful throughout the whole range of social studies. Sociology might be called the study of civilization itself if civilization were defined as the sum of the arts which make it possible to live together comfortably in large numbers.

Living together in large numbers requires certain specialized types of behavior. The degree of civilization any group can attain depends upon its capacity and willingness to adopt these ways of behaving. Here, again, all things tend toward a balance. The very first requisite for civilization — *i.e.*, for living comfortably in a large group — is the ability to secure subsistence for a large population.[1] The population is in definite relationship to the kind of economy. If a tribe maintains itself by hunting, its population must be small. However expert the hunters may become and however diligently they may hunt, they cannot, in the nature of the case, support large numbers of people. Unless they are able and willing to abandon their traditional methods of production, their civilization is doomed to low limits. It soon reaches its level. It may not be pleasant to surrender the freedom of the wandering life for the settled, monotonous existence of an agricultural society. But this is the price to be paid for an advancing civilization. And when once the group has made the transition, then again it feels that any further change is a further surrender of freedom. An agricultural life, which to the hunter seemed a life of drudgery, appears to certain modern idealists a life of freedom and "communion with nature" when compared with "slavery to the machine."

The plain fact is that agriculture uses the land more productively than hunting or herding. It will support a greater population. Therefore it is a superior system, economically, and economic forces will make it prevail. Agriculture will drive herding from land which is suitable for tillage. Similarly, machine work is more productive than hand work; it produces more from the same expenditure of human energy. It permits more people to live and to live better. Therefore, wherever it is possible, it will drive out hand work. And, finally, industry can support a larger population and support it more comfortably than agriculture. We do not, of course, ignore the fact that agriculture is absolutely essential for food. Unless a country

[1] Cf. the author's *The Economy of Human Energy* (The Macmillan Co., New York, 1924), chs. I, II, III.

finds it both possible and wise to import its foodstuffs it must devote considerable human energy to producing them. Nevertheless the fact remains that the nation with industrial resources and skill can ordinarily exchange its machine products for much more agricultural produce than it could have grown for itself. And even though it devotes part of its energy and land to agriculture, it will find it economically advantageous to devote as much as possible to industry, exchanging the products of its indoor industries for the products of outdoor industries from countries that are less expert mechanically.

Thus it is seen that civilization progresses as the methods of production progress. That group has survived which has been able to support larger and larger numbers, and the support of larger and larger populations has depended upon better and better uses of land and human energy. A glance at the history of the American frontier reveals in modern form the struggle between the rival economic systems. Gradually the herdsmen were driven farther west; the picturesque, freedom-loving cowboy could not withstand the assault of the plodding plowman. And later, people in the East who had supported themselves by the plow were replaced by those who built factories or worked in them. The forces determining the size of population and the forces at work in the economic system find an equilibrium.

It will be observed that these various ways of making a living upon which the size of the population depends require varying degrees of division of labor. It is somewhat like the reversal of Adam Smith's dictum, that the division of labor is limited by the extent of the market. Probably as hunters or herdsmen became farmers there was a transition period when each family, if not each individual, divided its energies between the two occupations. But gradually the greater effectiveness of specialization and coöperation would assert itself, and the group would become more productive as it became more interdependent. Division of labor has at present proceeded farthest in industry. The intricacy of a complicated machine, its many parts fitting perfectly and acting simultaneously, is an idealized picture of an industrial society. In the machine each part has its specialized function, and upon the accurate performance of each and the coördination of all depends its smooth running. An equilibrium of physical forces is involved.

Since productive efficiency depends to a considerable degree on specialization, since specialization means interdependence, and since interdependence requires dependability, it is apparent that dependability is a limiting factor in productivity. A country can be civilized in the sense of being able to support large numbers in a high state of comfort, only on condition that its people are sufficiently dependable to make specialization possible. In this very important sense, therefore, the level of civilization is determined by the degree of dependability existing among the people.

They who, for example, follow a highly specialized occupation on which everybody else depends, may discover that this gives them great power of extortion. Forgetting that they are also dependent upon others, they may not be able to withstand the temptation to use their power. If this idea spreads among all specialized occupations, it becomes self-destructive. Everybody loses and nobody gains. Civilization has reached its level and can go no higher.

One fundamental characteristic of a civilized man is that he substitutes usefulness for force, fear, or fraud in his economic life. He does not expect to secure what he wants through deception or through making it dangerous to refuse his demands. Rather he expects to make himself so useful to others that they willingly pay him for his work or his product. The test of usefulness is one test of the capacity for civilization. The group whose members gain prosperity through usefulness is to that extent civilized.

One type of occupational organization — usually called professional organization — expects to gain by setting high standards of service, believing that the public will pay well for service of higher quality. A society of engineers, for example, is interested in improving earnings of the profession, but it proceeds on the theory that the civilized way to succeed is to set a higher standard of engineering service. It belongs to the standard-setting type of organization. There are also fighting organizations which hope to gain, not by setting higher standards of work, but by making others afraid to refuse what the organizations demand. The level of civilization depends on which type of organization predominates.

It would be a very convenient sort of world if we could all do exactly as we please, working when we liked and playing when we liked, never doing hard or disagreeable things — provided, of course, that we could at the same time acquire the goods we desire. As a matter of fact, our world is not built that way. We are faced daily with the choice between doing what we like and getting what we want. Here again there is an equilibrium. If we insist upon "self-expression," in other words, upon following our "natural" inclinations, we soon find that we are depriving ourselves of goods to satisfy our "natural" desires. A balance is struck in each case between the unpleasantness of doing what we do not like to do and the unpleasantness of doing without things which we want. We stop a disagreeable or fatiguing activity when its unpleasantness just equals the unpleasantness of doing without more of the commodity or service which the activity is securing for us. By this compromise we obtain as much satisfaction with as little cost as possible. Thus self-expression must be balanced by self-discipline, in the first place, for the benefit of the individual himself.

We have just seen, however, that an additional emphasis is placed upon self-discipline by the needs of society, and that this need increases as civilization advances. When any group passed from the hunting to the agricultural stage of economic life, there were doubtless individual hunters who rebelled. They could not bring themselves to endure the quiet life and hard work of a settled existence. They refused to modify their accustomed self-expression by self-discipline. Such individuals were the enemies of progress. If they were not killed as outlaws, they were eventually eliminated by the economic process. Although their resistance to the life of the "clodhopper" might be defended by the romanticist, the final test of survival proved them unfitted for an economically developed society, or, in other words, for a high state of civilization.

The capacity of an individual to discipline himself, to adapt himself to the needs of his social group, is his capacity for civilization. That group whose members possess considerable capacity for adaptation can go far. It must drop by the wayside any individuals who cannot or will not discipiine themselves for the new life. Our society today has undergone a transition from a hand economy to a machine economy. This makes new demands upon individuals for the surrender of some opportunities for "self-expression"; it offers in return the possibility of more and better goods. There are many who rebel at the thought of fixed hours, routine, specialized work, mass production, factory life. They refuse to be "slaves to the machine." They say machine production destroys all creative work.[1] Such persons are really rebels against progress, against a new method of production which enables more people to live and to live better. They are the modern misfits. If they cannot adapt themselves to the new situation they thereby prove themselves incapable of more civilization, and are to be eliminated for the sake of social advancement.

The question, how much civilization can we stand? is important for every group.[2] It must find some means of encouraging those individuals who have powers of adaptation to a disciplined life, particularly those who have the characteristics of dependability. Others, who cannot discipline themselves sufficiently for a high degree of interdependence and responsibility are to be eliminated, either by an active or a passive social process. But, as a matter of fact, there is no reason, apart from the consideration of humanitarian sentiments, why the elimination of individuals unable, through a lack of capacity of their own, should not be considered essential if only social advance would thereby be enhanced. One of the direct ways by which such

---

[1] See discussion on this subject in *Problem Economics* by Keezer, Cutler, and Garfield (Harper & Bros., New York, 1928), p. 63. Also Arthur Pound, *The Iron Man in Industry* (Atlantic Monthly Press, Boston, 1922).

[2] See the author's *Economy of Human Energy, op. cit.*, ch. VII.

individuals may be eliminated is by killing their germ plasm. As F. W. Westway [1] puts it, " 'The survival of the fittest' is a hateful idea to democracy, but apparently it is inevitable as long as human nature remains what it is. . . . The one thing that matters is the quality of the human stuff, and therefore the development of the best stocks and the restraint of the unfit are essential. But democracy objects. . . ."

The question may arise, Does "democracy" object, or is it only the kind of democracy with which we are familiar? It is conceivable that there might be a democracy which would recognize the fact that one man could do a certain kind of work better than another man. If the masses want that kind of work done, they might prefer to have it done by the one who can do it best. This may apply even to the work of governing. Of course a question would arise as to the meaning of the word "best" as applied to the work of governing. If it meant governing in such a way as would be most pleasant to the existing majority, it might be a very bad government from the standpoint of the great majority which does not vote for the reason that it is not yet born. Rather obviously, the term "best" should be applied only to that way of governing which considers the interests of those not yet born as well as those of the generation which is now voting and clamoring for bread and circuses. It is not inconceivable that a democracy might support such a government.

But there are other kinds of work besides governing which the masses, if intelligent, would desire to have done by those who were best fitted for the task. Their wages depend on the skill and efficiency with which they are equipped and directed by their employers. Third-rate employers can pay only third-rate wages. Laborers need first-rate employers and, if intelligent, will desire them.

As to the extermination of the germ plasm of the least fit, the masses, if intelligent, would favor that. The multiplication of the feeble-minded is a menace to the mass of laborers. The

---

[1] *Scientific Method* (Blackie and Son, Ltd., London, 1924), p. 420.

progeny of morons and high-grade imbeciles are just efficient enough to glut the market for manual labor and not efficient enough to relieve that congestion. There is hope for democracy yet, but that hope depends on the ability of the masses to see that the term *survival of the fittest* has in it more that is favorable than unfavorable to themselves.

This process of selection is always going on. No one is completely adapted to his physical and social environment. And if he were, this desirable situation would be of but brief duration because the environment itself is ever changing. Although there may be no cases of perfect adaptation, some are much better than others. Specifically, individuals are likely to be best adapted to the requirements of the civilization of their group if that group has advanced gradually to its present state. If its environment and its economic system have changed so slowly as to permit a more or less normal adjustment, it will probably find few glaring deficiencies among its members. Selection will be no less sure; only less painful. It is when a very rapid transition takes place, as for example in the case of the industrial revolution, that the evolution of human nature lags far behind, and society is full of tragic misfits. Even those whose natures are best suited to the requirements of the machine age cannot get wholly away from the physical and psychological heritage of the past. The soul of their hunter and fisher ancestors is still within them, and its call may become irresistible at certain times of the year. Then a period of nomadic life is indulged in to compensate for the humdrum of industry; for a short time the arduous work and privation of camp life seems pleasant, but only for a short time.

Francis Galton called attention to the fact that the process of natural selection has fitted any long-established race to the conditions under which it has lived, and that civilization is a new condition imposed upon man just as new conditions are imposed by a geological change.[1] He says that when the changes were sufficiently slow and the race sufficiently pliant, the nature

---

[1] *Hereditary Genius*, rev. ed. (D. Appleton & Co., New York, 1883), pp. 336–350.

of the race was modified; when the changes were abrupt and the race unyielding, it was destroyed. This is what has happened in the case of certain savage tribes, which have been introduced to western culture.

The two characteristics of savages which most unfit them for civilized life, according to Galton, are their love of a wandering, independent life, making steady labor impossible, and their impulsive, uncontrolled nature. The former lives on in numerous modern Englishmen, but not unopposed by many "civilized cravings"; and both cannot be satisfied. "This is a serious calamity, and as the Bohemianism in the nature of our race is destined to perish, the sooner it goes, the happier for mankind. The social requirements of English life are steadily destroying it. No man who only works by fits and starts is able to obtain his living nowadays; for he has not a chance of thriving in competition with steady workmen." Gradually the characteristics of British workmen are becoming just the opposite of those of the savage nomad. The second savage characteristic, an impulsive and uncontrolled nature, Galton thinks even more alien to civilized life.

A civilized man must bear and forbear, he must keep before his mind the claims of the morrow as clearly as those of the passing minute; of the absent, as well as of the present. This is the most trying of the new conditions imposed on man by civilization, and the one that makes it hopeless for any but exceptional natures among savages, to live under them.

Upon his theory of a human nature which has not been able to keep up with the development of our civilization, Galton bases an interesting explanation of a sense of sin. It results, he says, from an inner conflict between man's aspirations and his fickle inclinations. He feels his nature to be inadequate to his social needs. Thus the Negroes who have been transplanted suddenly from a primitive to an advanced civilization,— so that the discrepancy between their nature and their moral requirements is great,— are oppressed with a feeling of their moral inadequacy, which theologians call a sense of sin, and are easily stirred by a preacher. The Chinese, with a long, slow development and adjustment behind them, can scarcely be ruffled.[1]

We have seen that a group is composed of a great variety of individuals, some adapted to group life and others not, some contributing to the stability and growth of the group and others hindering it. The group becomes strong to the extent that the latter can be eliminated, or their influence minimized. There must be the unity which comes of interdependence and coöperation. We have seen, similarly, that an individual is composed of numerous impulses and desires, some social and others not, some contributing to his usefulness in an advancing civilization and others retarding such development. Every individual, being an heir of the past, is possessed of some impulses that war against his moral or social ideals. If he is able, by self-discipline, to produce a kind of unity within himself, a balance or equilibrium of the various forces of his personality[2] in relation to the social forces about him, he makes himself an asset to his group. If he indulges some one impulse which is anti-social in its expression, he is to that extent an enemy to his group.

Society has at its disposal two means of getting men to do what they do not like to do. These are rewards and compulsion. Our society has adopted the first to a large extent, and in economic life it takes the form of paying men for doing useful work. The operation of this system is left to the voluntary activity of individuals. Each is willing to pay a certain amount or do a certain amount of work in order to obtain a particular commodity or service; any one who is willing to produce the commodity or perform the service for the reward offered is free to do so. In turn, with the reward — or pay — received, he is able to buy or hire a commodity or service which he wants. Thus is developed a system of voluntary contract, whereby each

---

[1] *Ibid.*, pp. 349–350.

[2] E. B. Holt speaks of personality as an integration of behavior into a single course of action, *i.e.*, the transition from *behavior* to *conduct*, and to *moral conduct*. He says, "The more integrated behavior is harmonious and consistent behavior toward a larger and more comprehensive situation, toward a bigger section of the universe. It is lucidity and breadth of purpose. . . . In short, all of the more embracing behavior formulae (functions) are moral." *The Freudian Wish* (Henry Holt & Co., New York, 1915), p. 197.

performs productive service and each obtains goods to satisfy his own needs.

Under this system, goods may be said, figuratively, to circulate by suction rather than by pressure. More literally, they move in response to the price offered rather than in response to commands given. In a military organization, supplies move in response to command rather than in response to demand. If society did not thus allow economic interest to guide the activities of men in making a living, it would have to compel them to work by threats of punishment. For the work must be done or the people will starve. Most men prefer to choose their own kind of work and receive rewards for it from their fellowmen, rather than to be assigned to certain tasks by authority.

Although the system of rewards marks a higher civilization than the system of coercion, only a society of completely socialized individuals could wholly dispense with the latter. Even in the economic realm society finds it advisable to limit the activities of individuals in certain details, as is evidenced by a government postal service, the Interstate Commerce Commission, pure food laws, and divers other regulated matters. These are cases where the freedom of the majority is protected at the cost of the freedom of the few, for a proper amount of regulation produces greater liberty on the whole. In other cases, for its own sake society must often resort to compulsion, as when it decrees that all children under a certain age shall attend school. There is a point, however, where compulsion gives way to reward, and students continue their education far beyond the legal requirements. It is a nice point for a society to decide where, in each activity, rewards cease to be adequate and coercion must be used. A balance has to be struck between the two. And when a group reaches a point where it cannot be further stimulated by rewards, or where it will endure no more compulsion, it has reached the limit of its capacity for civilization.

6. *The Balance Between Passive and Active Adaptation.* The largest and most striking phase of social equilibrium is found in the extent to which men are able to carry the active rôle in

the process of adaptation. As pointed out in a previous chapter, the active and the passive rôles are alternatives and, in an important sense, each is a substitute for the other. That is, in so far as a creature becomes passively adapted there is no need for active adaptation, and in so far as it can succeed in actively adapting the environment to itself, there is no need for further passive adaptation. Each form of adaptation has its own special form of cost. The cost of passive adaptation is the extinction of the unadapted individuals. This is likely to be a painful process, involving much sickness and suffering as well as a high death-rate. The cost of active adaptation is eternal vigilance, eternally looking ahead, planning, and working.

There is always a limit beyond which the individual or the group will not attempt to carry the process of active adaptation. In a rather fundamental sense, it is a problem of comparative costs. When the cost of active adaptation outweighs, in the minds of those concerned, the costs of passive adaptation, the process of active adaptation stops. When this point is reached, the group has reached the limit of its capacity to be civilized. From that time on, it will submit to the painful processes of natural selection, of survival and extinction, rather than carry on the still more painful processes of thinking, planning, and working which are involved in active adaptation. The group has reached its level of civilization. Further civilization "isn't worth the trouble" until the quality of the race so improves as to make civilization seem more worth while or less trouble.

The level of civilization thus becomes, as suggested above, a question of comparative costs. So long as the cost of active adaptation seems less than that of passive adaptation, the group continues to advance toward greater and greater control over its environment, to make an environment which will more and more conform to its own needs. But everything has its limits. That applies to the capacity of every race, including ours, to carry on the rôle of active adaptation.

Doubtless every one has been moved to ask, when reading how many thousands die of snake-bite every year in India, why don't the people of India exterminate poisonous snakes, once and for all, and be rid of the scourge? An Indian would assign a religious reason for this strange tolerance. If he were to put it on rational grounds, however, he would probably answer that it would be impossible, meaning that it would be too much trouble, or that it wouldn't be worth the trouble. The labor and expense involved and the shock to their feelings seem greater evils than the danger of snake-bite.

But the people of India are not different from other people. Every race and every nation has scourges which it accepts in preference to the cost of elimination. The house-fly and the mosquito probably cause as many deaths in the United States as snakes cause in India. We are likely to say that it is im-

DIAGRAM V

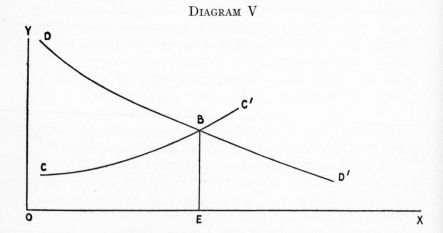

possible to exterminate the house-fly, which is an absurd statement. All it means is that we don't think it worth the cost. We would rather take our chances of dying of fly-borne disease germs than to do the thinking and planning, or to pay the taxes which would be involved in a successful anti-fly campaign.

The cases of snakes in India and of mosquitoes in America are only two among thousands which might be cited to show that there are phases of active adaptation which, though desirable in themselves, are yet too costly to seem worth while.

This diagram is designed to represent to the eye the balance of cost and utility involved in efforts to eliminate or minimize pests. Let us measure the effort required for the extermination of venomous snakes in India or mosquitoes in America along the line OX, and the cost of the effort as well as the desirability of its results along the line OY. Let the curve CBC′ represent the increasing cost of successive units of effort. This cost may consist in part of the increasing irksomeness of increased effort, and in part the increasing sacrifice involved in surrendering successive rupees or dollars of tax money. Let the curve DBD′ represent the decreasing danger as snakes or mosquitoes are thinned out, or the decreasing utility to be derived from further efforts at extermination.

When they are so thinned out as to cease to be a serious menace, it is pretty certain that a time will come when it will seem like a waste of money and effort to try to thin them out still more. The chance of being bitten becomes so remote, and the cost in effort or taxes becomes so great, as to outweigh the danger of being bitten. In the above diagram, efforts at extermination would be limited to those measured by the line OE. Beyond this point, the cost curve CBC′ rises above the danger curve DBD′. Up to this point, the danger weighs more heavily in the minds of the people than the cost. This is represented by the fact that the danger curve DBD′, up to point B, is higher than the cost curve CBC′.

A more vigorous or a less vigorous race might evaluate the relative costs differently. The reaction of a more vigorous race would be represented by lowering the curve CBC′ in the above diagram, and that of a less vigorous race by raising that curve. In other words, a more vigorous race would carry its war against snakes or mosquitoes beyond the point E on the line OX, and a less vigorous race would not go quite so far.

The same diagram could be used to represent how far we can go in the extermination of the house-fly, the corn-borer, the boll-weevil or any of the thousands of disagreeable things in our physical environment. It can also be used to represent how far we are willing to go in the prevention of crime, or any other disagreeable thing in our social environment.

If asked how far the government should go in the prevention of murder or any lesser crime, the average person would probably say that it should prevent all murder. In so far as that answer merely intimates a desire that all murder should cease, no criticism can be offered. In so far as it means that governments should spare no effort and no expense, but should, regardless of all costs, absolutely prevent all murder, it is going too far.

Along the line OX of the same diagram measure the efforts which might be made for the extermination or reformation of all murderers, actual and potential. Let the curve CBC′ represent the increasing cost of these increasing efforts, and let the curve DBD′ represent the decreasing danger of being murdered as murderers are thinned out, either through being exterminated or reformed. When the danger becomes sufficiently remote, and the cost of further prevention sufficiently high, every society is likely to call a halt. The average citizen, especially the average tax payer, would rather run the remote risk of being murdered than to pay the heavy additional taxes necessary to reduce danger still further. What is here said of murder and its prevention can also be said of all other crimes. There is apparently no crime which we consider it worth while to prevent. We are satisfied if we can keep it within such bounds as to give us that degree of safety for which we are willing to pay.

Safety from the depredations of criminals may be considered to be a form of utility as danger is considered to be a form of cost. The principle of marginal utility and the equilibrium between utility and cost applies to safety as to other desirable things. If a desirable thing may be had without cost, it will, of course, be used to the point of satiety. If, however, it is costly, it is never sought in such quantities as to satiate completely the desire for it. It is sought so long as each increment of utility is considered greater than its cost. Beyond that point we prefer to deprive ourselves of additional units of utility rather than to incur additional units of cost.

Safety from the depredations of criminals is not to be had without cost. Absolute safety, while in itself desirable, is not generally considered to be worth all it would cost. The standardized cost and utility curves of the economist illustrate the balance of crime — the prevention of it and its cost — as well as the balance of cost and utility in the production of wealth.

7. *The Limits of State Interference.* This method of analysis throws new light on the old and much discussed question of the proper limits of state interference. Instead of saying that certain things are "proper" subjects for state interference, and others "improper" subjects, the suggestion is that the whole question be put on a cost and utility basis. Anything is a proper subject for state interference which, if permitted, would result in social disutility. The only question should be, will it pay to interfere with or repress it, that is, will it bring about a degree of social utility greater than its cost?

If, to take an extreme case, it were scientifically determined that chewing gum or high heels were, on the whole, injurious rather than beneficial, their use would be a "proper" subject for state interference. But the propriety of interference would not justify state interference. There would be a considerable cost involved in repression. The cost would include not only a waste of man power in the form of police and court officers and other tax-eaters, but also a great deal of espionage and other irritating factors. In all probability the cost of repression would be greater than the cost of permitting the undesirable thing to continue unabated.

Even when, as in the case of murder, arson, or theft, there is universal agreement as to its injuriousness, and as to the advantage of interference, we still have to face the question as to how much interference the evil calls for, and how much the interference will cost. As shown above, complete prevention would not pay. More technically, if efforts at prevention are carried too far, the marginal cost will exceed the marginal utility achieved or the results of the marginal effort will not be worth what it costs.

This method of analysis provides a sufficient answer to the frequently used formula, "There ought to be a law against it." The question is never whether the thing in question is undesirable or not, but whether its suppression is desirable enough to justify the necessary cost. Drunken driving of automobiles undoubtedly kills more people than snake-bites in India. If it could be stopped by the mere passing of a law, without further cost or effort, its stoppage would pay. But there are other costs. Rather than pay these costs, the average citizen, apparently, would rather permit thousands to be killed and to run the chance of being killed himself. If that be true, then, on that point at least, we have reached our level,— the point beyond which we are unwilling to assume the active rôle and prefer the passive one.

In every phase of the problem of assuming the active rôle of molding our environment or the passive one of being molded by it, there is a point beyond which we will not go. This is only one manifestation of the universal tendency toward a balance or equilibrium of social forces. We saw in the chapter on Moral Adaptation that there is no survival value in being morally perfect in the purely idealistic sense of being immune to temptation. When we are "good" enough to respond favorably to such stimuli as the group can bring to bear upon us, we are as "good" as the group cares to have us. We then respond to the temptations to be "good," that is, to do socially desirable things rather than to the temptations to be "bad," or to do socially undesirable things. Even though the temptations to be "good" consist of rewards and punishments, both immaterial and material, if they are effective in getting the kind of behavior which the group wants, we are just as "good,"— that is as desirable to the group,— as though we did the same things instinctively or automatically. If we build a system of control which provides us with adequate aids to social "goodness" we have assumed the active rôle. We have made it unnecessary to be so passively modified as to need such aids to "good" behavior. We have succeeded in directing the course of social evolution.

CHAPTER X

CREATING A PHYSICAL ENVIRONMENT FAVORABLE TO HUMAN LIFE

1. *Power.* The process of remaking our environment necessitates the moving of matter on a fairly large scale. It has been pointed out many times that all we do in this world is to move pieces of matter. Whether we are constructing huge buildings, irrigating dry land, draining wet land, chiseling marble, painting a picture, or writing a book, our work essentially consists in the moving of physical objects, of shuffling them about, reassembling them according to our own ideas. In order to move a physical object power is necessary. No piece of matter was ever moved through an inch of space without physical power of some kind or from some source. To move these objects on such a vast scale as to make over our entire physical environment requires huge expenditures of power which can be measured in footpounds. Power is, therefore, next to intelligence, the most important factor in the process of adaptation.

The only source of power over which we have original and primary control is that which is developed in our own bodies and exercised through our own muscles. This source of power, however, is very definitely limited and would be wholly inadequate to the performance of the huge tasks which modern civilized men have accomplished. To economize and utilize this power to the maximum requires the exercise of a high order of intelligence. In fact it is probable that more intelligence has been used in the economizing of our muscular energies than on all other problems combined. Practically every tool or implement that was ever used or devised had the specific purpose of economizing muscular power, of enabling men to accomplish more, that is, to move larger masses of matter, or move them further and faster, with their limited source of power than would otherwise have been possible. The use of such primitive mechanical devices as the lever, the inclined plane, the wheel, the elasticity of the bow, the momentum of the hammer and the axe, were not only means of economizing muscular power, they were also the beginnings of science.

This point has seldom been more clearly stated than in the *Book of Knowledge:*[1]

> Here are we human beings, who could not live for a minute without the motion of blood in our bodies; and we are become the lords of the earth; we have changed its surface so much that men upon the moon could see the difference we have made. We rule other living creatures; we have built great cities and ships; have learned many of the secrets of the stars. And yet when we look upon ourselves and ask what it is that we can do, what it is by means of which mankind has done and will do everything, the answer is simply that we can move things. That seems absurd at first, but it is absolutely true. There is nothing that any human being has ever done, or ever can do, that does not depend upon his power to move things. All he can really do is to move his own body, in part or as a whole, and so, by pushing against other things outside him, he can scoop a hole in the earth and live in it, or put together machines that will build a palace.
>
> We move our chest, and lips, and tongues, and so we speak, or we move our bodies to get something that will make a mark; we move our fingers around that something and thus move it on something else, and so we write. We have done wonders, and we shall do much greater wonders yet; but all we can do is to *move things*.

Such primitive mechanical devices as were mentioned in a preceding paragraph merely enable men with their muscular power to accomplish greater results in the way of moving pieces of matter than would otherwise be possible. Of vastly greater importance in the economy of human energy is the tapping of other sources of energy than that generated within the human

[1] Arthur Mee and Holland Thompson, ed. (The Grolier Society, New York, 1918), p. 3428.

body and exercised through human muscles. The history of human achievements in this direction gives a better clue to the rise and fall of civilizations than the history of any other subject whatsoever. The use of wind for the propelling of ships, of falling water for the turning of wheels, and of the muscular power of domestic animals for carrying and drawing loads, antedates all historical records. It is a peculiar fact, however, which may be of some importance, that they were confined to Asia and its promontory, Europe. Neither the Africans south of the Sahara, nor the aboriginal Australians or Americans seem to have used wind or falling water as a source of power. With the exception of the llama which was used to a certain extent as a pack animal by the Peruvians, no animal power was used by any of these races. The Indian elephant, the camel, the Asiatic buffalo, the horse, the ass and the ox were all used as sources of power by prehistoric Asiatics and Europeans. The man who first tamed an elephant and made it do his work must have had courage at least as high as the man who first ate an oyster.

It is not always understood that the reason for the superior economy of machine production lies mainly in the fact that coal and petroleum are cheaper than human food, or that water power will supply footpounds of energy at a lower cost than muscular power can be developed from human food. Even the displacement of the horse by the tractor on our farms is traceable to a similar fact, namely, that gasoline is cheaper in proportion to the energy contained than hay and oats. The horse is, as Mr. Ford has said, "a hay motor"; he is also a good one. He makes good use of the kind of fuel he was built to consume. It is no fault of the horse that hay costs more per unit of energy than gasoline. In a country where men are willing and able to work on a kind of food that is cheaper than coal or petroleum, human power is not displaced by mechanical power from these sources. In some of the overpopulated and poverty-stricken parts of the Orient, men are seen pulling plows. Under certain conditions this is economical. A horse will eat as much as five men, and five men can do as much work as one horse. If men are willing to live on food which is as cheap as horse feed, it is economical to use human power. Where they demand more expensive food than the horse, horse power is cheaper than man power in certain kinds of work.

We are sometimes reminded that the average American has the equivalent of thirty slaves working for him in the form of engine and water power. But there would be no great advantage in having slaves unless the slaves could live on less, or could be made to live on less, than the free American was willing to accept. One might as well do one's own work and produce correspondingly less as to have a lot of slaves, each one of whom required as expensive a standard of living as the owner. In other words, in all our discussions of the superior efficiency of machine production, and in all our complacency over the fact that we have so many mechanical slaves working for us, we should not lose sight of the basic fact that a dollar's worth of coal or petroleum will furnish more energy than a dollar's worth of bread and meat or potatoes and beans. This more than anything else accounts for this age of power-driven machinery and machine production.

The harnessing of mechanical forces to power-driven machinery has been going on for a long time but the last century has seen a great acceleration of the process. Aside from wind and water power, the invention of gunpowder was the only important discovery of new sources of energy before the invention of the steam engine. The great acceleration in the process of harnessing mechanical forces to man's service is probably the result of the invention of the steam engine, which in turn resulted in cheap transportation. The steam engine enabled us to tap those vast stores of cheap power that were latent in the coal beds. Transportation has made this cheap fuel available over wide areas. At a later date the discovery of petroleum and the invention of the internal combustion engine have increased the rate of acceleration in the use of mechanical power.

Aside from the cheapness of fuel there are certain technological advantages in mechanical power. Thirty, sixty, one hundred or one thousand horses, no matter how cheap their food, could never give us the speed or convenience of an automobile or locomotive, to say nothing of the aeroplane. Ten thousand men or one hundred thousand, no matter how cheap their food, could not concentrate enough power on a set of rollers to roll a single steel girder. Some huge and powerful machines driven by mechanical power we should probably have no matter how cheap food became nor how scarce and dear coal, petroleum and other fuels became; but we should not see power-driven machinery displacing hand work in such a multitude of operations as we are now witnessing.

There is no doubt that in this present stage of civilization, while we are tapping these vast reservoirs of energy which were stored in the earth's crust in past geologic ages, we shall continue to substitute mechanical for muscular power on an increasing scale. This will mean an increase of product per worker and, under sound statesmanship, a higher standard of living for all workers. Even after these reservoirs are exhausted, there will be water power, wind power, and no one knows what other sources of power, to relieve human muscles. The incalculable and mentally paralyzing quantities of energy that come from the sun will be harnessed by solar engines under two conditions: first, that we have intelligence enough to devise solar engines; second, that we are willing to undergo the mental hardships of hard study and hard thinking, rather than the physical hardships of want and penury. Even if other sources of energy should not be discovered, we must remember that there have been noble civilizations where there were no mechanical sources of power other than winds and falling waters utilized by means of sails and water wheels. Much concern has been expressed lest this harnessing of mechanical power to our service should destroy our civilization. On this point, however, one of the greatest apostles of the aesthetic life, Oscar Wilde, says sanely:

The fact is, that civilization requires slaves. The Greeks were quite right there. Unless there are slaves to do the ugly, horrible, uninteresting work, culture and contemplation become almost impossible. Human slavery is wrong, insecure, and demoralizing. On mechanical slavery, on the slavery of the machine, the future of the world depends.[1]

[1] From *The Soul of Man Under Socialism* (Thos. Mosher, Portland, Maine, 1905).

Culture did not depend wholly on human slaves before the age of mechanical power. Animal slaves played their part in relieving human muscles of drudgery and fatigue. The yoking of the ox was one of the more important events in the history of man's use of power. In its day it was probably as significant as the invention of the steam engine or of the internal combustion engine at a later day. Taking the world as a whole, ox power is still the principal form of animal power, and animal power was, until recently, the principal form of power used by man. Besides, ox power was used on a vast scale for countless ages before steam power was thought of. When we consider how much longer men of Europe and Asia used oxen than they have used steam or gasoline, it is probable that the ox has played as large a rôle in the conquest of nature as either steam or gasoline.

Every shift from one source of power to another, like every mechanical improvement, has had its advantages and its disadvantages. The advantages are on the side of mechanical efficiency and the increase in the productivity of labor when products are measured quantitatively. The disadvantages are the unsettling of habits, the displacement of workers, and the loss of certain customary sights, sounds, and experiences which have become hallowed by time, and have therefore acquired a sentimental or an aesthetic value. The passing of the ox is one of the numerous illustrations of the cost or penalty of progress. It is one of the cases where our aesthetic feelings, which are of historical growth, are sacrificed to productive efficiency as measured by the quantity of product. Oxen at work are more decorative than tractors, perhaps even than horses. They give one the impression of irresistible power. There is something primitive about the way they are yoked and their power applied. The very slowness of their movements, the way they lean against the yoke and the way the yoke creaks under the strain, all heighten the effect. There are men who are never able to pass a pair of oxen at work without stopping to watch them and without a sigh of regret at the thought that they are a passing phenomenon. The countryside is losing one of its charms as oxen go out of fashion. Besides, skill in driving oxen is becoming one of the lost arts. Regret in this case, however, is futile, but it is of the same kind as regret at the passing of the handicrafts, of the domestic arts and even of some of the domestic virtues, in this period of active adaptation by means of mechanical power.

Significant as was the yoking of the ox, which may be taken as representative of the use of animal power through the enslavement of animals, a greater revolution in the use of power came with the discovery of the terrific power of expanding gases and the invention of contrivances for utilizing that power. Gunpowder and other high explosives, followed by steam and gasoline, have enabled men to move pieces of matter at higher speed than would otherwise have been possible. The reason seems to be that this form of power is more concentrated than others. An engine capable of developing thousands of horse power units occupies only an infinitesimal fraction of the space required by the number of horses exercising the same power. Where concentrated power is not necessary the ancient world did rather well in moving masses of matter and reassembling them according to their own tastes. The large blocks of stones in the Pyramids and the massive ruins of ancient temples in both hemispheres testify to the fact that ancient peoples could move apparently as large pieces of matter as we can, or at least as we have cared to move. But the ancient peoples took their time. They moved matter slowly, they had no means of propelling a missile through the air more swiftly than they could throw a spear or shoot an arrow. They could not move their own bodies faster than their legs or those of a horse could carry them. Doubtless we could, if we tried, move even larger masses of matter than they did but we are more interested in speed than in massiveness. Which is the better choice might be difficult to say. Certainly there was no merit on the part of the ancients in choosing massiveness rather than speed. They had no choice since they had no means of achieving speed. We have a choice in the matter and we have chosen speed.

A million slaves, with ten million oxen, equipped with levers, pulleys, windlasses, rollers and skids, could not greatly increase the speed with which any object could be propelled, but they could move and assemble heavy objects on a vast scale. Give them time — and they had plenty of time — and they could erect pyramids, hanging gardens, temples and cathedrals, but they could not travel many miles a day. Moreover, with this kind of power, they could produce approximately as much food from an acre of land as we can, though they could not cultivate so many acres per man, nor bring food so swiftly from distant lands. We must admit, in view of their achievements, that they used rather well such power as they had.

And yet we have at our disposal vastly more power than they and we could, if we cared for such things, outdo them in the erection of huge piles of magnificence. The simple fact is that we care more for other things and prefer to spend our energies in other directions. The reason the ancients achieved what they did was because they cared enough for what they were doing to give up other things. If the people of Athens had not cared to adorn the Acropolis they could have "saved" a great deal of money and man power for other purposes. They might have used these resources for the purpose of providing themselves with more luxurious food, more expensive clothing, or they might have amused themselves in more expensive ways. They probably could not have travelled so swiftly as we, but there were other ways of using up their energies.

At almost every stage in the modern development of mechanical power, men have been puzzled to know what to do with it. Periodically, during the last hundred and fifty years, it has been stated that our productive power was running away with us; that production was increasing faster than consumption, and that ruin lay ahead. Yet we have always found ways of consuming our surplus, or of using up our surplus energy. It is highly probable that we shall continue to do so, though our gift of foresight does not always enable us to see in advance just how. Thus far our preference seems to have been for speed rather than for magnificence as an outlet for our increasing energy. One begins to wonder how much further we can go in that direction. If we ever turn toward magnificence as a national ideal, there are boundless opportunities for the use of all the power we can develop. Is it conceivable that we shall ever care as much for magnificent buildings as we now care for travelling at high speed? It is not likely that we shall ever care for great mausoleums. No one seems to care enough for religion to want to spend much money or man power on temples. There is one thing, however, for which Americans really care and which, more than anything except speed, expresses the American spirit. That is the school. It is not inconceivable that we may care enough about our schools to pour our abounding energy into school building. If we do, we may leave to future civilizations examples of school architecture which shall eclipse the religious architecture of preceding civilizations.

2. *Organization.* We have seen that the problem of living together comfortably in large numbers is largely a problem of economizing human energy. Except for the limitations imposed upon the physical scientist by his special technique, this problem might very well be included under physics or studied by the physicist. It might come under that branch of physics known as energetics and might be called, to give it a human flavor, human energetics. In so far as economizing of human energy is accomplished by means of mechanical devices and mechanical power, it is a technological problem for the solution of which the physical scientist is equipped. If that were all there would be no need of the economist or the sociologist. But there is more to the problem than that. The great problem of organization is quite as important as the problem of mechanical equipment. Included under organization are such things as government, markets, media of exchange, laws, moral standards and a great many other things which help us to live and work together in large groups. For the study of these problems a training is required which is somewhat different from that of the physiologist, physicist, or technologist.

Every textbook in economics dwells at considerable length on the advantages of the division of labor, which involves specialization and exchange. The advantages need not be repeated here. They are an important phase of social organization and an important means of economizing human energy. Organization, however, is something a little more positive than the mere fact of specialization. It involves the active coördination of efforts of different kinds, performed at different times and places. How does it happen that men can be working at different times and places, totally unaware of one another's existence and under no one's command, on different parts of the same ultimate product?

One of the first things to be learned by the student of sociology is that organization may be very complex and highly efficient under either of two widely different systems. One system may be called, for convenience, the military system of organization; the other, the industrial system of organization. Under the military system the planning and coördination of effort are effected by those in authority. Those who carry on the actual work operate under command. Obedience is their first duty. Under what, for convenience, we have called the industrial system, contract or mutual agreement takes the place of authority and obedience.

One fundamental difference between the two systems of organization is found in the fact that under voluntarism everything is initiated by some individual's desire for a utility or a good. Under the authoritarian system everything is initiated from the high command. Under the voluntaristic system every producer anticipates the desire of some consumer for some article or means of satisfaction. Chronologically this power of anticipation complicates the problem of causation. Through this peculiarly human power of anticipation, production may start chronologically before a desire is actually felt. This sometimes seems on the surface as though it reversed one of the popular ideas of causation, namely, that the cause must precede the effect. It does not actually bring about this reversal when we trace all the links in the chain. The effective and immediate cause of the initiation of a productive process is the producer's desire for the product or the price of the product. With this desire as his own motivation he foresees a consumer's desire for the product and thus starts producing.

One of the great discoveries of the human mind,— a discovery that should rank with the alphabet and the multiplication table,— is the fact that large enterprises involving the united efforts of large numbers of individuals can be initiated and carried through by voluntary agreement among free citizens, and without the use of authority and obedience. In its widest sense this is coöperation, though that word is sometimes restricted to a particular form of organization, namely, an organization in which every participant has an equal vote regardless of his contribution. In the larger sense coöperation means working together voluntarily rather than working together under authority as conscripted workers driven by the fear of punishment. The nexus which binds the parts of the coöperative organization together into a unified whole is the hope of mutual benefit rather than the fear of authority.

This hope of mutual benefit may seem almost as mysterious to a sociologist as gravitation, surface tension, or chemical force does to the physicist; yet there can be no more doubt as to the reality of the hope of mutual benefit, or as to its effectiveness in uniting men for coördinated effort, than there is as to the reality and effectiveness of those physical forces. The lure is, in a sense, an attraction, and the idea of attraction is probably more difficult for the physicist to grasp than for the economist. Probably no one quite realizes how, if at all, a particle of matter can possibly be affected by another except by physical contact and pressure. We cannot put ourselves in the position of a particle of matter. We know by experience, however, how a human being can be attracted by something desirable, or by the anticipation of a pleasurable sensation through the contact of food upon the organs of taste. In this particular at least the economist has a slight advantage over the physicist.

3. *The Scope of Organization.*

A. *In Space.* Technological improvements have enabled the modern world to extend the scope of organization both in space and in time. Through improved means of transportation and communication the efforts of men widely separated in space may be coördinated. This is sometimes called "the territorial" and sometimes "the international" division of labor. Without these modern means of communication and transportation such territorial division of labor would be limited, in the main, to small communities. One aspect of this extended territorial division of labor is the widening of markets. The widening of markets, in turn, has made large-scale production possible. Where transportation is difficult and costly, the local producer for a local market would, of course, have a great advantage over a producer located at a distance. In most cases every producer would be limited to a small local market, and would find it useless, even if it were possible, to produce on a large scale. Those phases of the capitalistic system known as world markets and large-scale production are clearly the products of the technology of transportation and communication, literally of steam railways and electricity.

B. *In Time.* Even more striking is the extension of the scope of organization in time. Territorial division of labor is mainly contemporaneous, that is, it is the coördination of labor performed at approximately the same time but in widely separated places. There is another kind of division of labor which consists in the coördination of labor performed at widely different times. This form of coördination requires, for its extended application, durable pieces of matter. To be sure the labor of two men may be coördinated when that labor is performed at different times, if one will listen to the advice of another or in some way correlate his work at one time with that which the other man has previously performed. A certain amount of technical lore may be handed on from father to son or from generation to generation by oral tradition. The technical wisdom of one generation, acquired by experience, when thus transmitted to future generations may be regarded as a coördination of labor performed at different times. Later generations literally work with earlier generations.

If, however, that technical wisdom takes the form of recorded speech,— chiselled on stone, baked in tablets or printed on paper,— we have the other condition referred to above, namely, that of a coördination of labor performed at different times. In this case a durable piece of material carries the impression of one man's labor to another and later worker and thus facilitates the coördination of labor of a later time with that of an earlier time. The "art preservative of all arts" adequately expresses the function of the printing of books. It is a piece of durable material serving as a connecting link between workers of different times. Again, a composer of music might transmit to a singer his composition by the process of vocalization on the part of the composer and imitation on the part of the singer; but the possibilities in this direction are very limited. One evidence of this is the extremely limited knowledge we have today of the music of the ancients. Such knowledge as we have is derived from the very few written documents or musical scores which have been found. If more of their scores had been written on more durable material, singers of today might be rendering, in popular concerts, music composed two thousand years ago.

Printing, however, is not the only means by which the labor of the present may be coördinated with the labor of the past. A musician of today may play on an instrument made several centuries ago, in which case the labor of the instrument-maker and of the performer are adequately coördinated. Nor is it alone in the field of art that this form of coördination takes place. It is one of the striking characteristics of modern industry, quite as striking as the widening of the scope of territorial division of labor through transportation. It is sometimes called the lengthening of the process of production, sometimes the round-about process of production. This lengthening of the process of production means that the worker of today is working with or, more literally, his work is coördinated with, labor which was performed in the past by the inventors and tool-makers, by the extractors of raw materials from which tools are made, by the makers of the tools which aided in the extraction of raw materials, etc. etc.

This mass of durable objects which carry the impress of one group of laborers to another and later group, and enable both groups to coördinate their efforts, is, in industry, called capital. It is not difficult to see, however, that fundamentally it is like the musical instrument, the printed book or any other means by which the labor of past generations is carried on to later generations, permitting later generations to work with those that have passed and gone. The difference between a book of instructions for the guidance of a cook or a mechanic, and the implements with which the cook or the mechanic works is a difference of form and not, from the point of view of the present discussion, a difference of quality. The book of instructions and the implements are alike in that they are durable substances which carry the impress of former labor and transmit it to later labor, and literally permit labor performed at widely different times to be correlated and coördinated in the performance of the same essential line of production.

As stated above, it is modern technology that has widened the scope of this form of division of labor among workers who live and work at widely different times. The printed book is a technological product; the printing press, with movable type, was one of the first of that large number of technological products which make possible quantity production with interchangeable parts. In some respects the printing press is the most perfect example of this highly modernistic process. But practically every advance in modern technology is also a lengthening of the process of production, a means by which labor performed at widely different times,— that of the tool maker and of the tool user,— may be coördinated. It was the technologist who showed the world how this form of coördination could be effected. In other words, it was the technologist who made possible this modern phase of the capitalistic system.

While the technologist was an essential factor in making possible this modern capitalistic system, he was not the only factor. It would be very strange indeed if anything so vast and complicated as the capitalistic system could be accounted for on the basis of a single factor of causation. Another factor is the willingness and the ability to wait or to postpone the enjoyment of the products of present effort to a future time. To begin with, the mere preservation of the materials on which laborers of a former time have worked requires motive and purpose. If no one had the motive or the purpose of preserving such things and making them available for future laborers, such things would not be preserved or devoted to that purpose. Not even a book or a violin would be preserved unless some one had a motive for preserving it. Such preservation has to be done either by individuals or by groups of individuals in some organized capacity. Whether the preservation is done by individuals or by groups, the thing done is precisely the same. Where it is done by individuals or by voluntary groups, we have what is called private ownership of these durable materials. Where it is done by governmental or compulsory groups we have public or government ownership. Whether we have private or public ownership, the thing done is equally useful. The only real question is whether it can be done better under one system or under the other.

Under whatever system the preservation and utilization of those durable objects on which earlier laborers worked are preserved and utilized, there has to be definite ownership; that is, some individual or some organization, either private or public, must have a motive for their preservation. If the object is not owned, either by private persons or public organizations, it is soon lost, destroyed or dissipated, provided the supply is not indestructible and inexhaustible. Even books which nobody owns are soon lost or destroyed (it is to be observed that public ownership is *ownership*).

Under the present capitalistic system, which permits private ownership, the actual process by which labor performed at different times may be coördinated is somewhat varied. It may take the form of the continued ownership by the laborer himself of a piece of material on which he has worked. In such a case the maker of a tool, the writer of a book, the one who has improved the piece of land, retains his ownership and permits some other laborer, at a later time, to make use of his product. The former may rent it to the latter or may hire the latter to work on it or with it.

Again, the maker of a tool, or the one who has worked on a durable piece of material, may sell it directly to the laborer who intends to work on or with it at a later time. In this case the process of bargain and sale is an effective link in the chain which binds together, under one plan and purpose, laborers who work at different times. Again, a third person who may be called a merchant or a middleman acquires ownership in a piece of durable material, hires a worker to work on it at one time, and, still retaining ownership in the object, which now carries the impress of a worker, hires another worker at a later time to add his impress to the same piece of material. There are various other ways by which the process of coördination may be carried through. The point to be emphasized is that some form of ownership, either private or public, by the workers themselves, by merchants or middlemen, or by public agencies, is necessary for this form of coördination.

In all these cases it is evident that there is a postponement of enjoyment of the fruits of labor. Where the maker of a tool retains ownership in it, he has expended time and energy in making it and must wait until some product which is enjoyable can result from the use of the tool. In case he sells it for cash to the laborer who intends to use it, he (the maker of the tool) is relieved from further waiting; but the laborer who advanced the cash must now wait. He has, for the time, given up the opportunity to purchase articles of consumption and has bought, instead, an article of production, which yields no immediate enjoyment but which he expects to yield him an income in the future. In other words, the necessity of waiting is not removed by the immediate sale of a tool by its maker. In the case of a middleman, there is still an act of waiting or postponement of consumption. When he hires the first laborer to work on the piece of material and pays wages in cash, the first laborer is relieved of waiting as truly as he would be if he made the tool on his own initiative and sold it for cash. The middleman also relieves the second laborer of waiting because it is not necessary for the second laborer to advance cash to the first laborer; that has already been done by the middleman. This particular type of middleman in the modern industrial system is called the capitalist. His peculiar function is to coördinate labor which is performed at different times.

We have already seen that human labor consists in moving pieces of matter through space. Labor, in other words, changes the space relations of things but labor alone cannot change the time relationship. This requires an act of waiting. We may summarize the foregoing analysis by the rather brief statement that labor changes the space relationship; waiting changes the time relationship of things. Or, to put it a bit more concretely, laborers change the space relationship of things by moving things about from place to place, re-shuffling the physical objects with which they have to do. The capitalist, by the process of waiting, or investing, changes the time relationship of things and makes it possible for labor which is performed at widely different times to work together toward an intelligent and ultimate purpose. Both functions are necessary for the most effective organization of industry and for the greatest economy of human energy in the process of active adaptation, of mastering the physical environment and molding it to suit our own needs and purposes. This mastery of the physical environment, relieving us of the necessity of being molded by it, as lower organisms are; this process of making the seemingly rigid environment plastic to our touch is, in reality, all that is meant by the somewhat impressionistic formula, the victory of mind over matter.

4. *Motivation.* An unsatisfied desire of any kind is a form of discomfort and an evidence of maladaptation. The more intense the desire which is unsatisfied the greater the discomfort and the more extreme is the maladaptation. Two definite alternatives present themselves to any one who feels an unsatisfied desire: One is to suppress the desire, or, in general, to bring his desires into harmony with the environment; the other is to reshape the environment to bring it into harmony with his group of desires.

This is the first great alternative which presents itself to beings with the capacity for economizing, for adapting means to ends, for bringing about a state of adaptation between themselves and the conditions under which they are compelled to live. Two widely different philosophies or attitudes toward life develop under these conditions. One pursues the path of self-discipline, self-repression, glorifies the simple life, condemns the feverish pursuit of objects of desire, seeks blessedness in emancipation from craving, and, in the last extreme takes the road to Nirvana. The other seeks to kill desire, but by the opposite method, that is, by satiation. When a desire is satiated, it ceases to exist as desire. It is temporarily as dead as though it had been rooted out of one's system or erased from one's consciousness. Satiation, however, requires the multiplication of goods or desirable objects, and this requires work; and it also leads to rivalry for the possession of goods, to competition, to conflict and even to war. In order to keep this conflict within a social group from destroying the group, concepts of justice have to be formed and machinery has to be instituted for establishing and enforcing such ideals of justice as are developed.

As pointed out in an earlier chapter, a great deal of the work of the world is done for the sheer pleasure of working. If enough work could be done for the pleasure of working to satisfy or satiate all desires, none of these problems would arise. Every one could do that which he found pleasurable and he would not even experience a desire for leisure or a change of activity. At the same time all his desires would be satisfied or satiated and there would be no unsatisfied desire as an evidence of maladaptation. Men would fit into their environment perfectly and the environment would fit them perfectly, there would be no maladaptation to be corrected, no motive for progress, the goal of progress having been reached. But no actual environment ever responded so favorably to human effort and no group of human beings ever fitted so completely into their environment as that. Work which was disagreeable has had to be done and even after it was done there were unsatisfied desires to irritate men. Fatigue or some other form of irksomeness presented a disagreeable evidence of maladaptation; unsatisfied desire presented another. If we may use the word evil as a general term to convey the idea of maladaptation, then there are two evils in the world: fatigue and unsatisfied desire.

The whole world without exception is engaged in fighting one or the other of these forms of evil. The seeker after Nirvana fights it by trying to eliminate desire. The economic producer fights it by trying to increase the goods which are desired. The former is the method of old civilization where men have for centuries been baffled by, or convinced of the futility of satiating all desires. "As riches increase, they are increased that eat them and what profit is there under the sun." Seeing no possibility of counteracting the tendency of all animated life to increase beyond the means of satisfaction, convinced of the futility of ever producing goods fast enough to keep up with the rate of multiplication, or with our ever expanding desires, men drop into an attitude of pessimism. The other attitude is characteristic of new civilization in an expanding environment. Through colonization and commerce they bring subsistence from wider and wider sources and are, for a time at least, encouraged to believe that they can catch up with the ever expanding multitude of desires. This optimistic attitude will probably last as long as the areas from which food is to be secured expand more rapidly than population. When the limits of expansion are reached, this optimism may give way to pessimism. Then the control either of population or of desire will seem like a more practical policy than the multiplication of goods. We of the Western World are still encouraged in our optimism by the continued expansion of the geographical sources of raw materials. If desires multiply we hustle about to find new means of satisfaction. We have been measurably successful. We have been able to take land away from weaker people. We have been able to exchange cheap gewgaws for the objects of our desire and have found the way of satiation much more pleasant than the way of repression.

No matter which alternative is chosen the people generally succeed in developing a religion, a moral code, or a technique of idealization to help them to success. Where the way of repression seems the better alternative, asceticism is idealized both by religion and morals. Where the conditions are such as to make the way of satiation seem more feasible as well as pleasant, both morals and religion idealize work. Instead of extolling the virtues of self-repression, these psychological helps to adaptation idealize feverish activity, both mental and physical. To be forever doing something useful or practical for the alleviation of want, for the satisfaction of desires, is the ideal of practical sainthood. Asceticism, unless it be the asceticism of hard work and frugal fare, does not appeal to the buoyant Western mind.

One kind of Western asceticism includes not only hard work and frugal fare, but the augmentation of one's power to work by means of physical and mental training. As soon as men come to understand what tools are for, they will realize that it is quite as consistent with asceticism of the working sort to augment one's working power by means of tools as by means of training. Even the vow of poverty may permit the ownership of tools, even of large tools, by means of which one may work more effectively. But tools are an important form of wealth in the modern world. The vow of poverty does not preclude the ownership of this kind of wealth.

The Western World, having chosen the way of satiation rather than the way of repression, has had to face another alternative. The way of satiation requires a great deal of work that is not in itself pleasant, at least not pleasant enough to serve as a motive. Other motives have had to be found to induce men to work. In a simple, self-sufficing economy an adequate motive is found and provided by the simple rule that each shall have what he produces, and shall be protected in its possession and enjoyment. Where that rule prevails the desire for goods may provide a motive strong enough to overcome the individual's dislike for work. In a more complicated economic system, sometimes called market economy, where the average individual does not produce what he consumes, but specializes on what he can produce to the best advantage, and expects to exchange his product for the products of other specialists, a close approximation to the same result is secured when each individual is adequately protected, first, in the possession of that which he has made, and second, in the possession of that which he has secured by peaceful and voluntary exchange. In both conditions the worker is lured on by the hope, first, of his own product and, second, of the product which he can secure in exchange for his own. In other words, it is the lure of earning a desirable object and not the prod of authority which motivates his work.

No sooner is one great problem solved than another appears. In fact, the solution of one problem seems to create several others. The solution of the problem of production, of finding ways and means of getting from the earth enough for everybody, lifts society to a higher level where new problems arise to puzzle us. The technology of moving pieces of matter by means of mechanical power has enabled us to remake our physical environment. We have not been able to remake our social environment on a similar scale.[1] This is the great intellectual problem of the present and must occupy the minds of those intellectuals who are not content to "loaf and invite their souls." It is the field of study which calls for the endowment of schools and of research fellowships in the future as the field of technology did in the past.

We return now to the starting point of this chapter. The task of remaking the physical environment requires the moving of matter. Moving matter requires mechanical power. Our only original source of mechanical power is our own muscles, which, unaided, are utterly inadequate to the task. The problem then becomes one of economizing our muscular power, and applying it in ingenious ways in order to increase its results. Mechanical devices are used, new sources of power are tapped, and men are organized on a vast scale. Organization involves specialization or the division of labor. Work done in different places and at different times must be coördinated and made supplementary and mutually helpful. Coördinating labor performed in different places requires com-

[1] Cf. *infra*, Chapter XIII.

munication or transportation. Coördinating work done at different times requires foresight, waiting, and durable materials capable of preserving the impress of earlier labor in order that later labor may be added.

All these ingenious ways by which muscular power can be economized require motivation on the part of the men who are to initiate and complete them. One effective form of motivation is to guarantee to every one either the thing which he produces or the equivalent of the value which he adds to the thing which he handles or manipulates. Another effective form is to command him to work under direction and punish disobedience. A motive is needed for waiting as well as for working, for changing the time relationship as well as the space relationship of things. Motivation is closely associated with valuation. How to evelute products, services, and men is a problem for the future. The problem is to find what a man is worth, to assure him as much as he is worth, and yet make him worth enough to enable him to live in comfort on what he really earns. That will be the topic of the concluding chapter of this book as it must be of every book on economics or sociology that is not a waste of ink and paper.

CHAPTER XI

CONTROL OF POPULATION

A. CONTROL OF NUMBERS

1. *The Man-Land Ratio.* Very early in the development of group life men discovered the necessity of maintaining what Sumner and Keller have called the man-land ratio. Too many hunters in the same territory will thin out the game, either by killing it or driving it away, and those dependent upon the hunters will consequently suffer want. Too many herdsmen will overstock the pasture lands and ruin the business of herding. The search for grass explains the migrations of pastural people. Too many farmers result either in extreme *morcellement*, or an oversupply of agricultural workers. In either case the product per worker diminishes and the standard of living falls. Too many competitors in any industry result in hard conditions. The struggle for land, either in the form of hunting grounds, pasture lands or plow land, is one of the earliest forms of inter-group struggle.

Where, in any limited area, there are more people than can live comfortably, one remedy is emigration. So long as there were unoccupied lands, this was an easy solution. When, however, all productive land was once occupied, the migration of one tribe meant the dispossession of another tribe. The other tribe, in order to protect its source of subsistence, had to repel the invaders. In other words, the hunting tribe had to protect its hunting grounds; the herding tribe its pasture lands; the agricultural tribe its plow land. It was "fight or starve." However, any assertion of a special claim to hunting grounds, pasture lands or plow land, was an assertion of a claim to tribal property and a negation of any ideal of world communism. Such a tribe was facing a situation, not a theory.

Any idealist who would then have lifted his voice in protest against tribal property and in favor of world communism would have been promptly silenced. World communism would have made it impossible for any individual tribe to safeguard its own standard of living. Any tribe that tried to build up a higher standard of living by conserving its game, its pasturage, or its soil fertility, would have found its efforts nullified by the immigration of tribes with a lower standard of living who would soon eat the intelligent tribe "out of house and home." Any tribe that undertook to keep its numbers within such limits as could be amply supplied or supported on a high standard of living would find its efforts nullified by the invasion of other tribes that spawned as do the plants and animals. In short, the very idea of a standard of living, either on the part of the family, the tribe, or the nation, involves some control over the sources of livelihood, which is a negation of communism,— world communism in one case, national communism in another case. For even within the tribal boundaries the entire subsistence of the tribe is, under communism, thrown open to the progeny of the spawners. Neither continence, celibacy nor birth control would save the more intelligent from want, or a reduction of their standard of living.

The human race has had enough experience with a shortage of game or a shortage of grass to be convinced that if numbers increase beyond certain rather definite limits they cannot live so well in a given area either by hunting or herding. Those who have studied the problem closely and analyzed the factors involved are also convinced that the same rule holds true of tillage as of hunting and herding. However, so many new factors enter into the determination of agricultural productivity as to complicate the problem and make its solution somewhat obscure. New discoveries are continually increasing the productivity of labor on land. A few have increased the productivity of land. This fact has sometimes been used as an argument to show that the old law of diminishing returns which applies to hunting and herding does not apply to agriculture. Such a conclusion, however, is based on defective analysis.

A sentimental objection is sometimes raised against the law of diminishing returns from land. It is said that it "closes the door of hope" to mankind, or that hopelessness is inherent in a world of diminishing returns. Now the law of diminishing returns "closes the door of hope" to the social reformer only in the sense that gravitation closes it to the aviator; and hopelessness is no more inherent in a world of diminishing returns than it is in a world of gravitation. Gravitation has actually closed the door of hope to many a visionary aviator who could not get his device to work successfully because of the stubbornness of gravitation. It has not, however, closed the door of hope to those who took gravitation into account, adjusted their devices to it, and devised machines that could overcome it. Gravitation doubtless closed the door of hope to Darius Green, but not to the Wright Brothers. Similarly, the law of diminishing returns most effectually closes the door of hope to the Darius Greens of economic reform, but not to those reformers who take this and other laws of economics into account and plan their economic systems in conformity therewith.

Another mistake, commonly made by those who resent the existence of the law of diminishing returns, is to ignore the one important part of every definition of this law. Every correct definition limits its application to a given area of land. To point out, therefore, that by commerce and transportation a country may bring food from the outside and increase its population beyond the capacity of its own agricultural soil to feed, is not a negation of the law of diminishing returns. The question may legitimately be asked: why is it necessary to resort to commerce and transportation systems to bring food from wider areas? The only answer is, because the law of diminishing returns applies to the original area of the country in question.

Since the law of diminishing returns from land assumes a fixed quantity of land and a variable quantity of labor, it resolves itself into something fairly definite and concrete. It may be stated, and has been stated, in several different ways. Moreover, it has been tested in various experiment stations by various methods. It has been reduced to mathematical exactitude.[1] It has also been stated clearly without the use of mathematical symbols. It may be illustrated in the following way.

Let us assume a given field, say of ten acres, to which varying quantities of labor are applied in the cultivation of maize or Indian corn. Let us use, as our unit for the measurement of labor, a day's work of a man with a team and appropriate tools. One day's work applied to the whole field would probably produce no crop at all. Five days on the same field would produce a crop, but a rather poor one; ten days, possibly more than twice as large a crop as five days, and so on, according to the following table. Sooner or later, the point is reached beyond which additional units of labor do not add proportionately to the crop.

DIAGRAM

Day's Labor of Man and Team with Tools	Total Crop in Bushels	Bushels per Day's Labor		Marginal Returns per Day's Labor	
1	0	0		0	
5	50	10	Increasing	12	Increasing marginal returns
10	150	15	average	20	
15	270	18	returns	24	
20	380	19		22	
25	450	18		14	
30	510	17	Diminishing	12	Diminishing marginal returns
35	560	16	average	10	
40	600	15	returns	8	
45	630	14		6	
50	650	13		4	

[1] Cf. John D. Black, *Production Economics* (Henry Holt & Co., New York, 1926).

By comparing the third and fourth columns it will be noticed that there is a wide difference between the marginal returns and the average returns from labor. The terms increasing and diminishing may apply either to average or to marginal returns. When we try to find an answer to the question: how many people can be fed from a given area of land, diminishing average returns are more important than diminishing marginal returns. When we try to find out what determines the wages of agricultural labor, and the rent of agricultural land, the fourth column is the important one.

The law of diminishing returns from land is, as is well known, only one phase of a more general law relating to the combinations of factors. In any combination, if one factor is increased while all the others remain unchanged, the product does not necessarily increase in exact proportion as the one factor is increased. The product may increase at a higher rate, at the same rate, at a lower rate, or not at all. Where the one variable factor is so small in quantity as to be ineffective, any increase in that small quantity may result in a more than proportional increase in the product. When the variable factor is of sufficient quantity to reach its maximum efficiency in the combination, any further increase will be followed by less than proportional results. When the quantity of this factor is so large as to saturate the combination, any further increase in its quantity may actually reduce the total product or diminish the total result.

There are very few, if any, results that come from a single factor working alone. If there were such a case, any increase in that factor would probably result in a proportionate increase in the result. But in cases where the desired result is the product of a large number of factors working in combination, there would be no reason to expect that you could double or quadruple or sextuple the result by doubling, quadrupling or sextupling one factor in the combination. If every contributing factor, without any exception, could be doubled, quadrupled or sextupled, presumably the product would increase correspondingly. The phase of this general law, known as the law of diminishing returns, as originally stated by economists, applied to the application of labor and capital to the cultivation of land. It was merely an observation of the fact that when one or more, but not all, of the factors are increased, the product does not necessarily increase in proportion as the few variable factors are increased.

When thus understood, the law of diminishing returns becomes one of the greatest facts in human history. It explains the migrations of peoples as well as many of the conflicts of interests within the same national boundaries. It explains the spread of population across the continent of the United States and the dispossession of the weak proprietors of the soil, the American Indian. The peoples of Western Europe and the Americans may feel that they have little cause for alarm over the increase of numbers, but the reason is a rather gruesome one. They feel competent to take land away from the weaker races in the future as they have in the past, which means the extermination of those weaker races. The very complacency with which people under our western civilization view the problem of over population is, and (did they understand it) would be, a cause for acute concern on the part of the weaker races of mankind. It spells their doom. It is the principle of diminishing returns that makes the problem of immigration, or the shifting of populations, of such vital importance even to the peoples who live under our western civilization. Their standard of living is as definitely menaced by the existence of overcrowded areas in distant parts of the world as that of a hunting or herding tribe would be by the existence of neighboring tribes whose game or grass was running short.

The relation of the problem of population to the law of diminishing returns is a vital one. As pointed out in the chapter on The Balance of Social Forces, a standard of living of a population and its general well-being depend, in the last analysis, upon a balance between the productivity of land and the number of people to be fed. The importance of this balance may be summarized as follows:

1. That there are powerful motives which if not counteracted by prudential reasons, will lead to marriage and the begetting of offspring is a matter of experience.

2. That in a prosperous country the average pair is physically capable of producing, bringing to maturity and marrying off more than two children, is a matter of observation.

3. That if they continue to do so, each succeeding generation will be more numerous than the preceding, is a matter of arithmetic.

4. That, in any given state of scientific knowledge, there is a limit to the quantity of food that can be grown on a given area of land, is a matter of geometry, that is, of the limited space in which plants can spread their roots in the soil and their leaves in the air and sunlight.

5. That long before this absolute limit is reached, the returns from increasing efforts to increase the yield of a given area of land begin to dwindle, is a matter of experimental proof, having been demonstrated over and over at various agricultural experiment stations, besides being one of the largest facts in history, explaining, as it does, most of the migrations of peoples and struggles for markets.

These five verifiable propositions are the basis of the current theories of population. They are all truisms and therefore uninteresting to the newsmonger; but truisms are at least true, which is more than can be said of many interesting and original statements.

On the basis of these truisms one must conclude, if one is disposed to reason about them, or one can determine empirically if one prefers that method, that every population inhabiting any given area must eventually do one of two things, it must either become stationary or it must manage to draw its subsistence from wider areas. It can become stationary only by balancing its birth rate and its death rate. This can be done either by decreasing its birth rate or increasing its death rate. It can draw its subsistence from wider areas either by migrating to those areas, or by extending its markets, that is, by selling to the inhabitants of sparsely populated outside areas the finished products of indoor industries in exchange for the food and raw materials produced on those outside areas.

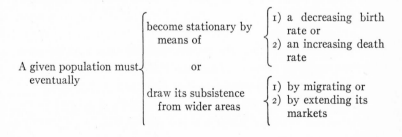

A given population must eventually

become stationary by means of
1) a decreasing birth rate or
2) an increasing death rate

or

draw its subsistence from wider areas
1) by migrating or
2) by extending its markets

Empirical observation shows that populations usually follow all these tendencies, though one or more may become dominant. On the basis of their dominant tendencies they become either pent up or expanding, that is, they continue, in the main, to live within their historic boundaries, or they tend to expand either their ownership or their commercial influence over wider and wider areas. Those which live the pent up life either reduce the birth rate as in France, or they suffer from over population and a high death rate as in China and India. Those who live the expanding life either migrate to new areas, as did the Greeks when their civilization was expanding, and as English speaking peoples have been doing for the last three hundred years, or else they develop their indoor industries, as England herself has been doing for a hundred and fifty years, bringing raw materials from sparsely populated areas, working them over in her indoor industries, selling the finished products back to the inhabitants of the sparsely populated areas and living on the profits of the transaction,— taking the profit largely in the form of food, also imported from sparsely populated areas.

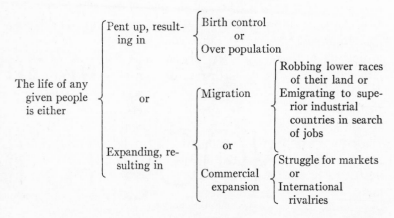

2. *Congestion.* While none of the western countries is suffering from general overpopulation, every country, without exception, is suffering from the congestion of population in one form or another. Congestion may be either local or occupational. There may be local congestion in a country which, as a whole,

is rather sparsely populated. Of course local congestion is not measured by the density of population, or the number per square mile. From the economic point of view, congestion is measured by the relation between the number of people and the opportunities for making a living.

Occupational congestion is a present reality in every civilised country with the possible exceptions of the United States and Canada, and even these countries are not wholly free from it. By occupational congestion is meant a condition in which certain occupations are over-manned. This usually means that certain other occupations are under-manned. In other words, it means a lack of balance among interdependent occupations, and all occupations are becoming interdependent. For example, if in any community there should happen to be more hod carriers than are needed to work with the existing number of brick and stone masons, that community is overpopulated with hod carriers, however sparsely its territory may be populated. Moreover, hod carriers would suffer from low wages or unemployment and be about as badly off as they would be if the whole region in which they lived were too densely populated.

At the basis of the general population theory is the important factor of balance between land and people. Too much land and too few people mean, of course, a low state of civilisation. Too little land from which to draw subsistence, or too many people dependent upon it means, on the other hand, an intense struggle for existence and a low standard of living. This idea of balance among the different factors is capable, however, of much wider extension. In these days of highly organized industry there is the same need for a balance between different kinds of labor as there is between labor and land. This was acutely illustrated in the days immediately preceding the so-called industrial revolution of the eighteenth century by a lack of balance at various times between weavers and spinners. At one time there were not enough spinners to supply yarn to the weavers. At another time there were not weavers enough to weave the yarn supplied by the spinners. In these modern times of extreme specialisation the illustrations could be multiplied by thousands.

Occupational like local congestion is a physical fact which lies deeper than forms of social or industrial organisation. It is as likely to exist under communism as under capitalism. The remedy is the same in all cases. The congested occupations must be relieved of their excess numbers. This can be done in either of two ways. First, by thinning out the numbers in the overcrowded occupations; second, by increasing the numbers in the undercrowded occupations. In the case of the hod carriers in the above illustration the remedy would be either to decrease the number of hod carriers or to increase the number of brick and stone masons.

In general, the occupations requiring little skill or special training tend to be overcrowded and those requiring much skill and long courses of training to be undercrowded. The most acutely undercrowded are the higher managerial positions, which, for purposes of this discussion, shall be called those of invention, investment and management. This is not a necesssary situation, but its remedy requires a more far-reaching and constructive programme than most of our statesmen or social reformers have yet been able to plan.

Undoubtedly one cause of the lack of occupational balance is the differential birth rate. The inordinately high birth rate among the ignorant and the unskilled, and the low birth rate among the business, professional and scholarly classes would naturally, in the absence of a sound system of popular education, tend to keep the lower occupations overcrowded and the higher ones undercrowded. By a sound system of popular education is meant a system which enables every person to acquire the training and skill necessary for success in the highest and most remunerative occupation for which his natural or inherited ability would make it possible for him to be properly trained. Even where such a sound system exists, the differential birth rate throws a heavier load upon it than it would have to carry if the birth rate among different classes could be more nearly equalized. It is in this connection that birth control bears on the only really acute population problem, namely occupational congestion.

As already indicated, a sound system of popular education is a means of restoring an occupational balance. The most important element in such a system is commonly overlooked. It is not enough merely to enable unskilled manual workers to become skilled manual or even clerical workers. It is most important that as many as possible be trained for those occupations where men are scarcest, that is, for the highest occupations. So far as industry is concerned, these are those of the investor, the inventor and the manager. The scarcity of first rate inventors, investors and managers is everywhere the limiting factor in industrial expansion. Any country in which this scarcity is acute will always show a congestion of the manual trades, as evidenced by low wages, unemployment or emigration. Any country in which inventors, investors and managers are numerous and of high ability will show an active demand for workers in the lower grades. That is, there will be high wages, general employment, or immigration.

One of the most specific cures for low wages and unemployment in England would be for Oxford and Cambridge to start first rate graduate schools of business, and to use their vast influence to turn the best minds of England for a few generations toward business pursuits. If the country could mass its best intelligence for a few generations on industrial problems, its industries would so expand as to employ at high wages all its working population and to attract immigrants from other countries. It would then have an immigration rather than an emigration problem. On the other hand, one of the surest ways to create unemployment, low wages and poverty is to develop a supercilious attitude toward business, to turn the best minds of the country into the so-called genteel professions and to leave industry to second and third rate minds. Second and third rate minds can never run first rate industries nor pay first rate wages to large numbers of workers. Whatever else a country might achieve which turned its best minds away from industry, or failed to give them adequate industrial training, it could never achieve the elimination of low wages, unemployment and poverty except by wholesale and forced emigration or drastic birth control among the manual workers.

Occupational congestion is similar in certain fundamental respects to local congestion. As pointed out above, local congestion is a lack of balance between two factors, workers and land. Occupational congestion is a lack of balance between different kinds of labor. Local congestion may be cured in either of two ways; first, by reducing the number of workers; second, by increasing the amount of available land. Occupational congestion may likewise be cured in either of two ways; first, by reducing the numbers in the overcrowded occupations; second, by increasing the numbers in the undercrowded occupations.

The possibility of overpopulating the world, while a real one, is too remote to interest the popular mind. Local congestion is a present reality only in certain oriental countries and does not excite the western mind except when those old countries threaten to flood the labor markets of the western countries with cheap labor, which would result in occupational congestion even in new and sparsely populated countries. Occupational congestion is an acute problem, or threatens to become acute in every industrial nation. The fear of it is at the basis of all laws for the restriction of the immigration of laborers.

It should be pointed out that there is another kind of immigration problem besides that of the immigration of laborers. There has been some immigration into Mexico and the Philippines from the United States, but the immigrants have not been wage workers and they have not competed with wage workers of those countries. The immigrants from the United States have been inventors, technicians, investors and managers. Instead of competing with native laborers, they have increased the demand for and raised the wages of the native laborers. The only ones with whom these immigrants have competed were the limited number of native inventors, technicians, investors and managers. These are the only ones who have objected to these immigrants. The reason for this opposition has been similar in principle to that for the opposition of American wage workers to immigrant laborers. If immigrants to the United States had been mainly of the employing class, that would have changed the occupational balance in favor of American laborers. It would have tended to congest the higher rather than the lower occupations.

This proposed refinement of the theory of population, throwing the emphasis upon occupational rather than territorial congestion, is important not only for the clarification of theoretical discussion, it is also intensely practical. It points the way to the only constructive or permanent remedy for low wages, unemployment and mass poverty. If this problem can be intelligently handled there will be no more underpaid occupations. The only cases of poverty which will remain will be those individual cases of incapacity or misfortune with which charitable organisations have to deal, and even these will be greatly reduced in number.

3. *Mobility.* It is rather obvious that the mobility of the population, where such mobility exists, is the remedy for congestion. Local congestion can be relieved by geographical shifts of population. Occupational congestion can be relieved by vertical shifts of the working population.[1] The most effective agency for promoting this vertical shift is the school. It, more than any other social institution, more than anything in fact,— unless it be a democratic tradition that accepts merit wherever it is found and encourages every one to rise as high in the social scale as his ability and character will permit,— moves men upward in the economic and social scale. This relieves congestion in the lower occupations.

Geographical shifts of population are of great historical importance, probably of greater importance than any other phenomenon connected with human history. In so far as these are international movements they have been adequately treated by historians. There is, however, another geographical shift which is equally important; that is the shift from country to city. It is not, as some have been led to suppose, a distinctly modern

[1] See Sorokin's remarkable study entitled *Social Mobility* (Harper & Brothers, New York, 1927).

movement. It seems to have existed as far back as there were cities, or as there has been a difference between country life and city life.

According to Greek legend, the prehistoric Athenians were at one time, when Athens was a country village, compelled to send a periodic tribute of youths and maidens to feed the fabulous Cretan bull known as the Minotaur. It will be remembered that Crete was full of cities while the mainland of Greece was still a land of farms and villages. It will also be remembered that the bull plays a part in Cretan symbolism somewhat similar to that of the eagle in American and the lion in British symbolism. In view of these facts, we may be excused for using this legend as symbolic of the city as the devourer of youth — the hungry monster levying its annual tribute of rural youth, always receiving, never giving, and yet never full.

Rural migration is one of the oldest of all social phenomena, yet in the last few decades it seems to be accelerated by some special factors. The purely economic factors in this present migration are so well known as to have become commonplace. They may be summarized under two main propositions. First, the demand for the great staple products of agriculture seems to have about reached the limit of its expansion except as population increases. Second, the product per worker in agriculture has enormously increased and seems likely to increase still further.

So far as a strictly economic analysis throws any light on the problem, there is no convincing reason to expect any reversal of the process of rural depopulation. If the product per worker engaged in agriculture should continue to increase through the use of power-driven machinery, and if the per capita consumption of farm products should fail to increase, we should be compelled to conclude that a smaller and smaller proportion of the total population would be required in agriculture. This would seem to mean that a smaller and smaller proportion of our people would live in the country, and a larger and larger proportion in the city. This conclusion, however, rests on another assumption not strictly economic in character and somewhat startling in its implication. That assumption is that nobody is going to live in the country who is not compelled to do so by the circumstances of his occupation; or that every one who can possibly do so will live in a city. This virtually resolves a rural community into a penal colony. It is with this assumption that the rural sociologist should be principally concerned. Why must we make this assumption?

So long as it remains true that no one will live in the country except those who are condemned to it by the fact that they are farmers, not much can be done for farmers. When the time comes, if ever, that men and women who are not farmers and who can choose their own places of abode will, in considerable numbers, choose the country or the country village rather than the city, we may expect the lot of the farmer to be improved. Something may be done to bring this about through the rebuilding of the country village, the reconstruction of the rural school, a national system of country roads built to serve farmers, hospitals and clinics within reach of all farm homes, and a wide distribution of electric power.

The human race as a whole is a village product. Both scattered farms and large cities are rare and unnatural phenomena when we consider the entire history of the human race. We are all, even the most urbanized, essentially village minded and we shall never feel at home except in a village environment. When we awake to that fact and try to build villages to suit our needs, the rural village may take on a charm which will lure us as effectively as the bright lights of the cities now do.

In the older parts of Christendom the church was the nucleus around which life centered — village life as well as urban life. The school is already beginning to displace the church as a nucleus of rural life. When we realize the ideal school system, under which every rural child shall have within easy reach as good a school as is provided for the city child, the school may function as the church once did as the center of an agreeable and profitable rural life.

In our recent road building enterprises we have, to a considerable extent, merely imitated the Romans in connecting large towns and cities with great highways. Farmers who happen to be favorably located can, of course, use these highways, but little has been done to build first rate roads primarily for the convenience of farmers.

Rural communities, especially those which consist of scattered farms, are inadequately served by medical and sanitary science. They are likewise poorly provided with urban utilities, commonly miscalled public utilities, such as power light and water systems. These services, like those of religion, education and medicine, go to the highest bidders, and the cities can out bid the rural communities. So long as that is true, no one will live in the country except those who cannot make as good a living anywhere else.

B. The Quality of the People

1. *Human variations.* An eastern potentate, invited to witness a horse race, is said to have excused himself for his lack of interest by saying: "It is already known to me that one horse can run faster than another." That may or may not have been a valid excuse, but there can be no difference of opinion as to the fact stated. A similar and equally valid remark might be made with respect to the unequal ability of human beings in any field of endeavor. In fact, one of the most universal of all observations, both scientific and popular, is that no two things are ever exactly alike. When a number of them resemble one another in one particular sufficiently to serve the purposes of classification, they may be catalogued as belonging to the same species, variety, or class. But even within the same species, variety, or class there will always be individual differences. This great fact of variation, even within the species, is what makes evolution possible, for without variation there could be no natural selection of favorable variations. It is also a necessary condition of plant and animal breeding, for without variation there could be no artificial selection. The human species is no exception to this universal rule. No two individuals are alike or even so nearly alike as to be indistinguishable by those who know them well. The differences, how-

ever, are sometimes so minute as to escape the notice of any but close observers, though they are generally so wide as to be obvious to anyone.

Another fact of observation is that these differences among individuals are, as a rule, less among those who are closely related by heredity than among those who are not closely related. Generally speaking, or speaking statistically, the closer the relationship the less the differences both physical and mental. But even in the case of identical twins, the closest of all hereditary relationships, there are always minor differences. This fact that those who are closely related differ less among themselves than from others less closely related, is what gives importance to heredity. It is briefly and popularly expressed by the saying that like begets like. This is another fact which, in combination with the fact of variation, makes both natural evolution and animal and plant breeding possible. Except for this fact we should not be surprised to gather grapes of thorns or figs of thistles. If we did not believe that like begets like, we should trust wholly to chance to breed race horses, dairy cows, or orchids, and pay no attention to pedigrees or parent stocks. While, of course, there is no certainty that the progeny of pedigreed animals or plants will equal their parents, we are never in any doubt as to whether they are more likely, as a general rule, to resemble their own parents than other parents, or that we are more likely, as a betting average, to breed able performers from able parents than from inferior parents.

All this is of vital interest to the sociologist because he realizes that individual human beings are the units which have to be organized into societies. Some are more organizable than others. Some, when organized, make greater contributions than others to the life and success of the group. While it is true that the behavior of the individual is a kind of response, more or less automatic, to the stimuli of various kinds which come to him from his social environment, yet it is also true that, so long as individuals are different, they will respond in different ways to these stimuli. The success of the group depends upon the ways in which individuals respond to such stimuli as it, the group, can provide. It is highly important, therefore, that it be made up of individuals of a kind which will respond in ways that are favorable to group life rather than in ways that are unfavorable.

So far as this part of our argument is concerned, it does not seem to make much difference what view we take as to the so-called freedom of the will. Even if we accept the view that all human actions are automatic responses to stimuli, it does not follow from this that all responses to the same stimuli must be alike. If there are differences among the automata, their responses may also differ. One automaton may respond in one way, and a different automaton may respond in a very different way to the same stimulus. It is quite rational, therefore, to speak of good or desirable and bad or undesirable automata. The difference between a "good" automaton and a "bad" one is that a good one responds in the way you want it to respond, and a bad one in the way you do not want it to respond. From a social point of view, a good automaton is one which responds in a way which promotes the strength and survival of the group. Since it is the group which sets the standard of individual fitness for survival it should be the purpose of the group to set a standard of fitness in terms of its own interest. From the standpoint of such a group, the individual is fit to survive who responds to such stimuli as the group can bring to bear upon him in such ways as will make the group itself fit,— that is,— able to survive.

As to the unfit, or those who do not respond favorably, it is not enough to say that if other stimuli had been brought to bear upon them, they might have responded favorably. There is at least the possibility that, in providing the kind of stimuli that would have produced favorable responses in those who are now responding unfavorably, others, who are now responding favorably might begin to respond unfavorably. In short, we must accept the great and universal fact of variation among individuals, even in the ways in which they respond to social stimuli. The group which hopes to survive must find ways of stimulating individual behavior which will secure favorable responses from the general average of its individuals. There will always be individuals who vary so widely from the mass as to respond unfavorably to the same stimuli which produce favorable responses from the general average. These extreme variations or exceptional individuals are the criminals, who will exist even in the best governed societies. So long as they are the exceptional individuals, we have strong empirical evidence that the group is reasonably well, or at least efficiently, governed. That is to say, it is succeeding in getting the great mass of its individuals to behave as it wants them to.

Much mental legerdermain has been used to confuse the public mind as to the efficacy of our criminal laws as preventives of crime. That they do not prevent all crime is, of course, admitted. It does not follow from this that they do not reduce the sum total of criminal acts. Against this possibility, however, it is argued that since human behavior consists in automatic responses to stimuli, it can not be controlled by law. This, however, overlooks the rather obvious fact that laws, and the punishments provided for their enforcement, are themselves stimuli. By applying such artificial stimuli, your human automata may be stimulated to respond — automatically of course — in desirable rather than in undesirable ways.

The engineer, desiring to move an inert piece of matter, applies physical pressure. The object moves, automatically of course, in response to sufficient pressure. The physiologist, desiring a certain response from a muscle or an organ, applies a stimulus. The muscle or organ responds, automatically of course, if the stimulus is sufficient. The sociologist, asked how to secure certain behavior from an individual, could likewise recommend a stimulus. The individual behaves (let us say, automatically, for the sake of argument) as the sociologist predicts, provided the stimulus is sufficient and of the right kind. The difference in the three cases is not necessarily in the automatic nature of the responses, but in the mechanism of the responses and the kind of stimulus applied. The inert object can respond only to physical pressure, which can be measured in foot pounds. The sensitive organism can move in response to an irritant or a stimulant with which it comes in some kind of physical contact — sight, hearing and smell, as well as taste and touch, being considered as forms of physical contact. A mind, even of a rudimentary sort, can move in response to an anticipated stimulant or irritant, even when there is no actual physical contact. The promise, for example, of a future reward or threat of a future punishment, is a stimulant to a creature with some power of anticipation.

A social group, desiring its individuals to behave in certain ways, and to refrain from behaving in certain other ways, may make use of all these systems of motivation, though its main reliance must always be on its power to move the individual through his power of anticipation. It can, for example, through its constituted agents, the police or the militia, physically propel the individual from place to place, or incarcerate him so that he can not move from place to place. In this respect, his response is, like that of an inert object, a mere response to foot pounds of pressure. The group may also, with a minimum of pressure at the point of a bayonet, or the lash of a whip, cause the individual to propel himself from place to place, or refrain from moving. In this respect, the individual's behavior is like the response of a muscle or an organ to the irritant applied by a physiological experimenter. In the main, however, the group must depend upon its power to influence the individual through his power of anticipation. An anticipated prick of a bayonet or sting of a whip lash may cause him to react as violently as an actual application of acid to a frog's muscle. An anticipated sensation of pleasure can also secure active responses from an intelligent creature with some power of anticipation.

As a matter of fact, the whole theory of punishment as a deterrent is based upon the theory of automatic responses to stimuli. The belief that behavior is at least partially automatic and therefore partially predictable is the only belief on which punishment could be considered as a deterrent. Punishment as a mere temperamental expression on the part of the governing power of dislike for certain acts, need have no theory of deterrence back of it. But punishment as a means of reducing the number of undesirable acts is a different thing altogether. Every law passed with a view to reducing the number of acts of a given class assumes some degree of power on the part of the lawmaker to predict human behavior. If he did not believe that the passage of a certain law, with penalties for its infraction, would decrease the number of acts of a given kind, there would be no sound reason for passing it. The belief that the law will decrease those acts is a kind of prediction. Such prediction would be impossible except on the assumption that men will, in general, respond in predictable ways.

The fact that they do not all respond in one identical way is merely an evidence that men are not all alike and do not all respond in exactly the same way to the same stimulus. In short, we are here dealing with the great fact of variation. But while emphasizing the great and universal fact of variation, we can not ignore the other great fact of resemblance. While no two individuals are ever exactly alike, it is equally true that they are all very much alike. They are at least human, and all humans have certain common characteristics. There is no contradiction in affirming both facts. "Alike as two peas" has a real meaning in spite of the fact that no two peas are ever exactly alike. They are at least enough alike not to be mistaken for beans, acorns or pebbles. All human beings are likewise enough alike not to be mistaken for elephants, mice, clothespins or anything else. This general resemblance applies also to the way in which they respond to certain stimuli. If they are enough alike to respond, most of them, in the same way to a certain appeal, the group can get the kind of conduct it wants from most of them. The fact that a few respond otherwise is no indictment of its system of motivation. If, as suggested above, it were to adopt a system of motivation which would get desirable behavior from the few who are now misbehaving, the probabilities are that some of those who are now behaving desirably would be motivated to misbehavior. Whether individuals are free or determined in their actions and choices, it is evident that the strength and survival or a group depends on the kinds of behavior it succeeds in getting them to carry on. This, in turn, depends as much on the kinds of individuals they are as upon the kinds of stimuli the group brings to bear upon them. Our first problem, therefore, is: what determines the kinds of individuals in a group, their characters, qualities, and capabilities?

It is generally admitted that the character of the individual is determined by two main factors, heredity and environment, sometimes called nature and nurture. The individual's heredity includes more than those physical and mental qualities with which he was born. It includes all the potentialities of growth and development with which he was born. He was, for example, born without teeth, but that does not mean that he acquires teeth from his environment. He was born, if normal, with the capacity to grow teeth in any kind of environment in which he could live at all. He was born with very little intelligence and no knowledge at all, but if he is normal, or possessed of five senses, he was born with the capacity to develop intelligence and acquire knowledge in any kind of environment in which he could keep alive. It is true that he learns from contact with his environment, physical and social; but he would learn nothing from any environment if he did not have the inborn or inherited capacity to learn. "To Newton and to Newton's dog, Diamond, what a different pair of universes!" The dog lacked the inborn power to develop the intelligence which could learn what Newton learned, though at birth the dog may have been the more intelligent of the two.

The mere fact that all babies are at birth very much alike, sometimes presented by the unthinking as evidence that their future intelligence depends wholly on their environment, is singularly inconclusive. Inherently, it means no more than to say that because none of them can run at birth, therefore their speed as runners will depend wholly on their environment as they grow up. It is akin to the fallacy that because a baby has no knowledge at birth, and that all that it ever knows it learns from contact with its environment, therefore its environment is the sole factor in determining what it will know when it is mature. This overlooks the observed fact that the power to learn is a factor quite as important as the opportunity to learn. There is, as a matter of fact, no reasonable doubt that heredity and environment are both essential factors in determining the quality of the mature individual. The whole matter was put rather conclusively in the famous answer of Themistocles to the Seriphian who was abusing him and saying that he, Themistocles, was famous, not for his own merits but because he was an Athenian: "If you had been an Athenian," said Themistocles, "and I a Seriphian, neither of us would have been famous."[1]

As to which of two essential factors is the more important, there is no method known to gods or men that can find the answer. If, without either factor, the product could not be had at all, both are absolutely essential and there is no comparing of absolutes. Air, or the oxygen in it, is as essential as fuel or the carbon in it, to the making of a fire. Neither can be said to be more important than the other. Air is more abundant and therefore cheaper than fuel in most situations, and unanalytical minds are sometimes misled into thinking that it is therefore less important than fuel. It is, of course, more important that one should conserve the factor which is scarce than the one which is abundant. This has an important bearing on the theory of value, but it can throw no light whatever on the relative importance of the two factors themselves.

Much futile discussion has been directed toward the question of the relative importance of heredity and environment in the determination of character. There is no possible answer to such a question. When it comes to a practical question as to what we are to do in a given situation, there is an answer, and it is usually fairly clear. As in the case of the two factors, air and fuel, in the making of a fire, it is usually clear that fuel is scarcer and harder to get. It absorbs the attention of anyone who wants to build a fire, not because it is the more important of the two but because it is the scarcer of the two. Instead of wasting time discussing the relative importance of the two

[1] Cf. *The Republic.* The Dialogues of Plato, Jowett's translation (The Clarendon Press, Oxford, 1871), p. 148.

essential factors, heredity and environment, we shall do well to follow that form of empiric wisdom called common sense, which will frequently tell us what to do in an actual situation. For example, when a child is born, its heredity is already determined and nothing further can be done about it. The only possible problem, so far as these two factors are concerned, is that of providing a favorable environment. It is difficult, perhaps impossible, to find out just what a good environment is,— what is good for one individual not being necessarily good for another,— but every one knows enough not to waste time trying to improve the heredity of the generation which is already born. Most social agencies, including schools, are concerned with the problem of environment, not because of any abstract notion that environment is more important than heredity, but because the environment is the only factor in the character of the present generation over which we can exercise any control. It is only when we begin to consider future generations that it becomes important that we should consider the problem of heredity.

It is interesting to note that certain authors who have studied human weaklings, or those who are presumed to be weaklings because they have not made a success of their lives, generally stress the importance of environment in determining the failure or success of the people whom they are studying. On the other hand, certain students of genius are equally inclined to stress heredity. Dugdale in his study of the Jukes [1] concluded that even heredity was the organized result of environment, but he wrote before Weissman had made his epoch-making discoveries as to the nature of the germ plasm. Dugdale found, for example, that for several generations the Jukes had lived in bad social environments. He found, likewise, that it was hard to make good and successful citizens out of members of the later generations. Therefore, it seemed to him that the bad environment had degenerated the stock, until weakness had become

[1] *The Jukes:* A Study in Crime, Pauperism, Disease and Heredity (G. P. Putnams, New York, 1877).

hereditary.[1] Galton,[2] on the other hand, after studying a number of geniuses, concluded that environment had very little to do with the production of genius. If a man was a born genius, he would show himself to be a genius regardless of the kind of environment in which he lived. The weakness of the argument, however, from the standpoint of evidence, lies in the fact that he could study only known geniuses. The known geniuses were those whom environment had not prevented from becoming known. It is like proving that laws against and penalties for crime do not deter men from committing crime by studying criminals. That method studies only the cases which were not deterred from crime. Such a method could not possibly show whether thousands of non-criminals were or were not deterred by respect for law and fear of punishment. Similarly, the study of known geniuses could not possibly discover whether there were or were not thousands of potential geniuses who were prevented by a bad environment from achieving rank as actual geniuses,— who were, in fact, born like the flower, "to blush unseen, and waste its sweetness on the desert air."

It is natural, however, that those who study human weaklings should be impressed with the importance of environment for the excellent reason that weaklings are the sport of circumstances. On the other hand, it is natural that one who studies men of great power and ability should be impressed with their power to rise above their environment and to succeed in spite of it. It seems to the casual observer that weaklings are made or unmade by their environment. When all the circumstances of his life are favorable, a weak individual may get on fairly well. When he is sheltered from exposure and contagion, a physical weakling may live a long and reasonably healthy life, but when not thus sheltered he dies. Therefore, says the unanalytical mind, it is all a matter of environment. It may not occur to such a student to ask how the weakling became a weakling and thus liable to be carried off by exposure or con-

---

[1] See also *Jukes-Edwards*, by E. A. Winship, and *The Tribe of Ishmael*, by Oscar C. McCulloh.

[2] *Hereditary Genius* (D. Appleton & Co., New York, 1870).

tagion. A mental weakling, when properly schooled and surrounded, may be trained for some simple but useful work by which he can make a living, marry and raise children. Improperly schooled and surrounded, he would fail and become a public charge. Again, it looks to some as though it were all a matter of environment. Others will ask, how did he come to be so weak as to require such long and careful training to make him even passably successful? A moral weakling, sheltered from competition, temptation, and bad example, may lead a decent and useful life; unsheltered, he becomes unmoral or even criminal. Again, some will say, it is all a matter of environment, until some troublesome person asks, how did he become a moral weakling and so easily influenced by his environment? It looks as though we could not explain the facts without the factor of heredity.

Let us take a non-human illustration. If one were studying jelly-fish, one might easily, though somewhat superficially, conclude that they were the sport of circumstances. If the waves, tides, and currents are favorable, even jelly-fish live, flourish and multiply. If the environment is unfavorable, they drift helplessly, are thrown up on the sand or meet with some other disaster. It looks as though the fate of the jelly-fish was altogether a matter of environment,— until we come to inquire: why are they jelly-fish? The answer is: they were born so, which means that heredity, after all, had something to do with their fate. On the other hand, a student of sharks, finding them able to swim against waves, tides and currents, might easily and superficially conclude that environment had very little to do with their success or failure. They are not victims of the same set of circumstances as determine the fate of jelly-fish. They overcome such circumstances because they were born sharks and not jelly-fish. Their heredity seems to determine their fate or, more accurately, to overcome the particular circumstances in their environment which would be likely to destroy jelly-fish. The environmentalist, however, could suggest a great many other circumstances which even a shark could not overcome.

It is probably not carrying our illustration too far to suggest that there are human weaklings who seem as helpless as jelly-fish, and other human beings who seem as self-determined as sharks. The student of human jelly-fish is likely to be impressed with the power of environment over them — until he inquires how they came to be human jelly-fish. The student of human sharks or of geniuses, on the other hand, is impressed with their seeming ability to flourish in any environment, until he is reminded that he has no means of finding out how many potential geniuses were spoiled by bad environments. No matter how far we carry the analysis, we never seem to get away from the fact with which we started, namely, that both heredity and environment are necessary to the production of human character. If we consider the individual as mere wax to be molded by his environment, we do not even then get away from the fact that if the individual is born wax, even that is a matter of heredity. If he had been born flint, he would not be so easily molded. He may be as clay in the hands of a potter (the potter being the environment) but flint in the hands of a potter is a different thing. Something even depends on the kind of clay.

One of the great facts of human ecology is that men mold their environment almost as much as the environment molds them. Nor is the molding of the environment confined to the physical side. Men create for themselves a social environment which is quite as artificial or man-made as the new physical environment which they build around themselves. One weakness no environmentalist has yet overcome. No one is able to say what a good environment is like, because no environment is good for everybody. Biologists have found out a few things about heredity; sociologists have found out very little, if anything, about the way any given environment affects character. That which is a good environment for one person is a bad environment for another. The impressions one individual receives from a given set of circumstances are different from those which another person receives.

Another physical illustration may help to clarify this point.

Two men plunge into ice-cold water. One comes out with a chill, the other with a glow. It was the same water with the same temperature, yet it affected them differently. The difference was in the men. To one ice-cold water was a bad environment. To the other it was a good environment. One did not, and the other did, have vitality enough to get a favorable reaction from the contact of his skin with cold water. Two children were born into a slum environment. So far as anyone can tell, the influences brought to bear upon one were as bad as those brought to bear upon the other. One responds favorably and becomes a good and desirable citizen. The other reacts unfavorably and becomes an undesirable citizen.

It may be objected that no two environments are ever exactly the same in all respects. One may have received impressions or made contacts which the other never received or made. True enough, but there is nothing in that fact to show that these unseen and unmeasured factors in the environment of the one who became the desirable citizen were, on the whole, more favorable than in the environment of the one who became the undesirable citizen. To say that they *must* have been better in the one case than the other because, otherwise, there would have been no difference between them when they reached maturity, is to beg the question. It is to assume that environment alone is the determiner of character and that heredity has nothing to do with it, which is the question at issue. The fact is that, so far as we have any real evidence, the environment was as good or as bad in one case as in the other. That there were differences may, of course, be assumed, since no two things are ever exactly alike. But there is an even chance that these unobservable differences were worse in the environment of the individual who turned out well than in that of the individual who turned out badly. Unless we are willing to beg the question, we must assume that, in the absence of positive evidence to the contrary, the chances were equal.

The same argument may be repeated with respect to two individuals who grew up in what, so far as general observation goes, looked like an equally good environment. They do not turn out the same. No one is in a position to say, on the basis of factual evidence, that the environment was either better or worse in the one specific case than in the other. To point out the accepted fact that no two individuals ever could have environments which were exactly alike in all respects, falls far short of proving that the environment of the one who turned out well was the better of the two environments. The chances are exactly equal that it was the worse of the two.

The height of absurdity is reached when it is argued that an individual who grows up in a slum environment can never have anything but slum incidents in his memory background, and that he is therefore a slum product. To begin with, it is a rather large assumption that a slum environment is necessarily a bad one. When sociologists learn as much about environments as biologists already know about heredity, not so many assumptions of this kind will be made. In the second place, there are all sorts of incidents in any environment, some tending to produce favorable, some unfavorable reactions in any individual. Even in a slum environment there are incidents, acts, and examples which could be expected to inspire the socially useful virtues of chastity, sobriety, generosity, courage, chivalry, and devotion, as well as incidents which might be expected to stimulate the opposite vices. In the third place, the same incident or succession of incidents which produce unsocial reactions in one individual frequently produce social reactions in another individual. The difference seems to be in the individuals rather than in the incidents. Examples are not wanting. Sons of a drunken father sometimes turn out to be drunkards, sometimes total abstainers,— even sworn enemies of the business of selling liquor. Some of our finest characters and most useful citizens are, in so far as one is the product of his environment, the products of slum environments. If all that some of the more extreme environmentalists insist upon were true, all products of the slums should show the injurious effects of the slum environment. Sons of non-drinking fathers sometimes remain non-drinkers, sometimes not. There is nothing to show that those who yielded to drink were under stronger temptation than those who did not. Children growing up in the most cultured homes, amid surroundings which we, with our limited understanding, are in the habit of calling good, sometimes turn out as badly as any of the products of the slums.

When we consider the two great facts, first, that there are good and bad incidents in every social environment, however good and however bad the environment as a whole may seem to be; and second, that no two individuals are ever alike and that they do not react alike to the same incidents, we shall see how weak is the position of anyone who ignores either the factor of heredity or that of environment. An individual in any possible environment will witness incidents which any sociologist would call good, or designed to stimulate favorable reactions, and other incidents which anyone would call bad, or designed to stimulate unfavorable reactions. Which class of incidents impress or stimulate an individual most will depend somewhat on the kind of individual he is. Foul language will disgust one and create in another the desire to imitate. Observing brutal behavior will shock one and turn another into a bully.

Another complication arises when we try to find out what a good environment is like. That which seems good for the individual may prove bad, or at least degenerating, to the race. A general situation in which physical weaklings may survive the dangers of disease may fill the land with physical weaklings. One which enables moral weaklings to avoid crime may fill the land with moral weaklings. One which enables mental weaklings to escape want may fill the land with mental weaklings. We have the observed fact that some strong races and some high states of culture have developed in harsh physical environments. Palestine and Greece may be put alongside of the fertile regions of Egypt and Mesopotamia. Scandinavia, Scotland, Ireland and New England compare well with milder and more fertile regions as racial breeding grounds. England's harsh criminal law probably improved the moral qualities of the English people by exterminating the intractable and rebellious. All these considerations leave us very much perplexed in the face of the question: What is a good environment?

2. *What kinds of men are needed?* If, now, it is reasonably clear, that heredity and environment both are factors in determining the kinds of citizens a country is to have, our next question is: What kind or kinds of individuals does a country need? This is somewhat more fundamental than, or at least it is preliminary to the technical questions of genetics and eugenics. What kinds of individuals does a group need is a sociological question; how to breed them is a biological question, and how to train them is an educational question. In a treatise of this kind, therefore, rather more attention must be given to the sociological than to the biological or the educational question. To spend time studying the technical side of eugenics and give no attention to the question of what manner of man we want to breed would seem somewhat illogical. Even an animal or a plant breeder generally knows what kind of animal or plant he wants to produce.

Assuming that a great society is interested in its own preservation, survival, growth, power, and prosperity, it will naturally want to breed the kinds of individuals who can contribute to those ends. The Indian chief who said that the good was that which kept the tribe alive, would have no difficulty in defining a "good" man. He is the man who helps to keep the tribe alive. Being in a position of great responsibility, and forced to think seriously in the face of many dangers which threatened the life of his tribe, our Indian chief worked out a positive theory of morals which has not been and can not be improved upon. It is final, complete, and comprehensive. It is also the final word on the question: what kind of men do we want to breed? The eugenist must take that answer as his starting point.

The kind of man needed to keep the tribe alive depends somewhat on the kinds of dangers which threaten the life of the tribe. If the chief danger comes from human enemies who are seeking to exterminate the tribe in order to gain its land, the best fighter is the best man because he does most to ward off that danger. If the chief danger is lack of subsistence, the best man is the best producer, the best hunter, herdsman, farmer, mechanic, manager, investor, etc.

It is commonly assumed that fighting as a means of keeping the tribe alive is of little value in our stage of civilization. That assumption should not be too easily made. The nations who are now in the lead because of their advanced technology have had little occasion to try to get land away from one another. It has been so easy to take it from less developed peoples in the Americas, Australia and Africa, that there has been little temptation to try to rob one another of their lands. The supplies of land in savage hands are not inexhaustible. There may come a time when the pressure of population on land will make it necessary for even civilized nations to safeguard their boundaries against invaders. In that event, even cannon fodder will have its value. Again, even within the most peaceful nation there is always incipient rebellion. While the average citizen may be quite content to stake his chance of making a living on his ability to do something which somebody else wants done and would be glad to pay for, there are always those who see, or think they see, easier ways of getting what they want. In order that the average man may have a fair chance of making a living by useful work, the violent minority must be held in check. They can only be held in check by superior power. That power can only be exercised by fighting men. When there are no fighting men among or on the side of the peaceful workers, men of violence will take charge of public affairs and civilization will collapse.

However, it is safe to say that the predominant need today is not for fighting men but for men who can do other things which the country or the society needs. In a large sense, it may be said that the country needs producers, but that statement is likely to be challenged by those who do not understand its full meaning. The statement is frequently made that we have too many producers. However, that is never true until every one has all the goods that he needs. We may have too many of certain kinds of producers. We do not have enough of those producers who can see ways to organize other producers and such productive agents as land and capital, and direct them successfully in the production of utilities which people want and at prices which the people can pay. The average person will say that that is an impossible task. It is impossible for the average person, but it is being done all the time by extraordinary persons. If we could manage to breed or develop a few more such extraordinary persons, a few of the unemployed workers of other kinds would be employed on some of the land which is now idle, or equipped with capital which is now seeking investment, in the production of goods and utilities which are now wanted by multitudes of people. If we could breed or develop enough of these extraordinary persons we should solve the unemployment problem. This suggests an economic test of fitness.

3. *An Economic Test of Fitness.* That the object of an eugenic program is to breed the kind of men who are most needed is probably clear enough by this time. The eugenist's first task must be to find out what kind of men are of most value. Before answering that question he must decide upon some test of a man's value to society, or, more specifically, to the nation. The only test now in actual operation is that of market value or price. It is admittedly crude and inaccurate, but is there any other standard which could be depended upon to produce less crude and inaccurate results? Let us examine the proposition that one way to find out what the people need is to find out what they are willing to pay for.

The first objection is that people do not always know what they need. They only know what they desire, and desires are sometimes vicious, either because of ignorance or of depraved appetites. Where there are vicious desires, those who pander to them may be well paid. The price which panderers get is no indication of their social value. Where people are ignorant they are easily imposed upon. The methods and devices for separating fools from their money are more numerous and varied than those for pandering to the vicious. The dime museum freak may achieve economic success by exhibiting his physical abnormality to the ignorant multitude and charging admission, but that could hardly be considered as an evidence of eugenic fitness. Novelists, dramatists and artists of a certain type may, if sufficiently ingenious, achieve a similar success by exhibiting their mental and moral abnormalities to a blasé public.

These considerations suggest the most fundamental of all objections to the market test of eugenic fitness. Novelty itself will have its market value so long as curiosity is a human trait. But an object or a faculty which derives its value from the element of novelty speedily loses its value as soon as it is generally reproduced, the reason being that as soon as it is generally reproduced it ceases to be novel. Consequently, if we set out to breed people whose sole market value lay in their abnormalities, the market would soon turn sour. A little mustard is an appetizer, a little more becomes an emetic. The demand is soon glutted.

But granting all that can be said against the price of a man's product or of his work as a test of his value to society, the question still remains, is there any other test which is any less objectionable? While men do not always know what they need, they sometimes do. Even in those cases where they do not, the question arises, who knows what they need any better than they themselves? Until we can find a person or a group equipped to act as censors, and to decide what people need, we may be compelled to leave such matters to the people themselves.

In evaluating men as in evaluating commodities, the question of oversupply and undersupply must be taken into account. If there are more men of a certain type than can be used in combination with the existing number of other types, there are social reasons for decreasing the number of the first type and of increasing the number of the other types. This must be a purpose of every sound system of education as well as of eugenics. In the community which we have assumed, in which the desires of the people are rational, and in which the market prices, wages and salaries are good indices of social values, the educational system must aim to give the kind of training for which there is an undersupplied demand, that is, in which earnings are high.

On the other hand, educational statesmen who are convinced that popular desires are not always rational, may well give their attention to supplying the kind of training which is needed, even though it has no market value. The missionary, for example, is not desired by the people to whom he is sent. He is sent because some one else thinks that the people need his service in spite of the fact that they do not desire it. In all these cases, the eugenist may well be guided by the same considerations as guide the wise educationist.

In another type of society, where desires are pretty generally irrational or vicious, no one need pretend that market values and social values are alike. The kind of talent which has high market value and whose possessors therefore have high acquisitive power, is not the kind needed. But, even in such a society, what is there which may serve as a better test of eugenic fitness than market value? A wise and benevolent dictator might, of course, arrange a better test than that of the market. But, dictators are seldom either wise or benevolent. In a democracy, the people who do the buying also do the voting. If their desires are so vicious as to lead them to buy unwisely, those desires will also lead them to vote unwisely. If the prices they pay on the market are no valid test of social values, neither are the things for which nor the men for whom they vote a test of social or of eugenic values. Even in such a community, there seems to be no better, or less inaccurate test of social values than market prices.

Individual philanthropy could, in such a community, if not suppressed by an intolerant authority, either autocratic or democratic, provide a kind of education that was needed, even though the populace would not pay for it. Such, of course, is all missionary activity. The field of eugenics does not seem to hold out similar opportunities for philanthropic action. Even mild attempts to extend birth control to the unfit arouses opposition and gives the unscrupulous demagogue an opportunity to play upon popular feeling. Therefore, even philanthropy may be prevented from making effective use of a better test of social fitness than the market test.

Individual cases can be cited both for and against that proposition. They who object to the test of marketability as a means of determining the social value of a man's services or the eugenic value of the man himself, can cite cases of geniuses, starving in a garret, for lack of appreciation of what they gave to society; that is, because their services, though great, had no marketability. On the other hand, saints have been persecuted for righteousness' sake by political authorities. "Crucify him" is the cry of a democratic mob appealing to a political authority rather than the reaction of the market to the offer of a service. It was not because his teachings had no marketability (for they had considerable market value) but because they had no political popularity or acceptability, that led to the execution of Socrates. When it comes to citing cases, as many can be cited for as against the proposition that the test of marketability is as accurate a test of social value as the test of political acceptability.

Probably no single principle of selection could be rigidly followed without modification to suit individual cases. However, it is proper to consider, tentatively, certain possible principles. Accepting the test of marketability, for want of a better, how would it work if reasonably applied? In order to apply it there would have to be a restriction of marriage to those who could show an actual earning capacity of some accepted minimum — say, for example, four dollars per day. Illegal unions would, of course, have to be rigidly suppressed. Marriage and the raising of a family would become a right to be achieved by some kind of marketable work, and not a privilege of every one. The eugenic or dysgenic results of such a rule are our sole consideration in this discussion.

These results are not to be determined by citing individual cases. They are to be determined by the law of averages. The question is not whether such a rule might prevent some thoroughly fit person from reproducing his kind, or permit some unfit person to reproduce, but whether the general average of all those prevented by such a rule would be below the general average of the whole population, or whether the general average of all those permitted by such a rule to multiply would be raised above that of the whole population. If so, it would be an eugenic rule. That conclusion is a mere matter of arithmetic.

How to determine the question of fact is difficult to say. No statistical records exist from which one could get any evidence on this point. We are thrown back on general observation and reasoning. The question is, is the average eugenic value of those who are unable in normal times to earn four dollars a day in some legal occupation inferior, equal, or superior to those who are able to earn that much or more? If the former are inferior to the latter, debarring the former from marriage would raise the average of all who were permitted to marry. If both groups are equal, the results would be neutral. If the former are superior to the latter, the results of such a rule would be dysgenic.

There can be no doubt that the labor of those who are unable in normal times to earn four dollars a day is less appreciated by the general public than is the labor of those who can earn that much or more. Is that appreciation an indication that those who are able to earn it are worth more, on the average, than those who are not? If not, our general population must have rather perverted notions as to what is of real worth. In that case, nothing can be done for the improvement, eugenically or otherwise, of our branch of the human race, and the sooner it is displaced by a superior race, the better world this will be. On the other hand, if those who are able to win such appreciation for their work or their products as will enable them to earn four dollars a day or more, are really worth more to the country than those who are not, there would seem to be good eugenic reasons for breeding more of the former and less of the latter. In the absence of positive evidence, each student will have to make up his own mind as to whether, according to his own observation and experience, those individuals of mature years who are never likely to be able to earn as much as four dollars a day are, on the average, as capable and valuable to society as those who are. If he does not think so, he will at least be acting consistently with such an opinion if he supports some measure for limiting marriage to those who show that degree of earning capacity.

Such laws as the minimum wage law, if rigidly enforced, have some such eugenic effect. Rigid enforcement of such a law would make it illegal for any one to be employed at less than, say, four dollars a day. As a general rule, though with many exceptions, men will not marry, or women will not marry them, unless they have some kind of remunerative employment. A minimum wage law would exclude from employment, and therefore from marriage, most of those unable to earn the minimum wage. The general effect of such a law would be to prevent many of the less fit from marrying.

While adhering to the general proposition, stated earlier, that the kinds of men a society needs to breed are those which will contribute most to the life of the group, we can, perhaps, venture a little further with our specifications. One outstanding fact in these modern days is the increasing displacement of physical by mental power. The need for muscle is rapidly decreasing and that for intelligence increasing.

Those incorrigible individualists who refuse to look at any problem from the social point of view, will, of course, insist that a man is a man, and that if society has no use for him, so much the worse for society. It is not necessary to argue that question. It can be made pretty clear, however, that, whatever a man may be worth in other senses, he is not worth much to his fellow citizens unless he can do something which they would like to have done. They are not likely to see any other reason except charity why they should support him. If he can do something which they need very much to have done, they will see an excellent reason why they should pay him well for doing it. If he can not, the only ground which they can see for supporting him, aside from private charity, is public charity supported by compulsory taxation. Society is made up of his neighbors and fellow citizens, and society as a whole is likely to look at the matter very much as his individual neighbors do.

On the whole, probably the best way to determine the value

of a man to those who are not bound to him by personal ties of affection is to apply the logical method of difference. How much difference does it make to the rest of the world whether he works or not, or even whether he lives or not? If his withdrawal would result in a great loss, that is, if he had been doing work which others wanted done, and his withdrawal would deprive them of that valuable work, he is obviously a valuable person. If, on the other hand, there is a superfluity of his kind, his withdrawal could make little difference to the rest of society. If there are already more of his kind than are needed, society could not possibly have any interest in breeding more of the same kind.

Another and more subtle objection to the marketability of a man's work as a test of his fitness to marry, is found in the fact that not all his fellow citizens have the same purchasing power. Catering to the whims of the very rich may be highly remunerative. Supplying the fundamental needs of the very poor, who have no money to pay for what they get, may prove unremunerative. Yet, it is argued, the latter is a far more valuable service than the former. That may be true and yet it may not. Something depends upon why the rich are rich and why the poor are poor. If we make a somewhat popular assumption that all the rich are predatory, and that all the poor are honest, we should reach one conclusion. But if we admit the verifiable fact that some rich men have earned and deserved their riches, and that some poor men deserve to be poor because they have done nothing of value, we reach a different conclusion.

In so far as our economic and legal systems permit men to get rich by accident or by predation, there is need of economic and legal reform. But this fact should not prevent eugenic progress. In so far as it is now possible for men to prosper or fail according to the value or lack of value of what they do or produce, our economic and legal systems may be said to be functioning normally. Under such normal functioning, the following considerations are suggested.

It is to the interest of society that persons capable of rendering valuable service should be adequately motivated by making it possible for them to get what they want in return for their service. He who supplies them with what they need, or with what will motivate them to exercise their capacity beneficially, is also rendering a service to society. What is done for a person engaged in highly productive work is not absorbed by that person, but is passed on to others. On the other hand, there is no great gain to society in supplying or motivating one who is incapable of rendering useful service. He absorbs whatever is done for him and does not pass it on to others. Charity may require that he be supplied, but the community does not get much back for what it gives him. There is more gain to the nation, or to society, in supplying those who act as transmitters of what is done for them, than in supplying those who are mere absorbers. What you do for one of the latter you do for him alone. What you do for one of the former you do for the whole of society. If society could speak as a personified entity it could say, in a literal and positive sense, "Inasmuch as ye did it unto one of these [highly capable producers] ye did it unto me."

Those who have learned to think in terms of the social good rather than in terms of individual needs, will have no difficulty in applying analogies. They who would rather see the whole community lose than see a single useless individual forced to accept charity will, of course, repudiate the whole idea. It is, by way of illustration, a waste of good fertilizer to apply it to a tree which cannot respond with good fruit. It is likewise a waste of good services or valuable goods to apply them to persons who can never respond with useful work. In the case of an unfruitful tree, it can be cut down. Not so with an unfruitful individual. Again, it is a waste of good fuel to stoke an inefficient engine which can not develop power. It is a waste of good feed to feed an animal that can give nothing in return. In both cases it is obviously better to stoke a good engine, or to feed a productive animal.

This is not to decry charity. Charity is necessary to the maintenance of our human quality of preference for our own species, upon the maintenance of which our whole social fabric depends. But eugenics is one thing and charity is another. Those whom we permit to be born we must take care of. But when we are discussing the question of what kind of people we desire to be born, we should reason as clearly as we would on the questions, what kind of trees shall we plant, what kind of engines shall we build, what kind of animals shall we feed? In general, we want the kinds that respond vigorously with something desirable to the fertilizer, fuel, or feed which we give them. Correspondingly, it pays society to offer adequate rewards or means of motivating those who, when motivated, respond with valuable service.

But how do these ideas harmonize with humanitarian principles? Does not the "brotherhood of man" require us to treat all men alike? He is no friend to man who also befriends the enemies of man. If there are human enemies, they must, in the interest of "man" be either converted into friends, restrained, or exterminated. He is no true "friend to man" who would behave otherwise. He who befriends these human enemies to man is very much like the one who befriends sub-human enemies. To be sure, they are all "God's creatures," as certainly as men are. The brutarian is even broader-minded than the humanitarian, and it would be as logical for the one to befriend the brutes who prey upon men as for the other to befriend the human beings who prey upon other humans.

"Doing good to good-for-nothing people" has its philanthropic justification, but that can scarcely furnish a reason for breeding more good-for-nothing people to do good to. No one should pose as a humanitarian or a "friend to man" who is willing to see that burden upon humanity grow heavier from generation to generation, even though it would greatly enlarge the opportunities for the capable to "acquire merit" by contributing to the support of the incapable. A genuine humanitarian naturally desires his race to become as fine a race as possible. That can scarcely be achieved by bidding the feeble-minded and the incapable to be fruitful and replenish the earth with their own kind. The young, the aged, and those incapacitated by accident or sickness must, of course, be served whether they are, for the time, capable of transmitting the service or not, but there is no good reason for adding to the list of absorbers. The ideal of a fine race is one in which every mature individual is capable of transmitting in large degree the service which he receives. A great society, if it were capable of thinking in its own interest, would try to breed such a race. A national group, whose every individual is capable of adding during his lifetime to the life of the whole more than he subtracts from it, has unimagined possibilities of progress.

So far as strictly economic progress is concerned, a simple formula can describe it. When production exceeds consumption there is progress. When consumption exceeds production, there is retrogression.[1] So long as production exceeds consumption, every generation is adding something to the national equipment. It is leaving the country not less but greater than it found it. Capital accumulates, durable goods of all kinds multiply. When, on the other hand, consumption exceeds production, each generation leaves the country poorer than it found it. Capital diminishes; durable goods wear out and are not replaced.

The individual who consumes more than he produces retards the economic progress of his country. Only those who produce more than they consume are the contributors to that progress. If we want to find out what the average man is economically worth, the way to proceed is to find out how much the real wealth of the country is increasing, year by year. It is not a simple task, but a rough approximation could be reached. After the annual increase is determined, it is simply a matter of long division. Divide the annual increase by the population, and you have the net annual value of the average person to the country. If the annual increase is a billion dollars (corrected, of course, for all the inaccuracies involved in the estimate) and the population (in round numbers) 125 million, the annual value of the average person is $8. Capitalize this at 5% and you get $160 as his permanent value.

If the average person's annual contribution to the life of his

---

[1] See Edward Van Dyke Robinson, "War and Economics," *Political Science Quarterly*, vol. xv, pp. 581–622.

group is only eight dollars more than his subtraction, his value may be stated in the formula: $V = P - C = 8$. (His value is equal to his production minus his consumption: which is $8.) Let us grant that there are other values besides economic value. Nevertheless, it still holds true that the individual who during his lifetime subtracts more than he adds to the sum of all human values is worth less than nothing. Unfortunately, it is not possible to measure, or to express quantitatively, other than economic values. Nevertheless, it would probably be agreed that some individuals contribute more human values in general than do others. The eugenist would be interested in breeding the kind of people who would contribute most to the sum total of all these values,— if he could only find out what they were.

4. *Eugenic and Dysgenic factors.* While biologists are making some progress in their study of the question; what determines variation, not much has yet been discovered that can be used by any society to control the variations among its individual members. The eugenist must, for the present, wait for spontaneous and, so far as we can yet determine, sporadic variations to take place. It seems somewhat easier to control the selective processes. If any progress in practical eugenics is to be made in the near future, the selective forces must be modified or controlled in such ways as will lead to the survival of such variations among those that actually happen as are desired. This conclusion is emphasized by the fact that, while it is not known that any social institution produces or causes variations, it is known that many human institutions cause the failure and extinction of certain variations, and the survival of others. In other words, society does actually select and exterminate, even though it does not consciously cause variations.

The selective factor most discussed is war. It is generally agreed that primitive warfare selected eugenically while modern warfare selects dysgenically. In primitive warfare there were no recruiting officers to select the finest specimens from among the youth for military service and reject the others. There was no recruiting because every male of fighting age was a member of the fighting force. Moreover, a battle was a series of personal combats in which the strong, agile, alert, and shrewd came off victorious more frequently than the weak, slow, dull, and stupid. Again, primitive warfare did not keep the fighting force in the field for long periods of time, separated from their wives and families. Finally, most primitive warriors were polygamous. At least, polygamy was permitted to its most distinguished warriors, doubtless supported by the old sentiment, however recently expressed, "None but the brave deserve the fair." Thus the greatest fighters had ample opportunity to multiply their talents through their progeny.

It may be questioned, of course, whether this is really eugenic selection. It does, of course, encourage the multiplication of men with fighting ability, but is that the same as race improvement? To begin with, in a time when fighting was necessary to keep the tribe alive, the men most needed were fighting men. From the standpoint of a tribe that needed fighters, it was eugenic selection when the best fighters survived and the poorer fighters perished in battle, and when the victorious fighters had many wives and many children. In the second place, fighting ability was correlated with several other kinds of ability. Fighting with hand weapons required muscular strength, skill, precision, and adroitness. The man who possessed these qualities could, if occasion required, turn them to many other purposes. A superior fighter was a good all-round man.

In modern warfare, on the other hand, most of the factors of selection are dysgenic. In addition to the recruiting officer, there is the selection of the battle field. Courage, strength, skill, and adroitness give one no advantage in a rain of bullets, shrapnel or high explosives. Size is a positive disadvantage for the geometrical reason that a large object is more likely to intercept a bullet than a small object. Courage certainly does not make for survival in such a situation. While the sentiment still holds that "none but the brave deserve the fair," in other words, while a soldier is still popular with girls, yet monogamy limits the eugenic beneficence of that sentiment.

A remnant of eugenic value remains in that sentiment even under monogamy to offset the many dysgenic tendencies of modern war. The popularity of the soldier gives him some advantage in choosing a wife, though the chief advantage probably lies with the men who can exhibit trophies of economic rather than of military prowess. In so far as soldiers are able to have their choice and to choose the most attractive women, it probably works to the eugenic advantage of society. In the first place, the work of the recruiting officer makes it certain that the average soldier is sound and reasonably capable, both physically and mentally. In the second place, women who are attractive, even though unlearned and ignorant in the academic sense, are more intelligent than those who are unattractive. It appears that the old saying that beauty is only skin deep is only a skin deep saying. Beauty is correlated with general health, strength, and intelligence.

In 1926, Messrs. Wechsler and Carter "gave intelligence tests to fifty actresses and chorus girls in the New York theaters of Messrs. Shubert and Ziegfeld, where the most beautiful girls are supposed to be gathered. The scores made by the girls were extraordinarily high, averaging 128 as compared with 127 made by college men in the United States army test and 130 made by college women in similar tests."[1] To the question, why, then, do these girls show such a lack of interest in intellectual or even serious subjects, the answer seems to be that they are intelligent or shrewd enough to know that men do not care for women who are interested in intellectual subjects. These chorus girls are smart enough to know what men like, and to assume the virtue of ignorance which they do not possess. Their display of ignorance is a kind of window-dressing. It is their skill as actresses which enables them so successfully to assume a rôle of shallowness. This, combined with the intelligence to know what men like, should have prepared us for the discovery that these women show I. Q.'s much above the average.

The popularity of soldiers in uniform with girls, giving the soldier an advantage over the civilian in the choosing of a wife, may be said to offset, in part at least, the dysgenic selec-

---

[1] Quoted from *The Builders of America*, by Ellsworth Huntington and Leon F. Whitney (Wm. Morrow & Co., New York, 1927), p. 151.

tion of the recruiting office and the flying missiles of the battle field. When the superior men chosen by the recruiting office for the wearing of a uniform, themselves choose the most attractive women, who turn out to be the most intelligent, the results of such matings must be eugenic rather than dysgenic. Yet when the total effects of military selection are summed up, the weight of opinion seems to be that the net result is dysgenic rather than eugenic.

On this subject Seeck [1] contends that war has the most detrimental influence on the growth and development of civilization in general as well as on that of the particular race or nation. The downfall of the Ancient World is, according to him, due primarily to the extermination of the best. The civil wars of Rome in particular were destructive not only in the conscription of soldiers and the destruction of life on the battle field, but in the wholesale proscriptions by which multitudes of the leaders of the beaten side were destroyed by the victors. He concludes that it was no accident that Roman civilization declined. He holds that the destructive influence of war and revolution on civilization persist even to the present day. Despite the fact that modern warfare is carried on by machinery, it is still the best of the nation that is called forth and exterminated. His words are strong, pointed, and apparently well supported by historical fact.

Next to war, the most discussed factor in the modern problem of race improvement or degeneration is philanthropy in its various manifestations. The arguments for the dysgenic effects of philanthropy are fairly simple and direct. The effect of philanthropy, it is argued, is to enable many people to live who would otherwise die of starvation, bad sanitation, the lack of medical attention, bad habits, and bad morals. On the assumption that those who would succumb to these enemies of life and longevity are, on the average, inferior to those who would survive, the conclusion would be that by preserving the less fit, philanthropy tends to degenerate the race. If philanthropy is undiscriminat-

---

[1] Otto Seeck, *Geschichte des Untergangs der Antiken Welt* (Siemenroth & Worms, Berlin, 1895), vol. I, bk. II, pp. 257–300.

ing, there is no very convincing argument to the contrary. There is, however, the possibility that philanthropy may become sufficiently discriminating to make it a eugenic rather than a dysgenic factor.

It has been pointed out many times that natural selection is somewhat haphazard and inaccurate. A million codfish may be born in order that one may survive and reproduce. There is no certainty that the survivor is absolutely the most vigorous; there is only an actuarial probability in favor of that conclusion. In the long run, that is, over millions of generations, that actuarial probability becomes, of course, a certainty. If there were some method of artificial selection by which the one who was absolutely and unqualifiedly the best of his generation could survive, evolution could proceed at a more rapid rate than under the haphazard method. Instead of waiting millions of generations for the actuarial probability to become a certainty, it would be a certainty that the best in each generation would survive.

Even vice may be defended as a moral agent if it can be shown to be effective as a fool-killer. If it is a means of selecting for extermination those who are morally weak,— that is, those who have little power of rational self-direction,— it would unquestionably be a factor in the building up of a moral race of men. Eventually the race might become so immune to all temptation as to need no social admonitions, no sanctions for good or rational behavior. Moral reforms, therefore, it may be argued, which aim to change the social environment so as to remove the temptations to vice may merely result in the survival of the morally weak and the propagation of their kind. But the selection for survival of the morally strong and the extermination of the morally weak proceeds, as does natural selection in its other phases, in a somewhat haphazard and inaccurate way. There is no certainty that every individual who survives is actually strong or that those who succumb are actually weak. There is only an actuarial probability in favor of that result. True, over long periods of time, the actuarial probability becomes a certainty, and moral progress is made in that way. If, however, the selective power of vice could be made to operate a little more accurately, with less of accident in it, the rate of progress could be accelerated by merely improving the environment.

The chauffeur who destroys his dependableness through his own vice may occasionally injure himself, but he is rather more likely to injure other people. The locomotive engineer who becomes incapacitated through any kind of vice or bad habit may occasionally destroy himself, but he usually destroys a number of others in the process. The motorman, the train despatcher, the surgeon, the drug clerk, and a multitude of others who are in responsible positions — and in our interlocking civilization we are all coming to hold responsible positions — imperil others quite as much as themselves if they ever become irresponsible and undependable through drunkenness or any other vice.

Let us grant for the sake of argument that fool-killers are needed to prevent the world from being filled with fools, and let us grant also that certain vices function as fool-killers. Still, we should have a right to insist that the fool-killers should work accurately rather than inaccurately; that is, that they should kill only the fools and not endanger the lives of others. Any agent of selection that works inaccurately works inefficiently, from the standpoint of race improvement.

This may be illustrated arithmetically by means of the following table:[1]

[1] See the author's *Principles of National Economy* (Ginn & Co., Boston, 1921).

I	II	III
10	10	10
9	9̸	9
8	8	8
7	7	7
6 ⎫ Average 5.5	6̸ ⎫ Average 6.6 of	6 ⎫ Average 7 of the
5 ⎬	5 ⎬ the survivors	5 ⎬ survivors
4 ⎪	4̸	4
3 ⎪	3	3̸
2 ⎪	2̸	2̸
1 ⎭	1̸	1̸

Let us assume that we have ten individuals, graded numerically, according to their relative wisdom or foolishness. At the bottom of the scale we rank those graded as 1, 2, 3, etc., whom we may designate as fools. We ascend through the moderately wise to the very wise, whom we will grade as 8, 9, and 10. The average of the whole group will be 5.5, as shown by averaging the first column of the above table. Now let us suppose that an inaccurate and ineffective fool-killer is at work, as shown in column II. Instead of canceling only numbers 1, 2, and 3, he cancels 1 and 2 and also 4, 6, and 9. Here is a rather wholesale slaughter, involving a death rate of 50 per cent, and yet the average is raised only from 5.5 to 6.6. This is a pretty heavy price to pay for so slight an improvement. If, however, the fool-killer worked accurately, as shown in column III, canceling only numbers 1, 2, and 3, the average of the survivors is now 7. Here we have a much lower percentage of slaughter, resulting in a much higher improvement in the average. There is something to be said for a fool-killer that operates so accurately as this. There is a great deal to be said against the one that operates so inaccurately as the one in column II.

Now the question is, does the vice in question operate accurately or inaccurately? If it works inaccurately, there is at least the possibility that some philanthropic endeavor, either on the part of the state or by private agencies, may increase the accuracy of selection. If the more fit individuals (6 and 9 in column II) can be protected against the destructive effects of the vice, and only the palpably unfit (1, 2, and 3) be permitted to succumb, there is a positive gain, both from the standpoint of emotional sympathy and eugenics.

This possibility was clearly presented by the late Amos G. Warner who defined true philanthropy in terms which would satisfy the sternest of eugenists. Properly understood and administered, philanthropy is merely a means by which those who, from the standpoint of race improvement, are fit to survive may be enabled to survive the accidental misfortunes of time and place, while those who, from the standpoint of race improvement, are unfit to survive may be enabled to pass out of existence with the least possible suffering. Probably, all things considered, including apprehension and anticipation, the most humane means of putting a man to death is by old age. It is as deadly and certain in its effects as chloroform. If the individual is segregated, his germ plasm is as effectually destroyed as though he were himself put to death.

Under this ideal of philanthropy, no individual is to be condemned to extinction until he has been given a chance to demonstrate his fitness or unfitness. Having been saved from the dangers of childhood, which, in the absence of care, would certainly carry him off, and having been given a reasonable opportunity for training and preparation for earning a livelihood; if, then, the individual shows himself unfit, his germ plasm must be killed. But this can be accomplished as effectually by institutional care and segregation as by lethal methods.

Whether the problem is that of protecting moral weaklings against the attacks of destructive vices, or physical weaklings against the physical dangers of accident or disease, the effects of philanthropy may be the same. There is no doubt that natural selection will do its work in either case, but it is a costly process. Artificial selection is vastly superior — if we know what we want. Animal and plant breeders can direct evolution by means of variation and rational selection and get quicker results than natural selection can bring. Philanthropy may, if wisely directed, improve on natural selection or, if unwisely directed, interfere with natural selection and offer nothing in its place, in which case it becomes positively dysgenic.

Adaptation to a physical environment carries with it the ability to escape the dangers which lurk in it. This ability to escape takes on many forms, depending upon the character of the danger. Where the danger is in the form of large and destructive enemies, wariness,— or the power to evade them; physical strength,— or the power to fight them off; protective coloration, or a protective shell;— are well known means of escape. Where the dangers take the form of unseen or microscopic enemies, protection usually takes the form of immunity.

The organism evolves the power either to throw off or to resist bacterial disease. In a parallel sense adaptation to a social environment involves the power to escape the enemies which lurk in it. This power may take the form of immunity to the evil which is present. On this point Galton made an interesting suggestion to the effect that if some of our streams and springs flowed alcohol instead of water, a race, in order to survive in such an environment, would either develop wisdom enough to avoid the danger, or the power to drink alcohol without serious injury. The one escape would be through wariness; the other through immunity. Apparently some progress has been made in parts of the world in both directions. When alcoholic drinks are introduced to a new race not having contact with it before, it proves peculiarly destructive. The case is somewhat parallel to that of a new disease like that of the sleeping sickness introduced to a new tribe which has not yet become immune to it. That race that has lived in contact with alcohol for a great many generations finds it somewhat less destructive than is the case when it is first introduced to a new, non-immune race.

This presents an important phase of the problem of active versus passive adaptation. Is it better for the race that has not yet acquired partial immunity to alcohol, to permit that danger to flourish as a part of its social environment and wait for the process of natural selection, through the elimination of its weaker members, to bring about immunity; or is it better to keep that enemy out of the social environment? A similar problem, of course, is presented by a new disease. Is it better for a tribe to whom smallpox is highly destructive to let that disease do its work until eventually the tribe acquires partial immunity to it; or is it better to control the physical environment and shut out the disease?

Every form of philanthropy presents a somewhat similar question, but the answer cannot be found until we can decide what traits or characters we desire to evolve or breed into the race. If the most desirable character is immunity to smallpox, then, of course, to interfere with the process of weeding out those who lack immunity would be a dysgenic factor. If, however, the qualities which we desire in our people have no correlation with immunity to smallpox, then it would not improve our breed to permit smallpox to do its work and it would not interfere with the improvement of the breed to stop the ravages of that disease. With respect to the so-called eugenic effects of vice, the same question arises. If the qualities which we desire to breed into our race are those that are always correlated with the ability either to resist opium or to use it with impunity, then the active sale of opium, by exterminating the people whom we do not want, would be a eugenic agency,— otherwise not,— and philanthropic endeavors to safeguard against the ravages of the dope-seller would not be dysgenic.

By far the most important question in the whole field of eugenics is what is commonly called the differential birth rate. By this is meant the observed tendency of the more intellectual classes to marry late and have small families, and of the less intellectual classes to marry early and have larger families. At one extreme we have celibacy; at the other extreme we have the planless, non-rational multiplication of the feeble-minded who multiply as automatically and as impulsively as the lower animals. As to celibacy, Francis Galton [1] has this to say:

The long period of the dark ages under which Europe has lain is due, I believe, in a very considerable degree, to the celibacy enjoined by religious orders on their votaries. Whenever a man or woman was possessed of a gentle nature that fitted him or her to deeds of charity, to meditation, to literature, or to art, the social condition of the time was such that they had no refuge elsewhere than in the bosom of the church. But the church chose to preach and exact celibacy. The consequence was that these gentle natures had no continuance, and thus, by a policy so singularly unwise and suicidal that I am hardly able to speak of it without impatience, the church brutalized the breed of our forefathers. She acted precisely as if she had aimed at selecting the rudest portion of the community to be, alone, the parents of future generations. She practiced the arts which breeders would use who aimed at creating ferocious, currish, and stupid natures. No wonder that club law prevailed for centuries over Europe; the wonder rather is that enough good remained in the veins of Europeans to enable their race to rise to its present very moderate level of natural morality.

[1] Hereditary Genius. Quoted also in T. N. Carver, *Sociology and Social Progress* (Ginn & Co., Boston, 1906), pp. 641–642.

A relic of this monastic spirit clings to our universities who say to every man who shows intellectual powers of the kind they delight to honor, "Here is an income of from one to two hundred pounds a year, with free lodging and various advantages in the way of board and society; we give it you on account of your ability; take it and enjoy it all your life if you like: we exact no condition to your continuing to hold it but one, namely, that you shall not marry.

The high prestige of the author of these words and their intrinsic value to the sociologist amply justify their quotation in full. No more weighty message to the modern world was ever written. Galton goes yet further in his condemnation of the superstitious mediæval Europe.

The policy of the religious world in Europe was exerted in another direction, with hardly less cruel effect on the nature of future generations, by means of persecutions which brought thousands of the foremost thinkers and men of political aptitudes to the scaffold, or imprisoned them during a large part of their manhood, or drove them as emigrants into other lands. In every one of these cases the check upon their leaving issue was very considerable. Hence the church, having first captured all the gentle natures and condemned them to celibacy, made another sweep of her huge nets, this time fishing in stirring waters, to catch those who were the most fearless, truth-seeking, and intelligent in their modes of thought, and therefore the most suitable parents of a high civilization, and put a strong check, if not a direct stop, to their progeny. Those she reserved on these occasions, to breed the generations of the future, were the servile, the indifferent, and, again, the stupid. Thus, as she — to repeat my expression — brutalized human nature by her system of celibacy applied to the gentle, she demoralized it by her system of persecution of the intelligent, the sincere, and the free. It is enough to make the blood boil to think of the blind folly that caused the foremost nations of struggling humanity to be the heirs of such hateful ancestry, and that has so bred our instincts as to keep them in an unnecessarily long-continued antagonism with the essential requirements of a steadily advancing civilization. In consequence of this inbred imperfection of our natures, in respect to the conditions under which we have to live, we are, even now, almost as much harassed by the sense of moral incapacity and sin as were the early converts from barbarism, and we steep ourselves in half-unconscious self-deception and hypocrisy as a partial refuge from its insistence. Our avowed creeds remain at variance, with our real rules of conduct, and we lead a dual life of barren religious sentimentalism and gross materialistic habitudes.

The extent to which persecution must have affected European races is easily measured by a few well-known statistical facts. Thus, as regards martyrdom and imprisonment, the Spanish nation was drained of freethinkers at the rate of 1000 persons annually, for the three centuries between 1471 and 1781; an average of 100 persons having been executed and 900 imprisoned every year during that period. The actual date during those three hundred years are 32,000 burnt, 17,000 persons burnt in effigy (I presume they mostly died in prison or escaped from Spain), and 291,000 condemned to various terms of imprisonment and other penalties. It is impossible that any nation could stand a policy like this without paying a heavy penalty in the deterioration of its breed, as has notably been the result in the formation of the superstitious, unintelligent Spanish race of the present day.

David Starr Jordon [1] includes among the dysgenic factors affecting the Spanish population the colonial policy of Spain after the discovery of the New World. The conquest and the exploitation of the new countries drained away from the mother country multitudes of the strongest, the most enterprising and courageous. Even in the Spanish colonies, it may be remarked, the Spanish blood was diluted by mixture with that of the natives. This seems to have been dysgenic.

At the opposite extreme, the menace of the feeble-minded is a very real one. Every old community is finding the burden of feeble-mindedness an increasing one. In a pamphlet entitled "The Menace of the Feeble-minded" by G. C. Hanna, Superintendent of the Minnesota School for the Feeble-minded, this danger is set forth very clearly. He points out [2] that medical science has as yet little to offer in the building up or restoration of intelligence in the mentally deficient. He states that the prison populations contain from 30 to 80 per cent who are feeble-minded. Others, however, find among certain prison populations, such as our federal prisons, a much lower percentage,— probably because counterfeiting, smuggling, and other crimes for which one gets into a federal prison are crimes that call for a good deal of shrewdness, which is a kind of mentality. After presenting other facts and figures to show the extent to which feeble-mindedness is becoming a burden, Hanna goes on to say that it is highly hereditary. Eminent men rarely fail to show family trees containing other eminent persons, whereas the family trees of most feeble-minded indicate that

[1] *The Blood of the Nation* (American Unitarian Association, Boston, 1902).
[2] *Eugenical News*, February, 1926.

feeble-mindedness is a legitimate fruit of the tree which bore them. "Society," he says, "must consider means of drying up the spring which is the source" of many of our social ills. He suggests, among other remedies, life-confinement of those who escape sentence on the plea of mental deficiency, a more adequate examination of immigrants, marriage certification, sterilization of mental defectives, discontinuance of parole during the child-bearing years, etc.

Between the extremes of celibacy on the one hand, and the spawning of the feeble-minded on the other, the differential birth rate shows itself. How damaging it may become over long periods of time will be shown later in this chapter. The question is sometimes asked, however, are not many highly productive individuals born from parents who were low producers or even economic failures in life? The answer is yes. The further question then arises, do not these distinguished children of obscure parents add appreciably to the total numbers of our successful producers, even to our men of genius? The answer to this question also is yes. If, however, the question is asked, do the children of low producers add to the *percentage* of high producers in our entire population, the answer is not so clear, and it is probably no. It depends upon whether a larger percentage of the children of parents who are relative failures in life turn out to be high producers than of children of parents who are relative successes. This is the really important question.

The proportions in which the different classes and grades of ability are combined in our population has a great deal to do with the success of our industrial system and with the distribution of the products of industry among the different classes of the population. To use a simple illustration: A community which has more ditch diggers than it can use in combination with its limited supply of competent engineers will always be in a bad way. Any process of multiplication which will increase the proportion of engineers to ditch diggers would be an eugenic program. Any process which would increase the proportion of ditch diggers would have to be called dysgenic. The question becomes, therefore, are we likely to get as large a proportion of competent engineers from the progeny of ditch diggers as from the progeny of engineers?

In the situation which we have assumed, the productivity of a ditch digger is low because he is superfluous. From the standpoint of the community it makes little or no difference whether he remains or emigrates. But, under the same conditions, the productivity of the engineer is high because he is indispensable. It would make a great deal of difference in the quantity or quality of the work done whether he remained or emigrated.

In the following discussion we shall use the term high productivity to include all the kinds and qualities of ability of which, because it hasn't enough, the community stands in great need. The term low productivity will be used to include all those kinds of skill or ability of which, because of their superfluity, the community does not stand in need.

How does the rapid multiplication of those who are economically superfluous and therefore relative failures, and the slow multiplication of those who are economically scarce and therefore relatively successful, affect the relative proportions of the two classes in the same community? It seems to depend upon the percentages of economic successes among the children of the two classes. This, in turn, seems to depend upon the extent to which the qualities which made the parents high or low producers are transmitted to their children.[1] The observed fact of biological variability is somewhat confusing, and requires some explanation.

From one point of view the fact of variation may be regarded as an evidence of imperfect heredity. It might be claimed, for example, that if heredity were one hundred per cent perfect, children of the same parents would not vary at all, but would all be exactly alike. It could hardly be claimed that they would be exactly like their parents, because they have two parents

---

[1] The most thorough-going investigation up to date of this problem has been by Professor F. W. Taussig and Dr. Carl S. Joslyn in a study entitled *American Business Leaders:* a study of Social Origins (The Macmillan Co., New York, 1932).

and if they exactly resembled one they would have to differ from the other. There might conceivably be a blending of the characters of the two parents, but, if so, the characters should be blended in exactly the same proportions in all the children, so that they would all be exactly alike. The fact that they are not may be said to show that there are still unaccountable factors in the determination of the inborn traits of each individual, and that, except within rather wide limits, these traits are unpredictable.

However, in this as in a great many other cases, it is sometimes possible to predict percentages when it is utterly impossible to predict individual results. Statisticians may be able to predict with a high approximation to certainty, what percentage of those now living in any country will die within a year, without being able to make any prediction with respect to any individual case. Similarly, it may be possible, when enough information is gathered, to predict what percentage of those born to successful parents will themselves be successful, but no amount of information available to the statistician will ever enable him or any one else to predict with respect to the success of any given child, present or prospective.

Let us grant also that the combination of traits which go to make up what we have called productivity is an exceedingly complex one, more complex, probably, than that combination which goes to make an athlete, or even a fighter. That would tend to make prediction still more difficult in the breeding of producers than in the breeding of athletes or fighters. Nevertheless, within wide limits it may yet be possible to predict as to the percentages of those born to parents who are high producers who will themselves be high producers and the percentage of children born to low producers who will, in spite of their unpromising parentage, prove to be high producers.

How strikingly a relatively small difference in marriage customs may affect the population may be shown by the following arithmetical illustration. Let us take two distinct classes, such as engineers and ditch diggers, architects and hod carriers, or, in general, enterprisers and manual laborers. Let us, first, assume that the average individual in both classes brings to maturity and marries off the same number of children, say four, so that the number in each class doubles in each generation. But, suppose also that in the higher economic group, marriages take place later in life and that the generations are further apart. In the higher economic group which we shall call group A, generations are $33\frac{1}{3}$ years apart, while in the lower economic group which we shall call group B, they are only 25 years apart. We should then get some such results as these:

	1900	1925	1933	1950	1966	1975	2000
Group A	100		200		400		800
Group B	100	200		400		800	1600

Let us assume that Group A and Group B start with equal numbers, say 100 each in the year 1900. Group A will then have in 1933, 200; in 1966, 400; and in the year 2000, 800, having doubled three times in a century. Group B will have in 1925, 200; in 1950, 400; in 1975, 800; and in 2000, 1600 having doubled four times in a century. Thus, in the short period of one century the final progeny of Group B will be twice as numerous as those of Group A.

If now we consider the probabilities of the case, it is extremely improbable that the number of children per marriage in Group A will be as large as in Group B. Where marriages take place relatively late in life there are two important reasons for expecting small families. First is the arithmetical fact that the child-bearing period of the female is materially shortened by late marriages. Second is the biological fact that the period of greatest fecundity is from the age of eighteen to twenty-five. Instead, therefore, of assuming that Group A as well as Group B will double in each generation, it is nearer the truth to assume that Group A will merely maintain itself; that is, that each pair will bring to maturity and marry off only two instead of four children. In that case, in the year 2000 the progeny of Group A will still number 100, whereas the progeny of Group B would number 1600.

So far we have been considering the physical progeny of the two groups. Nothing has been said regarding the distribution of this progeny as between the two occupations. Very naturally some of the progeny of original Group A will have gravitated to a lower economic group and some of the progeny of the original Group B will have climbed into the higher economic group. The question of relative occupational congestion will depend somewhat on the proportions in which the progeny of the upper group has gravitated downward and the progeny of the lower group has climbed upward. The original groups, it will be remembered, were assumed to be equal in numbers in 1900. What will be their proportions in the year 2000? This can only be determined by counting cases. Meanwhile, we can speculate as to the probabilities in the case.

If it should turn out to be true that fifty per cent of Group A have succeeded in maintaining themselves in the upper group, whereas the other fifty per cent has gravitated downward into Group B, and fifty per cent of Group B has succeeded in climbing to Group A, leaving the other fifty per cent in Group B, the ration in the two occupations would remain as in 1900. But if there is a slight difference in the rate of sliding downward from the upper group and of climbing from the lower group, the proportions would be changed and there would be some degree of occupational congestion in one or the other of the two occupations.

For a simple illustration let us assume that only 25 per cent of the progeny of the original Group B has succeeded in climbing into the higher occupation and that 75 per cent are still concentrated in Group B, while, of Group A, 75 per cent has maintained its position and only 25 per cent has fallen to the economic level of Group B. In that case the ratio would be changed. In the year 2000, 425 total progeny of both groups, numbering 1700, would be found in occupation A and 1275 in occupation B. This would fall far short of restoring the original balance between the two groups as it existed in 1900.

The dysgenic effects of such a differential birth rate might be for a short time, partly overcome by the superiority of schools and educational facilities, but there is always a limiting factor at work here. If the capacity of the great mass of the people to be educated is declining, then no matter how rapidly the schools may be improved, eventually they will reach a very definite limit beyond which they cannot train successive generations. What is more likely to happen is that the mass of the voters in later generations will have so little interest in education as to be unwilling to tax themselves in support of the excellent and expensive schools that would be necessary to train succeeding generations to a high degree of proficiency. Under such circumstances it is only a question of time until education would fail to correct the effects of the dysgenic differential birth rate.

Monogamy is so deeply embedded in the mores of Europe and America as to make any discussion of its eugenic or dysgenic effect a purely academic exercise. It is frequently hinted, however, that polygamy might help to correct or offset the dysgenic tendencies of the present time. If highly capable men, it is argued, were permitted to use a part of their surplus earnings in the maintenance of a plurality of wives and families instead of being compelled to limit themselves to expensive habits of consumption, yachts, race horses, art collections,[1] etc., it might help. The antimonopolistic sentiments of modern democracy might intervene and create more resentment than is now created by the lavish consumption and elegant leisure affected by our more successful money makers.

In a highly militant state of society, when every male of fighting age was pretty constantly engaged in military affairs and many were being killed, the inevitable scarcity of men and superfluity of women was probably a sufficient reason for polygamy without regard to the eugenic or dysgenic effects. However, whether it was planned or not, it seems highly probable that the effect was eugenic. As a rule, the most powerful chiefs

---

[1] Spending vast sums in purchasing ancient works of art is sometimes assumed to be promotion of the fine arts. As a matter of fact it merely magnifies the prices that have to be paid for old masterpieces and is no help to struggling artists of the present.

were those who were most successful in fighting, and fighting of the kind then practised required great physical strength and some mental ability. Polygamy was generally confined to the more powerful war chiefs. They were thus enabled to multiply their numbers at a somewhat higher rate than would have been possible under monogamy. Even in the pastoral and agricultural stages the results may have been somewhat similar, especially when we consider that an outdoor life, with vigorous muscular work, seems to be accompanied by a high degree of masculine potency. When, however, these occupations give way to sedentary and indoor occupations, and polygamy ceases to be a military or economic necessity and becomes a mere form of sensual luxury, it seems to lose some or all of its eugenic value. It is doubtful, therefore, whether in our state of civilization there would be any eugenic gain from the adoption of polygamy even if it were socially and politically possible.

Is there any hope for a civilization in which the dysgenic tendencies are so much greater than the eugenic tendencies as they seem to be in our present so-called Christian civilization? There is probably none. The extension of information on the subject of birth control to the less intellectual classes may reduce somewhat the tendency of their progeny to overwhelm the progeny of the more intellectual classes. But even this knowledge is effective only among people who have some degree of prudence and foresight. Among the feeble-minded who have none of these, no desirable results can be expected. Nothing except sterilization or a positive prevention of marriage, by segregating both sexes, can arrest the tendency of feeble-mindedness to multiply itself. Among the more intellectual classes there appears to be nothing except possibly a revival of religion or the development of a social sentiment and a social outlook which will increase the rate of multiplication where such increase is needed. The solution of this problem must be left to the moral leader, the rationalizer of standards, or the makers of ideals.

It is conceivable that a new aristocracy may develop on a somewhat more rational foundation than that on which any old aristocracy was built. Every noble aristocracy is based on family building. There is a noble aristocracy wherever it is the chief ambition of noble minds to found a noble family or to continue a family already nobly founded. Nobility, however, may be conceived as consisting in social usefulness rather than military prowess. Social usefulness consists in giving people what they need — not always what they clamor for. It does not preclude charging what the service is worth from those who are able to pay for it.

The difference between family builders and spawners is an important and a vital one. The family builder makes it his chief ambition to found or perpetuate a family with noble traditions and standards. As one of the means to that end, there must be a career and an income. But a career to the family builder is not an end in itself, it is a means to a higher and nobler end — the building of a family. He measures his success not by his career but by that for which the career is a means, namely, his family. If his family is of great social usefulness, he is a success, whatever he does or does not accomplish in his business, profession, occupation or calling. If his family is a failure, he is a failure, whatever eminence he attains in business, profession, politics, scholarship or art.

The differential birth rate is partly accounted for by a tendency, on the one hand, to honor mere fecundity in the poorer classes, a quality possessed by rabbits and guinea pigs, and, on the other, for the more intellectual classes to regard family building as secondary to some other career. One leads to spawning on the part of those who are not able to do much else, and who, in particular, are not able to take care of their progeny. The other leads men to devote all their attention to other careers and to regard marriage and a family as minor matters. Relegating family building to a secondary position as compared with a career in business, art or scholarship,— as a thing which must not interfere with the career,— results in the dying out of families. No genuine aristocracy, intellectual, cultural, capitalistic or military was ever built in that way.

Galton called attention to the vicious practice of certain universities which require celibacy as a qualification for a fellow-ship. An even more vicious practice is found in the habit of certain universities which select members of the faculty who have made a failure of the task of bringing up their own children and inspiring them with high ideals of character and scholarship, as heads of houses where they are supposed to inspire other men's sons with high ideals. If close contact with a professor is good for a student, the professor's own son should have profited by that contact. If he did not, it would seem somewhat hazard-ous to subject other young men to the same contact.

For the failure of the intellectual classes to multiply, the endowment of motherhood is sometimes proposed as a remedy. To begin with, it would not correct the difficulty unless it were accompanied by a fine or some other penalty for bringing into the world children of a kind that is already too numerous. How to select the mothers who are to be endowed, and the fathers of their children, is a task of great difficulty in a democ-racy. We must not overlook, however, a system for the en-dowment of motherhood which is already in operation in our own social system. It is connected with the formula: "With all my worldly goods I thee endow." The man who pronounces these words but has no worldly goods, and no prospect of ever having any, does not exhibit a fine sense of humor. The intel-lectual woman who permits those words to be said to her, but never intends to have any children is not socially minded, though she may harbor the notion, usually mistaken, that she can do more for society in other ways than by training its future leaders.

This plan of endowing motherhood by billeting the future mother on the father of her future children is entitled to some consideration. It has much to commend it, even though it is not working as well as could be desired at present. The reason it is not working is that it is not understood, or is not taken seriously by those who are under verbal contract to endow motherhood. As a matter of fact, it is working excellently among those who understand it and take it seriously. These do not figure in exciting news items, but they form a more numerous class than is ordinarily appreciated in these days of high divorce rates and marital instability. After all, most marriages are satisfactory and, in most cases, both husband and wife in the great but uninteresting middle class take seriously their task as family builders. We are easily misled by news. The fact that scandals and divorces are still news is somewhat reassuring. If a time should come when news gatherers would go looking for cases of domestic happiness, or would publish as news the fact that a family had been found where there was no scandal, we should be in a bad way.

The greatest derelicts in the matter of family building are found at the opposite extremes of society. The higher intellectual classes, who are most capable of handing on to future generations their intellectuality, not only fail to multiply but fail to take parenthood seriously, preferring to leave their more or less accidental progeny to the care of servants. The least intellectual classes, not capable of planning intelligently for the future of their children, merely give way to their animal impulses and multiply without regard to their ability to care for and educate their children.

5. *Race Mixture.* A sapient senator once opposed the restriction of immigration to this country on the ground that his grandmother used to change roosters in her flock of poultry, believing that an infusion of new blood would invigorate the stock. Before accepting this as conclusive proof of the advantage of race-mixture among human beings, several questions need to be asked. First, did the lady select her roosters, or did she accept any that came? If she selected them, that could scarcely serve as an argument for indiscriminate race-mixture. Second, if she selected her breeding stock, did she select superior individuals from the same breed as her hens, though from different flocks, or did she mix breeds? If she selected from the same breed, it could scarcely be used as an argument for race-mixture. Third, if she mixed breeds, we need to know what the results were. Did the mixing of breeds improve the stock or did it tend to mongrelize it? Until the answer to this question

is found, the lady's practice can scarcely be used as an argument for wholesale and indiscriminate race-mixture.

A scientifically planned mixing of races is one thing, and indiscriminate mixing is a very different thing. Selected individuals from two different races might, when mated, produce offspring possessing many desirable qualities. That would prove nothing as to the results of indiscriminate mixing. Again, if the immigrants of another race are among the finest specimens of that race, that is, if they are the most intelligent, courageous, resourceful, and well behaved of their race, the results on the national stock might be favorable, but we can not be certain that the same results would follow if the immigrants were among the poorer specimens of their race. Immigrants who are driven from their homes because of their revolt against an irrational or superstitious religion, because of an intolerable political situation, or because they are persecuted for their righteousness, presumably represent the best of their race. Immigrants who come because they have failed to make a living in their own country, are not likely to be the most capable and resourceful citizens of their home country.

French Protestants who fled to England and Prussia in the 18th Century, German revolutionists who came to this country in the forties and fifties of the 19th Century, Puritans who left England for the New World in the 17th Century, Russians who fled from the Bolshevik terror in the 20th Century, doubtless contributed vigor and intelligence to the countries to which they fled. Two things prevent this from being an effective argument in favor of indiscriminate race-mixture. To begin with, none of these migrants belonged to a race different from that of the countries to which they fled. They were all of the same race, though of different nationalities. Second, the fact already referred to, that where wholesale and unselected immigration is permitted, the immigrants who come are not likely to be the finest specimens of the country from which they come.

The fact that there was considerable mixing of nationalities in this country in Colonial times does not throw much light on the problem, much less does it furnish any evidence in favor of the mixing of widely different races. There are individuals of old Colonial stock who number among their forbears representatives of every nationality of northwestern Europe. But northwestern Europe is not a large territory, and its people are all of one race, as race is now understood. Whether the mingling of the blood of several of the nationalities of northwestern Europe was eugenic or dysgenic, it can throw no light upon the results of mingling the blood of white, black, red, and yellow races.

The supposed mingling of races in England turns out to be no such thing. "Saxon, Norman and Dane are we" is supposed to indicate a favorable result of cross-breeding. Such a supposition will not stand examination. Who were the Saxons and from what locality did they come? Who were the Danes and from what locality did they come? They were more closely related than the Dutch and the Danes of today and came from almost the same locality. Who were the Normans, and from what locality did they come? They were first cousins to both the Saxons and the Danes, and came from the same locality, though by a roundabout route, through northern France. There was no race-mixture in any true sense when those three peoples mingled, probably not as much as when people from Cape Cod and Cape Ann intermarry. As to the mingling of the Saxons with the British, there is not much evidence. Historians have given us the impression that the Angles and Saxons drove the British before them into Wales and Cornwall, though it is scarcely possible that there was not some intermarrying.

It seems as though the Anglo-Saxons had shown a rather pronounced intolerance in their attitude toward other races and even other nationalities. If the historians have given us a correct impression, they seem not to have mingled very freely with the natives of Britain but to have pushed the natives before them. They seem not to have inter-married to any great extent with the native women but to have brought their own women with them. It may not, of course, have been so much due to the intolerance of the men of Anglo-Saxon blood as to the unwillingness of their women to be left behind. That is, it may have been the result of the spirit of the Valkyrie embodied in the Anglo-Saxon women which led them to prefer the adventurous life of pioneers to the sheltered life of their old homes. Other migrants from the north into the various parts of the Roman Empire seem to have shown no such intolerance. They seem to have mingled rather freely with the native populations, and even to have adopted the language and the civilization of the countries into which they came as conquerors. The Anglo-Saxons not only retained their own language and institutions, but apparently retained the purity of their stock,— at least relatively so in comparison with other migratory tribes of the same period.

The same intolerance was shown by their descendants when they migrated to the Western Hemisphere. The French colonists to North America seemed a little more willing to marry and mingle with the native stock than the English colonists did. The Spanish colonists and to a certain extent also, the Portuguese, in Mexico and Central and South America, were exceedingly liberal in their attitude; they certainly showed much less narrowness or intolerance in the matter of marrying with the natives. The English settlers in Canada and in the present territory of the United States pushed the Indians ahead and did not mingle with them to any great extent. They brought their own wives with them, or, as in the first colonization of Britain, it may have been that the women would not stay behind, preferring the hardships and adventures of pioneering life to the comforts and safety of their old home. Whatever the reason, the British in America kept their stock relatively free from admixture with the native stock. Whether from a eugenic point of view this was wise or unwise may be open to question, but there can be no doubt that, down at least to 1880, the racial stock of the inhabitants of the United States and of English-speaking Canada was relatively less mixed than that of the French, Spanish or Portuguese-speaking peoples on the same continent. Even in the South, where the presence of the Negro has made race-mixture possible, it has been resisted vigorously and with partial success by the rigid, uncompromising intolerance of the whites toward mixed marriages.

The eugenic or dysgenic effects of race-mixture are still under investigation. Opinions are many and diverse, but verifiable facts are few. Such indirect light as can be thrown on the problem by the experience of animal and plant breeders is, from the eugenic standpoint, unfavorable rather than favorable. It is true that some remarkable results have been obtained by experiments in cross-fertilization and cross-breeding. From the human standpoint, however, these favorable results are of little value. The plant or animal breeder is privileged to experiment boldly and to destroy all the unfavorable results of his experimentation. If a hundred experiments in cross-fertilization produce undesirable results, there are no evil consequences because they can all be destroyed. Progress can be made if one experiment in a hundred, or one in a thousand, should result in something desirable. The one favorable result can be preserved, and the unfavorable ones are not left to cumber the ground. This, of course, can not be done with human beings. The unfavorable as well as the favorable results of cross-breeding are all preserved and perpetuated.

It is not improbable that, in time, it may be found that certain race mixtures produce desirable crosses and others not. Until we can determine with some degree of certainty by scientific experimentation or observation just what race mixtures are favorable and what are unfavorable, there is one unanswerable argument in favor of maintaining race purity for the present and opposing race-mixture. Let us assume, for the sake of argument, that the chances are about even that wholesale and indiscriminate race-mixture would be beneficial, or that the likelihood of such mixture being eugenic is equal to that of its being dysgenic. The argument, then, proceeds somewhat as follows: If, during this period of ignorance, racial purity is maintained, it will still be possible to change our attitude and resort to race-mixture if or when it is discovered that race-mixture is eugenic. That is to say, we can correct our mistake by initiating a policy of race-mixture. If, on the other hand, it should eventually be discovered that race-mixture is dysgenic, no mischief has been done; we can continue pursuing the more eugenic policy of maintaining race purity. But if, in this state of ignorance, we resort to race-mixture, we shall never be able to correct the mistake, if it should prove to be a mistake. If, after having proceeded with race-mixture, it should finally be determined scientifically that race-mixture is dysgenic rather than eugenic, we cannot reverse our policy. The mischief will have been done; the races cannot be unmixed. It is always easy to scramble; it is always difficult to unscramble eggs or races. Therefore, the safer policy seems to be to maintain racial purity until we have convincing evidence that race-mixture is desirable.

The eugenic or the dysgenic effects of race-mixture are not the only things to be considered in our attempts to solve the problem of race relations in a country occupied by considerable numbers of people of widely different racial stocks, such as whites and Negroes, whites and Indians, whites and Asiatics. Even granting that amalgamation would have slightly dysgenic results, the refusal to amalgamate might produce social results even more undesirable.

Race-mixture, or the amalgamation of two races living in the same territory, can be prevented only by continued dis- like,— probably by cultivated dislike. This dislike is certain to result in friction between the faces. This friction may produce hostility,— sometimes even race war,— and nothing could be worse than this. Some of the darkest pages in human history are those which describe race wars; other dark pages describe the persecution of the weaker by the stronger race when both try to live together in the same territory.

However, the alternatives are not agreeable to contemplate. There appear to be only three alternatives to amalgamation. or, if we include amalgamation, four possible outcomes of the attempts of different races to live together. Amalgamation solves all other problems except that of race degeneration which, if it should eventuate, would be the worst disaster that could happen to a race or to its civilization. Any of the other alter- natives, however objectionable, would seem less bad. One possibility is occupational separation. This seems intolerable,— at least to those with democratic ideals,— because it involves a system of caste. Occupational separation means that certain occupations shall be set aside for each race, and there shall be no competition between the two races within the same occupation. If the two races perform complementary functions in society, then each race needs the other. They do not compete but they complement each other. While this solution of the race problem sounds harsh to democratic ears, it is at least a means by which race war and race hostility may be either eliminated or greatly softened.

If neither amalgamation nor occupational separation seems tolerable, a third alternative is territorial separation,— that is, the two races should give up the idea of trying to live together in the same territory. Complete territorial separation is difficult to achieve after the two races have acquired a home in the same country. It may be preserved by the exclusion of immigrants across racial boundaries or across boundaries separating widely different races. The prohibition of the importation of African slaves into the territory of the United States, if it had come early enough, would have preserved territorial separation, but it offers no easy solution of the problem of dealing with the millions already here. Complete territorial separation was doubtless in the minds of those who promoted the acquisition of Liberia with the idea of wholesale colonization, but the ideal of complete territorial separation by this means has not been realized. It is also involved in Zionism. Partial territorial separation, however, is found in such expedients as the Ghettos of European cities under which there was at least local segregation. While these expedients did not cure the anti-Semitic feeling of those cities, they appreciably reduced it. Something of the same kind exists in this country in the Negro quarters in most of our cities, and in the Chinese and Japanese quarters in the cities on the Pacific Coast. In fact where complete territorial separation has not been found expedient or practicable, there is almost always some attempt at partial territorial separation as a partial solution of a difficult problem. This has seemed obnoxious to people with democratic ideals, but it is probably better than race war, and in the present state of ignorance as to the eugenic or dysgenic effects of amalgamation, it is undoubtedly better than amalgamation. The fourth alternative is continued race friction which seems, if possible, worse than any of the other possibilities.

There does not seem to be a fifth possibility though there are many who will vociferously assert that there is, or that it is possible for two widely distinct races to live and mingle together in the same territory without amalgamation, without occupational separation, without even partial territoriral separation and without friction but in a state of peace and harmony. This, however, is absurd on the face of it. If two races live together in the same territory and mingle together freely, there is only one possible way of preventing amalgamation, namely, to cultivate or at least to preserve dislike. If dislike is not preserved, there is nothing that will prevent young people from falling in love and marrying, and that results in amalgamation. If dislike is preserved there will, of course, be race friction and in extreme cases, race war.

When, in previous generations, the Quakers desired to prevent their young people from marrying worldlings, they found it impossible except by cultivating a dislike for worldlings. Very naturally the dislike was reciprocated, and, since the Quakers were a small minority, the dislike took the form of persecution. If they had been strong enough to avoid persecution, it would have taken the form of religious hostility,— possibly religious war. The initial step in the persecution, it should be remembered, was taken by the Quakers themselves in their determination to prevent amalgamation. The same thing happens in those countries where the Jews have been persecuted. The persecution is traceable to the determination of the orthodox Jews not to amalgamate with the Gentile population. They realized that nothing could prevent such amalgamation except the studied cultivation of a dislike of non-Jews. Nothing except dislike, and a cultivated dislike at that, could prevent young Jews and Gentiles from falling in love and marrying. The cultivation of a positive dislike was very naturally reciprocated, with the result that, in a country where the Jews were numerous enough to make an impression on the public mind and yet not numerous enough to be strong, they were persecuted and subject to pogroms.

The following graph indicates a method of approach to so complicated a problem as that of race relations. It shows how a few of the unifying and divisive factors combine to produce diverse results.

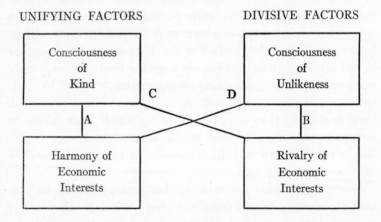

We may list as the principal unifying factors first, consciousness of kind, second, harmony of economic interests. Among the divisive factors, the principal ones are consciousness of unlikeness and rivalry of economic interests. In the above diagram an attempt is made to visualize the possible combinations of the unifying and divisive factors. Combination A is most favorable to peace and harmony. Combination B is least favorable. Combinations C and D are somewhere between the two extremes.

As applied to race and class problems, these four combinations show with some degree of historical accuracy the possibilities of inter-racial or inter-class relationships. In the early New England factory towns, employers and employees were of the same race, language, religion, had read the same books, in many cases had attended the same schools. Therefore a consciousness of kind tended to unify them. While there was not a complete harmony of economic interests, it was still true that each group needed the other. Obviously a class war, under such conditions, would have been impossible. Later, however, when the working population was largely immigrant, combination A was changed to combination D. There was a consciousness of unlikeness, together with a certain degree of harmony of economic interests though not a complete harmony. Class consciousness and class hostility became a possibility, but not a certainty. A somewhat better illustration of combination A was found on the farms of the Middle West during the greater part of the nineteenth century. The farm owners and the farm hands belonged to the same class, had the same outlook on life, the same ambition, the same loyalties. There was no class conflict, there could have been no class war. Later, when farm labor was supplied by Mexican peons, immigrants from southern Europe, or by migratory and casual labor, commonly known as hobo labor, a consciousness of unlikeness developed between employer and employee. In other words, the combination A of our diagram gave place to combination D. Again on the cattle ranches of the Far West the ranch owner and the cowboy were of the same stock, had gone through the same experiences, had ridden, herded, and fought together; there was complete consciousness of kind. Later, when ownership was transferred to Eastern companies, the employers and employees had different cultural backgrounds, spoke different languages, and had different standards and ambitions, the relationship between employer and employee became that of combination D of our diagram.

As already suggested, combination B is the most destructive of the four combinations, and provides the least possibility of peace and harmony. This is the combination found where people of different races compete for the same jobs. There is a consciousness of unlikeness and a direct rivalry of economic interests. It is this which produces such bitter feeling between the white working people of the south, including the working farmers, and their negro rivals. Combination D, however, is found in the relationship between the aristocratic, land-owning and professional classes of the south, and the negro. There is the same consciousness of unlikeness between these two classes as between the working class and the negro. But, instead of a rivalry of economic interests, there is a certain degree of harmony. Each class needs the other. While, therefore, the aristocratic element of the south will have no such thing as social equality, there is, nevertheless, a very kindly feeling toward the negro — *in his place*. It is to be observed, however, that the negro's "place" is, in the opinion of the class in question, where he does not compete with its members.

Lest it be inferred that the reason for the tolerance for the negro, and the kindliness of the educated and professional classes of the south toward the negro, is the result of their education and culture, it must be pointed out that there is no indication of tolerance or kindliness toward those educated negroes who try to enter the learned professions or to compete with the wealthy whites in business. If there is any difference between the educated and the uneducated whites of the south in their attitude toward the negro, it is that the educated classes are more intolerant than the uneducated, where the circumstances are the same. The circumstances are not the same, except where the negro competes. Where the negro competes with the white working men, the white men's labor union sometimes exclude negroes. Where the negro competes with the white professional man, the white men's profession excludes negroes. The Bar Associations exclude negroes as rigidly as any trade union. In short, the attitude of white lawyers to negro lawyers is the result of Combination B of our diagram. The reactions of southern whites of the United States to negro competition is not in any sense unique. The relations of Germans toward Jews is the same and may be illustrated by the same diagram.

There are not so many good illustrations of Combination C as of the other three. Where competitors are all of the same race, language, culture and religion, even though they are competitors for the same jobs, the rivalry or the antagonism is not so very intense. Jewish merchants compete bitterly with other

Jewish merchants. Jewish workers strike against Jewish employers and Irish workers against Irish employers, and it sometimes seems as though such conflicts were fully as rancorous as similar contests between different racial stocks or religious groups. There is observable, however, a distinctly greater tolerance on the part of a group of workers for other workers of the same racial, linguistic or religious types than for "outsiders." This sometimes results in the practical exclusion from certain employments of all except those who are members of the same religious faith, nationality, or language.

We may summarize our conclusions by repeating that there are four possible race relationships: 1) amalgamation; 2) occupational separation; 3) territorial separation, *a*) complete, *b*) partial; 4) continued race friction.

The problem of race relations is, therefore, an extremely complicated one. Where two distinct races are already separated geographically, the easiest and most satisfactory solution seems to be to maintain that geographical separation, that is, to check wholesale migration of either race into the other's territory. Where that solution is rejected, or where the migration has already taken place, there is still possible a partial separation, called segregation. This means a ghetto, a "Chinatown," Negro quarters, or some other form of localization. It is not a satisfactory solution; but, if complete geographical separation is not possible, such as Zionism, Liberian colonization, or repatriation, there are only three other solutions of the problem and they seem even less satisfactory than segregation. Amalgamation is rejected by the orthodox Jews for religious reasons, and, from a eugenic standpoint, is at least hazardous in the case of other race mixtures. If amalgamation is rejected there are only two remaining alternatives — both bad. One is occupational separation to avoid direct competition. This shocks our democratic sentiments and our desire for fair play. If this is rejected, there remains only one alternative, namely, race friction and misunderstanding.[1]

[1] The idea is somewhat widely propagated that in Hawaii different races mingle in a state of complete amity, without amalgamating, without segregation, and without occupational separation. Facts are constantly leaking into the news, however, which flatly contradict any such statement.

The problem of the eugenic or dysgenic effect of race mixture is complicated in other ways than those described above. If there is such a thing as a superior race, it is quite possible that the results of crossing may be definitely superior to the lower of the two parent stocks. Whether there is such a thing as a superior race or not, there is, without question, such a thing as a dominant race in a given territory. The race which, because of its superior numbers or its superior organization, is in a dominant position will generally regard itself as superior. Members of this dominant race are likely to regard a blend of the two races, while undesirable in the abstract, as superior in fact to the other parent stock. This may account, in part, for the fact that the average success of mulattoes in adapting themselves to the white man's civilization is somewhat higher than that of the pure Africans.

On the whole, it is probably safer not to assume that one race is, in any absolute sense, superior to another. That does not in any sense deny the thesis that one race may be somewhat different from another. Whether these differences constitute superiority or inferiority would depend upon what was expected of each race. It is quite conceivable that one race would show superior adaptability to one environment while another race would show superior adaptability to another environment. To an evolutionist it would seem strange if this were not true. A race which developed in an African environment would presumably have become somewhat better adapted to that than to an entirely different environment. Besides, it would be strange if it did not show greater adaptability to that environment than would be shown by a race which developed elsewhere under widely different conditions and was lately transplanted to Africa. Immunity or partial immunity to tropical diseases is a form of adaptation to a tropical climate. Immunity or partial immunity to the diseases bred in the closed and ill-ventilated rooms of cold climates is another form of adaptation. Races developed in different climates presumably develop immunities of different kinds.

It would be a biological miracle if a race which has become

adapted to a tropical climate could be transplanted to a cold climate and not show considerable susceptibility to the diseases which afflict the dwellers in cold climates. It would also be a biological miracle if Europeans could be transplanted to tropical Africa and not show somewhat greater susceptibility to tropical diseases than the natives. But, as we have seen, adaptation to a social environment is quite as necessary as adaptation to a physical environment. It is at least conceivable that a race which has developed its own civilization and created its own social environment,— its mores, standards, and behavior patterns,— may have developed a certain degree of adaptation to that social environment. It is also conceivable that members of a race which has been transplanted to a new social environment which was created by a different race, may have some difficulty in adjusting themselves to it. The problem of moral adaptation is quite as difficult as that of physical adaptation.

This may explain every known fact regarding the difficulty which the Negro, the Indian, or the Malay has in adjusting himself to the white man's civilization. It is not necessary to assume inferiority as an explanation, and such terms as superiority and inferiority may well be excluded from the vocabulary of those who discuss the problem of race relations. A higher or lower degree of adaptiveness to a given set of conditions will serve the same purpose.

It need not surprise us, therefore, if mixed bloods show a higher degree of adaptiveness to a given set of social conditions than the less adapted of the two parent stocks. This would mean that mulattoes show greater adaptiveness than Negroes to the white man's climate and civilization. With this understanding, we may proceed to consider some problems to which it gives rise.

The problem of the double standard of morals is involved. From the standpoint of the race which regards itself as superior or which, more scientifically, has a superior adaptability to the conditions of its physical environment and of the civilization which it has built, there is a mathematical justification for the double standard. Assuming that it is desired to "breed up" in the direction of adaptability to the conditions in question, the thesis can be sustained that unions of the "superior" male with the "inferior" female tend to breed up toward the level of the superior or more adaptable race, whereas unions between the "superior" female and the "inferior" male tend to breed downward. Every animal breeder recognizes this and acts upon it. He is in no doubt about it because he knows definitely what he considers the superior and what the inferior breed of livestock.

The issue turns upon the fact that the female is the limiting factor in the birth rate. A single female can give birth to a very limited number of offspring; the male can engender an almost unlimited number. When, therefore, the "inferior" female gives birth to offspring from a "superior" male, it reduces definitely the number of offspring that can be born of inferior fathers. Every mixed child, potentially at least, displaces a pure bred child of the inferior breed. On the other hand, where a "superior" female gives birth to a child by an "inferior" male, it limits the possible number of purebred children of the superior breed that can be born, and every mixed child, potentially at least, displaces a pure bred child of the superior breed.

When two races live in the same territory, the dominant race feels just as certain as the animal breeder does that it knows what a superior race is. Applying the same arithmetical principle to the problem of race mixture, it finds vastly less objection to the crossing of the superior male on the inferior female than to the opposite cross. Assuming, as it does, its own superiority, it follows logically that the one cross is eugenic and the other dysgenic. Whether this conclusion is reached by the process of arithmetic or not, the results are much the same. The emotional reaction is on the side of eugenics. The abhorrence in which one cross is held and the tolerance or milder abhorrence in which the other is held, operates very much as they would if they were the results of arithmetical calculations.

Wherever there is a definitely superior class or stratum of society or a class that regards itself and is generally accepted as superior (as in the case of a military aristocracy or a ruling caste as among the Spartans) the same double standard is tolerated, apparently for the same reasons. In so far as the assumption of superiority is based on fact, even the *jus primae noctis* probably had a eugenic value.

It ought to be apparent to any unprejudiced and thinking person that the success of a great society, as of an athletic team, depends somewhat on the quality of its personnel. An athletic team which relied wholly on its system of training, and paid no attention to the native capacity of those selected for membership would stand a poor chance against a team which both chose and trained its members wisely. There are only two ways by which the members of the great team called society, tribe, state, or nation, can be chosen, one is by infanticide, destroying, as Plato suggested for his ideal republic, those adjudged unsuitable for citizenship. The other is by preventing the birth of those likely to prove unfit because of the undesirable quality of their potential parents, and encouraging the birth of those likely to prove fit because of the desirable quality of their potential parents.

Can democracy adopt and carry out such a rational system of selection as the latter? If not, democracy is self-destructive. It can last until, under an enlightened dictator, an efficient system of eugenic selection can be adopted and carried out somewhere in the world. When that happens, the weak democratic nations must give way to the stronger nation which selects its personnel. That is as certain as that athletic teams which do not select their men must, in the long run, be beaten by teams that do.

In any democratic nation, the opponents of eugenic selection may win in the windy contest of demagogy, but their victory in this contest will bring defeat in the larger contest of intertribal or international rivalry, if there is wisdom enough anywhere in the world to build a tribe or nation on eugenic foundations. The only real question is: What is an efficient method of eugenic selection? How can we tell who are the fit and who are the unfit? Up to the present, no better test than that of the market has been presented.

If we could get over the absurd notion that everyone has an

inalienable right to multiply, and could adopt the reasonable idea that the right to marry should be achieved by doing well something that the group wants done, we should have made a start. This rule would, of course, need to be modified in some particulars, but as a general working plan, it could not be opposed except on sentimental grounds. If an individual is of no use to the group, as shown by his inability to do what anybody wants done, there is no good reason why he should be encouraged to beget more of his own kind. Even sterilization is less shocking than the bringing of children into the world to live lives of ineffectiveness and misery.

CHAPTER XII

THE CONTROL OF INDIVIDUAL BEHAVIOR

1. *Sanctions.*[1] The control of behavior is what is commonly called government. There is always danger that students of government will spend so much time on the technique of government, or the refinements of the governmental functions as to forget that for which government really exists. The student of sociology should not be so much interested as the student of government in forms of government, the division of functions, or the technique of administration. He should be even more interested in the relation of government to his own peculiar problem, that of living and working together comfortably in those large groups called societies. In beginning the study of the relation of government to the problem of living and working together, we need to begin with some very elementary facts and ideas.

The primary function of government is to govern. Whatever else a government succeeds in doing, if it fails to govern it is a failure in the essential thing for which it exists. To govern is to control, or at least to modify the behavior of some of its

---

[1] "The constraining principle; that which impels to conformity to a command or judgment. That which makes virtue morally obligatory, **or** which imepls, finds, or furnishes a motive for man to seek it."—Standard Dictionary.

citizens. It must have some definite ideas as to what kinds of behavior are beneficial and what kinds are harmful to social life, and it must take measures to increase the kinds that are beneficial and to decrease the kinds that are harmful.

One way to increase the kinds of behavior that are beneficial is to see that they are adequately rewarded. One way to accomplish this is to protect the producer of useful things in the possession and enjoyment of his product, and the doer of useful work in securing and enjoying the equivalent in value of the useful work which he has done. Wherever this is accomplished, men will have an adequate motive for the kind of behavior which produces useful products and does useful things. Wherever a government fails to accomplish this, men will lack adequate motives and this kind of behavior will not be so general as to promote the maximum growth, prosperity and power of the social organization to which they belong. Since well-being depends upon the number of useful products that are produced and the number of useful things that are done, well-being is promoted in proportion as producers and doers are adequately motivated.

One way to decrease the kinds of behavior[1] that are harmful is to see to it that every act so classified is followed by unpleasant rather than by pleasant consequences to the doer. One unpleasant circumstance which sometimes follows such an act is the loss of social esteem. In very small groups this is often effective; in large groups, especially in groups that are conglomerate as well as large, it is ineffective. In a small family group, the misdoer may be "sent to Coventry" and rather promptly brought to repentance. When the individual culprit finds that no one will talk to or play with him, his inherently social nature (*sic*) finds the situation unbearable and is sooner or later tortured into seeking reinstatement into full membership in the group. Small tribal or village groups also make effective use of the same form of punishment. The system breaks down, however, when the group becomes large enough

---

[1] For a classification of the kinds of behavior, see the outline in Chapter II.

to have two culprits at the same time. When two are sent to Coventry, they can combine and have a good time,— better perhaps than the ninety and nine that need no repentance. As the number of offenders to be punished increases, the method becomes more and more ineffective, and something a little more positive in the way of unpleasant consequences becomes necessary.

This applies to all forms of control through the granting or withholding of popular esteem. In a large and composite population, there are enough criminals to form their own social groups, provide their own social esteem, and even find in the esteem of the only group for whose esteem they care an added motive for criminal activity. Emulation among wrong doers to win the applause or esteem of a society of wrong-doers becomes an incentive to rather than a preventive of crime. The loss of the esteem of those parts of the general public whom the criminals despise is also an incentive to crime.

That elusive thing called public opinion is even more ineffective in a large and composite population. To begin with, there is, in such a population, no real public opinion. There are a great many publics, each with its own body of opinion. Political corruption, or even organized crime, has its own public which approves of its predatory activities. Spoiling the Egyptians may have resulted in the loss of the good opinion of the Egyptians, but it won the good opinion of the Israelites. Soaking the rich may lose the good opinion of the rich, but, where there is class consciousness, it may win the good opinion of the poor. Since the poor have most of the votes, public opinion may increase rather than decrease the depredations of the grafting politician. Vituperating the Methodists, or baiting the Jews, may offend the sensibilities of some but win the applause of other groups, and the politician whose votes come from the latter will be incited by the only public opinion for which he cares to exercise his vituperative powers.

In those communities where there is unity of religious belief, with a single religious organization to give expression to that belief, excommunication, or even the loss of good standing in the church, may be sufficiently unpleasant to serve as a deterrent to misconduct; but excommunication loses some of its terrors when there is just as good society outside the church as in it. It loses the rest of its terrors when there is no longer any fear of the occult. In those strata, or social sets, of a great society where there is unity of opinion as to what is orthodox, as to what is morally right, as to what is in good taste, or as to what is authentic "finish" under the name of education, the fear of losing social standing may serve as a deterrent until it is discovered that there are just as desirable people, with just as rational opinions, just as good morals and manners, and just as good taste (though widely different) in other social strata as in the stratum from which one is in danger of being ejected.

More and more, as societies grow larger in numbers, more complicated in structure, and more conglomerate in composition, it becomes necessary to resort to other sanctions than public opinion as means of influencing individual behavior. Some other form of unpleasantness must follow forbidden acts than the supposed unpleasantness of losing the good opinion of that part of the public for which the misbehaving individual does not happen to care. The habit of pouncing upon or pommelling the offending person is a habit which does not lose its effectiveness with the mere increase of numbers. While it is said that misery loves company, it does not follow from this that we like to be made miserable merely because others are miserable. Physical punishment does not lose its unpleasantness, as being sent to Coventry does, merely because of the numbers that are punished.

In its elementary forms and stages, the infliction of physical punishment was, apparently, as spontaneous and unpremeditated as the depriving of social esteem. There is no reason for believing that primitive men reasoned that, unless the offender was deprived of social esteem it would encourage a repetition of the offense, or that they said, even in effect, "Go to, now, we must deprive this fellow of our esteem in order that he and others may be deterred from repeating his offense." It was probably more spontaneous than that. They simply did not like what the offender did and showed their dislike, in one case, by refusing to have anything to do with him, in another case, by pommelling him. It was spontaneous and temperamental expression of dislike or anger at what had been done. Even so, when the individual learned that these outbreaks of dislike or bad temper were not wholly sporadic, but were regularly to be expected after certain acts, and could safely be counted upon not to occur after certain other acts, he could then, if discreet, so order his conduct as to avoid being sent to Coventry or being pommelled. At that stage, individual behavior began to be controlled, modified or influenced by the group.

This hypothesis as to the primitive beginning of punitive justice is not altogether guesswork. We see it in operation among the higher mammals, and also among unsophisticated human beings. Anyone who has seen a mother cat disciplining her kittens, or a mother bear her cubs, must have been impressed with the temperamental character of the process. It would be difficult to imagine that either mother has a reasoned theory of deterrence. So far as we can interpret her actions, there are certain things which she likes and certain things which she dislikes, in the behavior of her offspring. The youngster, who, however unintentionally, offends her gets his ears cuffed. He soon learns that certain behavior is followed by unpleasant results. He learns it by the same process that he learns not to play with fire. His mother is an important factor in his environment which may hurt him under certain circumstances. He learns to avoid those circumstances. Even a human mother with a brood large enough to compel her to be extremely practical, that is, to get the largest results with the minimum of mental and physical effort, is also likely to use the same methods. Maternal wrath, the youngsters soon learn, is a thing to be avoided and maternal approval a thing to be coveted. They also learn, empirically and thoroughly, that the one may be avoided and the other obtained in certain specific ways. There are reasons for believing that individuals learned in the same rough and ready ways how the wrath of the group might be avoided and its approval won. The belief is strengthened by those outbreaks of primitive passions called mobs. Here there is certainly no reasoned theory of deterrence. It is sheer anger at a piece of behavior which arouses strong group disapproval.

However, as men become more sophisticated, and as their manners soften, these spontaneous expressions of social approval and disapproval become somewhat less pronounced. Men at least persuade themselves that they are more rational in their efforts to control behavior, though the rationality of their efforts is frequently more apparent than real. Unless there is a pronounced hatred of crime and criminals, efforts at deterrence are usually half-hearted and "sicklied o'er with the pale cast of thought." The people forget that the purpose of government is to govern; legal procedure is designed more for the protection of the criminal than for the suppression of crime; pettifogging lawyers work upon the sympathies of jurors; the poor criminal, rather than his poor victim, becomes an object of concern; and the will to justice becomes paralyzed. In the last analysis there is no real substitute for parental wrath in the government of a family or for public wrath in the government of a great society.

But the question arises: does punishment really deter? The study of criminals cannot possibly discover the answer to that question. The answer must be found from a study of those who do not commit crime rather than from a study of those who do. There is as much room for a science of noncriminology as for a science of criminology. The study of the sociology of crime should find the answer to two equally important questions: first, Why do criminals commit crime; second, Why don't the rest of us commit crime? The intensive study of criminals may throw a good deal of light on the first question, but it can throw very little light on the second. In order to find the answer to this question, it will be necessary to make an intensive study of non-criminals. Morality needs explaining just as definitely as does criminality, and moral people are surely as worthy of study as criminals.

If one were to make an intensive statistical study of the

inmates of state prisons, or any other group of persons who have been convicted of crime, one would necessarily get a one-sided view of the problem of crime. If such an investigator were an amateur logician, he might easily reach the conclusion that the fear of punishment did not deter men from committing crime. All that his method could possibly prove, however, would be that the persons whom he was studying had not been seriously deterred, at least not prevented, from committing crime by such fear of punishment as existing laws inspired. To conclude that, because such persons had not been deterred by such fear, therefore no one is ever deterred by any fear of punishment is obviously going too far. To conclude that those persons who actually committed crime in spite of laws and penalties were not effectively deterred by the fear of punishment is certainly not a profound discovery. We don't need a criminologist to tell us that; we knew it already.

Another logical error of the same kind is made by those who insist that criminals are of a special mental type. Even if this is statistically demonstrated, it can only apply to actual and not at all to potential criminals. Let us assume, for the sake of argument, that actual criminals are of a special mental type, and that this mental type is not deterred by the fear of punishment. All that this could possibly prove would be that those persons who are of a different mental type from criminals, a type which is really deterred by fear of punishment, do not commit crime. Again, this is not a profound discovery. We have long suspected that to be true, and we may thank our stars that it is true.

When men of wide discretion, men who figure carefully on the consequences to themselves of what they do, turn to crime we shall be in a bad way. Such discreet persons may turn to crime if, as the result of careful study, they can figure accurately that crime will be followed by no unpleasant consequences to themselves. So long as such persons are deterred it will, of course, be true that actual criminals will be limited to those mental types which are not deterred by punishment. The latter will constitute the so-called "criminal type." If there were no punishment to be afraid of, it is by no means certain that actual criminals might not include a good many of a different mental type. We might have to include in the criminal class not only those impulsive, indiscreet, weak-minded, or depraved persons whom we now include, but also some of the highly discreet people who are now excluded by the fear of unpleasant consequences.

Something has certainly been achieved if our penal system has succeeded in limiting crime to the narrow fringe of persons of a peculiar mental type whom punishment cannot deter. If we have done that, the problem of crime is at least half solved. The other half will be solved when we can find some way of dealing with that fringe,— with the so-called criminal type. They constitute a special problem, but we must have a care that in dealing with them we do not create a new class of criminals of a different type altogether.

Until we know more than we now do about the deterrent effects of punishment upon the discreet and non-criminal portion of our population, we shall do well to adhere to the policy of punishing criminals, not, of course, for vengeance but for deterrence. Furthermore, a punishment must be certain enough and severe enough to convince even a moderately discreet person that crime does not pay. This policy must be persisted in even though we are convinced that it will be ineffective with a narrow fringe, sometimes called the lunatic fringe, of indiscreet persons which some call the criminal type. New methods of dealing with such persons, when such methods are discovered, should be supplementary and not antagonistic to our penal system.

But why are sanctions of any kind necessary? A musician does not need any other motive than his own love of harmony to keep him in tune with the orchestra or the chorus of which he is a member. The idea of setting up another system of rewards for keeping in tune would seem absurd. Those who are well trained in the principles of good breeding need no system of punishments to keep them from behaving like cads. Neither do those who appreciate good English need any special motive to keep them from slovenly or ungrammatical speech. Similarly, it might be said that a good citizen should need no other motive than his love of harmony to lead him to behave in harmony with the great society to which he belongs. Unfortunately, however, no society has yet achieved a harmony which is comparable to that of an orchestra or a chorus. The answer to the question at the beginning of this paragraph is that we have not yet bred up a population with a "sense" of social harmony comparable to the sense of musical harmony possessed by the trained musician. If it were desired to prevent all raucous and discordant singing it would be necessary to provide punishment or some other sanction or preventive than the undeveloped sense of harmony of many of our citizens, for even the sense of musical harmony is not very wide-spread. If there is a "sense" of social harmony it is not widely enough distributed to make sanctions unnecessary.

2. *Intolerance.* No discussion of social evolution would be complete without a consideration of the sanctions by means of which a group, particularly the great group, creates in its members the feeling of *oughtness* and of *mustness*. These feelings can be created, or at least intensified, by the attitude of the group toward various forms of behavior and those who do the behaving. Before the group can act in these matters there must be general approval of certain types of behavior and disapproval of others. Approval may be positive or consist merely in toleration. Disapproval must be positive but may vary in intensity. Intense disapproval partakes of the nature of intolerance, and intolerance is sometimes considered a vice. However, very few are tolerant toward the more repulsive forms of misbehavior, such as killing, kidnapping, rape, stealing, lying and cheating. While we all pay lip service to the virtue of tolerance, there are many minor offenses toward which we find it difficult to avoid intolerance.

All liberal-minded persons are supposed, as a matter of course, to possess the virtue of tolerance. This may or may not be a virtue, according to circumstances. It is easy, for example, to be tolerant toward others whose opinions and reactions differ from your own if the point at issue is one that does not interest you, or toward which you are indifferent. The difficulty arises when they oppose you on some point, or interfere with some purpose, for which you care intensely. It is not easy, for example, for one who cares for his wife to be tolerant toward one who slanders her, nor is it much easier for one who cares for his country to avoid intolerance toward one who seeks in any way to injure it or bring it into bad repute. It is not inconceivable that one might care so much for his church or his religion as to show something resembling intolerance toward those who try to undermine it. Even anarchists have been known to care so much for anarchy as to be bitterly intolerant toward the restraints of government and the officers who enforce these restraints. Possibly no one ought to care for wife, government, church, or anarchy, and quite possibly, also, one ought to care for some of these things and not for the others; but that is another story.

We may as well be honest about it, and admit, to begin with, that no one ever is and no one ever can be tolerant on any subject for which he cares intensely. The scholar who cares intensely for scholarship is intolerant not only toward a student who cheats, but also toward one who does inaccurate and slovenly work, and the artist is equally intolerant toward bad art, though both the scholar and the artist may be very tolerant on every subject except his own. Even in the general field of scholarship, scholars are sometimes known to be tolerant of slipshod work in every special field but their own. The linguist may be tolerant toward bad reasoning in economics, the economist toward bad linguistics, and both toward poor work in mathematics; but neither, if he has a high standard, will tolerate poor or dishonest work in his own field. The cultured person who takes his culture seriously is generally intolerant toward vulgarity, even though he is tolerant toward everything else, the reason being that culture is the only thing that seems to him worth while. The man who prizes his honor is intolerant toward aspersions and will fight his defamers.

If we would stop praising tolerance and condemning intolerance in general, and begin to use some discrimination, we should soon be asking ourselves some such question as; Is there anything that is really worth caring for, or should we develop a calm indifference toward everything? If we decide to do the latter, and succeed, the question of tolerance will take care of itself. We shall then be so indifferent toward everything, including even tolerance and intolerance, as to avoid the sin of intolerance in ourselves. But if we decide that there are a few things that are really worth caring for, and succeed in caring intensely for them, there will be an end of tolerance so far as those things are concerned. We ought, in that case, however, to have the grace to be frankly intolerant on these subjects, and not pretend to a virtue we do not possess.

It must be admitted that well-meaning people have in the past cared intensely for a great many silly things that clearly were not worth caring for. This made them so intolerant toward other equally well-meaning and equally worthy people as to produce some of the bitterest controversies, not to say the worst crimes in history. The superlative foolishness of these controversies is nowhere more vividly pictured than where Lemuel Gulliver tries to explain the religious wars of his own people to the Houyhnhnms:

Difference in Opinions hath cost many Millions of Lives: For instance, whether *Flesh* be *Bread*, or *Bread* be *Flesh;* whether the Juice of a certain *Berry* be *Blood* or *Wine;* whether *Whistling* be a Vice or Virtue; whether it be better to *kiss a Post*, or throw it into the Fire; what is the best Colour for a *Coat*, whether *Black*, *White*, *Red* or *Gray;* and whether it should be *long* or *short*, *narrow* or *wide*, *dirty* or *clean*, with many more. Neither are any Wars so furious and bloody or of so long continuance, as those occasioned by difference in Opinion, especially if it be in things indifferent.

Everywhere we find men getting excited over trivialities and waging bitter warfare over trifles. This has produced so much unnecessary intolerance as to provoke a natural reaction in the form of a general dislike, especially among the three-fourths-educated classes, toward anything savoring of intolerance. Some have even prided themselves on their general attitude of indifference toward everything. A little more intelligent thinking is needed to save them from that form of nihilism that declares that nothing is worth while.

The fact that men have often cared for worthless things does not prove that nothing is worth caring for. It does prove, however, that we ought to exercise great care and wisdom in deciding what is really worth caring for. If we can once assure ourselves that certain practices endanger civilization, or the welfare of society, we should be very unwise if we were to show tolerance for them. It is not easy to be certain on everything that bears upon so large a question, but there are a few things upon which one may be reasonably certain.

Every civilization and every really comfortable society is characterized by minute interdependence of parts. We are all mutually dependent upon one another, and we are growing more so as civilization advances. But there can be no interdependence of parts where there is no dependability of character. To be concrete, unless we can depend upon the doctor and the druggist not to poison us, we must get along without doctors and druggists. Unless we can depend upon merchants not to swindle us, we must either get along without merchants or we must become so expert in buying everything that no one can swindle us. Either plan involves wasted effort. Unless we can depend upon locomotive-engineers and switch-tenders not to get drunk, we must stop traveling.

In our interlocking civilization, every position is becoming a responsible one. Unless we can develop responsibility and dependability of character, we must go back to a more primitive state of society where every one lives to himself alone. That would mean so much wasted effort as to result in wholesale starvation, or such a thinning out of the population as would make it possible for the remainder to live on the reduced productivity of industry. Consequently, honesty, sobriety, fidelity, and every other quality necessary to give dependability to human conduct, lie at the very foundation of civilization. Their opposites — namely, dishonesty, drunkenness, and infidelity — will destroy those foundations and with them civilization itself.

The race that shows tolerance for such things will soon exterminate itself.

We have long recognized the necessity of extreme fidelity for
men in highly responsible positions. The sentinel who would
desert his post, the switch-tender who would leave his work
when a train was due, a pilot who would desert his ship before
it had passed the danger point, the physician who would abandon
his patient before the crisis was passed, would all be regarded
with a feeling of abhorrence. We are not tolerant toward such
unfaithfulness. But all positions are becoming highly responsible positions and must become increasingly so if civilization
is to advance. When our ways of thinking catch up with the
development of modern society, we shall begin to regard with
the same abhorrence the miner, the carrier, the plumber and
every one else upon whom we have come to depend, when he
deserts his post and leaves us in the lurch.

3. *Political Power.* The agency through which the great
society creates the feeling of *mustness* is government. Government consists of those who can get political power. They may
get it by military force, by chicanery or by popular vote. Whoever gets actual political power has the power of physical compulsion over others. Government is good or bad according as
this power is used. Its goodness or badness is not determined
by its origin as its source.

One of the most fascinating pursuits is the study of social
origins. Historical sociologists and anthropologists have carried
on prodigious labors in this field and are still extending the
limits to be explored. The origin of the family, of government,
of religion, of property, and of innumerable manners and customs will furnish themes for doctor's theses for many decades
to come. The dynamical sociologist, however, is less interested
in the historical origins of institutions than in the functions
they perform, or their place in the great human problem of
living and working together in large groups.

There is as yet no certain way of finding out exactly how,
when, or where government first originated. We have a fairly
clear idea as to what it is and what it is for, and that is of vast

importance. In fact, as has already been suggested, there is no good reason for believing that government always and everywhere originated in the same way. It may have originated independently and in a good many different ways in different times and places. The famous *Mayflower* Compact is a good enough illustration of the way the government of the Plymouth Colony began, but it throws no light on the origin of Government. There are reasons for believing that governments sometimes grew out of the family, but it does not necessarily follow that all government originated in that source. It is not unlikely that governments may have originated here and there because some strong man wanted to be boss, to be cock-of-the-walk, King of the Wood, tyrant, imperator, or merely the leader of a gang of toughs. Wherever he was able to achieve his desire there was government. Some one told the rest of a group what to do and they did it. The reason they did it was that they feared what might happen to them if they didn't.

However government originated, it could not have survived had it not been for the fact that it increased the chances of group survival. However humble or ignoble the origin of government, it seems to have had survival value in a sufficient number of cases to have enabled those who were well-governed to multiply and to occupy the earth to the exclusion of those who were not well-governed. It is necessary to put the emphasis on the term "well-governed" because government as such has no survival value. Like religion, government may be a handicap rather than a help to the people who are governed, even when, or if, government was an outgrowth of family life. If the rule of the benign patriarch was whimsical and irrational, it would result in the extermination rather than the preservation of the family. Even though government originated in the desire of an overbearing bully for power, if, having achieved power he ruled in such a way as to contribute to the strength of the group, his government would have a good chance of surviving.

If the overbearing bully were far-sighted and intelligent, he would have a motive for governing well. Let us assume that his motive was a purely predatory one and consisted wholly in the desire to rob his subjects. An intelligent despot of this kind would soon discover that his own income was limited by the quantities of desirable things of which his subjects could be robbed. If they were poor, his own income would be small; if they were rich, his pickings and stealings would be good. An intelligent despot would soon recognize the principle "poor people, poor king, rich people, rich king." He would find it to his own interest, therefore, so to rule as to make his people rich,— at least potentially so. The opportunities for constructive statesmanship were open to the robber baron or the overbearing bully as well as to the *pater familias* or the benign despot.

Many a beneficient institution has had unidealistic origins. Marriage by capture (rape) and marriage by purchase have had something to do with the family. Cunning priestcraft, profiting from the superstitious fears of the people, may have had something to do with the beginnings of religion. Robbery and exploitation may have had something to do with the origins of government. None of these institutions is to be judged today by its origin. They are to be judged by the functions they now perform, by their helps or hindrances to the great problem of living and working together in groups.

When, for example, small bandits fight among themselves, the weaker are eliminated, and the stronger grow greater in the number of their followers and in power. The more successful may attain to the rank of robber barons. The process of elimination goes on until the most successful emerges as King or Emperor. Then we have a great dynasty which may attain respectability by success. The great dynasty may rule well. Under its beneficient rule, the people prosper and multiply, adding still more to the power of the reigning dynasty.

4. *Bigger and Better Bandits.* It would doubtless seem very strange to some people if some gangster should take over the government of a great city, transferring its seat from the City Hall to his own stronghold. It would seem still stranger if the people should learn to like it and, instead of calling the gangster harsh names, should learn to revere his name as the founder of a great dynasty. But it need not seem so very strange because

the same thing, or something very much like it, has happened in so many times and places as to have become quite commonplace. Most great dynasties have been founded in this way, and they have become so respectable as to make it seem almost irreligious to refer to their founders as gangsters. In this as in most other cases, the new is that which has been forgotten.

Of course this cannot really happen in any misgoverned American city. We all prize the word "democracy" so highly as to be willing to fight and to suffer a good deal in other ways rather than to give it up.[1] Besides, country people would probably come to the help of any large city which was threatened with a despotism. However, there can be no possible harm in letting one's imagination play around the idea. Many good men, from Plato to Bellamy have amused themselves by picturing impossible states of society. Most of these Utopian dreams, however, resemble nothing which ever was on land or sea. The picture of a great American city under a dynasty founded by a super-bandit would resemble some of the best and most durable governments of the past, and would probably reproduce the primitive origin of all governments which did not happen to grow out of the enlargement or a family.

Let us suppose that some gang leader in any great and misgoverned city should turn out to be a great man,[2] vastly superior to his rival gangsters in intelligence, courage, initiative and all that goes to make a great character. Such a man would organize and discipline his own retainers into a superior fighting force and equip them with superior technological devices. He would make short work of all his rivals in the profession of robbery, and exterminate all gangs except his own. Having achieved peace through victory, by means of swords or machine guns, he could then turn his attention to the constructive problem of making his business more profitable.

If he were as intelligent as we have assumed him to be, he would soon conclude that there was more money to be made by accepting regular and calculable tribute from the peaceful

---

[1] At least we used to care a great deal for democracy.
[2] Such, for example, as Dionysius, tyrant of Syracuse.

citizens than from the sporadic and uncertain profits of violence and rapine. The peaceful citizens on their part, especially if they were as peaceful and non-resistant as some of our pacifists think we all ought to be, would find it much cheaper to buy immunity by regular tribute than to run the risk of sporadic and unpredictable violence. Even if they were not extreme pacifists, they might find it advantageous to pay this tribute if they found that the super-bandit was more efficient in suppressing other criminals,— his rivals,— than the city government had ever been.

Having discovered that peaceful citizens are willing to pay pretty heavy tribute, or taxes, if they are certain of being left in undisturbed possession and enjoyment of the rest of their incomes, our super-gangster must next turn his attention to the problem of increasing their incomes. "Poor people, poor gangster; rich people, rich gangster." How to make the people prosperous is an economic problem, and our gangster must either study economics, or capture an economist.[1]

His captive economist would tell him that the first step in the solution of the problem of increasing the prosperity of his new subjects had already been taken. When he suppressed all other thugs, together with thieves and swindlers, and when he accepted regular tribute in place of loot, he gave his subjects that feeling of security in the enjoyment of the fruits of labor which is at the basis of all prosperity. In the administration of justice he would be especially efficient because he would not be much puzzled as to what was wanted of the courts. Such abstract terms as personal liberty, the rights of man, moral responsibility, and freedom of the will would not be permitted to confuse the minds of thick-headed judges and juries. He would instruct tribunals to find out: Is the behavior of the person before the court useful or harmful, does it increase or decrease the social income (the source of my income)? If the

---

[1] When Diogenes was sold as a slave to Xeniades, and was asked his trade, he replied that he knew no art but that of governing men and begged that he might be sold to a man who needed a master.

former, free him; if the latter, punish him sufficiently to prevent a recurrence either on his part or that of others.

People who have lived in India tell us that it is practically necessary to pay tribute to various guilds of thieves. The payment is ostensibly to hire a watchman to guard your property against thieves, but the watchman does not watch. The fact that you have paid your tribute and recognized the guild is enough. You are let alone by thieves, or at least the guild will discipline any individual thief who molests you. It is found that an organization of thieves provides better and cheaper protection than the government itself.

In America we boast that we do things in a "bigger and better" way. However, our methods are frequently crude and lacking in finesse. Our banditry followed, for a time, the general rule. The period following the Civil War was a period of violence, especially in the then wild and woolly West. It was the time of the Younger Brothers, the James Brothers, the Daltons, Billy the Kid, and a host of other names now passed into romance. John Younger or Jesse James could have given any modern gangster some points on courage, resourcefulness and gun play. It was a time of train robberies, stage coach hold-ups, and the "shooting up" of towns. The more successful bad men of that day rode horses instead of automobiles. They operated in the open country and small towns rather than in the great cities. They were not so very successful in cities. The honest men who then lived in cities had a way of dealing with bad men — when they became too bad. When the city government showed its complete inability to control the criminal element, the vigilantes took charge. It was a crude method, but it was effective.

The period following the World War is also a period of violence, but the crime frontier is now in our great cities. The bad men of the older day were of "good" American stock. Foreign names dominate in a list of present-day gangsters and racketeers. The bad men of the older day learned their badness in the rough and tumble life of the frontier, of the cattle trails, the buffalo camps, the mining towns and the railroad construction camps.

The bad men of today seem to have learned their trade some-where else. Just where they learned it would make a good subject for a Ph.D. thesis. Most of them came from countries where banditti and brigands had flourished for generations. Paris has long had a deadly warfare between the forces of law and order and certain organized gangs of criminals whom the Parisians have called *Les Apaches*. Naples has had a similar war. Even within the memory of men now living, travel was unsafe in Greece and Southern Italy because those countries were infested with banditti who not only robbed, but kidnapped and held for ransom.

America is a land of mergers, of vast combination, of coördi-nation on a huge scale of a multitude of functions under one organization. Banditry is following the general trend of other businesses. Here among our gangsters we have a combination of the subtlety and finesse of the thieves' guilds of India, the brilliant strategy of the Apaches of Paris, the sneaking mean-ness of the Black Hands of Italy, the calculating shrewdness of the Brigands of Greece, the dare-devil hardihood of the desper-adoes of our western frontier, and the constructive imagination of the trust magnates of modern business. It is no wonder that business men find it cheaper to buy immunity and protection from these criminal organizations than from their own govern-ment. This policy of buying immunity is extending not only to business but to private life as well. Possibly the next stage will be an economic discussion of the superior economics of large-scale banditry. Mergers in this field may be shown to reduce the price of immunity to the purchaser. Bigger and better bandits may become a slogan.

5. *The Science of Demagogics.* Two questions present them-selves to the would-be ruler and statesman. First, how to get and hold power; second, what to do with power after it has been secured. There are two answers to the first question. One is to inspire fear and make the people afraid to disobey. That is the method of those super-bandits who formerly founded great dynasties. The other is to inspire hope, or the belief that the people's own interests are to be furthered by obedience to

law and support of the government. Throughout the greater part of the history of human government, there is not much doubt that the former of these two methods of securing power has predominated. Even in the most advanced governments of the present day, the element of fear is still present. No government has ever been able entirely to dispense with its power to inspire fear. Fear, however, is of various kinds — the fear of the hangman is still more or less effective; the fear of the loss of popular esteem is somewhat more effective where there is a uniform public opinion. Where public opinion is sharply divided, where there are all sorts of population groups more or less hostile to one another, the fear of loss of popular opinion has little or no effect in the control of behavior.

The problem of getting and holding power has been neglected by most writers on the subject of government. Machiavelli [1] is a brilliant exception. Realizing the futility of beneficient designs for the betterment of social conditions unless one can get the power to make and administer the laws, Machiavelli devoted his great talents to the solution, in an academic sense, of the problem of getting and holding power. The gangster, the robber baron, the Italian prince solved it in a practical way. Machiavelli as an academic theorist went about the study of the problem in the same cold blooded way as the practical ruler. He had in mind, of course, the conditions in an Italian city of his day. The late D. MacGregor Means, writing under the pseudonym of Henry Champernowne,[2] showed a remarkable parallelism between the conditions in a modern American city and those of a mediæval Italian city. He likewise showed a very close resemblance between the methods of the Italian prince of Machiavelli's day and the American boss of the present day. In their special studies both Machiavelli and Means showed a more intelligent grasp of the fundamentals of government than most other writers in this field.

[1] *The Prince and other Pieces*, from the Italian of Nicolo Machiavelli, with an introduction by Henry Morley (London and New York, G. Routledge & Sons, 1883).

[2] Henry Champernowne, *The Boss* (George H. Richmond & Co., New York, 1899).

Educators will generally agree that there should be more university men in government work. Legislation no less than administration needs men of scientific training. Why, then, should educators and educational institutions neglect the one means of accomplishing what they all desire? If scientifically trained men are to fill government positions, they must manage to get elected or appointed. Departments of Economics, of Government, and of Sociology may teach men what the Government should do. Their graduates may know what to do when or if they ever get into public office; but unless they are also taught how to get elected or appointed, these departments will have little influence on government.

In those times when advancement in public affairs came through the royal favor it was not thought beneath the dignity of gentlemen or even of scholars to try to win that favor by paying court to the sovereign person. Now that such advancement must come from the people, why should it be thought undignified for gentlemen, or even for scholars to pay court to the sovereign people? It savors of sour grapes for educated men to despise public office. They know that they could not get elected nor could they deliver enough votes to get appointed by some one who has been elected to high office. With all their learning they have never learned the first essential of public service in a democracy, namely, how to win popular support.

Why not be frankly realistic about this question? We have had enough experience already to convince us that the office does not seek the man. So long as educated and virtuous men play the rôle of the shrinking violet, public offices will be filled by the uneducated, the self-seeking and the corrupt. There is no hope for democracy unless intelligent and honest men run for office. They will have little success in the race for office unless they are trained for it. They will not be well trained unless colleges and universities train them.

A department of demagogics is much needed in every great university. It would fill a gap quite as important as that filled by existing departments in the general field of the social sciences. It will be fully as scientific as any of the social sciences. How will a published suggestion affect the popular mind? How many votes will it precipitate? These are scientific questions, capable of study by the scientific methods of experiment and observation. How can enough votes be won for this desirable policy? is an important problem in applied science. Unless men who are trained in the social sciences pay some attention to such problems, their studies are not very fruitful, and should be listed among purely cultural studies.

6. *Checks on Political Power.* When Aaron the Just was Caliph of Bagdad he was, according to the Arabian Nights, anxious to be fair to his subjects. In order to find out what they wanted he used to disguise himself as a private citizen and mingle with the people on the streets and in the bazaars. By engaging them in conversation and listening to what they said he learned many things about his own government which he would otherwise never have learned.

Why was it necessary for him to go to all this trouble to find out what the people wanted, and whether they were satisfied or dissatisfied with his government? The answer is: because his government did not provide the machinery by which his subjects could give expression to their wishes, their satisfaction, or dissatisfaction. In spite of the democratic instincts and purposes of the ruler, the form of government itself was not democratic. If the ruler found out how the subjects felt about any public question, he had to initiate his own inquiries. Under a ruler less just than Aaron, or less resourceful in methods of gathering information, the people would have had no legal means of making their preferences known. Satisfaction could only be expressed by acquiescence, and dissatisfaction by rebellion or assassination.

Such a government was analogous to a physiological organism with no sensory system. It had means by which the commands of the ruler could be carried to the subjects, as the commands of the brain are carried by the efferent nerves to the body cells. It lacked the means for carrying the wishes of the subjects back to the ruler as the conditions of the body cells are carried back to the brain by the afferent nerves. His government lacked sensitivity as truly as the body would if the afferent nerves were to cease to function. He could still govern, that is, he could send out his commands, as the brain could still govern the body by sending its messages over the efferent nerves. The citizens lacked legal means of making the ruler aware of their conditions as the body cells would lack means of making the brain aware of their conditions if there were no afferent nerves to carry their messages back.

This analogy pretty clearly illustrates the real difference between a democratic and an undemocratic government. The real difference is not that in a democratic government the people really govern themselves and in an undemocratic government they are governed by some one else. We are as truly governed in a democracy as in a monarchy. We have rulers and they rule us. They make laws and administer them, punishing those who disobey. In the strictest possible sense, self-government is no government at all but anarchy. The real difference is that in a democracy they who govern are made sensitive to the wishes of the governed. Moreover, this sensitivity does not depend upon the good-will of the rulers, nor upon their anxiety to find out how the subjects feel. Legal machinery is provided by which the subjects may, on their own initiative, make the rulers aware of their feelings.

There is a real difference between self-government and the ability to make the government aware of your wishes. The body cells do not govern themselves, though they can make the brain aware of their conditions. They do not govern or control the brain though they can influence it. Neither do the subjects of a democratic government actually govern themselves or control the government. They merely have the means of forcing the government to consider them. Having considered them, it may ruthlessly sacrifice their interests unless their dissatisfaction assumes such proportions as to bring a majority vote against the government.

If any one is under any illusion on the subject of self-government, or is in doubt as to whether he is governed or not, let him try an experiment in self-government. Let him ignore a command of a police officer, of a magistrate, or even of a legislative body. He will find that he must obey in a democracy as well as under a monarchy. The only difference is that he has in a democracy several legal ways of expressing his dislike, if he dislikes the way he is ruled. This is a privilege of immense value to people in general, though it is not of much value to the individual who happens to be in too small a minority to actually reform the government. Democracy is the best form of government there is, but it has its limitations and we must not expect too much of it. There is no use in demanding better bread than can be made from wheat.

The most that can be hoped in the development of democracy is that adequate means shall be found for making those in authority sensitive to the wishes of the governed. The progress of democracy can be measured in terms of that increase of sensitivity. The right of petition is one legal means of making the government aware of the wishes of the governed, but the ballot is by far the most effective means to that end. Nothing has ever been invented which so effectually compels those who govern to give attention to the wishes and even the whims of the governed as the ballot. That being the case, it is not surprising that the popular mind should have fixed its attention upon the ballot as the safeguard of its liberties. The Almighty Ballot, even more than the Almighty Dollar, has become an object of an almost idolatrous worship. It is also natural that the popular mind should have come to believe in the ballot as an end in itself, and that it should have forgotten what the ballot is really for, that it is merely a part of the mechanism for creating sensitivity in government.

A great many writers on politics and morals periodically disapprove of popular whims; and, recognizing that the ballot is a mechanism designed to make popular whims talkative, they denounce, in their discontent, not only the whims, but the ballot. The people are not intelligent enough to know what is good for them, the argument runs. The argument may be valid in reference to such devices as the initiative and referendum; it may still be valid in reference to Mr. Lippmann's criteria,[1] concerning the proper subject matter of a ballot. It is quite possible that the people are capable of saying Yea and Nay only to the overt and external behavior of their officials. It may be that it is not for the public to judge the executive acts of their rulers, or the intrinsic merits of a political question; it may be that they cannot anticipate, analyze, and solve public problems. Possibly the public can merely judge whether the actors in political controversy are following a settled rule of behavior — serving a public interest — or their own arbitrary desires.

Mr. Lippmann's argument is at least the subject of debate. His question: What constitutes the subject matter of a good ballot? has at least two sides. But the ballot as a pure mechanism of sensitivity — the importance of that to a democratic people is beyond question. Negatively viewed, it saves them the expense of rebellion; but positively it allows them self-expression. Indeed, the power of self-expression — of self-discipline and individual choice — is personality; and loyalty to an ideal of personality-value we early defined as the essence of democracy.[2] Democracy has, in fact, been called self-government. The term is not quite accurate, if we understand self-government to mean the absence of any power controlling the individual; it is accurate, if we believe it to mean simply the capacity of the individual to have a voice in choosing the power that should rule him.

Why is the ballot so necessary in order to give sensitivity to government? Largely because government is by nature monopolistic and compulsory. Government is monopolistic in the sense that it tolerates no rivalry in its own field. The individual has no choice except both to obey and to support his own government. A rival government is an insurrectionary or a

---

[1] See especially *The Phantom Public* (The Macmillan Co., N.Y., 1927), pp. 144–145. Also *Public Opinion* (Harcourt, Brace & Co., N.Y., 1922), ch. xiv.

[2] We may even take a numerical view of personality-value, as Mr. Lippmann does, when he remarks (*ibid.*), ". . . majority rule is not an ethical superiority, but a necessity to find a place for force in the weight of numbers." As Sir James Mackintosh remarked, "Counting heads is cheaper than breaking heads."

rebellious government. A citizen has no choice but to accept the service of his government, whether he wants it or not, and to pay for it, whether it pleases him or not. Without the ballot he would be in a peculiarly helpless position. He could not express his dissatisfaction either by refusing to accept the service of his government, by transferring his allegiance to a rival government, or by refusing to pay for the unwelcome service which his government forces upon him.

This peculiarity of government may be made clear by taking another organization that does not have monopolistic or compulsory power. Let us take, for example, a religious organization which has no temporal power, no power to tax, no power to compel allegiance. Such a religious organization would be dependent upon voluntary membership, voluntary attendance and voluntary contributions to its support. Whether the members of that church vote or not, the church itself must be peculiarly sensitive to their desires and even their whims. If they are dissatisfied with its service they can refuse to attend. If this church has no power to suppress rivals, its members can transfer their allegiance to other churches. If it has no power to compel financial support, its members can merely withhold financial support. Such a church must be delicately sensitive to the slightest wishes or whims of its membership. Even though the church is autocratic in form, with a personal head and with no voting whatsoever on the part of the membership, it dare not lose its popularity. It may have the outward form of an autocracy but it must be in fact exceedingly democratic. It cannot ignore its humblest members. Its very continuation depends upon its sensitivity.

The membership, on the other hand, have very effective means of making the management of such a church aware of their feelings. Instead of voting ballots, they can vote or refuse to vote their dollars. Voting and refusing to vote dollars is quite as effective a means of expressing satisfaction and dissatisfaction as the voting of ballots. The members of such a church can be as free from tyranny as the citizens of the most democratic government that ever existed, or that can ever by any possibility be created.

Take another non-compulsory organization such as a great mercantile establishment: having no power to compel customers to trade with it, or to suppress rivals, its only chance of success is to please customers. It must be sensitive to their slightest wishes and desires. Its customers do not need a ballot to safeguard them against economic tyranny. They have a more effective weapon even than the ballot in this case, and the management is likely to be more sensitive to the wishes of customers than the most democratic government ever was or ever can be to the wishes of its citizens.

If the church of the above illustration, or the mercantile establishment, had power of compulsory taxation and could compel financial support, even on the part of people who do not want its service, the ballot would be the only effective safeguard against tyranny. It was this profound sociological fact which our forefathers so forcibly expressed in the misunderstood proposition that "taxation without representation" was tyranny. No more profound or far-reaching principle was enunciated during that period when many principles of government were enunciated. It goes to the very heart of the problem of democracy. As a corollary, however, of that proposition is the proposition that where there is no compulsory support, representation, in the political sense at least, is not necessary to prevent tyranny.

In discussing the sensitivity of a merchant to his customers we were considering one actual relationship. There is another relationship that needs some attention. That is the relationship between the merchant and his employees. Similarly in discussing the relation of the government to the citizenry, we were ignoring the relationship between the government and its employees. How can the government be made sensitive to the interests of its employees — the employees, let us say, in the City Hall, in the State Capitol, or in the National Capitol? That is similar to the problem of the relationship between a mercantile establishment and its employees.

Two things are to be said about this secondary relationship,— one is that the primary purpose of government is to serve the citizenry and not its employees, except as they share in the general benefits that come to all citizens. The government is democratic in the fundamental or primary sense if it is highly sensitive to the interest of all its citizens. It would not necessarily become more democratic if it became especially sensitive to the interests of a special group called employees. In other words, if the employees in the City Hall or the State or National Capitol should insist upon some special power over or privilege under the government, that would not necessarily make the government more democratic. It might in some cases even make it less democratic in that it would make it less sensitive to the interests of those for whom it primarily exists, namely, the general citizenry. The same is true of a mercantile establishment. It exists primarily for the benefit of the people who need the service which mercantile establishments render. If it is sensitive to the needs of those who need the mercantile service, it is democratic. It would not necessarily become any more democratic if it becomes peculiarly sensitive to its own employees. If they should assume some special power or control over the establishment, that establishment would not necessarily become more democratic. It might even become less so. It would become less democratic if, through their control over it, it served its customers less well or became a little less sensitive to their interests while trying to cater to the interests of a special class, namely, its own employees.

7. *The Extension of Suffrage.* The voting place and the ballot are as essential to voluntarism in government as the market place and money are to voluntarism in industry. As the study of economics centers in markets, prices, and money, so the study of democratic control must center in the machinery for the exercise of that control. The ballot is the most important piece of machinery ever invented for the exercise of democratic control. The ballot, therefore, and that for which it stands, must receive attention comparable to that which the

economist gives to money and markets. This is the justification for the long discussion which follows.

The view expressed in the previous section that the function of the ballot is to give sensitivity to the government, naturally raises the question, How far must the ballot be extended in order to provide either the maximum or the optimum sensitivity? The doctrine that the ballot has a function carries with it the idea that it has an instrumental rather than an original value. It is good for something and not a good in itself.

The ballot itself, either for men or women, is not justified merely because men like to have it, or because they derive a pleasurable sensation from dropping pieces of paper in a box. If men had demanded the ballot merely because they felt that they were just as good as the king, the nobles, or any others who were participating in government, this would have been a natural feeling and one which we should all share; nevertheless, it would scarcely constitute a reasoned argument in favor of the ballot. Envy of others, covetousness toward something which others possess, or the desire to possess something merely because some one else possesses it, while it is one of the most natural things in the world, being one which shows itself very early in the lives of young children, does not seem to take the place of a reasoned argument to show why we should have it.

This feeling with respect to the ballot would, on the contrary, furnish a pretty good reason to show that we were not fit for it, though if we were quite as fit as those who already possessed it there would have been no particular reason why we should not have had it. It would signify a wrong attitude toward the ballot and a misunderstanding of its meaning and what it stands for. It would indicate that we looked upon it as an end and not as a means to something else, as a source of direct personal satisfaction and not as a tool for the accomplishment of a certain large purpose, as a toy with which to please ourselves and not as a means of doing things, as a privilege and not as a burden, as a right and not as an obligation. No one, either man or woman, is fit to vote in any rational scheme of things who has this attitude toward the ballot. Any one who takes the ballot seriously and tries to use it properly knows that it is not a privilege but a burden, not a right but an obligation, not a thing to be sought as a source of personal satisfaction, but, like a sword or a rifle, to be taken seriously as a tool or a weapon, and to be used for certain large national ends.

The only sound reason why we should have the ballot at all, that is, the only reason which can be made a part of a well-reasoned system of political thought, is that with the ballot we can have better government than without it. If it can be shown that extending the ballot to any group, class, or considerable number of individuals who do not now possess it would probably secure us better government in the long run, that would be a good and sufficient reason for so extending the ballot. Let it be shown that by taking the ballot away from any group, class, or considerable number of individuals who now possess it, we should have better government in the long run, that would be a good reason for so restricting the ballot. If it can be shown that by giving the ballot to some and taking it away from others we should have better government, that would be a good reason for so extending the ballot on the one hand, and so restricting it on the other. This would place the ballot where it belongs, as a tool to be used and not as a toy to be played with, as a sword and not as a plume, as a burden and not as a privilege, as an obligation and not as a right. It should go to those who can use it effectively for the good of the nation.

More of the faults of modern governments are due to this mistaken notion as to the nature and meaning of the ballot than to any other single cause. Men who do not take the ballot seriously as a burden and an obligation, who go lightly to the polls and cast their ballots as a privilege or a right, and then come away feeling proud of themselves because they have exercised one of the "sacred rights of citizenship"; do not, in nine cases out of ten, know what they are voting for nor why. The writer can testify that when, some years ago, he began to examine himself and to analyze what he did on election day, he began to feel like a complete humbug. He found that he had simply gone into a booth and placed a mark opposite a certain number of names which meant nothing to him, and had deposited the ballot so marked in a box. If, on emerging from the booth, he had met the bearer of one of the names against which he had made a mark, he would not, in nine cases out of ten, have known the man from Adam. He then began to realize that he had voted without any intelligence whatsoever; that a blind man, or an illiterate man could have voted exactly as intelligently as he. He had not taken the ballot seriously enough. He had not spent weeks of his time trying to find out for himself about the respective merits and qualifications of the various candidates. To have done so would have been a great burden, would have taken time and energy away from other things which he wanted to do, and would, in fact, have been a heavy tax. He began to realize that the ballot was no more of a privilege or a right than, and quite as much of a burden as, the paying of taxes or performing military service. This is probably true of the average voter. If he votes intelligently, or even honestly, he must spend a great deal of time and energy in preparing to vote, and this will cost him more than all his taxes.

The average ignoramus, who knows that he is an ignoramus, is usually honest or naïve enough to acknowledge his dependence upon party symbols or upon the advice of some one whom he regards as an expert on political questions. He frankly acknowledges that he does not know how to vote, or for whom, therefore he will ask Mr. So-and-So; he knows. But the average educated man is not generally conscious of his own ignorance of political matters, or if he is conscious of it, is ashamed to reveal it, or not honest enough to acknowledge it. In most cases he is exactly as ignorant of the personality, the programs, and the political ideas of the candidate for whom he votes as is the illiterate man. It did not take a great deal of honest self-examination on the part of the present writer to convince him that the above statement applied to him in a most literal sense. The reader who will cross-question himself and find out what he really knows at first-hand about the various candidates for whom he voted at the last election, may learn something to his own advantage. Let him set down in one column the names of those candidates concerning whom he had enough first-hand or even second-hand knowledge to enable him to vote confidently, and in the other column the names of those concerning whom he lacked adequate knowledge. He will then, unless he is a very uncommon person, probably understand why a party machine or a boss has been a necessity even for him.

But if men misunderstand the nature of the ballot and therefore misuse it, have not women as good a right as men to misunderstand and misuse it? Certainly; but this is a sort of negative right and not a positive right. This desire to do what others do is another of the most "natural" things in the world. If some one else is doing badly, haven't I as good a right as he to do badly? This question is asked frequently by every child and by many grown-ups. It does not seem to satisfy the demand for a reasoned philosophy.

This presents one of the deepest moral problems of life. In every time and place there are people who are actuated mainly by the sense of their own rights, their wrongs or their grievances; there are others who are actuated mainly by the sense of their own obligations and opportunities for usefulness. How much there is in the life of any time and place which is constructive, noble, or worthy of remembrance, depends upon the number of people who fall in the latter class. When the former class dominates the situation we have nothing but quarrelling and bickering, scrambling to get feet in troughs, resentment at the success of others, covetousness, and jealousy. When the latter class dominates the situation, we have public spirit, construction, generous rivalry in well-doing, willingness to bear burdens, the joyful baring of breasts to receive the blows of fortune, the absence of self-pity and squealing.

The leaders of the world fall into two classes according as they appeal to the one spirit or the other. The easy way to achieve political leadership in a community made up of the former class is to tell the people a great deal about their rights, their wrongs and their grievances, and to play upon their sense of self-pity which, by the way, is the most demoralizing and despicable of all mental conditions. If, however, you will study the example of any one of the half dozen greatest popular leaders of the world, leaders whose influence lasts over centuries and millennia, you will find that none of them ever told the people to whom he spoke a single word about their rights, their wrongs or their grievances, but a great deal about their opportunities and their obligations; never played upon their sense of self-pity, but tried to create in them the power of self-abnegation. It is only where this kind of an appeal is successful, where the leader is great enough to lead, or the people responsive enough to follow in this direction, that great things have ever been done. When the people forget to be sorry for themselves, and begin to rejoice in their own burdens, then and then only, are noble things accomplished.

Voting is not a question of the deserts or of the rights of this or that class of voters. Women neither have a "right" to vote nor have men a "right" to keep them from voting. It is wholly a question as to what system of voting will give us the best government. With respect to the ballot, men should neither ask themselves what do women deserve, or what are their rights, nor what are men's deserts and rights in the matter. Whatever is best for the nation as a whole we must do if we have a proper sense of our own honor and of our own opportunities and obligations.

Why, then, it may be asked, should we have general rather than restricted manhood suffrage? In the first place it is restricted to men who are twenty-one years of age or over, and also to those who are either citizens (native or naturalized) or have been enfranchised by special state legislation. However, these restrictions may be considered unimportant. Manhood suffrage is so little restricted as to be generally called universal. In the second place, there is only one sound reason why it should be so nearly universal as it is, but that one is quite sufficient. It is highly important that every interest should be safeguarded and that it should have an equal chance with every other interest to be heard and considered by the government authorities. If one interest were heard and another not, however fair-minded the government might try to be, there would be great danger of its being sensitive to the interest which had an open and recognized channel of expression, and insensitive to the one which had no such open and recognized channel. That would be bad government.

This right to have one's interests fairly considered along with and on a parity with all rival interests comes as nearly being inalienable as it is possible for a right to be. After one's interests have once been fairly considered, it may be necessary for the government to sacrifice them and to take action which will work to the disadvnatage of one and to the advantage of another. In that case, one must submit, and can not thereafter claim that any fundamental right has been sacrificed. It would be practically impossible for the government to take any action whatever that would not be more advantageous to one man than to another, or that would not lay greater burdens on one man than on another. The one thing which a just government must always and everywhere be careful to do is to see that every interest concerned with its action is fairly considered. Having done this, it must take such action as will favor the largest number of interests, and work to the disadvantage of the smallest number.

There appears to have been a positive reason for that so-called historical accident which made the male rather than the female the voter of the family unit. It apparently grew out of the militant stage of social development. The gradual change from turbulence to law and order was the result of the concentration of greater force on the side of law and order than on the side of turbulence. Whenever the turbulent elements again exercise greater force than the law-abiding elements, the change will proceed in the opposite direction.[1] The male rather than the female was the sex which used force, both on the side of turbulence and on the side of law and order. The victory of

---

[1] For example, in March, 1934, the Attorney General of the United States stated that the criminal elements had more men under arms than the Federal government had.

the forces of turbulence, whenever they were, or are, or shall be victorious, is a masculine rather than a feminine achievement. Likewise, the victory of the forces of law and order, whenever they have been victorious, has been a masculine achievement. This has been true in the past, whatever may be true in the present or in the future. Historically, it was the law-abiding masculine element which brought under control the turbulent masculine element, and established something which could be called government. Government was, in that state of social development, a masculine rather than a feminine affair. Just as there were reasons why we should have turned to the right rather than to the left on the road, so there appear to have been reasons why the male rather than the female should have been concerned with affairs of government. Similarly, just as the reasons why we should turn to the right rather than to the left have disappeared with the lapse of time, so the reasons why the male rather than the female should run the government *may* likewise have passed away. This conclusion, however, depends upon a number of circumstances.

If there is any place left on the face of the earth where there are turbulent elements, made up mostly of males, who will not submit to the law of the land, who will use force to resist the enforcement of law, one of two conditions must result. There will be anarchy — that is, no government, or there will be government by force. Law and order will then prevail, if they prevail at all, by reason of the fact that the side of law and order can exert more force than the side of turbulence. In such a community, if such there be, government will, even now, be more of a masculine than of a feminine affair, on the supposition that males are, on the average, somewhat harder fighters than females. This assumption can scarcely be invalidated by pointing out that some women are better fighters than some men. That question could only be decided by the method of trial and error, which might have unpleasant results. The question as to who are men and who are women is easily settled. The question as to who are good and who are poor fighters is not so easily answered. Since the male seems to be, in general, the fighting animal, he must be relied upon mainly to suppress turbulence where it exists.

It will be observed that the word "ought" has not been used in this discussion. The writer has not said that people "ought" or "ought not" to vote because they can or cannot fight. That is not the argument at all, and no one is quite truthful who travesties the argument in that way. The argument is wholly concerned with the relation of cause and effect. What is the effect of the votes of non-fighters in such a community as we have assumed? The answer is that they have no effect whatsoever.

These considerations, of course, have no bearing on the question of suffrage in any community where people are all so civilized as to abide peaceably by the decision of a majority vote, and to wait for what they want until the majority peacefully votes to give it to them. They have a bearing on the question in any community which has not yet reached that condition. In a community where government is practically self-operative, where voting consists merely in registering opinions, where elections are necessary merely to ascertain the weight of opinion, and where minorities will gladly and spontaneously support any opinion or policy as soon as the votes have been counted and it has been ascertained that the majority favor it, there is no reason why non-fighters should not vote. There is no reason for believing that they could not, if they put their minds to it, register as intelligent opinions on public questions as fighting men. But if government is not yet self-operative, if there are minorities who will resist law and its enforcement, or who will try to get by force what a majority has not yet voted to give them, then government is still a matter of force, and is mainly a masculine affair. This opinion does not ignore such superb and conspicuous fighters as Mrs. Nation; it merely regards her as an exception and not as a representative of the average woman. If women were generally such Amazons as she, and men were generally non-fighters, then one would be forced to the conclusion that government in a turbulent community was a feminine rather than a masculine affair.

Have we reached that state of civilization in which government is self-operative, where law does not have to be enforced, where every one gladly and spontaneously supports the will of the majority as soon as it is determined, and waits patiently and peacefully for what he or she wants until a majority can be peacefully and lawfully persuaded to vote to give it to him or her? There are reasons for doubting it. Not all the suffragettes themselves have reached that plane, and if they have not, what can we expect of less advanced men and women? We have apparently reached a stage in which, on the common run of unimportant questions, a majority vote is practically self-operative, where a minority will gladly support the decision of the majority as soon as it is ascertained. On a good many other questions a majority of this minority would, if necessary, rally to the support of the government to help enforce a law against which they had themselves voted. In all such cases, a woman's vote would be as effective as a man's. Most of the men even who did not like the way in which women voted would still help the police and the militia to enforce a law which was carried mainly by women's votes. But in some other cases where vital interests are at stake, or where political passions are aroused, minorities are not thus easily won over to the support of laws which they do not like, or which, in their opinion, operate against their vital interests and what they call their sacred rights. If this minority should happen to include most of the fighting men, while the majority which passed the law should happen to be made up mainly of women, there is not the slightest reason for believing that the law would ever be enforced. In such a case, their votes would do the women no good whatsoever.

When, in a previous age, fighting was a technical trade and fighting men a distinct class, trained and equipped for the fighting trade, they could not have been governed by non-fighters. The ballot would have done the non-fighters no good. The professional fighting men could easily have ignored any law they did not like and defied any who tried to enforce it. In that situation, the question of the right to vote would not have seemed very important to the non-fighters. Their votes would have been about as effective as the famous vote of the mice that the cat must wear a bell. It is well known that gun powder had a great deal to do with making democracy possible. It gave to men untrained in the technique of equitation and swordsmanship a weapon which made them almost equal to the professional fighters.

But can not a majority of non-fighters hire policemen and militiamen to do their fighting for them? Yes, so long as the turbulent element does not greatly outnumber the police and the militia. Even where this element outnumbers all the officers of the law, it will not openly rebel or resist the law if it knows that, back of every policeman and militiaman there are a hundred determined and courageous fighting men who will rally to the support of the police and militia whenever it is necessary. This turbulent element will then realize that it will eventually be suppressed, even though it should for a time succeed in beating the police or even the militia.

The experience which this country has had in trying to enforce laws that were unpopular with the turbulent element, will, if we think clearly and do not give way to envy, teach us that the ballot is a serious matter and not a thing to be liltingly fluttered and daintily dropped into a box. The difficulties which police have had in coping with organized crime may teach citizens that protection can not always be hired, and that they may themselves be called upon, as in time of war, to fight a public enemy. There is not and never has been a well governed democracy except where those who vote are also willing and able to fight for the enforcement of the laws for which they voted, and in support of the officers whom they elected. In the absence of that fighting force, turbulent minorities have always defied the laws and its executives. It looks as though no one should vote for anything for which he would not fight if there is resistance. Otherwise, government becomes a soft, ineffective, and useless thing.

Why should there be democracy at all? Is not the development of democracy a counter-current or a backwash in the general process of social evolution? Everywhere we see differentiation and specialization. There are fewer and fewer things which everyone does for himself, and more and more things are done for him by specialists. Why, it is asked, should government be the one general exception to this rule? Why should the average citizen pretend to a knowledge or expertness which he does not possess? Is not monarchy or a dictatorship a more highly evolved form of government than either a republic or a democracy?

The answer is found in two large facts already mentioned in this work but frequently overlooked. The first is that, strictly speaking, the people do not govern themselves even in a democracy. They are governed as truly as in a monarchy, and they are governed by men who are, for the time being at least, set apart for the special work of governing. Presidents, governors and other administrative officers, legislators, judges, and all those who really do the governing, are specialists in a democracy as truly as in a monarchy; that is, they are specialists in the sense of being permitted to give their undivided attention to the work of public office and are not compelled to divide their attention between public office and some other occupation by means of which they could make a living. That is as much as can be said of those who govern under a monarchy or a dictatorship. From the standpoint of specialization, therefore, there is no essential difference between monarchy and democracy.

The real difference, as pointed out already in this chapter, is that under any form of popular government, the people who are governed have provided for them the machinery by means of which they can express their assent or dissent, their satisfaction or dissatisfaction with the way in which they are governed. In this respect a popular government is a more highly evolved form of government than any form of autocracy. A biological organism which lacks a sensory system or is devoid of afferent nerves by means of which every part of the body can register in the brain,— the governing part,— its comfort or discomfort, would not be a highly evolved organism. The organism with a sensory system is, from the evolutionary point of view, a higher organism. Similarly, a social organism in which there is something to correspond to the sensory system of the physical organism is more highly evolved or, from the evolutionary point of view, a higher form of organism than one which lacks a sensory system.

Apologists for dictatorships always point out that there must be a head to every organism and to every effective organization. They do not take the trouble to point out that every organism which has evolved far enough to have a head has also a sensory system, a mechanism by which the governing head can be made aware of the feelings of the most distant parts of the organism. The analogy between a state and an organism with a head is not complete until the state develops a mechanism for the same purpose. That mechanism is the ballot, or some similar system for enabling the citizenry to register their feelings or wishes. That mechanism would destroy a dictatorship.

8. *Representation.* A question on which both political theorists and practical politicians are very much divided relates to the function of a representative. It need not be said that direct government by the people themselves becomes impossible when they live too widely scattered to permit them to gather in one place or when they are too numerous to crowd into a space small enough to enable them to hear one another. The election of representatives seems to be the only solution of that problem. But how shall the representative represent? Shall he serve merely as a rubber stamp to register the opinion of the majority of his constituents, or shall he use his own judgment and intelligence? The theory that he should record by his vote the opinion of the majority of his constituents, or vote as they would if they were physically present in the legislative hall, is known as the democratic theory. That he should actually deliberate and reach a conclusion by using his own judgment and intelligence is known as the republican theory. The drift is undoubtedly toward the democratic theory.

One evidence of this drift in the United States is found in the behavior of the electoral college which technically elects the president. It was established for the purpose of deliberating, looking the candidates over, and actually choosing a president. Technically, therefore, the president is not elected in November, but at a meeting where the votes of the electors are counted. Actually, however, the president is elected by the people at the November election. The newspapers correctly publish the news, the morning after election, that so-and-so is elected President. Actually the electors do not deliberate, they do not choose, they are virtually so many rubber stamps which record what the voters have decided.

There was a time when United States senators were not elected by the people but by the State legislatures. For a time the legislature really elected. The members deliberated, debated, and exercised a real choice. Gradually, however, in most of the states, the party candidates for senator were nominated by party conventions, and candidates for the state legislature were pledged to vote for the party nominee. A situation was reached where the newspapers, the day after the election, announced that so-and-so was elected senator. When the legislature met months later, there was neither deliberation nor choice. In the formal election of a senator, the members of the legislature exercised no more discretion than the members of the electoral college in the choice of a president. When that stage was reached, the logical thing was to have the senators formally as well as actually elected by popular vote. The spread of such things as the initiative, the referendum, and the recall is a further evidence of the drift toward the democratic theory.

Yet there is much in the republican theory to recommend it. It recognizes that the average man is fully occupied with his own affairs and can not, without neglecting these affairs, devote enough study to public affairs to decide most of the questions that come before a legislative body. It holds that the average men, thus occupied, should pick out some one in whose wisdom and honesty he has confidence, and say to him, in effect, "We will pay you a salary so that you can be relieved of these daily worries which keep us occupied; in return for this, you are to devote your time to public questions. We select you as our expert, or as one who may become an expert, on public questions.

We expect you to meet with other experts similarly chosen, to confer with them, deliberate, discuss and debate, and reach the wisest decision within your power. We will not tell you what you must do, for we do not know; but we will know whether we are comfortable or not, or whether we are prospering or not. So long as we are comfortable and prosperous, we will keep you as our representative. When we become uncomfortable and unprosperous, out you will go."

Under the democratic theory, on the other hand, such a thing as deliberation or debate in legislative halls is out of place. What has a representative to deliberate about except to find out what his constituents want? To debate a question, and try to persuade a fellow representative to vote other than his constituents wanted him to vote, would scarcely seem honorable.

Under the democratic theory a vicious circle is likely to develop. If representatives are to be merely rubber stamps or megaphones to express the wish of constituents, men of high character, independent judgment, and trained intelligence are not likely to accept the position of representative. Only men who are so anxious for jobs as to be willing to be rubber stamps in return for a salary will fill our legislative bodies. When legislative bodies are filled with such men, the public will lose confidence in them and wish to have safeguards in the form of the initiative, the referendum, and the recall. The more such safeguards are used, the less attractive the position of representative becomes to men of character and intelligence, and so things go from bad to worse. If, instead of this vicious circle, it were possible to get men of sound judgment and dependable honesty into legislative bodies, the public would not feel the need of so many ways of interfering with them.

In the final analysis the problem depends upon the question whether the public at large can secure better legislation by trying to legislate directly than by entrusting the function of legislation to such experts or near-experts as it can manage to elect. Ideally, of course, every difficult task should be performed by the most expert person who can be found. The average man, it would seem, might almost as well try to be his own physician, lawyer, or plumber as to try to be his own legislator. He might, however, be compelled to perform these functions for himself if his experience showed him that professional physicians, lawyers and plumbers could not be depended upon. A society, however, in which there were no dependable experts would need something more than the initiative, the referendum and the recall. Of course there is a difference between legislators and some other experts, but this difference is not where it is ordinarily expected. The public has a way of licensing or otherwise sifting out those who pretend to be experts in some of these fields. It does not trust the average person to pick out his own medical or legal adviser or even his own expert mechanic. He can only choose from an accredited list,— members of the bar, men licensed to practise medicine, or to carry on any other technical or highly skilled occupation. There is no workable plan for a similar accredited list of candidates for the citizen vote. Therefore it appears that the choice of legislators must be left to the discretion of the citizenry at large. These, as suggested above, have the two alternatives: first, of selecting men whom they believe to be capable and honest and then leaving the work of legislation to them without interference, very much as they leave any other expert workman to do his work in his own way without meddling; second, of electing men who are so anxious for office as to accept the rôle of a larynx to vocalize the ideas of the constituency, and then control the representative, as the brain is supposed to control the larynx.

The drift toward the democratic theory explains the general decline in the quality and character of legislators. While there are still noble exceptions to the rule, in every legislative body there is a tendency to elect men of weak character whose sole qualification for office is their ability to keep their ears to the ground, or to trim their sails to every shift of public opinion and who are blown about by the contrary winds of political doctrine. Even the public which demands this kind of service of its legislators soon learns to despise the very men whom it chooses for that undignified rôle.

g. *Political unity.* Unity, continuity and sensitivity — these three things are the essentials of democracy. How can they be best assured? The first two of these, namely unity and continuity, are achieved by other forms of government as well as—possibly better than — by democracy. Democracy alone can achieve sensitivity. There is danger, however, that a government which shows a high degree of sensitivity may lose something in the way of unity and continuity. Governments, like individuals, may try to please everybody and actually please nobody. In efforts to follow the popular will it may vacillate and accomplish nothing. Blown about by all the contrary winds of conflicting opinion it may dissipate its energies and that of its people, to no purpose. The problem of democracy, which must possess sensitivity in order to be a democracy, is to find ways of combining it with the factors of unity and continuity.

There is one word, namely loyalty, that is rather vital to the answer; but it has not a reputation for being especially scientific. Loyalty is not precise in its connotation; it covers too many virtues all at once. Political scientists prefer to talk of "patriotism"; sociologists, with fraternal understanding, have coined the phrase "ethnocentrism." Even the metaphysician refuses to talk indiscriminately of loyalty.

Josiah Royce, for instance, believed that a man might be loyal to an idea — a cause — a superpersonal thing; but affection for a human being — devotion to pure personality — he called simply love.[1] Professor Royce was doubtless making a distinction which, to the intellectual, has great significance. Yet, to the vast majority of men, loyalty and love are not vitally separable. Loyalty, to them, is a passionate attachment, an habitual complex, an emotional attitude of devotion to — anything. The philosopher might argue that the soldiers of Napoleon were in reality not loyal to him, but to the cause for which he stood in their minds — France, or glory, or what you will. But the soldiers did not care whether Napoleon was merely a cause, or whether, in fact, the cause was Napoleon;

[1] See the *Philosophy of Loyalty* (The Macmillan Company, New York, 1920), p. 20.

it was, in any case, the little grey corporal whom they followed to battle and to death. Followers of Andrew Jackson have now decided that it was not Andrew Jackson but the principles for which he stood, to which they are so loyal. That, however, is probably an afterthought. It was Jackson's personality which inspired so much enthusiasm among his followers and gave that unity and coherence to the Democratic party which still holds it together in spite of fundamental differences within it.

Loyalty, then, is a great love for or devotion to anything. If a number of people are loyal to the same thing,— the strip of land where they were all born, the same man, the same purpose,— their common loyalty is a unity of will which is a basis of control over them. If their common attachments are more important to them than their less vital, personal, and conflicting desires, they will submit to any agency which promises in some way to make it possible for them to live together. The more loyalties they have in common the less difficult will be the task of establishing a unified and continuing government and social life among them.

The argument that political power,— absolute and unlimited,— entered the world as a mystic force at its creation or at some primeval disarmament conference when it was decided that much was to be gained by limiting the war of all against all, is antiquated. Political power originates as a psychic force created by a social and economic situation. Governing power, which in the end is the power of the mass over the individual, is built upon loyalties. These loyalties fuse the conflicting wills of large numbers of individuals into an organic, or quasi-organic unity. This makes the mass, thus unified, irresistible in its power over the individual. Whoever can, by whatever means, wield that irresistible power is in fact the ruler. If he succeeds in coercing the mass to act under his will, woe unto the weak individual who opposes him. If he can persuade the mass to believe in his divine commission to govern, he can still, because of the mass power under his control, crush opposition. If he can make himself so popular with the mass that they will act under his direction, he can still govern as ruthlessly as in either of the other cases.

That common loyalty which fuses the conflicting wills of the mass of men into a kind of unity, is helped and hindered by a multitude of factors. A common language makes it easier, while a diversity of language makes it harder for them to think, feel and act together. A common literature, religion, and culture likewise contribute to unity, while differences make it harder to achieve unity. Racial unity is also a help while racial disunity is a hindrance. Territorial unity, that is, the occupation of a compact territory, all contiguous, is likewise a help. The greatest possible unity is found where all the unifying factors are in combination. Where there is not only territorial unity, but also racial, cultural, religious, and linguistic unity, the problems of governmental unity are greatly simplified. Where none of these bases of unity exist, there is no unity of any kind.

In the life of men who inhabit the same bit of the earth, who are of the same race, of the same religious faith, who possess a common literature and speak the same language, who have experienced a common struggle, there is a unity of purpose that is born of their common loyalties. They are so strongly bound that they can even agree to disagree on loyalties that do not threaten to destroy their essential unity, but woe to the individual who threatens their major loyalties.

There are three objects of loyalty that are of particular interest to the sociologist. Loyalty to a person, loyalty to an organization and loyalty to a principle was probably the primitive root of government. It all began when some strong man found that he could impose his will on his poor, stupid relatives. Obedience on the part of the weak was either a fear or an inertia reaction. The group, however, which acquiesced to control — even in the way most of us obey a man with a pistol — was more successful in combating its enemies and in procuring a food supply than other groups which had not the same unity of will imposed upon it. Loyalty to a personal leadership, even though it were forced and even though it seemed chiefly to redound to the advantage of the leader, had a survival value for the group. The disloyal were killed off in the course of evolution because men capable of loyalty survived.

Yet government based upon the physical or economic strength of a man and his ability to command loyalty is not a very stable form of government. The governed must be ready to shift their loyalty at a moment's notice — whenever the power to control them is in dispute or whenever death shows itself no respector of despots. Certain Latin American countries, in the past, have suffered from the instability of government, because their loyalties were so intensely personal. There has been no object of loyalty strong enough in its appeal to cause the followers of rival leaders to act together in the service of common love. Revolution and counter-revolution have characterized the history of some of those unhappy countries.

A much more lasting form of government is based upon loyalty to an organization. When no man is strong enough to command the obedience of a group, but control is divided among a number of men according to a recognized division of power, the division of power,— the organization of control, it limits and methods of application,— are much more vital to the governed than the particular men who hold sway for a time. If the king has his court, and his successor assured, if the King already lives, though the King is dead, what does the death matter? The subjects of a King are loyal to kingship — and kingship does not die in many generations. Tammany Hall, the Republican or the Democratic Party, the D. A. R., the Catholic Church, the Checka — these can command a more lasting loyalty and unity of will among their followers than any personality in the seat of power.

Loyalty to ideas or principles, however, gives greater unity and continuity to government than loyalty to persons or organizations. If men are bound by a common principle, kings and organizations must be themselves bound by the same loyalty, or they will be unable to command the obedience of the governed. The rulers and the ruled are not merely loyal to each other; they are bound by a common loyalty to something more than the personal desires of either. If the people are loyal to a principle, they give their obedience to the agency which cherishes the principle, not to the agency which simply gives them their money's worth of soldiers and police and law courts and public baths. The rulers and the ruled will quarrel over method; but they will be so vitally bound by the common principle they serve that they cannot be disloyal to each other. The passions of party and faction will not destroy the constitutional morality of the people.

It is difficult to persuade the mind that has freed itself from all emotional attractions and abhorrences to care for an ideal of personal sacrifice. "Society," de Maistre is said to have remarked, "is an association of the living with the dead and the unborn." What way can be found to persuade those at any time living to safeguard the interests of unborn generations? Surely the most hedonistic calculator must recognize that the greatest number of men are not yet born. Unless the living had been motivated to produce more than they consumed, so that their posterity could have a better start in life than they, there would have been no such thing as the economic progress of which the twentieth century boasts. As the late Edward Van Dyke Robinson sagely remarked "When consumption exceeds production, there is retrogression." But why should anyone care for progress — why should anyone care for the dead or the unborn?

The world at least, belongs, as though by a law of nature, to peoples who are moved, in some way, to act as if they cared for all these. The people who manage to live and work together efficiently in large numbers, and who act as though they were tremendously interested in the unborn, will outlast those who say, "what has posterity done for me?"

The Japanese have for centuries reverenced their ancestors. One of their great poems reads:

> Our fathers precepts
> Handed down from ages past
> By rulers holy
> Have become a nation's treasure
> Held in reverence closely claspt.

Ancestor worship produces an interest not only in the past, but in the future, for the desire to deserve the reverence of posterity becomes a motive to one who himself bows before the memory of his ancestors. The Japanese found in their religious faith a loyalty which gave tremendous unity and stability to their government.

Democracy has, in its idealism, the essence of a religious faith which is capable of binding men together in a lasting loyalty. Democracy is more than a form of government; it is a faith in the potential power of personality. The mature democrat does not believe that all men are equal or that one man is as good as another; he does believe that all men must be given a fighting chance to display the good that *is* in them. A people who are loyal to the principle that the desires of every citizen have a potential value will be ruled by any agency which respects what most men desire — including, among most men, a reasonable proportion of the dead and the unborn.

There has probably never existed a people completely bound together by loyalty to such an ideal as democracy upholds. The word has always had to become flesh, or most men are incapable of loyalty at all. Yet the religion of democrary is being preached all over the world today, even though the world's interest is dying out. The machinery is being created to make rulers sensitive to the desires of the ruled. Unity and continuity of will among the governed are vital to all government. But it makes a difference how these are secured. Democracy secures them principally by the common loyalty of a people to an ideal of personality. It requires that anyone who wields power over men must respect their personality — their insistent desire.

People who can only be loyal to a person will be governed by a succession of persons. The person who governs at any time may be a military despot, a hereditary monarch, a political boss or a popular dictator. People who have developed only to the point where they can be loyal to an organization will be governed by an organization. The organization may be a military caste, as in Sparta or Prussia, it may be Tammany

Hall in New York, the G. O. P. in the North, the Democratic Party in the South, or the small communist party in Russia. People who are capable of being loyal to a principle are capable of popular government in its best sense. Even the rulers must be loyal to this principle if they are to retain power.

The future of government depends, in a rather vital sense, on the proportion of the people, in any country, who belong to those three loyalty groups. In a country where the great majority are capable only of loyalty to a person, democratic government will be a personal affair. A dominating personality will rule. Where the great majority are capable of being loyal to an organization, government will be dominated by political machines, men will believe, more or less blindly, in some organization and will vote accordingly. But where the majority have reached the point where they can be loyal to a principle, government will be dominated by principles or ideals. Men may come and go, parties and organizations rise and fall, but the people will still insist on a government which carries out their ideals and principles.

Most of us, nowadays, without critical examination, associate a definite bit of territory, with definite boundaries, and a definite name, with every government, and assume, as a matter of course, that all who live within those boundaries are subjects of the government. For administrative purposes, the people are grouped in smaller territorial units, rather than in class groups, religious groups, or occupational groups. This territorial basis of government has not always existed and is, even now, criticised. It is an unusual, but still a pertinent question; why should the fact that we happen to live within the same geographical limits subject us to the same government? Why should those who have common class, religious, or cultural interests not be grouped in administrative units? or, why should not all who profess a given religion, belong to the same labor organization, or speak the same language, have their own government, and be independent of all territorial governments?

There is one economic factor of such fundamental importance as to deserve the most careful attention of students of sociology.

That is the extreme difficulty and the supreme importance of protecting a high standard of living.[1] In the more primitive stages of social development, the standard of living was mainly a question of food. How to conserve and safeguard an adequate food supply was a problem of major importance. Since food came from land, the conservation and protection of the food supply soon came to mean the control of a strip of land. Intertribal communism in land gave no tribe an opportunity to safeguard its own food supply. No matter how careful it was not to kill more game than it needed, nor how frugal it was in consumption, nor how constructive its policy with respect to pasturage and herding, and no matter how prudent it might have been with respect to its birth rate, it could gain no advantage from its own wisdom and frugality so long as its hunting or herding grounds were left open to the less wise and thrifty tribes around it. Its own food supply, however carefully conserved, was open to the most lavish consumers and the most reckless breeders among its neighbors.

There was only one possible solution to that problem. That was to claim a strip of land for its own, to establish boundaries to its hunting or herding grounds, and to keep others out. Here was an assertion of a right of property on the part of a tribe or a considerable group. On what ethical principle could such a right be claimed? By none, unless the preservation of the life of the tribe be called an ethical principle. The tribe was facing a condition and not a theory, and every tribe that ever grew into a great nation has acted in much the same way. It has done the obvious thing, and has controlled a strip of territory in order to safeguard its own food supply.

But the necessity of controlling a strip of territory has not disappeared with the development of agriculture, manufactures and commerce. With the increase of the standard of living it has come to include many things besides food. There is no way by which we in this country, with all our urbanization and with all our transportation and international trade, could long

[1] *Supra*, Chapter IX.

maintain a higher standard of living than Europe or even Asia except by controlling our own territory and being able to say who should be permitted to enter it. With our own territory under our own control it is possible by wise policies to build up a high standard of comfort for our own people regardless of what the rest of the world does. Without that control it would be impossible no matter how wise our policies might be in other respects.

This fact is so patent, it has been acted upon by so many thousands of years of human experience, as to have pretty definitely established the principle of territoriality as the basis of statehood. The territorial state is not likely to be easily superseded by any non-territorial organization. Men have been thinking geographically for too long a time to be easily persuaded to give up the idea of country and begin to think in terms of class, caste or culture as a sole basis of unity. Besides, even if they could change their psychology and begin to think in non-geographical terms, it could only bring disaster. Changing their psychology would not change the economic facts which gave their present psychology its survival value. The behavior of things is quite as important as the behavior of men. In certain aspects, things are less plastic than men and serve as the mould which gives form to human nature.

Let us assume that any group, whether a hunting tribe, a herding clan, an agricultural or a manufacturing nation, has succeeded by conservation of resources, by a prudential birthrate, and by superior productivity, in building up a higher standard of comfort than its less intelligent neighbors. What is to prevent those neighbors from hunting on its preserves, pasturing on its range, plowing up its fields, and working in its shops in such numbers as to reduce the standard of living of the superior tribe to their own low level. One thing, and one thing only can prevent it, and that is, control of its own territory. No tribe ever did or ever could build up and maintain a superior standard of living without that territorial control. Any theory of internationalism which ignores this elemental necessity can only benefit the most backward and the most degenerate races. It must be destructive of civilization, because it merely throws the results of superior culture open to the depredations of the least civilized peoples.

With a geographical psychology built up by millions of years of human experience, it does not seem likely that it can be changed by a few years of preaching of loyalty to non-territorial groups. Men are likely, for some time to come, to think geographically, or in terms of geographical groups. Party organizations are likely to reflect that habit of thinking geographically. One who understands this principle need not expect to see representation changed from geographical to class groups. Neither religious groups, occupational groups, income groups, nor cultural groups are likely to displace geographical groups as the basis of government.

10. *The Limits of Control.* "There ought to be a law against it!" is an expression too frequently heard. So long as it is understood to mean nothing more than: "Such a thing ought not to be done!" it can do no great harm. It is merely one way of expressing disapproval of what some one else is doing. But when voters and law makers take it literally and begin trying to legislate against everything that any of them dislikes, it is certain to do a great deal of harm. He who happens to be in a minority on any question affecting his liberty will then find himself controlled by an unrestrained majority. Any citizen is likely to be forbidden to say or do anything that does not happen to please the majority. Neither freedom of speech, freedom of consumption, nor freedom of business can long survive in such a community.

In a democracy the majority has unlimited power — no monarch ever had greater. As in a monarchy, so in a democracy, a constitution may place hindrances in the way of an abuse of power, but these are only temporary and may be removed, if they are not ignored by a determined majority. At most they can only compel a majority to go slowly. Except for provisions in our federal and state constitutions, the majority could curb freedom of speech and of the press, and even disfranchise the minority, as easily as it can regulate trade and commerce.

Revolutionists who would overthrow the government and the constitution should ponder this. Without this safeguard, coupled with the temperate use of power by majorities, they would not be allowed even to speak in public, nor, for that matter, would any other unpopular minority. Better even than written constitutions, however, are the spirit of reasonableness and the habitual self-restraint of the people, leading to the temperate use of power by majorities.

One of the best safeguards against the intemperate use of power is the prudent habit of counting the cost of every proposed undertaking. The costs of government repression, especially when there is determined opposition, are many and far-reaching and the prudent citizen will not favor it except where the evil to be repressed is so definite and so great as to make its repression almost a matter of necessity, in which case its importance outweighs any possible cost. Repression requires the exercise of physical force, besides much espionage, and many arbitrary and wholesale rules that work hardship to the innocent as well as to the guilty. Of course, when the citizen has carefully calculated the cost and voted for the repression of a given abuse, he ought to bear his share of the cost and not try to shirk it, even though it leave its marks on his own body.

To say that it may not pay to do a thing is not the same as saying that it is not desirable that it may be done. It may mean only that it is not worth what it will cost. This should be applied to every problem of government regulation or repression. The opponent of any piece of government regulation is too often accused of believing that everything is working perfectly or that there is no need of a change. He may be merely the prudent man who counts the cost while his accusers are determined to get what they want regardless of cost.

No economist has ever questioned the necessity of some government control over the activities of individuals. It is made necessary, first, by the fact that human interests are sometimes antagonistic and require an umpire with power to enforce his decisions, and, second, by the fact that certain individuals of immature or unsound mentality are obviously incapable of looking after their own interests as intelligently even as the officers of government can look after them. So much is generally admitted. How far the state should go in its regulation and control of individual conduct is a matter upon which there is a wide difference of opinion. One school has inclined toward a restriction of government control to a few of the most important cases, leaving individuals of mature years and sound minds to find their own place in the economic system and to make their own economic adjustments with their fellows on the basis of voluntary agreement or contract. Other schools advocate a general extension of the authority and control of the government over more and more of the affairs of individuals, gradually enlarging the field wherein things are done under the system of authority and obedience and narrowing down the field wherein they are done by voluntary agreement among free citizens. The term *laissez faire* is sometimes applied to the former school, implying that its followers believe in the "let go" or "let alone" policy of government. Various names are applied to the other schools, depending upon how far they propose to extend the field of authority and obedience, or to restrict the field of voluntary agreement or free contract.

This section is concerned with the *laissez faire* school and the underlying assumptions on which its policy must be based. There has been much misapprehension on this subject and not a little misstatement. A recent book, "Economics for the General Reader," by Henry Clay,[1] states four assumptions as underlying the *laissez faire* policy: (1) the assumption of rational self-interest, or "that individuals in their economic relations can be relied on to pursue their own interest, and that their action will be rational and informed"; (2) that competition leads to the survival of the fittest, or "that competition in industry will result in the survival of the socially fittest"; (3) that wealth will ordinarily be the result of social service, or "that *as a rule* private wealth or property will be acquired only by service"; and (4) that market values and social values are

---

[1] The Macmillan Company, New York, 1919, pp. 370-371.

identical, or "that market values correspond roughly with social values, and are an adequate indicator of need for production to follow."

It may be true, at least one would be bold who would deny, that there have been advocates of a *laissez faire* policy who have made some or all of these assumptions. If one believed that government was omniscient and omnipotent, and could without difficulty and without cost, either in the form of money, man power, or irritation, control human conduct in any way it saw to be wise, then the best reason one could give for the government's keeping its hand off or letting things alone would be that things were working well enough anyway and could not be improved even by such an ideally perfect government. If any one saw anything going wrong, or any one doing that which was socially inexpedient, and if he understood that an all wise and all powerful government could, without cost or disadvantage of any kind, compel the individual to do that which was expedient, he could not reasonably do other than ask that the government act in the matter and correct the evil. If, for example, he were convinced that, on the whole, the cigarette did slightly more harm than good, and that, if it could be eliminated without cost or disadvantage in any form, that more good than harm would result from its loss, and if he believed that the government could eliminate it without harm or disadvantage of any kind, he would, as a good economist, demand that the government act in the matter and eliminate the cigarette. But if he believes that the government is not able to do any such thing without a great deal of cost, in the form of money, man power, irritation or something else, it is an entirely different story.

With such a view of government one may believe in a *laissez faire* policy without making any of the assumptions mentioned by Clay. It would be quite as near the truth to charge the advocates of government interference and regulation with assuming (1) that voters are dominated by rational self-interest or that individuals in their political relations can be relied on to vote for their own interest, and that this voting will be rational and informed; (2) that political competition or politics will result in the election of the socially fittest; (3) that public office and political power will ordinarily be the result of social service, or that *as a rule* public office and political power will be acquired only by service; and (4) that political values,— that is, power to get votes,— and social values are identical, or "that political values correspond roughly to social values and are an adequate indicator of need for legislation to follow."

A man may have a rather poor opinion of the average individual in business and his ability to pursue his own interest on the market; but if he has a still poorer opinion of the same average individual in politics and his ability to pursue either his own or the public's interest at the polls, he will very consistently prefer not to have average citizens in politics interfering too much with average citizens in business. Again, he might be exceedingly pessimistic as to the results of economic competition, believing that rascality and predation frequently succeed as against honesty and production; but if he is still more pessimistic as to the results of political competition, believing that rascality and predation succeed as against honesty and production even more frequently in politics than in business, he will consistently regard unregulated economic competition as less evil than wholesale government interference. Again, he may believe that property and wealth frequently accrue to men who have not earned them by any corresponding social service; but if he believes that government offices and political power and influence still more frequently go to men who have not earned them by any corresponding social service, he may consistently prefer the results of economic competition to those of control by politics or by those who manage to get elected to office by political methods. Finally, he may see very clearly that market values and social values are frequently far apart; that many things of little real worth sell on the market at a high price, and others of great worth at a low price; but if he sees equally clearly that ideas of no social value frequently have high value as vote-getters, he may very consistently consider market values as a less unsafe guide than political values.

The question is not how much confidence one has in the wisdom or disinterestedness of the people, but whether he thinks the people show greater average wisdom in their economic than in their political activities or vice versa. The believer in a *laissez faire* policy may merely believe that men generally show more wisdom or less unwisdom in their business dealings or economic activities than in their political activities; whereas the believer in a general policy of regulation must believe that men show more wisdom or less unwisdom in their political than in their business activities.

An illustration is furnished by the question of foreign trade. It is doubtful if many free traders would insist that every buyer of foreign goods buys wisely in every case, even from the standpoint of his own advantage, much less from the standpoint of the general advantage. The writer is of the opinion that an omniscient and omnipotent government, could, if it were benevolently disposed, place many restrictions upon foreign trade that would be advantageous even to those who would like to buy foreign goods, and also to the general public. But in view of the fact that the government is run by men who are neither omniscient, omnipotent, nor benevolent, in fact no wiser or more benevolent than those who would like to buy foreign goods, it is extremely improbable that the government could interfere with foreign trade to the advantage of anybody, except, possibly, in extreme cases. This, in the writer's opinion is a sufficient reason for being a free trader, in spite of the fact that there are many theoretical possibilities of advantageous interference.

The question of freedom of speech will serve as an example. It would be absurd to charge the advocate of freedom of speech with assuming that every one who talks will talk intelligently, or that his talk will be "rational and informed"; that competition in speech, that is, discussion, will always or generally result in the survival of the fittest ideas; or that talk which results in the greatest profit to the talker, either in the form of money or popular esteem, will ordinarily be the most useful to the community, etc. He may believe none of these things; he may

be convinced that a great deal of foolishness results from freedom of speech; that infinite harm is done by some talkers who
mislead the people. Probably no one would seriously contend
that false or misleading talk or teaching does less harm than
predatory business, and yet one may be a firm believer in free
speech merely because he thinks that attempts by the government to interfere with it result in even greater harm. The
argument may not be convincing when one is told that the
government represents the people, and that the people will vote
for those officers who suppress certain talkers and against those
officers who let them talk. One may not believe that the people
voted wisely when they elected these official censors, or refused
to elect officers who would not act as censors. He may believe
that the result of the peoples votes in such cases will be worse
than any that would be likely to follow the policy of letting the
talkers alone, that is, a *laissez faire* policy with respect to speech.

No one need claim that men, left to themselves, will always
do what is right or socially useful. They will do many things
that are socially useless or even harmful. But to say that a
thing is harmful, or that it ought not to be done, is not the
same as saying that the government should repress it. Government repression requires the use of force, generally a good deal
of prying and espionage, in order to find evidence. We may
try to rob these things of their repulsiveness and make them
as attractive as possible by introducing a kind of ceremonialism
into judicial procedure, but they are still repulsive and are to
be used only where the thing they are trying to prevent is more
repulsive than they. In many cases, a socially harmful thing
really does less harm if let alone than the government would
do if it tried to repress it. Any one who is convinced of this
may very consistently favor a *laissez faire* policy with regard
to the thing in question. In short, the only necessary assumption of a *laissez faire* policy is that government regulation or
repression costs something. With this assumption agreed upon,
the question then becomes: are the results of repression or
regulation worth as much as they cost? A more accurate and
detailed statement of the question would be: are the evils to

be repressed greater than those that accompany the work of repression, and are the evils to be removed by regulation greater than those that accompany the work of regulation? When it is once understood that this is the question, the method of procedure must be to consider it and compare the evils on both sides.

Unfortunately there is no instrument of precision by means of which we can weigh or measure these evils. The appraisal must be largely a matter of judgment, and judgment must be largely a matter of temperament, sometimes of prejudice. Those who temperamentally or otherwise care greatly for freedom of consumption, and see no serious evils connected with freedom to consume whatever one likes, may decide against sumptuary regulations on what to them are purely utilitarian grounds. Others who see, or think they see, that certain forms of consumption are doing great harm, may with equal consistency decide in favor of the regulation or repression of those specific forms of consumption as less evil than the thing to be repressed. Again, those who prize greatly freedom to talk, or who think that it does not matter much if people are misled by bad talk or false teaching, will very likely decide either against any regulation or to restrict regulation to the most extreme cases, where, for example, the very life of the nation may be at stake. Others who do not see that freedom to talk is so very important, or who believe that great harm results from bad teaching may be a little more liberal in their use of political power in the repression or regulation of speech. Finally, they who do not care greatly for material wealth, or who do not see that any great harm is done if a few men here and there do get more than their just share, may decide that the evils of unregulated business are not great enough to justify a large amount of interference, whereas those who care greatly about such things, who are deeply resentful if someone gets more than his share, or, if not resentful on their own account, simply feel that it does great harm if a man here and there is getting too much, will naturally go in for more regulation. On the other hand, something will depend also upon one's temperamental attitude toward government and its agents. One who does not feel that it is a very serious thing to have police officers and other agents of the government prying around, gathering evidence regarding possible violation of sumptuary regulations, espionage laws, factory acts, etc. are likely to be very complacent toward rather minute regulations. Others, who feel differently toward government and its agents are likely to feel more or less impatient toward any except the most necessary regulations. These temperamental and emotional differences will always make it difficult for people to agree on the precise limits of government interference, but it is worth something to have the problem stated in terms of comparative cost, and divested of unnecessary assumptions.

CHAPTER XIII

CREATING A SOCIAL ENVIRONMENT FAVORABLE TO THE INDIVIDUAL

1. *The Fitness of the Social Environment.* The average individual in any highly developed society gets most of the things he needs from his social environment. That is, he gets them from other individuals and not directly from physical nature. His success or failure depends more on his ability to fit into a social than into a physical environment. In a peaceful society he must develop the kind of skill or adaptability which will enable him to get what he needs from other people with their consent. If he fails, the fault is either in his own lack of adaptability or in the nature of the society in which he lives. There is something to be changed, modified or corrected in this situation quite as truly as would be the case if the isolated individual found himself unable to get from his physical environment what he needed. In the latter case he would either have to change his ways of doing things or manage in some way to change or modify his physical environment, as Robinson Crusoe was rather successful in doing.

The great problem of adjustment between the individual and his social environment has two aspects, suggested by the analogy of the isolated individual. The individual in society who is not getting what he needs must either reform himself, reform society, or fail to earn a living. There are, therefore, two great classes of reformers: those who are by education or evangelism trying so to change individuals as to fit them into their social environment, and those who are trying to change the social environment in order to fit it to the individuals who compose it.[1] What constitutes individual fitness for a social environment was discussed in Chapter VIII on MORAL ADAPTATION. What constitutes a suitable social environment, adapted to the needs of men, is the subject of this chapter.

In cases where there is obvious maladjustment between the individual and his social environment there are many shades or variations of maladaptation. In some cases the difficulty is obviously with the individual himself. It may be difficult to draw the line between those individuals who are unfit for life in any society and those who are unfit for life in the particular society in which they find themselves because the society itself is badly organized. However, there are certain cases, commonly called pathological, where the individual could scarcely be said to be fit for any social environment whatsoever. There are other cases, presumably not pathological, but nevertheless unfit, because of laziness, feeblemindedness or such low mentality as to lack all power of adaptation. There are also many cases which are difficult to classify. In a society where there are no known or available sources of mechanical energy, mere muscular power has its value. A man of low mentality but high muscularity might be adapted to life in such a society because there might be a market for his muscular power. In a society, however, that has learned to tap other and very cheap sources of energy such as coal and petroleum, the amount of mechanical power that can be generated in any human body may have a very low market value. The individual who has only muscular power to sell may not be able to sell it for enough to maintain his power through the purchase of food. In a peaceful society where violence is suppressed, such an individual would be a failure.

The question could be argued, with much to be said on both sides, whether the fault or difficulty is with the individual or

---

[1] It is sheer fanaticism to assume either of two extreme positions, (1) that in every case of social maladaptation it is the fault of the individual, and (2) that it is necessarily the fault of the social group, the great society, or the social order.

with the kind of society in which he happens to live. The individual himself might say that it is no fault of his that coal and petroleum are cheaper than the food which is the source of his energy. On the other hand, any representative of the society in which he lives could say that the members of that society have no motive for paying this muscular individual a high price for his muscular power when they can buy all the power they need at a lower price. Sympathizers with the individual will, of course, inveigh against this cold-blooded way of calculating the value of muscle. Those who are so very careful of the individual and careless of the interests of the group as to call themselves socialists will say that the muscular individual should be supplied with sufficient food to maintain his muscular power because he needs it, regardless of whether he is worth that much to anybody else or not. Those who are willing to sacrifice the individual in the interest of the group and who are, therefore, frequently called individualists, will reply that they are willing to contribute to the support of this muscular individual but that they do it out of charity and not because of any worth or merit on his part. There are many other misfits found in every existing society whose cases are as difficult to explain as that of the individual who has only muscular power to sell.

There are also in every society misfits where the fault is obviously with the society in which they are trying to live. In a state of semi-anarchy, where violence is unrestrained, the individual who is highly competent to supply what other members of society need, or to do many things which would be to their benefit, but is so weak physically or so lacking in pugnacity as to be helpless,— like a sheep in the midst of wolves,— is un, adapted to a society of that kind. An individual who is honest-innocent, and unsuspecting is not adapted to a society of swindlers. He may make valuable contributions to the life and well-being of his fellow citizens but be regularly cheated out of the rewards which he legitimately earns for such service. However well he might be adapted to life in a decent society, he is unadapted to life in a society where fraud is not repressed. There are also, even in fairly decent societies, misunderstood geniuses, men ahead of their times, whose services are not appreciated or paid for.

Where different members of the same society have different standards of conduct, those with the higher standards are generally at a disadvantage as compared with those with lower standards or with no standards. A gentleman whose words are "yea, yea, and nay, nay," who tries to treat others not according to their deserts but according to his own honor and dignity, is at a disadvantage in a group of blackguards, especially when it comes to a verbal argument. These differences are peculiarly apparent in a conglomerate population made up of sections with widely different standards. In competition for employment, laborers with low economic standards can underbid laborers with high economic standards. In politics men with low standards of morality or culture may succeed and generally do succeed, not because they are superior but because they will stoop to demagogical tricks to which men of higher standards will not stoop. In business, men with high standards of business honor are sometimes beaten by men with low standards, not because the latter are more efficient business men but because they will stoop to business practices to which a man with high standards of honor will not stoop.

2. *Poverty as maladaptation.* The most wide-spread form of maladjustment between the individual and society is that which goes under the name of poverty. Under the market economy, poverty is the result of the individual's inability to sell his labor or his product at a price which will enable him to live in comfort or decency. Such an individual is unadapted to a society in which there is no demand for his labor or his product, or his society is not adapted to him. He must either learn to do or produce something for which others are willing to pay, or others must learn to appreciate and to pay for what he can do or produce. Otherwise the maladaptation remains unmitigated. When large numbers of individuals find themselves in this unfortunate situation, it presents the greatest and most perplexing problem of maladaptation.

The persistence of poverty in the midst of plenty is the most humiliating as well as the most baffling fact in modern social life. It is the fact which, more than any other, justifies the study of economics. Except for the possible light which it may throw on this problem, economics becomes merely a technical aid to business and its study might as well be relegated to business and trade schools. Modern civilization must stand or fall on its ability or inability to solve this problem of poverty. The challenge has been issued by revolutionists like Karl Marx, and by reformers like Henry George, one insisting that the problem could not be solved without a complete overthrow of the present economic system and starting over again with a new system, the other suggesting that the problem could be solved by the simple expedient of a single tax on land rent.[1] There are also other plans, but none of them has yet been tried on a comprehensive scale, mainly because there are so many influential people who want cheap labor in their factories or on their plantations, or cheap help in their homes. Cheap labor means mass poverty. Russia is trying the Marxian plan. Meanwhile, the problem remains unsolved because no country has seriously tried any rational and comprehensive plan.

The problem of poverty presents itself in two aspects, somewhat different but closely related. One aspect is the occasional (not periodic) lapse of all industry into a state of stagnation, when practically every one is reduced to a lower economic condition; where, in short, every one grows poorer. Those who were near the level of poverty are pushed below it. Those who were below that level are pushed further down, and many who were never near that level find themselves dangerously near it. The other aspect is the persistence of considerable masses of poverty even in good times. The mass grows smaller in good times, larger in bad times, but there is always a mass of it. These two aspects of the poverty problem call for two different solutions. The one calls for a stabilization of business

---

[1] The problem which Henry George set out to solve was: Why does poverty increase in spite of increases in productive power? The answer which he thought that he found was in the power of land rent to absorb all the gains from mechanical improvements. The obvious remedy, he thought, was for the government to take that rent in the form of a tax, to the exclusion of other taxes.

which will prevent the recurrence of those industrial cataclysms which depress all classes alike. The other calls for a reduction in the inequalities which exist all the time among different classes or occupational groups.

A condition in which a whole nation is plunged into a state of real and prolonged want has never failed to produce international wars. A condition which plunges large classes of the same nation into hopeless misery has seldom failed to produce revolutions or class wars. The only question is, How large is the group or class which finds itself in a condition of hopeless misery? When a whole nation becomes land-hungry, or when its people realize that they have not land enough or knowledge enough to support their numbers, they are likely to try to get more land if there is more to be had. If there is no land to be had by conquest and colonization, they become merchants and traders, or emigrants and colonists, thus extending the area from which they may draw their sustenance. But class groups are quite as covetous and unscrupulous as territorial groups. A large class, finding itself in a state of hopeless poverty while other classes are living in wealth and luxury, will carry on forays over the class boundaries as certainly as a territorial group will carry on forays over the territorial boundary under the circumstances.

The law of class struggle is so definite and calculable as to be startling in its arithmetical simplicity. The same facts which increase the poverty of an occupational group also increase its political and military power. The same condition which gives an occupational group low bargaining power on the market gives it high voting and fighting power. Therefore, the deeper into poverty it sinks the greater its physical power becomes. The greater its poverty, the greater becomes its motive for a revolution, the greater its fighting power, and therefore the greater the likelihood of succeeding in a revolution.

The reason, under our economic system, why a whole occupational group or class grows poorer is that there are too many in that class, but that fact increases both its voting and its fighting strength. When manual workers become too numerous, many will be unemployed, and wages, even for those who get wages, will necessarily be low. It can not be otherwise under any voluntaristic system. As soon as those who are in that situation realize this fact, they will desire another system in which wages and employment are not reduced by an oversupply of workers. As soon as they think that their numbers are large enough not only to keep them in misery under our system, but to enable them to overthrow the system, the system will be overthrown. There are reasons for believing that, in the long run, even the masses who overthrow our system and set up another will lose by it. They can, however, dispossess and impoverish the few who are now rich, and thus get rid of class distinctions based on differences of wealth. They will have no one to envy, which may be some compensation for the increasing misery in which they find themselves.

In the United States, the first of the two above-mentioned aspects of the poverty problem, that which comes with depressions, is as acute as it is anywhere and as it ever was. We have made no contribution or approach to the problem of stabilizing business and preventing these great unevennesses in business activity, sometimes mis-called business cycles. Our depressions are as pronounced as they are anywhere. If our misery is less, it is because poverty of the other kind is not so deep as in other countries. But this aspect of the poverty problem should not be confused with the second aspect, that of a permanent over-supply of the lower grades of labor, and the permanent poverty of the masses. We, in the United States, have made some slight contribution to the solution of the latter problem, but, because of a confusion of thought, the fact of industrial depressions is sometimes said to negative that statement. On this point, the workers themselves are more clearheaded than some of their self-appointed champions. In times of depression they seem to realize that it is not so much the result of injustice, or of discrimination against themselves, as of a general world condition which affects all classes alike. It would be difficult to explain, on any other ground, the strange lack of revolutionary

activity when there is so much poverty as there is in a time
of depression.

The two principal grounds on which the present economic
system of the Western World is indicted are, therefore, its instability and its inequality. The indictment is well grounded
and every advocate of our economic system must plead guilty
in the name of his client. There is a great deal of instability
and a great deal of inequality. A market is an unstable thing;
prices fluctuate, and everything in our system seems to be in
a state of flux and flow. Under a military form of organization
the individual would at least feel certain of his rations, but if
he chooses the military régime in order to attain that feeling
of security, he must accept everything that goes with the military scheme of things, including subjection to authority.

Neither system can be said to be absolutely better than the
other for everybody. No matter how well the military system
operates it will work to the disadvantage of some, and these will
have an interest in changing to the voluntary system. No
matter how well the voluntary system operates, there will always
be some who would be better off under the security of the military system. Even though the great majority of the people
would rather live under the voluntary system, even though they
could feel so secure in the midst of price changes and wage
fluctuations as to be unwilling to surrender their freedom for a
slightly greater degree of security, there is likely to be a small
fraction of the people who feel so insecure under this system as
to prefer the security of the military system, even at the cost
of subjection to authority.

Whether the Western World will be able to maintain its system of voluntarism, or suffer a revolution and a reversion to
the military system, will depend upon the relative percentage
of its people in the two classes. So long as the overwhelming
majority feels secure enough, under our system, to prefer it to
the system of authority and obedience, our system is safe.
When, however, a majority finds itself so insecure as to be
willing to surrender the doubtful privilege of bargaining for itself
in return for the greater security of a rationing system, there

will undoubtedly be a revolution. One of the great problems, therefore, for those who feel a preference for the system of voluntarism, is to reduce the instability of the system and to reduce the number who feel any great degree of insecurity. In other words, this is one of the major problems of statesmanship.

3. *Justice.* We have seen that in the more advanced stages of social development the individual must get what he needs, if he gets it at all, from his social environment, that is, from other people. Under the market economy, he gets in exchange for what he gives. As social life becomes more and more complicated it becomes more and more difficult to make sure that each gets as much as he gives and no more. This is the problem of distributive justice. The problem is, more specifically, to secure for each participant in every industry the equivalent of what he contributes to the productivity of the industry, and for each worker who performs personal service the exact value of his service.

If that can be achieved, we shall have taken the first and the most necessary step toward creating a social environment favorable to individual success. Any falling short of that ideal must necessarily reduce the chances of success for the average individual, or decrease the number of individuals who can succeed in getting what they need. The realization of this ideal of justice will also insure the maximum success for the group as a whole. When each and every worker can feel certain of getting the equivalent of what he produces or the exact value of his service he will have the strongest possible motive for producing and serving up to his capacity. When he gets the value of his service or his product he can then use what he gets for the benefit of those for whom he cares most. When he is compelled to share with people for whom he does not care he has not the same motive.

In a simpler economy, where there is little division of labor, it is generally assumed or admitted that justice requires that each worker should have the exact things which he produces. When he exchanges his products for the products of other workers, if the exchange is a fair one, he gets the equivalent in value of what he produces. In a more complex economy, where several workers take part in the production of the same thing, we say that justice is done if they all share in the product, or its value, in proportion to the value of the labor which each contributes.

While justice is the first step, and a necessary step, justice alone will not eliminate poverty. Other steps are necessary. Justice will not help any one whose product or whose service is not worth anything to anybody. If it is not worth anything to anybody, nobody will have any reason except sympathy or charity for paying him for it. In such a social environment, such an individual can not be a success. He is as helpless as a man in a physical environment like that of a pioneer in a wilderness without the resourcefulness of a pioneer. He must either learn to do something for which there is a market, or a market must be created for what he can do if he is to avoid poverty.

That there are many poor people who do not get as much as they need is well known. That some people get more and some less than they earn is equally well known. It is easy to assume that those who do not get as much as they need are identical with those who do not get as they earn. If that assumption were true, it would only be necessary to guarantee every one what he earns in order to eliminate or at least to alleviate poverty. But suppose the assumption to be untrue. Suppose that those who do not get what they earn are an entirely different group from those who do not get as much as they need. In that case, guaranteeing to every one what he earns would not help those who do not get what they need. In other words, such a guarantee would not even alleviate poverty. If we assume a middle position, namely, that in some cases, but not in all, those who do not get what they earn are identical with those who do not get what they need, then to guarantee every one what he earns would help some cases of poverty and leave others untouched.

But what is justice in the distribution of the products of industry? There are three different and irreconcilable answers.

One is that each should get the value which he produces, or what his work is really worth. Another is that each should be given that which he needs regardless of the service he renders. Another is that each should be rewarded according to the sacrifice he makes.

The second of these answers can be eliminated. To give to a person that which he needs, because he needs it, and without any regard to what he does or how much his work is worth, is not justice but charity. The motive for giving it is love, sympathy, or anything but justice. To give to a person because he has earned it or because he deserves it is justice. The motive need be neither love, sympathy nor charity, but a desire for fair play.

But when does a person deserve or earn a reward? The first and the third of the above answers bear on this question. Does one earn a reward or a share in the products of industry merely because he has borne fatigue, endured hardship, or made a sacrifice, or does he earn a share because his work was useful, because he helped to make the product, because he contributed to the total product? Something depends upon what we want to motivate by our rewards. Do we want to motivate usefulness and productivity, to the end that there may be the largest possible amount of useful things produced? If so, reward men in proportion to their usefulness, or the usefulness of the things which they do or produce. Do we want, on the other hand, to motivate sacrifice? If so, to what end?

It is sometimes argued, however, that we might adopt a plan which would give equal material rewards to everybody and supply such immaterial rewards as laurel wreaths and other expressions of public esteem. In other words, we could motivate men to special service by social esteem rather than by money or things which money will buy. To begin with, there is no reason why we might not continue to use both forms of reward, as we and every civilized society have always done. Both forms of reward may turn out to be more effective than either of them alone would be.

If immaterial rewards, such as popular esteem, are universally effective, that is, if everybody cares intensely enough for such rewards to be willing to work hard in order to win them, the problem of distributive justice still remains. If some receive large and others small rewards or none at all, there will be great inequality. Under the assumption that everybody is eager for such things, there will be the same discontent as the result of this inequality as results from inequality of pecuniary rewards. Of course, if only a few care for these non-pecuniary rewards there will be no widespread discontent if the rewards go only to a few, but, as we have seen, if that were true, these rewards would be ineffective motivators. The rankling sense of injustice would not be widespread, but for the same reason, the motivating power of such rewards would be negligible. In short, if non-pecuniary rewards were effective as motivators they would not solve the problem of distributive justice at all. If men desire public esteem as much as money, those who get little or none of it will feel as dissatisfied as those who get little or no money.

This presents a problem in distributive justice whose statement is quite as clear-cut and whose answer is quite as baffling as the problem of distributing pecuniary rewards. We complain of the injustice of having paid Caruso so much more money than other excellent tenors, and Babe Ruth so much more than other excellent batters. We contend correctly, that the differences in the pecuniary rewards of these "firsts" and those of other performers who are nearly as good, are all out of proportion to the actual differences in performance. Sometimes we go further and say that these differences of pecuniary reward are contrary to all sound ideas of distributive justice.

Be that as it may, it cannot be said to be peculiar to the money economy, or to the system of pecuniary rewards. Other rewards are distributed in much the same way. Applause, social esteem, newspaper space, public honors, high political offices, popularity, power, and prestige are never distributed on any theory of equality. These things are probably distributed even more unequally than material rewards, though the exact degree of inequality would be difficult to measure.

No informed person will contend that we are in practice approximating very closely to that ideal of justice which requires that each should get in proportion to the value he gives in the form of service or product. However, it is an ideal to strive for. Moreover, it is the ideal toward which the modern world has been steadily approaching. But the problem is not a simple one. How much does a man earn? What incomes are earned and what are unearned? These are difficult questions.

All wealth may be classified under three heads: earnings, stealings, and findings. Earnings may be defined as wealth which the owner has himself produced, or which he has bought and paid for out of the price of his own useful labor. The more a man gets by this method the richer he makes his country or the world. Stealings may be defined as all that any one gets by methods which injure or tend to impoverish the rest of the people. They include not only all gains from robbery and fraud, but also those which result from illegal monopoly and from taking advantage of the ignorance or weakness of others. Selling smallpox-infected blankets to Indians, or other harmful or worthless substances to other people, would come under this head. All such transactions are fundamentally alike.

Findings include all wealth that comes to any one through sheer good luck. Stumbling on a gold mine, or an oil well, inheriting a fortune, and benefiting through a rise in the price of an old masterpiece, of an autograph of John Milton, or of a parcel of land, all come under this head. Many fortunes are made up of mixtures of earnings and findings; some undoubtedly include an element of stealings.

How to deal with earnings and stealings is an easy problem so far as the principle is concerned. There are difficult problems of a practical or administrative nature, but the principle is clear. Earnings must be safeguarded and stealings must be suppressed. That statement needs no qualification. It is the problem of findings which gives us trouble. Shall the lucky individual who, through no fault or merit of his own, comes into possession of riches, be permitted to keep them?

On the one side it can be said that he has not deprived any

one else of anything that was rightfully his. No one else can claim any right to what the finder has found or come into possession of. The rest of us may envy his good fortune, but we cannot claim that he has robbed us of anything that was ours or that we have produced or earned. On the other hand, the lucky person cannot claim that he has earned his wealth. Instead of putting on airs he should walk humbly, and thank not only his stars but the people who let him keep his wealth. Our present policy is to let the lucky finder keep what he has found. It is the principle of "finders, keepers."

The worst danger which may come from this principle is that the fortunate person may go to waste. Having enough to live on, he may stop working, in which case a unit of man power is wasted. Instead of trying to show his appreciation of his good fortune by working and by making his wealth work also, he may act as though he was doing the world a favor by living in it. As a matter of fact, such an idler would do the world a favor by leaving it. His fortune would remain, the world would still have it, and would be rid of an unproductive consumer.

So long as finders in general comport themselves humbly, and use their powers and their wealth productively, they will probably be left in possession of their findings. When they become arrogant, idle, or snobbish, they will probably be dispossessed by the masses who hold absolute power over such matters.

When we are considering the distribution of wealth as though it were a question of distributing rewards, justice seems to require that they be distributed on the basis of service or productivity. There is another aspect of wealth, however, which is growing in importance. An increasing proportion of the wealth of all industrial countries is coming to consist of producers' goods, sometimes called capital goods, or simply capital. In fact there is high and respected authority for regarding all wealth as tools, potentially at least, or as power to be used in the service of society. In the Parable of the Talents, this is the clear meaning. From the standpoint of the group, or its best interests, productive instruments should go to those who can use them most productively.

Wealth is rather frequently, if not generally, thought of as means of self-gratification. If we start with that idea, the Parable of the Talents is an absurdity. It would be monstrously unjust to take wealth away from the man who had only one unit and give it to the man who had already accumulated ten. But wealth may also be thought of, not as means for the self-gratification of the owner, but as instruments of production, whose function is to serve. That is the idea of wealth which the author of the Parable of the Talents always tried to teach. He applied it to wealth as well as to personal powers and capacities.

Now the function of an instrument of production is to produce. In proportion as instruments of production are wasted, in that proportion will the nation remain poor. In proportion as instruments of production are put to work producing things that are needed, in that proportion will the nation prosper. In proportion as instruments of production are permitted to remain in the possession of men who do not use them, in that proportion will they go to waste. In proportion as they are put into the hands of those who will use them, in that proportion will they perform their function and contribute to the welfare of multitudes of people.

It is all as clear as addition and subtraction when you start with the idea that wealth is to be regarded as a mass of productive agents. The obvious thing is to make them produce. One obvious way to make them produce is to put them under the control of those who can use them most productively. If a legal and harmless way can be found to transfer them from wasters to users, their productivity and the general prosperity of the group will be increased.

There may be many ways of effecting this transfer,— of taking productive agents from those who permit them to go to waste and giving them to those who will use them efficiently. One tolerably good way is to let men bid for these productive agents. The man who can grow a better crop with a given quantity of labor and land can afford to pay a better price for both than the man who can only make them produce a poor crop. The man who can manufacture a better, or at least a more saleable product with the same men and machines can outbid others for both.

It sometimes happens, under this system, that productive agents are taken away from wasters or ineffective users and put under the control of more efficient users. This results from the simple fact that the more efficient users can buy out the less efficient, or pay higher prices for productive agents than their less efficient rivals can afford to pay. There may be better ways of giving additional talents to those who use them well and taking them away from those who waste them, but the transfer has to be made in some way in any country which hopes to prosper.

This happens to conform to the principle that wealth,— certainly productive wealth,— should go to those who can use it. It is a perversion of this principle to say that no one should have more than he can consume. Men do not consume land, tools, and other productive agents. To use such things is to make them produce. Such things should obviously go to those who can use them in this sense. When the talent was taken from the man who did not use it and given to the one who had shown his capacity to use talents productively, it was in strict accordance with this principle. Competitive bidding for instruments of production tends in the same general direction.

This is not so hard on the one-talent man as it may at first seem. His own working capacity is one of his talents. If he cannot direct his own working capacity as well as some one else can direct it for him, he may be better off if he gives up trying to be his own boss and puts himself under the direction of a more efficient boss. Under better management he may produce more and get more than he could get if he tried to direct his own labor and got the entire product.

The only real problem is to find the best way of taking wealth (talents) away from the inefficient users and giving it to the efficient users. If a better way can be found than the method

of competitive bidding, of course we want it. It is not enough
to show that this method works crudely and inaccurately. That
could be said of any method. What we need is a method which
works less crudely than the present method. That method has
not been found.

4. *The Market Economy.* As already suggested, our present
method of distributing the products of industry is the method
of marketing, of buying and selling, sometimes called the market
economy. In a balanced market, where buyers and sellers are
well informed, and where fraud is prevented, it has been generally assumed that products and services would sell for about
what they were worth. If that were true, justice would result.
We know, however, that it does not always result. There must,
therefore, be something wrong with the market economy. In
so far as justice is defeated by fraud, monopolization and other
ways which we have classified under the general name of "stealing," a more efficient administration of justice would bring a
cure. There would still result many hardships which we shall
discuss under the two headings: A. *Stabilization*, and B.
Equalization.

A. *Stabilization.* The more complicated a machine or an organism, the more things there are to get out of order. A thousand things may go wrong with an automobile; not so many
could go wrong with a wheelbarrow. The ice-man reminds us
that a block of ice never gets out or order; he leaves us to infer
that electric refrigerators "are not so." There is a long list of
maladies that may afflict the human organism. It does not
seem possible that so many things could go wrong with an
oyster. The same rule seems to apply to economic systems.
The less complicated the system, the more stable; the more
complicated, the less stable. All highly organized machines,
organisms, or economic systems are alike in that in each one
there is great interdependence of parts. Each part does something on which every other depends. If one part fails to do its
work, the whole machine stops, the organism is sick, and the
economic system is thrown out of balance.

The simplest of all economic systems is what some German

writers call the "natural economy," that is, a system in which there is no division of labor, but where every one produces what he consumes and consumes what he produces. The next simplest economic system is what is known as the barter economy. Under this system, there is a great deal of swapping, or of trading without the use of money. Each family and each neighborhood now become somewhat dependent on others. Whatever affects the prosperity of one begins to have some effect upon the prosperity of others.

While the fact of barter would introduce an element of instability not present in the "natural economy," this is still a relatively stable system. There would still be no price revolutions because there would be no prices or price levels. There might be overproduction of certain things, but there could not be overproduction of everything. The reason is that the supply of one thing would be an immediate demand for something else. Offering one thing would be an attempt to purchase something else. If there was nothing else to be bought with one product, that would be an undersupply of other things as truly as an oversupply of the one.

The next stage is the money economy, a system in which products are sold for money, and the money received by one producer is later used to buy the products of other producers. The use of money introduces another element of instability. A variable interval of time may come between the sale of one product and the purchase of another. With money, the purchase of the other commodity may be delayed a longer or a shorter time. If the interval between sale and purchase is shortening, business is speeding up. If the interval is lengthening, business is slowing down. It is now possible to have rising and falling price levels. Nevertheless, so long as all sales and purchases are cash transactions, and there is no credit, the business instability cannot be so very great.

Next comes the credit economy under which we are now living. This introduces still another element of instability. Whereas, under the money economy, one could not buy another product before he had sold his own, under the credit economy one may buy another product long before he has sold his own. This makes it possible, for a time at least, to accelerate purchasing vastly more than would be possible without credit. So long as men are generally accelerating their purchasing, business is booming. But when they begin slowing down their rate of purchasing, business stagnates.

Even buying on credit or with credit instruments would not create such instability as we have been having were it not for speculation. Speculation is buying, not for current use, but in anticipation of a rise in price, or selling in anticipation of a fall in price. When men imagine that they are endowed with the gift of foresight they are likely to try to cash in on it. When they think that the price of something is about to rise, they are tempted to buy it, whether they want it or not, merely for the purpose of selling it again at a higher price. By means of credit they can do vastly more speculating than would be possible if all business were done on a cash basis. This combination of the credit economy and the speculative spirit makes possible a speculative mania.

These speculative manias are frequent, but so far as any one can discover, they are sporadic. There does not seem to be anything cyclical about them. They are all alike in certain particulars, so also are all epidemics, all wars, and all earthquakes. So long as we have a credit system, it will be possible for people to buy more than their current income will pay for. When large numbers do so, it makes temporary prosperity. Later, when they begin paying for what they bought the year before, they must cut down current purchases. That makes a depression. When a speculative mania seizes large numbers of people, they strain their credit to the limit, buying vastly more than they can pay for. Later, everybody stampedes to sell what he had bought but hadn't paid for. We are all so dependent upon one another that even those who had neither speculated nor over-strained their credit, are affected. The innocent suffer with the guilty. The question is, What can the innocent do about it?

We saw, in an earlier paragraph, that much of the instabiliy of modern business is directly connected with the widening or narrowing of the interval of time which elapses between the sale of one commodity and the purchase of another. Hoarding money widens the interval in one direction. That is, it increases the lag, or lengthens the distance with which a purchase lags behind a sale. Buying on credit decreases the lag until it becomes a minus quantity. Whereas in strictly cash transactions, each person must sell something for money before he can buy anything, under credit he can buy one commodity before he has sold anything to get the money to pay for what he bought. The hoarder holds the money received from the sale of one commodity a long time before purchasing another. At the opposite extreme, the man who uses his credit may buy another commodity a long time before he sells his own. Thus there is a possible variation of years in the interval between sale and purchase. During the period of lengthening or shortening that interval there may be wide fluctuations in the quantities of goods any one or any population can purchase. Here is a factor in the problem of business booms and depressions which is too little understood.

The abnormal unemployment of a time of depression arises from two distinct sources. One source is the displacement of men by machines; the other is the shrinkage of credit and purchasing power. The one is now called technological unemployment, and is the one most talked about. The other, which is vastly more important, reduces, for a time, the effective demand for goods and for the labor which produces them. The one makes it possible to produce a given quantity of goods with less labor; the other reduces the quantity of goods that can be sold. When the public buys fewer goods than before, and when each unit of goods requires less labor for its production, it is obvious that there must be a pronounced decrease in the demand for labor; and, unless the supply of labor can be reduced, there must be wholesale unemployment.

Technological unemployment affects directly only the kind of labor that can be displaced by machines or superior mechanical processes. The unemployment which arises from a shrinkage in the effective demand for goods affects all kinds of labor, mental as well as manual, administrative as well as technical. This is the kind of unemployment from which a country suffers most acutely in a depression.

There is no reason for believing that the rate of technological unemployment has increased in recent decades. It has existed ever since the introduction of steam-driven machinery. Dire prophecies as to the collapse of capitalism through technological unemployment have been made so often as to leave us skeptical. If the effects had been cumulative, all the dire prophecies of the last one hundred and fifty years would probably have come true. But the effects have not been cumulative because a curative process has been going on. Every decade has seen a certain amount of displacement of men by machines, and every normal decade has seen a certain amount of reabsorption into industry of the men who were displaced. In good times the reabsorption is rather prompt, and technological unemployment does not impress the public as an acute problem. In hard times, the reabsorption slows down, the unemployed accumulate, and the public is impressed by the so-called technological unemployment, which is not technological unemployment at all but is, in reality, unemployment resulting from the instability of our credit system.

The process by which displaced labor is reabsorbed is not very difficult to understand if we approach it in the right way. When the production of a commodity is cheapened by a labor-saving device, one of two things must happen. The commodity is either sold to the public at a lower price, or, through monopolistic control, the old price is maintained and profits increased. If the price falls, the public can either buy more of it, or save money for the increased purchase of other things. In either case the displacement of labor is halted by the increased purchasing of goods. If consumers buy enough more of the commodity in question, it may take as many men with the new machines to supply the new demand as it took before with the old machines to supply the old demand. If they buy the same quantity as before, at a reduced price, their power to purchase other things is increased by the amount of money saved. This increased purchasing of other things will stimulate the demand for labor in other industries and tend to reabsorb in those industries the labor which was displaced in the industry in which the technological improvement took place.

This explains why it is that, though men have been displaced by machines every year for the last one hundred and fifty years, nevertheless the total amount of unemployment does not increase over long periods or time, however much it increases during depressions. Of course it is a real hardship for laborers to be displaced by machines, even for short intervals, and be forced to find new jobs. Those of us who never have to compete with machines, who gain the benefit of cheapened goods but escape the burdens of technological unemployment, who enjoy all the advantages of improved technology but incur none of the penalties, may find it economical to purchase self-respect by taxing ourselves to help the technologically unemployed. However, the problem is not acute in good times when displaced labor is quickly reabsorbed and the interval between losing one job and finding another is short. It becomes acute in hard times, but, as shown above, the acuteness arises not from a more rapid displacement of men by machines but from the slower reabsorption of displaced labor into industry. This slow rate of reabsorption is the problem to which attention should be given.

So far as the problem of normal technological unemployment is concerned, it presents no great difficulty. The easiest temporary expedient is the sharing among all workers of such employment as there is at any time, and also of such wages as can be paid. This avoids several glaring mistakes sometimes made by advocates of the shortened day or week. This plan does not assume that it can increase the sum total of employment. It merely shares such employment as there is. It does not assume that men are to be paid the same wage for a short week as for a long one. Wages as well as work are to be shared. It recognizes the fact that if labor works shorter hours or fewer days, capital must also work shorter hours or fewer days, unless some plan can be devised to avoid this difficulty. Accordingly, a rational plan includes double shifts whereby capital works longer hours while labor works shorter hours.

To attempt to pay the same wages for a reduced product per worker would, of course, mean an increased labor-cost per unit of product. This would necessitate either a higher price to the public per unit of product, or it would mean bankruptcy for the weaker employers. A higher price to the public would mean that less could be purchased and less labor hired to produce the diminished product. Bankrupting the weaker employers would throw men out of work. Hence a rational plan includes a reduction of wages in proportion as the product per worker is reduced. Even then, if capital works fewer hours, there will be an increased capital cost. This, like an increased labor cost, would necessitate either a rise in the price of the product or the bankruptcy of some factories. In either case it would decrease employment. Hence a rational plan provides for a double shift in order that the capital cost may be reduced rather than increased.

One difficulty remains, however, and needs to be considered. We must realize that not all industries are run on a competitive basis. In some of the larger industries there is some degree of monopolistic control. This is the era of great business combinations, federal reserve systems, and price stabilization policies. It was proclaimed a few years ago that these new factors would stabilize business and employment. This doctrine was based on the belief, which was wide-spread even in high financial circles, that one way to stabilize industry was to stabilize prices. It is demonstrable, however, that the stabilization of prices through monopolistic control increases the instability of industry, that is, the instability of production and employment. These methods of big business, strictly speaking, do not stabilize industry at all; they have been a leading factor in the growing instability of modern industry.

In order to stabilize prices in a monopolized industry, production must be controlled. When the demand for its product begins to fall off, instead of lowering the price to stimulate buying and maintain the rate of production, the monopoly curtails production in order to maintain its price. In order to curtail production it must fire men, close plants, and stop buying raw materials. If, instead of pegging its price at a fixed level, it would let the price come down, it would not need to curtail production so much, fire so many men, close down so many plants, or cut its purchases of raw material to such an extent. In other words, by permitting the price to be flexible, industry and employment would become somewhat less unstable.

This does not imply that the stabilization of prices is, in itself, a bad thing. It merely means that monopolistic control of production is diametrically the wrong way. In order to stabilize prices in this way, it is necessary for the monopolistic power arbitrarily to increase or decrease production, which means the unstabilization of employment. But there are other ways of stabilizing prices. If, for example, credit can be stabilized, it will help to stabilize prices without arbitrarily expanding or contracting production and employment. Prices could, under stabilized credit, be stabilized without arbitrarily increasing and decreasing employment. So long as credit expands and contracts so violently as it has been doing during the last century, prices will automatically fluctuate. To try to prevent this fluctuation by monopolistic control of production is to begin at the wrong end of the problem and to make a bad situation worse.

Seeing that the private management of business results in so much instability, the suggestion is made that government planning should be substituted. It is natural, of course, when anything is not working satisfactorily, to try something else. If the new experiment does not work we can go back to the old one. It looks, however, as though the only plan for government stabilization which could be expected to work would be a general plan of licensing and rationing, which we might not like any better than instability. This would require a planning board that was empowered to license all producers and ration all consumers. Such a board would be able to adjust supply to demand and demand to supply,— provided it were given ample power and endowed with the somewhat rare gift of omniscience. Unless we are ready to entrust the direction of industry to a board with such extraordinary powers, we shall do well to hesitate before we add another useless board to the number now existing.

A certain wholesome skepticism is needed as to the superior wisdom or efficiency of government boards. There is no reason to believe that the government could get abler men on such a board than industry can now get on its governing boards. Grant that industry has shown mismanagement, that the greatest business magnates have shown an utter inability to grasp the larger facts of the present situation and of that which preceded it. The same is true of political magnates and government heads. Government has to be carried on by the same kind of men as run our businesses. Politics is not an alembic in which stupidity and selfishness are distilled into wisdom and virtue.

We need to go deeper into the question as to why industrialists overbuild factories, why farmers develop too many farms and why miners open too many mines. The principal reason is that they are misled by the strange behavior of our credit system over which they have no control. When credit is expanding, purchasing power is increasing abnormally. It is increasing abnormally because every one whose credit is expanding can purchase more than his income will pay for. When credit in general is expanding, the whole nation can buy more than its entire income will pay for.

During the period when credit is in process of expansion, the abnormal demand for goods stimulates production. More than that, short-sighted business managers who imagine themselves to be far-sighted, plot curves to show the current increase in demand,— say for automobiles,— and then proceed to project that curve into the future. "Far-sighted" promoters proceed to promote new construction to prepare for that future demand. But they are misled by the abnormal demand. The future increase in demand fails to materialize for the excellent reason that credit cannot go on expanding forever. When it stops expanding, even if it does not begin to contract, the abnormal demand falls off and the industry finds itself overbuilt and overequipped.

Another factor of instability is found in the growing importance of the investors' market. An investors' market is a market
where producers' goods, generally summarized under the word
"capital," are bought and sold. It is distinguished from a consumers' market where consumers' goods are bought and sold.
In actual fact the distinction, though valid, is not very sharp
because, on the border line, the two kinds of markets are somewhat mixed. Wheat, for example, as it is dealt in on the produce exchange, though destined for consumption in the form of
bread, is still an article of merchandise, a form of raw material,
and therefore a producers' good. At the extremes, however, an
investors' market is very different from a consumers' market.
This furnishes a distinction which is clear enough for the present
discussion.

The clearest example of an investors' market is, of course,
the stock exchange. The things bought and sold on that market
are producers' goods. The transfer of a share of stock is essentially a transfer of an undivided share of some agent of production or producers' good, such as a railroad, a factory, or a mercantile establishment. The investors' market is notoriously
unstable. Prices on the stock exchange fluctuate over a wider
range and with greater violence than on the consumers' market.
In other words, the prices of shares are more unstable, and
fluctuate more violently, than the prices of food, clothing, and
other consumers' goods.

Why should the prices of producers' goods or capital, as they
are sometimes called, fluctuate more violently than the prices
of the consumers' goods which they help to produce? Because
the entire value of a producers' good is based on the relatively
small margin between the price at which its product can be sold
and the cost of operation.[1] A slight rise in the price of the
product may easily double or quadruple that margin, and a
slight fall in the price of the product may wipe the margin out.

With the growth of mechanical invention has come a vast increase in the volume of producers' goods. Modern inventories

---

[1] This point is elaborated in the author's *Principles of National Economy* (Ginn
& Co., Boston, 1921), p. 436.

show that the greater part of the tangible wealth of a country consists of producers' goods. Before the age of mechanical invention, and today in countries where mechanical invention has not progressed, inventories of the riches of rich men would show a smaller percentage of producers' goods and a larger percentage of consumers' goods. Aside from land, there was not much that a rich man could own except consumers' goods. Gold, silver, precious stones, palaces, and other articles of adornment and ostentation were the forms in which wealth was embodied.

The vast increase, both absolutely and relatively, in the volume of producers' goods, and the fact that their value is necessarily unstable together constitute one of the major factors in the instability of our economic system. Even durable consumers' goods, such as dwelling houses, furniture, and jewelry fluctuate less than durable producers' goods. No matter how low the price level, durable consumers' goods can still be enjoyed by consumers, and they always have *some* value. A producers' good, however, may become a liability rather than an asset and become worth less than nothing. When it no longer produces a product than can be sold for as much as it costs, the producers' good has lost all its value, except as junk. When so much of the wealth of a country consists of goods whose values fluctuate so violently as is the case in any highly industrialized country, the system necessarily becomes somewhat unstable. The stock market, where producers' goods are bought and sold, merely reflects that basic instability.

There is still to be considered the problem of speculative prices. Speculation may be defined as buying and selling in the hope of gaining something from a favorable turn in the market, that is, by a rise or fall in the market price of the thing dealt in. It differs from a normal mercantile transaction in which the hope of gain is in the normal difference between wholesale and retail prices. It differs from investment in which the hope of gain is in the income, in the form or interest or rent to be derived from the purchase. Needless to say, it differs from the purchase of raw materials where the hope of gain is in the difference between the price of the raw material and that of the finished product. It is speculation only when the dealer bases his expectation of gain on a change in the market price of the thing in which he deals.

There is, of course, a speculative element in almost all buying and selling. The man who buys a suit of clothes might decide to buy at a time when he thought bargains were good, say just after Christmas. However, speculation is not the main purpose of his purchase. His main purpose is the use of the suit of clothes. The manufacturer may also buy his raw materials at a time when he thinks the market is favorable, but again, speculation is not the main purpose of his purchase.

Since the main purpose of speculation is to profit from a fluctuation in the market price of something, it is natural that speculation should be most active on those markets which are most unstable, and in those things whose prices fluctuate most widely and most violently. That is why there is more speculation in producers' than in consumers' goods, and in equities than in unmortgaged forms of property.

As to the effects of speculation on the instability of markets and prices, there is a difference of opinion, the reason for which may be that the effects of speculation differ with circumstances. It is generally believed that an active speculative market for wheat tends to reduce the seasonal variations in the price of wheat. That is, when there are active speculators ready to buy indefinite quantities of wheat whenever it shows signs of being cheaper than the conditions of supply and demand would warrant, this active buying tends to raise the price of wheat. Similarly, when the price of wheat appears to be higher than the conditions of supply and demand would warrant, there is active selling of wheat. This speculative buying and selling, it is argued, keeps the price from going so high or so low as it might go if there were no active speculators watching for a chance to make a speculative profit.

Some of the weight of this argument is borrowed from the effect of storing wheat, which is partly but not wholly a speculative transaction. Storing wheat, like storing ice, is a physical process, and preserves a commodity from a time of superabundance until a time of scarcity. Of course, if no one were willing to store wheat from the time of threshing until it was needed, the price of wheat would be very low in August and September, and very high in February and May. The motive for storing is the hope of a rise in price between threshing time when it is bought and stored, and a later time when it is sold for consumption. This, undoubtedly, has an element of speculation in it, but it is not mainly speculative. It is like buying a raw material at a low price and selling it in finished form at a higher price, or buying at wholesale at a lower price and selling at retail at a higher price. In both these cases a utility is added, in the one case by processing, producing form utility, in the other case by transferring a good from a person who does not need it to a person who does, thus creating personal utility. Storing a good from a time when it is not needed until a time when it is needed creates time utility, and the profit on such a transaction is not really a speculative profit.

When we consider the vast amount of speculative buying and selling of wheat which has nothing whatever to do with storing, the argument is not so clear in favor of the proposition that speculation tends to steady prices. The important function of hedging by which the miller and the shipper may insure themselves while carrying on the useful business of grinding wheat into flour or shipping wheat from an area of surplus to an area or scarcity, does not reduce fluctuations in price. It merely insures the miller and the shipper against loss through fluctuations of price.

However, the weight of the argument seems to be slightly in favor of the proposition that a large amount of active speculation tends to reduce somewhat the ordinary variations in price, and to spread over longer periods of time the effects of changes in demand or supply. The mere anticipation of the results of a partial crop failure, for example, causes prices to rise long before the scarcity of the product becomes acute. Buying increased quantities now, in anticipation of a future scarcity, is a form of speculation. It causes the scarcity, when it comes, to be less acute than it would be if prices were to remain low, and consumption were to proceed at the old rate until the supply was exhausted.

There is another phase of the question of the effect of speculation on prices which is too generally overlooked. When the price of anything, whether a producers' good, a consumers' good, or land, has been tending upward or downward for a considerable period, a peculiar attitude develops among people with speculative tendencies. If the price has been rising, the belief seems to spread that it will continue indefinitely to rise. This leads to accelerated buying in anticipation of that further rise. This accelerated buying causes the price to rise still faster. This, in turn, stimulates still more rapid buying, etc. etc. until the market becomes an assemblage of whirling dervishes.

In quite similar manner, when the trend has been downward for a time, the belief develops that it will continue downward. Accordingly, those who accept this view refrain from buying as long as possible, waiting for a further drop in price. The more they refrain from buying, the faster the price falls; and the faster the price falls, the more they refrain from buying, etc. etc. until complete stagnation is reached. These are cases where speculative buying and selling, as distinguished from buying and selling for use, undoubtedly increase the instability of markets.

B. *Equalization.* The problem of improving the market for the kind of labor that generally sells at a low price is different from that of stabilizing the market. In fact, some very stable countries have such chronic oversupplies of labor as to leave the masses in a permanent state of poverty. In most parts of the world, particularly in the Orient, this presents a more acute problem than that of instability. The United States is one of the few countries where the opposite is true. We have made some progress in the solution of the problem of chronic poverty. We have made no progress toward the solution of instability, partly because the problem has not been studied intelligently.

The problem of equalizing prosperity is a problem of equalizing earning capacity,— first, as between occupations; second, as among individuals of the same occupation. Both are real problems though the world has scarcely begun to think about the second. Most of the dissatisfaction grows out of the fact that some occupations are poorly paid, while others are relatively well paid. So far as present indications go, there would be little dissatisfaction if each occupation were, all things considered, about as well paid as any other. If within the same occupation one worker earns more than another, there would apparently be little social discontent. Individual jealousies would doubtless exist, but until the general public discovered a new grievance there would be no public agitation for the alleviation of this kind of inequality.

The problem of occupational inequality appears to be mainly a problem of occupational congestion, on the one hand, and of the undermanning of other occupations. Until this occupational congestion can be relieved, or until the working population can be redistributed occupationally, there will continue to be occupational inequality.

Just what is meant by equality of economic rewards among different occupations? Of course allowance must be made for differences in the cost of training. To pay equal wages, or allow equal incomes, to occupations which require widely different training, involving different costs in the form of time and money, would not be equality but inequality. Allowance must also be made for the chances of failure. An occupation in which there is a high percentage of failure must afford at least a few large prizes, otherwise it would fail to attract workers.

It need not be pretended that the present differences of income earned in different occupations in any country bear any relationship to the actual differences in the cost of training. There is a difference which may well be called the "rent of personal ability" which is quite analagous to the economic rent of land. An arithmetical illustration ought to be convincing.

Let us suppose that two young men, A and B, aged eighteen, decide upon different occupations. A goes at once into a manual trade which requires no more preliminary training than he has had. B decides upon a profession which requires four years in college and three years in a professional school. He spends $2000 a year for living and tuition. Let us suppose, further, that A earns $4 a day or $1200 a year for forty-seven years, retiring at the age of 65. His total earnings are $56,400. If B also retires at 65, he must, in forty years, earn $56,400 plus the $14,000 which he spent on his education, or a total of $70,400. In other words, he must earn an average of $1760 a year. If, however, B had to borrow the $14,000 at 6 per cent to pay for his education, he would have to amortize his debt in forty years. In that case he would need to earn roughly $2660 a year in order to be on an equality with A.

There are not many professions that would consider the difference between $1200 and $2660 an adequate difference between a professional income and a manual worker's income. In other words, most professional men expect a rent of personal ability, in addition to an adequate allowance for the cost of training.

As already suggested, allowance must be made for the risk of failure. If, in one occupation, any one with average health, ability, and industry, can succeed, while in another, only the exceptional men really succeed and the others fail, no one except a gambler, or a very adventurous person, would choose the latter occupation unless there were at least a few exceptional prizes to be won.

Of course all occupations involve more or less risk. From the nature of many of our modern business arrangements, however, there is one occupation or group of occupations which involve somewhat greater hazards than the others. This occupation or group of occupations may be called that of the independent business man, the entrepreneurs, or the enterprisers, as they are variously called. A business arrangement could be made, and was actually made in the old whaling industry, in which the risks were distributed among all the participants. Under this arrangement, every one,— laborer, officer, and owner,— took a percentage of the proceeds. No one received a fixed wage, a fixed salary or a fixed interest rate. All shares went up and down according to the state of the business.

Under the common arrangement, however, the enterpriser undertakes to pay a contractual income to others, and accepts a contingent income for himself. Whether he gets any income or not depends upon whether anything is left after all contractual incomes are paid. Under this arrangement, the enterpriser's position is somewhat more hazardous than that of those who receive contractual incomes. Unless there were possibilities of making large gains no one would choose the hazardous occupation of the enterpriser. The fact that increasing numbers of young men of ability and training, in seeking a career, choose positions which promise contractual rather than contingent incomes would seem to indicate that even the considerable prizes won by a few successful enterprisers were not sufficient to compensate for the risks of failure.

When we consider the differences in the cost of training, and the differences in the risk involved in different occupations, it may seem impossible to define equality of occupational rewards or earnings. Probably the most satisfactory test of equality or inequality is to consider the relative attractiveness of different occupations. When a young person of good ability and judgment begins looking for a career, if he has difficulty in deciding between two occupations,— that is, when he balances all the advantages and disadvantages, they seem equally attractive, it would indicate that the two occupations offer approximately equal rewards, material and immaterial. If all occupations appealed to all young persons of good ability as equally attractive, we could at least rest easy in the feeling that no occupation was being unfairly treated or inadequately rewarded. Under such conditions, if a tendency showed itself for too many to enter one occupation, the difficulty of finding work would prove a deterrent and discourage others from entering it. Thus a balance among occupations would be preserved.

When, on the other hand, there are large numbers who have no choice but to enter occupations which are already overcrowded, no such occupational balance can be established or maintained. Whether those who have no choice of occupations are handicapped by lack of native ability or lack of opportunities for training, would not make any immediate difference. The occupations into which large numbers were forced by either reason would be overcrowded and poorly paid. The remedy, however, would be different. Where the handicapped individuals suffer from lack of inherited ability, the only possible remedy is in the eugenic control of population. Where the difficulty is in the lack of opportunity for training, the remedy lies in superior educational facilities in the form of free schools. It is probable that both remedies will have to be applied before an occupational balance can be reached.

Are not machines displacing men to such an extent as to make unskilled labor forever a drug on the market? Not necessarily. The advent of power-driven machinery is undoubtedly disturbing the balance, reducing the demand for muscular labor relatively to that for certain other kinds of labor. But there is and always (probably) will be a considerable demand for unskilled labor, and this for two reasons. First, no machine can use discretion. Even the moderate discretion necessary to distinguish between a weed and a useful plant has to be exercised by a human being. There are multitudes of other operations which call for human judgment. Second, it does not pay to make a machine to perform any operation unless the operation has to be exactly repeated a great many times. There are multitudes of operations, sometimes called chores, which do not call for such exact and frequent repetition as to make machines profitable substitutes for human hands. Even though the demand for muscular labor is reduced by machines, that demand is not destroyed.

With the demand for muscular labor considerably reduced, relatively to other forms of labor, the market can be balanced in one of two ways. One is to decrease the use of machines, the other is to reduce the proportion of workers who are capable of doing only muscular work. Reducing the hours of work does not touch the problem because it affects all kinds of work, muscular as well as mental, and does not change the ratio. It also reduces the hours during which machines work unless there is an increase in the number of shifts which might increase the working hours of machines while reducing those of men. In this case, there is an increased motive for substituting machines for labor.

It looks as though there were no third choice. We must either stop the progress of invention or we must reduce the numbers who have only muscular labor to sell. The latter can be accomplished, to a certain extent, by better schools. If, as some would have us believe, all children are born with equal capacity for training, education would be enough. If that is not true, eugenics would have to be added to our program.

The nineteenth century saw a great outburst of educational enterprise in every democratic country. Men pinned their hopes to their school systems as agencies for human betterment. That some disappointment should result was only to be expected. This disappointment shows itself, however, in very different ways. Some are encouraging those who are unadapted to a machine age to be fruitful and multiply and cumber the earth, and then propose to take care of the unadapted by government support, by reducing the hours of labor, or by returning to more primitive methods of work. Others are proposing eugenic programs for the elimination of the feeble-minded and the near feeble-minded, of the criminal types, and of the unadapted in general. The twentieth century may see a development in this direction, paralleling and supplementing the educational development already under way. If not, the twentieth century will be a period of recession as the nineteenth was of advancement.

In order that there may be no counsel of despair, no turning back, let us consider what possibilities lie ahead on the road we have been travelling.

Honor nourishes art [wrote Cicero[1]], and glory is the spur with all to studies; while those studies are always neglected in every nation which are looked upon disparagingly. The Greeks held skill in vocal and instrumental music as a very important accomplishment, and therefore it is recorded of Epaminondas, who, in my opinion, was the greatest man amongst the Greeks, that he played excellently on the flute; and Themistocles some years before was deemed ignorant because at an entertainment he declined the lyre when it was offered to him. For this reason musicians flourished in Greece; music was a general study; and whoever was unacquainted with

[1] *The Tusculan Disputations*, Yonge's translation (G. Bell & Sons, London, 1878, bk.)

it, was not considered as fully instructed in learning. Geometry was in high esteem with them, therefore none were more honourable than mathematicians; but we have confined this art to bare measuring and calculating.

This quotation introduces the first proposition, that in any large population of a reasonably capable race there is enough latent talent to develop any of the arts or sciences provided the proper stimulus is afforded and sufficient time is allowed for its proper development. The second proposition is that if enough talent of high quality is turned into industrial pursuits, industries will so expand as to furnish adequate employment at high wages for all who want them. In the present stage of thought, the second of these propositions is the more important, not from the standpoint of pure logic, but because the public mind is less prepared for it.

The whole modern educational system is really based upon the first of these propositions. Poets may be born and not made, but it is believed that we can make more competent lawyers, doctors, preachers, engineers, farmers and mechanics if good professional and technical schools are provided than if they are not. Otherwise such schools would be worthless. The same remarks may be made of schools of business. It is also necessary, if we are to have good business men, that men of talent should want to be business men. Who wants to be a business man in a country where business is despised, or looked upon as distinctly less respectable than the so-called learned professions, or than literature and art? If you want capable men to do any particular kind of work you must give them, as a reward, what they want. Most men want to be well thought of by their fellow citizens. If business men are not well thought of you must either get along without good business men or you must bribe them with high profits. Moreover, high profits will be certain for those few who do bring great ability into business because they will have very little competition. In addition, wages will be low because there will be few well managed industries, and therefore few industries in which the product per man would be high enough to make high wages possible. On the other hand, where constructive business men are held in the highest esteem, where the best products of the universities are encouraged to go into constructive business, and where there are large numbers of high grade professional business schools, the opposite conditions will prevail.

If a great deal of high intelligence, thoroughly trained, can be brought to bear on business problems, the probabilities are that difficult business problems will be solved at a rapid rate and industries will expand at a corresponding rate. This expansion of industries will require larger and larger numbers of workers to man them. In other words, the increase in the number and quality of men available for the higher industrial functions creates an increasing demand for other men to perform what are now considered the lower industrial functions. This increase in the demand for what may be called the common laborers tends to raise their wages and to improve their general economic condition.

Great social results are never achieved by an academic formula and seldom by a stroke of genius. An industrial system which is capable of paying high wages to large numbers is the result of the massing of a large number of intelligent minds for long periods of time on industrial problems. By this massing of the national intelligence, every phase of the problem is studied intensively, a multitude of minor corrections, improvements and adjustments are made, and, in the course of time, a highly efficient industrial system is built up. It is safe to say that no workable system was ever built up in any other way.

This view is opposed to the heroic theory on the one hand, and to the accidental theory on the other. By the heroic theory is meant the theory that some great super-mind conceived and planned the whole thing and set it working. Such things do not happen in real life and it is extremely unlikely that such a thing will ever happen, though utopian writers will probably continue to divert us.

Even mechanical results are achieved in the same way. No genius ever lived who could have planned and built even a tolerably good automobile. It took thousands of highly intelligent men working incessantly by the method of trial and error for at least a generation, learning from one another, each one correcting his own mistakes as well as those of his fellows, to arrive at the present stage of development in automobile building.

By the accidental theory is meant the theory that these things just happen, or that they evolve of themselves. They happen because a vast amount of high intelligence is bent on making them happen, they evolve because intelligent men in large numbers are using nature's method of trial and error, variation and selection, to direct their evolution. Nor is it true that these results are achieved by ordinary minds working in combination. They are achieved by extraordinary minds working in combination. Tens of thousands of ordinary minds with ordinary training never could have made a workable automobile, much less a workable industrial system.

How did it happen that such large numbers of highly intelligent and highly trained men worked so intensively for so long a time on the construction of automobiles in the United States? Partly, at least, because this work was appreciated by the American people and they were willing to give honor and glory, power and dominion, and even hard cash, to any one who could build a first-rate automobile at low cost. For much the same reason, the Americans have built a highly efficient industrial system.

Here the following analogy suggests itself. The Germans built what was probably the greatest fighting machine the world has ever known. There is no reason to believe that the Germans ever developed a greater military genius than the French, the English, or even the Americans; but from the time of the Great Elector down to the reign of the recent Kaiser a military career has been the most honorable career within the gift of the government or the people. The best talent of Germany, or at least more than a fair share of the best talent, sought military careers. By the sheer process of massing a vast amount of high intelligence on the problems of military organization, the result was achieved. The English people have probably built the most efficient government in the world, at least if we forget all our ideals except that of sheer efficiency in the control of human conduct. There is no reason to believe that the English people ever developed a greater political genius than the French, the Germans or the Americans, but during the last century, at any rate, the most honorable career open to an Englishman was in the field of politics, of government service, or the judiciary. Consequently the best talent, or more than a fair share of the best talent, sought government careers and thus the result was achieved. In the United States neither military life nor politics has been quite so honorable as business. There is no reason to doubt that out of our hundred-odd millions, potential military geniuses or potential political geniuses may have existed, but they were not discovered in large numbers, and consequently we have not succeeded in massing a vast amount of high intelligence on either the army or the government. Business, on the other hand, has always been respected, has never been despised as in certain old, aristocratic countries, and our people have shown a high appreciation of any one who could build and manage a productive industry. Consequently we have succeeded in massing a fair share of our best talent on business problems. For this reason primarily, we have succeeded in building the greatest industrial machine the world has ever seen.

The only thing that ever cured any man's unemployment was giving him employment. The only thing that ever cured any man's low wages was paying him higher wages. The expansion of industry is what gives employment to more and more men. The increase in the productivity per man is what makes possible higher and higher wages. Second- and third-rate managers, technicians and investors never succeeded in expanding the industries of any country, or in increasing the productivity per man. First-grade managers, technicians and investors make first-rate industries possible, and only first-rate industries can pay first-rate wages. These are almost truisms, but after all the most difficult problems in the world are solved by getting back to a few obvious principles.

The principle involved here is one of the simplest, and at the same time one of the most far-reaching, in the whole field of economics. It is called by various names, but it simply means that where several factors are necessary to the getting of a good result, if one of those factors is scarce or of poor quality, this fact tends to make the others useless or of little effect. This principle applies to the simplest as well as to the largest and most complicated of all combinations of factors. To take a simple case, sugar and lemons are both necessary to the making of lemonade; the scarcity of sugar tends to destroy the demand for lemons. To take a somewhat more complicated case, labor, land, and tools are necessary for the growing of crops. Where land is scarce or poor, labor and capital are not very effective and must be content with small returns. Give the same labor and capital an abundance of fertile land, and they become more effective and receive larger returns; or vice versa, land and tools would be of little use where labor was scarce or of poor quality, and the land owner as well as the owner of tools would have to be content with small returns. Balance the land and tools with an abundance of competent labor, and they become more effective and the returns larger. Thousands of other illustrations of the same principle could be given.

We now come to some still more complicated cases. Manual labor alone can produce little or nothing. It takes a great many different kinds of labor nowadays to produce anything. If any one necessary kind of labor is scarce, all the others will be made ineffective and must be content with small returns. Management is just as essential nowadays as any other kind of labor. Where the kind of labor called management is scarce, or of low quality, all the other kinds are made ineffective by that fact and the returns will be small. Any policy which will supply an abundance of managing ability of high quality makes all the other kinds of labor more effective and increases their returns. A firm grasp of this principle, and a clear knowledge of its consequences, is the key to all effective programs for the raising of wages, the elimination of poverty, and the general improvement of the conditions of the laboring classes.

Not only management, but investors, inventors, and technicians are needed in order to increase the productivity of manual labor. The world over, wherever these are scarce or of low quality, manual laborers are poorly paid for the sufficient reason that the product per worker is small. The world over, wherever managers, investors, inventors, and technicians are numerous and of high quality, wages are high. There is no exception to this rule. The first thing to do, therefore, if it is desired to substitute high wages and prosperity for low wages, unemployment, and poverty is obviously to turn as much as possible of the best talent of the country into industrial careers, to increase the number and improve the quality of the managers, investors, inventors, and technicians.

The next thing to do is to see to it that the rest of the world does not shift its burden of unemployment and poverty upon us. If we merely expand our industries we may merely give employment to increasing numbers of Oriental coolies, Latin-American peons and other low-wage laborers from countries where men of high ability have chosen to cultivate the arts of elegant leisure rather than to solve the problem of poverty. In short, we must restrict immigration and stop importing poverty if we would eliminate poverty on our own soil.

One of the most difficult phases of the problem of poverty is that which grows out of the sheer fecundity of mankind. In other words, it is the population problem. In many parts of the world, the pressure of population is so great as to almost cause a student to despair of any improvement in the general condition of the people. On this subject E. A. Ross in his book entitled *Standing Room Only*[1] has this to say:

. . . During the sixty years 1860–1920 the peoples in the tropical colonies and dependencies of the great nations added to themselves *105 millions* — a twelfth of mankind in 1860 and equal nearly to the present inhabitants of the United States, yet a population uncontemplated and unwilled, a chance by-product, so to speak, of capitalistic industry in the tropics.

During forty years of British rule in Egypt, 1882–1922, the population doubled. In the Nile Valley to-day there are not far from seven million souls who might well regard the British as their godfathers. But for the Occupation most of them would never have been called into life, or else would have quitted it before the census-taker made his rounds. Galled

[1] New York, The Century Co., 1927, pp. 93–98.

by a sense of inferiority, the more self-conscious Egyptians "compensate" by furious anti-British agitation. Few of them realize that most of the Egyptian population is due to factors which the British introduced and that widespread misery attended by decline in numbers is inevitable unless the Egyptians can handle police, justice, railways, and irrigation works *about as well* as the British have been handling them.

Since the fall of Napoleon III the natives of Algeria have doubled. Thanks to the cultural elements the French introduced among this hidebound people, three millions are engaged in the Great Adventure of living who otherwise would be moldering under the sand, or else would never have been summoned from the limbo of the unborn. It is safe to say that few natives ever reflect that half of them all dwell not on the familiar natural soil but on a mole of added production and trade built by French ability, science, and capital.

In view of the terrific fecundity of mankind, is it possible to make headway in our fight against poverty? Obviously not unless we can isolate it and prevent it from spreading. If the over-fecund races can be confined to certain areas, the other peoples who gain some control over population will be able to deal constructively with the problem of poverty. If not, that is, if the more fecund races are permitted to spread to countries which have succeeded in raising their standard of living, there can be no possible solution of the poverty problem. The fecund race, transplanted to a region of high wages, can multiply as the European rabbit in Australia or the English sparrow in America. The fight against poverty then becomes as hopeless as Dame Partington's famous enterprise.

One question remains. Is the abolition of poverty a worthwhile enterprise? Will it be worth what it will cost? It will be necessary, first, for the universities to turn larger numbers of their most brilliant students toward the higher business careers. This may cause the arts and sciences to suffer. If so, the cost of the attempt to abolish poverty would be heavy, yet we may well consider the question, Which is more important, the development of esoteric culture along with a great mass of poverty and squalor, which seems to be what some of our frank Mediævalists would like to have, or, on the other hand, actually to achieve for once at least in the history of the world the abolition of poverty and squalor, even at the expense of that kind of culture which requires a leisure class for its cultivation? We may not be compelled to take our choice between these two extreme conditions, but even if we were, we should certainly not be ashamed of our country if we somewhat neglected the finer cultures of the past and achieved nothing except such a diffusion of material prosperity as would lift even the common laborers into a condition of universal well-being. We would at least have achieved something unique in the history of the world. We would have removed the scandal of poverty which has disgraced every civilization up to the present moment.

For the benefit of those who think that the solution of the poverty problem is an unworthy aim for an educational system, the following quotation from a writer who can hardly be accused of underestimating the value of culture may be considered. That writer is John Ruskin, who wrote as follows:

One day last November, at Oxford, as I was going in at the private door of the University galleries, to give a lecture on the Fine Arts in Florence, I was hindered for a moment by a nice little girl, whipping a top on the pavement. She was a *very* nice little girl; and rejoiced wholly in her whip, and top; but could not inflict the reviving chastisement with all the activity that was in her, because she had on a large and dilapidated pair of woman's shoes, which projected the full length of her own little foot behind it and before; and being securely fastened to her ankles in the manner of moccasins, admitted, indeed, of dextrous glissades, and other modes of progress quite sufficient for ordinary purposes; but not conveniently of all the evolutions proper to the pursuit of a whipping-top.

There were some worthy people at my lecture, and I think the lecture was one of my best. It gave some really trustworthy information about art in Florence six hundred years ago. But all the time I was speaking, I knew that nothing spoken about art, either by myself or other people, could be of the least use to anybody there. For their primary business, and mine, was with art in Oxford, now; not with art in Florence, then; and art in Oxford now was absolutely dependent on our power of solving the question — which I knew that my audience would not even allow to be proposed for solution —"Why have our little girls large shoes?"[1]

---

[1] *Fors Clavigera*, vol. II, letter, XXXVII.

INDEX

561